EXPERIENTIAL EDUCATION

and the SCHOOLS

Second Edition

EDITED BY

RICHARD J. Kraft
University of Colorado

and

JAMES KIELSMEIER
University of Minnesota

Association for Experiential Education
Box 249-CU
Boulder, CO 80309

Copyright by: A.E.E.
All rights reserved.

1986

PREFACE

The Association for Experiential Education is committed to furthering experience-based learning in a culture that is increasingly "information rich, but experience poor." A growing body of evidence, including the reports of five different national commissions, indicates the need to incorporate direct experience in education. The AEE's mission is:

1) to empower individuals by helping them assume responsibility for their own learning and personal development, and to contribute to the quality of life in their communities;
2) to promote definition, application, and evaluation of experiential learning; and
3) to support and guide Association members and other practitioners in their efforts to develop experiential learning within human service programs.

The Association is an international network of individuals, schools, and other educational organizations which share a common interest in and commitment to experience-based teaching and learning. The AEE was incorporated as a not-for-profit organization in 1977 and offers both individual and institutional memberships.

The articles found in this anthology were originally published in the Journal of Experiential Education, the official publication of the Association. Special thanks are due the editors of the Journal for their careful selection and editing of the original manuscripts. Dan Madden (1978-79), Anne Wasko (1980-81), Pamela Wood (1982), and Peggy Walker Stevens (1983-Present)

Among the benefits of membership in the Association for Experiential Education are the following: A subscription to the Journal of Experiential Education; a membership handbook; reduced rates at the annual conference; reduced rates on the Jobs Clearing House; a membership directory; consultant network. network resource assistance; and reduced rates on Association books and other publications. Interested persons should write to the AEE at Box 249-CU, Boulder, CO 80309.

TABLE OF CONTENTS

1984: The Orwellian Year of Educational Politics and
   Reform, by Richard J. Kraft..............................1

THE NATIONAL REPORTS..3

The Establishment Critics: A Summary of the Major Reports
   on Secondary Education in the 70's, by Richard A.
   Zajchowski..5
A Summary of the Major Reports, by Richard J. Kraft........13
A Nation at Risk: Another View, by AEE/CAEL/NSIEE.........20
A Conversation with Theodore Sizer, by Peggy Walker
   Stevens..23
A Nation at Risk Report: Is It Good for Students,
   by Diane Hedin...29
A High School Principal Looks at the National Reports,
   by Arnold Langberg.....................................35
Two Perspectives on the Crisis in Education, by Homer
   Page...39

GENERAL THEORY...43

Stress, Burnout, and Culture Shock: An Experiential,
   Pre-Service Approach, by Samuel J. Mungo...............45
Experiential Education: A Search for Common Roots, by
   Greg Druian, Tom Owens, and Sharon Owen................50
Designing Experiential Curricula, by Jed Williamson........56
A Marriage Proposal: Competency Based Education and
   Experiential Learning, by Sherrod Reynolds.............60
Challenging the Past, Present, and Future: New Directions
   in Education, by Arnold Shore and Ellie Greenberg.....66
Looking for Experiential Education in the Elementary
   School, by Casey Murrow................................71
Forum for Teachers, by Shirley-Dale Easley.................73
The Ultimate Challenge for Experiential Educators:
   Navigating into the Main Stream, by Albert M.
   Adams, II..75

CULTURAL JOURNALISM/FOXFIRE..................................89

A Look Back: The History of the Cultural Journalism
   Movement, by Murray Durst..............................91
Beyond Foxfire, by Elliot Wigginton........................94
English in the Treetops, by Peter G. Beidler...............98

EXPERIENTIAL LEARNING AND THE CLASSROOM.....................107

Experiential Components in Academic Courses, by
   G. Christian Jernstedt................................109
A Turn Down the Harbor, by Peter G. Beidler...............118
Do Your Homework: A Guide for Starting an Experiential
   Program in a School, by Peggy Walker Stevens..........127

Experiencing History, by Adolf Crew, James Brown, and
    Joyce Lackie..131
Experiencing History, by Raymond H. Muessig..............140
Melding Classroom Instruction with Real-World Problem-
    Solving, by John E. Gannon and G. Winfield
    Fairchild...143
The View from the Classroom, by Peggy Walker Stevens.....147
Experiential Learning in Political Studies, by
    David M. Purdy..151

SERVICE LEARING..155

Reclaiming a Wasted Resource: Youth, by Jim Kielsmeier..157
Return from the Mountain, by Alec Dickson................161
Fanning the Flame, by Lyn Baird..........................171
The Changing Role of Service in Outward Bound, by
    Robert S. MacArthur..174
Project Leadership Pairs Youth with Inner-City
    Children, by H. Dean Evans and Roberta Bowers.......180
"YES"-Upbeat Project Buoyed by Student Initiative,
    by Joy Hardin...183
Seeking Roots from Hahn to Greenleaf, by Anthony
    Richards..188
Fight Illiteracy with Volunteer Youth, by Jonathan
    Kozol...192

INTERNS AND APPRENTICES..197

Internship Education: Past Achievements/Future
    Challenges, by Tim Stanton.....................................199
An Introduction to Internship Education: New Roles for
    Students and Faculty, by Dennis Pataniczek and
    Carol Johansen..202
Educating Interns in a Child Life Program: The Agency
    Supervisor's Perspective, by Joan M. Chan...........206
Perspectives on Learning in Internships, by David
    Thorton Moore...213
Integrating the Traditions of Experiential Learning in
    Internship Education, by Jon Wagner..................218

RESEARCH AND EVALUATION..227

National Assessment of Experiential Education: Summary
    and Implications, by Dan Conrad and Diane Hedin.....229
The Judicial Process as a Form of Program Evaluation,
    by James Ellsberry...244
How to Creatively Evaluate Programs, by Alan Warner......248
Practical Evaluation for Experiential Education, by
    Judith Kleinfeld..254
Research Update: The Effects of an Experiential
    Aerospace Program on Career Maturity, by Betty
    Burkhalter and James P. Curtis.......................257
Johnny Says He is Learning...Through Experience, by
    Diane Hedin and Dan Conrad...........................258

Evaluating Experiential Learning Programs: The Case
    Study Approach, by Robert Stevenson..................263

PRACTICAL IDEAS..267

How to Process Experience, by Larry K. Quinsland and
    Anne Van Ginkel.......................................269
Chicken Gizzards and Screams in the Night: The Making
    of a Successful Simulation, by David Morrissey
    Moriah..275
Designing Processing Questions to Meet Specific
    Objectives, by Clifford E. Knapp......................278
Using Initiative Games to Assess Group Cooperation,
    by Alan Warner..281
Some Simple Initiative Tasks, by Jeff Witman..............283
The Idea Notebook...284
Organizing Brainstorms, by Kate Friesen...................288
The Idea Notebook, by Bert Cohen..........................291
The Idea Notebook, by Sherrod Reynolds....................292
Idea Notebook: The Encouraging Teacher, by Mike Pegg....293

BOOK REVIEWS...297

Book Review: Experiential Education Policy Guidelines,
    Experiential Education: A Primer on Programs,
    reviewed by Mary Jensen...............................299
Book Review: The Experiential Taxonomy: A Different
    Approach to Teaching and Learning, reviewed by
    Barbara Shoup...300
Book Review: Cheez! Uncle Sam: What Price Justice?,
    reviewed by Al Adams..................................301
Books in Review: Cognition and Curriculum: A Basis for
    Deciding What to Teach, reviewed by William G.
    Larmer..303
Books in Review: Teaching as a Conserving Activity,
    reviewed by Bert Horwood..............................304
Book Reivew: Growing up Suburban, by Peter T. Klassen...306
Books in Review: Educating for a New Millennium: Views
    of 132 International Scholars, reviewed by Dan
    Conrad..307
Guest Editorial: Becoming "High-Risk" Educators, by
    Maryann Hedaa...310
Books in Review: Mindstorms, reviewed by Peggy Walker
    Stevens...311

HIGHER EDUCATION...312

Impelled into Experience: The United World Colleges,
    by David Sutcliffe....................................315
Student Orientation in Wilderness Settings, by Michael
    Gass and Pamela J. Kerr...............................320
Are Good Teachers Born or Made? A Canadian Attempt at
    Teacher Midwifery, by Bert Horwood....................331
PROBE: Problem-Based Teacher Education, by Richard J.
    Kraft, John D. Haas, and Homer Page...................334

Editorial

1984: THE ORWELLIAN YEAR OF EDUCATIONAL POLITICS AND REFORM

by Richard Kraft

In 1957, the Soviet Union launched Sputnik I, providing the impetus for a massive Federal involvement in education in the United States. President Eisenhower and Congress vowed that we would catch up with the Russians in science and technology. The National Defense Education Act (NDEA) provided billions of dollars over the next decade to train teachers, conduct research, and develop curriculum materials in the natural and social sciences, mathematics and foreign language. Upon his election, President Kennedy announced plans to put a man on the moon by the end of the decade, but neither side in the Cold War was willing to admit publicly that the only thing really proven by the Soviet "first in space," was the superiority of their German scientists over our German scientists, rather than superior or inferior educational, political or economic systems.

A quarter of a century later, President Reagan has once again brought education to the forefront of the political agenda. The purpose is no longer to keep up with the Russians, as the massive defense budget is doing that quite well, but rather to "catch up to the Japanese," whom the President, many governors and other politicians consider to have a superior educational system. Educational cycles in the Twentieth Century appear to have about a 25 year lifespan, and it is time for another round of reform. The early years of the century were ones given over to massive expansion of secondary education and the education of the millions of immigrants. The 1930's were a time of battles over progressive education, while World War II and the GI Bill saw mass higher education become the order of the day. The educational reform movement of 1983-84 is not unexpected, given that twenty-five years have passed since the failures of the Sputnik reforms. Without question, 1984 is the year in which more good and harm can be done in education than at any time in the past 25 years, and quite possibly at any time in this century.

If experiential educators are to have an influence on the direction of public and private education in the closing years of this century, it is critical that we act now. If 1983 was the "Year of Educational Reports," then 1984 is surely to be the "Year of Educational Legislation." In the State of Colorado alone, there are over 90 bills before the House and Senate to "improve" education. The Federal Congress has numerous bills before it, particularly in science, mathematics and technology education. President Reagan and every state governor have made education their number one priority for the 1984 legislative session and the campaign to follow.

As a member of the Colorado State Board of Education, I have been privileged and condemned to sit through one of the most intense years of educational lobbying in decades. Almost every state and local board of education in the nation is now faced with a reform agenda, and thousands of rules and regulations affecting every child and young person in this country will be decided in the coming months. The following abbreviated list is but a small portion of an array of issues now before your state and local boards.

1) Tenure, merit pay, and career ladders for teachers.
2) Certification and recertification reforms for elementary and secondary teachers.
3) State mandated graduation requirements for high school students.
4) Minimum competency tests for high school graduation.
5) Competency tests for future and practicing teachers.
6) Expansion of the minimum hours per day and the length of the school year.

Dick Kraft is the Executive Director of AEE and an elected member of the Colorado State Board of Education from the Second Congressional District.

7) More requirements in writing, mathematics, science and technology, with greater use of computers and other high tech equipment.

If history teaches us anything, it is that educational reform is painfully slow. John Goodlad, whose report, *A Place Called School*, is reviewed later in this issue, details how little the classroom environment has changed throughout most of this century. Seventy years ago, most classrooms were characterized by teacher-talk, and in spite of computers, simulations, laboratories, movies, slides, discussion techniques, and countless experiential in-school and out-of-school activities, most classrooms today at both the elementary and secondary levels are still dominated by the teacher lecturing, giving instructions, disciplining, or testing.

Because much of the public sees the school in crisis and recalls how much better things were in the "good old days," the national, state and local reports tend to emphasize traditional, back-to-the-basics. The progressive ideas represented by the experiential education movement have never been tried on a mass scale, and if we are to impact what happens to the 50 million children in our schools, it is critical that we act immediately. The following suggestions are ways in which you can act to improve education in the coming months.

1) Run for your local Board of Education. It generally takes very little money, and in most communities a few well organized and committed friends can get you elected.

2) Offer to write a weekly editorial on education for your local newspaper. At the very least, write letters to the editor.

3) Call up the education writer or a general reporter from the local or regional paper and share with them your ideas, dreams, programs and plans. Send them a copy of the Joint Statement of Reform by AEE, CAEL and NSIEE published in this issue of the *Journal*. You would be surprised at how few people take the time to help "create" news for reporters.

4) Call your state Department of Education and ask to be placed on the mailing list for their State Board agendas. Hearings are held almost every month on changes in rules and regulations governing schools, and often few if any citizens appear to testify. This also can and should be done at the local level.

5) Lobby members of your local and state boards of education and members of the legislature. On most issues, no one bothers to contact us with the pros and cons, and a well stated argument often wins the day.

6) Offer to serve on local and state task forces on topics of interest and concern to you. There are over 175 state educational task forces operating during the spring, 1984, and thousands of local ones. Even if you can't serve on the task force, be sure to give testimony. Disgruntled citizens and ideologues with an ax to grind too often dominate these meetings.

7) Get to know your state representative or senator, and those that control the education and budget committees. I have never known one of them who was not willing to talk extensively on education. Education in most states takes up well over half of the state budget, and all legislators want to see those billions of dollars better spent. Monitor bills as they enter the legislative arena, and offer testimony before house or senate committees.

8) Conduct basic research or collect previous research on critical topics before Board and Legislatures. "The research says," is still one of the most powerful phrases in any hearing, and can often carry the day.

9) Join a political party, attend your local caucus, and get yourself elected to attend the county, district, and state conventions, where you can have input into the party platform. Although platforms are often ignored by candidates and the public alike, they are a good place to begin to surface your critical educational agendas.

10) Don't give up hope. Although educational change and reform is slow, all good ideas began small and then spread from class to class, school to school, state to state and eventually nation to nation.

We must act now. 1984 cannot go by without the ideas of the experiential education movement getting a hearing. Most of the rhetoric of 1983 was by the "back-to-the-basics" crowd. Although we too are for the Basics, we can ill afford to have the tried and disproven ideas of many of the national reports put into state law, and local and state board rules and regulations. We must offer progressive alternatives now, or we shall surely live to regret our inaction for another quarter-century.

I. The National Reports

THE ESTABLISHMENT CRITICS: A SUMMARY OF THE MAJOR REPORTS ON SECONDARY EDUCATION IN THE 70's

by RICHARD A. ZAJCHOWSKI

The critics of education in the 70's are a new breed advocating changes with far-reaching implications for experiential education. This article examines five major reports.

Less than a year ago, Neil Postman in an aritcle entitled "Where Have All the Critics Gone?" lamented the absence of serious criticism of education in the United States today. Having looked back nostalgically at the "tough, reality oriented critics" of the 60's — Holt, Kohl, Kozol, Hentoff, Herndon, Dennison and Silberman — Postman commented:

> And then suddenly it was over. The situation had not been much improved or even very much clarified. Everything, as of today, looks quite the same as before... What happened? Where did all the critics go?[1]

---
[1] Neil Postman, "Where Have All the Critics Gone?" *The Education Digest* XLIII:6 (February 1978): 20. The article is condensed from *New York University Education Quarterly*, IX (Fall 1977): 28-31.

Postman's contention that education has not changed much in the past decade is certainly debatable, but more to the point is the fact that critics of education — at least of *secondary education* — are still very vocal, if not as visible. The critics of the 70's, however, are a new breed. They sit on commissions and study groups sponsored by prestigious philanthropic foundations, government agencies and profesional educational organizations. These present day critics have been influenced by the critics of the 60's, or at least they express in a less strident and colorful way the same desire for significant change in the nature of secondary education that sparked the criticism of the 60's.[2] Indeed, it seems to me that unless one insists that the medium is the message, we have redical educational thought in the 70's without the radical expression of the 60's.

The work of these establishment commissions and panels in the 70's led A. Harry Passow, Jacob H. Schiff Professor of Education, Director of the Division of Educational Institutions and Programs, and Chairman of the Department of Curriculum and Teaching at Teachers College, Columbia University, to write in 1976:

It could well be that a combination of forces including better communication media, a press for community involvement and control, a youth population which differs from its predecessors, a new or at least different teaching profession, and better insights from the social and behavioral scientists could produce the conditions necessary for change being advocated. If so, the prospects for reforming secondary education are good — or at least better than they have been at any time since we began shaping America's high schools. Surely the need for reform has been established.[3]

Passow's remark concluded a review of the reform literature of the 70's, and his conclusions are the more potent because Passow is no millenialist.

I have quoted and alluded to scholars of education because it seems to me necessary to make a case — not a case for reform, but the case that the reform movement has continued and is underway in the United States today. The activity and ideas of this movement have not been widely publicized in the mass media. Even most educators, if asked about a reform movement in the 70's would probably, somewhat reluctantly, refer to the "back to the basics" movement. Basics are certainly a concern of the moment, but alongside of this thrust in education today there exists another — a quieter force but a significant one — that continues to insist that major changes are necessary in the *nature* of secondary education, and that these changes will lead us more in the direction of "experiential education" than is commonly realized or acknowledged. The reformers believe they are talking about basics in education too, but basics of a very different sort.

How has "the need for reform been established?" Between 1972 and 1976, five reports were published which made the case for reform in the mid-70's. These reports in turn spawned numerous, significant and independent commentaries, and new study groups. I will not attempt to summarize in this article the work of these "second generation" responses, though an annotated list of some of the most important ones appears at the end of this article. It is sufficient here to note that all of the responses to the five original reports, even when critical of specific proposals or sections of the reports, have tended to support the basic assumptions and recommendations of the original reports. What follows is a summary of the five original reports that set in motion and defined the reform movement of the mid-70's.[4]

"It could well be that a combination of forces including better communication media, a press for community involvement and control, a youth population which differs from its predecessors, a new or at least different teaching profession, and better insights from the social and behavioral scientists could produce the conditions necessary for change being advocated. If so, the prospects for reforming secondary education are good — or at least better than they have been at any time since we began shaping America's high schools. Surely the need for reform has been established."

Richard A. Zajchowski *was a faculty member of the Emma Willard School in Troy, New York, for fourteen years. Last year he worked for the Commission on Educational Issues, Newton, Massachusetts, as director of a project which produced an independent school commentary on recent reform reports on secondary education. He is a member of the Academic Committee and the Board of Directors of the National Association of Independent Schools, and is presently on the faculty at the Maumee Valley Country Day School in Toledo, Ohio.*

---

[2] See Lawrence Cremin's interesting analysis of the reform movements of the 60's and 70's in *Public Education* (New York: Basic Books, 1976), pp. 9-19 and 61-69.

[3] A. Harry Passow, *Secondary Education Reform: Retrospect and Prospect* (New York: Teachers' College, Columbia University, 1976), p. 54. This booklet provides a thorough and readable history of American educational reform. The observation that the case for reform has been established is also made by William Van Til in "Reform of the High School in the Mid-1970's," *Phi Delta Kappan* 56:vii (March 1975): 493. Van Til emphasizes that the recommendations of the 70's critics carry the weight of the prestigious group which sponsored their work. Van Til will be quoted below; his "editorial" is the best short piece (two pages) I have seen on the reform movement of the 1970's.

[4] My summary of the reports is taken *verbatim* from my summary which appears in *The Expanding School Environment* (Commission on Educational Issues, 1978), pp. 2-12, and is little more than abstracts and collations of numerous summaries of the reports, especially those of John Esty "Emergency Reform Movement in Secondary Education," a conference working paper, Educational Development Corporation, May 23-24, 1974; and Gordon Cawelti, *Vitalizing the High School*, Association for Supervision and Curriculum Development, 1974.

YOUTH: TRANSITION TO ADULTHOOD

A Report of the Panel on Youth of the President's Science Advisory Committee

James S. Coleman

This Coleman report (sometimes called Coleman II, to distinguish it from Coleman's earlier report on inequality) is the key document in the 70's reform movement, perhaps because it moved the focus of discussion away from the high school. The Coleman panel — composed of sociologists — set out to study youth, not schools. Its report is the most comprehensive and carefully reasoned of the national reports.

The Coleman report is a study of the age group 14-24, and of the social context in which this age group matures. The panel studied trends since the 19th century in age grouping, the legal rights of youth, demography, the economics of youth, and educational institutions, in addition to examining the youth culture and the biological, psychological and socio-cultural aspects of adolescence and youth. The Coleman report documents in a powerful way the changing social context in which youth has matured, and offers some tentative and qualified recommendations for changes in the education of youth based on these social changes. Subsequent responses to this report have questioned methodology and interpretation, but few to my knowledge have seriously questioned the general drift of the panel's observations on changes in the social context of youth.

Coleman's panel seeks to identify those environments in which youth can best grow into adults, in all ways, not merely intellective ones, and it begins with the assumption that school as now constituted is not a complete environment "for the accomplishment of many important facets of maturation." On the basis of its research it finds:

- Historically, work — economic productivity — has been a significant factor in youth's transition to adulthood. Recently the young have been kept out of production in order to increase their eventual opportunities. Therefore schooling has become a more significant factor.
- Youth spend more time in school and away from adults than in years past. Within the school, age segregation is the usual form of organization. Both age integration within the school and more contact with adults would be more desirable.
- Although there has been an evolutionary increase of rights for young adults, there is still much overprotectiveness.
- Young people are responsive to shifting job opportunity patterns, but there is little assurance that there will be sufficient professional jobs for the increasing number of college graduates.
- The 60's were unique in the heavy concentration of population in the 14-24 age group, and this bulge led to a strain on institutions serving this group.
- High schools have become too large and homogeneous; higher education has become more diverse and accessible. These factors have contributed to the restiveness of youth.
- The biological development of youth has accelerated but does not appear to have had much effect on schools' expectations of them, or on their psychological maturity.
- The youth culture now seems to have these characteristics:
  — inward-lookingness
  — close "psychic attachment" of youth to peer group
  — "press toward automomy" which leads to challenging of adults
  — frequent concern for the underdog

The Panel recommends, on the basis of research and discussion:

- More specialized schools, and free choice in pursuit of appropriate alternatives to the comprehensive school.
- Smaller schools to encourage age integration and improved interpersonal relations.
- Introduction of roles other than the "student" role within school. Assignments to tutor younger children, for example, would encourage responsibility and helping relationships.
- School as an agent for placing students in out-of-school learning sites such as museums, libraries, work or public service opportunities.
- Encouragement of work-study programs, and experimentation with half-day school/work patterns.
- Encouragement of work organizations that incorporate youth and provide structured learning experiences for youth at the work place.
- Establishment of youth communities or organizations which are largely self-

- Expansion of federally funded public service programs to promote public service and contact with adults for years 14-24.
- Research on existing institutions and on programs proposed by the Panel to determine effectiveness as youth environments.

It cannot be emphasized too much that Coleman's intention in *Youth* is to raise questions and initiate debate. The Panel makes recommendations in the hope they will clarify or particularize the larger issues raised by the study and in need of public discussion. For it does believe "it is time to reappraise the contexts of youth, to question even the most accepted and ordinary aspects of their current institutional settings, and to consider the reformation of existing structures and if necessary the creation of new ones."[5]

THE REFORM OF SECONDARY EDUCATION

A Report to the Public and the Profession, by the National Commission on the Reform of Secondary Education, Sponsored by the Charles F. Kettering Foundation

B. Frank Brown

Coleman's focus is primarily on youth, and secondarily on schools; Brown's emphasis, indeed the committee's charge, it clear from the title of the report. The Commission was established to "make a comprehensive examination of secondary education and provide the American public with a clear, factual picture of their secondary schools, indicating where and how they can be altered to better serve the nation's young people."[6] In a sense, the report outlines the ways schools can accommodate to the observations of Coleman, as well as to additional observations about schools made by the Reform Commission itself.

The Brown report is comprehensive, perhaps too much so, for it makes very specific recommendations on a wide variety of subjects and issues in too cursory a fashion at times. The report is organized so that each of 32 recommendations is followed by the rationalization for it, and this presentation is in strong contrast to Coleman and its slow accretion of a case for reform. It should be noted, however, that the case for reform in Brown has a broader base of support to begin with, for it was built on monthly hearings throughout the United States and tested on national panels of teachers, parents, students and administrators.

Brown's view of the state of secondary schools is a sobering one and must be understood to appreciate many of the Reform Commission's recommendations. Brown finds:

- in roughly ten years, the costs of operating high schools has doubled.
- student populations are coming from more diverse or "inconsistent social" backgrounds.
- schools are becoming "the victim of an economy of declining populations," having been the country's fastest growing enterprise.
- we have moved quickly from teacher shortage to teacher surplus, and the result will be an older teacher force.
- a decade of change and innovation in the schools had little or no lasting effect on the content of school programs or the quality of teaching and learning."[7]
- absence, tardiness, and class-cutting are rampant; crime is increasing in the schools. High schools are "beleaguered institutions" with some urban systems "on the verge of collapse."
- the pressures of marked social change and resultant sudden and traumatic changes in mission exhaust "the strength of the high school as an organized institution."
- the "deschooling" of society cannot be taken very seriously; the high school is still the key educational institution.

The thirty-two recommendations of the committee vary considerably in magnitude, and I will summarize only those which add to Coleman's recommendations in a significant way.

- Schools and communities in partnership should develop new statements of goals, and work together to achieve them.
- High schools should not be "required to perform purely custodial functions."
- Performance-based instruction which necessitates specific detailing of objectives should be the basis of curricular revision.
- Career education should be expanded with community help, with actual job experience and ex-

---

[5] James S. Coleman, et al., *Youth Transition to Adulthood* (Chicago: University of Chicago Press, 1974), p. 3.
[6] B. Frank Brown, et al., *The Reform of Secondary Education* (New York: McGraw-Hill, 1973), p. xiv.
[7] Brown, et al., pp. 7-8.

panded job placement part of the 11th and 12th grade program.
- All secondary students should receive a basic global education which stresses the globe as a human environment requiring interdependency.
- Alternative paths to a diploma should be available and fully supported, with students assuming responsibility for formulation of educational goals, developing their own learning activities and appraising their progress.
- Scheduling and accrediting of learning must be made more flexible.
- Secondary schools should establish extensive credit programs for accomplishment or work outside the school.
- Research should determine the influence of television on student's lives, values, and learning, and television should be exploited as an educational medium.
- High schools should stop calculating student rank in class.
- Every school should develop a code of student rights and responsibilities, and schools must grant and respect rights of youth.
- Compulsory attendance should be eliminated and the formal school leaving age should be dropped to fourteen. Only eight years of schooling should be compulsory, although every citizen should be entitled to fourteen years of tuition free education, available when he chooses.

THE EDUCATION OF ADOLESCENTS

The Final Report and Recommendations of the National Panel on High School and Adolescent Education

John Henry Martin

As the title of this report suggests, the panel focuses on both young and schools, though youth from 14-18, not 14-24 as in Coleman. The panel takes a broad view, moves easily between the nature and needs of youths and schools, and develops a smaller number of issues in individual chapters more thoroughly than Brown. It takes a very sympathetic view of the high school, seeing its shortcomings as inherent in the many demands made of it. It proposes a narrower role than at present for the high school in the future, and a greater role for the community in the education of youth.

Two other observations seem relevant, and may reflect the panel's charge to advise the Office of Education on the role the federal government should play in assisting or promoting change. The panel is very sensitive to the organization and management of the school, and sees organizational and management problems, caused largely by factors outside the school, as the source of the schools' present condition. Second, if Coleman focuses on youth, and Brown on schools, one comes away from Martin with an awareness of the community as an educational resource, though the interrelationship of youth, school and community becomes the subject of each of the three reports.

Martin's panel discovered that:

- in the pursuit of universal education we have concentrated on administrative and managerial problems.
- in our desire for diversity of offerings, our responsibility for all-day supervision, and our concern for class integration we have centralized high school education into ever larger plants.
- organizational assumptions, particularly the idea of the comprehensive high school and its necessarily large size, are responsible for many of the problems identified, e.g., age segregation, resistance to change, student alienation; the priorities of management have precluded adjustment to changing student characteristics or societal conditions, and even make human consideration of individuals difficult.
- we have innocently believed that the high school "could serve as a major if not sole instrument with which to cure our social ills" and this faith in the school as "cultural carrier and therapy agent" has weakened the intellectual function of the school. Schools are over-burdened because we fail to plan "multiple programs of education through other agencies and media."
- the custodial responsibilities are a great burden to schools and vital to their effectiveness.
- in keeping the schools free from political influence we have reinforced the isolation of the schools from all other educational enterprises.
- by concentrating education in the high school, we have isolated adolescents from younger children and adults.
- despite the evidence of earlier maturation of adolescents, schools as an institutional imperative tend to prolong dependency.

- responsibilities for broadening educational opportunities should not be imposed on the high school, but shared with other community institutions working in a coordinated relationship with the school. Reform thus far has been intramural, rather than community based, and therefore lacking in public support or commitment.
- the skills of systems analysts and designers should be used in a responsible way to bring a holistic view to the change process and to improve the nature and quality of research and organizational practice.

The Martin panel recommends that:

- we replace the concept of the comprehensive high school with that of comprehensive *education* which can be provided through a variety of means and in a variety of institutions.
- we create educational programs and institutions *in the community* in the arts, vocational education and local government (laboratories for citizenship) in which adolescents and adults will jointly participate.
- *ad hoc* specialized schools be created and staffed by professionals in the community.
- compulsory daily attendance in schools be reduced to 2-4 hours a day, and complementary education activities in the community with adults be made available.
- "the basic role of the high school as society's only universal institution for the education of the intellect be re-emphasized" and that basic competencies — including media literacy — be taught.[8]
- a "Community Guidance Center" independent of the school be created to coordinate the educational activities of schools and other agencies, and to arrange, schedule, evaluate and monitor services as well as record and communicate information about a student's program.
- the preceding recommendations be viewed as working hypotheses "to be rigorously tested through small scale adoptions, careful monitoring and ruthless evaluation."[9]
- we facilitate the earlier and increased entry of youth into the work force.
- we undertake "critical research . . . into the social and cultural roles and educational effects of the mass media."[10]
- we change accrediting procedures to accommodate experience and training outside the school and classroom.
- citizen and adolescent participation in planning and reviewing programs be required.
- the Office of Education and National Institute of Education sponsor research on the change process, especially on programs which are peer centered and democratic, and programs which will assist schools in planning.

[8] John Henry Martin, et al., *The Education of Adolescents* (Washington D.C.: U.S. Government Printing Office, 1976), p. 13.
[9] Martin, et al., p. 15.
[10] Martin et al., p. 106.

AMERICAN YOUTH IN THE MID-SEVENTIES

A Report of a Conference Sponsored by the National Committee on Secondary Education of NASSP (National Association of Secondary School Principals) and Financially Supported by the Stone Foundation, the U.S. Office of Education, the U.S. Office of Economic Opportunity, the White House and ACTION.

As Coleman was making the case that schools isolated youth from opportunities and experiences needed for adulthood, this conference was proposing that action-learning was one possible solution to this isolation. Action-learning was defined as follows:

Action-learning is learning from experience and associated study that can be assessed and accredited by an educational institution. It may be in paid jobs, in non-paid volunteer work, or in personal performance, as in publishing, art, drama or music in which participant learning is an objective. Action-learning has an element of novelty; it is not menial or repetitive. It is not classroom work; it takes place in the company of other performers. Part-time action-learning programs will usually complement formal study in school or college. Full-time assignments may involve guided study on the job.[11]

The papers given at the conference were in four categories: (1) the need for action-learning programs; (2) institutional views on action-learning, including unions, state educational agencies, and public agencies; (3) action-learning research and evaluation; and (4) action-learning project examples.

Many of the observations on youth in schools and youth in the work force duplicate those of the commissions described above, but a few are of special interest.

- a survey of three dissimilar American cities reveals enough workplace openings for teenagers on a part-time basis.

[11] *American Youth in the Mid-Seventies* (Washington D.C.: National Association of Secondary School Principals, 1972), p. vi.

- there is not yet much empirical evidence that action learning produces significant affective growth in teenagers.
- there is little evidence that action-learning produces an increased sense of civic responsibility.

Specific recommendations to the National Committee on Secondary Education of the NASSP all dealt with ways of publicizing and forwarding the action-learning concept. Of more relevance for our purposes might be the following conclusions of four working seminars of the conference:

- action-learning is useful and desirable and should be integrated into the total educational program of a community.
- the criterion for validating action-learning projects should remain flexible to foster a variety of programs.
- action-learning should receive graduation credit — both in high school and college — and should have the same status as academic learning.
- individual schools should assume primary responsibility for formulating goals, objectives and design of programs.
- possible legal problems, such as child labor laws, accident liability and insurance, and workman's compensation need to be explored.
- more research and evaluation must take place, both in terms of the process taking place and the outcomes in the lives of the students.[12]

THE GREENING OF THE HIGH SCHOOL

A Report on a Conference, Sponsored by the Education Facilities Laboratories and IDEA

Ruth Weinstock

[12] American Youth in the Mid-Seventies, pp. 97-100. Much of the wording in the summary of conclusions is that of the original report.

The report of this conference gives good examples of action-learning programs in high schools, because the conference was called to present non-conforming models of programs and settings, and to discuss alternatives and options. The report is a discursive one, often iconoclastic and irreverant in tone, but important because the model programs described are appealing and show that significant alternatives are possible and do exist. The report includes in an appendix a persuasive keynote address by Harold Howe entitled, "How you gonna keep 'em down at the school after they've seen TV?"

At the conference there was general agreement on:

- the need to "dejuvenilize" the school by granting youth more responsibility.
- the need for those with knowledge and experience of new programs and young people to make their knowledge known and operable.
- the need to honor the individuality of every young person.
- the need to reorganize and integrate the vast amount of education that goes on outside the school.

There was disagreement on:

- whether disadvantaged youth are not better served by traditional programs.
- the socializing and learning from peers that might be lost as more out-of-school learning took place.

The center portion of the report describes eight educational programs that take youth out of the school, bring the community into the school, or modify the schedule or organizational arrangement significantly.

* * * * * *

William Van Til, Coffman Distinguished Professor in Education at Indiana State University, has provided the best single par$graph summary of these five reports that I have seen:

> The mid-1970's high school reform proposals encompass a variety of problems and are naturally different from each other to some degree. *In general*, however, the reports are critical of contemporary high schools as too-large, age-segregated, overly separated, quasi-custodial environments for adolescents which do not sufficiently provide youth a transition to maturity and the adult world of work and community participation. *In general*, the reports support smaller, more diverse, age-integrated, and community-related schools characterized by both academic and action learning and supplemented by alternative paths to maturity through experiential learning by way of business-industry work organizations, social involvement opportunities, and community education centers.[13]

The critics of the 70's all agree on the need to devise new ways of assisting youth in the transition to adulthood. All are concerned with the "non-intellective" growth and with breaking down the isolation of the schools. Whether they speak of *participatory education* — learning by doing what is socially useful, personally satisfying and health-supporting for the individual and community (Martin); *action-learning* (NASSP); or *career-education* (Brown), they promote learning which is a combination of action and reflection, and which they believe will become more vital and appropriate to needs of adulthood by becoming less abstract and vicarious. What emerges in the reports are proposals for a wide diversity of options; most all of which would take youth into the community: "alteration of school and work, work-study programs, public service or social service programs, action-learning experiences, educational travel, cross-age tutoring, education in specialized high schools or alternative schools, work organizations that would combine working-learning-teaching experiences and would terminate with GED school equivalency tests. Many of these experiences would be on an 'in-out' basis."[14]

If the "reformers" have their way — and we are not talking now of the angry critics of the 60's but the establishment ones of the 70's — experiential education will be an integral part of every young person's education in the future. It is, therefore, incumbent upon those of us who support experiential education to draw public attention to the reform reports, and ironic that most experiential educators are unfamiliar with them. Experiential education is the keystone of current educational reform literature. If it is to become central in the educational *practice* of our schools, experiential educators must ally themselves with the establishment critics — an unexpected alliance perhaps, but one in the service of necessary changes in American education.

A Selected List of Responses to the Reform Reports

Catholic Secondary Schools and the Educational Reform Movement in American Secondary Education. Washington, D.C.: National Catholic Educational Association, 1976. In this special bulletin issued by the Secondary School department of the NCEA, Brother Victor Hickey reviews and reacts to the five reports. He is especially critical of the definition of purpose and of the relatively superficial concern with values education, the curriculum, and the school climate.

Cawelti, Gordon. *Vitalizing the High School: A Curriculum Critique of Major Reform Proposals.* Washington, D.C.: Association for Supervision and Curriculum Development, 1974. This pamphlet is a thorough summary and critique of the reform reports. The final chapter contains provocative sections entitled "Present Curriculum Deficiencies" and "Toward a Purposeful Curriculum Organization."

Gibbons, Maurice. *The New Secondary Education.* Bloomington, Indiana: Phi Delta Kappa, 1976. This Phi Delta Kappa Task Force Report moves from a consideration of compulsory education to the creation of an educational program which develops a "learning lifestyle." By far the most imaginative and exciting of the reports provoked by the reformers, it takes the reformer's thinking to a logical and comprehensive conclusion.

New Dimensions for Educating Youth. Washington, D.C.: U.S. Department of Health, Education and Welfare. 1976. This report of a Bicentennial conference co-sponsored by the Office of Education and the National Association of Secondary School Principals covers a wide range of concerns. It includes adaptations of general session addresses, reports on 20 workshops on specific topics, and descriptive articles.

Porter, John W., et al. *The Adolescent, Other Citizens, and Their High Schools.* New York: McGraw-Hill, 1975. This report is the work of Task Force '74, a National Task Force for High School Reform, assembled by the Kettering Foundation to follow up on the work of B. Frank Brown's National Commission on the Reform of Secondary Education. Task Force '74 focused on the issues of community involvement, collective bargaining, student responsibilities, and alternative programs as options.

The Rise Report. Sacramento, Calif.: California State Department of Education, 1975. This Report of the California Commission for Reform of Intermediate and Secondary Education is "a framework for overhauling education" in California. It makes clear that, in California at least, the reformers have been heard.

This We Believe, Reston, Virginia: National Association of Secondary School Principals, 1975. This report, prepared by the Task Force on Secondary Schools in a Changing Society, focuses in depth on the educational program of the secondary school. The Task Force confronts directly the need for flexible and diverse school programs.

Timpane, Michael, et al. *Youth Policy in Transition.* Santa Monica, California: The Rand Corporation, 1976. This report, commissioned by the Office of the Assistant Secretary for Planning and Evaluation, HEW, analyzes the reform reports in the light of recent research in the social sciences and suggests their policy implications. By far, this report is the most rigorous analysis of the reform reports.

The University of Chicago *School Review,* 83:1, November, 1974. This issue, devoted to a symposium on Coleman's *Youth: Transition to Adulthood,* contains some good criticism and a spirited and articulate defense by Coleman.

Zajchowski, Richard A., et al. *The Expanding School Environment.* Newton, Massachusetts: Commission on Educational Issues, 1978. An independent school response to the reform reports in which six school heads explore the need for and nature of the expanding school environment called for by the reformers.

---

[14] Brother Victory Hickey, "Review of the Five Reform Reports," *Catholic Secondary Schools and the Educational Reform Movement in American Secondary Education* (National Catholic Educational Association, March, 1976), p. 21.

A Summary of the Major Reports

by Richard Kraft

In 1978, Richard Zajchowski examined five major reports on education for the *Journal of Experiential Education*. Those reports, almost without exception, were supportive of experiential education in its many forms. They advocated improved transitions-to-adulthood, service learning, work-study, internships, flexible scheduling, consideration for student interests and needs, alternative paths to graduation, action-learning, a reduction in compulsory attendance rules, and a host of other "progressive" ideas. The educational critics of the 1970's recognized that much of education, particularly at the secondary level, was not functioning, and that the solutions lay not in a return to the past, but rather to a major restructuring in what happens to children and adolescents, both in and out of school.

In 1983, the "Year of the Public Schools," educational critics once again were out in full force, but this time most of the voices were raised in favor of traditional educational ideas. In this article, we shall summarize the major recommendations from the various studies. Few recommendations from the 1970's Task Forces were ever implemented on a large scale, and many of those that were tried were destroyed in budget cutbacks and the cries of "back-to-the-basics." Ignoring this fact that the "crisis" in which we find ourselves is due to the old ways in which we have been doing things, and not to "progressive" ideas which have never been implemented, many of the national and state reports call on us to return to the way we imagine things used to be.

The concern for education should be welcomed by all of us, as it contains the greatest possibility for change than at any time in the past quarter century. Those of us committed to experiential education can ill afford to remain on the sideline, while legislatures, governors, and state and local boards of education mandate major reforms. Political activism in 1984 is mandatory, if we are to move forward rather than backwards in our educational systems. An important place to start is with the national reports themselves.

Dick Kraft is the Executive Director of the Association for Experiential Education and also serves as Director of Teacher Education at the University of Colorado-Boulder.

A Nation at Risk

Without question, the most highly publicized educational report of 1983 was *A Nation at Risk*. This document was the result of a Task-Force appointed by President Reagan and Secretary of Education Bell, and was the first of the major reports. The document defines the crisis in extremely powerful terms.

"If an unfriendly foreign power has attempted to impose on America the mediocre educational performance that exists today, we might well have viewed it as an act of war." (National Commission, 1983,5)

"Each generation of Americans has outstripped its parents in education, in literacy, and in economic attainment. For the first time in the history of our country, the educational skills of one generation will not surpass, will not equal, will not even approach, those of their parents." (National Commission, 1983,11)

Such rhetoric captured the headlines of newspapers and the attention of educatonal decision-makers at all levels. Although the accuracy of some of the statistics given in the report has been questioned, the following "indicators of risk," have served as a major impetus for new legislation rules and regulations.

1) On an international comparison of achievement, American students were never first or second, and ranked last seven times.

2) Twenty-three million American adults are functionally illiterate.

3) Thirteen percent of all 17 year-olds are illiterate, and among minority youth, illiteracy is as high as 40 percent.

4) Test scores have been dropping for two decades.

5) Remediation is costing universities, businesses, industry, and the military millions of dollars.

6) Gifted students are not being challenged, and science and mathematics achievement continues to drop.

To deal with these and other problems, the National Commission on Excellence made the following recommendations.

RECOMMENDATIONS

1. Strengthen high school graduation requirements through 4 years of English, 3 years of mathematics, 3 years of science, 3 years of social studies, and 1/2 year of computer science, along with 2 years of foreign language for the college-bound.

2. Schools, colleges and universities need to adopt more rigorous and measurable standards as well as higher expectations for academic performance and student conduct.

3. More time needs to be given to learning the "New Basics" through better use of the school day, a longer school day, or a lengthened school year.

4. The schools need brighter, better educated, and better paid teachers and administrators.

5. The schools need better leadership from principals and superintendents, and the local, state and Federal governments must provide the leadership, fiscal support, and stability to bring about the reforms.

The Commission on Excellence conducted hearings throughout the country and commissioned many studies, but appears to have ignored what it heard and read, in favor of a more politically palatable attack on public education, with a call to do more of the same. The report has done a major service in laying out the problems, but is the most conservative of the national reports in its recommended solutions. Experiential educators can use the statistics and powerful rhetoric to help build the case for needed educational reforms, but will find little support for its underlying philosophy or educational methods.

The Commission comes down squarely on the side of learning taking place within the formal educational institutions of the society, rather than through informal or non-formal experiences. Interdisciplinary studies are hardly mentioned in the recommendations to require more of each of the "Basics." Acquisition of measurable content is the major, if not only, mechanism for measuring achievement, and little value is placed on the needs or interests of the students. The authoritative and authoritarian role of the teacher and principal underly much of the report, rather than an emphasis upon all participants being both learners and teachers. Vocational education, work-study, internships and other experiential modes of learning are hardly mentioned, and certainly do not play a prominent role in what the Commission sees as necessary for the reform of education in this country.

High School

While the President's National Committee on Excellence has received the most publicity and has served as the major impetus for reform, the Carnegie Commission report, *High School*, is likely to turn out to be the most influential of the year. In addition to a careful diagnosis of the various problems facing secondary education, Ernest Boyer and his staff have produced a document filled with positive suggestions for change. While the President's Commission tended to ignore the research and reports of the past decade, the Carnegie Commission built on those studies, and added careful observation of its own. Rather than producing a political diatribe, Boyer and his staff conducted a careful field study of 15 high schools, using knowledgeable observers and researchers.

After a description of the research leading up to its conclusions, the Commission concludes with the following recommendations.

RECOMMENDATIONS

1) High Schools must have a clear and vital mission. Goals must be clearly stated and shared by teachers, students, administrators and parents.

2) Language, oral and written, is central to the success of all students.

3) A core of common learning is essential. This core should be expanded to include up to 2/3 of the required units, and should contain work on literature, U.S. history, western civilization, non-western civilization, science and the natural world, technology, mathematics, foreign language, the arts, civics, health, and work.

4) High schools must help young people make the transition from school to the world of work or higher education. The last two years of schooling should contain an elective cluster helping students to explore a career option or do further study in selected academic subjects.

5) A new Carnegie unit in SERVICE should be part of all high school student requirements, to help students meet their social and civic obligations.

6) Working conditions for teachers must improve, with a better reward structure, recruitment incentives, and better training programs to attract better qualified persons.

7) Instruction must be improved through the use of a variety of teaching styles. There should be a particular emphasis upon the active participation of the students.

8) Technology, particularly computers, should be used to enrich instruction and extend the teacher's reach.

9) Flexibility in schedules, size of classes, size of schools and types of programs should characterize secondary education in this country.

10) Principals must be more than administrators. They should be the educational leaders of their schools.

11) Connections to lower and higher education, business and industry must be strengthened.

12) Support for the schools must be strengthened at the local, state and national levels.

The Carnegie Commission is not just making recommendations, but is putting millions of dollars over the coming years to help implement them. Recognizing that education reform is best done at the local level, it is providing initial seed money for hundreds of secondary schools to explore ways of bringing about one or more of the reforms.

For experiental educators, the Carnegie report is like a breath of fresh air in its call for community involvement, oral and written literacy progams, the importance of a transition to the world of work, the formation of a service ethic in our youth, an experiential base for teacher training, the active participation of the student in his/her learning, and the need for flexibility in schedules, class sizes and programs. The report is based on the real world of adolescents, rather than the mythical past or technocratic future, and experiential educators would do well to use it in bringing about reforms in their local schools.

The Paideia Proposal

For over half a century, Mortimer Adler has been an advocate of a classical education for all young people. As

chairman of the Paideia Project, a group made up of university scholars and public school administrators, Adler has authored the most scholarly of the numerous educational reports. Some basic assumptions underlie the *Paideia Proposal*: the tracking system is inherently unequal and must be abolished in favor of quality education for all young people; all children are capable of learning, regardless of background or ability; and schools must help to create lifelong learners who have the ability to learn on their own.

Education should have three basic goals:

1) Every child should be able to look forward to a lifetime of personal growth or self-improvement - mental, moral, and spiritual.

2) The schools should cultivate appropriate civic virtues and an understanding of the framework of our government and of its fundamental principles.

3) Young people should be prepared to earn a living, not by training for a particular job, but by possession of the basic skills common to all work.

To achieve these goals, Adler and the Paideia Group advocate the same course of study for all children for 12 grades, with only one exception - the choice of a second language. The proposed curriculum depicts in three columns three distinct modes of teaching and learning. The three columns are integrated and rise in complexity and difficulty throughout the twelve years of schooling.

The Same Course of Study for All

	COLUMN ONE	COLUMN TWO	COLUMN THREE
Goals	ACQUISITION OF ORGANIZED KNOWLEDGE	DEVELOPMENT OF INTELLECTUAL SKILLS – SKILLS OF LEARNING	ENLARGED UNDERSTANDING OF IDEAS AND VALUES
	by means of	by means of	by means of
Means	DIDACTIC INSTRUCTION LECTURES AND RESPONSES TEXTBOOKS AND OTHER AIDS	COACHING, EXERCISES, AND SUPERVISED PRACTICE	MAIEUTIC OR SOCRATIC QUESTIONING AND ACTIVE PARTICIPATION
	in three areas of subject-matter	in the operations of	in the
Areas Operations and Activities	LANGUAGE, LITERATURE, AND THE FINE ARTS MATHEMATICS AND NATURAL SCIENCE HISTORY, GEOGRAPHY, AND SOCIAL STUDIES	READING, WRITING, SPEAKING, LISTENING CALCULATING, PROBLEM-SOLVING OBSERVING, MEASURING, ESTIMATING EXERCISING CRITICAL JUDGMENT	DISCUSSION OF BOOKS (NOT TEXTBOOKS) AND OTHER WORKS OF ART AND INVOLVEMENT IN ARTISTIC ACTIVITIES e.g., MUSIC, DRAMA, VISUAL ARTS

THE THREE COLUMNS DO NOT CORRESPOND TO SEPARATE COURSES, NOR IS ONE KIND OF TEACHING AND LEARNING NECESSARILY CONFINED TO ANY ONE CLASS

Like the ancient Greek model on which this proposal rests, all students would be required to take physical education and participate in intramural sports. Manual activities such as typing, cooking, auto repair, and maintenance of household equipment would also be required for part of the time, along with career exploration.

As if speaking directly to experiential educators, Adler clarifies Dewey's oft-quoted maxim that "learning is by doing."

"*What John Dewey had in mind was not exclusively physical doing or even social doing-engagement in practical project of one kind or another. The most important kind of doing, so far as learning is concerned, is intellectual or mental doing. In other words, one can learn to read or write well only by reading and writing... To learn how to do any of these things well, one must not only engage in doing them, but one must be guided in doing them by someone more expert in doing them than oneself.*" (Paideia, 1982, 52)

Like the other reports, the *Paideia Proposal* also speaks to the training of teachers, the role of the principal, and the better use of school time. It is the least specific, however, on how reforms should be implemented. It is perhaps best seen as a plea for the liberal arts and the passing on of the intellectual and aesthetic heritage to all children, regardless of ability, social class, race or other differences which have traditionally separated them. Such a goal is admirable, but when considering how feasible it will be to implement such a system, this report sounds utopian compared to the others.

A Place Called School

The most carefully researched of the 1983 reports on education is John Goodlad's *A Place Called School*. The research on which the book was based involved 38 schools in 7 states, and included 1,350 teachers in 1,000 classrooms. Over 17,000 students participated in the study and 8,600 parents were surveyed and interviewed. Unlike the Carnegie report, Goodlad's study covered education from kindergarten through grade 12. This book is by far the most detailed of any of the reform documents due to the extensive research which went into it. Unlike most of the reports, however, the recommendations for reform are scattered throughout the four hundred page report, and are so numerous that the following listing is limited to the major and most provocative reforms.

As an educator, Goodlad recognizes the difficulty in bringing about rapid educational reform, and continually cautions against quick fixes mandated by the state or federal government. He also recognizes that most meaningful reform must come at the local school level and must involve all the participants, or it is doomed to almost certain failure. *A Place Called School* is unique among the various reports in giving a detailed description of what actually occurs in the schools and individual classrooms throughout the United States, and it does an excellent job of pointing up the failures and weakneses of traditional education today. Rather than making global prescriptions for more mathematics, foreign language, or other subjects, it speaks in great detail about how the total educational environment or ecosystem can be improved to meet social, civic, personal, and cultural goals.

RECOMMENDATIONS

1) More time needs to be spent on teaching higher order skills, rather than the current emphasis on factual information.

2) Too much time is spent on "teacher talk." Other teaching methods more actively involving the students must be used. Specifically, discussion, writing, problem-solving and analysis are recommended.

3) A core curriculum made up of a common set of concepts, principles, skills and ways of knowing should be developed. This is not a core of topics or subjects, as most other reports have recommended.

4) Mastery learning, which can significantly improve achievement and cut down on failure, can be a valuable tool in improving the schools.

5) Vocational education which does not train for work should be eliminated, and hands-on experiences should be more extensively used.

6) Tracking and minority overrepresentation in vocational programs must be eliminated. The best education for the world of work is still a general education.

7) A better use of instructional time is critical in improving the schools. Too much time in many schools and classrooms is spent on housekeeping chores, discipline, getting the class started etc. All schools should aim for a minimum of 25 hours of actual instructional time per week. The concept of "engaged" time is of critical importance, rather than just spending time in a classroom.

8) The curriculum should aim for:

a) 18% of student's time on literature and language
b) 18% on mathematics and science
c) 15% on social studies and society
d) 15% on the arts
e) 15% on vocational education and career preparation
f) 10% on electives of the student's choice

9) Most of the top-rated schools in the study were small. Where small schools are impractical, schools-within-schools should be created. Non-graded mini-schools with four teachers and 100 students should be developed.

10) Teachers need a career ladder to provide an incentive for

excellence (head teachers, residents, interns).

11) Schooling should occur in four phases: Ages 4-7, primary; 8-11, elementary; 12-15, secondary; and 16-18, service and work/study. Compulsory education should start earlier and end earlier than is currently the case.

12) Better use of technology should improve education, and partnerships and networks with business, industry and the community must be developed.

Experiential educators would do well to make Goodlad's book required reading. Not only does it detail the significant problems to be found in our schools, and the failure of the traditional ways of teaching, but it makes countless suggestions for the teacher or administrator on how to change and improve. The book is short on political rhetoric and long on research based reform, and as such should be welcomed by all who are committed to improving the ways that children and adults learn.

Other Major Educational Reports

Space does not permit us to go into detail on the other national and state reports, but all agree with Governor Hunt of North Carolina, who chaired the Educational Commission of the States Task Force on *Education for Economic Growth*;

"We have heard now from many directions about the problems of our schools. We have had an abundance of research, a plentiful supply of analysis and an impressive piling up of reports. Public concern is rising. What is needed now is action: action for excellence." (Education for Economic Growth, 1983)

His task force concentrated on ways that governors, legislators, educators and business and industry can collaborate to improve education at the state level. Governors concerned about balancing their budgets made up a large number of the Task Force participants, so it is not surprising that the emphasis of the report is on mathematics, sciences and technology. Improvements in these areas are seen as a way out of economic stagnation and will lead to a more competitive position in the international marketplace.

The *Business-Higher Education Forum* document was prepared at President Reagan's request and focuses attention on industrial competitiveness. Like the Economic Growth Task Force, it focuses on science, mathematics, engineering, and collaboration between business, industry and education. It calls for retraining through a national displaced workers program using educational vouchers, and individual training accounts (ITA's) to give incentives to individuals to save for their training and retraining needs. Tax incentives, scholarship programs, and other economic incentives form the basis for much of the report.

The *Twentieth Century Fund* report calls for a new Federal policy on elementary and secondary education. While many of the other reports concentrate on what can be done at the state and local level, this report concentrates on Federal policy, and calls on the Federal government to meet the special needs of the poor, the immigrants, the bilingual, and handicapped populations. It calls for a core curriculum of reading, writing, calculating, computers, science, foreign languages and civics, with a strong emphasis on mastery of oral and written English.

The National Science Foundation report titled, *Educating Americans for the 21st Century*, concentrates its recommendations on the improvement of science and mathematics instruction from kindergarten through higher education. All students should take three years of mathematics and science and technology in high school, and schools should emphasize higher level problem-solving skills. The report spends a good deal of time on teacher recruitment, training and compensation, and calls for higher pay for math and science teachers, career ladders for teachers, raising standards to enter the profession, and many other related ideas. It also calls for massive Federal intervention in K-12 and higher education to improve the quality and quantity of science and mathematics training in this country.

Other Reports Completed or Due in Early 1984

The College Board
The Southern Regional Education Board

The Association for Supervision and Curriculum Development
The Northwest Regional Laboratory
The National Association of Secondary School Principals and the National Association of Independent Schools
The National Academy of Education
The Congressional Office of Technology Assessment
The National Institute of Education and the Ford Foundation
Stanford University

Summary and Conclusions

Many themes appear throughout the various reports. On the subject of teachers, they call for recruitment incentives to attract higher quality personnel, better pay, career ladders, revision of tenure laws, improved teacher training, and better working conditions. On curricular matters, most call for a diminution in the number of courses offered, a required core curriculum, better use of technology, particularly computers, a clarity of goals, greater variety in instructional procedures, and vocational education more closely tied to the real world of work. The school principal is singled out in most of the reports as the key individual, and most call for an expanded instructional leadership role. While some call for an extended school year and school day, most agree that better use of school time is essential. The role of the Federal, state and local governments in school reform differs in the various reports, but all call for greater connections between the schools and business, industry, higher education, and the community.

More good and harm for education is possible in the next year than at any time in the past twenty-five. The American schools have been dramatically successful in educating millions of students, but their failures are all too evident, and we must continue to speak out on the role of experiential learning both in and out of school.

References

- Adler, Mortimer J. *The Paideia Proposal*. New York: Macmillan Publishing Co., 1982.
- Association for Supervision and Curriculum Development. *Redefining General Education in the American High School*. Washington, D.C.: ASCD, 1983.
- Boyer, Ernest L. *High School: A Report on Secondary Education in America*. New York: Harper and Row, 1983.
- Business-Higher Education Forum. *America's Competitive Challenge: The Need for a National Response*. Washington, D.C., 1983.
- College Entrance Examination Board. *Academic Preparation for College: What Students Need to Know and Be Able to Do*. New York:, 1983.
- Goodlad, John I. *A Place Called School: Prospects for the Future*. New York:, McGraw-Hill, 1983.
- Joint Economic Committee of the U.S. Congress. *Computerized Factory Automation: Employment, Education and the Workplace*. Washington, D.C. (Spring, 1984.)
- Kennedy, Donald. *The Study of Stanford and the Schools*. Palo Alto: Stanford University. (1985).
- National Academy of Education. *An Education of Value*. Washington, D.C., 1984.
- National Association of Secondary School Principals and the National Association of Independent Schools. *A Celebration of Teaching: High School in the 1980's*. Washington, D.C.: NASSP. (Spring, 1984).
- National Commission on Excellence in Education. *A Nation at Risk: The Imperative for Educational Reform*. Washington, D.C.: Government Printing Office, 1983.
- National Institute of Education and the Ford Foundation. *Education, Character, and the American Schools*. Syracuse: Good Schools Project, 1983.
- National Science Board Commission on Precollege Education in Mathematics, Science, and Technology. *Educating Americans for the 21st Century*. Washington, D.C.: National Science Foundation, 1983.
- Northwest Regional Educational Laboratory. *Goal-Based Education Program*. Portland: NREL, 1983.
- Southern Regional Education Board. *Meeting the Need for Quality: Action in the South*. Atlanta, Georgia, 1983.
- Task Force on Education for Economic Growth. *Action for Excellence: A Comprehensive Plan to Improve Our Nation's Schools*. Denver, Colorado: Education Commission of the States, 1983.
- Twentieth Century Fund. Report of the Twentieth Century Fund *Task Force on Federal Elementary and Secondary Education* Policy. New York, 1983.

A Nation at Risk: Another View

A Joint Statement of
The Association for Experiential Education (AEE)
The Council for the Advancement of Experiential Learning (CAEL)
The National Society for Internships and Experiential Education (NSIEE)

The leadership of AEE, CAEL, and NSIEE met this past October at the Lake Geneva AEE Annual Conference to discuss ideas for collaboration on various projects. A collective response to A Nation at Risk was deemed worthy and a committee representing the three organizations set about the task. What follows is the product of several drafts and many hours of labor by the group.*

AEE members who support the statement are encouraged to "release it" to local media outlets, include it in newsletters and other publications, or reproduce it as a handout for friends and colleagues. Wide dissemination is the goal of the committee who drafted the statement.

Jim Kielsmeier, AEE President

1983 was the year to look at excellence. Thomas J. Peters and Robert H. Waterman, Jr., wrote about excellence in corporations in *In Search of Excellence*. George Keller wrote about excellence in institutions of higher education in *Academic Strategies*. The National Commission on Excellence in Education published its recommendations for excellence in the American educational system in *A Nation at Risk: The Imperative for Educational Reform*. All three studies seem to agree on some basic ingredients of a quality institution:
- a clearly articulated goal,
- the investment of all of the players in the (shared) goal, and
- attention to available, relevant research.

We, representatives of AEE, CAEL, and NSIEE, are concerned that the National Commission seemingly lost sight of these basic ingredients as it prepared its plan for ensuring quality in American education. The report does not address its original goal of educating to improve quality of life; instead, it focuses more on beating the competition in high technology. It virtually ignores the primary players, the students, as it focuses on teaching rather than learning. Finally, it ignores the large body of research about how and why individuals learn, how they develop cognitively, morally and socially, and how they differ among themselves. Instead, it makes recommendations for more homework and longer days for everyone.

We submit that there is a need to look again at what we are educating for, and to create learning environments which are attentive to students' and teachers' attitudes and which maximize the potential for learning despite individual differences. We believe that a major component of such learning environments must be opportunities for not only abstract but also experiential learning; that is, learning in which the learner is directly in touch with the realities being studied rather than simply reading about, hearing about, or talking about these realities.

A Sound Goal, A Flawed Strategy

The beginning of *A Nation at Risk* clearly articulates a goal for American education: "...that all children by virtue of their own efforts, competently guided, can hope to attain the mature and informed judgment needed to secure gainful employment, and to manage their own lives, thereby serving not only their own interests but also the progress of society itself." (p. 4) We applaud the implications of this statement, namely:
- that equity of educational opportunity be guaranteed,
- that individuals must assume responsibility for their own learning,
- that learning can be guided, facilitated, and
- that education is important not only to fulfilling career goals but also to enhancing the quality of life of individuals and ultimately of society.

We do not believe, however, that these goals will be realized if the strategies for reaching them are limited to more classroom experiences, longer hours in school, and more homework -- more of the same types of learning experiences with which many students and teachers are dissatisfied. Current research suggests that excellence in productivity results from close attention to the people in the organization -- how they feel about what they are doing and about the organization. *A Nation at Risk* ignores the fact that many of our students do not see their schools' programs as relevant in their lives, and many teachers feel they have no control. Longer days and merit pay will not change these attitudes, will not increase productivity. *The need is to change the environment.*

Changing the educational environment means acknowledging what research has proved: a) that genetic and environmental factors influence learning, b) that not everyone learns everything in the same way, and c) that learning is ultimately self-directed, an individual matter, and occurs best when motivation and interest are internal. A critical task of educational institutions is the design of learning environments and teaching strategies which allow for the differences in learning styles and which build up the intrinsic interests of the learners.

Toward a Better Strategy

We offer no nostrum for what is patently an enormous and a complex undertaking of the American educational system. But, quality in education is not primarily a matter of such things as time spent in class, of subject matter covered, or of teacher compensation. The most crucial factors in learning are strength of motivation, appropriateness of learning resources to the learning tasks, choice of strategies of inquiry, and the climate of the learning environments. If a genuine, lasting, and pervasive change for the better in American schooling is to be achieved, it will have to grow out of more thoughtful attention to these crucial factors.

For many learners, from the youngest to the oldest, the learning of certain concepts is most interesting -- and most successful -- when it comes through concrete experiences and involvement in practical problems (as confirmed in the work of Jean Piaget, James Coleman, and David Kolb). We "experiential educators" therefore advocate a mix of abstract and experiential learning. An environment providing this mix includes the laboratory as well as the classroom, includes occasions in which the teacher is primarily a facilitator rather than information-giver and includes occasions which are student-centered rather than teacher-centered. Sometimes the laboratory is a classroom, more often it is an environment more suited to the learning; e.g., the mountains, the inner city, a museum, a corporation, a government office.

We strongly recommend that a variety of forms of non-classroom, experience-based learning (e.g., internships, cooperative education, practica, clinics, outdoor education, service-learning, work-study) become part of the required curriculum of American schools and colleges. Across the country the experiential approach is proving successful in motivating students to learn and develop those skills, strategies, and attitudes which will enable them to be productive and responsible adults. There are clear reasons for the success:

The experiential approach is a powerful motivator for learning because it is positive, and meaningful, and real. The learning environment is success-oriented rather than competitive. It offers opportunities for real-life problem solving in which feedback is uncontrived and immediate and in which results are real-life physical and emotional consequences. Because the learners participate in the design, implementation, and management of their own learning, they are invested in the goal, hence internally motivated.

That motivation frequently transfers back to the traditional classroom as students recognize the need for more theoretical background, as they try to draw inferences and conclusions from their experiences, or as they find reasons to improve their basic skills. The need to write becomes important when one needs to write a report or proposal for a community organization. The need for theoretical understanding of human relations becomes important if one is helping in a crisis intervention center. Understanding of motivation is important when marketing a new product.

Additionally, by providing for integration of ideas and actions into the larger community, experiential learning facilitates the transition to adulthood and develops skills for responsible citizenship. Documented outcomes of experiential learning include concern for fellow human beings; the ability to get things done and work with others; self-motivation to learn, participate and achieve; an improved self-concept, confidence, competence, and awareness; responsibility to the group or class, openness to new experiences, and a sense of usefulness to the community.

Finally, experiential education contributes to the preparation of a well-educated and productive workforce. If our goal were merely to beat the Japanese in the high-tech race, we could train our students to be crack technicians through classroom experiences in math, science, and computer technology. If our goal is to prepare an enlightened citizenry to lead productive and purposeful lives and to contribute to the growth and development of society, then we must insure that they learn how to learn, how to grow and adjust to change.

Workers of the future need both generalized competence and specific job skills which may not apply to their future job requirements. Future jobs will require different skills, and workers must be prepared to meet the changing needs. We must teach students how to reflect on their experiences, define their learning goals, and independently manage their own learning. These outcomes require an education which combines experiential learning with abstract learning.

For more information consult one of these organizatons:

Association for Experiential Education (AEE), PO Box 249-CU, Boulder, CO 80309. (303) 492-1547.

Council for the Advancement of Experiential Learning (CAEL), 10598 Marble Faun Court, Columbia, MD 21044. (301) 997-3535.

National Society for Internships and Experiential Education (NSIEE), 124 St. Mary's Street, 2nd Floor, Raleigh, North Carolina 27605. (919) 834-7536.

Contributors to the statement were Jim Case (Ohio), John Duley (Michigan), Morris Keeton (Maryland), Jane Kendall (North Carolina), Jim Kielsmeier (Minnesota), Dick Kraft (Colorado), Barbara Leahman (Texas), Joan Macala (Illinois), Peggy Walker Stevens (New Hampshire), Don Vogel (Illinois)

A Conversation with Theodore Sizer

Interviewed by
Peggy Walker Stevens

Horace's Compromise: The Dilemma of the American High School, by Theodore R. Sizer, was published in March by the Houghton Mifflin Company. It is the first of three reports based on a five-year study of American high schools co-sponsored by the National Association of Secondary School Principals and the National Association of Independent Schools.

Theodore Sizer, director of the study, is a former dean of the Harvard Graduate School of Education and former headmaster of Phillips Academy in Andover, Massachusetts. As part of the study, he visited 80 schools in the United States and Australia in an attempt to get "the essential 'feel' of high schools." The book presents his findings and recommendations for reforming the schools.

Stevens: Why did you title the book *Horace's Compromise?*

Sizer: The book is about 40% stories because some of the subtler things I wanted to say about teachers and teaching are easier said with word pictures than with expository prose. Furthermore, books about education are terribly dull and story books are a little more fun. All of the portraits are real people, but some are composites; that is, I invented a 53-year old English teacher at a suburban public high school whose name is Horace Smith, a bad joke on Horace Mann. I describe at length how this composite character spends his day. Pieces of the day are all real classes taught by different people, but I've strung them all together in a kind of fiction/nonfiction way. The lesson which comes out of the extended anecdote of how Horace spends his day is that he has to make a whole lot of compromises. I mean, all of us have to make compromises in life. It's just that the ones he's forced to make by the system are really intolerable, and he knows that in the pit of his stomach although he doesn't like to express it.

Stevens: How does your report differ from the others?

Sizer: It's much narrower. The focus is just on high schools and primarily on the insides of high schools - teachers and kids. So it doesn't deal with a whole lot of other issues like teacher education, school finance, state role and all those other things, except by inference. It rests very heavily on a lot of listening to teachers and kids. The priorities for change are different in our case than those in many of the other reports. To oversimplify, I find the structure of the school not only remarkably pervasive across the country but also getting in the way. It's forcing Horace to make compromises that he shouldn't have to make. If you have 150 kids a day, 5 classes of 20, 30, 40 kids, there's no way you can get to know them. And if you can't get to know them, how can you figure out how their minds work? And if you don't know how each kid's mind works, how do you get them to think clearly? It doesn't need an awful lot of research - you just have to be able to add and multiply. The typical city high school teacher has, by contract, 5 classes a day, 35 kids each. Now, if you spend 5 minutes a day, even 5 minutes a week just reading the homework or talking outside of class to each of those students, you're talking a dozen or more hours. That system is the problem. Not the only problem, but certainly a fundamental problem, and you're not going to change the schools until you change the compromises that are made in the school. That's our message and it's not

> "Narrowly defined experiential education has suffered at the senior high school level because much of the important work... is, necessarily, abstract. You just can't do it very well."

the message you're hearing from some other quarters. It is the message we're getting from John Goodlad. And it is not for nothing that his research and ours, although quite different in the way we proceeded, are heavily field-based rather than holding hearings and that sort of thing.

Stevens: You would say, then, that all these reforms about increased teacher pay, increased graduation requirements, etc. are beside the point?

Sizer: They're not beside the point - teachers need to be paid more. Some of the diploma requirement improvements make some sense, but why add 20 days to the school year when the teachers are already incapable of doing the job in 180 days? Why make it 200? If you have 180 days of low quality, you're just adding 20 more low-quality days. It's missing the point.

Stevens: You say that your ideas will require new teacher behaviors. What are the types of roles that teachers will have to learn?

Sizer: Less talking and lecturing. Much more coaching where kids will be expected to do the work and the teacher will support that. This is where John Goodlad's research is so devastating. A large percentage of the time in classrooms that he and his army of people observed with their little stopwatches was spent in teacher talk, not surprisingly. If you have 5 classes a day, 175 kids, you don't have time to do anything else but talk. But people don't learn by being told things. I can lecture to you about how to write, but until you write you're not going to learn how to do it. So much more coaching is necessary and it's hard. For many teachers it's a new kind of pedagogy, and in many ways a very boring pedagogy.

Stevens: Why do you say it's boring?

Sizer: Well, you get 100 papers every other day - misspelled and silly prose - and you write all over it, trying to get kids to do better the next time. You give the papers back to them and two days later get another 100 papers. It can be pretty devastating But important! It's tough work. A lot of people like to stand up and talk about Marie Antoinette and they think that's teaching. You can tell about Marie Antoinette a little bit, but if you do nothing but tell stories... Some people get a kick out of pretending they're Herr Doktor Professor, lecturing. I think it will be really hard to shift teachers to coaching.

Stevens: What kinds of things would help teachers to make the shift?

Sizer: On-the-job training - teachers helping teachers. The best kind of thing is workshops using real kids, the real youngsters you're teaching, the department you're working with - that's the way to do it. It's going to be slow.

Also, people say, "Well, let's cut the teacher's load by 5%" Forget it. You have to cut it in half. Then you'd get somewhere. And the only way you can do that is by making some compromises on the other side. You can't double your teaching force. People aren't going to pay for that. So you have to give up some things. Right now we're compromising the wrong things. We're compromising on teacher load in order to provide a whole raft of good [subject] specialties and we can't afford to do that any more.

Stevens: In your article, you state that you found students to be docile and compliant.

Sizer: If you're being talked at all the time you can just sit there. [The teachers] have to start saying, "I'm not telling you the answer. You've got to find it and I won't even tell you the answer once you show me the work. I'll ask you a whole lot of questions about the steps you went through and ultimately you've got to tell me 'By God, *that's* the right answer' and then you have to figure out how to prove it.''

Stevens: What kinds of activities do you see students doing in this ideal school?

Sizer: There'd be a lot more hands-on kind of work. The easiest to describe is science and the most difficult is history. History is my own subject and in many ways the hardest to teach in school because it deals with this abstraction called time past. For a kid to get a sense of abstraction of what time is, you get them writing their autobiographies and the biographies of other people and then they begin to realize that history is nothing more than a collective biography. I think we can waste an awful lot of time thrashing around trying to make them pseudo-historians. There are certain kinds of "play" history and you can go too far in that direction, spending all of your time on some little local thing. You have to have balance. There is an awful lot of information out there that the kids ultimately should and will want to know and you can just tell them. The point I'm making is that we need a lot more balance. The example that I've always found telling is in teaching the Civil War - Pickett's charge. Pickett's Brigade had a lot of teenagers in it the same age as the students. And yet, knowing full well that they were going to charge across an open field into an absolute hail of gunfire from well-protected Yankee soldiers, they still did it. You ask the kids "Would you do it?" "Oh, no, I wouldn't do it. No way!" "Well Pickett's men all charged." "They all charged?" "Yes, they did." "Did they get killed?" "Yes, they did." "Why do you think they charged? What is it about a 19-year old in Pickett's Brigade that made him fix his bayonet and run right to certain death?" You try to create a sense of empathy for the values of the time. And that's history. That's real history. You have to give some sense of what it was like to be 18 or 19 in 1863.

Stevens: I've always found in teaching

cult to make it experiential because in both subjects you are vicariously experiencing someone else's life. Subjects like science and government lend themselves more readily to experiential education.

Sizer: Yes, it's like the advanced sciences. There is an abstraction and in many ways the abstractions of science are more difficult to empathize with than the 19-year olds in Pickett's Brigade. That's why narrowly defined experiential education has suffered at the senior high school level. Much of the important work at the senior high level is, necessarily, abstract. You just can't **do** it very well. At least it's not obvious. The hands on exercises are not obvious, or if they appear to be obvious they're spurious. When you set up a mini-government in your school and play United States Congress, it's a joke. And the kids know it's a joke.

> "Why add 20 days to the school year...? If you have 180 days of low quality, you're just adding 20 more low-quality days."

Stevens: That's also one of the reasons why people often only let you do experiential programs with the non-college-bound students. There's a sense that anything you do with them is more than they were doing before.

Sizer: That's right. And isn't that a sad commentary? We call them the "unspecial" majority.

Stevens: Do you see a role for experiential education in high schools?

Sizer: It depends on definitions. As John

> "Get the diploma connected to kids actually showing they know something, rather than serving time."

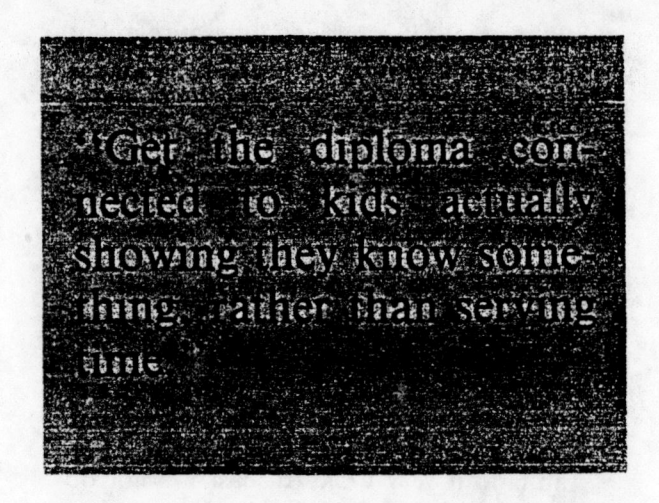

so the experience of thinking hard about some knotty problem is a form of experiential education, as all good education is experiential at one level. Without experience there wouldn't be learning. But that's not what you mean. It's narrower. My view is that a lot of what we now try to and often succeed at organizing as experiential education in fact is exploding in acceptance outside of the schools; the most important of that being work. One of the least expected facts that we are now confronted with in our work is the percentage of kids who work regularly for pay for strangers. The Coleman *High School and Beyond* data show that 60% of high school kids have jobs or are seriously looking for them. We've been in high schools where, particularly among twelfth graders, the kid who doesn't have a job is considered some kind of freak. Well, those kids are getting a lot of "experience," some of it quite demanding, much of it totally undermining the athletic and activities programs of the schools. A lot of schools essentially shut up at 2:30 and everybody, teachers and kids, go to work. That is a relatively new phenomenon; it wasn't the case in the sixties. There's not much demand for some kind of organized connection between that youngster [who works] and the real world - that youngster is deep into the real world... There may be stronger arguments for more organized, off-campus, experiential education at the middle school level than in the senior high school because many of those [older] kids are already out there.

To me, the trick in experiential education is not to let them get over their heads where they have some experiential assignment quite beyond their competence and they either end up faking it or making fools of themselves. You never want to exceed the kid's grasp. And to come up with a problem that the kids can solve in a legitimate way, not a fake way - that's hard to do. That's why the kid's own employment is probably the richest soil for careful experiential education... If a student has a demanding job, we can ask "How can we extend your knowledge in general by using the material you have to use in order to master your job?"

Stevens: But most kids don't have those kinds of demanding jobs.

Sizer: No they don't. Most have jobs at check-out counters, but there's a lot even in those jobs. All you have to do is watch them. Go to a mall after school and watch the kids. There's a lot of engagement there. There's a lot of things to work with. I mean, just dipping ice cream and putting it on ice cream cones for the people that come up involves a lot of facing of humanity. You deal with all kinds of people. You might be able to do very interesting things in the humanities with kids who have to see the public all the time. How do you deal with the making of an ice cream cone for the terribly crippled person? How do you help a person who is semi-senile make up her mind what flavor she wants? We've all seen people who can't make up their minds. What do you do? Yell at them? What do you do? And what does it mean? What is the paralysis, the inability to select an ice cream cone? What is it like for the person to be in a place in life where he can't do that? Oh, there are all kinds of things you can do to get kids thinking, reflecting.

Stevens: In your study, did you find that the kids who work don't value learning but want to have the diploma in case they need to get a job someday?

Sizer: That's why we think the diploma's so important. Get the diploma connected to kids actually showing they know something, rather than serving time. Then you get everything lined up right. Now a kid can work the 3 to 11 shift and do virtually no homework, show up regularly, be relatively orderly, and get a diploma even if that youngster's semi-literate. And that's too bad, that's cheating kids.

Stevens: How would a diploma based on achievement work?

Sizer: There would be what we call an exhibition. When a lot of people hear that they say, "Oh, great. We'll just give them machine-graded exams, a three-hour exam, and that's it." That's too narrow. To pass a test tells you something, but not everything. I think there ought to be a variety of ways that the kids can exhibit their mastery of the work. Some people display their knowledge better orally than in writing. People have to be able to lead with their strongest suit. There ought to be a variety of ways of showing off. There ought to be a limited amount of specific subject matter and a maximum amount of demonstrated skills. Subject matter you forget; skills are what you retain. It's a matter of indifference to me whether a youngster studies Modern European History or Modern Asian History. What I'm more concerned about is whether he can deal with some historical phenomenon that doesn't relate to his immediate American past. So I can see quite flexible areas set up where kids can show in a variety of ways how they do well in each of those areas. Complicated. Very complicated, but time spent setting up those exhibitions would be well spent. It would force a lot of issues and would give the kids a sense of what they needed to do. Then if they didn't do any homework and sat like munching cows in class, they would suddenly realize that the only loser was themselves. Kids want the diploma. If you set up incentives so they have to work to get it, they'll work. If you set up the incentives so that can just sit and be entertained, they'll sit and be entertained just like we would.

Stevens: In your study, you talk about making the curriculum more simple and reducing the number of subjects studied. Could you explain your ideas about this?

Sizer: There are many ways of making the curriculum more simple and the idea I've been fussing with is only one. The point is to say you have to simplify; you have to take our best understanding of different modes of inquiry or subjects or disciplines [and see how they] can be grouped in useful ways. For instance, literature and the arts [the art of language, the art of the visual realm, the art of music] have a great deal in common. They are the aesthetic realm. Right now we teach them in separate little specialized boxes: English, art, music, drama, public speaking. We fractionate them, split them up, and I'm sugesting that we put them all together. The same with the forms of expression of which writing and speaking are obviously important, but there are other forms of expression - gesture, use of a foreign tongue, painting, drawing, music. They're all aspects of expression and the sensible way to help a person who is learning how to express himself or herself, is to give them these various forms of expression in a connected way, not a disconnected way. So I approve of a curriculum which would consist of four areas: forms of expression and inquiry, math and science, history and philosophy, literature and the arts. Basically it's going back and thinking through the relationships of areas of knowledge with the imperative always behind you that you have to simplify. You no longer have the luxury of breaking things into further and further little pieces. You're going to have to go the other way. You're going to have to find what is important, what's at the core.

> "People say, 'Well, let's cut the teacher's load by 5%.' Forget it. You have to cut it in half. And the only way you can do that is by making some compromises on the other side."

> "The teacher must be coach, critic, cajoler, supporter, harasser, lover."

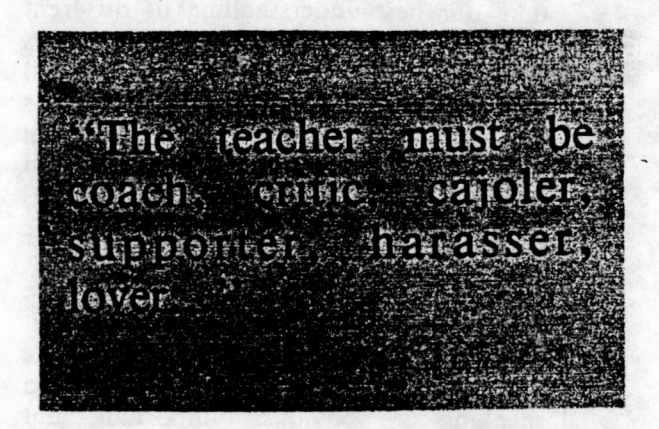

Stevens: What would you envision students doing in an inquiry and expression class?

Sizer: That has to be heavily, if you will, experiential. The only important thing is how the student uses her mind, not how I tell her to use her mind. You have to get the kid to [solve problems] and the problem may be an abstraction: "I want you to describe for me and define for me the concept and the word called cruelty. I want you to write me a paragraph, I want you to write me two bars of music, I want you to draw me a picture." The kid is dealing with an abstraction, but that's the kid's work. I just don't lecture, "Write after me: cruelty is..." and read the Webster's dictionary to the student.

Stevens: Doing something like that would be good for students. I know that I can feel a little panic in my gut at the thought that someone might ask me to draw my concept of cruelty, when my idea of myself is that I couldn't possibly draw anything.

Sizer: Just think of the kid who can draw but can't write. That kid has been humiliated every day in every school. Ours is a culture of words. It would be good education [for teachers to try things they aren't good at] because every teacher is going to be a klutz somewhere and it would be good for kids to see that teachers can be klutzes and aren't afraid to exhibit klutziness, if that's a word.

Stevens: One of your statements, that we must stop thinking of how to present materials to kids, struck me hard because when planning my teaching, I often think "How can I best present this material?" and I've never questioned using those words.

Sizer: Well, if you want to tell somebody something, that's a good question. If the person wants to be presented the material and the person understands the context in which I'm making the presentation, then it's a good question to ask, "How do I present it?" But, if the kid doesn't understand the context or if the kid doesn't want to be lectured at, you've got a prior job to do. The context is important because any one of us have to know why something is important before there's any energy to learn it.

Stevens: You see the teacher, then, as a problem-poser.

Sizer: That's right. Coach, critic, cajoler, supporter, harasser, lover, all of that. But the kid has to be the worker. We have to stop thinking of the schools as a deliverer of instructional services. That's nonsense. Nobody ever learned by being delivered knowledge on a platter. They have to experience it.

Continued from page 2.

Most experiential educators espouse not only alternative educational methods but a variety of alternative visions, and with this Journal, AEE comes out of the closet to articulate something of our vision. I hope you will read this issue critically and let us know your reactions to it and to the current educational debate, and, more importantly, that you will take Dick Kraft's suggestions in the editorial to heart and become politically involved this election year.

I believe that the Association's programs and people offer the beginning of answers to questions about how to prepare children for an uncertain future. Let us continue to confer together, laugh together, and create together. Let us also envision and build a world worthy of our children.

Jim Kielsmeier
AEE President

A NATION AT RISK REPORT:
Is It Good for Students?

by Diane Hedin

A Nation at Risk, the report of the National Commission on Excellence in Education has been lauded by many of the participants in public education -- teachers, principals, school board members, faculty members of colleges of education, parents' groups, and professional associations of educators. Often the report is praised effusively by the very people who are being held responsible for "the rising tide of mediocrity." They seem to be so relieved that someone in Washington is finally paying attention to them that they have themselves joined the chorus of those condemning the schools they have created. Do professional educators really support the recommendations for more homework, more requirements, and more time in school? It's difficult to know because so many of their public statements tend to gingerly avoid discussions of the substance and recommendations of the Report (except for higher salaries) and instead confine their remarks to gratitude about "putting education on the national agenda again."

Where do the other key participants in public education, the students, stand on these issues? Merely asking the question reminds us that they have had almost no input in this debate. While the Commission had its one token teacher, they apparently didn't deem it necessary to have a student member. Their decision may have been a wise one because the lone voice of an adolescent among presidents of universities and chairmen of corporations might not have been heard anyway.

Since the publication of the Commission Report, I have informally discussed it

Diane Hedin is Associate Professor at the Center for Youth Development and

group of students in Minneapolis shared their critique of the report, which I find so persuasive that I have included it in this article. Prior to publication of *A Nation at Risk* in April 1983, I conducted a study entitled, *Minnesota Youth Poll: Youth's Views of School and School Discipline,* (Hedin and Simon, 1983), which covered some of the same issues about the state of American education. Approximately 900 9-12th graders around the state of Minnesota participated in the Poll. It is from these perspectives that I comment on whether the Commission Report reflects the concerns of American adolescents about their education.

"It is difficult to understand why adolescents would study hard and retain information and knowledge they believed to be useless."

I will first present student reactions to the Commission Report according to the same four categories the Commission used: content, expectations, time, and teaching.

Content

The Commission's major criticism was that there was too much student choice within a "curricular smorgasbord," and that too many of the credits earned in high school were in "questionable" areas such as physical and health education, work experience, and "personal service and development courses, such as training for adulthood and marriage." (NCEE, p. 19)

Young people tend to strongly disagree with this criticism of public schools. In fact, many believe that more student choice is needed, and suggest that an active interest in what is being learned is crucial to real learning. In my 1983 study of youth and their schools in Minnesota, students were asked to grade their schools from A to F. For a school to receive an A or B, it almost always had to have a wide and varied curriculum, with extensive opportunity for students to choose courses in which they were interested.

Some students also cautioned that the Commission's recommendation to have more required courses in English, math, science, social studies and computers was likely to backfire. They argued that forcing students to take courses for which they had little interest or ability would have the effect of further watering down the curriculum. The student who was required to take biology and didn't know his beet roots from his Greek roots and didn't care about the distinction would hold the better students back and make the teaching of biology far less productive for both the teacher and the science whiz kids. Precisely the opposite effect that the Commission hoped its recommendation would have!

In the Minnesota Youth Poll on Schools, students were asked to assess how well the school curriculum had helped them prepare for adulthood and for their current status as adolescents. By far the most frequent response was that the school is most effective in promoting personal and social development. The most important learnings gained are *social skills* (such as getting along with people, working in groups, fulfilling one's obligation to the school and community) and *personal skills* (such as becoming independent and responsible, learning to use free time wisely, gaining self-control, and decision-making). It was obvious from their responses that young people do not equate learning with what is taught in the formal curriculum. Thus, the Commission's narrow focus on academic achievement (defined as standardized test scores), and the "Five New Basics" seems to miss entirely what many high school students view as a far more *basic* educational goal -- gaining the basic personal, social and intellectual skills to function as a competent adult.

Specific courses or content which student respondents thought to be least important were those which they felt would not be used in the future or applied to problems of everyday living right now. Included most often in this list were algebra,

English, literature, history, grammar, geometry, physics, chemistry. The students' list of "unimportant courses" sounds surprisingly similar to the Commission's "New Basics." Others offered more general categories such as "Learning lists of stuff that you memorize and forget the next day," or "Classes that concern things that have happened thousands of years ago when we should be learning to handle the future." Overall, the students took a pragmatic view of what is worth learning, with knowledge, skills and attitudes related to earning a living and coping with personal and social relationships being high on the list. These comments point to one of the key problems with the Commission's findings and recommendations about curriculum: student motivation. It is difficult to understand why adolescents would study hard and retain information and knowledge they believed to be useless.

Expectations

The Commission found serious deficiencies in the amount of hard work, self-discipline and motivation students devoted to their studies. They were highly critical of the lax standards, easy courses, and low-quality of textbooks. The students tended to agree with many of these criticisms, particularly those related to disciplined study. In fact, in the Minnesota Youth Poll, students said that the biggest problem in schools is boredom and disinterest in academic work. When asked to characterize the day-to-day reality of going to school, boredom and lethargy were the dominant themes. The lack of genuine engagement and excitement about learning on the part of *both* students and teachers was viewed as the most serious problem in public schools. Students commented on their own contribution to these problems:

"Some students don't care about the future and don't respect students who want to learn."

"Kids just really don't care."

"Lack of enthusiasm about learning and lack of motivation is one of the biggest problems. Teachers have a very hard time getting students interested in studying."

High school students, however, recommended very different ways to deal with low motivation for learning than did the Commission. While the Commission recommended some sort of nationwide system of achievement testing and upgrading textbooks, students were more likely to suggest changes in school rules, a wider variety of teaching methods, and improved relationships between teachers and students as a way to increase student motivation for learning. These will be discussed in more detail in the section on Teaching.

"The Commission ... neglected to use one of the key principles of our chief educational and industrial competitor: the Japanese concept of quality circles."

Time

The Commission found that American students spend less time in school than do students in other countries and not enough homework is assigned. They recommended this situation be remedied by assigning far more homework, lengthening both the school day and year, and using the time in school more efficiently. Of all the recommendations of the Commission, these seem most directly in conflict with student perceptions. In the Minnesota Youth Poll, the most frequent complaint about school was its length. Students thought the school day was too long, there was not enough time between classes, not enough time for lunch, classes were too long and there was not enough free time. It is likely that school seems to last so interminably long because of what students said earlier about boredom and the monotony of classes. From the students' responses, merely lengthening the school day and year would contribute little toward improved academic achievement without significant changes in the learning and teaching process.

Teaching

The Commission found that the academic quality of teachers was low, that salaries needed improvement, and that there was little opportunity for advancement in teaching. Student perceptions about the problems with teachers and the methods they used focused on very different issues. Students thought that the relationship between students and teachers played a crucial role in learning. In fact, students consistently stated that when there were empathic and respectful relationships between students and teachers, students worked harder and achieved more academically. This was an issue that *A Nation at Risk* never addressed.

Closely related to this concern about more positive interactions between staff and students was the issue of school rules and policies. The most frequent suggestion for improving the quality of education had to do with changes that would give students more control over their lives and education. They argued that because they felt so regimented and infantalized, they often spent an inordinate amount of time focusing on unimportant rules, rather than learning. As one student put it, an open campus policy would make students behave more responsibly:

"We feel an open campus policy would help alleviate skipping out and other irresponsible actions by kids. It would show the responsibility of students about use of free time -- in preparation for college. Mistakes now could help us learn for the future."

The readers of this journal will, no doubt, agree with the students' recommendations about how to improve teaching in secondary schools. More experiential learning and student participation was the most frequent suggestion:

"Less lecturing, more group discussions, more field trips."

"More learning by doing, like in our community service class where we help people, and learn from helping them."

These are ideas and recommendations that approximately 900 high school students in Minnesota have about their high schools. They often differ dramatically from those of the members of the Commission. Another perspective about what can be done to improve secondary education was offered by a group of high school students at the Learning Lab, an innovative academic program at the Children's Theatre School in Minneapolis, Minnesota. The students studied the Commission report and discussed it extensively among themselves and with their teacher and principal, Dan Conrad. Because they were so convinced that the Commission was moving in the wrong direction, they decided to write to the education committee of their state legislature, which was supporting many of the Commission's recommendations. The chief author of the letter is 16-year old Sarah Corzatt, but the comments reflect ideas of other members of the Learning Lab as well. The letter is printed in its entirety below:

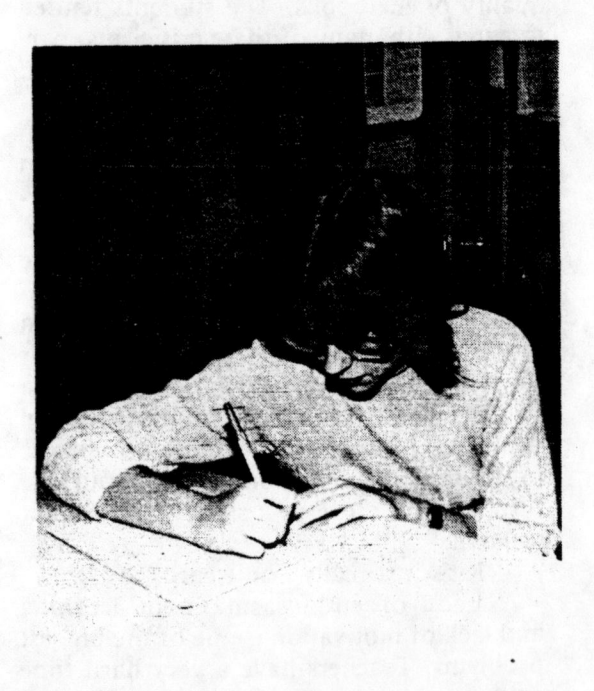

As high school students concerned with the standard of education in our state and nation, we are writing to you in order to voice our opinions and disagreements with measures now being taken to improve education. We feel that if people (such as the House Education Committee) intend to make changes in the school system, they ought to speak with those most closely connected with the schools, the students and teachers, to gain an insider's view of what needs to be done.

First of all, from information gathered from newspapers and the radio, we have deduced that the House Education Committee and yourself seem to favor recommendations given by the National Commission on Excellence, namely things like more homework, longer school days, and heavier requirements. Our first questions for you are: why do you favor these recommendations? what exactly are the problems you see in our present system of education? and why do you think that the recommendations will work? We think that if we understood your point of view better and where your proof is gathered from we would be able to address these specific points better. As it stands now, we don't feel enough research has been carried out to prove that more homework, requirements, etc. are a valid solution. Perhaps everyone is confused as to what the actual problem is.

As we see it, the problems are not with the things we're teaching and the time spent teaching these things, but with the whole way we teach and the mentality of the American public regarding the purpose of education. Think about it; have the skills of teachers and the methods and materials they use actually declined in the past twenty years? We don't think so. In our minds, the problem lies in the fact that things are the same -- methods of education have stayed the same when everything else is quickly changing and moving forward. If it has indeed been shown that our nation is at risk and that students aren't learning as much as they used to, doesn't it follow that we have gone beyond and above our old educational patterns and need something new? Is the solution to do more of what we've found isn't working now (i.e., homework, requirements, longer school days)? It's the same type of thing we've been doing for the past 20 years and more of it. We need to re-evaluate our entire viewpoint on education.

We feel that what education should do is to prepare students for life; interesting, creative life. It is to give them skills they can apply. To meet these goals, schools should offer courses in a wide range of subjects to stimulate the curiosity of many different types of people, and to equip students with life-long learning skills. It is NOT to turn kids into robots programmed with loads of useless information that they don't understand, can't apply, and can do little more than rattle off unintelligibly.

The recommendations we have are as follows:

1) That students be allowed to progress in school not according to their age or the number of credits they have built up, but instead by ability and achievement, perhaps as measured by competency achievement tests or by other means. This would, eventually, phase out the current norms of grade-age standing.

2) We also believe, as stated earlier, that the curriculum should be strengthened, but not by forcing people to take more required courses such as math, English, and science. If people who are now unhappy and lost taking these courses are forced to take even more of these undesired courses, will that make them any more willing or desirous to do the work? No. And isn't that part of what education should ideally be about, helping kids to enjoy and relish learning and want

> to continue learning their whole life through? In our opinion, the best way to help people do this is to offer a wider range of elective courses (and by saying elective, that doesn't automatically mean easy or fun). Covering more things that students have an interest in would make learning more enjoyable by letting us learn what we want. Requirements are necessary in some ways, but perhaps they would be better utilized if present in earlier education and greatly reduced in higher education. Students then could take courses in areas of their own interest. Those who want a well-balanced education will take a wide range of courses whether required or not and won't be held back by those taking the course only because of a requirement. This would be better for all students and teachers.
>
> 3) Schools should make as much use as possible of varied resources around the community and put more emphasis on learning through experience and doing rather than pure textbook learning. Learning from reading and hearing lectures, we will admit, is a valid and good way to learn -- some things. However, rather than spending lots of money on big new textbooks, why not learn by actually going to museums, visiting historic sites, attending plays, going to radio and TV stations, participating in actual EVENTS? To us this seems a powerful and interesting way to learn and to also acquire lifelong learning skills.
>
> 4) Our last recommendation deals with teachers, and a way of changing our present view of them. To have good schools we must, as a base, have good teachers who enjoy teaching, who can help students to be more independent and to grow emotionally, and who will act more as guides and mentors to the students rather than as authority figures with whips. We think to get teachers like this, the profession must attract the top students from graduating college classes rather than the poorer ones who will take whatever pittance they can get as a teacher. To be able to offer more to the teachers as incentive, the public must realize what a very important job teaching is, and that it should be highly respected -- a change of view that will take no short while to accomplish.
>
> Representative Nelson, we hope you will consider these recommendations, especially as they are coming from members of a little-heard-from group -- high school students. We would also relish the opportunity to serve on or testify before one of the state education commissions, as we feel that student input on these matters is very important.

The perceptions and recommendations of one of the group most intimately involved with American high schools, students, differed dramatically from those much further from the day-to-day reality of schools, the members of the National Committee on Excellence in Education. It is surprising that the Commission, being so attuned to the educational practices of other countries, neglected to use one of the key principles of our chief educational and industrial competitor; the Japanese concept of quality circles. Had the Commission done so, they would have never ignored the experiences and ideas of the most important actor in the learning process, *the learner*. The Japanese model is built on the belief that problems can best be dealt with by involving the persons closest to the problem in its solution. The letter from Sarah Corzatt and the students of the Learning Lab of Children's Theatre is dramatic testimony that the Commission report would have been a more useful document had they done so.

References

- Hedin, Diane and Simon, Paula. *Minnesota Youth Poll: Youth's Views on School and School Discipline*, Minnesota Report 184-1983, St. Paul: University of Minnesota, 1983.
- National Commission on Excellence in Education. *A Nation at Risk*, Washington, D.C. Department of Education, 1983.

A High School Principal Looks at the National Reports

by Arnold Langberg

When I looked over the notes I had taken while reading *A Nation at Risk*, I found myself thinking back to my attempts to take up the game of golf many years ago. I had had occasional flashes of brilliance; a long straight drive, an accurate approach, a perfect putt. These seldom occurred on the same hole, however, and for each outstanding shot that I made I would have six or eight miserable dribbles. The report from The National Commission on Excellence in Education is right out there on the fairway with its definition of excellence:

"At the level of the individual learner, it means performing on the boundary of individual ability in ways that test and push back personal limits, in school and in the workplace. Excellence characterizes a school or college that sets high expectations and goals for all learners, then tries in every way possible to help students reach them."

It's on the edge of the green with its statement that

"For our country to function, citizens must be able to reach some common understandings on complex issues, often on short notice and on the basis of conflicting or incomplete evidence."

And the report is on the lip of the cup with its concern that

"An over-emphasis on technical and occupational skills will leave little time for

---

Arnie Langberg is the Principal of the Jefferson County Open High School in Evergreen, Colorado. JCOHS is in its tenth year as a public alternative high school using extensive experiential education and walkabout concepts.

studying the arts and humanities that so enrich daily life, help maintain civility, and develop a sense of community. Knowledge of the humanities...must be harnessed to science and technology if the latter are to remain creative and humane, just as the humanities need to be informed by science and technology if they are to remain relevant to the human condition."

These statements, however, are rare moments of insight that are almost lost within a context that is elitist, chauvinist, and a bit paranoid. The tone is set in the very first paragraph.

"Our nation is at risk. Our once unchallenged pre-eminence in commerce, industry, science, and technological innovation is being overtaken by competitors throughout the world."

The metaphors that are employed shortly thereafter are so materialistic that I find them ludicrous.

"Knowledge, learning, information, and skilled intelligence are the new raw materials of international commerce and are today spreading throughout the world as vigorously as miracle drugs, synthetic fertilizers, and blue jeans did earlier."

(During my first year as a teacher the school board rejected our request for a salary increase and then added funds for fertilizer for the playing fields. Now, twenty-eight years later, we have finally achieved parity!) To make it perfectly clear that the humanistic statements shouldn't be taken too seriously, the "fertilizer" quotation continues as follows:

"If only to keep and improve on the slim competitive edge we still retain in world markets, we must dedicate ourselves to

the reform of our educational system....;"

I have chosen to deal with this report the same way as I do with golf. For the few moments of value, I don't dismiss it entirely, but on the whole there are more fruitful ways to spend my time and energy.

My response to *High School*, The Carnegie Foundation Report by Ernest Boyer, was much more enthusiastic. I enjoyed the irreverent statistic in the prologue that puts our last national reaction to an educational "crisis" (the response to the launching of Sputnik) in perspective. "Nearly 5,000 objects are now orbiting the earth; more than 3,400 of them are officially listed as debris." This report has a global approach that transcends the petty nationalism of *A Nation at Risk*. The prologue continues with the statement:

"If education cannot help students see beyond themselves and better understand the interdependent nature of our world, each new generation will remain ignorant and its capacity to live confidently and responsibly will be dangerously diminished."

This larger viewpoint is not, however, allowed to eclipse the fundamental purpose of education, "to enrich the living individuals," nor can the push for excellence permit us to ignore the needs of less privileged students. "Clearly, equity and excellence cannot be divided."

As the Principal of an alternative school I find fault with both studies. *A Nation at Risk* makes no mention of alternatives at all, while *High School* suggests only that such schools "might be organized to give intensive, continuous help to some high-risk students." It is my belief that implementation of the changes recommended by Boyer, most of which I support, would require alternatives to the present system for *all* students. On page 147 he poses the following three questions:

"How can the relatively passive and docile roles of students prepare them to participate as informed, active, and questioning citizens? How can the regimented schedule and the routinized atmosphere of classrooms prepare students for independence as adults? How can we produce critical and creative thinking throughout a student's life when we so systematically discourage individuality in the classroom?"

I believe it will take more than a mere reform of the present system to answer these questions. It will take a radical departure from our reliance on grades, Carnegie units, and even classrooms. I shall give a brief description of how Jefferson County Open High School (JCOHS), though differing in some basic assumptions from his report, puts into practice Boyer's recommendations.

The "Walkabout" Program

JCOHS, currently in its ninth year, serves 210 students who, with their parents' permission, have chosen to enroll there rather than in one of the twelve conventional high schools in the district. Approximately one-third of the students would characterize themselves as "high-risk," another 20% would probably be called "gifted," and the remainder, almost half the school, came to "Open" to avoid the impersonal, alienating social conditions in the large, comprehensive high schools. The

> "Our notion of school, classroom, and teacher is broad."

curriculum structure at JCOHS is a "Walkabout" model which considers high school years as the rites of passage to adulthood. (The name "Walkabout" refers to the Australian aborigine's rite of passage to adulthood.) Students, with the help of faculty advisors, develop individual programs to master some fifty "pre-walkabout" skills before embarking on their passages: challenging projects that will demonstrate their ability to use their skills in the real world.

When students enter JCOHS, their first quarter is spent on personal and social matters. In an environment where they feel they can be themselves, they can confront who they really are and what they would like to become. In small groups, with veteran students and staff members, they spend one week camped out in the wilderness and one week living in the inner city. This is vital in helping them change their notion of school to include any environment in which they are learning. Here, too, they are introduced to our evaluation system, one of our most important structures for emphasizing Boyer's prime concern, literacy. They are required to write about their experiences, what they learned and how they feel about it, and these are responded to, in writing, by the teachers. Instead of a computer printout with grades and credits, a student's record at JCOHS is a collection of such self-evaluations and teacher responses. During their beginning quarter all the new students get to work with every staff member to some extent, thus enabling them to choose the advisor they want to help them through their walkabout. The second phase at JCOHS, building a foundation of skills, could last anywhere from one to three semesters, depending on a student's background and motivation. The list of skills includes all the conventional subject areas mentioned in *A Nation at Risk* and *High School,* but it also includes such skills as: "Be able to clarify values and understand principles for making moral decisions" and "Be able to apply previously acquired knowledge to a new situation." Most students find that they have already mastered some of these skills and they just need to convince their advisors through adequate documentation or demonstration. For working on the remaining skills, students may create pro-

other institution, trips, apprenticeships, and independent study.

Classes at JCOHS have many of the attributes desired by Boyer. They are small, informal, interdisciplinary, and they usually meet two or three times a week for from one-and-a-half to three hours each time. Quite often there is more than one teacher and all the students are expected to do independent work and to share their learning with the class.

Graduates of our school, rank the trip program as equivalent to the advisory relationship in its educational value. Instead of an interscholastic athletic program and other conventional extracurricular activities, we use the equivalent money to purchase and maintain vans that allow us to travel throughout North America. Our Mexico Work Trip is a good example of how we "link our curriculum to a changing national and global context," to quote again from *High School*. During Holy Week, when their schools are closed, we live in a small village in Mexico to which we are assigned, and we refurbish their school. We paint it, inside and out, sand the desks, and repair the plumbing and electricity. The villagers have a fiesta for us and we have one for their children. When the work is done we get to play at the beach for a few days before returning home. The preparation for such a trip includes basic conversational Spanish, a study of the social, political, and economic situation in Mexico and the relationship with the United States, and an introduction to Mexican culture including music, art, social customs, and food. Our students learn almost as much from living closely and intensely with thirty of their peers for two weeks as they do from being non-tourists in another country.

Apprenticeships, which we call community learning, range from working one day a week in our student-run food service or helping in our pre-school, to spending fulltime for one quarter of the school year with a local sign-maker and then using the newly-acquired skill of wood carving to make a sign for the school. Other community teachers with whom our students have worked are: lawyers, social workers, special education teachers, veterinarians, chefs, potters, architects, physical therapists, journalists, and many more. Our notion of school, classroom and teacher is broad.

When the student and advisor agree that the foundation of skills is sufficiently strong, the student enters the final phase by proposing a first passage, a project that will demonstrate the application of these skills. There are six passage areas: career exploration, creativity, logical inquiry, practical skills, adventure, and global awareness/volunteer service. Students must cover all six areas but they are encouraged to combine them rather than do six separate projects. This phase may take from two to four semesters and it is here that our program offers a model for many more of Boyer's recommendations such as: "All students should complete a senior independent project, there should be a smooth transition from school to adult life, students should be given more responsibility for their education, and there should be a service requirement."

Among the more recent passages was an adventure wherein a student who had learned sign language had a doctor fit her with ear plugs for one week so that she could truly feel what it was like to be deaf. She spent part of her week with hearing people and part with deaf people and the most frequent entry in her journal was the word "lonely." Global awareness passages have included studies of aging, hunger, acid rain, hazardous waste disposal, immigration, alcoholism, and nuclear weapons. Service projects that have resulted from these studies ranged from helping an elderly person do her weekly shopping to working in the office of the freeze campaign to writing newspaper articles to making presentations at our school and other schools and organizations in our community.

In attempting to respond to two of the many criticisms of American High Schools, I have described JCOHS in what I hope is adequate detail. I have done this because I think it is a more complete model for the future of secondary education than can be found in either of the studies. *A Nation at Risk* proposes a form of "educational rearmament" to mobilize our youth against the threat of foreign competition. This would be accomplished by increasing the dosage of narrow academics, the failure of which has led to these studies in the first place. *High School* does a more creditable job, with emphasis on equity, as well as excellence. Experiential education makes at least a token appearance in Boyer's study, although it must happen on the students' own time. *High School* is worth reading, because it asks many of the right questions, and it does offer some innovative solutions. I only wish it had gone a few steps further and questioned *all* of the "givens" of our current educational system.

Two Perspectives on the Crisis in Education

by Homer Page

Americans have a passion for self-doubt, and when that doubt is especially intense, they look to education to overcome their real or imagined ills. Thus, Horace Mann and John Dewey and the men and women of their generations turned to education in order to address the problems brought about by industrialization, urbanization, and immigration in the changing America of their day. The men and women of the age of Sputnik and the Black civil rights movement, similarly turned to the education system for answers to troubling questions.

The most recent cycle of doubt and reform came to an end in a deeper mood of criticism of the whole American reliance on education than had ever previously occurred. The educational system was called racist, bureaucratic, sexist, and stultifying. The faith and hope in education and educators that has been a trademark of American culture faded away with the fall of Saigon, the Nixon presidency, and the worldwide supremacy of the U.S. auto industry. Russian missiles and Japanese computer chips, Iranian fanaticism, and Korean steel and ship building have all assaulted the American psyche and generated a deep and pervasive self-doubt. The conservative reaction, which swept Ronald Reagan into the White House, draws its energy from what it perceived to be the failure of liberals to keep the faith of the American dream.

Once again, Americans are turning in a time of national doubt to education to locate blame and to find strategies for cor-

Homer Page is the director of the Office of Services for Disabled Students and an Education Professor at the University of Colorado in Boulder.

recting the wrongs of the past two decades. In the last year, a number of reports have been issued that purport to evaluate the quality of American education, and provide recommendations for overcoming major deficiencies. It is the argument of this essay that there are two distinct perspectives which are emerging out of this critical analysis of American education.

Since we Americans place such a serious emotional, political and cultural investment in our educational institutions, it is incumbent on us to understand those perspectives, their underlying value assumptions, the way in which they state the problem with education, the methodologies they use, and the recommendations they make.

Two reports will be examined to demonstrate the two divergent perspectives. They will be the report of the National Committee on Excellence in Education, *The Nation at Risk*, and the study conducted by John Goodlad, entitled *A Place Called School*, both summarized in a prior article in this *Journal*.

I. A Nation at Risk:

The overriding theme of the report is that in order to arrest the decline in American power and prestige around the world and restore the domestic economy and society to health, a way must be found to achieve a new excellence in education. The Commission report is grounded in a particular world view that must be understood if we are to be able to assess the report. The following propositions attempt to summarize the structure of that perspective on the world:

1. The U.S. is caught up in a bitterly competitive world. Our survival as a great nation is at risk.

2. Participation in the world of tomorrow depends on the possession of technical knowledge and skills. The possession of such knowledge and skills is widely distributed throughout the world.

3. It is the role of education to teach the basic knowledge and skills needed by individuals to be successful participants in the world, and for the nation to be successful in the competition with the world of today and tomorrow.

4. America is losing the struggle for predominance in the world, and education must bear the brunt of the responsibility for the failings of the nation.

The primary value in this perspective is winning. The world is filled with hostile forces and it is the patriotic duty of all to aspire to do their very best so that the nation may be sustained as the pre-eminent world power.

If one starts with the above mentioned world view, the problem for study is, logically, what is wrong with education and how do we fix it? It is not surprising that the Commission found that American education is lax to the point of moral decay. Academic standards are unconscionably low. The content of the curriculum of our schools is pure fluff. Students are allowed to pass through school spending little time on school work, and the quality of teaching and teachers is abominable.

It should not be surprising, either, that the report recommends more time be spent on academically challenging curriculum, standards for measuring achievement be raised, and teacher qualifications upgraded. The anecdote to laxness is to re-invigorate education with a challenging, demanding school experience.

The Commission studied education by setting up a series of public hearings, taking testimony from panels of experts, soliciting papers from experts in the field of education, receiving and reading unsolicited letters, and doing a general review of the literature. The report documents the failure of American education by pointing to falling scores of American students on standardized tests, by poor performances on standardized tests when compared with students from other countries, by levels of functional illiteracy in the American population, and by the need for remedial instruction by persons entering college, business or the military.

The methodology chosen by the Commission fits well with the world view which is held. Test scores have fallen. In a competitive world, this measurement of competitive performance provides a guideline by which we can assess whether or not we are winning the war. Since no original research was conducted and since no attempt was made to understand in any systematic way what goes on in the schools, the Commission was in a position to pick and choose among the experts and citizens who provided an input to the study. The world view governing the Commission's report provided the criteria used to select relevant testimony, which in turn determined the findings of the Commission. The findings then governed the recommendations.

The Commission ignored important educational issues such as the youth culture, family environment and structure, declining economic expectations by this generation of students, and the impact on teachers of the educational culture of the schools. These are issues dealt with extensively by John Goodlad, who works from a different set of values. We shall now turn to an examination of the Goodlad analysis of American society.

II. A Place Called School:

Few book titles are more descriptive of their content than is John Goodlad's book, *A Place Called School*. The title has meaning at several levels. *A Place Called School* refers to the idea that education should be studied as a place where a process occurs. School is a clearly defined ecological system. It has its own culture and must be studied as a social system in order to be understood. *A Place Called School* also refers to the idea that the basic unit for educational analysis and educational reform is the individual school.

Goodlad argues that four major purposes should characterize the educational enterprise. They are: intellectual development, personal growth, civic involvement,

"The emotional tone of schools...is neither warm and exciting, nor cold and oppressive. It is simply flat."

and vocational direction. While these goals are not new, Goodlad believes that they are the crux of the educational enterprise, and that a tremendous gap exists between the ideal for education that they represent and their implementation in the schools of America.

Goodlad argues that the measurements used to evaluate education are primarily ones which assess the purpose of intellectual development. Real evaluation of the three remaining purposes is never done. His research indicates that parents, students and teachers all feel the other purposes are quite important. In fact, those schools which are rated highly by those who participate in them go beyond simply the academic area to attempt to achieve the full development of each student. Those schools that demonstrate a caring attitude toward their students are the ones that are considered to be most satisfactory to students and teachers alike.

The basic underlying value that permeates Goodlad's work in *A Place Called School* is that of the full self-realization and self-direction of each individual in our society. Goodlad is critical of schooling in America because all too often it fails to achieve this end. He is also critical of a great deal of reform proposals that have been directed too narrowly to the academic area because they do not recognize the larger needs of students and teachers. Schooling in America is textbook and teacher centered. Little time is given over to the active involvement of students in their own learning. Minority and lower social economic class students are too often tracked into educational programs that will direct them toward the most dead-end, menial occupations. Torn away from family ties and other adult institutional relationships, a youth culture has developed in opposition to the formal school culture. Finally, the emotional tone of schools, according to Goodlad, is neither warm and exciting, nor cold and oppressive. It is simply flat. All of these findings mitigate against students achieving the level of self-realization which they are capable of achieving. The central problem for education from Goodlad's perspective is how to get elected officials, school administrators, teachers, parents, and students to all work in a coherent way to narrow the gap between educational purposes and educational realities.

The book, *A Place Called School*, is itself a major methodological tool which Goodlad wishes to use to address the educational problem as he sees it. It is written at a level which he hopes will be relevant to decision makers. Therefore, it is not simply a research report. Goodlad relates comments made to him, by friends and potential financial supporters, which encouraged him to forget about spending several years studying the schools. These persons argued that he already knew enough about the schools and should spend his time trying to change them. He did the study and wrote this book, however, because he wanted a thorough, systematic appraisal of what the schools were really like, as they are experienced on a day-to-day basis by those who actually live out their lives in them.

He and his team conducted extensive research. They interviewed and surveyed thousands of teachers, students, and parents. They spent thousands of hours in classrooms observing the workings of the schools. They talked to school administrators and elected officials. The Goodlad team sought to capture the culture of schooling.

Recommendations flow from the value commitments, the statement of the educational problem, and the methods used by Goodland. The recommendations seek to provide the basis for establishing a self-renewing process within the educational system. This includes the involvement of parents, administrators, teachers and public officials in the search for a consensus on purposes for education. State officials would plan for the implementation of agreed upon purposes and have access to thorough research on the success of the schools in implementing those purposes. Parents would be more directly involved in the education of their own children. Students would have access to a full and balanced curriculum, designed to allow maximum participation on their part. Teachers would have greater control over the curriculum and funds spent for instruction. Administrators would be better trained for their role and would have more direct involvement with the educational process itself. Self-direction and self-fulfillment would be achieved in the context of a coherent, dynamic, educational system.

Summary and Conclusion:

Dimensions of the Comparison	A Nation at Risk	A Place Called School
Underlying primary value	Winning in a worldwide competitive struggle.	Self-fulfillment in a dynamic environment.
The educational problem	Why is education failing? How can we overcome the failure?	How can we activate the actors in the educational system to create a dynamic self-fulfilling environment?
Methods	Selected expert testimony.	Original culturally oriented research.
Recommendations	Overcoming laxness through higher standards and greater commitment of time and an establishment of a new basic curriculum.	The creation of a dynamic self-renewing process within the educational system which activates all individuals to participate in an accountable, responsible way.

Most, if not all, commentators on American education see serious problems. However, these problems and the recommendations which flow from them are framed in distinctively different ways.

The authors of the Commission report, *A Nation at Risk*, argue that American greatness is at stake in a worldwide competition with both friends and foes. American security, prosperity and civility are threatened by what they view as the collapsing American educational system. Reforming education is a patriotic duty which should be taken up by all Americans.

John Goodlad's view of the world is quite different. There is a pervasive sense of atrophy and fragmentation of the basic American institutions. The educational system is impacted, significantly, by this breaking apart of the cohesion of the American culture. This atrophy and fragmentation also characterizes the internal life of American education. He believes that only as education, as an institution, can renew itself and recover coherent purposes can it accomplish its primary goal which is to assist in the development of fully human, self-directing individuals.

Both these perspectives point to a dim picture of American education and American life. Each calls for reform and citizen involvement. Citizens must decide first if they agree that education is in crisis, and then they must decide what view of the world constitutes their emotional and intellectual consciousness. And then they must decide if they really want to be involved. These decisions will determine the future of education and, probably in similar ways, the future of the American civilization.

II. General Theory

Stress, Burnout, and Culture Shock:

AN EXPERIENTIAL, PRE-SERVICE APPROACH

by Samuel J. Mungo

Stress and burnout, as any casual review of the literature will reveal, is a topic of great concern to educators today. For those of us working in teacher education and preparing students to work in cross-cultural settings, a related topic--culture shock--is an additional concern. Unfortunately, the literature on these topics also reveals that the major emphasis on finding solutions to these concerns seems to be centered on activities for the individual on the job. (Randall, 1980) There are, however, excellent opportunities at the pre-service level to address these problems in a unique and meaningful way.

It is the purpose of this paper to explore the various aspects of stress and burnout, show the relationship of these aspects to culture shock, and describe an off-campus field-based model that is being used as a preventative approach at the pre-service level. This program adapts the Outward Bound model of using a controlled amount of stress as a growth-producing experience.

First, let us look at a representative sample of what the literature has to say about stress and burnout:

Stress begins with anxiety . . . a disturbance arising from some kind of imbalance within us . . . this anxiety leads to tension. Tension is a physical reaction to the anxiety. When we are tense, nervous impulses cause changes in our body. When tension reaches a degree of intensity that has adverse effects on the body . . . we are under stress. (Sparks, 1981:2)

. . . anxiety arises when the person's feelings

Samuel J. Mungo is Associate Professor of Curriculum and Instruction at Illinois State University

of self-adequacy and security are threatened. (Sinclair, 1974:241)

Two kinds of situations lead to stress:
1. the individual's skills and abilities are not sufficient to meet the perceived or real demands of the job.
2. the individual's work does not meet his/her needs or values. (Derlman, 1980:8)

A main effect of stress is loneliness, a loneliness related to the fact that often there is little community or feeling among fellow teachers. (Jersild, 1955:15)

Burnout--a person is attempting to perform a job by merely going through the motions. (Rickon, 1980:21)

Beginning teachers suffer a great deal of anxiety stemming from the discrepancy between their ideal roles and the roles they find themselves following in their practice. (Jersild 1966:43)

Following is a sampling of what the literature says about culture shock:

Culture shock--the massive physic reaction which takes place within the individual plunged into a culture vastly different from his own. (Anderson, 1971:21)

Culture shock--primarily a set of emotional reactions to the loss of perceptual reinforcements from one's own culture, to new cultural stimuli which have little or no meaning. (Adler, 1975:18)

The one common element that is found in all the preceding citations is the reference to undue *anxiety,* caused by any one or a combination of the following: low self-image, threat to security, fear, inadequate skills, helplessness, defensiveness, role conflict, loneliness, unfamiliarity, and frustration. Whether brought upon by culture immersion or other situations, these aspects seem to lead to the anxiety that leads to stress or to culture shock.

Now that we have identified these

aspects, we can describe our model, indicating where these aspects are addressed.

Model

The model, an adaptation of an existing program at Illinois State University, is a pre-service field experience program prior to a student's full-time internship or student teaching. The need for placing it at the pre-service level is supported by studies that indicate that students participating in off-campus field experiences benefit from an enhancement of their capability to cope with stressful situations. (Bernstein, 1974)

The location of the model program is in a community with a diverse cultural/ethnic population. Not only is self-concept enhanced by experiences in such varied settings, (Harty, 1976) but among the approaches suggested to overcome culture shock--exposure to many types of people and ideologies--seems to make it advantageous to locate in a diverse community. (Barra, 1976) It is not necessary to have a wide range of non-white ethnic diversity; cultural diversity in its broader sense refers to diversity in religious populations, the white ethnics, the aged, handicapped, etc. As the field experience component of the model is described, the use of this broad view of cultural diversity will be made clear.

Component One--Orientation

It is essential that students go off campus, into the agencies and programs for first week orientations, so that they can begin the steps toward familiarity and the reduction of fear and anxiety. It is during this week that the development of the concept of social support, to be described in component three, begins. Experiences of sharing feelings, questions, and apprehensions take place, and the idea of the program as a growth experience is presented. Although not all anxiety and uncertainty is alleviated, a beginning is made that will continue over the remaining weeks of the program. The concern constantly addressed this week is very well stated by Maslow. (1976:64):

The human being is very apt to repress his anxieties and fears and even to deny to himself that they exist. To such a person, the unfamiliar, the vaguely perceived, the mysterious, the hidden, the unexpected, are all apt to be threatening. One way of rendering them familiar, predictable, controllable, i.e., unfrightening and harmless, is to know them and to understand them. This knowledge may have not only a growing forward function, but also an anxiety-reducing function.

"Students experience, in a controlled environment, some of the aspects of culture shock and stress."

Component Two--Field Experiences

Nine-Week Block. The field experiences take place primarily in non-school settings, including whatever social agencies, mental health facilities, alternative schools, drug and alcohol centers, geriatric units, correctional facilities, etc., are available in the given community. The main concern is to provide experiences in programs and agencies that will be culturally/ethnically diverse. The specific assignments are made by the Director, based on knowledge of students' skills and backgrounds, and the needs of the community-based programs. These assignments, in order to provide the kinds of experiences that will accomplish the goals of prevention of stress and burnout, are characterized by three elements: time, variety, and challenge.

Time. In order to insure the intensity needed to gain not only the maximum from the experiences, but to set up stressful settings, the students' day is full, going from 8:00-8:30 a.m. to 10:00 p.m., with the time being divided among three different assignments--full-time, 8:00-3:00; part-time, 3:30-5:00; and evening, 6:00-10:00. Seminars and classes with the Director fit into this schedule.

Variety. Students will be assigned a

minimum of three separate assignments per day, with a total of 7-10 experiences throughout the program. Assignments are determined by three criteria: skills and background of the student, needs of the agencies and programs, and areas of experience needed by the student. Each student is given at least one assignment per day in a setting that will be culturally unfamiliar, or work with a population that is

> "The director...takes the role of the Wizard Gandalf of the Hobbit Trilogy."

ethnically different. Priority is also given to agency needs, so that in some cases students will be assigned to activities that are foreign to them and seem to have little relationship to teaching. What they will have relationship to, however, will be their growth and awareness of role differentiation, both professionally and culturally.

Challenge. Due to the above two elements, students should find themselves in some unsettling, stressful, and unfamiliar settings. This element of challenge is essential if students are to experience, in a controlled environment, some of the aspects of culture shock and stress.

So that the reader does not think that participants in this model are going to be subjected to an unnecessary trauma haphazardly, this approach is based partly on research done on the Outward Bound participants, which supports the approach using controlled challenging and stressful experiences. These studies, among other findings, indicate that mental and emotional stress was extremely valuable in causing participants to examine their own behavior and learn about themselves. It is important to keep in mind, throughout students' stress-related experiences, that stress can have motivating powers as long as the stress or crisis is not allowed to develop debilitating qualities. (Richards, 1977) In addition, researchers, such as Adler, have found that having students experience culture shock can actually contribute to their learning:

1. Learning involves change and movement from one cultural frame of reference to another. Individuals are presented with changes in cultural landscapes.
2. Culture shock assumes unique importance and meaning to the individuals. Individuals undergo a highly personal experience of special significance to themselves.
3. Change becomes provocative. Individuals are forced into some form of introspection and self-examination.
4. Adjustment is extreme in its ups and downs. Individuals undergo various forms of frustration, anxiety, and personal pain.
5. Confrontation forces personal investigation of relationships. Individuals must deal with the relationships and processes inherent in their situation as outsiders.
6. New ideas force behavioral experimentation. Individuals must, of necessity, try out new attitudes and behaviors. This becomes a trial-and-error process until appropriate behavioral responses emerge.
7. The results from step 6 present unlimited opportunity for contrast and comparison. Individuals have at their disposal an unending source of diversity with which they can compare and contrast their own previous experiences. (Adler, 1976:14-15)

It becomes obvious that you do not just "drop" students into these challenging situations, but to maximize their learning and analysis of their experiences, it is necessary to provide support and feedback. The following two components provide just that.

Component Three--Social Support

Social support, as used in this model, is: *Information leading one to believe that he/she is cared for and loved, esteemed and valued, and belongs to a network of communication and mutual obligation that emphasizes the individual's perception that support is available when needed. (Cobb, 1976:312)*

This network is the participants themselves. In order to survive the challenging experiences, the culture shock, and the stress they will initially be exposed to, students must develop into a close-knit, cooperative, caring unit. Various devices designed to promote "groupness" are used during orientation and throughout the program. These include group work projects, sharing sessions, and cooperative assignments. Although the Director is available, more and more of the ongoing support--the "soft shoulder" and the "sounding board," must be seen as coming from within the group. This is essential for the mitigating of stressful life events. (Rhoads, 1980) As students share experiences, switch assignments, and thus face similar challenges, the quality of the emotional support increases--and the means of reducing anxiety are increased. As the Outward Bound Research states:

> As members generally identify their common problems, learn to express and utilize observational and feelings data, and build a group organization, individual anxieties reduce, and the individual moves toward a less defensive behavior. (Richards, 1977:64)

These strategies--support systems, sharing with others, caring and cooperating with peers--can be carried over beyond the program. Once experienced and found to be successful in a limited, controlled environment such as the program provides, these approaches and strategies can be used by future teachers when they face similar anxieties on the job.

Component Four--Seminars and Feedback

The Director holds weekly seminars and has periodic individual conferences with participants. These meetings, coupled with the use of feedback cards or diaries, provide an opportunity for two-way feedback between the Director and participants. Staff from community agencies are often invited to participate in seminars. Opportunities for clarification of cultural confusion, analysis of experiences, and discussion of role determination can take place at these sessions where both student and agency personnel can openly discuss concerns. One of the most beneficial approaches used during these sessions is relating Lauderdale's four stages (1982) leading to burnout (enthusiasm, stagnation, frustration, and apathy) to the students' current experiences. They are asked to identify the stages they feel they have experienced albeit at minor level, and then discussion develops around intervention methods for these stages. Since the type of experiences and the length of the assignment lend themselves very well to this type of analysis, valuable insights into preventative inter-

> "To survive challenging experiences, students must develop into a close-knit, cooperative, caring unit."

ventions to be used once out in the real world can be attained.

Although the Director is available for individual conferences and the seminars, in regard to the day-to-day contact with students in their assignments, he takes the role of the Wizard Gandalf of the Hobbit Trilogy. The Wizard sets the characters on the path, sending them forth toward unknown challenges, then fades into the background, returning at times of intense crisis to help alleviate the difficulty and set them again on another challenging path. The Director will visit sites as necessary, but the role is not one of "protective overseer." If he is perceived as the "Wizard," he can be more successful in encouraging the use of the support systems alluded to earlier.

In conclusion, although this model allows for much flexibility depending upon the population of students and community resources available, the components as structured do address the aspects of the anxiety leading to stress and culture shock listed at the beginning of this paper. This model, used at the pre-service level as suggested, enables students to experience stress and culture shock in a controlled environment. It allows them to experience the benefit of strategies involving support systems in overcoming these stresses and anxieties, and can lead to overall growth in positive self-image and coping skills. In the final analysis, it will enable the participants to experience

> *Recognition of the growth inspired by overcoming the difficult, awareness of the self that comes of a person "meeting himself" in crisis, and the compassion and understanding fused into the minds of people who overcome adversity together. (Richards 1977:60)*

References

- Adler, Peter S., "The Transitional Experience: An Alternative View of Culture Shock," *Journal of Humanistic Psychology*, 1975, 10 pages.
- _____, "Culture Shock and the Cross Cultural Learning Experience," in R. Brislin and P. Pederson, *Cross Cultural Orientation Programs*, New York: Gardner Press, Inc., 1976, 223 pages.
- Anderson, Barbara Gallatin, "Adaptive Aspects of Culture Shock," *American Anthropologist*, 1971, 5 pages.
- Barra, LaRoy, "How Culture Shock Affects Communication," ED 184909, 1976, 20 pages.
- Bernstein, Judith, "Urban Field Education: An Opportunity and Structure for Enhancing Students' Personal and Social Efficacy." Paper presented at Philadelphia, Great Lakes Colleges Association, Urban Semester, 1974.
- Cobb, S., "Social Support As a Moderator of Life Stress," *Psychosomatic Medicine*, 1976, 15 pages.
- Derlman, Baron, "An Integration of Burnout into a Stress Model," ED 190939, 1980, 30 pages.
- Harty, Harold, "Preservice Teacher Self Concept from the Campus Through Early Field Experiences in Multicultural Settings," ED 179630, 1976, 16 pages.
- Jersild, Arthur, *When Teachers Face Themselves*, Columbia University: Horace Mann Lincoln Institute of School Experimentation, 1955, 10 pages.
- Lauderdale, Michael, *Burnout: Strategies for Personal and Organizational Life*, Learning Concepts, Austin, Texas, 1982.
- Maslow, A. H., *Toward a Psychology of Being*, New York: Van Nostrand Co., 2nd Ed., 1968, 225 pages.
- Randall, William, "Stress Management for Educators: Resource Guide," ED 193788, 1980, 110 pages.
- Rhoads, Deborah, "Life Change, Social Support, Psychological Symptomology: A Search for Causal Relationships," ED 190922, 1980, 18 pages.
- Richards, Gary, "Some Educational Implications and Contributions of Outward Bound," ED 194266, 1977, 270 pages.
- Rickon, Robert, "Teacher Burnout: A Failure of the Supervisory Process," *NAASP Bulletin*, March 1980, 13 pages.
- Sinclair, K. E., et al., "Anxiety and Cognitive Processes in Problem Solving," *Australian Journal of Education*, 1974, 15 pages.
- Sparks, Dennis, "Helping Clients Manage Stress: A Practical Approach," ED 195923, 1981, 55 pages

Experiential Education: A Search For Common Roots

by Greg Druian, Tom Owens and Sharon Owen

Do experiential programs have any common elements? A comparison of some successful programs indicates that there are some essential similarities.

Do experiential education programs have more in common than coincidental resemblances? There are compelling reasons for starting to look at common features. As long as programs operate in isolation from one another, they will be vulnerable to the chipping away that accompanies economic hard times. In order to overcome their isolation, they need to learn more about the purposes, outcomes and techniques of similar programs. In this way, good programs will be able to present a stronger front and will be more likely to sustain the momentum generated over the past decade. An understanding of features held in common by successful programs could strengthen the case that any specific program might make for continuance; it could lead the way to standards for quality in experiential education; it could help in the adaptation of programs by assuring that site-specific conditions and needs are attended to; and it could facilitate the integration of new elements into an ongoing program, thereby offering an alternative to the establishment of new programs.

The main purpose of this article is to offer a framework for identifying essential elements of three experiential education programs: Experience-Based Career Education, Foxfire, and Outward Bound. A second purpose is to select elements that we believe to be essential to effective experiential education. After review of pertinent literature and our discussions with staff in the three programs, we chose the following nine categories as most likely to contain essential program elements: purposes; setting; characteristics of participants; learning strategies; student roles; instructor roles; product of learning activities; management and support; and program outcomes. Experience-Based Career Education, Foxfire and Outward Bound were chosen because they have been around long enough to have become stable, each was developed in response to a different set of needs, all three have separate and clear identities, they have reasonably clear and well articulated principles and procedures, and each has been widely imitated and adapted.

Greg Druian, Tom Owens and **Sharon Owen** conducted their research at the Northwest Regional Educational Laboratory in Portland, Oregon.

Experience-Based Career Education (EBCE) is a program that began in 1971 for high school juniors and seniors, and has since been adapted to many other groups of people, including adults. It provides students with a comprehensive, fully-accredited education that emphasizes community-based learning. EBCE staff are learning managers and facilitators; no classes in the traditional sense are offered, although seminars are frequently used. The learning managers help students design and follow individualized learning plans that incorporate basic skills, life competencies, and career development. Students profit from the chance to explore various careers of interest in the community; many are helped to prepare for adulthood and economic self-sufficiency as well as to interact with adults in natural work settings. EBCE was developed by four regional educational laboratories with funding from the National Institute of Education, and EBCE projects are now operating in over 200 school districts throughout the country.

Typically a wilderness experience, Outward Bound is an educational process in which students find meaning through group and individual encounters with unfamiliar environments that provide physical stress.

Foxfire, by contrast, began with one man's effort to design a curriculum that would draw upon the unique resources of the local community. Eliot Wigginton, faced with a class totally turned off to the traditional approaches to learning English, one day simply asked his students in Rabun Gap, Georgia, whether they wanted to write a magazine. Today there are programs similar to Foxfire operating in approximately 145 schools across the nation. Most cultural journalism programs engage students in developing and publishing a journal that reflects the cultural pluralism of the community in which they live. Many related activities may be pursued in conjunction with the journal. For example, in some cases videotapes replace the journal as a project. Students do most of the work associated with whatever project they happen to be working on. Thus, Foxfire tends to be comprehensive in the kinds of activities it offers students. It has been implemented in colleges, high schools, junior high schools, even elementary schools.

Like Foxfire, the Outward Bound program may be implemented for practically any age group. Typically a wilderness experience, Outward Bound is an educational process in which students find meaning through group and individual encounters with unfamiliar environments that provide physical stress. The focus of Outward Bound is on building self-confidence, trust, and acceptance of personal responsibility. Since 1962 when the Outward Bound movement began in this country, having been imported from Great Britian where it was started in 1941, Outward Bound has expanded to six schools, a center based at Dartmouth College, and a national organization based in Greenwich, Connecticut. Outward Bound also has been implemented in conjunction with school programs at the high school and college levels, as well as outside the educational system with people of various ages. In a typical Outward Bound course, participants might spend the first few days together coping with relatively unfamiliar tasks, learning new skills, and developing greater physical stamina. Next they might spend two to three days on a "solo," alone with few resources and no responsibilities except to reflect on their experience. Finally, participants might spend the remaining time on an expedition they carry out themselves without instructors. Characteristic of the Outward Bound experience is a powerful sense of accomplishment--often preceded by extreme frustration. Having experienced and successfully coped with one's physical limitations, and with limitations of self-awareness and of group responsibility and identity, participants emerge with new confidence in their abilities.

In the remainder of this article, we will describe what we believe to be common elements of these three programs, following the nine categories listed above. Then in Table I, we distill the elements we hypothesize as essential for experiential education.

1. Purpose

Successful experiential education programs have clearly articulated purposes that are interpreted similarly by program participants. It is reasonable to suppose that stated program purposes both reflect needs of a group of learners and imply a certain program content. In successful programs, the relationship of program purposes to educational need and program content are demonstrable.

2. Setting

Setting refers to the physical and psychological environment in which the learning takes place. If more than one environment is involved, setting also refers to the manner in which the environments are controlled so as to maximize learning. Characteristic of experiential settings are four essential factors: realism; challenge; an appropriate level of risk; and diversity. A setting has *realism* when the learner thinks it is not contrived. A realistic setting may be either natural (e.g., wilderness) or man-made (e.g., the workplace or a person's home). In both cases the setting is not artificially developed as a place for student learning. The setting is viewed as *challenging* because there are adults there who are engaged in dynamic activities. The presence of psychological or physical *risk* often motivates the learner to maximum performance. In Outward Bound the natural environment provides physical risk, which is

---

A setting has realism when the learner thinks it is not contrived.

---

kept at a manageable level by the presence of a highly trained leader. In EBCE or Foxfire the anticipation of first voyage into the community to meet an unknown adult is a psychological risk for an adolescent. Finally, in cases where a *diversity* of settings is part of an experiential education program, activities within these settings are integrated. In Foxfire and EBCE, in-school activities are integrated with community activities through a process of analyzing which academic skills are needed for task accomplishment. A major purpose of these programs is to combine learning activities inside and outside the school into a balanced, comprehensive, and individualized program to help high school students prepare for the demands of adulthood. Outward Bound, on the other hand, is not generally geared to combining in-school with out-of-school activities. A main purpose of Outward Bound is to use the outdoors to help participants develop personal skills such as self-confidence, team work and self-understanding, which will contribute to success in adulthood.

The learner in Experience-Based Career Education spends time in at least three settings. First is the workplace, where the student may either be performing real work or learning about a job through observation or "shadowing." The second is a learning resource center where students work with a learning manager to plan, monitor, and assess their activities. At the learning center, skills can be practiced and developed; it is also a place

---

Research related to this article was supported by the National Institute of Education under Contract NE-C-00-4-0010 as part of the work of the Education and Work Program of the Northwest Regional Educational Laboratory (NWREL). The opinions expressed or implied in this article do not necessarily reflect the position of the National Institute of Education or of NWREL.

where seminars may be held to discuss issues. The third setting is the classroom. Some programs offer a part-time EBCE program with students attending regular classes the rest of the time. The EBCE learning manager is able to help the student coordinate the activities in each setting by helping to develop a learning plan that specifies objectives appropriate for the student.

In Foxfire there are two settings that relate to the program. One is the community. In Foxfire this means anywhere in the community where something is going on that the learner thinks is important. Frequently this means going to meet people and interview them in their homes. In other cases it may mean visiting their places of business. The second setting is the in-school location where the information gathered in the community is processed and turned into a written, taped or printed product that can be shared with others.

Outward Bound programs use learning settings in still a different way. The setting, normally in the outdoors or wilderness, is treated as a challenge to be overcome. In the overcoming of challenges, the learner's self-image, sense of responsibility and will to achieve develop steadily. It is expected that there will be a carry-over effect; a learner who sees how to overcome an obstacle during a rock climb will use similar strategies to solve problems encountered in the classroom—or, for that matter, in life. The outdoors and the wilderness are treated as a metaphor, standing for something that can be anticipated to occur after the program is over. At the same time, the immediate sensory appeal of the outdoors is exploited in

---

In the overcoming of challenges, the learner's self-image, sense of responsibility and will to achieve develop steadily.

---

the Outward Bound program. Intense experience over a short time period is the goal. Unlike the other two programs, there are usually no multiple learning settings to be integrated during the time period of the program. Outward Bound does, however, concern itself strongly with the question of how learning during the wilderness experience can be transferred back home and how learning relates to the individual's own development.

3. Characteristics of Participants

We are referring to the types of students involved in experiential education programs, particularly to learner characteristics such as sex, age, ethnic background, economic status, preferred learning style, level of academic, moral and psychosocial development, and reasons for joining the program. Elements hypothesized as essential are voluntary participation and diversity of participants. The fact the experiential learning strategies may be effective for some students does not imply that they would work best for all students. Foxfire, EBCE and Outward Bound involve only students who voluntarily join the program. In each case, participants reflect all segments of the population from gifted and talented

---

The fact that experiential learning strategies may be effective for some students does not imply that they would work best for all students.

---

students to mentally retarded youth. Often a program will try to establish a diversity of students so that those less advanced in some areas can profit from the help of their peers.

4. Learning Strategies

"Learning strategies" has to do with the sequence and interrelationship of learner activities. There is greater congruence of approach among the three programs in this category than in any other. The common sequence of the learning process characteristic of these programs is:
- Assessment and goal setting;
- Negotiation and planning;
- Engaging and experiencing;
- Reflecting and evaluating;
- Sharing and publishing;
- Application and generalizing.

Though the names of the steps may differ, each program uses a version of the above steps. All three programs begin with an assessment of student needs, along with some kind of determination of where the student would like to go. A set of activities is planned or negotiated that both student and instructor believe is likely to lead to the desired goal. All three programs involve the student in the negotiation and planning step, although the degree of implementation of this step varies.

The next step is engaging in the experience itself. Following engagement, the learner reflects on the activity through a personal journal, group discussion, discussion with the instructor, or by other means. This step often merges with the next, which involves transforming the raw material of the experience through reproducing it in a form that can be shared by others. This is a crucial step of experiential education programs and what differentiates experiential learning from the mere having of experiences. Both immediate and delayed transformations occur. As part of the program, EBCE students transform their experience into a project portfolio or journal; in Foxfire, raw material of interviews and photography is transformed into a magazine; in Outward Bound groups, rap sessions and personal journals are used. Finally, this "thing" created out of the experience is tried out in a new situation. This last step may not be part of the experiential education program itself--although it certainly is in Foxfire as the magazine gets marketed, people purchase it, students receive feedback, and ideas for new projects are generated.

All three programs provide an opportunity for students to renegotiate their learning plans and to learn from unplanned experiences. The latter is important since all three programs operate in the real world where the environment cannot be entirely predicted or controlled. The strength of all three approaches is linked with certain assumptions about how people learn. Without documenting fully, it seems safe to list the following assumptions about learning as among those shared by EBCE, Foxfire and Outward Bound. First, people learn best from doing real tasks. Second, young people carry serious consequences. Third, everyone learns best by following a systematic process that leads them from where they are to where they want to go. Fourth, adolescents can learn or reinforce basic skills as effectively out of class as in class.

5. Student Roles

Student roles are extremely important in experiential learning programs. The key questions here are what roles

TABLE I
ESSENTIAL ELEMENTS OF EXPERIENTIAL EDUCATION

Program Categories	Essential Elements
Purpose	1. Purposes reflect learner needs 2. Purposes imply program content 3. Clearly shared and understood purposes
Setting	4. Setting considered realistic by the learners 5. A physical or psychological challenge is provided by the setting 6. An appropriate degree of risk exists 7. Diverse settings are integrated
Participants' Characteristics	8. Voluntary participation 9. Diversity of participants
Learning Strategies	10. Based on an explicit theory of learning 11. Encourage young people to perform tasks normally given to adults in our society 12. Emphasize a balance of action, reflection, application 13. Provide learning experiences that are individualized, sequential, developmental 14. Involve frequent structured interaction between student and instructor 15. Provide opportunities for unplanned learning from new experiences
Student Roles	16. Active student role in planning and carrying out activities 17. Chance to experience various roles—leader, team member, employee, tutor, etc. 18. Assuming responsibilities for one's own actions 19. Opportunity to interact with various adults as well as with peers
Instructor Roles	20. Help students plan and carry out their activities 21. Provide role model as participant in the learning process 22. Monitor progress, assess and feed back information to students 23. Provide motivation and encouragement 24. Model skills in planning, empathy, communications and resource sharing
Outcomes of Learning Activities	25. Outcomes of learner activities are perceived as real and important by students and others 26. Students feel ownership for the outcomes
Management and Support	27. Locating community resources for student learning 28. Forming positive relationships with external agencies (such as may be needed in awarding regular school credit for program participation 29. Obtaining funding and community support 30. Recruitment and selection of staff who are committed to using experiential learning strategies
Program Outcomes	31. Increased student self-confidence and ability to relate to others 32. Staff and students are involved in assessing effectiveness of program 33. Openness to looking at both positive and negative outcomes and in examining areas for program improvement

are played by students and with whom does the student interact in each role. In experiential learning programs, it is worth investigating when students are learning primarily alone, in interaction with one adult, with peers, or with a diverse group of people. It is also important to know whether students are learning from people with backgrounds similar to or different from themselves, since the latter provides greater opportunity for growth in empathy with others possessing different values. Furthermore, experiential learning programs may show important differences and similarities in the extent and the conditions under which leaners are expected to play the roles of leader, tutor, active learner, observer, employee, advocate and entrepreneur.

The elements of this category that we consider essential are an active student role in planning and carrying out activities; a chance to experience various roles; the assumption of responsibility for one's own actions; and the opportunity to interact with adults as well as with a variety of peers. In the three programs described here, students' roles are different from those they play in the traditional classroom. In Foxfire students may serve as reporters, photographers or local historians. To the extent that some students instruct less experienced ones in darkroom techniques, they also share the role of a teacher. Outward Bound participants have the opportunity to serve as team member and leader during certain phases of their program. In EBCE students often take on the role of employee and have responsibilities similar to other employees in the organization. They sometimes serve customers, handle money or equipment, or coordinate the activities of others.

6. Instructor Roles

Effective instructors help students plan and carry out their activities while also serving as a role model of an active, involved learner. They monitor student progress; they assess and feed back information to students. Effective instructors motivate and encourage students, demonstrating skills in planning, empathy, communications and resource sharing. Instructional roles in the programs under discussion require similar skills, knowledge and attitudes. The instructor functions as a facilitator of learning, rather than primarily as a dispenser of knowledge. This attitude is a mixture of sensitivity to individual needs and of conviction that engagement with unfamiliar but feasible activities can meet those needs. The instructor must have imagination to use the immediate environment as a learning resource to provide that unfamiliar but feasible task. In EBCE the learning manager needs to show the same kind of skills in helping students formulate individual learning plans. In Foxfire it is crucial to have students do things for themselves, showing each other how to accomplish tasks that have been mastered by others before. And Outward Bound instructors must not only be sensitive to the needs of the individual; they must also know how to guide the development of a group of individuals engaged in their common wilderness task and how to implement the safety requirements.

Interpersonal skill is required of instructors in these programs. Empathy, individual and group communication, and the ability to elicit response are skills that instructors in these programs use regularly. A further characteristic is the ability to function as a resource person able to link the student with appropriate people, things or pieces of information. This ability may be described in terms of the instructor having knowledge about knowledge--how it is obtained, how to gain access to it--rather than simply having knowledge about one subject matter area.

7. Products of Learning Activities

In successful experiential learning programs, students exhibit a high level of ownership of their products. Similarly, successful programs exhibit a high degree of student responsibility for the consequence of activities undertaken by the student. The Foxfire magazine or videotape is the group product of the program; Foxfire as a concept or a project is a product of student energy and group decision making. In fact, the responsibility for managing the project makes for unique kinds of student involvement. With EBCE the products usually reflect individual rather than group effort and consist of written reports or other presentations for which individual academic credit is awarded. In Outward Bound there is more engagement and commitment to process outcomes than to a tangible product; in this respect it differs from Foxfire and EBCE.

8. Management and Support

Management and support contribute to the climate of the program: sponsorship, program image, support services, relationship to other aspects of the school system, staffing patterns, funding, and community support. We consider four elements to be essential within this category: locating community resources for student learning; forming positive relationships with external agents (such as may be needed in awarding regular school credit for program participation); obtaining funding and community support; and recruitment and selection of staff committed to using experiential learning strategies.

Successful EBCE programs usually have a strong program identity that is manifested in a distinctive name and the evolution of unique habits and routines that convey the message, "This is how we do it." The same characteristics may be seen in Foxfire. Foxfire-like programs have been adapted in numberless ways, but one of the surest ways of identifying them is by a name that refers to a forgotten folkway, artifact, or custom of the region. The concentrated nature of the Outward Bound program appears to result in students identifying closely with the group that develops over the course of the program.

Each of the three programs is sponsored and financed differently. Foxfire receives much of its funding from sales of its publications. Outward Bound generally charges a tuition, offers scholarships to those without funds, or is subsidized by special project funds, such as those for helping to rehabilitate youth offenders. EBCE programs are usually funded by the school districts adopting them, often using state or federal support for career education, vocational education, CETA funds or categorical aid (as for the gifted or handicapped).

9. Program Outcomes

Although Foxfire, EBCE and Outward Bound have developed independently of each other, they contain some common program outcomes. Each develops self-confidence in young people and an increased ability to relate to others. Each is concerned about both the short- and long-term effects on students. In each, some short-term effects are seen as instrumental for longer term effects. In EBCE the students' exploration of a particular career is intended not only to learn about that one job, but also to gain a broader perspective for looking at other occupations. Outward Bound students use initiative groups, climbing exercises and other experiences to examine how they react to metaphorically similar situations in their lives. Foxfire students learn camera and darkroom techniques that can be used to produce a magazine and also to promote social and cultural values. Foxfire and EBCE share a characteristic of being broader than a single subject area. Thus, the experiences learned may be

While these essential elements represent a beginning in the task of building bridges between experiential education programs, much remains to be done.

translated by school staff into academic credit in language arts, social studies or elective credit. In Foxfire and EBCE the mode of experiential learning is sometimes used as a vehicle for broader curriculum reform. Both provide a model of integration of separate subject content to blend in with the interests of the students. The final essential element hypothesized for this category is that students and staff are involved in assessing the effectiveness of their program, using both positive and negative outcomes for program improvement. Because EBCE programs are often publicly funded, the evaluation process is more formal than that of Foxfire or Outward Bound. Comprehensive summaries of EBCE evaluations have been done by Bucknam (1976) and Crowe and Adams (1979), while Shore (1977) has analyzed numerous evaluations of Outward Bound.

Summary

In this article, we have suggested essential elements of three experiential education programs. We grouped these elements in nine categories that can be used to describe programs. Thirty-three elements were hypothesized within these nine categories, as shown in Table I. While these essential elements represent a beginning in the task of building bridges between experiential education programs, much remains to be done. The nine categories may need to be refined. The number of essential elements probably needs to be reduced to be useful to practitioners. Before these refinements can take place, other experiential education programs should be studied. The categories and essential elements listed here will, no doubt, be tried out on selected programs over the next several years. Out of these studies we expect not only to refine our findings, but also to collect practical examples of ways in which essential elements are made manifest in successful programs. Ultimately these examples will serve as point of reference for anyone interested in experiential education, whether in developing new programs or in improving those that already exist.

REFERENCES

Bucknam, Ronald B. "The Impact of EBCE—An Evaluation Viewpoint," **Illinois Career Education Journal**, 33, No. 3, Spring, 1976.

Crowe, Michael R. and Adams, Kay A. **The Current Status of Assessing Experiential Education Program**. National Center for Research in Vocational Education, Ohio State University, March, 1979.

Hagans, Rex W. "What is Experience-Based Career Education?," **Illinois Career Education Journal**, 33, No.3, Spring, 1976.

McBee, Duchess. **"Finding Yourself in the Wilderness,"** Passages (Magazine of Northwest Orient Airlines), 10, No. 11, November, 1979.

Reynolds, Sherrod. "Golden Hindesight, Homespun, Logniappe, et al." **Teacher**, Vol. 96, No. 7, March, 1979.

Rice, Berkeley. "Going to the Mountain," **Psychology Today**, 13, No. 7, December, 1979.

Shore, Arnold. **Outward Bound: A Reference Volume**. Greenwich, Connecticut: Outward Bond Inc., 1977.

Wigginton, Eliot. **Moments: The Foxfire Experience**. Kennebunk, Me.: Star Press, 1975.

DESIGNING EXPERIENTIAL CURRICULA

by JED WILLIAMSON

Public schools can involve students, parents, community and school board in the design of experience-based learning. The author describes one such program, The Mt. Cardigan Environmental Unit.

The purposes of this article are first to provide a framework which contains what I believe are some essential understandings for allowing one to think experientially, and second to suggest some strategies for implementing activity-centered and community-based curricula within a typical public school context.

The Framework

Among the goal statements in every school district with which I have come in contact can be found tenets upon which the experiential process is based. These goals include the following, usually stated in this format:
- to provide students with the skills necessary for coping with a changing world;
- to teach students how to solve problems;
- to provide students with challenging and real learning experiences;
- to meet the individual needs of students;
- to help students learn how to communicate effectively with each other;
- to prepare students for living in a society founded upon democratic principles.

It is not essential for the purposes of this article to list those goals which specifically pertain to "demonstrated competence" in basic skill areas, although they must be addressed through the curricula. Keeping all of these goals in mind, I will state the framework for learning experientially, be it for a 40 minute class, an eight-week unit, or an entire year. First, (1) the learners must be placed in a problem situation which calls for individual or cooperative actions; these actions and their attending consequences are then (2) observed and reflected upon, and from these reflections the learners (3) review the appropriateness of their actions and attitudes and postulate what changes might be desirable in a similar problem solving situation. Then, (4) learners are placed in a new problem solving situation in which to test any desirable changes.

Diagrammatically, this cycle can be represented as follows:[1]

```
                    Actions Consequences
              (1)  ↗
         Concrete Experience
       ↗                    ↘
   (4)                       (2)
Testing Concepts in      Observation
New Context              Reflection
       ↖                    ↙
              (3) ←
         Formulation of
      Concepts and Generalizations
```

To foster this process in any school setting, certain preconditions are desirable. Generally, the faculty would view the school building as primarily the place where steps two and three occur. The direct, concrete learning experiences would take place as much outside of school as inside school. Additionally, the faculty would view the role of the teacher as being the problem poser rather than the problem solver, as someone who establishes clear objectives which focus as much on what is happening, and how, as on content. In short, the teacher is a process expert as well as a subject matter expert. The concern is to help learners

---

JED WILLIAMSON *teaches at the University of New Hampshire's Department of Education. He is co-developer of the Live, Learn, and Teach program, which is a seven week summer course in designing experiential curricula followed by a full year internship, leading to an M.A.T. or M.Ed. degree.*

---

[1] This diagram is a combination of ideas taken from models of experiential learning by James Coleman, et al., in "The Hopkins Game Program: Conclusions from Seven Years of Research," *Education Researchers*, August 1973, and David Kolb, et al., in *Organizational Psychology*, Englewood Cliffs, NJ: Prentice-Hall, 1974. The groundwork was done by John Dewey, as stated in his *Experience and Education*, New York: Collier Books, 1963; and by Kurt Lewin, in *Field Theory and Social Science*, New York: Harper, 1951.

achieve a personal high standard of comprehension and perception of their outside world and inward lives. The school curriculum would have an emphasis on integrating disciplines, and, thereby, for collaborative teaching. With interdisciplinary units and a core of faculty working with one grade or one group of students, the 45 or 50 minute class period could be shortened or lengthened, and class sizes could vary according to need. Learning situations would stress involving students physically, mentally, and socially in direct, active experiences.

Designing Experiential Units

Whether one teacher wants to devote fifteen minutes a week to experiential learning or a team of teachers wants to develop a ten-week interdisciplinary unit using an experiential approach, the process for design and implementation is the same. The following three tables are illustrative of how this process is accomplished in the Live, Learn and Teach program. Table A, "A Checklist of Factors in Planning for Experiential Learning — A Planning Format," is a fairly typical lesson planning format, while Table B is a very specific and detailed expansion of Step IV, "The Planning Process," from Table A. Table C is but one method of determining if a given unit meets the criteria for experiential learning. In keeping with the goal of involving learners, all three tables should be viewed as instruments to be used by both teachers and students.

Table A: A Checklist of Factors in Planning for Experiential Learning — A Planning Format.

I. Theme of the plan
  Rationale including overall purpose
  Desired results
    Cognitive
    Affective
    Behavioral
II. Resources and needs
  Personnel
  Materials and geographic locations
  Budget
III. Logistics
  Dates and Places
  Transportation
  Emergency procedures
  Permission/medical requirements
IV. Planning Process (See Table B for detail.)
V. Assessment procedures for student learning (consider pre- and post-test/assessment).
VI. Journal observations and conclusions

Table B: This is a sample of how the Planning Process in Table A, Item IV, might appear for a beginning lesson on orienteering.

IV. PLANNING PROCESS

OVERALL PURPOSE: A growing sense of competence in dealing with the environment

ACTIVITY: Orienteering
DATE:
NAME:

RESULTS	PROCESS	PROCESS CHECK

What the learner-centered teacher seeks to accomplish. Think in terms of affective, cognitive and behavioral growth.
 	
1. -reduce potential threat
   -remove mysterious aspects
   -create a sense of comfort/ease
   -gain attention of learners
2. -provide sense of all learners becoming involved
   -provide initial success experience
   -provide acquisition of skil in reading compass, setting compass dial
	What actions the learner-centered teacher takes to achieve the desired RESULTS. Consider also resources, logistics, and budget.
	
	1. Introduce activity by: (10-15 min.)
	   -Holding up grapefruit as representation of world
	   -Describe where poles and magnetic pole are located
	   -Describe characteristics of compass while handing out compass (one for every five)
	   -Break into small groups (4-5 each group)
	2. Go to point from which prearranged sitings have been made and:
	   -Have groups together
	   -Have them turn dial to 42° and site most significant object in distance
	   -Have them turn dial to 203° and do same
	   -Continue above process until learners have "got it"
	3. Pacing and distance
	4. Short course
	5. Larger course
	6. Post activity discussion
		What behaviors during the PROCESS will verify if the activity is succeeding or if any adjustments in actions are needed.
		
		1. Are learners exhibiting ease, understanding? (Look for relaxed facial expressions, physical proximity, minimal movement. Listen for relatedness of questions and conversation.)
		2. -Are learners in small groups with friends or strangers?
		   -Are all individuals involved with task?
		   -Are learners siting correctly?

EVALUATION How many of the desired RESULTS were attained? How much of the OVERALL PURPOSE was achieved? Which teacher actions must be changed to achieve the desired RESULTS?		

> **Table C: Sample of an Experiential Class Assessment Format**
>
> 1. This class had the following experiential components (on a scale of 1 to 10):
>
>   ____ students actively involved — physically
>   ____ students actively involved — mentally
>   ____ students actively involved — socially
>   ____ teachers actively involved
>   ____ teachers set up problem
>   ____ others
>
> 2. The teachers (on a scale of 1 to 10):
>
>   ____ were well organized
>   ____ were aware of students' abilities
>   ____ were aware of students' concerns
>   ____ made good use of resources
>   ____ made good use of time
>   ____ communicated well with students
>   ____ were enthusiastic about what they were doing
>   ____ did not get between the students and the learning situation
>   ____ other:
>
> 3. The students (on a scale of 1 to 10):
>
>   ____ liked the lesson
>   ____ understood the lesson
>   ____ were fair to the teachers
>   ____ cooperated with each other
>   ____ learned something
>   ____ other:
>
> 4. The things I liked most about this class:
>
> 5. Something which could be improved:
>
> 6. Something I did not like or which made me uncomfortable:

As an example of what is possible in a typical American public school, I will describe how an eight week interdisciplinary unit, the Mt. Cardigan Environmental Unit, emphasizing a study of the natural environment has been developed over the past six years at the McKelvie Middle School in Bedford, New Hampshire. As a supervisor of graduate interns in that school for the past several years, my first-hand experience has shown that the usual roadblocks and constraints, such as lack of money, community involvement, or support, can be surmounted.

In its current stage of development, the unit works in the following manner. During the late spring, parents of seventh grade students and the students themselves are given a presentation and description of the unit. This occurs at an evening meeting, with teachers and administrators present, and includes video-tape and slide presentations, a question and answer session, and information handouts. Over the summer, the eighth grade teachers finish the current year's revision of the Field Study Manual, which becomes the guide book for each student throughout the unit. This guide book contains a great variety of problems to be solved, with considerable latitude for each student to identify his or her own particular area of inquiry. The manual is meant to serve as a journal, as a guide to inquiry, as a means to record observations and as an aid to posing and solving problems.

For the first six weeks of school, all eighth grade students (the number has ranged from 125 to 160) and their teachers prepare for a week of investigation and exploration on and around a mountain in northern New Hampshire. The skills which the youngsters learn prior to the trip include water testing, soils testing, flora and fauna identification, mapping, orienteering, archeology, camping, first aid, weather observation and prediction, food preparation, and photography. All of these skills are taught through actual field problems set up in the school, on school grounds, and in the community. Steps one, two and three of the experiential process are engaged in daily, with step four presenting a real and immediate prospect in mind. From the first day of school, students work in groups of twelve with at least one adult in each group. School subjects such as physical training, writing, and social studies are integrated as a result of the kinds of problems that must be solved throughout the unit.

By the time students embark on their trip to the mountain, they have encountered in a direct and personal manner the problems they will be solving in the new setting. Although the students are structured into activities such as a beaver pond study, a plant succession observation, an archeological dig in an old farm house cellar hole, and a stream flow study, there is also an individual focus which each student has chosen, and which will result in a culminating project synthesized during the final week, then presented to parents and the communtiy. Such projects have included making scale models of the 25 square mile study area, picture displays, written and pictorial reconstruction of farm life 200 years ago, a video-tape production depicting the entire unit, flora and fauna guides for the area, and a booklet designed to help other teachers and students start such a unit. All but a few students choose to work on these projects collaboratively. Teachers and students assess whether learning goals have been met both by the projects and the continuing work in the Field Study Manual.

It is hoped this brief sketch of a fairly complex unit will give the reader one indication of the kind of experiential approaches possible. In addition to the pre-conditions stated at the end of the first section, some specific details need attention. These details are revealed through the following interview, which Greg Kniseley, a graduate student intern, conducted with the school principal, Robert Little:

> The science Curriculum Coordinator had the task of reviewing and revising our science curriculum five years ago (1973). Ray Landry, and the other science teacher, Dick Janelle, wanted to provide an exciting 'hands on' experience for the eighth grade class. In a brainstorming session during an eighth grade team planning period, the teachers conceived the idea of involving students, parents, and community leaders in developing an interdisciplinary unit of instruction, which has now come to be known as the Mr. Cardigan Environmental Unit. Ray also involved the Assistant Superintendent, Rod Mansfield, in the preliminary stages, and this proved to be an important step in gaining support for the idea. During the summer, Ray, with input from his peers, used the vehicle of the summer Curriculum Development Committee to have the program come far enough along in its design that first year so that it

was included as part of school district policy. As principal, I directed as much funding as I could towards the project.

As is the case in most innovative or new projects, one person really has to get turned on to an idea and then develop the plan. In this case, Ray Landry was the person. In addition to the steps mentioned, he built an evaluation model and kept the right people involved and informed throughout.[2]

Implicit in his statement are some important factors essential to the success of such a venture:

(1) The project began with a few dedicated teachers, low-key in their approach, and a principal, willing but thorough in matters of an exploratory nature, spending the time in and out of school to launch the project, taking care to involve all of the necessary people.

(2) The teachers began with modest, step by step experiments. At first, the unit focused entirely on science and math, and did not include all teachers in the eighth grade. Year by year, the unit expanded to include the other subject areas. The current level of complexity is a healthy indication of the support and involvement of many adults in the community and of agency participation.

among the essentials.

During my five year tenure, I have observed some positive changes in attitude and involvement on the part of staff, and I believe this is attributable to the fact that the learning experience has been so obviously successful, as determined both by academic achievement and by student and teacher attitude. At this point, not only are the academic subject matter teachers involved; the nurse, secretary, home economics teacher, and physical education teachers have joined the effort. All staff have galvanized — in spite of obvious and expected differences in style and approach — around the task of preparing for the week in the mountains. It is a time they enjoy, as do the students.

Although some of the students feel that the Field Study Manual is really just another workbook to be completed, most students use it for what it is — a guide to give substance to their observations and discoveries. The blend of experiential and pencil/paper learning is achieved through necessity and natural inquiry. This is not to say that students can choose to do nothing. Rather, it is to say that there are more options than might be found if they were pursuing a curriculum in a more traditional manner.

During my five year tenure, I have observed some positive changes in attitude and involvement on the part of staff, and I believe this is attributable to the fact that the learning experience has been so obviously successful, as determined both by academic achievement and by student and teacher attitude.

---

(3) The teachers' primary motive was to create an interesting set of learning experiences from which observable and measurable skills would generate. Like their students, these teachers have developed a keen sense of ownership of the teaching materials and the learning experiences — which is not a typical response when using prepared texts.

(4) Teachers ensured that lines of communication remained open with all the people concerned. Written information to parents, presentations to school board and community, slide and videotape documentations, student projects, parents' meetings and continual program evaluations are

As to student-teacher relationships, it would be apparent to an observer that a positive tone for the school year is generated through the shared learning and living experiences.

It is encouraging to see the many schools which have developed units of a similar scope. The message which comes through from each of them is that the development of experiential approaches is limited only by temporary constraints, most of which are within the people doing the developing. As the network of teachers who are currently able to use these approaches becomes more sophisticated and as more articles on this topic are written, it is hoped there will follow a substantive increase in the use of experiential curricula.

---

[2]*Autumn Adventure — An Eighth Grade Environmental Experience*, Greg Kniseley, et al., Published by McKelvie Middle School, Bedford, New Hampshire, 1978.

A Marriage Proposal:
Competency Based Education and Experiential Learning

By Sherrod Reynolds

The tide of Competency Based Education (CBE) is rising nationwide, pulled by the force of demands for accountability and a return to basics. To date, some thirty-eight states have bowed to public pressure by legislating some form of minimum standard testing to be carried out by the schools. Truly a "popular" reform movement emerging largely from forces outside of education, CBE has drawn fire from many professional educators who fear the back-to-basics thrust will have a meat cleaver effect on programs deamed "non-essential" and may result in a contracted version of the goals and aims of public education.

The verbal barrage that has occurred between protagonists and antagonists of the movement has resulted in confusion and anxiety among school people who are expected to fulfill the mandates meted out by the states. Those teachers whose goals are more liberal than literal, and whose approaches are more child-centered and experience-oriented than subject-centered and results-oriented, are especially troubled by the "basics" pressure. It is not surprising that experiential educators have squared off in anticipation of another educational fracas, prepared to fight for their very existence. The polarity that has been assumed between CBE and experiential education is a reactionary and unfounded response to the stated goals of the competency movement. CBE has marched into the public schools carrying the seed of reform. But the seed will not bear fruit without a help-mate capable or nurturing the idea into fruition. Experience-based education has the potential of becoming the needed help-mate. The wedding of these two notions of education—the one built on the rock of basic skills, the other on the belief that learning requires accompanying experience in order to be fully effective—offers a creative and powerful approach to the implementation stage of CBE.

The Problem:

Falling SAT scores, reports of declining ability among young people entering the work force, evidence of functional illiteracy among high school graduates, lowered entrance standards in colleges and universities to accommodate lower achieving student populations, and a general belief that young people coming out of public schools today simply are not getting a good foundation in basic skills have all contributed to the vengeance with which CBE has been advocated by the tax paying public and the legislators. "Minimum competency laws are attractive because they put the focus on what most people see as the 'bottom line' of education—whether students can read, write and calculate. They are thus a dramatic and easily understood—albeit imperfect—response by legislators to the public's frustration."[1]

Critics of CBE fear that minimum competencies, met with the minimum compliance of unenthusiastic teachers, will yield minimum education—the antithesis of the stated goals of Competency Based Education. They warn that school response to CBE will result in teaching to the test and a responding narrowing in curriculum. In his *New York Times* column, Fred Heckinger states this view:

> A program stripped to the basics usually does not provide much real education, even in the basics. If reading and writing are to have strong appeal, children must be interested in them as tools with which to tackle a world that seems interesting to them. Bare literacy, without the development and enjoyment of those other skills—in music, the arts, an understanding of a variety of people and cultures—offers little incentive to put the basic skills to work.[2]

---

[1] Chris Pipho, "Involving Yourself in the Minimum Competency Testing Movement," in *Teacher* 97 (11-12, 1979): 60-64.
[2] Fred Heckinger, *New York Times* (Nov. 9, 1976).

Sherrod Reynolds *has worked for* **Foxfire** *and recently received her M.Ed. from* **Harvard Graduate** *School of Education. She is presently working as a consultant in Boston.*

When society places the emphasis of education so decisively on the outcome rather than the process of education, then teachers will build their curriculum around the requirements of the test, because the signals suggest that test results are more highly valued than less measurable outcomes. Historically this has been the case, as reported by Madaus and Airasian in their study of certifying examinations in the United States, Australia and Europe:

> Faced with a choice between one set of objectives which are explicit in the course outline and a different set which are explicit in past certifying examinations, students and teachers generally choose to focus on the latter. This finding holds true over different countries and over many decades . . . Most studies have found that the proportion of instructional time spent on various objectives was seldom higher than the predicted likelihood of their occurrence on the external examination. (Madaus and Airasian, 1978).[3]

CBE generally does not create an atmosphere conducive to taking many educational risks. Teachers are told what must be taught, with an implied threat of punitive action if they fail. This puts the teacher in the role of a technician in what Isreal Scheffler terms the "transmission model" of education.

> The transmission model of education, coupled with the drive for increased efficiency, tends to foster the view of the teacher as a minor technician within an industrial process. The overall goals are set in advance in terms of national needs, the curricular materials prepackaged by the disciplinary experts, the methods developed by educational engineers—and the teacher's job is just to supervise the last operational stage, the methodical insertion of ordered facts into the students' minds.[4]

The pressures to become a technician are great, and the underlying uncertainty teachers feel in the face of society's demands for accountability tend to leave them more cautious and more likely to build curriculum around test requirements. In order to avoid this trap, teachers must feel they have support from administrators to continue experimentation and innovation around the stated demands of CBE.

The message is clear, and is repeated over and over again in the critical writing on CBE: beware of the temptation to teach to the test, to focus on pragmatic and practical competencies to the exclusion of a more liberal education, to eliminate those outcomes of education which are difficult to measure, to sacrifice "humanistic concerns" to the rigid demands of "accountability." These are the voices of the prophets warning the people against seeking simple solutions to complex problems at the risk of losing sight of the goal. Competency Based Education may prove a useful tool for working at the larger problems of public education, but like any tool, it is worthless unless put to good use by a skilled hand.

No one can justifiably argue with the premise from which Competency Based Education operates: that after twelve years of schooling a student should be able to demonstrate a mastery of the "minimum skills necessary to enable further learning and social functioning," as the State of Vermont phrases it.[5] That has always been a partial goal of education. It is also important to note that the literature of CBE says nothing about eliminating anything from the curriculum, in fact the opposite is true. Information disseminated to local districts cautions school people **not** to take identified competencies as the sum of educational expectations, but only the minimum, the floor of what schools should accomplish.

The stated goals of Competency Based Education are simple and straightforward: "To improve instruction for each student," and "to ensure that all pupils attain and maintain basic skills."[6] The movement represents a concerted attempt by the public and the profession to connect learning outcomes to life roles, and to require successful demonstration of these outcomes prerequisite to graduation from high school.[7] It is society's attempt to pump some meaning back into a high school diploma, to shore up the sagging beams of public education, to insure future grist for America's mills.

Competency Based Education is an obvious example of what society wants schools to produce. The onus for incorporating society's goals into the broader educational framework falls on teachers and administrators. It is a reasonable and logical union, but school people, specifically teachers, must be very firm in their guidance of the process, despite the fact that the impetus was external. To borrow Machiavelli's advice to the prince, "we must see which way they are going and place ourselves at their head, for we are their leaders." The objective should be to take advantage of the opportunities CBE presents to create stronger linkages between the "real world" and the school, to establish the validity of learning skills by doing them, to focus in on individual needs of more students. It is commonly believed that young people need opportunities to make the most of their human potential, and that basic skills are necessary for accomplishing that goal. How this is put into practice is left to the peculiar resources and ingenuity of each teacher, guided and supported by administrators, and augmented by

---

[3] Vito Perrone, "Competency Testing: A Social and Historical Perspective," in **Educational Horizons** 58 (Fall, 1979) p. 5.
[4] Israel Scheffler, **Conditions of Knowledge** (The University of Chicago Press, Chicago, IL, 1965) p. 61
[5] **Basic Competencies**, "A Manual of Information and Guidelines for Teachers and Administrators," Vermont Department of Education (March, 1977).
[6] "Study of Minimum Competency Testing Programs," p. 673.
[7] **Competency Tests and Graduation Requirements**, The National Association of Secondary School Principals (Reston, VA, 1979), p. 9

the conscious help and opportunities available through the community.

It is the purpose of this essay to present a case for the proposed marriage: Competency Based Education and experiential education. In order for the seed of this reform movement to bear fruit, it must 1) engage both teachers and learners in the enterprise, 2) be integrated into a broader educational context rather than isolated out, and 3) focus on demonstrated competency through actual experience in a real situation.

A Practical Union:

Competency Based Education means that competency must be demonstrated, it emphasizes showing a skill, the ability to do rather than simply being exposed to something. When applied to learning, this can only mean that the learner is actively engaged in doing the skill in order to master it, rather than simply studying about it. Experiential educators have always demanded demonstrated mastery of minimum competencies in their programs as a way of preparing for the experience. In some cases the competencies will include knowing how to tie into a belay using a bowline, how to load and use a camera, basic survival skills needed for winter camping, being able to recognize poison ivy and dangerous snakes before taking a field trip through the woods, learning interview techniques before doing field research in oral history, being able to use video equipment effectively before taping a community event, and so on. Experience-based education places learning into a meaningful framework. It is based on the age old wisdom that when there is a need to know, people will learn. Using planned experience as an integral component of the curriculum is a logical and accessible way of establishing a need to know.

Beyond setting up a reason for learning a skill, the act of going through an experience which is new and open-ended provides a personal challenge to the learner. Meeting and overcoming that challenge will produce results that could never be duplicated in the classroom. This aspect is referred to as a "reality base," meaning that the learner's performance has ramifications beyond the superficial assigning of a grade. For example, if a student is to speak before a meeting of community leaders on a proposed activity in an attempt to raise funds, the presentation will acquire a more significant weight than doing a book report in front of his classmates. It matters whether he does well or not. His self-concept and self-esteem are involved. He becomes "invested" in the learning.

Another important aspect of experiential education is the fact that it occurs in cooperation with others which allows the development of interaction skills. It is extremely important for young people to learn how to work well in groups, how to discuss rationally, how to respond to others, how to reach consensus in a difficult situation, how to work toward a common goal. To learn skills and be able to demonstrate competency in isolation is not giving the student a realistic idea of his or her ability. Driving a car in the practice lot, while far better than trying to learn how to drive from a manual, still does not equip the student with the necessary know-how to deal with rush hour traffic. The idea of group interaction is built into the process.

A third touchstone of the experiential process is a strong emphasis on community. The community becomes more than a resource, it becomes the classroom, the laboratory, pulling the outside world into the school milieu. Eliot Wigginton, the founder of the Foxfire program, built his successful project around the idea of using the community as a rich learning environment. In his introduction to **Foxfire 2** he discusses his conviction about the validity of a community base:

> I believe that in most cases the most rewarding and significant things that happen to a kid happen outside the classroom: falling in love, climbing a mountain, rapping for hours with an adult who is loved or respected, building a house, seeing a part of the world never seen before, coming to some deep personal empathy with a kid from another background and culture, or genuinely understanding some serious community or national problem.
>
> These are all things that may later give him the motivation necessary to want to be able to write correctly and forcefully, or want to know history, or want to understand the complexities of nature and man through biology, botany, psychology, anthropology, or physics. But we too often ignore these events, seeing them as "irrelevant" or "froth." Until they are acknowledged as important and relevant to the student's existence, all he does inside those walls is doomed to seem meaningless and without reason . . . the world must be their classroom, the classroom a reflection of their world.[8]

It is encouraging to note that in official quarters the idea of making greater use of community resources is receiving more support. The National Association for Secondary School Principals made the following recommendations in **This We Believe:**

> The Association believes that the secondary school curriculum should be redesigned and placed in a more comprehensive setting. Opportunities for service and work, serious contact with adult institutions, and experiences which span age and ethnicity need to be a part of secondary education. Thus would schools become less exclusively cognitive, egotistic, and segregated by age and culture.[9]

---

[8] Eliot Wigginton, **Moments: The Foxfire Experience** (IDEAS, Inc. Star Press, Inc., Kennebunk, ME, 1975) p. 126.
[9] **This We Believe,** NASSP Task Force (Reston, VA, 1975) p. 17.

One of the positive results of CBE is the receptiveness of schools toward using off-campus activities for school credit. Vocational education has done that for years, but it has taken some time for the idea to spread into other branches of the school.

Another side of the argument for moving more into the community has to do with the concept of shared responsibility for education. It is to the society of local communities that young people go upon leaving high school; it is the community that needs "fully functional adults" who will be able to participate as citizens, workers, parents, and consumers. In an age of shrinking resources, greater demands on schools from the federal and state levels, the eternal problem of having to do more with less, schools are going to have to turn to local resources in order to do the job adequately. One of the problems with schools today is that they have become increasingly isolated from the surrounding community. The more schools distance themselves from their environment, the less relevant their lessons will seem to students. Conversely, the more isolated schools are, the less responsibility non-parent members of the community will feel toward supporting the school. It is critical for this trend to be reversed, for communities to become re-involved with education and for young people to believe that they have a viable role in community life. The shared responsibility of training students in basic skills coupled with setting up experiences in the community to exercise these skills could be a direct and meaningful way to begin this process.

In addition to establishing a motivation for learning by presenting an experience, creating an opportunity for personal challenge, encouraging the development in interpersonal communication skills, and working out of the community context, experiential education incorporates two other themes: the importance of problem solving and the necessity of thoughtful reflection on experience. Basically, the experiential process follows these steps:

1. The theme of the experience is chosen with learner participation.
2. Basic skills needed for the experience are learned.
3. Learners are placed in the situation, which always involves some problem, and requires the cooperative efforts of the group.
4. The experience is discussed and reflected on in class.
5. Learners review the appropriateness of their actions and consider how the experience might have been handled differently.
6. The learners are placed in a new problem situation in which to use their new knowledge in a different setting.

Competency Based Education represents an effort to make schools responsive to the needs of society by turning out young people who are capable of carrying out the work of that society. In addition to learning literacy skills, states are variously requiring schools to teach life-role skills such as communication skills, self-understanding, career development, life long learning, leisure, citizenship, family life, health, environment, personal finances, problem solving, social sciences, and so on.[10] These are not simple skills, but complex combinations of abilities which build on a number of lesser skills. George Klemp states that:

> Competencies do not exist in isolation from each other, nor does a person use only one competency when responding to a situation . . . Competencies should be assessed not in a vacuum, but in the context of a situation in which a cluster of competencies are involved and must be demonstrated.[11]

If CBE is to make a positive and effective impact on public schools, then teachers, administrators and community members must be willing to work with students to render the identified skills meaningful, useful and applicable through experience. By allowing teachers the freedom within the demands of the curriculum to use the experiential model, they become a part of the process. Rather than simply fulfilling the technician's role, they participate in setting up the hypothesis, attempting the experiment, observing the results, reframing the hypothesis with the provided feedback, attempting another experiment: the Deweyian approach to curriculum. By integrating the identified competencies into a broader curriculum package, using an experiential component, the tendency of teaching to the test is lessened. By using the experiential process, difficult to measure outcomes like group interaction, personal responsibility, completion of tasks, development of self-concept, a sense of community are actively encouraged and valued.

CBE and experiential education may not be a marriage made in heaven, but it is decidedly a practical union. The key to making the combination work is a strong commitment on the part of school administrators to support and encourage this kind of extension into the community, a willingness on the part of teachers to invest their time and energy into learning a new approach and incorporating it into their curriculum, and a receptive attitude in the community. There would certainly be problems, but the end result would justify the difficulties in implementation. CBE has marched into the schools carrying the seed of reform. If it is planted in fertile soil and nurtured by a broad base of human knowledge and understanding, it will produce healthy fruit. The needs of society will be met, as well as the needs of the children. If CBE meets only grudging compliance and is left to grow on fallow ground, the seed will bear stunted, misconceived fruit. We can ill afford such a harvest.

---

[10] Georgia State Department of Education "High School Graduation Requirements."
[11] George O. Klemp, Jr. "Identifying, Measuring, and Integrating Competencies" in **Defining and Measuring Competence**, p. 49.

Two Examples:

In this section two examples of successfully integrated programs will be presented. The first is a total school effort which is built around a core of competency requirements; the second is a curriculum piece demonstrating ways of building required competencies into an experience. Both illustrate how minimum competency skills can be incorporated into an experience-based curriculum.

The St. Paul Open School has designed a competence based curriculum which demonstrates a successful union of experience-based education and competency-based education. The administrators and teaching staff, working with members from the community, evolved a statement of what young people should be learning in schools:

> First, the process of learning from experience should be primary. Through experience, students would be expected to acquire communication skills in ways beyond the usual printed routes—perhaps by photographing, debating, appearing before the city council, or interviewing total strangers. They needed to calculate accurately, from measuring a room for a rug to mastering a short income tax form. They had to learn how to draw information from all kinds of sources and also to protect themselves and others as consumers. They must be able to get and hold a job, pursue a career, and make reasoned decisions. They should give something back to the school and community. They needed to learn how to keep physically fit. And they should study at least three cultures, including their own.[12]

These skills have been organized into three broad categories: career education, community involvement and current issues; consumer awareness, cultural awareness, information finding; and personal and interpersonal skills. In order to graduate from the St. Paul Open School, a student must demonstrate strong competency in at least half of these areas and some degree of competency in the remainder. Students are also expected to pass a staff created math exam by the 11th grade. In this program, students are required to design their own program of study to meet the stated competencies. A careful system of checks has been established to assist each student in designing and meeting their personal program.

Once the student has designed his or her plan, s/he is responsible for fulfilling the contract and securing individuals to serve as validators to certify their mastery of a given competence. "Validators are people who have worked with a student and/or who because of their education, training, skills or knowledge are qualified to make informed believable judgements about a competence which a student claims to possess."[13] The validator is asked to submit a letter following set guidelines stating the ability the student has demonstrated.

The emphasis is placed on "what a student can do as a result of having taken a class, completed a project, interned at a business, or participated in on-the-job training."[14] Prior to graduation, students must write a three year educational summary outlining the work they have done while at the Open School. This report includes letters from validators, as well as any other supporting data the student wishes to include. It is on the strength of this summary that the graduation committee decides whether the student is qualified to receive his or her diploma.

While the St. Paul Open School is a unique situation, the model is useful. Schools should carefully consider the idea of making students partially responsible for mapping out their own course of study around specified requirements. Every community offers opportunities for student involvement in areas where basic skills are required, and it makes good sense to create avenues to allow those resources to be used. And in areas where colleges, universities or community colleges are nearby, students could be encouraged to make use of those facilities on a mutual credit system.

Most schools will want to begin on a much smaller scale than St. Paul Open School. The following curriculum unit shows how minimum competency requirements and experiences can be incorporated into a history class, a journalism class, English, social studies or current affairs class. It is built around the theme of the Great Depression and how that event affected the local community. Students are expected to research the Depression from the national perspective, and then take their exploration out into the community to interview people willing to share their own experiences. This information would then be collated and condensed into a single article for the local newspaper, or, if the information proved rich enough, a series of articles.

---

[12] **Breaking Loose: A Competence Based Graduation Process,** The St. Paul Open School, (St. paul, MN, 1979).
[13] Ibid. p. 16.
[14] Ibid. p. 17.

Goals

1. Academic concepts will be presented in an inter-disciplinary way.
2. Students will actively participate in the learning process
3. Students will be placed in a new and challenging situation which will create opportunities for personal growth.
4. The community will be used as a primary resourse.
5. Students will gain a new understanding of their community culture and history through the experience.
6. Students will acquire and use skills necessary for functioning as a productive citizen such as initiative, leadership, flexibility, following through on commitments, working in groups.

Activity	Skills
1. Students will research the Depression through at least three sources, the library being one.	Learning retrieval skills through READING
2. Students will team up and decide on a community contact.	
3. Students will telephone their contact and request an interview.	Demonstrate ability to get information by SPEAKING on the telephone.
4. Students will learn how to use a tape recorder and proper interview techniques. Team teaching will be employed.	Given directions to explain a process, students will do so demonstrating organization, sequence, clarity, and accuracy in SPEAKING.
5. Students will go into the community and interview their contact.	Ability to introduce him/herself. Student will participate in a conversation, making suitable responses, and SPEAKING clearly and loudly.
6. Students will transcribe the interview, using proper grammar, spelling and punctuation.	Student will demonstrate ability to WRITE in complete sentences, to proofread carefully, to use punctuation.
7. Student will edit transcript, organizing the material and providing bridges between material when needed.	Student can observe and report data from an experience.
8. Students will make an oral presentation to the class on their project, using both the interview and the researched information.	Student can distinguish between statement of fact and statement of opinion.
9. Student will listen to the reports of their classmates and note important similarities and differences.	After LISTENING to a report, student will summarize the essential details of the presentation.
10. Students will identify the problems which led up to the Depression	Student can identify the PROBLEM or issue presented in an experience.
11. Students will suggest possible causes and draw analogies to the present economic situation.	Student can suggest possible CAUSES. Student can identify similarities and differences between situations.
12. Students will combine the information into an article	
13. Students will write a business letter to the newspaper requesting that their article be reviewed.	Students will demonstrate ability to WRITE a business letter
14. Students will write a friendly letter to their contact thanking them for their help and include a copy of the finished article.	Students will demonstrate ability to WRITE a friendly letter.

CHALLENGING THE PAST, PRESENT, & FUTURE: NEW DIRECTIONS IN EDUCATION

Articles by ARNOLD SHORE and ELLIE GREENBERG

A two-part article focusing on where we've been, where we are, and where we're heading in experiential education.

Part I: The Past and Present
By Arnold Shore

There are a number of ways to have a conference:
- We can celebrate ourselves;
- We can celebrate ourselves and note several topical issues as they emerge;
- We can celebrate ourselves and take seriously the issues that seek our attention.

In all three cases, we no doubt celebrate ourselves. In the last case we do so seriously and search for broad distinctions, broadly applicable to our pursuits and interests. The celebration is the convening of this conference. The seeking of broadly applicable ideas to take away with us has been the work of every session. For those of us who have been asked to articulate these ideas in this concluding session, the process may have begun earlier than we would like to admit.

Before I came to Asilomar, I jotted down several topical concerns; I wrote:
- Can we integrate with conventional education? I started to doodle with distinction of timing, pace, and duration. In passing I noted that the vertical scheduling of experience-based programs was never imagined by those who studied time in relation to traditional education programs. I noted, too, that time was on our side. We have had little of it for our programs, thus alleviating the problems and disappointments associated with being the central consumer of this all-encompassing resource.
- I asked myself about the differential applicability of experiential education. I reasoned that not all of us can invent the calculus; then, we are concerned with a variety of categories of learning, from discovery to re-discovery to invention to creation. Having these types of learning in mind and the style of experiential learning, can we develop a pedagogy of experiential education? Dare we contemplate a philosophy of experiential education?
- I wondered about staff training. Who are the staff of these programs? How are they trained? How are they kept trained?
- I wrote the word "schools" and followed with financing and cost issues and curriculum. Since I had just thought about staff training, I wondered about the fate of those who repeat the over-stimulating experience that attempts to teach lifetime lessons in short order. What of the routinization of excitement in a system of education which pursues excellence intensively and delivers that service day after day?

Then I came to the conference and tried to put aside my pre-conceptions and take notes on things as they happened. Being all too human, I could not completely put aside my pre-conceptions but I could organize them along with the observations I made at the conference and reflect on how I saw things after participation.

From the seminar on issues held in advance of the conference (the four sections on outdoor pursuits in higher education, corrections, outdoor leadership, and teacher training); to the happening of Durst, Nold, and Unsoeld (which showed us what we could be like if we worked hard and long in experiential education); to sessions on evaluation and administration — from all of these I noted high points. Then I struck a theme and did not try to note everything nor encompass it all. And I got on with the business of getting beyond my pre-conceptions.

Arnold Shore, *is vice-president of the Russell Sage Foundation.*
Ellie Greenberg, *is the Director of the University Without Walls, Loretto Heights College.*

I began with the idea that experiential education is a movement. Its genesis I freely depicted as follows:

In the beginning we sought ourselves: better, Outward Bound sought itself to understand itself better by sharing experience among compatriots.

Then we conceived of something *un-defined* that was larger but closely related, that is, experiential education. Not unlike the bead game in Hesse's *Magister Ludi*, this central concept can remain un-defined with its purpose yet safe — to get us beyond ourselves to something which must be grander.

Then we began to ask about our place in the scheme of things educational, about the relationship between the education we impart and that imparted by others.

As is the case in some areas of study, a few sentences are worthy of more extensive commentary.

The movement is young. Its parts are not sure of their place. Since no one has defined it nor described it satisfactorily, can we, all of us, really be in the business of experiential education? Some of us, more concrete and specific about our work in experiential education, may seek separate association (here I include corrections and higher education).

Being young, just beginning to consider where there is receptivity to experiential education, organizations like IDEAS are spawned to help new programs get established on a firmer basis. We are consulting to ourselves: those who have survived fifteen years are available to help new programs survive the first few very bumpy years.

Being young, we are idealistic. We believe that adversity can lead to gain:
- We believe that the shortage of dollars will lead to an honest use of community resources;
- That an aging faculty (aging too soon and too fast, some would say) can be renewed;
- that the school system, broadly speaking, needs us in our various incarnations of "hands-on";
- that problems as seemingly intractable as racism in the United States have appeal, since we seek out and work with social diversity.

What have we done? I do not mean concrete achievements, which are all too shaky. I do mean, What have we done of a more lasting nature?

We have re-defined things: therein lies our advantage.

All education must have something to do with the relationship of older to younger (of older people to younger people, older ideas to younger ideas), time, resources, place and society. Previously we termed these teachers, pupils, curriculum, finances, school, and community. Now we see things differently:
- Now, the teacher is one who knows how to face learning without a fully laid-out plan, one who guides, one who is in league with students;
- the pupil is the one who is newer at this relationship;
- the ideas are all around us, outside and inside of books;
- time is truly flexible;
- resources are those we find in a spirit of cooperation;
- the place has been the school, then the wilderness — now we find it most anywhere;
- and the society is the group experience we emphasize as one of many tasks and activities.

I stopped myself and looked around for idiosyncracy, for that further characterization which helps make gross generalizations more palpable. I picked on two things — corrections and certification. Why? Because they relate back to the movement notion I propounded a few paragraphs ago.

In almost every seminar where practical details were in short supply, lingering doubts about one's professional status, one's future, the future of experiential education and the future of education in general were expressed and re-cast in terms broadly philosophical. People spoke of values and value sets in ways which revealed a disturbing uneasiness about their positions as professionals and about the day-to-day task of getting other educators to see the need for experience-based education.

Not so in corrections where individuals spoke of constructing a civil society for those who have never experienced it. They were comfortable with themselves, just mentioning in passing, but not dwelling on it, that some would say they were involved in manipulation. I listened to individuals who had learned how to apprehend

> *"A movement starts out with dedication and then, if it is to survive, faces success with noble resolution to deal with the discomforts of size, with the need for professional recognition, with issues of recruitment, training, the development of curriculum, the business of doing business and the insurance and management expertise this requires."*

needs, to construct programs around basic activities of living, something many would have a hard time doing. But were they professionals? I would immediately say, yes. What would others say? Coming face-to-face with dedication and skill, I would wager they would *want* to say, yes. Alas, these practitioners should be proud of their achievements and require professional recognition for accomplishing what others have not.

* * * *

A movement starts out with dedication and then, if it is to survive, faces *success* with noble resolution to deal with the discomforts of size, with the need for professional recognition, with issues of recruitment, training, the development of curriculum, the business of doing business and the insurance and management expertise this requires. Then, when it regains poise, it seeks broader goals to put it once again on the margin of survival so as to assure excitement and service and rediscover relative youth. This is the paradox of growing up as a movement. For now, we consolidate and face the task of learning more about ourselves, our needs, our abilities at concerted action. Tomorrow we seek tasks now unknown or decline gently, or not so gently, as but one more movement in education.

Part II: The Future
By Ellie Greenberg

What I want to share with you is my thinking and writing in the sun yesterday...

I am sixty-five year old now. And it is 1997. The year we always talked about — 2000 — is upon us. Soon we will be in the 21st century — a fact not nearly as strange as we once thought it might be.

Not too long ago, sixty-five year olds were forced to retire, to stop productive employment. But the cost of this nonsense finally changed the law. Since more than one third of our population is now in this age group, the other two thirds simply cannot afford to support such a large number of people. Besides, what would we do with our energies and accumulated expertise for the next twenty good years? We have come a long way from being the wasteful nation we were between 1950 and 1980.

I, along with a few thousand others, have gathered for the *25th Annual Conference on Education for the Future*. We are all feeling a bit sentimental, returning to Asilomar for the fourth time in twenty years — and, sitting around in the lounge sipping warm tea, apple juice, throughout the world associated with Interversitas. There are others, of course. And the original names of the organizations have almost been forgotten; and almost all these titles have changed as well.

But what is important about this 25th Anniversary Reunion Conference in 1997 is that we have become such a powerful force in American education during the past quarter of a century; and that we sense a need to return to our roots, to assess our impact, and to think ahead to the celebration of the year 2000 AD — which really means the celebration of our survival as a people as well as a dynamic movement for creative change.

I remember that my own learning agenda back in 1977 at Asilomar was a kind of 'internal solo'. I needed to get out of the stress of the prior weeks and months, and I sought aloneness in the midst of six hundred persons. The sea helped; the quiet deer helped; the sun helped; and the gentle people helped. I centered, gaining equilibrium for my next venturing. I listened. I walked. I wrote. I tried to learn how not to feel lonely in my aloneness, a mellow goal for that transitional phase of my life. I experienced my detachment positively.

I recall the Conference as good. People smiled, I re-

> *"I recall the Conference as good. People smiled, I remember, and hugged. They also paid attention to the workshops and speeches and became involved in their own learning — a search for both rationality and synergism. After serious wrestling with some specific educational concerns in small 'Advanced Issues' groups, the people came from everywhere, and seemed glad to be here."*

and mellow sherry in front of the fire — we are being a bit indulgent with our memories... And thinking back to 1977 in November, when we first gathered here and had just formed an organization known as the Association of Experiential Education. Of course, we are a different group now; and this *Cooperative Congress on Education for the Future* (CCEF) has long been a reality and a significant force in this country and throughout the world.

It took a bit of doing to lay aside provincial politics and personal ambitions. But, after five years of effort, and with the help of computers and telecommunications (which we finally decided were our helpers and not our enemies), we were able to connect and form a living network with a number of other groups: the Council for the Assessment of Experiential Learning, the Union for Experimenting Colleges and Universities, the University Without Walls, the Council for the Advancement of Small Colleges, the Society for Field Experience Education, the Teacher Corps, the Fund for the Improvement of Post-Secondary Education, the network of centers called Empire State College, a number of organizations representing Teacher Education and Secondary School Principals, and individual experimental educators

member, and hugged. They also paid attention to the workshops and speeches and became involved in their own learning — a search for both rationality and synergism. After serious wrestling with some specific educational concerns in small 'Advanced Issues' groups, the people came from everywhere, and seemed glad to be here.

The opening experience I recall with great pleasure. Three men, who had found each other through a group now known as *Learning Unbounded*, shared their individual and collective warmth and power in a way that was then uncommon for adult males. A lasting memory for me is that they projected significant role models for the majority of younger men and women in their twenties and early thirties who were there. The characteristics they revealed were: camaraderie, affection, informality, verbal and intellectual competence, humor, joy, parallelism in their career changes and personal development, common work and problem-solving experiences, shared values and ideals, a searching attitude toward life, an ability to learn through experience and study, good looks, their own adult journeys and transitions and sufferings, an openness to their audience, and, most of all — a kind of graceful, gentle, intensity — not without tears. Each represented lives well-lived with optimism and humor. Each had been self-directed, erected their own barriers, and chose to find ways to surmount them. And, in each victory, each mountain climbed, each challenge taken on — survived — and grew — and became more integrated with themselves, with others, and with the world.

In them was the essence of 'educatedness' — a zeal for learning, a thirst for experiencing, a capacity for loving. And because they influenced the lives of others by revealing themselves, they were, indeed, role models and facilitators for others Yes, they appeared to be teachers, in a true sense.

In the days that followed, men and women moved from workshop to workshop — some terrific, some falling short — but all done in earnestness, attempting to get at the issues and experiences that helped us to be better at our own lives and programs. A great deal was happening throughout the country. Programs, once new, were gaining stability. Persons, once novices, were gaining experience. Outdoor people were coming indoors and indoor people were moving outdoors. Women were becoming increasingly vocal and assuming leadership roles. There were even "alumnae" around — a symbol of the maturity of an idea.

solar, nuclear, hydrogen, and all. But more importantly, we are managing our lives more simply in everyday ways.

Personal energy has become a key concept. And those with it have prospered; while those without sources for personal energy renewal have become overwhelmed and alienated, and have often had to retreat to a mental health support home.

We've learned to collaborate better. It's a curious thing, but as with Yin/Yang, Black/White, and complementaries of all sorts, we seem to be at our best as human beings when both our individualism and self-directedness are combined with our cooperative and collaborative skills. I've personally worked hard at this for twenty years. It's been a struggle; for I had been so well schooled for competitiveness. Even visiting China didn't prove to be as helpful as I had hoped. And, being a Jew, trust in outside groups was not one of my positive historical experiences. But, our schools now state self-directedness as well as collaborative skills as primary behavioral objectives. And it pleases me as an educator, to travel across the country observing small groups of learners working at real community problems together throughout the day.

I recently visited an Education Center (they used to

"In them was the essence of educatedness — a zeal for learning, a thirst for experiencing, a capacity for loving. And because they influenced the lives of others by revealing themselves, they were, indeed, role models and facilitators for others. Yes, they appeared to be teachers, in a true sense."

As idealism became balanced with the hard realities of research, funding, management, accreditation, and staffing issues, a kind of new professionalism was becoming evident. This was a professionalism compatible with valueing excellence. For a true professional is one who expects more from him or herself than others would ever dare to expect or could capture in a licensing procedure. It had always been curious to me to consider whether those who chose to be in this business of change and program development were mavericks, missionaries, or masochists. I think we had more than a touch of each back then in 1977. And, during the past twenty years, a sense of mellowness has been added to our zeal, as well.

Personally, I feel — now, twenty years later, both satisfied and tired.

We have lived through and survived a series of small scale nuclear wars, not the least of which was in the Middle East. Economics and the uneven distribution of resources were at the root of most of these skirmishes; although sheer power for the previously powerless certainly figured into the African and Asian conflicts.

Energy has been a key word for at least twenty-five years now. Yes, we have found new sources of fuel —

be called schools) in the Midwest where a group was meeting in a small octagonal building, not unlike some here at Asilomar. The age range in the room was about twelve to seventy. The group leaders were a local Anglo male farmer and a black female computer technologist from a nearby industry. There were five or six men and women between twenty-five and fifty, who were on sabbatical leave from their jobs; four youths between twelve and twenty, who were completing phases three through five of their Learning Credentials ladder; and two persons between fifty and seventy, who, acting as mentors to the group, were charged with the responsibility of transmitting the pertinent history to the group and providing for the recording of the history the group will generate. It was a pleasure to observe the practicing scientist, farmer, young people, on-leave professionals from education, law, and medicine, along with the electro-transitcar operator and the telefood programmer discussing approaches to developing a new cultural arts program and wilderness excursion combination. This was to be proposed to the Community Forum soon.

The Education Center's core of Learning Advisors will work individually with the twelve to twenty year olds, who are each working on different levels and credentials, and will have learning plans, product outcomes, and process analyses ready to present to a Learning Credentials Committee within four months. The twenty-five to fifty year old group will produce what we used to call a 'slide show' for their colleagues, when they return to work in a few months. This will be presented during the 'refreshment periods', spaced twice throughout each work day. And the fifty to seventy year old mentors will be responsible for recording the project in the community's computerized archives for easy retrieval by the next group, which will build on this group's work.

Yes, it seems to me that we have made considerable progress on new learning designs which are life-long, self-directed, collaborative, trans-disciplinary, practical as well as theoretical, and both process and content rich. The levels of excellence have risen; and our test scores show it. But even more importantly, we, as a society, seem finally to be getting a handle on the 'quality of life and learning' issues that preoccupied us so at the Conference in 1977. Evidence of this is that:

- Ethnic minority members are visible at our meetings and in all sectors of our society now. City-burning and ghetto riots are truly ancient history.
- Our older citizens stay in the community; and health home facilities are reserved only for the physically dependent.
- Our Mental Health Support Centers house people for shorter periods of time and actually spend less money.
- Our prisons house only a small portion of legal offenders and others who have been unable to live constructively in the community. They are part of the Education Centers during the day and live together in Support Homes at night until they can return to their families or living groups.
- Men and women can choose short term legal marriage, long term marriage, temporary group or paired living, or single living arrangements.
- Children now draw on a wide array of persons for nurture and support, freeing their biological parents for self-development and collaborative community endeavors.
- Women and men have made peace about their differentiated, but equal, roles. And gender does not seem to be as significant a factor in power distribution as it used to be; although we still have a way to go in this area before inter-personal relationships consume less of our emotional pre-occupation...

I could go on. But it's time to get on to the Conference to plan the celebration of 2000 A.D.

It is now 1997. And the memories of 1977 are a bit cloudy. I smile as I think of the energy that went into helping the Association to become a real movement; and recall the paranoid feelings we all had that what we were doing needed acceptance by others. Well, now it seems we were as right as we thought we were.

It's hard to believe that I am sixty-five years old now and that it is 1997. Looking back, I am pleased with my work and with my life. It is a good feeling to have been part of the beginnings of what is now the basis for our entire educational system.

"It is now 1997. And the memories of 1977 are a bit cloudy. I smile as I think of the energy that went into helping the Association to become a real movement; and recall the paranoid feelings we all had that what we were doing needed acceptance by others. Well, now it seems we were as right as we thought we were."

Whether we want to think about it or not, the future goes right on arriving day by day. And each day's future is ours to live fully and with style. We continue to be able to choose which poetic dream on the human agenda we will dream.

And the dream that seems the most worthwhile to me is the dream
  of climbing
    and of reaching
      and of growing
        and of making meaning
          and of helping justice to happen
           in the world —
believing, as always, that 'anything is possible.'

Focus: CLASSROOM TEACHING

LOOKING FOR EXPERIENTIAL EDUCATION IN THE ELEMENTARY SCHOOL

by Casey Murrow

I stood in a spacious outdoor play area of a California public school, talking with the father of a six-year-old there. He had been questioned by another father about why his daughter was not yet reading. "Well," said the second father, "your daughter can't read at all, can she?"

"No," said my acquaintance, "but she can still draw." This man knew, of course, that the drawings were expressions of his daughter's experience. He understood the power of that experience in the girl's overall development, beyond one specific skill.

In a very different community in central California, I spoke with a man who has worked extensively as an artist in the schools through the California Council on the Arts. He was worried about what he saw. "By the fourth grade," he said, "they're so tight, they can't feel anything."

The memory of these two conversations touches me deeply when I think of elementary school students across our country. These are children who are facing more of the basic competencies push than high school students. In the elementary school, the pressure to teach skills can be intense and the

Casey Murrow is an Assistant Professor of Education at the University of Vermont's Southeast Continuing Education Center in Brattleboro, Vermont.

student must grasp all this from one teacher whose own skills cannot span all fields adequately.

Elementary schools permit the best and the worst of instruction to flourish, in adjacent classrooms or adjacent school districts. Consider, for example, reading.

Some schools and teachers focus on reading above any other skill. Repeatedly, I have seen classrooms where the teachers say with pride that they work on reading for 2½ hours per day. Remember that most of this time pertains to reading skills, not to the joy that many of us feel when we sit down with a good book for a long evening.

Yet, it is only infrequently that reading in school provides any link to the experience of the student. The book may be about trucks, or gardens, but it is very hard for the author to make strong enough links for an individual child to identify the book with his world.

In a few schools, reading is based on the children's writing: in other words, the recording they can do and want to do about the world around them, and the private worlds and fantasy worlds within themselves. In such classrooms, the writing is turned into books and other formats and shared with others in the class. Reading takes on a very important purpose, to learn and enjoy the experiences and imaginings of people you know. That is the beginning of ex-

periential learning and it ought to commence in the elementary school, not years later in high school when the first effort must be to fight the "tightness" established in the earlier years and so clearly observed by my artist friend in California.

Experience: The First Step

From the point of view of child development, the younger the child, the more his or her learning activities must derive from immediate experience. I have a seven year old son who fascinated his class last week with stories and drawings about building hand-made cardboard airplane models. He has done this with an older cousin whose creations include planes with four foot fuselages, complete with cockpit, seating, and galleys.

Yet, if you confront our son, Derek, with a book about planes he has little interest in much of it. The technical details are not yet important. The thing flies because he picks it up and runs around with it. That is his experience with building planes and that is what he wants to share with others.

Derek is lucky. His teacher knows how to capitalize on that interest—to make it a focus for his learning, not a momentary expression of interest by a seven year old, sandwiched between this reading period and the next.

The elementary classroom is the place to begin experiential learning, or, more realistically, to build upon the experiences that the child has had and will continue to have in his family—and the ones he may have had in nursery school or pre-school.

To do so is both easy and cheap, for it does not require elaborate facilities, or even transportation to unusual places. In the elementary school, the resources for experiential learning are there, around the school, in the local community. But time after time they go unused. Why?

These resources for rich experiential learning are ignored out of fear, confusion, and the lack of a coherent support system for teachers as professionals in their classrooms.

The fear is that of taking risks, of moving beyond the traditional curriculum and of becoming visible. The teacher who uses community resources as part of his or her curriculum will be seen around town. Children's work will be discussed and opinions aired. None of this will happen to the teacher who stands steadfast at the ditto machine and cranks out the worksheets. Some teachers can manage a community oriented experiential program alone, but most of us need a support system that works for us.

Support System

In order to circumvent these problems, we need a support system that communicates well with teachers and helps them to share their strengths. In a very few places, this happens through informal networks, or particularly supportive principals. In other areas, this can happen through the network of a Teacher Center, run by and for teachers, and espousing teacher developed curriculum and communication as major goals.

If experiential learning in the elementary school is to become a reality, we must undertake an effort with at least four facets. All must go on at once and be done by many people. I think they are as follows:

First, in-service education—staff development—for teachers must focus on the experiential opportunities that abound near a school and how they may be used. It takes a lot of "unlearning" as well as learning for many teachers to recognize the possible uses of a sanitary landfill, the school bus garage, or the patch of scrub trees and brush at the back of the school property. Staff development that concerns community resources is not a popular idea among many administrators.

I did a workshop on just this subject for the National Staff Development Council a year ago and met with substantial hostility because these administrators and planners said my approach had nothing to do with basic skills and competencies. We have come a long way in this country from the time when a basic skill was something you could do with your hands and your head.

The second of the four facets is communication and understanding among teachers and community members of the integration of experiential learning with conventional curriculum. Obviously, there are important links between the two and each can benefit from the other. Math is a fine example of this in which traditional instruction that focuses on skills remains vital, but experience and practical math situations become instructive as well.

The third facet goes beyond elementary schools to encompass virtually everything that concerns members of AEE, and that is greater popularization of the idea of experiential learning. As parents and others begin to understand the value of experience as teacher, there will be less resistance to experience-based learning during school hours.

Experiential learning, the oldest form there is, is poorly understood and supported in this nation of hierarchical schools and textbook salesmen. But the fact that we are here today is testimony to the growing professional and public interest in experiential learning. From here, with a lot of help from our friends, we need to slowly, confidently expand people's awareness of experiential learning—and, from my perspective, how it can affect young children.

These first three facets, in-service education, communication of experiential links with the standard curriculum, and popularization of the concept of experiential learning, are hard work for all of us. The fourth facet I propose is pure joy for a teacher.

It is the satisfaction that results from setting up an experience with kids and watching the motivation that grows in their faces and in their work as a result of that experience. Greater motivation of students is vital to the success of schooling. It happens through life experiences, applied to the work of learning in school. Kids own their own experiences. If the experience ties into school, then they begin to own their education.

When that happens, they do not become so tight by the fourth grade.

When that happens, they will read—for their own reasons—and they will still be able to draw. In experience, young students find motivation, ownership, and a reason to learn within the context of our schools.

Correction

In the Fall, 1981 issue of the Journal, an interview with Vito Perrone was published (page 46). Unfortunately, several changes and corrections were not made, the most glaring of which is Dr. Perrone's title and address. With due apologies, this is the correct title and address: Dr. Vito Perrone, Director of the Center for Teaching and Learning, University of North Dakota, Grand Forks, ND 58202.

Forum FOR TEACHERS

by Shirley-Dale Easley

The ball is bouncing up and back on the gymnasium floor, bouncing, bouncing, forever bouncing, and I can hear my voice over it all..."Pass, don't dribble, over here, over there, keep your head up, watch the windows, the lights..." All day the balls have been bouncing, and at night they bounce inside my head. It is hot and dusty and I wonder how many times I've said these words, how many times I'll repeat them. "Who's winning?", the children call over to me. "Who's ahead? What's the score?"

This is a good class. They keep in their lines...lines from the classroom, lines to the bathroom, lines for a drink of water. They will fit in well to real life situations; standing in lines at the supermarket, lines at the bank, lines at the fast-food take out. A good portion of our waking hours are spent in lines — and school for this class thus far has been one continuous line. Now they come bounding, charging into the gymnasium for physical education — but I insist they go to their teams, get in proper order, keep their places.

"Let's go out and play," I suggest.

"Play what?" they ask.

"Just play," I answer. "You know, like you do when you go out and play at home."

"But play what?" they repeat. "Play hockey? Play ball?"

Shirley-Dale Easley *is an elementary Physical Education teacher in a rural school in New Brunswick, Canada. She has developed many innovative approaches to "non facility oriented" physical education programs.*

We line up and go outside to the edge of a small stretch of woods left standing around the school. There are a few blow-downs, a little brook, some large low branches, and a forest floor covered with soft pine needles.

"There you go," I say. "Play."

They stand around me, shivering, looking up at me for more explicit instructions. This was the play space of generations of people before them but they cannot think of anything to do with it. Worse yet, I cannot think of anything to tell them to do. So we go back inside to our games, our scores, our lines.

I do not give up. Each day I take a class out to the woods for awhile — and I watch closely. It occurs to me that the super socialization, the super organization of the school system is being met by the super structure of organized sports. These children do not just go out and play; they play "something", with sides, with scores. They have access to swimming pools, rinks, gymnasiums with all the latest equipment, and maybe, just maybe, we should be providing play opportunities of a more interpersonal type.

But how do we begin to teach children to play in the out-of-doors? Or should I say, "re-teach" them to play, when for most of their years, we have been saying, "Come inside, it's too cold, too wet, too dirty, too hot."

A New Approach

As it happened, I learned from a group of children at our own school. This class of students had been particularly trying from the moment they came into grade one. With no indoor gymnasium available, we had to go outside for our lessons, yet I insisted on teaching the basics to organized sports. They just would not stay in lines. I would find them hanging upside down on things, swinging on branches, pushing each other off things and rolling, in the grass, the mud, even in the gravel. So why was I constantly fighting to put them in lines? Here was a class, a whole class of pre-teens, who still played with a rare blend of creativity and with what I will call "calculated abandon".

"Come inside, it's too cold..."

So I watched, and I used the inherent senses of these children in guiding their play activities. I stopped saying, "Be careful...you can't do that...come down" and began to say instead, "How did you do that anyway?"

Now, from the notes to myself written in the margins of dog-eared pages, let me share some of the activities I have tried and found successful.

First comes conditioning. Condition them to feel sun, rain, soil, air, to get wet, to get dry again, and to regulate the body heat with proper clothing — layering, use of a hat for heat control, dry socks, rain gear, old clothing that can get dirty.

Safety is important. They need a lot of experience in falling from various heights, fall with impetus, rolling, spotting, and trusting one another. Try trust falls and trust dives. Play "Electric Fence" where you fence

> "I stopped saying, 'Be careful'...and began to say instead, 'How did you do that!'"

them all into a clump of trees with a rope and they must help each other out without touching the fence. Play "Reach for the Sky" with a piece of chalk. Here they must work together holding each other, pyramid-style, up the side of a building to see how high they can place a mark.

Explore. Look over an area of woods yourself. The more large trees, boulders, and natural objects, the better. Tell the children to find a rocking log for balancing, a log over a wet area, a leaning log, a big tree, a tree with hanging branches, a crawlway, a tunnel. Go under something, go over something, through, around. Play follow the leader. Explore as a group and use the movement themes that automatically come to your mind — body awareness, flow, time, space, momentum. Let them explore in twos. Teach them the yell that carries in the woods, "the hog call". Hide on them and let them find you. Hide some balls in the woods, give them clues, and let them find them. All these things can cover a realm of learning experiences but with a sense of daring, a sense of adventure. Then ask each child to find a place of his own, a secret spot where he goes to be alone, to think, to be away from the others for a short while. This little time of solitude becomes very important to them.

Of course, the unpredictability of the weather is a major factor in lesson planning. The only answer is to wake up early enough to see the day and go from there.

It might be a day to build an igloo, or a quin-zhee, to throw snowballs at targets, make a snowman or a snow creature. Run under the first snowflakes and catch them on different parts of the body. Trample down a fresh blanket of snow in patterns. Play "Fox and Geese", or go sliding on cardboard.

Try teacing a winter survival course, make a survival kit, and go on a day hike — or perhaps you could plan to hike until lunch hour, then stop to boil a kettle in the woods for hot soup. The major watch-points will be for "hypothermia" and "frostbite".

Did you ever play TUBICIDE on a crust of snow? Take an old inner tube and punch, kick, push, or ride on it to the goal lines — no referees, no rules, no boundaries.

Try boot skating when there's a little rain on top of the ice in the school yard. Fly a kite when it is windy. Play "punctured drum" when it is too hot to do anything else — puncture an old drum at various spots and have the students try to fill it with water, using only body parts to plug the holes.

Outdoor equipment adds a great deal to the fun; canoes, kayaks, a parachute, orienteering equipment, skiis, snowshoes, bicycles, ropes for climbing, tires on ropes for swinging and dropping into targets.

There are so many kinds of days, so many kinds of people, that not all classes suit all people, but some come very close. The day of all days that stands out in my mind was one in early spring. The crust on the snow was hard and shining in the morning sun. I was standing on a knoll, looking down over the Nashwaak Valley and the little first graders in their slippery nylon snowsuits whizzed by me, doing curly ques, upside down and backwards. Every hill, every hummock, was transformed into a magnificent glistening slide for them and they were laughing.

If these children had a gymnasium in which to play, they could be taught a sound basis of game skills to take to junior high school. Outdoor physical education cannot take the place of these. Yet the students' fitness level is high as they have been encouraged to move a bit beyond their own limits. They have been learning that success or failure is not the only thing — trying is, making the effort is. They have been experiencing the same delight their parents did, their grandparents did, in the natural environment.

They will fit in well to real life situations; standing in line at the supermarket, the bank, the fast food take-out.

So, try throwing your lesson plan away for a day. Choose the kind of a day that strikes your fancy and go out and play. Try something old. Try something new.

THE ULTIMATE CHALLENGE FOR
EXPERIENTIAL EDUCATORS: NAVIGATING INTO THE MAIN STREAM

Albert M. Adams II, Ed.D.
Headmaster, The Cambridge School

I want to thank the AEE Board for inviting me to join you this week. It is wonderful to be among so many old friends. Although I left Colorado over five years ago, I have been with many of you in spirit and have continued to be inspired by you both indiviually and collectively.

It is clear that there are few in the audience today who need to be convinced of the legitimacy of experiential education. At the same time there is always a risk when speaking to the already converted of wallowing self-satisfaction while ignoring the hard questions which face us. In order not to fall into that trap, my goal for today is to induce many of you to stretch your limits--to take a risk, conceptually that is--by opening your minds to what may be a broader definition of experiential education than you are accustomed to. I acknowledge at the start that I am part of a distinct minority within the AEE constituency--since my work over the past sixteen years has been in the arena of formal schooling. My bias as a school person notwithstanding, I am among the first to wave the banner of experiential education in non-school settings. It goes without saying, in my mind, that those of you who commit your lives to experiential learning beyond the schools have chosen nobly and chosen well. At the same time, I argue that there is a difference in _kind_ between succeeding in these two domains of experiential education.

It is one thing to convince the public of the efficacy of experiential education when working with special populations in a society which is desperate for solutions, or when working with programs which are subject to being viewed as extracurricular and even luxurious or when working with avant-garde avenues to self-actualization or to corporate team-building. It is quite another challenge to fully integrate experiential learning into the main stream of American education--ultimately to the point where such approaches are no longer relegated to the periphery where, in times of cutbacks or conservative ideological shifts, they become expendable. So I maintain before you today that the most _formidable_ challenge facing experiential educators is to navigate our beliefs and our programs into the main stream of American education. I do so not with _any_ desire to further separate the school-based folks from the non-school-based folks in AEE. Instead I argue that all experiential educators can benefit from the lessons which continue to be learned in this most exacting of arenas.

My plan for the next half-hour is as follows:

First, I assess the place of experiential education in the current national debate about schools. Next, I provide snapshots of 45 experience-based courses or programs which have worked in school settings. Last, I briefly address the issue of how to market experiential programs in these conservative times.

I define experiential learning as (1) that which involves direct experience (including the hands-on use of various media), (2) that which is action-based, and/or (3) that which carries with it real, as opposed to abstract or contrived, consequences. Experiential approaches enable us to expand the standard learning format to address a wide range of learning styles and interests, to enhance the connections between schools and the real world, and to provide meaningful opportunities to apply acquired skills. In addition they provide us with unique tools to enhance self-esteem, to empower young people to take responsibility for their learning, to prepare them for and to impel them toward a risk-taking orientation. In the final analysis they help to unlock many of the subtle mysteries which promote self-directed and lifelong learning.

I believe that educators must attend in equal measure to five strands of individual development: physical, cognitive, moral, emotional, and aesthetic. I also know that individuals develop at different rates and learn best in a variety of ways. (On that score, I strongly recommend Howard Gardner's book, Frames of Mind: A Theory of Multiple Intelligences.) I also believe that it is individual developmental needs which should determine our teaching objectives and that it is these individually-prescribed objectives which should determine our teaching methods. The great diversity of needs and interests which we find in our classrooms cries out for a similar range of teaching methods. In most cases, however, the constraints of the Carnegie Unit and the limits of conventional wisdom snuff out the thought of such innovation. (It might interest you to know that the curriculum which we all experienced in school was first devised by the Committee of Ten in 1893. That definition of discrete academic disciplines has gone virtually unchanged for 92 years. Also, the creation of the Carnegie Unit in 1909 assured that all students would not only jump through the same hoops but that they would do so at the same rate and at the same time. Although such a system may well have been appropriate in an era when a small percentage of the population attended high school and when the main purpose of schools was to disseminate information, it is hardly a reasonable formula for shaping an appropriate education for the 1980s and 1990s.)

I was reminded by Adele Simmons a couple of years ago that the American public seems to develop deep concerns about, and interest in, education every fifteen years or so. Most recently we have been innundated by a virtual flood of education reports--nearly fifty in number--and I suspect that attention will soon wane and interests will be diverted elsewhere. Therefore, regardless of how one feels about the various reports, we as educators should be grateful that education continues to enjoy a place on the national agenda. We, as experiential educators, must seize this opportunity to become a voice in this debate.

The best known of the education reports is A Nation at Risk published two years ago by the Department of Education. Its conclusions are dangerously simplistic and have encouraged lawmakers around the country to devise any number of quick-fix schemes. I believe that A Nation at Risk ignores the complexities of teaching and learning in the 1980s and does little more than call for an enshrinement of "business as usual." I take particular exception with this report's myopic reverence for the "basics" (generally interpreted to mean the teaching of more facts), its conviction that the main goal of education is to drive the American economy, its belief in a top-down reform model emanating from state governments and its notion that a school's performance can be judged exclusively by quantitative measures. It neglects, in the words of Theodore Sizer, to make an intrinsic in addition to a utilitarian case for education in our society, to assess curricular substance rather than simply time spend in the classroom, to stress the interconnectedness of education with a broad social context and to reinforce the school's role in moral and ethical development.

In contrast, different voices have emerged from other high school studies. These voices often resonate with those of experiential educators. For example, Sarah Lawrence Lightfoot in her book, The Good High School, captures a richness, a complexity and a diversity among exemplary schools which absolutely defy simplistic characterizations. Likewise, John Goodlad, in A Place Called School calls for a major overhaul--not mere tinkering--of our schools. In his report, Horace's Compromise, Ted Sizer challenges what he calls the "regularities" of today's high schools: (1) age grading, which ignores the reality that people learn at varying rates and at different times; (2) the goal of time spent in school and on "task" which overshadows the goal of proficiency (residency vs competency); (3) the concept of "giving an education" and "taking classes" based on the assumption that teachers, rather than students, are the key workers in schools; (4) the centrality of the traditional disciplines, which devalues the arts, and fails to reflect real life while emphasizing the "covering" of subject matter rather than learning how to learn and; (5) the primacy of the Carnegie Unit daily schedule which severely limits the possibilities for employing innovative teaching approaches.

A second book has just emerged from A Study of High Schools, sponsored by the National Association of Secondary School Principals and the Commission on Educational Issues of the National Association of Independent Schools. It is entitled, The Shopping Mall High School: Winners and Losers in the Educational Marketplace and is co-authored by Arthur Powell, Eleanor Ferrar, and David Cohen. A recent issue of Education Week described this metaphor for today's schools this way: "The shopping mall works well because it is governed mainly by consumer preferences. Students who want to learn can usually do so, especially if they seek out "specialty shops" where a focused commitment to learning prevails. Students with less commitment can usually graduate in return for orderly attendance. Many different bargains or "treaties" to engage in learning or avoid it are accomodated. High schools solve many problems for themselves and their clients by saying, "it's here if you want it, but it's all up to you."

And just the previous week Frank Newman, the president of the Education Commission of the States, introduced his report "Higher Education and the American Resurgence." His conclusion--which will ring true to experiential educators--is that the entire educational structure of the nation is plagued by a lack of independent-minded participation. In fact, he estimates that students spend as little as 5% of classroom time in active discussion. He says, and I quote, "you've got an educational system that puts a premium on a student sitting in class passively, reading back exactly what was taught, giving you the interpretation that was given the student. It is not a system that puts a high premium on creativity; it is not a system that encourages risk-taking in any way." Newman goes on to say "the crucial issue is not whether we're going to have another computer scientist. It's whether the typical student coming out is prepared for a world of entrepreneurial change. That is to say: Are they risk takers? Are they creative?"

He goes on to say that the future health of the American economy depends on "just those sorts of people who can innovate--whose education has not stifled but enhanced their creativity. Needed, too, are the schools that produce such people. The economic climate has changed and the educational institutions must change with it. This is no longer the age of old brick schools that look just like the old brick mills turning out students willing to labor away in docile obedience. Our age has a different pace, a different texture. Success--or the sort of success that matters--appears less and less to come from abjectly doing what one is told. It seems nowadays to come from making bold connections, drawing large inferences, seeing new paths through old woods, and finding better ways to walk them."

Last, I want to share with you Earnest Boyer's prescription for improving our schools. Boyer is the President of the Carnegie Foundation for the Advancement of Teaching; his study, which was published two years ago, is entitled, High School: A Report on Secondary Education in America. Boyer and his distinguished panel argued for the following: (1) the need to clarify and to articulate schools' goals--stressing the mastery of language, a core of common learning, preparation for work and further education, and community and civic service; (2) a single academic track for all students, combined with elective clusters in the junior and senior years; (3) a service requirement and broad opportunities to become engaged in social and civic obligations; (4) the use of a wide variety of teaching skills; (5) greater flexibility in class schedules; (6) increased use of community resources in the curriculum and; (7) multiple connections among all levels of schools and between these levels and the business community."

In a 1981 AEE Journal article Sherod Reynolds and I argued that a thorough knowledge of the progressive education movement would help experiential educators to understand their roots and to develop effective strategies for the 1980s. I still believe that, just as I believe that a knowledge of Kurt Hahn's philosophy will assist each of us in furthering the cause of experiential education. At the same time, it is crucial that we be aware of the innovative thinkers on the educational scene today and that we recognize an ally when we see one, whether he calls himself a progressive or belongs to the AEE or not. There is grist for our mill and fodder for our cannon in many of these high school studies, and I admonish you not to miss the opportunity to integrate them into your thinking. If anything, living in these conservative times obliges us to speak out more persistently and more eloquently than we ever have. To do so requires that we understand both the context and the language of discourse which characterize the debate which we are a part of, whether we want to be or not.

Before talking about particular programs which have been successful, I should say that I am an advocate of bottom-up as opposed to top-down strategies for bringing about change within schools. This is not to say that school administrators cannot inspire change, and it is clear that few new initiatives will succeed without the support of the administration. At the same time, it is those who create the change at the grass roots level who are ultimately most responsible for nourishing it and helping it to grow. I should also note that I do not view experiential learning as an end in itself; rather, it is one component of well-rounded teaching. Maurice Gibbons, in his book The New Secondary Education, provides a very useful matrix for keeping the place of experiential learning in perspective. Down the side he lists three kinds of learning: by experience, by study, and by productive activity. Across the top he lists three modes of learning: the personal domain, the social domain, and the academic domain. Several of the points of intersection within the matrix call explicitly for experiential learning. Several others legitimately do not. Last, I must note, as did John Dewey, that experience per se does not necessarily represent good education. For instance, there are those today who might argue with James Coleman's premise that young people are currently information-rich and experience-poor. They might suggest that the vast numbers of teenagers working in fast-food chains across the country are having their learning enriched by real-world experience. I, in turn, would argue that this is not the quality of experience which good educators would advocate.

FROM THEORY TO PRACTICE

1970-1975 represented a momentous period of change at the Colorado Springs School. In 1972 several of us founded The Children's School, a kindergarten through sixth grade independent school whose program was patterned after the British Integrated Day philosophy. The following year we implemented a unique middle school program which featured the combining of 7th and 8th graders, team-teaching, individualized, interdisciplinary, and experiential teaching methods. By 1975 these changes partially bubbled up and partially took root on their own at the upper school level, and we implemented a very innovative module system.

It is often the first tentative steps, the pilot programs if you will, which teach us the most about the creation of more grandiose schemes. Among the early initiatives which led to the birth of the CSS middle school were the following:

* A 7th grade course in Anthropology and an 8th grade course in Urbanization and the Development of Technology which integrated hands-on projects, lengthy field trips, and various simulation games. One might think of this kind of innovation simply as the "enriched academic course."

* Pre-Algebra and Algebra classes which combined individualized teaching methods with an emphasis on applying mathematical skills and principles outside the classroom--for instance, doing math around the campus as well as designing and building a wide range of models and objects.

* English courses which required students to interview people in the broader community.

* Experiments with grouping patterns and with group dynamics--including group cooperation, active listening, and initiative games.

* Scheduling a 45-minute History class and a 45-minute English class back-to-back in order to pursue an interdisciplinary and team-taught study of Utopian communities. This particular course ended in a week-long trip into the mountains in mid-February with the objective of actually implementing the Utopian scheme which the students had devised. The first part of that week, I must confess, was relatively harrowing since, in our naivete, we never expected that this experiment with group living could turn into the Lord of the Flies.

Simultaneously, similar initiatives were surfacing throughout the upper school:

* English courses which featured role-playing, practice teaching, and writing from direct experience.

* A program of senior internships as well as broader opportunities for community service.

* Interim Weeks: These began as one week in the middle of the academic year devoted primarily to on-campus and academically-oriented pursuits of various topics. These quickly expanded to twice a year and took on much more of a wilderness-based focus ranging from river trips on the Yampa and the Greene to "conservative camping" outings.

* Faculty retreats: Somewhere along the way we, as a faculty, began to retreat into the mountains for two or three days prior to school each year. Thus we began to both experience and to model the approaches which we were increasingly promoting. In addition, many of our teachers benefited from Outward Bound's teacher practicum during this time period.

* First weekend: In 1974 we began to take the entire school to the mountains for three days prior to the start of the year--breaking up into 10-person groups with each group responsible for its own food and shelter, and participating in a wide range of challenge-oriented activities (including rock climbing, rapelling peak ascents, etc.).

I should add that it was at this time that Bob Godfrey, Jim Kielsmeier and others from Outward Bound worked regularly with our faculty on ways to integrate wilderness experiences with our academic program.

It was such embryonic programs which convinced us that we needed to construct a different time-frame for the operation of our school. The middle school, then, grouped 45 7th and 8th graders together with three teachers for 4-1/2 hours each day. The teachers were responsible for the math, science, English, and history curricula. At that time students continued to rotate out of the middle school for foreign language, physical education, and the arts. In later years these disciplines were also woven into the curriculum to varying degrees. By concentrating intensely on skill-building at the beginning of each day we were free to pursue our themes of study (core areas) for two to three hours each day. Each core area was designed to integrate at least two academic disciplines and to maximize the opportunities to apply cognitive skills in real settings. Among the most glamorous of the core areas were the week-long trips which we did twice each year:

* Santa Fe: To study westward expansion or cross-cultural relationships.

* Denver: To study urban planning or an analysis of public attitudes about different policy issues.

* Various mountain settings: To study environmental issues or the arts in nature.

It is important to stress at this point that these were serious academic pursuits and that the standards for participation and for the quality of work were every bit as high as in a conventional academic class. In addition, students were required not only to do extensive reading, writing, and arithmetic, but they were also required to speak, to present, to construct, to design, to draw, and to paint. One of the beauties of such an approach is that no one student or group of students can always be the best at everything. It is a wonderful way to publicly value individual strengths and to build self-esteem so that students dare to take risks in areas where they are not so strong. Examples of school-based or town-based core areas--which lasted from one to six weeks--included:

* Propaganda and advertising--which drew on
  numerous community resources.

* Human physiology--which included, among other
  things, the construction of a model of the
  human heart big enough to walk through.

* Design--which included the total renovation
  of our interior classroom space--including
  all elements of design, budgeting, and
  construction.

* The Stock Market--which centered around a
  powerful simulation game produced by Interact.

* A history of Old Colorado City--a full-fledged
  Foxfire-type oral history, with the final
  presentation being at a reception for the very
  people who had been interviewed.

It is impossible, given this short time, to adequately capture the richness and the diversity of the learning experiences which occurred in that little program, but I hope I have given you some sense of the ways in which we first carved out some wiggle space in a very conventional program and later, having established credibility, were able to shape it altogether.

In 1975 the Colorado Springs School implemented a module system which it had borrowed from the Cambridge School (where, coincidentally, I am presently employed). The Module System (called the Unit Session Plan at CSS) divides the academic day into three 90-minute blocks and divides the year into seven or eight (depending on the school) four to four-and-a-half week modules. Many courses meet for just a 90-minute period for four-and-one-half weeks, others such as lab sciences meet for three hours per day for nine weeks, and sequential courses such as beginning languages and introductory mathematics meet for four 90-minute blocks running horizontally across the year. There is no end to the experiential possibilities within all of those courses, given their intensive nature and the large block of time available. For our purposes today, however, I will concentrate on what CSS came to call Experience-Centered Seminars--that is, courses which run all day long for the entire month-long module. You can imagine how liberating it is to be able to take your class off campus for a day or for a month without having to clear it with other teachers first. Like the middle school core areas, the ECS also focuses on interdisciplinary study and the application of cognitive skills to real-world issues. A few examples are as follows:

* France and Mexico--a full module in one of these
  countries for advanced language students
  including extensive home-stays to insure
  complete immersion in the culture.

* Walden III (and IV)--a wonderful course designed
  and run by Roy and Susan Grimm located at the
  Outward Bound base camp in Marble, Colorado and

combining studies of English, history, and environment.

* Other Southwest study courses including Canyonlands and Immigration.

* New England--an English/History course for seniors which entailed a full month of traveling around New England (including doing college visits and interviews).

* Solar Hut--one of David Berger's many successes at CSS, where he and a group of students first designed and then constructed a solar building for the Sanborn Western Camps. He and the group lived on the site for the entire module.

Some examples of less exotic, more locally-based experience-centered seminars included:

* Aging and Adolescence--a study of these two stages of human growth which included not only interviewing elderly folks but also pairing individual adolescents and elders in intimate month-long relationships.

* Outdoor Service--a course devised by David and Molly Niven which first taught basic outdoor skills to students who then took the lead in working with special populations in outdoor settings.

* The Legal System--which included a mock trial overseen by a real judge and week-long internships in the courts or in law offices.

* Many other courses such as Economics or The Military and Society which made extensive use of the Colorado Springs community as a resource.

* Solar Greenhouse--the design and construction of a sizeable greenhouse addition to the Science Building.

I should also note that CSS has an extensive independent study program which enables students to pursue an almost infinite number of experiential interests.

Both at CSS and at the Cambridge School a study's interaction with the module system is, in and of itself, an important growing experience. Since every student could conceivably have a different schedule, the control that students have over their learning, and the choices which they make, are very real. The system is also very fast-paced and students need to learn early on that they must be fast starters. In addition, the intensity of their courses and their daily accountability make it all but impossible to play "the school game."

While similar to CSS in many ways, the Cambridge School is also unique. In particular, it is comprised of a higher percentage of urban students and it has much less of a wilderness focus than CSS. In addition, it is located in a highly competitive area where the pressures for academic excellence and college admissions border on the neurotic. The Cambridge School also enjoys a 100-year heritage as a progressive school in an area of the country which is very sympathetic to the role of independent schools. Some of the more notable ways that we at the Cambridge School are using the Module System include:

* Writing from Experience--a very creative introductory course for all 9th graders which exposes them to a wide variety of experiences within the community--especially in the areas of education, the law, and the arts. This course focuses a great deal on students' writing skills and helps them to make the transition into a system which expects them to take a great deal of responsibility for their learning.

* France, Spain, and Germany--language programs very similar to those at CSS.

* England--a potter's tour this year; a literary and historical tour last year.

* Marine Biology--based on Cape Cod.

* Research at the Kennedy Library--an opportunity to work with primary sources. You might be interested to know that 8% of all the research done at the Kennedy Library in recent years has been done by Cambridge School students.

* The Charles River--a team-taught course in Biology and History studying the development of technology along the Charles.

* The Dance Troupe--an opportunity for advanced dance students to tour over 20 schools and institutions within the module.

* Puppets and Players--a theatre group which also tours schools in the area. Due to Propositon 2-1/2 in Massachussetts these groups sometimes represent the only arts assembly which some of the school children see in a given year.

Other aspects of the Cambridge School program which may be of interest to experiential educators include the following:

* A requirement that every junior and senior fulfill at least one off-campus course--often individual internships--prior to graduation.

* Superb programs in the visual and the performing arts--an area too seldom embraced by experiential educators. It is difficult to imagine examples of more direct experience or more real consequences than those faced by artists.

* A Master of the Guild Program--where students accept the same level of responsibility as adults for various areas of the school.

* An annual School Service requirement--often times fulfilled through internships in our Day Care Center, working with the Maintenance Department, etc.

* An active commitment to social responsibility --whether involving active participation in STOP or marching on Washington as many students did last year.

* Students genuinely involved in decision-making --at all levels of the school including a monthly Town Meeting and two student members of our Board of Trustees.

* Notable speakers brought on campus--an area which many experiential educators would not consider legitimate experiential education. However, when General Tran Van Don came to talk to a class on Vietnam last year it certainly felt like a bona fide experience or when, in our course on the Holocaust, one of our parents came to speak about his experience in a Nazi concentration camp, we later learned that this setting was the first time his daughter had ever heard him speak of that experience.

One of the great benefits of experiential learning is that it goes beyond the mere acquisiton of facts and concepts to probe to the deeper level of values. In fact, one could argue that it has the potential to massage the spirit and the soul in ways that textbooks, lectures, and multiple-choice exams cannot. I have provided you with brief glimpses of some of the courses and programs which I have seen work at the 7th-12th grade levels. Karen Zapel Huff, the Director of the Childrens' School at CSS, could speak even more eloquently about the application of experiential approches at the K-6 grade level. Since nearly all of my professional work has been at the middle school and high school levels, I have chosen to limit my remarks today to those age groups.

You might well ask what evidence I have that this kind of program works. Since the inception of the Module System at both schools we have heard consistently from college representatives that our students come to them with cognitive skills which are at least as good as those from other good college preparatory schools. Beyond that, however, we hear time and time again that our students are distinguished from their peers in the areas of self-discipline, self-direction, creativity, and resourcefulness. In addition, we are told that they are critical thinkers who are not afraid to ask the hard questions; that they are risk-takers and that they are committed to participating fully in the democratic process. Most importantly, however, I am convinced that because they have been so intensely immersed in the process of learning they have an excellent chance of becoming effective and inspired life-long learners.

I have chosen examples today from my own professional experience, and therefore from the world of private schools--and even more, from the miniscule portion of that arena which thinks of itself as innovative. What I have not said is that I believe private schools, due to their independence, flexibility, and semi-precious stature, have an obligation to develop experimental educational models which might be of use to the educational community at large. In closing, then, let me sketch for you one vision of how the ideas which I expound might be applied in a public school setting. Recognize, of course, that many excellent public school models already exist, including the Mitchell High School Senior Seminar Program in Colorado Springs, the Evergreen Open Living School also here in Colorado, and Mosaic, an urban approach to Foxfire, run by Michael Tierney at South Boston High School.

My vision emanates from a deep interest and some experience in rural education. Specifically, I spend a good deal of time studying the impact of rapid population growth and very scarce financial resources on a small town in New Hampshire. In particular, I looked at the intersection between the schools and the community--especially with regard to how and why the tax payers voted on the school budget each year. To understand the intensity surrounding this vote each March it is helpful for you to know that New Hampshire ranks 50th with regard to the amount of state aid given to public schools (in fact, it also ranks below Guam and Puerto Rico in that Category). Therefore, over 85% of the school and town budgets derive from local property tax. Given the complex reltionships between natives, near-natives, and newcomers, the wide range of expectations placed on the schools, and the relentless cloud of austerity hanging over the town, school officials are faced with a marketing (or public relations) dilemma of monumental proportions.

It occured to me during my research that this town in particular, and probably most other towns could benefit from closer and more positive ties with all elements of its community. One prerequisite to enhancing school-community relations is to recognize, on the one hand, that education is the one profession about which most adults feel they are experts--the assumption being that since each of us attended school we know what schools should be like. Ironically, the local school budget is also among the few major areas of public policy where a voter can have direct influence. On the other hand it is important to understand that the criteria upon which most voters judge the worth of a school are relatively unsophisticated.

Most people believe that a school is effective if it has a minimum of public problems, if attendance records are good, and if students do a lot of homework. Additional indicators include whether the school's graduates attend college or get good jobs and whether students seem to reflect the values of the community.

I maintain that there are two keys to enhancing positive relationships between school and community. The first is to aggressively make students--in crassest terms, the school's product--visible in the broader community. This includes all students not just those in vocational education programs, and the primary objective is to allow these "products" to be seen as both competent and useful. The second is to demonstrate the respect which teachers have for the community by using it regularly as a valuable resource. There is no better reservoir of knowledge than that impounded by experiential educators to make these two things happen. Local history, academic internships, town-based courses, and community service are just a few of the ways that students are able to practice using their skills and enrich their life experience at the same time that they demonstrate their competence and perform a service for the community. Likewise, the regular use of parents and professionals as resources goes a long way toward breaking down the stereotypes about townspeople and school people which proliferate when the two worlds live apart from one another.

I wish I could adequately describe for you the enthusiasm generated among bankers and financial analysts when a group of high school students taking an economics course actually walk into their offices, or the same for lawyers and judges when they find that high school students have genuine interests in the American Legal System or among neighborhood organizers when they find young people eager to put their energies to work on behalf of the public-at-large. One of the fastest-growing groups in the New Hampshire town which I have described is composed of retired people. In a town struggling to fairly parcel out its meager resources, one would expect these people to vote for more social services and smaller school budgets. This suggests just one more reason to develop programs which will link adolescents with senior citizens. Clearly, pure marketing concerns are not enough reason to develop curricular programs. However, I argue that in virtually all of these cases, philosophical and marketing objectives can dovetail very nicely. I should also note in closing that marketing is not a dirty word and anyone in the field of education who thinks that he is not involved in marketing is naive. We have very direct accountability in the private school world and if parents and students do not approve of what we're doing they simply do not pay to attend. The dynamics in the public sector may be more complex and illusive but are every bit as real. Likewise, the longevity of your program within a school is very much dependent on how well you promote it. I see no reason why the marketing of experiential programs within schools and the marketing of schools within communities should not be mutually beneficial, and I hope that my talk has inspired at least some of you to re-think those connections and those possibilities in fresh and compelling ways.

: **III. Cultural Journalism/Foxfire**

A Look Back: The History of the Cultural Journalism Movement

by Murray Durst

"A Look Back: The History of the Cultural Journalism Movement" by Murray Durst is reprinted with permission from The Foxfire Fund, Inc. It was first published in "National Workshop For Cultural Journalism: Workshop Report", Jan. 1980. This paper is an edited version of a speech given by Durst at the National Workshop for Cultural Journalism Projects in August, 1979, St. Louis, Missouri.

It is very gratifying for me to be here speaking to you today. You represent, for me, the fruit of seed planted several years ago. You are the realization of a notion that many of us shared in the early days; a belief that **Foxfire** could spread and grow and thrive in schools just about anywhere. To be here just seven years later and see that you could be drawn together from around the country, because each of you is doing something we now call "cultural journalism" is very exciting.

There were times in the early going when we questioned whether the idea of **Foxfire** could be disseminated at all. But in fact, and most importantly I think, it has become self-disseminating. There is no need for one organization to lay claim as sponsor, to take credit for "spreading the word". Each of you, out of your own projects, is doing a great deal more for disseminating the idea today than those of us who worked to organize the effort in the beginning.

I am going to try to reconstruct a little bit about those earlier times so that you will have the sense of being part of a continuum. I will not say a great deal about the organizations or the individuals involved, because I don't think that was important. What was and is important, is that the idea moved. This importance is because we are talking about a fundamental idea in education that is deeper than the spread of **Foxfire**. We are talking about the whole concept of reinvolving kids in the joy of learning, in the excitement of self-discovery, in the proposition that one learns most deeply when one is wholly involved with learning—with hands, with ears, with noses, with feet, with being, as well as with one's head.

Foxfire itself was originated in the 1966-67 school year, as most of you know. Eliot Wigginton, "Wig", and

Murray Durst is the Director of the Collaborative for Experiential Learning and an instructional resource person for Appalachian State Univeristy in Boone, N.C. He is the former Executive Vice President of IDEAS.

his kids in Rabun County, GA, simply started doing something different for a ninth-grade English class. They didn't have a name for it. They surely didn't have a label for it as pretentious as "cultural journalism" at that time. They didn't know precisely where they were going, but it worked. Some **Foxfire** magazines were published, some people bought them and read them and became interested in the project. Subscription lists grew and came to be spread more widely outside **Foxfire's** home ground.

Along the way, one of the magazines ended up in a dentist's office in the Washington, D.C. area and Brian Beun, founder of an organization called IDEAS, read it while waiting for an appointment. IDEAS is an organization which, at that time, was concerned with economic and cultural minority development outside the United States. **Foxfire** struck Brian and others at IDEAS as a nonformal education process that might be appropriate in the international development field; or, if not there, perhaps in the area of cultural minority development in the U.S. With those interests in mind, IDEAS established contact with Wig. That was 1970, the third year of **Foxfire's** evolution in Rabun Gap.

At about the same time, others were discovering **Foxfire** and its potential for application in communities different from the Southern Appalachians. This is one of the unique things about the way the idea of cultural journalism was spread. No single individual or group; no calculatedness in itself was responsible for you folks being in this room in St. Louis. A mixture of accident and calculation led you here.

In New York City, a community group was at work in a predominantly Puerto Rican neighborhood. It happened that a woman working in the area was from Georgia and knew about **Foxfire**. She thought it might make sense to try something along the same lines in her neighborhood. This project came to be called the **Fourth Street i**. So, here was an independent, almost casual kind of seeding at the time Wig was making connection with IDEAS.

Wig became an associate of IDEAS for the purpose of disseminating the idea of **Foxfire** in 1970. Their first venture was to help initiate a project on the Ogalalla Sioux reservation in the Dakotas. **Hoyekiya**, the resulting project, began almost simultaneously with the independent development of the **Fourth Street i**. They were as far as we know, the first direct adaptations of the **Foxfire** idea.

In 1972 **The Foxfire Book** was published by Doubleday and that event was probably the most significant one in this whole chain. The book proved to be an extraordinary commercial success with hundreds of thousands of copies sold. An amazing number of people bothered to read Wig's introduction—most folks don't read introductions to books—and were excited to learn that high school students had written the book. Also, late in 1972, the Ford Foundation made the first of its two grants to IDEAS for the purpose of disseminating the **Foxfire** concept. Out of that effort helped by the success of **The Foxfire Book**, about a dozen additional projects were started during 1972-73. Those projects showed the original interests of IDEAS, which was to use the concept of **Foxfire** in work with cultural minorities. They were to serve as vehicles through which cultural minorities might build their own self-concept and build their own empowerment for dealing with the majority culture.

One of those projects was called **Angel Oak** and was developed on St. John's Island off the coast of South Carolina. This is an entirely black community, a community that, because of geography, economics and politics over the years, had lived in relative isolation for decades. **Angel Oak** was one of my favorites; and it did not succeed. I still hope that some day the project will be started again. You see, this special group of people are custodians of the remnants of the Afro-Gullah culture developed by enslaved black people as they were moved from their diverse homelands through the West Indies and into the United States.

Bittersweet is still going strong after seven years. It was started in Lebanon, MO, and is a project of the Ozarks.

Kil-Kaas-Git was another of the first dozen projects. It was developed off the coast of southern Alaska and served a population of Native Americans.

Nanih Wayia was established in Philadephia, MI, by a group of Choctaw Indians and has been in continuous operation for about seven years now.

Salt at Kennebunkport, ME, is one of the pioneer projects begun seven years ago. If you don't know about **Salt**, you may well know Pam Wood, its advisor, because she put together the student guide, **You and Aunt Arie: A Guide to Cultural Journalism.** Pam coined the phrase "cultural journalism" that we have come to use as the generic term for **Foxfire**-type programs.

Sea Chest is another project that is still going from those formed during 1972-73. It operates at the Buxton School on Cape Hatteras, NC. Again, this project served a culturally isolated population. If you have never been to Hatteras, you can not appreciate how isolated those folks are. But, through **Sea Chest** you can read about their lives on that shifting sand barrier jutting into the Atlantic.

Another of the early projects was started in Ramah, NM, by Navajo youth at the Ramah Navajo School. The project's name is spelled **Tsa'Aszi**, but it is pronounced "sa ze". It is operating still in a new graphics center where they do all their own printing.

A project that was not continued, **Dovetail**, was started at Ronan, MT, in Flathead Indian country. This was a conscious effort to bridge the gap between Native Americans and Anglo Americans who lived in the same community.

Then there was a project on the eastern shore of Maryland another relatively isolated cultural situation, called **Skipjack**. **Skipjack** developed well for a couple of years, then dropped out of sight for a while, and now is back stronger than ever.

There were two projects started outside the United States among those first ones. **Peenie Wallie** was in Jamaica and **Tim Tim** in Haiti. Those folks have been out of touch the last few years, but at last report **Peenie Wallie** was doing well.

Those were the first sponsored projects and they formed the base of experience from which a lot of other things followed. But, at the same time, some independent projects were getting underway. One of the intriguing ones was **Loblolly** in Gary, TX, a small town in the Piney Woods of east Texas. The idea for **Loblolly** was picked up by Lincoln King, a high school teacher, from reading Wig's introduction to **The Foxfire Book**. Starting off quite on its own, the students sold "stock" in their enterprise for which there would be no dividends paid excpet for the magazine itself. **Loblolly** had been going for about a year before any of us working on the spread of **Foxfire** were in touch with it.

Loblolly was a very significant event in my mind, because its success clearly demonstrated that the idea behind **Foxfire** could be picked up by teachers and students without an expensive workshop/teacher training/student training process that we had locked ourselves into initially. Our awareness of **Loblolly** came at about the time that we—Wig, Pam Wood, Ellen Massey and others involved with the first "sponsored" projects—were talking about putting together some written materials on **Foxfire** as a learning concept. Those written materials turned out to be two books: **Moments: The Foxfire Experience**, a teacher's guide written by Wig and **You and Aunt Arie**, a student guide written by Pam Wood. Both authors were helped by other advisors in the network. These books were finally published by IDEAS in 1975. Linc King of **Loblolly** joined in the helping process for writing the books, but even more important, **Loblolly** was the confirming experience that told us it was worthwhile to publish cultural journalism guide materials so any teacher or any group of kids could pick up the idea and run with it for about ten bucks—the cost of the two books.

About the same time, late 1974, a key operation called **Cityscape** got going in Washington, D.C. It too was rather independently started, though with discussion with those of us at IDEAS, due to our office proximity in Washington. **Cityscape** became the first really successful urban adaptation of **Foxfire** inspired projects. It has been in operation more than five years now, and it serves as the principal model for other urban projects.

By the end of 1974, there were about 24 projects underway. I have not kept close track of the expanding network since then. I understand that there are close to 150 projects that we know about today, and probably at least that number where people are working quietly in their own areas without being known by the network.

Importantly, we have moved beyond the proposition that it is necessary for anyone to have to sponsor or shove people into using the concept. Cultural journalism is being discovered and adapted widely now. And the fact that all of you are in this room from as far away as Australia and as close as downtown St. Louis is proof.

There are those of us who continue to work, continue to plant the seeds and continue to nurture the idea. Our goal is to broaden and deepen awareness for cultural journalism within education as a whole. We believe this is an extraordinarily important concept—this approach that has its roots in **Foxfire** and has spread and grown into a grass roots movement. It is example and part of needed reform in education.

Between 1970 and 1975 there were five major studies independently conducted in this country, all looking at the state of secondary education. Those studies comprise a body of information that is generally referred to as the "reform of secondary education movement." Every one of them said, in effect: "Look, we have got to open up secondary education. We have got to help kids become involved with their own learning. We have got to help kids be involved with doing self-recognized, responsible learning activities. We have got to help kids connect with the fact that they are part of a cultural continuum." Every one of those studies came essentially to the same findings. And, it was as though they were describing a need for **Foxfire**, for operating concepts like cultural journalism; the proposition that young people in this country can be and ought to be participants in documenting our cultural base by looking deeply into their own community roots.

Cultural journalism has demonstrated in high schools and junior highs and even elementary schools that it is possible for youth to be responsible researchers, recorders and reporters of their immediate community's culture. It has shown it is possible to have in schools that excitement, that joy, that opportunity for discovery which so often is missing in our large comprehensive schools. And, that those involvements can be generated through a curricular-based program that is tied to "the basics." Cultural journalism provides opportunity for self-discovery and cognitive learning in school as a part of schooling. And by example, it may open the door for algebra teachers to see how to teach their subject as though it had some real world meaning for students; geometry teachers who can appreciate that their subject is an applied mathematics form which can be taught through experience, perhaps better than through memorization. It might even suggest to a life science teacher trying to impart understanding of ecological cycles to get off his/her seat, find the nearest swamp, and wade into it with the kids, where all can muck around to find out about ecology at its base.

It is conceivable for cultural journalism to help those and other creative teaching approaches come about because it has **Foxfire** as a base. The **Foxfire** books are a phenomenon in the publishing world. Millions of the five books series have been bought and read by the public. There is a credibility derived from those books, now joined, incidently, by **Salt** and **Bittersweet** on the book sellers' shelves.

Given that base of credibility, it may be possible for colleges of education, the trainers of teachers, to start suggesting that the whole idea of using experience as a teaching method should be part of every teacher's professional "tool kit." Good teachers strive to produce learners who "know" more than the teachers. To do that, teachers need to be convinced that they are still learners, and it is okay to risk experiences with kids. All of those things are part of the concept that underlies **Foxfire** and cultural journalism. I am hopeful that your success may convince some colleges of education to seriously introduce these concepts into their curriculum and the curriculum intended to recertify teachers. There is *that* kind of power in the cultural journalism movement.

In the short span of 13 years, Rabun County, Georgia, has impacted a whole bunch of folks through its **Foxfire**. The potential for those folks to impact education through a national network of cultural journalism is considerable indeed.

BEYOND FOXFIRE

by ELIOT WIGGINTON

A penetrating look at why Foxfire has been so successful, how it is quietly revolutionizing the educational world, and its direction for the future.

On April 24, 1978, three men from out of town erected an eight foot high sign on state highway 23-441 five miles north of Rabun Gap, Georgia. The sign went up in front of a log building. It read, "Foxfire Homes."

That same day, people began to call the offices of The Foxfire Fund, Inc. which are located just south of Rabun Gap. First to call was Mrs. L.D. Hopper, a retired weaver who used to work for the Rabun Gap Craft Shop. So Paul Gillespie, vice president of the Fund drove north to have a look, and he returned to report to the staff.

The following day at the Rabun County High School, a group meeting was called of all the high school students involved in the activities sponsored by the Fund. They were presented with the situation, they discussed it, voted on it as a group, and that same afternoon eight of the students headed north on 23-441 in two cars. They walked into the offices of Foxfire Homes and delivered to the men there a simple message: take the sign down and change the name or be sued. It was April 26. And they weren't bluffing.

Since *Foxfire* Magazine began in 1966, it has grown into a operation that produces books, record albums, and television shows, and one that is involved in scores of activities in its home base of Rabun County, Georgia. The products and the activities are real, believing as we do that the best way to teach and hone the skills we want our students to have (whether grammatical or mathematical or physical or analytical or legal or creative) is by plunging them into real work that requires those skills. That focus of the operation

---

Eliot Wigginton, is the President of Foxfire Fund, Inc. and founder of Foxfire Magazine.

remains clear and unchanged from those earliest magazine days. If it were put into the form of a directive that all our staff members were to follow, it would go something like this: Before you start to do anything related to your work with this organization, ask yourself first why a student is not doing it instead. If you don't have a good reason, then go and find a student — perferably one who has never done it before.

The longer we continue operating, the more we realize that there are very few honest reasons any of us can come up with for a student *not* to do the job in preference to an adult. And if it's a job that has been done before and mastered by students that are still involved with us, we've found that it is often preferable to have them show the new ones how.

That's not the lazy way out. In fact, it's the harder way out. The job often takes longer. Mistakes are made. That, of course, is why an adult in most organizations usually does the job instead. Rule: An adult who habitually says, "This is a job that must be done, and must be done correctly and well, and therefore I must do it myself," must never be allowed to be a teacher. The only things left in his world for students to do are menial, meaningless tasks and exercises that have no real bearing or real consequence in the real world. A school full of teachers like that does not graduate competent, responsible, self-confident sensitive seniors. Ever. Except despite that school.

Rule: We have to have more confidence in our students than they have in themselves.

The reason for our organization's continuous expansion into projects other than magazine journalism is simple: if a magazine is all we have to offer, our students are being limited. There comes a point at which they say, "What

When a group of ladies from the Tiger, Georgia, Home Demonstration Club set up a quilt in the Foxfire classroom and set to work one morning to finish it, all the Foxfire students participated in the quilting itself, and in photographing and videotaping the process.

next?" And we don't know what to answer. They're ready to be stretched, and we can't accomodate them.

There's another reason, too. After years of teaching the same skills, the teacher stops learning. Whenever one of my old students comes back, he or she repeats, inevitably, the same refrain: "You know what was the most fun about those early days? And what I got the most out of? The fact that none of us knew what he or she was doing. We had to learn together." There was an excitement then, accentuated by that magical sense of risk and danger as we entered the unknown together, that only happens again, to us, when we begin something new. Then the senses are never more alive. The togetherness and the excitement is never more complete. And the learning that takes place is never more memorable.

On the last day of school this year, I shut the classroom door and walked out. On the way to my truck, I passed through the upstairs student commons area. Two students are working late with a Chicago muralist and friend of mine named John Weber. They are putting a coat of varnish on a mural eighteen feet high and twenty-two feet wide. With John's guidance, the mural has been designed, approved by the principal, transferred to the wall and painted by fifty high school students, most of who had never taken a high school art course. It took two weeks. Varsity football players who had laughed at the project at first had later changed their minds and decided they wanted one in the gym also. One of them is on the third tier of scaffolding painting at this moment. He has volunteered to organize the sports mural project this fall. The theme of the mural he is working on now is the passing on of skills and wisdom from the older generation to the young.

I go down the stairs into the commons area on the first floor and pass through the exhibit of student photography that Paul's classes put up earlier that week. My first impulse is to be amazed that not a single photograph has been marked or vandalized in any way, despite the constant traffic through that area. My next impulse is to get angry at myself for being surprised. What I was taught to expect from kids dies hard. . . .

I go out the double doors into the sunlight and past an empty space between two classroom buildings. In my mind, I try to imagine what kind of a park Bob and his Foxfire environmental classes will create there next fall. When our principal asked them to design and build it, he mentioned wanting a brick patio, benches, plantings. I know that whatever they do, it will be special because Bob is going to use a class of ninth graders that nobody wants — ones who have yet to pass a science course. This year, with Bob, they designed and laid out the nature trail that the biology classes use. . .

I get into the truck and shove a pile of finished layouts to one side to give myself more driving room. The layouts are for the new summer issue of *Foxfire* which includes articles

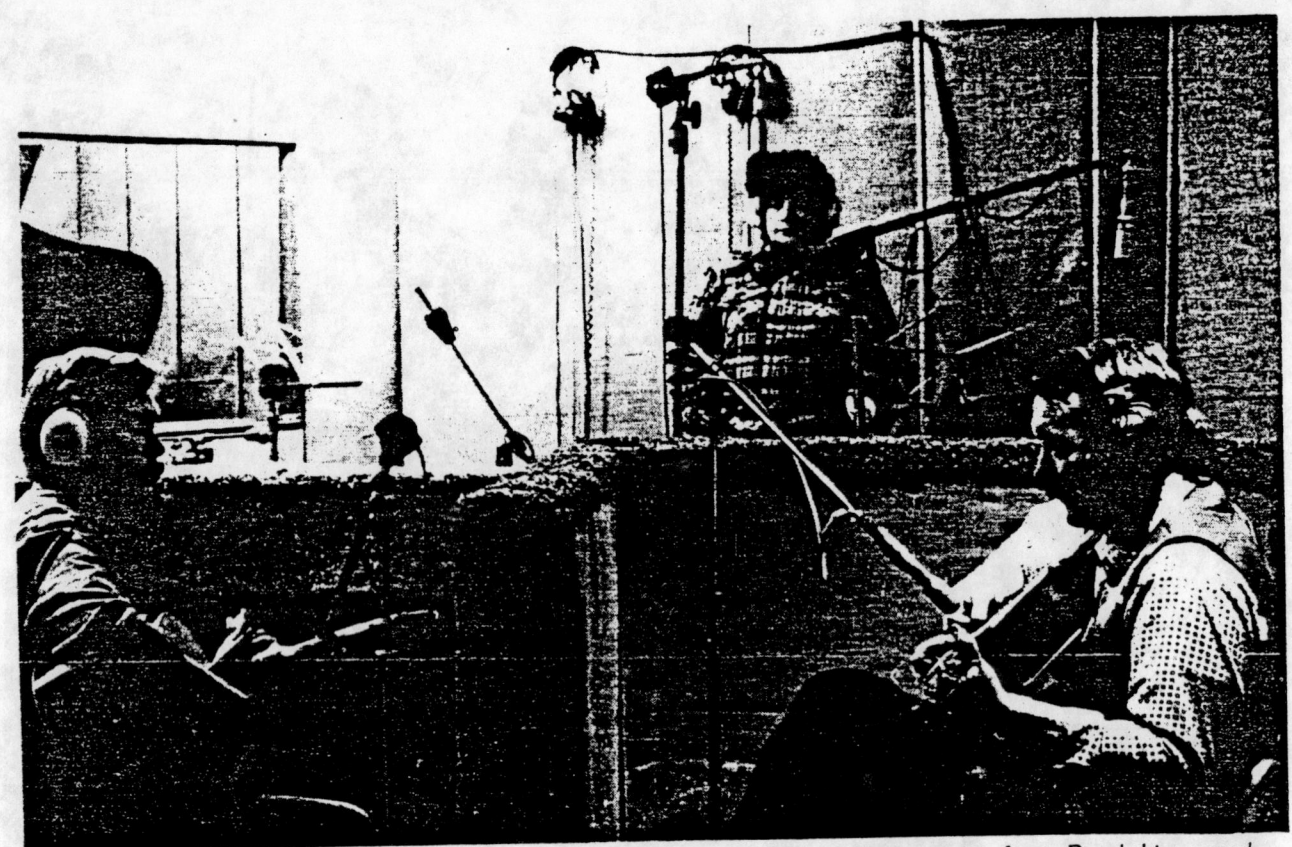

In the foreground, Foxfire's George Reynolds (left) and songwriter Ron Short help songwriter Joyce Brookshire record a song for her album, Foxfire's first. Students did the mixing for the album, designed the album covers and insert, and handled marketing and advertising.

about a mule swapper, a gold miner, a fur trapper, and an ax handle maker named Numerous Otis Marcus. It's a fine issue.

I drive down the highway and onto our land, past the environmental project's experimental garden — planted completely with seeds saved by local families for generations — and their American chestnut seed beds that contain over a hundred seedlings nearly ready to set out in the woods; and I park in front of a hundred-year-old log building that students helped community carpenters move, restore and convert into our editorial offices two years ago.

Inside, I find a message from Susan Cooper, the scriptwriter for Hume Cronyn and Jessica Tandy whose current Broadway hit, "The Gin Game," won a Pulitzer and a Tony this year. She will meet me in the Atlanta airport in three days on my way back from Nacgodoches, Texas, and come up with me to Rabun Gap to spend five days. Cronyn and Tandy's new play, now that students have approved the contract, will be based on material from the *Foxfire* books. The dramatic theme that holds the play together: an elderly Appalachian woman whose son has moved away and wants her to join him there so he can take care of her must decide whether or not to sell the family home place to a real estate developer who is pressuring her. It is the most common theme, in reality, in our part of the mountains, and I know students will be faced with some hard choices as they try to help Susan decide whether the woman will sell, or hold onto the land in the hope that some of her grandchildren will carry on.

George comes through the office. He is going to put his summer Foxfire students to work a week early recording for two new record albums. One will feature a local songwriter, and the other will be a traditional music sampler featuring four old-time musicians. I'll be working with four students restoring our collection of furniture and artifacts, cataloguing it, and arranging the items as they would have been over a hundred years ago inside the two log homes our students moved last summer and designated as museum buildings. Work will have to wait, though, until I return from an educational conference in California where I hope to pick up some new ideas for next year.

Environmental class trips to the ocean to compare ecology, student-written field manuals and texts, exchanges with Outward Bound (two of our students are on three-week Outward Bound trips this summer, and twelve of their students are coming down to spend a week with ours), budget meetings, weekly decision-making sessions with students from all the Foxfire divisions meeting together as a common group, full time cable television programming through an ARC satellite hookup — dozens of new projects being field tested, tinkered with, changed to fit our needs, and then discarded or added to our regular offerings. All are part of a continuing period of growth and experimentation. And all have common roots: students run the activities, basic skills are built in at every level to reinforce competence, and all the activities use as their motivating vehicle the concept of audience, and the past, present and future of an Appalachian community — its

Wig talking to the students at the dedication of the mural.

culture and its environment and its needs. And all take place naturally and easily within the context of an extremely traditional public high school. That's what twelve years of responsible action within the rules and boundaries of such a public school buys.

What's next! Celebrating the grand new experiments of other *Foxfire*-type groups for one, and learning from them. A new oral history/folklore project that's about to begin that will be run by deaf kids, for example. Or an antique air show run annually by the kids at *Skipjack*. Or the boat yard being run by the kids at *Salt*. Or the traditional farm being run by the elementary school students at *Homespun*. The list goes on.

Equally exciting for me are two new directions of ours. One is an extension of our activities downward into our local elementary schools where our students are designing and building playgrounds with elementary school students, and helping those same kids write and edit their own readers and texts, and produce their own slide/tape shows. Students in the Foxfire folklore classes are also doing fieldwork and collecting at the elementary school level in a fascinating extension of what used to be collecting only among the elderly.

Another is the extension of our work outward into the community itself where hundreds of former Foxfire students are now resident adults who could take the leadership of our community into their own hands. The first organization of such adults is now running a Reading Is Fundamental project through which every one of our thousand elementary school age kids will get five free books in October. Another group will help us make plans for a worker owned furniture factory we hope to build in the near future on a piece of land we have just purchased in Mountain City. And, hopefully, as their strength and confidence grows, men and women from such groups will move into our county's elective offices and begin to exercise a new breed of sensitive leadership and control. At that point, we will have come full circle.

For all of us who teach, there are moments of fatigue and frustration. This is as it should be — as it must be if we're doing our best. If our teaching doesn't make inroads into our personal lives, then we probably aren't doing a good job.

In times of such fatigue — in times when we get discouraged over the fact that schools don't seem to be getting much better, and problems don't seem to be getting solved much faster — it helps to know that there is a long history of struggle behind us, and that many of our new ideas were old ideas in the 30's. Knowing of this struggle helps us put our own struggle into perspective, and it helps to know that our role may be to keep alive a tradition of struggle that did not begin with us and will not end with us. And it helps to know that it may be enough, for now, for us to keep alive and nurture small islands of decency in an alien ocean while preparing for the larger fight.

And that struggle is nothing less than to change society itself, and to empower those who are powerless and to sensitize those who will lead.

To this end, we must all grow daily. And our teachers must be our kids.

English in the Treetops

by Peter G. Beidler

"I can't do it. I just can't. Don't make me try. It's too far down. Please don't make me go across." The horizontal 300-foot rope stretched in front of the waterfall and over the rocks a hundred feet below. It looked like a spider's filament, and Moji was scared.

I want to tell you about Moji, and about why she and eight other Lehigh University freshmen were with me in the woods in northern Pennsylvania on a chilly day in April, 1985, looking at a tyrolean traverse stretched across Angel Falls.

Vacations and Bad Teaching

I teach English at Lehigh University. I have done so for twenty years. One of my favorite courses is the one I teach almost every semester: good old English 1, the basic required composition course. I do not love grading papers, but I do love first-semester freshman students. Well, most of them.

The spring, 1985, course was a particular challenge. For one thing, with 27 freshmen it was too big for one section but not big enough for a split into two. For another, it was an uncomfortable mix of students. Approximately a third of the students were first-semester freshmen who for one reason or another had not enrolled at Lehigh in the fall semester. Another third was transfer students, and the final third had failed the course at least once and were trying again.

Majisola Shabi was one of these last. I later learned that Mojisola — who preferred to be called Moji — was born in Brooklyn to parents who had been born in Africa. She was an engineering student, and writing was **not** her favorite activity.

During the first week of classes I told my students my basic expectations in a freshman theme: a bold thesis, specific support for the thesis, and a clear organizational principle. Then in the second week I had my students write an in-class theme on one of several topics. The topic Moji chose to write on was "College: A Vacation from Home?" I reproduce the theme below, purged of the twenty-odd spelling and punctuation errors it contained:

College Is Not a Vacation

When entering college for the first time the college freshman is filled with anxiety, with exhilaration, and with anticipation.

And why not? He is about to embark on an experience which most likely will never occur again in his life. For the first time he is pretty much on his own. Even though mom and dad are a phone call away or a two-hour bus ride away, he is going to have to do things which he never had to do, i.e. the laundry, and make decisions he never had to make. The thought of all this is exciting so that it feels that one is on a vacation, on a break. Things like throwing out the garbage, walking the dog, or watching over the younger siblings are left ninety to a hundred miles away. One feels that this is the time for me and for me to do what I want.

A vacation, in my opinion, is a break; a break in a length of time or work. A vacation is used to relax, to enjoy, and most important to keep worries and problems out of one's mind. A vacation should be a selfish act in that it is a time for you and the ones you are with to pamper and enjoy themselves.

I'm sure most people would agree with me to a certain extent, from the busy executive to pressured student. But I feel college students, in particular, college freshmen, feel that the university is a "break" from the pressures and worries of home, but are rudely awakened by the fact that college is not quite a vacation and may present more problems than are at home.

But all this could be taken to an extreme. The freshman goes out every weekend and socializing and getting to know people become Priority One. He seems to forget why he is at college in the first and foremost place. But when finals and grades come around his memory is jolted if not kicked. This is the rude awakening. The freshman's retention in the university is at stake, which could trigger a chain reaction such as affect scholarships, future grants, and maybe his future in general.

Pete Beidler is an English professor at Lehigh University in Bethlehem, Pennsylvania.

Moji climbing to the high ropes course. "Now what?" (Tim Mayer)

After first semester of freshmen year he realizes the vacation is over. In college one would probably have to deal with more pressure than he will ever experience after school. So in actuality life is going to be the vacation from college.

It was easy enough to see why Moji had failed English 1 the first time. Because she did not get around to stating a thesis until the end of her fourth paragraph ("college is not quite a vacation and may present more problems than are at home") and then quickly abandoned it, her theme never got very far. Because she offered no specific evidence or personal examples to support any thesis, her theme failed to be convincing or memorable. Because she had no organizational principle, her theme wandered with no apparent aim. Because she never decided on a single point of view, her "one's" and "me's" and "you's" and "he's" competed for control. Her logic was faulty (is doing one's laundry an activity usually associated with vacation time?). Her antecedents were vague (just what is "all this" that could be taken to an extreme?). Her thought processes were undeveloped (just why, in that last sentence, is "life," whatever that is, going to be a "vacation from college"?).

Moji had a problem.

As her English teacher, I had a problem, also. How was I to help her to improve her writing? How was I to take a young woman who had so little to say and help her to say it better?

With twenty years of experience behind me, I had some ideas about how to proceed. The comment I wrote on that first theme turned out to be longer than the theme itself. I explained how Moji must state a thesis earlier in the theme. I wrote a new introduction for her, one which contained both a thesis statement and an organizational plan. I explained how she should draw from specific experiences she had had last semester that showed how unwise it was to consider college as merely a vacation from home.

My comments were useful, I think, and Moji's revision on that theme as well as her next theme on "bad teaching" were somewhat better than her first effort. Still, something was missing. There was no fire to her writing. It was heartless, perfunctory, and mechanical.

After several weeks of having to read heartless, perfunctory, and mechanical writing from Moji and her classmates, I decided that at least part of the trouble was the writing assignments I was making. How much fire could I expect from those same old theme topics? We English teachers are all familiar with such topics: peer pressure; television; my favorite teacher; my roommate; racism; campus sports; the food in the freshman dining hall. In the hands of our better students, those topics yield pretty decent themes. Each can be dealt with in a couple of pages. Each can be approached in many different ways. Each encourages students to draw from personal experience.

But I was getting bored with reading about such topics, and I sensed that my students were getting bored with writing about them. I decided it was time for a change.

The Call of the Wild.

As a result of a series of circumstances I cannot take the space to explain here, I had been invited to give a talk at the October, 1984, annual convention of the Association for Experiential Education at Lake Junaluska, North Carolina. While there I talked with a number of people about what experiential education was all about. I learned about things called Outward Bound and wilderness treks and high ropes courses. Even then I found myself wondering if there might be ways to work experiential education into the freshman English curriculum.

I knew that students often did their best writing if they wrote about what they knew best — their own personal experiences. In practice that usually meant having them draw from their memories.

Might it be a useful experiment, I wondered, if I provided experiences for my students that they could then write about in their themes? If so, then there would be no need to rely on fuzzy recall of unmemorable experiences.

I decided to talk with some of the people I had met at the Association for Experiential Education in North Carolina. I got in touch with Bill Proudman, director of the Quest Program at Bloomsburg University in northern Pennsylvania. The Quest people routinely organized adventure education courses for Bloomsburg students. They also did contract courses for people not associated with Bloomsburg. I asked Bill if he could help me provide some memorable experiences for some Lehigh freshman English students.

Bill had heard my talk at Lake Junaluska and with very little ado said, "Sure."

Further talks with him and with his assistant, Heidi Hammel, resulted in our reaching agreement on a two-day, three-night, course just before Easter. We would take a two-hour bus trip from Bethlehem to Bloomsburg on Wednesday afternoon and, after some orientation and get-acquainted activities that night, sleep in the main lodge of an unused girl scout camp near Bloomsburg. Later we would split into two groups. Each group would complete a team-building "get the group over the log" exercise, a trust fall, a two-person tight-rope balance, a low-ropes course, a high-ropes course, a tyrolean traverse. We would also have some individual time alone in the woods, as well as camping experience. At the end of two days the two groups would get together again to debrief, turn in their equipment, and leave Saturday morning. Bill Proudman would work with one group and Heidi Hammel with the other.

Having never done any of the activities Bill and Heidi described, I was not sure what I was getting us into, but it sounded like fun and it sounded like the kind of experience that could make for some interesting writing. I asked a few questions about safety, then told Bill and Heidi that I needed two weeks to work on it at my end before I would let them know.

Working on it at my end meant two things: money and students. My first task was to convince my dean and provost that the $65 per student (including instruction, meals, equipment, lodging and transportation) was something worth supporting. They replied quickly and affirmatively.

It was tricky business convincing my students that they should give up three days of their Easter break to join me in the woods to take part in some experiences seemingly irrelevant to freshman English. I think the worst moment came when I told them they would not be able to take a shower during the whole time. But, then, this trip was strictly voluntary and they were free to choose without reward or penalty. Those who opted for a traditional Easter vacation would return to a routine much as they had enjoyed since the beginning of the semester. For those who went to Bloomsburg I would cancel the next five regularly scheduled classes and see that they got credit for two themes from the experience: one would be for keeping a journal while at Bloomsburg; the other would be for writing a theme on something they learned there. Most of my students seemed interested but, at the same time, were puzzled and hesitant. I called Heidi and told her about the puzzlement and the hesitation.

Heidi Hammel suggested that if it would help my students understand what to expect, she could visit Lehigh to show them some slides, to explain more about the program, and to answer any questions they might have. I was happy to accept her offer because I had never met Heidi and I had a number of questions myself, the kinds of questions it is easier to ask face-to-face than over the phone.

She came to my class and we had a good session. Her slides were enticing but more than a little frightening. Heidi and I assured my students that none of them would be forced into any activity they preferred not to do.

In the end two-thirds of my students joined the Bloomsburg expedition. Of those who did not, several had religious conflicts; others had sports conflicts; one or two were afraid.

Moji was afraid, but she went.

From Dusk to First Light.

The bus ride to Bloomsburg was depressing for all of us. At four o'clock that Wednesday afternoon most of the other Lehigh students were heading home to their families, and here we were — off to the wilds. Although we had met together three hours a week for two months in the classroom, we did not know each other well. I was the only one in the class who knew everyone's name. We were sullen and quiet as we dutifully ate the dry turkey sandwiches and the apples that were to be our supper. Looking through the windows of the Lehigh bus, we watched dark clouds gather over a misty dusk.

Upon our arrival in Bloomsburg two hours later, Heidi greeted us. Soon she, Bill, two interns, and eighteen shy Lehigh folk stepped into two vans with overnight bags and headed toward the girl scout lodge.

Once there we played some ice-breaking games. While these made us feel silly at times and were a little threatening, we were pleased with our successes. Group members discovered that they had a lot in common.

Then we had a snack, unrolled sleeping bags and mattresses, and went to bed. We kept the lights on for an hour or so for those who wanted to begin writing in their journals.

Moji Keeps a Journal

Moji began writing that night, lying in her sleeping bag. I shall let her words tell most of her story, along with a few comments interspersed from me. Here is what Moji wrote that first night:

April 3. Hi there. I've decided to write my journal to someone. No one in particular, not even Prof. Beidler. But I think it will be easier for me to express myself if I think someone — anyone — will be reading this.

Well, I must say it has already been an interesting and thought-provoking start. The staff members, Bill, Heidi, Nancy, and Frances, are really nice people. They seem to have their act together emotionally and mentally. I mean, they seem very satisfied with what they are doing with their lives.

I can't say exactly how I feel about being here in Bloomsburg. Like Bill said, we could be worrying about the amount of work we have to do before school resumes. How do I feel about not being home and not **finally** seeing my friends from high school?

I feel excited. I've never done any kind of camping before. I can deal with sleeping on the floor, no shower or toilet, and no concept of time because it is like when my family and I go to Africa, where we live without any electricity at times.

The part that scares me is being able to handle the activities mentally and emotionally. Will I crack up and chicken out? Will I ever realize and utilize my potential? Now that I think about it that is what I am really afraid of. I have been told that I have potential to go far and do great things, but I never seem to get past the average. I hope I get past it during this trip. My arm is getting tired so I'll talk to you later. Bye.

The next morning we split into two groups. One group went off with Bill. I was in Heidi's group. So was Moji. Heidi's group headed off to the low ropes course. The low ropes course involved several group activities. We had to help each other climb over a horizontal log eight feet high. Then we did the "trust fall" in which each of us, in turn, stood on a four-foot high stump, closed our eyes, and fell backwards into the arms of others in the group.

The most memorable event in the low ropes course was the one we came to call "two on a tightrope." Two cables, three feet off the ground, were tied to a single tree at one end but to two different trees, some twelve feet apart, at the other end. The task was to start with a partner on separate cables at the apex of the "V" and gradually move outward. Moji and Christine were partners for this one, but had a hard time of it. When they fell off, Moji bruised her arm. Her second attempt with Tim was a little more successful.

Then we moved on to the high ropes course. Our task was to shinny up a steeply inclined log, climb some pegs to reach the proper level, then walk through a route in the treetops on steel cables. We were always secured by seat harnesses into safety cables so that if we fell off we would dangle rather than crash to the ground. Almost all of us — me included — fell off at least one of the legs of the course. But we had been trained how to pull ourselves back up again. I followed Moji, and I could see how scared she was. She really did not want to be on the high ropes. But she was up there, and she completed the course. She wrote the following journal entry immediately after she reached the ground.

A sigh of relief is the only sound I can make. The feelings I was going through just now I only remember feeling when I was little under the age of 10. During

Two on a tightrope. "Push down, Christine." (Tim Mayer)

that age period when I was told or saw something scary or frightening I would be terrified for lack of understanding or comprehension.

Later. I didn't finish my last entry because I was numb from the experience of the ropes course. Now I think I'm ready to write.

At times I feel stupid because I think everyone in my group must have done something similar to if not exactly like what we've been doing for the past couple of days. I mean, at one point during the ropes course I started to cry. I was terrified, even though I logically knew I was perfectly safe. I felt like a little child. I wanted to be safe on the ground hugging something like a tree or a stuffed bear or a person.

Later still. A lot of things that happened on the trip wills stay with me for a while. One thing I realized was that it was all right to cry. I'm the type of person who will not cry no matter what. I probably feel it is a sign of weakness or that crying is a stereotypical characteristic of women. And I don't like to be classified. But when I was on the high ropes and had to change hands on the "hourglass" part I felt like I was going to die. I thought, this must be what it feels like just before you die. That may seem a little harsh, but for some reason something told my mind that even though the high ropes course was probably 98.5% safe, I felt that the 1.5% danger would appear when I was up in the trees.

All this sounds ridiculous considering I was perfectly safe, but I took the course as more than just a game or exercise. It was a test, an aptitude test or a personality test. As for failing or passing, I think I passed with flying colors.

That night we slept at the camp site across a stream. We were not in tents. Our only cover was a large orange tarp strung over a rope between two trees, open on all four sides. We stayed mostly dry when it rained a little, but most of us were uncomfortably cold, even in our goose-down sleeping bags.

The next morning we got up at first light again, had a hasty breakfast of oatmeal and hot chocolate, packed up our gear, and began the one-mile trek to Angel Falls. When we got there we spotted the tyrolean traverse the other group had set up the previous day while we were on the ropes course. Moji panicked when she saw it. "I can't do it," she said.

April 4. My handwriting is messier than usual because I'm freezing. I just got off the traverse ten minutes ago. I am in shock. I'm shocked I actually went through with it and had a minimal amount of fear. I think I was more terrified on the high ropes course than on the traverse. The ropes course helped me deal with my fears.

I wish I wasn't so chicken. I'm not used to being a follower, but in this case I really have no choice. I guess one can't always be in the head. I don't think that anyone in my group thinks less of me because I am not the fastest or the strongest. If anything, they should be proud — no, I should be proud of myself — because I attempted and completed feats that I never really saw myself doing. I've always wanted to go camping and hiking and do almost dangerous things, but I just thought about doing them. "Someday I will," I said. But in the back of my mind I was really thinking, "Fat chance."

On the hike back from the tyrolean traverse we did a "blind man's walk." Moji paired off with Christine again. Moji put on a blindfold, and Christine took her by the hand and led her some 20 yards through the woods to a certain tree or rock. Moji was to play close enough attention with her other senses — to the terrain, to the sounds, to the feel of the rock or tree — that after having been led back to the point of origin, she could remove the blindfold and set out to find that same tree or rock. After Moji had successfully performed the experiment, then Christine put on the blindfold and Moji led her to a different place in the woods.

One of the best parts of the trip was the "time alone." Heidi took each of us to a place off the main trail where we were to spend nearly two hours alone, out of sight of, and unable to hear, anyone else. We were to think or write or listen to the sounds of the woods. Moji used part of her time to write:

I am now sitting all by myself in a clearing in the woods. Believe it or not, but I am not afraid. I like it a lot. I can talk out loud without anyone thinking I am crazy. I've been alone many times, for many reasons, but this is the first time I'm sincerely and truly enjoying it. I've always wanted to be alone in the woods and feel safe about it. There is something romantic and dramatic about just sitting and writing in the woods. It's like a scene from a movie or a play.

Friday night the two groups got back together and we were all asked to respond orally to several questions: What had we learned? What was the high point of our experience? What did we like best about the person sitting to the right of us around the circle? Moji was impressed with what the group revealed and managed to say a few things beautifully herself. At the final meeting she spoke with considerable eloquence about what the trip had meant to her. Some of that eloquence found its way into her journal:

I found that when I am faced with an obstacle that makes me hesitant, if I work towards getting past, over, under, or through the obstacle, I surprise myself. I find I have qualities and abilities I never put to use. From the beginning of this trip I was worried about making a fool of myself, of looking like a wimp, of failing. But even in the things I did badly I realize I didn't fail, because each time I learned something. Example: two on a tightrope. I think the reason Christine and I didn't do well, even when I felt calm and balanced, was that there was this small part of me which didn't believe I could do it. Even though I was, with all my might, trying to concentrate on balancing, this little voice said, "You'll never make it." But later, when I did make it halfway with Tim, I only felt confident when I look in his eyes. He was smiling and that smile was louder than the little voice.

I shall quote no more from Moji's journal. That journal was of particular interest to me not only because of what it said, but also because Moji was writing differently in that journal than she had in any other writing she had done for me that semester. Most of the awkwardness was gone. She wrote with feeling and conviction about an experience that obviously meant something to her. Did she write with grace, feeling, and conviction because, for once, she had experienced something that did mean something to her? Or was it simply that, freed from the necessity to write a theme, that artificial exercise with a thesis, support, and an organizational pattern, Moji's writing style was able to flourish like a tulip released from the burden of a flat rock?

From Journal to Theme

Naturally I was curious to see whether Moji would write as well when she did her theme based on the Bloomsburg experience. For this theme I asked my students to suggest several topics they would like to write on, and I would pick the one with which I thought they might best succeed with. Moji asked if she could write about her "internal metamorphosis." I told her I thought it would be a fine topic. Here is the theme she turned in.

Internal Metamorphosis.

When Pete first mentioned the trip to Bloomsburg I was filled with excitement and anticipation because I had never been camping before. But as the day of the trip got closer my excitement lessened and I became worried. I was worried about what this trip might reveal about myself because after Heidi's slide presentation I began to think of the Quest program as a type of self-awareness program. So with that thought in my mind I began to worry whether I would come out of the three-day excursion with anything worthwhile or if I would actually learn something. Well, I must say I returned from Bloomsburg with a lot in tow. Aside from my luggage, I came back with stories of a new and exciting experience, but most important I returned with a new me. No, it wasn't that I changed my hair or lost weight, but I was different inside. I was different in the way I acted, in how I felt, and in what I thought. Because of the trip I've returned to Lehigh with self-confidence, with a sense of appreciation of the things around me, and with a realization of my own potential.

When the bus left the front of Lehigh's University Center on that Wednesday afternoon, I was a girl who was lacking in self-confidence and who constantly wondered what others thought of her. Now I am someone who cares very little what others may think of how I look, act, or dress. I think this new confidence in me came from the support I got from group in Bloomsburg. When I was on the high ropes course I was ready to stop in the middle of the course and turn back. But each time I hesitated to go on I found myself surrounded by people who for some reason had faith in my completing the course. At one point in the course I was scared to move and just felt like crying, yet from behind me I had Pete telling me to take my time. I also had Tim ahead of me advising on what to do and the others on the ground yelling encouragement. At that moment I thought that here is a group of people who didn't even know me, yet were confident I could finish the course. I later realized that I couldn't always rely on others to tell me that I am capable. I had to tell myself. I had to develop the confidence.

After leaving Bloomsburg I became more deliberative. Instead of always looking as if I'm in a rush to be somewhere, I now take my time and am more observant. I'll stop and listen to birds or look more closely at clouds. This all may sound corny and not terribly profound, but the important thing is that I do stop to take notice. This probably grew from my blind walk in the woods because in that activity I had to be more aware of the little things in my surroundings, without sight. So when my blindfold was removed I had to find my way back to where I was previously led. In order to do so I had to recall things like bumps in the path and textures of bark. So now when I walk around campus my pace is less hurried and more leisurely.

I think the biggest change within me I've experienced is that I now realize my potential. For years, teachers and friends have told me I had such potential and that they could see me being famous and doing great things. Yet in school I only did a minimum amount of work and did well. And outside of the security of school I would hesitate in trying new things for fear of not being capable. But Quest helped me prove that I had capacities I had never used. The tyrolean traverse seemed impossible for me to attempt emotionally and physically. Yet when I was harnessed in and hooked on to the rope there was no turning back. I had no choice but to go forward. And when I finished exhaustedly I was amazed at how my terror before going across had turned into an exhiliration of being 100 feet in the air next to a waterfall. I have to admit my realization of my potential was forced upon me in that I was put into situations in which I had no choice but to go on. But the fact that I did go on and sometimes succeeded showed me that in my past there was something mental stopping me from attempting challenging endeavors, whether physical, social, or academic.

How else can I conclude other than saying I had a great time and even though I didn't act like it when I was in Bloomsburg, I would go through the experience all over again. I am pleased with the new me and I hope I can continue to develop outside of Bloomsburg, Pennsylvania.

Moji's theme will not earn her a Nobel prize for freshman writing. There were still some spelling and punctuation errors (which I have corrected for her above). There are more serious problems, as well, which almost any reader and, certainly, all more polished writers would notice.

Still, Moji's writing in that theme was far and away the best she had done that year. She had a thesis, a point to make. She used personal examples to support that point. Her theme was organized, with a single point developed in each paragraph. Best of all, she wrote as if she believed in what she was saying, as if she cared, as if she wanted to tell the world — even the narrow world of her English professor — about an experience that was important to her.

Moji was pleased at the grade she got on that theme. "It doesn't seem fair.", she told me. "I really sweated on those other ones and got those bad grades. This one was so **easy** and quick to write, and I got my best grade of the year."

Moji learned something about writing as a result of those days at Bloomsburg: that writing is easier if she has something she wants to say.

I learned something about the teaching of writing as a result of those days at Bloomsburg: that my job as a teacher of writing really extends beyond explaining the principles of writing, assigning topics, and commenting on the writing students do. Part of my job is to arrange experiences through which my students will learn enough about themselves or the world around them that they **want** to tell me about it in words they find are suddenly easy to write.

Thank you, Moji.

IV. Experiential Learning and the Classroom

Experiential Components in Academic Courses

by G. Christian Jernstedt

Although there has been a tendency to separate academic and experiential learning, the two can be successfully integrated.

The Goals of Education

For what do we educate? The introductions of diverse college catalogues describe goals of higher education that are remarkably consensual. The purpose of education "is to free students to explore, for a lifetime, the possibilities and limits of the human intellect."[1] Toward this end effective faculty "regard the mind...as a flame that is to be fed, as an active being that must be strengthened to think and feel..."[2] The mind, alight with learning, develops through "rigorous study and the acquisition of information and technique, on the one hand; and a sustained productive effort and vigourous personal expression on the other..."[3]

Aristotle alluded to this same dual nature of education in the fourth century, B.C.: "Their using the language of knowledge is no proof that they possess it...students who have just begun a subject reel off its formulae, though they do not yet know their meaning, for knowledge has to become part of the tissue of the mind..."[4] Thus, during the course of two millenia, we find an awareness that there are two elements to the state of being educated: the possession of skills and knowledge, and the expression of those abilities in intercourse with the world.

The Nature of Schooling

Cross-cultural studies of cognitive abilities suggest that certain unique attributes of Western schooling have had a profound effect on our use of language and, hence, on our modes of thought. This effect is quite complex, and involves a separation of language from its roots in everyday communication.[5] The advantage of such a formalization of language is its resultant power for deriving abstractions, rules, and general principles, and for logically manipulating facts and ideas. The danger in formalization and decontextualization of language is that knowledge may become separated from experience. Formal schooling may result in the development of skills appropriate to academic environments but ineffective in life situations.

G. Christian Jernstedt is associate professor of psychology at Dartmouth College. Active in Outward Bound, he currently serves as Chairperson of the Advisory Board of the Dartmouth Outward Bound Center and a trustee of Outward Bound, Inc.

Comenius, Dewey, Piaget, and Bruner have all voiced a similar concern.[6]

The most dangerous response to this dilemma of Western schooling is to propose an unreserved emphasis on relevance in institutions of higher education. The goal of colleges and universities must remain the nurture of the life of the mind. But if the mind is to function in the complex world community of the present, it must be equipped with the ability to bring its abstract, intellectual skills to bear on the realities of secular existence. For the educated world citizen, intellectual ability must be inextricably linked with a testing of that ability through life experiences.

> The most dangerous response to this dilemma of Western schooling is to propose an unreserved emphasis on relevance in institutions of higher education.

A serious problem with much of contemporary higher education is that students are tested on their acquisition of knowledge, with only the assumption that the use of that knowledge will follow its asquisition. What I propose is that we test our students' abilities to use their knowledge, realizing that successful use of knowledge proves the previous acquisition of that knowledge.[7] By training for

---

[1] University of Chicago, **The College** (Chicago: University of Chicago, 1971), p. 9.
[2] Williams College, **An Introduction** (Williamstown, MA: Williams College, 1979), p. 5.
[3] Bennington College, **Catalog** (Bennington, VT: Bennington College, 1978), p. 5.
[4] Aristotle, **Nichomachean Ethics**, in The Philosophical Foundations of Education, ed. Steven M. Cahn (New York: Harper & Row, 1970), p. 116.
[5] Ann L. Brown, "Knowing When, Where, and How to Remember: A Problem of Metacognition," in **Advances in Instructional Psychology**, ed. Robert Glaser, I (Hillsdale, NJ: Lawrence Earlbaum Associates, 1978), pp. 143-148.
[6] David R. Olson, "The Languages of Instruction: The Literate Bias of Schooling," in **Schooling and the Acquisition of Knowledge**, ed. Richard C. Anderson, Rand J Spiro, and William E. Montague (Hillsdale, NJ: Lawrence Earlbaum Associates, 1977), pp. 65-89.
[7] G. Christian Jernstedt, "PSI/T: Personalized Instruction with Emphasis on Extraclassroom Transfer," Paper presented to the Conference on the Keller Plan, Cambridge, MA, October, 1971.

knowledge and testing for use of knowledge, we simultaneously focus on the dual nature of education, stated as early as Aristotle and as recently as this year's college catalogue.

Teaching Methods

Though institutions of higher education serve many functions, their initial and fundamental activity is teaching. Preeminent among teaching methods is didactics, the imparting of knowledge, principally through books and lectures. Teaching is not limited to didactics, finding expression also in heuristics, the use of problem solving techniques, and philetics, the concern for the learner as person.[8] Yet comparisons of various teaching methods fail to find differential effectivenss. When educational outcome is measured by the average performance of students on final examinations, distinctly different teaching methods are found to produce similar scores.[9] We cannot, however, use these results to dismiss concern with teaching methods. Others have found that the grades which are based upon such examination performance do not predict later adult competence and may, in fact, predict psychological immaturity in adulthoood.[10] These data on teaching methods may best be interpreted as revealing that our attention should be focused on learning rather than teaching methods.[11] Apparently it is not what the teacher does, but what the teacher encourages or enables the student to do that determines what is learned.[12]

Learning Methods

Historically, memory researchers have focused their attention on the properties of the material to be learned more than on the actions of the learner. We must not forget, however, that active learning is more efficient than passive or highly directed learning.[13] Students who use information they are trying to learn, who challenge and grapple with their new knowledge, or who use it to solve new problems, tend to learn more effectively than students who passively read, memorize, or merely absorb that to which they have been exposed. Correspondingly, recent research on memory has shifted in attention from the material to be learned to the mental activities of the learner. We now know that learners remember not what they encounter while learning so much as what they do while learning.[14]

Furthermore, the research literature paints a surprisingly narrow picture of the impact of learning techniques on students. For a student to master a body of knowledge, the student must be trained in the task for which he or she wishes to use that knowledge. This conclusion is true for specific skills such as writing, for bodies of factual knowledge, and for such complex skills as problem solving. In each case, the most effective learning comes when the student, during the original learning, engages in the behavior which will later be used as test or example of the success of that learning.[15] Skills which are learned in classrooms may not simply transfer to life situations, whether those situations be the next course which the student takes or an event in his or her own life. The precise nature of the learning task is the determinant of the learning outcome. For example, reading and writing about material which one is learning produces different learning than reading about the material and studying for a test on it.[16] Neither method is better overall than the other; each produces particular benefits.

Operating in the domain of abstraction or pure knowledge may lead to an inability to use knowledge in situations other than those in which it was acquired.

We see that the purpose and structure of learning activities guides the acquisition of knowledge. Operating in the domain of abstraction or pure knowledge may lead to an inability to use knowledge in situations other than those in which it was acquired. To move toward a state of being educated by studying in a purely academic environment may be most effective for future college and university faculty, but for few other students.

To describe education as a state may, in fact, be to obscure its meaning. The educated mind has not only acquired a structure but also developed a set of processes. This argues for the introduction of experience into the academic environment, as a means of reconnecting the structure of knowledge with the process of using knowledge. Research on learning methods supports the argument. Tying information to be learned to experience, even when the experience is purely hypothetical, can preserve that learning within the mind and prime the

---

[8] H.S. Broudy, "Didactics, Heuristics, and Philetics," **Educational Theory** 22 (1972): pp. 251-261.

[9] David C. Berliner and N.L. Gage, "The Psychology of Teaching Methods," in **The Psychology of Teaching Methods**, ed. N.L. Gage (Chicago: University of Chicago Press, 1976), pp. 15-19.

[10] Douglas H. Heath, "Academic Predictors of Adult Maturity and Competence," **Journal of Higher Education** 48 (1977): pp. 613-632.

[11] Donald Dansereau, "The Development of a Learning Strategies Curriculum," in **Learning Strategies**, ed. Harold F. O'Neil, Jr. (New York: Academic Press, 1978), pp. 1-29.

[12] Christian Jernstedt and Wilfred K. Chow, "Lectures and Textual Materials as Sources of Information for Learning," **Psychological Reports** (under review).

[13] W.J. McKeachie, "Research on Teaching at the College and University Level," in **Handbook of Research on Teaching**, ed. N.L. Gage (Chicago: Rand McNally, 1963), pp. 1118-1172.

[14] Fergus I. M. Craik and Endel Tulving, "Depth of Processing and the Retention of Words in Episodic Memory," **Journal of Experimental Psychology: General** 104 (1975): pp. 268-294.

[15] G. Christian Jernstedt, "The Relative Effectiveness of Individualized and Traditional Instruction Methods," **The Journal of Educational Research** 69 (1976): pp. 211-218.

[16] Jernstedt, "The Relative Effectiveness of Individualized and Traditional Instruction Methods."

mind for new learning more effectively than other techniques.

A Proposal

In the context of what we now know about learning, we may formulate a proposal to meld the structures of knowledge with the processes of using knowledge. We must do this by retaining the accumulated strengths of classroom instruction and adding the breadth, mnemonic effectiveness, and active expression of life experiences.

By combining experiential components with academic courses, we may couple the acquisition of knowledge with the ability to use it. An experiential component is a part of a course which provides the student with what the dictionary defines as experience: "direct participation in events,. . .knowledge, skill, or practice derived from direct observation of or participation in events,. . . something personally encountered, undergone, or lived through. . ."[18]

I do not propose that we improve education simply by adding extensive practical or applied problem-solving experience. The life of the mind is nurtured by the study of abstract concepts, as well as by the application of those concepts to complex, life-like situations. What we must do is increase the number and quality of ways in which the developing mind can encounter and grapple with the worldly embodiment of its expanding knowledge. The classroom is the traditional locus of education because it can be very effective. Our task is to redouble its effectiveness with experience.

Techniques

How shall we introduce this element of experience into the academic course; must we redesign the course first? I think not. I have examined the use of experiential components in many, different courses, where methods of teaching have varied from the traditional lecture-reading-examination format to the innovative, individualized style

> *Experiential components seem to be effective regardless of the format or style of the teaching methods.*

of each student following a unique path through the course materials.[19] Experiential components seem to be effective regardless of the format or style of the teaching methods. In exploring the use of experiential components, my attention has been directed at two domains of experiences. On the one hand, I have examined experiences which occur or are presented within the classroom. Techniques in this domain include examples, modeling, and demonstrations. On the other hand, I have ventured outside the formal classroom to develop experiences which may then be related back to the classroom. Here I have considered experiential laboratories and extended group living experiences.

EXPERIENCES IN THE CLASSROOM

Experience by Example

The previously cited advantage of active learning over passive learning argues for direct rather than vicarious experiences. However, a full understanding of the impact of experience on learning requires an awareness of its limits. Accordingly, I began by studying such vicarious experiences as examples of others' behavior.

Printed Handouts. --The simplest and most direct way of integrating experiences into the academic course is through the use of printed examples. I have found that concepts which are taught with examples drawn from the natural environment are remembered more correctly and for a longer period of time than are concepts taught without such referents. I gave a group of students a simple list of examples of concepts that had been covered in a lecture. This is certainly the extreme point on the continuum of experiential learning, but these students performed better on a later examination than did students who had not received the example list. Not only had the students with exposure to the list learned the basic concepts better, but they also were more proficient at using the concepts they had learned.[20]

Now, I do not propose that such a procedure is an ideal one; it was created to examine the limits of introducing experiential-like materials. But handouts work. What they seem to do is cause the students to transform and extrapolate the principles being learned, so as to relate them to the examples in the handouts, and these transformational activities refine the intellectual processes occurring within the students' minds.

Recalled Personal Experiences. --It seems obvious, however, that reading another's examples should be less effective than using one's own. Consequently, I have used exercises in which students must take the concept being learned and apply it to an example from their own life. They are asked to describe a situation from their own experience to which the principle under study may be applied.[21] This is a more powerful and engaging activity than simply studying a list of examples. It, too, is very effective in enhancing learning, but it has a serious flaw which I have not been able to correct. The student must recall from memory the situation which is to be analyzed.

---

[17] John D. Bransford, Kathleen E. Nitsch, and Jeffrey J. Franks, "Schooling and the Facilitation of Knowing," in *Schooling and the Acquisition of Knowledge*, ed. Richard C. Anderson, Rand J. Spiro, and William E. Montague (Hillsdale, NJ: Lawrence Earlbaum Associates, 1977), pp. 31-55.

[18] *Webster's New Collegiate Dictionary*, 1975.

[19] The evaluations of the programs described throughout this report have been carried out through the Experiential Learning in College Project at Dartmouth. Particular attention has been paid to the methodological and statistical validity of the evaluations. All results reported in this paper are significant. Full details cannot be included because of space limitations, but are available in reports from the author.

[20] G.B. Northcraft and G.C. Jernstedt, "Comparison of Four Teaching Methodologies for Large Lecture Classes," *Psychological Reports* 36 (1975): pp. 599-606.

[21] G. Christian Jernstedt, *Learning: The Philosophy and Structure of a Course*, (Hanover, NH: Dartmouth College, 1976), pp. 13-33.

Memory is imperfect and often acts to make our recollections more consistent with our desires than was the original situation. The often distorted accuracy of these recollections is a serious impediment to their effective use. Since the instructor has available only the student's imperfect recall, we find a significant retardation in the learning of concepts when this method is compared with one in which there is a means of externally validating the information in the example. That is, the student's task is too simple. The original experience is recalled to fit the principles under study much more directly than true life situations fit. The result is a seriously limited ability to use the principle. To provide examples of real experiences but retain a means of externally validating the details of real experience, the instructor must provide the example.

Experiences in Novels. --With instructor supplied experiences, the goal is to provide each student with some form of life experience to which the concept being learned may be related. I have tried newspapers, magazines, novels, and films as resources for these experiences; novels are the most effective. A novel, if well chosen, provides the students with a stream of life situation events and concommitant mental images. Though the experience is vicarious, it is powerful, realistic, and emotionally involving. Critical to its success is the fact that the instructor and student each have full access to the record of the experiences and can and must confront the experience in a factual, undistorted manner.

The novel is used to provide resource material for the students' learning activities. As with the recalled personal experiences described earlier, the student may be asked to find an instance of a particular concept in the novel or to take a scene in the novel and analyze it in terms of relevant course concepts. This use of vicarious, but realistic, life situations can improve homework activities, examination performance, and class discussions, as well as the ability to speak or write intelligently about what one has learned..

Instructor Modeling. --A related use of vicarious experiences that is relatively unused in teaching, but which is powerful in its effect on learning, is modeling. I have found that modeling can bring not only improvement in learning but increased motivation to learn as well. Modeling involves having the instructor in the course actually engage in the behavior which the students are trying to learn. It resembles a test given to the instructor by the students.

Consider the following example. The instructor announces to the students that during the next class meeting he or she will accept problems from students and solve them in front of the class. The questions may range from requiring the writing of a paper on the blackboard to the solving of homework-like or exam-like problems. Critical to the success of this modeling is that the instructor does not know what he or she will be asked to do. In front of the students, the instructor then tries to prepare a good answer to the assignment. This may involve the use of resources such as the text or various heuristics, as well as false starts, incorrect solutions, and, usually, a successful solution.

An instructor needs a healthy sense of self-worth to engage in modeling. The results can be spectacular. Students who have languished with course materials can

---

The most experiential of all the options for engaging students' minds within the classroom is the use of demonstrations or simulations.

---

suddenly come alive. They have seen that their own weak attempts and wrong turns are not uncommon for even a skilled professional. Most importantly, they have a concrete expression of what it means to grapple intellectually with a difficult concept. (Do not forget for a moment that these student-provided questions will be tricky and difficult, though realistic.) I have measured a significant increase in student work level after such sessions and an increase in the quality of their thought about the course concepts. Once again, tying the mind to the reality of life enhances understanding and action.

Demonstrations. --The most experiential of all the options for engaging students' minds within the classroom is the use of demonstrations or simulations. I once asked my students to come back a year after the course and tell me what they remembered of the course. This was a most revealing experience for me as a teacher. My students did not remember what I said to them in class, did not remember what they said in class, remembered very little of the textbook, but did remember the writing that they did. What they remembered best, and still remembered five years after the course, were the demonstrations. In other words, they remembered what they did. They remembered their experiences, the events which engaged their eyes, ears, and bodies along with their minds.

One of the best remembered demonstration experiences I have used may serve as a brief example. I was attempting to show my students that some strongly held beliefs about human behavior might be unfounded. My efforts at verbally convincing them of this proved futile. Eventually, I arranged an experiential proof of my point. The proof involved creating a situation in which obviously supernatural powers of a person were clearly and dramatically exhibited to the class. Later revelation of the deception involved in the situation served as a most compelling example of how easily we can confuse the intensity of a belief with its validity. One must personally hold an intense belief which is then discovered to be invalid before one can fully understand how ubiquitous these beliefs are. In other examples, what we find is that when students adopt the role of a senator in political science, when they try to write a short story as Hemingway would write, or when they try to authenticate a newly discovered document in history, they learn.

We have since studied the use of demonstrations in lecture courses and find it is not the demonstration, per se, that produces the enhanced learning. Courses in which lectures are supplemented with demonstrations are not necessarily better than those without. The critical element is the manner in which the demonstrations are chosen. Courses in which the instructor focuses on choosing demonstrations that are interesting and relevant do not produce the same learning as those in which the instructor focuses on the concepts to be taught and then finds demonstrations to fit those concepts.[22] The effectiveness of experiences for courses is a function of the necessity for those experiences. Merely adding exciting or interesting experiences to a course does not lead to enhanced learning in our studies. All too often, we have found, instructors use demonstrations as motivating rather than intellectual devices. But the power of a demonstration to improve intellectual performance lies with its intellectual content and the necessity for the experience. The most effective procedure we have found for introducing demonstrations in a course is to have the instructor generate a list of ten most important concepts, the ten concepts which he or she wants the students to remember two years after the course. Then the instructor looks for the ten best, most interesting, and most enjoyble demonstrations which illustrate those ten concepts.

EXPERIENCES OUTSIDE THE CLASSROOM
The Experiential Laboratory

It may be clear at this point that many of the procedures I have outlined thus far involve attempts to simulate direct experiences within the confines of the classroom. For almost no courses, however, are we confined to the classroom. One might propose that the truly effective ex-

The purpose of the laboratory is to provide a planned experience in a prescribed environment that will serve as resource material for the intellectual content of the course.

perience should, as we have seen, be carefully designed by the instructor to fit with the concepts to be learned, and should, in addition, occur in a realistic life environment. In conjunction with the Dartmouth Outward Bound Center, we have developed the vehicle of the experiential laboratory to fulfill this purpose.[23]

Design. --The experiential laboratory is a 2 to 4 day experience participated in by a small group of students, the course instructor, and a trained leader. The labs occur during the weekend, with occasional overlaps into the week. The labs are optional, and typically about one quarter of the students in a course opt for the lab. The labs may occur at any time during a course, though they usually take place early in the term. Some courses have as many as three labs, while others have only one. Each lab group is limited to 10 students. Often the instructor will not participate in all groups or all labs. We normally provide specialized gear through the Outward Bound Center, but that is not necessary. The skilled group leaders, such as are provided by Outward Bound, are absolutely necessary.

The purpose of the laboratory is to provide a planned experience in a prescribed environment that will serve as resource material for the intellectual content of the course. The small group nature of the labs provides for personal encounter and group interaction. The fact that the labs occur away from the classroom and the campus provides a sense of privacy and isolation in which the forces that are designed into the experience may operate. The novelty of the environment in which the labs occur provides a case study of the novel environments into which we all are placed throughout our lives. The short duration of the labs allows an intense focusing on the experience for each participant and an openness to exploration and experimentation with oneself and one's ideas. The typical presence of stress, uncertainty, and the need for problem solving and immediate judgment provides elements in the situation which are present at many important points in each of our lives.

The design of these laboratories is never casual; it typically takes a month to develop a new laboratory. Great cooperation and energy is required of both the instructor and the laboratory staff. The staff must know the concepts which the students are learning in the course. They normally read the texts or have taken the course. The instructor must understand the dynamics of group growth and individual development. Plans are usually quite detailed, often by the ten minute block. The plans are not followed rigidly, but are absolutely necessary if the experience is to be effective for the course.

The laboratories require great attention to safety and exceptional sensitivity to personal mental health principles. I would hesitate to design such a laboratory without the full involvement of a staff as highly and specially trained as those of the Dartmouth Outward Bound Center. The results of this care have been exceptional.

An Example. --The best way to understand these experiential labs is to participate in them. In lieu of such direct experience, a description will explain their relationship to and impact on an academic course.

The most common lab is Rocks and Ropes. It is chosen by many instructors because it presents a novel, highly

---

[22] Bruce Smoller, "Short and Long-Term Retention of Classroom Learning," Senior Fellow Dissertation, Dartmouth College, 1979, pp. 86-109.

[23] G. Christain Jernstedt, "Learning about Learning: A Personal Guide," (Hanover, NH: Dartmouth College, 1977), pp. 15-16.

motivating, skill-requiring experience which relates well to a wide range of course materials. The lab requires one weekend. On a Friday afternoon, the participants engage in a variety of group initiative exercises designed to build interpersonal contact and trust. Retrieving the evening's food supply from a nearly inaccessible spot further develops this process and gradually introduces the feeling of isolation and privacy. The next day is spent in climbing and rappelling, climaxed by blindfolded climbs. On Sunday, a difficult ropes course is negotiated, involving both group supported and individual efforts.

Course material is deliberately not discussed during the weekend. Journals are kept and individual reflective time is provided. With the exception of training for ropes work, the instructors are present only to provide safety and challenges and see that the environment is structured to encourage the ultimate goal of the weekend. For this weekend, which is often used to introduce the laboratory idea and set the stage for later laboratories, the goals are simple.

The weekend raises the issues of why we must learn certain concepts and how the value of learning may only become apparent in the later expression of that learning.

The weekend raises the issues of why we must learn certain concepts and how the value of learning may only become apparent in the later expression of that learning. The climbing language is an excellent example of this. When first told of the series of commands and communications which climbers use, the group members feel self-conscious and awkward in using the language, especially while practicing on the ground. Learning of the language is typically minimal at this stage. When the group moves to the short cliff face used for intermediate training, the purpose of the language becomes clearer, but it is not yet needed and hence not fully learned. Finally, when climbing the steep rock face, when belayer is not visible to climber or when the climber is blindfolded, the full import of the language blossoms and it is learned. This example of a concept which cannot be understood fully until it is experienced serves well throughout the remainder of the course to illustrate the impact of motivation and action on the learning of knowledge and intellectual skills.

During the week after the experience, debriefing sessions are held. It is in these sessions that the direct connections to course materials are made. Here the students are asked to take the classroom materials and use them to describe, analyze, and predict their own behavior in the natural environment. The most obvious advantage of the experience that is revealed in these sessions is that students typically encounter in their courses only idealized examples of life situations. The natural complexity of the experiences in the labs make the application of course principles difficult and inexact, precisely the case when applying most abstract knowledge to natural situations. The most effective heuristic device which I have found to teach students the subtleties and complexities of

---

There are times when nothing in our environment happens as we expect it to.

---

translating academic knowledge to real world situations is this debriefing after the laboratory.

Representative Laboratory Themes. --These laboratory experiences are not limited to courses which deal with psychology. We have designed and used a wide variety of laboratories in which concepts critical to courses from many disciplines may be presented. We have classified the laboratories according to their dominant theme.

One of the earliest themes we developed was that of novelty. For this theme students are taken into the woods with sufficient gear for climbing and hiking and given 15 minutes to move their entire group into the trees for the duration of the weekend. Anything left from the group or anyone touching the ground after this period is removed. Establishing a community in the trees raises important questions about the skills which we have and can bring to new environments, about how easy or difficult we find it to change, and about what happens to individuals and groups when they are forced to make sudden modifications in their previously well developed habits.

A related theme, which has led to the development of a very powerful laboratory, is uncertainty. There are times when nothing in our environment happens as we expect it to. In such a situation, as soon as we have decided how to act, the environment changes and that action is no longer appropriate. We create this situation in an experiential laboratory by issuing, first, an unusual equipment list to the students. They are required to bring with them sunglasses, swimming suits, a down jacket, a textbook to study, heavy work gloves, or other such gear. Upon departure, two small groups of students are put in two vans, with no outside view, and driven toward their destination. Along the way they are required to select additional gear from that in the van, which includes snowshoes, an envelope of cash, climbing rope, a rubber life boat, and so forth. They have one hour to select about a third of what is available and to arrange to carry it all on their backs. Just when they have decided, the vans are stopped, and the groups are each split in half and rearranged in the vans. These new groups must then repeat the selection process since they do not agree. The groups continue traveling until they are suddenly told that in five minutes they will reach their destination. There they will have exactly 15 seconds to vacate the vans and be on their way, on their own. Anything not on someone's back or left in the van will be lost for the next two days. The vans then stop, the doors are thrown open, and the students burst forth with all manner of strange gear on their backs. They have been so intent on preparing for this moment that they have not listened to the sounds outside the van, and, as the van roars off, they suddenly become dramatically aware of the fact that they are standing in the middle of a busy intersection in a large city. Their first task, left in an envelope, is to find and join up with the other group, which has been left somewhere else in the city. Their only restriction is that they may not move above ground. For the next hours they travel on the subway, deciding on a strategy to locate the others, guessing the others' strategy, and collecting a list of items which their information packet requires that they present later for food and bedding, of which they have little. The list requires the names and birth places of thirty people on the subway, a surgeon's mask, sand from a local beach, a symphony ticket, a used ticket from the topless bar district, a pig's foot, and other such items. At two in the morning, when they have found each other and most of the items on the list, they are suddenly met by a leader and removed to the vans. An hour later, after being led blindfolded from the vans, they remove the blindfolds to see total darkness and discover that they are locked in a bomb shelter. The weekend continues.

As might be expected, this lab provides a full academic term's worth of experiences which are used in the course. Issues include the kinds of uncertainty which are most and least disruptive, the skills which can be carried from environment to environment, the nature of the adaptation process, the maintenance of stability in an uncertain world, and the assistance and comfort of others in times of stress. In fact, the urban environment has proven to be fully as effective as the wilderness for these experiences, though one typically does not think of programs like Outward Bound as providing an urban experience.

Equally powerful is a laboratory in the city in which many members of the group are handicapped, with limbs or senses immobilized for the weekend. With no food or money the group must seek work. The job leads provided by the leaders before the experience are discovered to be difficult to develop due to the group's lack of training. When a dirty job cleaning the subway is found, and long hours spent working in the filth expecting a few dollars for food, the refusal of the employer to pay because of the "poor quality" of the work adds to the sense of frustration and helplessness. Courses in religion, history, economics, education, literature, and even technology may use this laboratory to enhance the learning of their students.

Even the designers of the laboratories are often surprised at the impact of these experiences on the intellectual growth of the students. One laboratory, in which students had to travel by bushwhacking through dense woods and make a variety of tools and implements to barter for food, motivated the students through the promise of a chicken banquet at the termination of the laboratory. The fact that the chickens were live when the students arrived for the banquet provoked nearly half a day of discussion about food sources and ethics, about medicine and health, and, most interestingly to the designers, about the law (is it legal to kill chickens?).

Evaluation. --My evaluation of the laboratories has examined three points of their impact: the individual students who are attracted to the laboratories, the immediate outcomes from the labs, and the long-term results of the experience.

Interestingly, the prior grade point averages of the lab participants are typically higher than those of the other students.

As might be expected, the students who are attracted to the laboratories are different from those who are not.[24] Those who sign up for this option in the courses I have examined have had more experience with outdoor adventure programs than their peers have had. They enter the course, even before they know about the laboratory option, expecting the course to be more flexible and less oriented towards factual content than do their peers. Once these students know about the lab option, their attitudes change compared to the attitudes of those who know that they are not participating in the labs. The participants-to-be expect the course to be more exciting than they did when they enrolled or than their peers do. They expect to develop more self-respect and self-confidence than do the other students. Their expectations also move towards a more interesting, valuable, and application-oriented course. The picture emerges of a participant who has used experiences for learning or simple pleasure in the past, and expects that they will enhance learning in this course.

Interestingly, the prior grade point averages of the lab participants are typically higher than those of the other students. I have since discovered that this is an artifact. There is no grade point difference between those who want and those who do not want to participate in the labs. The difference arises from the fact that among the initial applicants only those students who have relatively high grade point averages finally decide that they can afford the time for three weekends away from their other studies.

---

[24] Amy Gillenson, Scott McGovern, and G. Christian Jernstedt, "Effects of Outward Bound Participation," (Hanover, NH: Experiential Learning in College Project, 1974), pp. 1-23.

Students who have experienced the labs and their associated debriefings perform significantly better on later examinations than do their peers without the experiences, even when the differences in grade point average are controlled. This performance improvement is quite specific. The experiential students do not know more facts or principles; they understand concepts better. In situations in which they are asked to recognize instances of concepts or to choose and apply concepts correctly to complex situations, these students are superior.

The affective impact of the experiences at the end of the course depends, in part, on the teaching methodology used in the course.[25] To examine the worst case in which experiential laboratories might be used, we studied them in a course taught with the traditional lecture-text-examination format, and taught with no attempt on the instructor's part during the course to integrate the laboratory experiences with the course work. The only point of integration occurred during the one hour debriefing sessions, in which the experiences were related to course material, following each of the three weekends. At the end of this course, the laboratory participants reported that the course was less difficult, less well integrated, less organized, less effective in teaching factual content, and less fair in grading than the other students reported. Interviews with the students suggested that these feelings derived from the contrast between the personal intensity and relevance of the laboratories and the more traditional nature of the course itself.

In traditionally taught courses and in courses with more innovative formats, when the labs are integrated with the course material by the instructor, this difference does not appear. In contrast, students in such courses who participate in the labs report feelings of better integration, organization, fairness, and so forth.

These differences between courses which integrate the laboratories and those which do not disappear by one year after the course. We questioned students 12 and 24 months after the courses, in order to observe how they felt after the experiences and the course materials had settled in their minds. Regardless of the nature of the teaching methods in the course, those students who had participated in the laboratories reported a greater interest in the course subject matter, a greater ability to approach new subject matter and use effective learning techniques, and a greater tendency to seek challenges in their lives as students. In addition, the laboratory participants reported the course, itself, to have been more challenging and more relevant than the other students reported it to have been.

Interviews again provided information to elaborate upon these findings. It appeared that the laboratory students, during the time since the course, had integrated the experiences with the course material and with their own lives. Their experiences in the laboratories had served as a bridge between the course content and their own experiences after the course. Because the laboratories were designed to illustrate course principles, and because the experiences of the labs had roots in common experiences in natural life situations, the labs aided the transfer of course learning to later life experience. It is important to realize that this transfer was accomplished by the students without the instructor, since it occurred after the course was over, but was apparent only for those students who had experienced the labs.

We are presently collecting information about the students' long-term retention of the course materials and about the actual behaviors in which they have engaged since the course. One early result suggests that laboratory participants are much more likely to engage in later experiential learning than are non-participants.

The same principle discovered with in-class demonstrations applies to the laboratories. They are only effective if the principles and concepts of the course are developed first and independently, and then experiences are designed to provide the necessary enhancement of the intellectual content.

Extensions of Experiential Components

Students who take an active role in the development of their own education and make aggressive use of the resources in their environment strengthen their cognitive and affective development and improve their intellectual disposition.[26] The success of the laboratories is due in part to their ability or tendency to attract active students and to

---

A natural extension of these critical dimensions is field experience education, in which an entire course moves into the natural environment.

---

their intensification of student-faculty interaction. A natural extension of these critical dimensions is field experience education, in which an entire course moves into the natural environment. Examples include internships and language study abroad programs. Although the research literature on field experience education is methodologically weak, field experiences seem to attract different students than do more traditional courses, and to impact on their educational growth.[27]

A different manner of integrating life experiences with academic studies is that of the Living/Learning Term developed by the Dartmouth Outward Bound Center.

---

[25] Amy Gillenson, Scott McGovern, and G. Christian Jernstedt, "Effects of Outward Bound Participation," pp. 1-23.
[26] Robert C. Wilson, Jerry G. Gaff, Evelyn R. Dienst, Lyn Wood, and James L. Bavry, **College Professors and Their Impact on Students**, (New York: John Wiley, 1975), pp. 178-182.
[27] Gregory J. McHugo and G. Christian Jernstedt, "The Affective Impact of Field Experience Education on College Students," **Alternative Higher Education** 3 (1979): pp. 188-206.

Participants in this option combine a normal academic term with small group living in a house on campus. The 10 to 12 participants organize and execute all logistics related to food, maintenance, and personal interaction. They take a full course load, sharing one course in common, and participate in all the elements of a standard Outward Bound course (initial expedition, rescue and service work, personal skill and fitness development, solo exerience, and final expedition). The focus of the Living/Learning Term is neither on the content of a particular course, as is the focus of the laboratory experience, nor on a particular environment, as is the field experience course. Rather, its focus is on the integration of a series of life exprience with a spectrum of classroom based courses. The impact of this long-range experiential program is complex and shares significant similarities with the laboratories and with field experience courses.[28]

Conclusion

What can we conclude about experiential components of academic courses? The techniques reported here are not radical. They make changes within the educational system as it now exists in institutions of higher education. It is obvious that the programs are more expensive than traditional teaching methods, but nearly all good, innovative methods require an increase in monetary or personal expenditures. These techniques are focused on two elements of learning which appear to be critical for the full development of the mind and the person: an active learner in interaction with his or her environment.

I have found that adding experiences, whether vicarious or direct, can lead to improvements in the learning which occurs in an academic course. Experiential learning tends to make greater use of the whole person than does traditional academic learning. In doing so, it appears to produce more accurate and more persistent learning. The results can feel better and last longer than purely academic learning.

The success of experiential components in academic courses rests on the development first of the intellectual content of the courses. Experiences which are not necessary or important to the development of course concepts may provide increased student motivation, but do not appear to produce better learning.

Learning should be a life-long process. Integrating the growth of the intellect in academic courses with life experiences can occur in college, improving the quality of education in the college years and building the foundtion for an integrated style of learning in later life.

---

[28] G. Christian Jernstedt and Gregory J. McHugo, "The Impact of Combined Experiential (Outward Bound) and Traditional Academic Programs on Personal Development," *Alternative Higher Education*, (under review).

REFERENCES

B.T. Johnson and G. Christian Jernstedt, "The Effects of Long Term Groups on Their Participants," (Hanover, NH: Experiential Learning in College Project, 1975), pp. 1-30.

Gregory J. McHugo, "A Multivariate Analysis of Self-selection and Change Due to College Experience," Dissertation, Dartmouth College, 1979, pp. 1-627.

A Turn Down The Harbor

by Peter G. Beidler

To my astonishment, I was informed on leaving college that I had studied navigation! Why, if I had taken one turn down the harbor I should have known more about it.

Thoreau, "Walden"

"Hey, Pete, we're looking for someone to work up a new kind of course--a sort of 'hands-on' course. We want someone who will get some students involved in doing-- not just studying about--some technological process, while considering it from a humanities point of view. Interested?"

"Sure, Ed." I always say yes to a new course. The best way to learn a new subject is to teach a course in it.

"Good. Can you get me a course proposal by Monday? I'll have to show it to the Steering Committee that afternoon."

That gave me four days to work up a plan for a new course in Lehigh University's Humanities Perspectives on Technology program. I started thinking fast.

I decided to start by sorting out my ideas about technology. I was pretty sure it was foolish to be against technology. After all, it had done wonders for the American way of life. Why, then, did I feel so uneasy about the astronomical increase in our use of technology and its products? Why did I not feel merely proud of America's technological success?

Part of my uneasiness grew from an awareness that all those machines and implements used energy, thus both depleting the earth's supply of fossil fuels and contaminating our air and water. But something else bothered me more: that the individual American had been transformed from a doer into a consumer. When the average American needed something, he said not "I'll fix it," or "I'll make it," but "I'll buy it." Indeed, the American economy very much depended on this almost automatic American response. When people retarded their buying impulses, the American economy went haywire. Surely it was a sad commentary on American life that those few Americans who still embodied the old, original, founding virtues of independence, ingenuity,

---

Dr. Peter Beidler is Lucy G. Moses Distinguished Professor of English at Lehigh University, Bethlehem, Pa. He wishes to express his appreciation to **Dan Meyer**, who solicited and excerpted this article from a 200-page privately-circulated account of the course, to **Teri Bloom**, who took the photographs, and to the 15 students with whose permission he has quoted excerpts from their journals.

and frugality had become a positive drag on the American economy, for that economy had come to rely more on citizens' ability to consume and spend than on their ability to do and save. How could Americans be expected to be self-reliant when the economy responded so recessively to. . .

That was it--self-reliance! Because of technology, things had become so complex that most Americans felt that they could no longer understand them. Capitalizing on people's ignorance, the American economy required that we all be one-thingers, experts in one small area, but reliant on experts in other areas for everything else. We were all trained to do our one little thing on the assembly line of life, and let the next man down the line do the next little thing. In this new course, perhaps I could. . .

I uncovered my typewriter and started typing. On Monday, I gave this proposal to Ed:

Course Title: **Self-Reliance in a Technological Society**

The gothic novel **Frankenstein** *was prophetic of twentieth-century life by showing the dangers involved when man creates a monster-machine he is unwilling to be personally responsible for. Contemporary human existence for most of us in America means moving from one kind of machine to the next one: we wake up to an alarm clock; cook breakfast in an electric frying pan; shave with an electric razor; watch the news on a television set; ride a car to work; lecture through a microphone to students who were assigned to our sections by a computer; figure our final grades on a pocket calculator, by the light of a fluorscent tube. There is no point in denying, however much we might nostalgically want to, that most of these machines are better than what we had before: they do their tasks more quickly or more reliably or more cheaply or more completely. The trouble is, however, that most of us do not understand the machines we rely on at almost every turn, and as a result, we are at the mercy of these machines. If the heating system breaks down we are cold; if the distributor points are corroded we are stranded; if the roof leaks we are damp. We are helpless until we can get in touch (assuming that the telephone still works!) with the appropriate specialist. Almost never have we built the devices we surround ourselves with, and almost never are we able to repair them when they fail us. We have lost the will, and therefore the ability, to do for ourselves the basic construction and maintenance of the paraphernalia of our lives.*

This loss of the ability to do for ourselves is generally not examined in contemporary educational circles. We are taught to respect, and quite rightly, the things humans make and the humans who make them, but we fail to consider what we pay for the services we do not provide for ourselves. Not only do we lose dollars when we hire someone else to repair that toilet or to build that home, but, more important, we lose the self-respect that comes from doing it ourselves. The course I propose would aim at examining some of the costs we pay for our highly developed role specialization in a technological world, and at demonstrating what can be gained by a more self-reliant attitude toward doing for ourselves.

This loss of the ability to do for ourselves is generally not examined in contemporary educational circles.

To be more specific, I have in mind a course which is part practical and part theoretical. For the theoretical part, my students and I will read and discuss a number of books. One of these would surely be Thoreau's "Walden" (1854), a book about one philosopher's experience in building for himself his own house (total cost, $28.12). Another might be Robert M. Pirsig's "Zen and the Art of Motorcycle Maintenance" (1974), a book about a wandering 46-year-old practical philosopher who repairs the machine on which he relies. Still a third book might be John Fire's "Lame Deer: Seeker of Visions" (1972), the spiritual autobiography of a Sioux Indian who sees various aspects of contemporary American life from the point of view of an outsider who refuses to be swallowed into the technological mainstream of American life.

The practical part of the course will probably consist largely of a building or remodeling project. The nature of the subject would depend in part on the size of the class and on the approval of the appropriate officials of the university. The objectives of this project would be (1) to give the students experience in the use of design techniques and tools; (2) to give them experience with building materials; and (3) to give them a practical basis for reflecting on the implications of doing for themselves.

I trust that it is clear that this will be an experimental course. I am not sure how it will work, or even that it will work. One danger is that the two parts of the course, the theoretical and the practical, may remain two separate parts, with the former being merely cerebral (no matter how interesting) and the latter being merely physical (no matter how much fun). I shall try to select readings, to provide activities, and to encourage discussions which will mesh the two parts, but I am not entirely sure what will come of it all. Want to take a chance on it?

The members of the Steering Committee weren't so sure they did want to take a chance on it. After they read my proposal they raised lots of questions. Was this an academic course? Did Lehigh University really want to get into the vocational-technical training the local high schools provided for the "nonacademic" students? How could we call this an English course? How could they scrape up enough students to take such a course? What if somebody cut off a thumb and sued the university? Finally a member of the committee spoke up: "I don't think the course will work, either, but this whole program was set up to encourage new ideas. Let's give Beidler his chance to fail. That's what experimentation is all about." The vote was taken and I was granted my chance to fail.

I thought I had the best chance of avoiding failure if I kept clearly in mind what my goals for the course were. First off, I was not out to train professional carpenters. I was not out to make a profit. And I was not out to convince my students that they should avoid either technology or its products.

No, my goals for this course were somewhat different, somewhat more basic--and more lofty--than those:

1. I wanted to offer a course which would bring the humanities and the sciences back together again. I wanted to show that learning need not be entirely compartmentalized, that there is a connection between thinking and doing, and that literature is connected to philosophy is connected to practicality is connected to self-reliance is connected to humanity. To study one is to study all.

2. I wanted to force my students in this course to question two rather contradictory attitudes that they probably held about physical laborers: first, that "blue-collar" workers, such as carpenters, do work that is somehow less sophisticated than the work which lawyers and doctors

And I was not out to convince my students that they should avoid either technology or its products.

and accountants do; second, that carpentry is so complicated and specialized that only professionals can do it.

3. I wanted my students to feel that rare feeling of pride and accomplishment that comes from doing something they didn't think could be done.

4. I wanted my students to have an organized forum for discussing a more intellectual aspect of self-reliance; the connection between imaginative literature and practical doing.

5. I wanted my students to see that college courses could deal directly with real problems. And I guess I also wanted them to see that professors were real people.

The more I thought about my lofty goals, the more I knew the course project had to be a big one. It would not do for us to remodel a campus storage room into a seminar room. Too easy. No risk. No, my potential failure had to be a potential big failure: a house. Thoreau had built one; why couldn't we build one--or at least remodel one? I vaguely remembered what Thoreau had said about not playing life, nor merely studying, but earnestly living it from beginning to end. Thoreau did not have a university that would give him a room to remodel, pay for his materials and his mistakes, and complete the project if he did not; why should we?

This was supposed to be a course in life, and in life we would have to do what anyone else who wanted inexpensive housing would do: find a ratty old house for sale cheap, then go to a bank and try to get a loan to purchase and remodel it. Why couldn't we do that? I thought some more, and came up with a hatful of real-life problems: What about the down payment? Who would keep the accounts? Where would we find a ratty old house? What about insurance if someone got hurt--would they sue me, or the university? What about the tax forms? And who were "we," anyhow? How could an English class buy a house? I decided I had better get a few answers.

Lehigh's insurance carrier said it would be no problem to attach a $25 rider specifically covering the students in this course.

A Lehigh alumnus who was practicing law in the area said he would be happily to explain to my class how to form a corporation and would help us file the right forms.

A local banker told me he thought the bank would go along with the project--provided it was handled like any other business transaction: "We don't expect to make much money on a deal like this, but we don't want to lose, either. If you can come up with one-third of the cash you'll need, we'll provide you with a short-term loan for the project--provided our inspectors think the house you buy has potential."

"I wouldn't want it any other way," I said.

"Good. Where are you going to get the down money?"

"Well, for the kind of place I'm thinking of, a total of $15,000 would probably do us. I'm prepared to use the money my wife and I were saving for a new car to make up the corporation's one-third. If all goes well, I'll have it back by next summer anyhow, in plenty of time to get the car."

"It is difficult to begin without borrowing, but perhaps it is the most generous course to permit your fellowmen to have an interest in your enterprise."

But the university, fearing that all might not go so well, and reluctant to have me risk my personal funds, insisted on loaning us the $5,000. At first I refused. "In real life we wouldn't have a university to loan us the down money," I insisted.

"In real life you wouldn't have an idealistic English professor risking his new car, either," they insisted. I couldn't fight that kind of logic. Besides, about then I remembered that even Thoreau had built his house on borrowed land and with a borrowed axe: "It is difficult to begin without borrowing, but perhaps it is the most generous course to permit your fellowmen to have a interest in your enterprise." I decided that ours would be a generous course so I accepted the $5,000 loan from the university.

There were other questions I had not asked yet, but it was preregistration time by now, and I had to write up an "official" course description for inclusion in the notice of new courses for the spring semester. This is what I came up with:

English 198. Self-Reliance in a Technological Society (4 credit hrs.)

Theory and practice of self-reliance in today's world. In addition to reading and discussing several pertinent books, the students will become members of a legally registered corporation set up just for this class. As members of the corporation, they will get a bank loan, purchase a run-down south-side house, work on redesigning and remodeling the house, then sell the house and divide the profits (if any). Not for cowards or cleanliness freaks. Both men and women welcome. Limited to 15 students.

The last phrase I added in as an afterthought just as the description was going to press. I did not expect even 15, let alone more than 15 students, but I wanted to protect myself just in case. It was good that I did. As soon as the notice appeared I started getting visits and phone calls. The course was filled by 9:30 on the first morning of preregistration week. By the end of the week, I had a waiting list of 45 names. I was told that it would have been longer, but that word had gotten around that the course had long since been closed, so people stopped coming.

This course had to begin early, well before the start of the semester, so I called my 15 students--eight men and seven women--together for a meeting with our lawyer. As we sat, in considerable awe, around the huge oak table in his library, the lawyer explained the forms that had to be filled out and filed in Harrisburg, and he explained the filing fees that were required.

Steve, a member of the class, took a break and posed for a photograph. The rubble surrounding him is debris from the old roof and inside.

To fill in the names of the corporation officers, we had to have some on-the-spot elections. I would have to be president of Self-Reliance, Inc., because I would have to be able to conduct the business of the corporation during vacation and breaks when the students were away from campus. Through a process of acclamation, finger-pointing, and modest assent, a pre-law student was named vice president and an accounting major became treasurer. The rest of the students were named to the board of directors. We left an hour later, grinning at each other, and feeling pretty powerful. None of us had ever been members of a corporation before.

Two weeks later the following notice appeared in the local newspaper and the county law journal, making us official:

> CORPORATION NOTICE
> NOTICE is hereby given that Articles of Incorporation have been filed with the Department of State of the Commonwealth of Pennsylvania at Harrisburg for the purpose of obtaining a Certificate of Incorporation of a proposed business corporation to be organized under the Business Corporation Law of the Commonwealth of Pennsylvania, Act of May 5, 1933, (P.L. 364) 15 P.S. Section 1204). The name of the proposed corporation is SELF-RELIANCE, INC.
> The purpose for which it is to be organized is for the corporation to have the power to buy or otherwise acquire hold, improve, develop, mortgage or otherwise encumber, deal in, sell, convey, exchange and lease real estate and personal property of every class and description.

We just wanted to buy and renovate a ratty old house, not "real estate and personal property of every class and description," but the lawyer said we had to use one of the standard categories. Oh, well.

The next major job was to find a ratty old house. I had already begun, and had had several disappointing false starts: price too high, house too far from campus, not available by mid-January, tenants who did not want to leave, fear that we would resell the property to "undesirables," distrust of students. When the real estate agents I talked with told me they didn't have anything else in my price range, I decided to start hoofing it in the little streets within five blocks of the campus. I knew what I wanted, and I knew when I saw it on one of my late-fall rambles.

It had no for-sale sign, no mail box, no house number. Clearly no one had lived there for years, for the "hedge" was a wild jungle, and honeysuckle vines all but obliterated the little porch on the south side. The ancient roof sagged under the weight of decaying slates, and it obviously leaked where some of the slates were missing. A couple of the windows were broken, suggesting that the house had been vandalized a time or two. The "yard" was overgrown with weeds and brush. The house was tiny, ungainly, and covered on three sides by shreading "insul-brick"--a fake fiber siding product in vogue 30 years earlier.

In short, the little bungalow on Vernon Street was perfect. I asked around, but the neighbors couldn't remember the name of the lady who lived there a couple of summers a decade ago. I went over to city hall and found the place on a big city map. Yes, the taxes had been paid. Yes, they were allowed to release the name and address of the owner.

I wrote her a brief note, telling who I was and asking if she might want to sell the little house on Vernon Street. I gave her my phone number and waited. Nervously.

Two days later she called. Yes, she would sell the place. She hated to, for it was a lovely little place and she had always hoped to fix it up. Real charm. Beautiful location there on the hill--fine view out over the city. Walking distance of Lehigh University. Nice yard.

"How much do you want for it?" The way she way talking I was afraid she thought she was selling a priceless house on a prime lot in Key West.

"I hate to sell it at all. I always wanted to fix it up. But my husband got sick. Then I did. And now I know I never will. I really love the place. If I hadn't gotten sick. . ." Here it came. Now she was playing on my sympathies. I wouldn't cheat a sick lady, would I? ". . .so I'll have to have what I paid for it, plus the repairs and taxes I've paid.

The bank inspectors weren't so sure the little bungalow would do just fine for anything but bulldozer food, but they admitted the price was right.

The one neighbor there wants it, but he just wants to tear it down to make a dog run for his German shepherd. I didn't want him to get it."

"I don't blame you. I think the house can be saved. How much do you have invested?"

"$3,800. That's the price."

I wanted to say, "We'll take it." Instead I said, "I'd like to see the inside. Do you have a key?" At that price we could scarcely go wrong, but I couldn't talk the bank into the mortgage if I hadn't even seen the inside.

The inside was as sorry-looking as the outside: no kitchen, a defunct toilet, a sagging, rickety stairway into a tiny head-bumper loft, a dirt-floored, no-head-room basement. . .yes, it would do just fine for Self-Reliance, Inc.

The bank inspectors weren't so sure the little bungalow would do just fine for anything but bulldozer food, but they admitted the price was right. The decided to take a chance on an idealistic English professor and 15 college kids who thought they could do, with little more than enthusiasm and guts, a remodeling project most professional contractors would not touch. A week after the bank inspectors came through the house, I got the bank's "letter of commitment":

> We have approved the loan of $10,000 to you for a period of one year to be secured by a first mortgage against the premises described above. The proceeds of the loan will be deposited into an escrow account at the bank. As construction progresses in accordance with amounts agreed upon between you and the bank, and after an on-site inspection of the work covered by said payout has been made by the bank, construction draws for renovations will be made.

I was feeling pretty good about things. The course had been approved, the money was available, 15 eager students were waiting to get started, and the little bungalow on Vernon Street was waiting for whatever hammers and enthusiasm we would bring to it.

Thus, puffed up with pride, I tried not to act surprised to discover on returning home one night, that **Time** magazine had called. "You're supposed to call back," my wife Anne told me. "It's about that self-reliance stuff." Stuff! Anne had to live with me, and had a good sense of when to start deflating my ego.

I knew how **Time** had heard about the course. Lehigh's Office of Public Information had somehow got wind of this "innovative" course I was organizing and had written up a short news release and sent it to around 400 local and national newspapers and magazines. I had already had a few phone calls from local dailies wanting to know a few more details. But **Time**! Goodness.

I called the number and asked for the name. The name, it turned out, belonged to an ex-philosophy teacher who had seen the Lehigh release and wanted to know if I had read a couple of recent books which showed that self-reliance was a dangerous and limiting trend in American history. I had to tell him that I had not. No? Well, had there been much controversy on campus about the course. You know, major committees or professors or administrators opposing such a course in the curriculum of a major university? I told him that there had been some scattered opposition, and that a lot of people had asked a lot of good questions, but no serious opposition seemed to have surfaced, at least none that I had heard about. Really? Well, he guessed that was it, then.

I hung up feeling the way my freshmen must feel after they get an "F" on that first theme. This fellow at big-deal **Time** had called to show off his knowledge and to sniff out some newsworthy campus controversy over my dumb little course. What could be less newsworthy than a non-controversial course taught by an uninformed professor? I had blown it.

Two weeks later Anne told me that there was a little piece about the self-reliance stuff in **Time**. I tore into the magazine and in the American Notes section found the following:

The Fourth R
"How could youths better learn to live than by at once trying the experiment of living?" asked Henry David Thoreau in "Walden," that celebrated text on the discovery of inner resources. That will be one of the many texts–along with "Moby Dick" and "Zen and the Art of Motorcycle Maintenance"–in a new English lit. course offered next month by Lehigh University of Bethlehem, Pa. The course: Self-Reliance in a Technological Society.

For lab work, students will form a small company, buy a run-down house, spend three hours a week fixing it up, and then try to sell it. The university aims to teach that "there is still worth in the old notions of independence, pride in workmanship and craftsmanship." Perhaps self-reliance is a trait that cannot be taught as a sort of fourth R, but a university determined to give students the broadest outlook could hardly try to teach anything more important.

That last sentence kept rolling off my mental tongue: "a university determined to give students the broadest outlook could hardly try to teach anything more important." No bad, either, referring to reliance on oneself as being as important as reading, writing and arithmetic. Yes sir. I was pretty terrific.

Anne brought me back almost to earth again by telling me that she was going to write an expose about her big-deal husband. The headline of her story, she said, was going to be, "Self-Reliance Professor Doesn't Wash His Own Socks." It was a headline I tried to keep in mind in the weeks ahead when program managers at both ABC-TV and CBS-TV called me. They had read about the course in **Time** and wanted to bring in some crews to interview some of the students and take some footage of them working on the house. Did I mind? I told them I'd take it up with the students.

By now it was late January, and the students were about to return for the start of the new semester. I called them together and we discussed whether we should let the TV crews come in. The students, generally, felt that as long as it did not interfere with our primary mission, we should permit television coverage. If we really did have something so original and exciting going on, why should we try to keep it to ourselves? If living a subject, not just studying it or testing in a mock or theoretical situation, was such an interesting idea, why not let the world in to see our experiment in self-reliance succeed--or fail?

There is just no way this "house" can be fixed up in a semester.

So the TV crews came down from New York City to run their cameras as we tore the roof off the old house--in a snowstorm, no less--and as we. . .

But I can't tell that whole story, here, of how we designed the new structure, how we got the materials, how we decided on color and texture schemes, how we worked in three three-hour "lab" sessions a week on the little house on Vernon Street. What is most important can perhaps best be told by the students themselves, in the form of excerpts from the journals they kept that spring as the course developed and as the house--and they--grew.

First class today. Prof. Beidler showed us slides of the house. Won't see the real thing until my lab tomorrow morning, but, my God, I can't believe it. The junk, the old sink, the crud, the sagging roof. There is just no way this "house" can be fixed up in a semester.
                                                            Peter, January 21

We cleaned up and departed. I was bone tired yet euphoric. I stalked proudly back to campus. The butterflies and excitement

122

were gone. My back and brow turned cold with sweat and dust, and dirt caked my lips and throat. My skin was chapped and reddish brown, like sunburn. My gait was long and forceful. My gaze and expression reflected my inward satisfaction. I think it's gonna work!

Simon, January 22

It rained today on our roofless house. A hard, steady rain. I felt awfully helpless about the house getting soaked.

Jeff, January 26

Lab today was just OK. I always enjoy being with the other kids and never fail to learn something new. Yet, I guess I'm bothered by the fact that I'm extremely slow to understand what is going on or what I'm supposed to do. I think I worry too much about messing something up. I liked removing the floor because not much can go wrong there.

Nat, February 4

Frani and George, members of the class, work together on wood to be used as a beam. (Notice that the stairs location has changed.)

I'm not much of a writer. I find it hard to sit down and pen the thoughts that fly by. Suffice to say that I think we're on the right track. My gut feeling is one of cautiousness, yet positive on all sides, but like Henry David says: Gotta do it, not think it.

Brad, February 8

I got sort of frustrated that I couldn't hammer any nails. It looked so easy when someone else was doing it. I feel rather stupid and slow doing everything, but I've got to remember that this is the first time I've done most of this stuff.

Nat, February 11

I couldn't sit down because I hurt. I loved this feeling because I felt like I had stretched and used my muscles and I knew why and I would be able to see my work in a finished product someday. I knew I was part of a growing, live thing.

Frani, February 13

I feel as though the house is pulling me by the bootstraps to some kind of rude awakening about "me" and "my life" at this point.

Jeanne, February 14

I am frightened to death of the circular saw. I feel it is too damned dangerous and I am really nervous when anyone uses it. Is this merely a coming to grips with technology, or what? I would prefer a good old-fashioned sharp hand saw. I'm afraid someone is going to get hurt. I don't want to think about having to get someone to St. Luke's Hospital in a hurry.

Simon, February 19

My parents came to school for a visit. I took them over to the house. We all climbed in the upper floor. "Hold on to the studs I put in, Mom. See the shelves I built." They were so impressed. I could see that they really felt I knew what I was talking about. They didn't expect it.

Frani, February 22

Last semester I would never have understood what the hell he was talking about.

When he told me what I would be doing, Pete spoke to me as he would Simon or John: "I want those 2 x 3 studs and a 2 x 4 plate with an angle cut here." I know that I am learning something despite my disappointment at not knowing much and being given minor chores. Last semester I would never have understood what the hell he was talking about.

Peter, February 26

Today was probably my worst day at work so far. Nothing seemed to go right. I couldn't understand Pete's directions well enough. I was unsure of how to cut the floorboard. Karen and I definitely screwed up the last square of foyer floor. I get embarrassed each time I look at it. I wish we had done it over. Working on insulation with Teri wasn't bad, but the glass fibers kept getting down my throat. Today I also smashed my thumb and crushed my fingernail and hammered myself in the knee. Good job, Frani.

Frani, March 4

The physical and the practical took up most space in most of the journals in the early weeks of the course. As the semester wore on, however, the students began writing about more intellectual and personal aspects—especially the books they were reading and the discussions of them which we were having in class.

In class this morning we talked over "Walden Two." I don't like Skinner's style. He seems to overanalyze every comment. Of the two Waldens, I find Thoreau's infinitely superior.

Jeff, February 18

In class we discussed "Walden Two." I felt it was a very good book but others felt just the opposite. Maybe I enjoyed it more than "Walden" because I don't like to be alone. I like cooperation and that is what "Walden Two" is centered around.

Karen, February 18

I have finally gotten into "Zen and the Art of Motorcycle Maintenance" and it frightens me a little because I feel like I've

been converted to all Robert Pirsig's beliefs. The book seems to be extremely controversial, especially in class.
Frani, March 16

A very important idea came out in discussion on "Zen and the Art of Motorcycle Maintenance"--the idea that a perfect picture will flow from you if you are perfect inside.
Jeanne, March 17

I got upset during our discussion of "Brave New World." I said that I didn't believe that anyone could be anything they wanted to be. Brad replied that he really felt sorry for me if that's what I believed. Brad really shouldn't feel sorry for me because I don't feel sorry for myself.
Nat, March 24

"One Flew Over the Cuckoo's Nest" has to be my favorite book. There is so much to it. I'm seeing in all the books we read lately a trend: the authors question sanity and insanity in the individual and society. I'm finding this question really intriguing.
Frani, March 25

About 20 minutes into the discussion of "Cuckoo's Nest" I realized I had read the book completely wrong! I was so interested in the way Kesey developed McMurphy that I really neglected the Chief and Big Nurse--two more important characters in the book's theme.
Peter, March 31

Insane asylum, fog machines,
Barbituates, amphetamines,
Indian plights,
Niggers and whites,
Sodomy,
Lobotomy,
It's all the truth even if it never happened.
Paul, March 30

It is so difficult for me to sit and write here. The emotions I feel are so strong. Why should women be denied the right to be self-reliant? I cannot be an individual and a woman according to societal definition. I am prepared to be alone. I always have been. It is my strength and source of self-reliance. But I truly care about things, people, feelings. I say excuse me to walls. I think of the girls in the course, and their own guilt feelings about lack of contribution to the house physically, and it absolutely tears me with frustration. It is through no fault of our own that we were stuffed away from physical reality, but as a result our ability to deal with reality is so limited. If we had been trained to deal with reality, how could or would any self-respecting woman accept a boring role as housekeeper, homemaker, child raiser? I must come together enough to handle being a woman. My feminity must add to my Self, not be denied by it. I want to be Jeanne first, then a woman.
Jeanne, March 17

I'm becoming a pessimist. It seems like we will never finish. There were nine hours put into plastering the joints in the sheetrock! I think that we will need to put in quite a few Saturdays. I just hope we can get it finished.
Wendy, April 17

Pete drove me over to see the former owner of the house. I asked her lots of questions about the history of the house and what she had done with it. Pete asked her if she would care to see the house. She quickly accepted the invitation. She was quite impressed with the work we had done and I, taking notes all along, recorded some of her comments: "Oh, I love it. . . Look at that view!. . .It's beautiful. Fantastic. . .Terrific!. . . Wonderful!"
Jeff, April 9

Cedar shakes are nice to work with. If you are careful they won't split. They look great, smell better. It was more demanding than I expected. It requires skill and thought to put them up so they look good. My respect for the "blue-collar" worker is growing--at least for the ones who give a damn about their jobs.
George, April 21

I did some varnishing above the steps. That was one thing that made me feel confident that I had changed during the semester. In the beginning I would never have gotten up on the ladder over the steps. It was probably because nobody would have expected me to or asked me to. I would be willing now to try many things that previously I would not have.
Wendy, April 24

In the beginning I was clearly the boss. The students would come to me--usually pretty meekly--in the "lab" sessions at the house and ask what to do and how to do it. As they grew more confident they needed me less. But as they needed me less, I found it increasingly difficult to control the class and the decisions we made. I know it should not have bothered me, for one of the goals of the course was to wean them from me. Still. . .there was the argument, for example, about whether to rent a floor sander and try to sand the floors ourselves or to hire a professional to do the job for us. I thought it best to hire someone. We had hired a few professionals for other parts

John, a member of the class, merrily nails a shingle into the house. The class decided to do the siding itself, instead of hiring a professional.

of the job--a plumber and an electrician, for example, because the city codes required licensing for that kind of work. Besides, it was getting late in the semester. We had plenty of other work to do without the sanding, and I wanted to get the house done by the end of the semester so we could sell it. Not everyone agreed.

> A hassle developed over sanding the floor. George, John, Paul and I make ourselves pains in the asses by saying that we would like to have a shot at doing the floor. We got shot down by the realist faction. I got pissed and made a snide comment about the tremendous self-reliance in the class, and a few of us got a little upset.
>
> Simon, April 21

> I name this "Black Wednesday." I'm bummed out that I am being forced to compromise my idealistic notions of achieving a stoic sense of self-reliance in this course for something as unimportant as a time factor. I say damn the time limit! If the class is unable to get the job done this semester, then I say lock the doors for the summer, give everyone an incomplete, and finish it up in the fall. It might not "look good" to the outside world, but at least we would be standing firmly beside our slogan of self-reliance, and we'd get it done ourselves. It is wrong to compromise ideals under pressure of external influences. Thoreau would back me on this.
>
> Paul, April 21

> We had our "first real fight" as Pete put it. Four boys in the class wanted to sand the floor themselves. The class voted to let a professional do it. I voted for the professional because I was afraid we would wreck the floor. I didn't want to chance it. Besides, it would have been a hell of a lot of work. The guys accused us of not being self-reliant--the most cutting of all cuts. It doesn't matter what I know in my head; he made me feel guilty anyway.
>
> Frani, April 21

I won that one, but not the next: whether to put in a brick patio or a gravel one. I wanted to get a big truckload of smooth river-stones, dump them in there, rake them level and call it a day. Some of the students thought that would look stupid and volunteered to work an extra Saturday to put in a brick patio. We voted.

> We talked about putting brick in front of the house. We all voted in favor of it despite Pete's objections. I think it will really clean things up in front of the house.
>
> Wendy, April 28

> Put in a brick patio out in front of Boardnail Villa today with some very nice help, thank you, from George and John. Got a lot done. The place is looking good. Might be a bummer to have to sell the place, but so it goes. No sense in letting sentimentality creep in at this point. But hell, if I ain't startin' to love the place and the people.
>
> Paul, May 1

It was, as Paul put it, a "bummer" to sell the house, but we had to sell it. We brought in an appraiser to give us an idea of how much to ask, then advertised an open house to let people come in and see our semester's work. It was like putting a baby on the auction block.

> The appraiser came to talk to us about how much we could get for the house. He said our little house was charming and sweet but it was only worth $14,500. It was hard to take because it seemed so low. Everyone in class tried to make him see the huge value of the educational factor, the uniqueness, the fine workmanship. He said yes, but the neighborhood, the ground. Doreen made a valid point in saying that we didn't take the course to make money. But after thinking about it I decided the real problem for everybody was putting a price on something they loved. It's hard for me to say that something I love and cherish can only be worth a measley $14,500. It's worth $100,000,000.
>
> Frani, April 21

> Today we had open house. It was usually possible to tell who the administrators from Lehigh were. They were the ones that asked questions about the strain the course was to us, what we learned from it, whether we thought it should become a part of the regular curriculum, etc. Some visitors thought the price was too high. Two engineers tried to figure out the price per square foot--nice way to judge the quality of our house!
>
> Wendy, May 9

At open house, we had a taker. He had to talk to a bank, of course, but he was a lawyer and he thought he could talk a bank into financing our asking price of $16,500. After the open house we had an end-of-course picnic. We enjoyed the hamburgers and the beer, but the finest moment came when the men, who had been treating the women as fellow men all semester long, working beside them in the dirt and mess, presented each of the women with a little bouquet of flowers.

> I had such a great time at the picnic. I never sat back to think that I really got to know those people pretty well--better than in any other class. Didn't want to leave at all. When the guys gave us the flowers I was never so shocked and so touched in my whole life. NEVER! I loved that moment.
>
> Karen, May 9

> Brad made a terse, heartfelt speech commending the durable spirit in our representatives of the fairer (but not weaker) sex. I think the others shared my massive emotion--a happy dejection or a sad jubilation.
>
> Jeff, May 9

That about said it, Jeff. Happy dejection and sad jubilation: happy because we had finished the house, because no one had gotten seriously hurt, because we had sold our pride and joy and even made a $3,000 profit on it; sad because it was over and because all 15 of us would probably never get together again, certainly never at our house. The end of the semester was upon us. We all looked forward to other courses and other friends, but would there ever be friends like these, or a course like this? The end of the semester was a time for summing up, looking back, for reflecting. At the picnic I asked the students to make whatever final entry they wanted to in their journal and hand them in in a day or two.

> What else can I say? For once in my life I've loved a course. No one forced me to do anything and I couldn't have done more.
>
> Doreen

Sometimes I forget that English 198 is even a course. If someone asks me what English it is, I never get the number right so I have to go into some long description of the course. Other courses I just know by their numbers and that's all they are for me—a number, nothing more.
                                                                    Nat

I'm not one for looking back too much, but this has been my most significant Lehigh experience: no regrets, no bad vibes, good job. But I question its overall value in the arena of life. We still had Lehigh to fall back on. I'm anxious to try it without having anybody to fall back on.
                                                                    Brad

I am no longer afraid to be soft and open. That will be my stronger self, for it is my inner self that I have been hiding. There is no shame in showing that you need to be needed. My new self-reliance is based on the fact that no one is self-reliant, and I am not afraid to admit it.
                                                                    Jeanne

---
If there's one thing I have learned this semester, it is that if something you want to happen is going to happen, you've got to make it happen.

If there's one thing I have learned this semester, it is that if something you want to happen is going to happen, you've got to make it happen.
                                                                    John

I'll never forget that first day. When I look back in my journal to my comments on that day, all I say is that it was cold, dirty and hard. What I was afraid to say then (I'm not afraid to say it now) was that I hated that day. I felt miserable. I was scared to admit it but it was horrible. The slate dust in my eyes was just too much to bear. And now I just sit here and laugh at myself.
                                                                    Karen

I would not only have the courage to take on a house-building project now if I had to, but I would also have enough faith in myself to attempt other, unrelated, tasks like fixing a car, flying a plane.
                                                                    Jeff

The class sort of adopted the term "Go for it!" while working around the house this semester. It's a term used by misty-minded surfers when they are talking about riding a big wave in. "Go for it. Take it to the limit." I guess we went for it this semester, and I think we got it.
                                                                    Paul

Thoreau opened "Walden" with the brash statement that he was going to "brag as lustily as chanticleer in the morning, standing on his roost, if only to wake my neighbors up." I, too, have done my share of bragging in this account. I may be forgiven, however, for quoting two more sentences from the journals my fellow students turned in, for they seem to require answers. First: "I hope we touched Pete like he touched us." You did, Simon, you did. Can't you see that you've proved Thoreau right when he said, "Age is no better, hardly so well, qualified for an instructor as youth, for it has not profited so much as it has lost." Second: "I wonder if my parents realize how great an effect Pete has had on me; he was the only adult who helped me grow and then accepted me as an equal." Thanks, Frani. I treasure those words. But you know that good people, like good ideas, don't wait for acceptance; they command it. From the beginning you were anyone's equal.

The house as a finished product, and as it was opened up for prospective buyers.

I guess that's about it. People keep asking when I'm going to teach that course again. Surely so successful a course will be repeated? No. It's against my principles to repeat any more than I have to. Learning to do one thing well and therefore continuing to do it well over and over is the basic premise of the assembly line system of American industry. Why should I turn that same bolt over and over again? Doing something well is the best reason for not doing it again; that way you can spend time doing things you have not yet done or done well. When Thoreau was asked why he left the woods after his successful two-year experiment, his answer became eternal: "I left the woods for as good a reason as I went there. Perhaps it seemed to me that I had several more lives to live, and could not spare any more time for that one. It is remarkable how easily and insensibly we fall into a particular route, and make a beaten track for ourselves."

Life is for beating tracks, not for following them. It is for turning down the harbor, not returning down it.

But I have this other idea about teaching novel-writing. Fifteen students and I would get together and spend a semester writing a novel. We would. . .but that will be another story.

Do Your Homework:
A Guide For Starting An Experiential Program In A School

By Peggy Walker Stevens

A college graduate at his first job, a woman in a traditionally male-dominated field, or an architect watching the building of his radically new design all feel the pressure of doing something new. Everyone is watching. Small mistakes will be noted; large ones will confirm traditionalists' belief that they should have stayed with the proven person, idea, or way of operating.

As an educator who has introduced eight alternative programs into public high schools, I feel the constant tension as well as the rewards of being labeled an innovator. My mistakes have sometimes been conspicuous, but through them I have learned that an experiential program must be better planned and more comprehensive than the regular school curriculum in order to gain acceptance. Anything that bucks a school's normal way of operating will probably be resisted unless problems are anticipated and minimized. This fact is true especially when starting a program that extends more than one class period, crosses over subject boudaries, involves more than one teacher, or engages students in concrete experiences.

Despite the extra work involved, there is a great need for programs which do exactly these things. It takes time for students to explore, to problem-solve, to understand the inter-relationships among things, to learn to become a constructive member in a group task. In a typical secondary school, students are lectured at and questioned by a random series of adults who specialize in certain subject areas. In a well-planned experiential program, academic knowledge in a variety of disciplines can be integrated with skills and experiences. This unified approach adds a rich dimension to the learning of all students. But such an approach should not be assembled haphazardly. Do your homework first.

1. Assess School and Student Needs

A look at the student needs that are not being met by present school programs will provide a good starting point for an experiential program. It is easier to get others to support your proposal if it is designed to help a group of students who obviously need additional motivation or an alternative approach. It isn't difficult to document your hunches about who this group might be with statistics usually available from secretaries, the guidance office, or the administration.

In one school where I taught, absenteeism, discipline problems, and failing grades all increased for the freshmen class by the end of the year. Few freshmen were involved in extra-curricular activities. For many students, this pattern continued throughout high school. I was able to document this problem and propose an experiential program that involved freshmen in a variety of activities, inside and outside of the classroom.

The needs were different in another school. Here, it seemed to me that the most uninvolved and troublesome students were enrolled in the school's "Level II" classes, designed for the "non-college-bound" student They called themselves "the rats" and could usually be identified by their dislike of school, their faded denim clothes, and their proximity to the school's smoking area. Using the school's computerized grade records, I found that "Level II" students had substantially higher failure rates than "Level III" students in many required courses. One percent of the students enrolled in Level III biology failed the course whereas fifteen percent of the students enrolled in Level II biology failed the course. By documenting examples such as these, along with comparative rates of absenteeism and suspensions, I convinced the administration that an alternative was worth trying.

The students whose needs you identify and document do not have to be those with many problems in school. You may demonstrate the needs of gifted students who need leadership training or of the senior class who generally get low grades during their last semester and who could benefit from concrete experiences in the community before graduation. If you want to avoid having your program labeled as one strictly for "troublemakers," you can combine students

---

Peggy Walker Stevens is coordinator of alternative programs at Merrimack High School, Merrimack, New Hampshire.

who cause a variety of problems in school with others who are more motivated and can serve as role models. Experiential programs often work well with students who are unsuccessful or difficult to handle in traditional school programs, but it would be unfortunate if those became the only students who are given opportunities to learn through experience.

2. Set Goals and Devise a Plan to Meet Them

Once you have chosen the student population for whom you will design your program, decide upon the major goals that you would like the programs to meet. These goals can relate to an improvement in student attitude and behavior or to growth in academic skills or knowledge. It is best to limit your goals to three or four and to state them so that you can measure what you have accomplished at the end of the year. "The absentee, suspension, and failure rates of the students will decline when compared to their previous year's records (or compared to a control group)" is better than "Students will do better in school." Combine data from school records with attitude surveys, student and parent comments, pre and post writing samples, and other, more subjective evaluations. Emphasize that you are willing to be held accountable for the results of your program. Evaluation can be an important selling point to the administration who will have a clearer picture of what was accomplished in your experiential program than is the case in a traditional history or science or physical education class.

If your program does not improve students' ability to read, write, solve problems, and think critically, it probably won't last long and doesn't deserve to.

Curriculum planning will be necessary if you are to meet your goals. It is not necessary to have the entire curriculum planned before your proposal is approved, but you should have an outline of the topics which will be taught and sample activities which indicate the nature of the experiences which you will incorporate into the program and the ways in which different disciplines will be related to one another. Perhaps you and another teacher already have a great idea for your classes or for an experiential program you'd like to start. If not, find teachers who experiment with new approaches and brainstorm what you could do together. Anything can fit into an interdisciplinary approach. Teachers have combined subjects as diverse as French and peace studies. In your school's curriculum guide, you can find courses or units that fit logically together. In one school, freshmen earth science teachers taught topographical mapreading and so did the freshmen geography teachers. They were able to combine the two and teach the skills outdoors in an orienteering unit. In another school, a look through the course selection guide revealed separate courses in New Hampshire geology, New Hampshire history, and New Hampshire literature.

Department heads and others will have legitimate concerns over the academic aspects of your program. While it is often true that students will not learn if they are bored, hostile, on drugs etc., changing attitudes and behavior is not enough. If your program does not improve students' ability to read, write, solve problems, and think critically, it probably won't last long and doesn't deserve to. This is true especially if your program is to be an alternative way of earning credit for required courses such as English rather than for physical education or general credit towards graduation. Bob Gillette of Fairfield, Connecticut has had a successful experiential program in a public high school for twelve years. His students represent a cross section of that school's population. They spend three periods each day in the program for both their freshmen and sophomore years. At the end of that time, his students are expected to do at least as well as their classmates in the traditional program on standardized achievement tests. Bob Gillette feels that not only do these standardized scores help to validate his program in the eyes of the school and community, but also that if he is going to involve students in a long-range program they must make academic progress.

3. Plan for the Necessary Resources

Another planning step is to determine what resources the program will need. You must first be realistic about your commitment of time and energy. Don't design a program where you promise to take students on one weekend trip each month, only to find that your family is resentful and you are exhausted. Taking twenty students backpacking, for example, requires hours of preparation. It is never relaxing because you are always alert and working to make the trip a

Programs that take an unreasonable amount of time from a teacher's personal life often don't last more than a year or two.

safe, enjoyable, and effective learning experience. Experiential programs take more time than more traditional classes in a number of other ways. Adapting a course so that it includes more "hands-on" activities takes time, and developing a whole new curriculum for a course that has never existed before takes even more time. Keeping track of equipment, recruiting for the program, talking and writing about the program to maintain good public relations, and supervising student money-raising activities are just some of the things that take after school and weekend time. Some teachers are reimbursed for this extra time by teaching half days or by being paid the equivalent of a coach's salary for after school activities done with students. How much you are willing to do with and without compensation is an issue that should be addressed in your original proposal. Programs that take an unreasonable amount of time from a teacher's personal life often don't last more than a year or two. It is up to you to assess your limits from the beginning.

It is also important to be realistic about the amount of money which will be necessary to carry out the program. Outside funding (grants, etc.) are helpful for getting a program started and for the initial investment in equipment. However, beware of making your program dependent for its operating expenses on funds outside of the school or district. The funds often dry up, as many programs are finding in this budget-cutting era. Think about what you can study which is close by. In one school, the original curriculum called for a study of a mountain area about 40 miles from the school. Just before the start of the new school year, the school board cut the field trip budget to zero. Even if they had been able to keep the original funding, they had severely underestimated the cost of transporting students on afternoon and weekend trips. When the teachers were forced to revise the original curriculum, they took advantage of a river environment within walking distance of the school.

Find out ahead of time the price of the books, backpacking equipment, printing costs, ropes course hardware, or whatever you will need. One hidden cost which teachers often overlook but of which administrators are very aware is teacher time. If a teacher earns $15,000 and normally teaches 5 classes, the cost to the school district is $3,000 per class. If two teachers ask to team teach the same group of students during a period, the cost of that class becomes $6,000. Their team teaching may also burden other teachers with a larger class load and may cause scheduling problems.

You must consider not only how much money you will need, but also from whose budget it will come. Find out how your school budget works if you have not had experience with it before. Are field trips, books, equipment, and supplies all separate parts of the budget? Would it be better for your program to have its own budget or for it to be part of another department's budget? The budget for a program at one school came from the physical education, English, social studies, and science departments. This approach had the advantage of keeping a lot of people involved in the ongoing process of the program, but it had a distinct disadvantage: sometimes the money for the experiential program was lost in favor of earth science textbooks or a new goal post. On the other hand, a well-established program in Massachusetts with a yearly budget of its own of over $50,000 was recently eliminated completely from the budget by the school board which found it an "extra" that the town could no longer afford. Consider the alternatives carefully before making your program a highly visible and very vulnerable budget item.

4. Sell the Program

Not only will it be necessary to plan appropriately, but you must also sell your program effectively. Decide who will have to approve your program and figure out what the concerns of each decision-maker are. Is the superintendent worried because too many freshmen are opting to go to private school instead of public school? Is the principal concerned about the number of suspensions? You can design your proposal to meet some of the legitimate concerns of influential people in the school and this increases the probability of them approving your program. It is also crucial for you to discern the actual decision-making hierarchy. Who makes decisions is often different in reality than it is on paper.

Don't be deterred by your own or the administration's initial reaction that your interdisciplinary teaching idea will be too difficult to schedule. You can work out numerous arrangements if you plan far enough in advance. One possibility is to teach two related subjects yourself so that you can have the students for more than one period. A course which teaches the scientific and social aspects of environmental problems is a good example of this arrangement. If two teachers want to work together, plan to team teach during the same period, occasionally or all the time, or plan the course together but teach the same students during different periods. Schedule your class at the end of the school

---

A reservation expressed to you in a discussion over lunch is better than one stated vehemently at a faculty meeting.

---

day and require students to stay after school one day each week, giving them extra credit for their additional time. The key is to be both flexible and persistent when convincing the administration to adopt your proposal.

An alternative way of designing a program that you would like to teach is to develop it slowly, over a number of years, from activities you do with a particular class. One of the more famous examples of this is Eliot Wigginton's assignment to his English class to interview some of the older people in the community. The assignment evolved into the **Foxfire** magazines and books. Other teachers have involved their classes in career internships, investigations in cities, and environmental clean-up projects and have seen the initial idea grow into a permanent part of the school's offerings. A program which emerges slowly has the advantage of "proving" itself as it goes along. It may, therefore, be less controversial than an entirely new program. However, it sometimes takes a great deal of negotiating to make changes once a program is established. Institutions often take even a new idea and quickly become rigid about the way it operates and fits into the budget and schedule. There are times when a bold proposal is approved more quickly and without compromising your vision of what the program could be. Whether to start slowly or boldly is something that each person must decide by assessing the school climate.

Anticipate opposition because you will be sure to get it. Try to figure out who will oppose your idea. Will it be the central administration, a school board member, principals, department heads, certain teachers? Find ways to involve these people in the planning or at least to discuss your ideas with them. You will probably feel like avoiding your opposition, but don't give in to this natural tendency. Find out what their concerns are. A reservation expressed to you in a discussion over lunch is better than one stated vehemently at a faculty meeting. In discussion, you can clarify misunderstandings and consider making some changes if the person's concern is valid. If a skeptic comes to respect you and sees how well planned the program is, he may be willing to let you give the idea a try. One of the advantages of planning a program which involves team teaching is that the enthusiasm of several respected teachers will carry more weight than that of a single teacher when a program is being considered.

By listening to your opposition, you will also have a more valuable critique of potential problems than you can get from more enthusiastic colleagues. If both the vice principal and the guidance counselor are worried about scheduling problems, maybe you need to revamp that part of your proposal. If that old-fashioned department head is concerned about basic skills, perhaps your program needs to be more specific about the ways in which students will be able to use and improve these skills.

Some teachers are uncomfortable with the idea of selling their program proposal. They see the process as "playing politics," something which they are reluctant to do. However, it is senseless to spend hours assessing student needs, deciding upon goals and curriculum, and finding the necessary resources if you don't spend an equal amount of time convincing others of the merit of your idea. An experiential program can be designed so that it fits almost any circumstances. Step-by-step planning at least a year in advance is the key to gaining approval for any experiential program.

EXPERIENCING HISTORY
Article by DR. ADOLF CREW, DR. JAMES BROWN, JOYCE LACKIE

An innovative graduate course in education devoted to the development of techniques utilizing direct experience in the history curriculum.

Introduction

In 1976 a private Washington-based organization took tentative steps toward creating an Experiential Learning Center for the State of Alabama. Some thirty interested Alabamians from a diverse geographical and institutional range were brought into contact, many for the first time, to listen to and talk with the creators of exciting educational programs including cultural journalism, traditional crafts-apprenticing, and adventure-based programs.

While planning and funding were still in the early stages, the group assayed a pilot program based primarily on local resources. The pilot was an inter-university, interdisciplinary course entitled "A Workshop in Experiential Education" and is the subject of this article. The course was offered for six hours graduate or undergraduate credit (three in Education from the University of Alabama, and three in History or Folklore from Samford University in Birmingham) and comprised six weekends over a six-month span during the summer and fall of 1977. Primary locale for the course was Tannehill Historical State Park, site of two impressive furnace structures of Civil War vintage and proposed site of the Learning Center.

The three themes pursued in the course were: 1) experiential learning techniques; 2) local cultural history; and 3) the local environment, in the ecological sense. Although the pilot in no way was a polished course, having been put together under time pressure and the uncertainties of new friendships, it developed a momentum that tended to leave its inventors behind. With some modification it might be applicable any place on most any level of education. The following is a three-part presentation of the course from the perspectives of Jim Brown, a historian and sometime folklorist from Samford University; Adolph Crew, Head of the Department of Secondary Education at the University of Alabama, and Joyce Lackie, a participant.

Dr. Adolf Crew, is Professor of Education at the University of Alabama.
Dr. James Brown, is Associate Professor of History at Samford University.
Joyce Lackie, is a doctoral candidate at the University of Alabama and an Assistant Professor of English at the University of Northern Colorado.

Part I: The History Component

To show how ecological consciousness and a range of experiential learning techniques can be linked in the same course by cultural history.

As a historian, I naturally saw chronology as the key to a course structure and lobbied for that sort of organization with my colleagues in Education. The general idea was to: 1) take a level of local cultural history on each weekend, 2) show how that culture related to and changed the land, and 3) whenever possible, communicate that with experiential learning techniques. Here is how it went, and on further reflection how it might go again.

WEEKEND ONE — Wilderness: Alabama on the Eve of European Settlement.

The first weekend the local cultural level was *Amerind:* in historic times in Alabama that means mainly Creek, with Cherokee in the north and Choctaw in the west. The ecological horizon was the well-nigh incredible southeastern wilderness as it was when Michaux and William Bartram, the first naturalists to describe it, came through in the 1700s. The major experiential learning techniques were adventure-based, taking place on a two-day backpack in the Sipsey Wilderness Area of the Bankhead National Forest.

Doug Phillips, University of Alabama, was the instructor and, judging by evaluations, it may have been the best one of the course, creating an initial bond among students as well as a lasting feel for the natural environment. The Bee Branch area of the Wilderness is a small canyon with one of the most remarkable forests left in Alabama, including one of the largest tulip poplars east of the Rockies. Doug spent a lot of time explaining primeval botany there and having us experience it. An introduction to the forest by a slow single-file walk keeping the person in front just out of sight; a blindfolded trust walk and a night hike; a map and compass exercise; a community bread bake the night before the trip; group packing and communal meals of natural foods — these were new and of real value to a class of twenty-five graduate students and active teachers.

In this instance local cultural history was not necessary

as a link between experiential techniques and ecological knowledge. Even here, though, thinking about the culture and its relationship to the environment is a good way to visualize that environment and begin seeing it in new ways. One of the many Indian statements on the relationship between a people and the land was read on a morning just after the group went down into Bee Branch; its message was clearer there than in a classroom. Another reading for the course was William Bartram's *Travels*. He cut across Alabama from central Georgia to Mobile, went a way up the Tombigbee and then back again to Georgia, in 1776 and 1777. The first naturalist to describe the interior of the State, Bartram ran out of superlatives. Despite the Latin lists of flora and fauna, his is a vivid, immediate look at the pre-European ecology and the Indian relation to it.

Finally, in Alabama as in much of the rest of the western hemisphere, Indian cultures were the foundation for the cultural evolution of the land no matter how overwhelming later cultural invasions may have been in numbers. The natives' relation to the land was intimate, of thousands of years accumulation. Some of their practices were necessary for the survival of all the early immigrant groups, even those of a higher technological level, and many are still visible in cultural survivals today. Controlled burning

> "One of the many Indian statements on the relationship between a people and the land was read on a morning just after the group went down into Bee Branch; its message was clearer there than in a classroom."

seems to have been the only major impact the Indians had on the local ecology, creating the extensive cane "meadows" and the first pasturelands hereabouts. There are many plants of known Indian usage and name; herb medicine as it survives in the remoter areas of the State has Indian overtones, as does folk cookery. Alabama place names are mostly Indian or translations of Indian names, especially rivers and other geographic features. Fortunately a dictionary of those names exists. It can be used not only to illustrate the land as the Indians saw it, but as a tool to uncover usable information. "Choccolocco" in Creek means "big shoal;" there must be half a dozen of these on detailed maps of the State. If you like rapids to fish or gig or float or whatever, here is a geographical index that is rich even after all these years. Of primary importance in the area of cultural survivals plus experiential education — each of the three major tribes of Indians has a remaining center: the Creeks around Atmore, Alabama; the Cherokee around Cherokee, N.C.; and the Choctaw at Philadelphia, Mississippi. All three, for example, still keep alive their traditional versions of dyed rivercane basketry. That craft would make a nice vehicle for a hands-on history and ecology lesson.

WEEKENDS TWO AND THREE — The Iron Age: From Indian to European Settlement Patterns.

The local cultural level was rural settlement from pioneer times which in Alabama amounts to the first two-thirds or so of the nineteenth century. The ecological horizon was the extensive European style farming of the land. The major experiential learning techniques were oral history and cultural journalism for Weekend Two, and for Weekend Three crafts-apprenticing.

These weekends were back to back in early August at Tannehill Park. Sessions went from 9:00 a.m. Saturday to 2:30 p.m. Sunday, most of the class choosing to camp together at the park. We had the run of a Pioneer Inn just being finished, and a spring-fed creek for swimming — in all a beautiful setting in a place historically connected with the period under discussion.

Eliot Wigginton came for Saturday of Weekend Two. We had in mind to listen to him for half the weekend and try to put out a small cultural journalism project in the other half. The *Foxfire* magazine and books had concentrated on the pioneer heritage of the Georgia mountain country, making it on the surface an ideal parallel for Alabama pioneer history. Wigginton's students had seemed to get interested in the present of their region through its past, and in its ecology through its people. True, Wig did come and talk about cultural journalism in particular and education in general in a powerful way. Better, he and two local high school students conducted a remarkable interview in class with Mr. Ray Farabee, a retired engineer who presided over the refiring of the Tannehill Furnace 110 years after it was shut down by Union raiders. The major difficulty was that cultural journalism is only a small part of what is included in the word "Foxfire," and the mountain community only part of the potential of cultural journalism. Wig had to caution us not to see a magazine as the end-all of experiential learning. In fact, our high-pressure crash course in magazine production evolved into several gentler seminars on photography, oral history, layout and such, and left some time for other things.

A minor part of the weekend was dealing with some oral cultural survivals from the pioneer period of Alabama history. I tried a class singalong and history lesson on the mountain ballad and fasola (Sacred Harp shaped note singing), the first a dying form and the second now resurgent. They are both of British origin and little-changed over the last hundred years. Essentially white forms, they are nice to pair with black shape note music, spirituals and down home blues. In rural Alabama all these nineteenth century forms are still come by. Singing the music is a good way to experience the hopes and fears of a bygone era; Laurie Seidman and Tony Scott are preaching that gospel nationwide now, with considerable success. In the same vein is the narrative — classic popular storytelling. Every region tucks its most powerful thoughts away in stories, of its strong men and women, tragic love affairs and supernatural happenings. We discovered later that Alabama's premier collector of ghost stories and a fine teller of tales herself had heard of our course and come to crash it, only to be turned away by someone who didn't know what she had to offer. Too, if this part of the course were to teach again, I would like to use Lyn Montell's Saga of Coe Ridge, a powerful oral history account of a small black Kentucky settlement, and talk about, demonstrate and have the class get involved in some Alabama parallels. The nineteenth-century settlement period is only a step or two back in folk memory.

Weekend Three featured Lance Lee, by general consensus the best teacher (and learner) most of us encountered in the course. Lance tried to communicate the mechanics and magic of apprenticing and the values associated with the old-time hand crafts. He not only discussed good and bad tools; we learned them by touch in carving models. A considerable historian and folklorist of the seafaring community of northern Europe and New England, Lance was quick to point out the Tannehill furnaces as the key to a nineteenth-century craft matrix. The iron and soft steel parts of woodcraft tools once came from here and similar places. Part of Lance's vision for the Learning Center is that Tannehill might produce them again, as part of an educational process, since the old quality tools are gradually disappearing. The role of education in community and the folk technique of education through apprenticing were the big lessons he taught. Small fragments of that are encapsuled in hard-to-forget phrases, like "those intricate tricks of self-sufficiency" developed by people in any traditional liflestyle. Lance Lee's message neatly fit the historical framework of the course, and called up all sorts of Alabama parallels. Regional folkcrafts are still alive in almost every Alabama county: split oak basketry, net tying, quilting and blacksmithing among them. Some of the same beauty, economy and strength of Maine wooden boat building can be found in a white-oak cotton basket from the deep South. Folk crafts of any region are an eloquent introduction to the land and the people.

In retrospect, the fate of the land got short shrift these two weekends. We tried a field geology trip to explain why Tannehill came about and how it led to the future steel industry of Birmingham; we seined creeks to identify local darters, sampled wild peppermint and such. But we did not document the extent of the change in the environment. The cotton lands of Alabama lost perhaps five feet of topsoil in the first forty years of farming. The fantastic population growth over the once stable population of 25,000 or so Indians meant more extensive as well as intensive farming. Siltation of rivers probably wiped out many species of fish before any biologist sampled the rivers: at least one of these, the Harelip Sucker, supported a sizeable fishery on the Tennessee River. The creeks at Tannehill, now blue-green, ran red as blood from the open ore pits that fed the furnaces, and the woods for miles around were cut down for charcoal. Early reports from the Geological Services of the State show that the great timber, pine and hardwood, fell to the saw by the turn of the century. The major predators were exterminated except in large swamps, and valuable game became more scarce as the century wore on. By 1920 beaver and deer were extirpated in most of the State. In north Alabama the chestnut blight seems to have cut into the squirrel population, a usually reliable food source for the marginal farmer. These scattered facts outline a massive change in the ecosystem. It is a familiar story in every State: when the culture changes the land, the land in turn restricts the possibilities of the culture. The bad news is that you can't find this kind of history in an Alabama high school or college text; the good news is that a class can build one from game wardens, gardeners, farmers and all the other people resources of the rural community.

WEEKEND FOUR — Urbanization & Industrialization: Alabama in Recent Times.

The local cultural level for this weekend was Twentieth Century Modern. The ecological horizon was the massive urbanization of the past century and the accompanying development of industry. The major experiential learning techniques developed in the context of a two-day adventure in downtown Birmingham, largest and most industrialized city of the State.

Ron Gager set this weekend up, with help from a part time class member who lives in the city. On Saturday morning we left our cars on a manicured suburban campus, walked four blocks and committed to mass transit for the weekend. There followed a morning-long cultural scavenger hunt in Southside, an old and ethnically varied neighborhood of the city. By early afternoon we moved base camp to a downtown church where we were to spend the night. We drew a "human interest map" of the area and listened to a dedicated church worker and enthusiastic city dweller talk about minuses and pluses of city life. Ron took us through a series of New Games in the city, fondly remembered in course evaluations later. The class members were mostly suburban or rural in origin, with a built-in distrust of anybody's inner city; but by the end of the first day a whole new attitude toward cities and city people was evident. The spark of city life that got struck several thousand years ago in the Near East is still very much alive in Birmingham. All of a sudden the city was seen as responsible for civilization (museums, zoos, great libraries, etc.), and as a place of unparalleled social variety and excitement. Having seen the attractions of city life, one had a more balanced view of the social price of late: white flight and inner city collapse, street crime and the like. The chief lesson learned was that the city is of fascinating potential as a setting for education.

We could and should have done the same thing with industrialization. Technology's attractions are powerful, in medicine, communications, luxuries and sheer physical capabilities. From UAB med school to the South Central Bell building, and from U.S. Steel to the new car dealerships, you can see it clearly in Birmingham. In this light, then, maybe the ecological change wrought upon the land by industrialization can be weighed as being either too expensive or a cheap price to pay. Because of the urbanization of the Birmingham area, the creek into which the Tannehill springs drain thirty miles away is often an open sewer; if the species of life in those springs are ever destroyed the way they were in the 1860s, they will not be restocked again from lower down the drainage. Because of the steel industry, part of the pure water that drains from the forest of the Sipsey Wilderness where we spent the first weekend goes into Village Creek in Birmingham in a state akin to liquid mothballs. The open waters, the underlying acquifers, the air and the soil have been drastically changed by urbanization and industrialization. For all the attractions of the city and technology, nothing in them replaces the wilderness. Mental health indices reflect that fact almost as surely as the particulate count. Maybe the beginning of wisdom is that this is not an either-or proposition. As Schumacher says in *Small is Beautiful*, the manner of technology can be changed so that the extreme ecological price need not be paid. Again in retrospect, we certainly should have made time to visit the Recycling Center operated by the Alabama Conservancy, the same group that spearheaded the drive to protect the Sipsey Wilderness.

WEEKEND FIVE — Regional Planning: Awareness of What is to Come.

The cultural and ecological level under consideration was the forseeable future. The experiential learning techniques were ways of community planning.

The second assigned text for the course was Ian McHarg's *Design With Nature*, read for this weekend. Professor McHarg approaches ecology and culture as units that are related, and he does it historically. On his faculty at the University of Pennsylvania he has assembled geologists, biologists, ethnographers and finally political specialists. In approaching an area, he begins with basic geology and climate, moves through natural flora and fauna, traces early settlement patterns through to the present. This identifies the directions of a community's evolution and its effect on the environment. This approach then enables a planner to say: 1) here's what you will look like in the year 2000 if you don't change your ways, and 2) tell us what you want to look like in 2000 and we'll tell you what you can do to achieve it, barring man-made catastrophes and acts of God. On Dauphin Island, where half the class spent a much-acclaimed optional weekend at the Sealab of the Marine Sciences Consortium, there was a perfect illustration of McHarg's introductory exercise on sanddunes. Some school keeper cut the beach grass to get a better view of the ocean or to tidy up, and the dunes are now covering the playground and threatening the building itself. Seining the marsh and noticing the beach erosion seemed to make several students appreciate the seriousness of McHarg's arguments.

Some of the tools of the planner should make great teaching techniques. McHarg makes use of the transparent overlay as a way to get social values into the planning process alongside purely physical and economic ones. If you are considering routes for a highway, make transparencies in suitable, marginal and unsuitable shades for areas of sinkholes, flooding, slope and other physical features. But don't stop there: consider recreational use, agricultural value, historic importance and all the other important social variables. By stacking the transparencies together you might be able to identify the wisest route for the road. I wanted the class to have the chance to try this technique in helping plan a part of the Learning Center at Tannehill, but fell down on advance preparation.

This weekend as special consultant we had Ron Thomas of Attic & Cellar Studios in Washington, a planning and environmental collaborative. After the class ended, Ron did double duty by working with the steering committee of the Learning Center. From him we got a professional's view of participatory design and cognitive mapping. Most impressive were his slides and explanation of a series of community planning projects across the country. He also brought a valuable bibliography in the form of a suitcase of books dealing with the planning process and some aspect of education.

Course evaluations indicated that we spent too much time indoors and not enough time in hands-on learning. One of the purposes of this last substantive weekend was to show that culture is always limited by the parameters of ecology, and that the future is to some extent controllable if we are conscious of that fact. On reexamination of that statement of purpose, it now seems to me that this weekend more than any of the others could have benefitted by in-the-field experience.

A CASE STUDY — Freshwater food fishing in Alabama.

This sort of integrated treatment of cultural levels, the environment and experiential learning techniques can work with smaller, more manageable units as well, in this example an occupational group.

Most of Alabama's rivers still support a population of commercial fishermen. Today they use nylon lines and chromium hooks, and those few who still tie nets use nylon needles and fiberglass hoops. They are a fascinating breed but vanishing fast because of social changes generally, perhaps, but more particularly because of siltation, chemical pollution in the form of oil, PCBs, heavy metals and insecticides, organic pollution from fertilizers and sewage, and new regulations for the benefit of sport fishermen.

So as a teacher you begin a time travel, first stop thirty years or so ago when the hoop nets were woven of cotton twine, put on white-oak splits made into hoops, and the whole dipped in tar. There are old-timers out on all the rivers who can teach you elementary net tying in an hour and how to make a functional net in a day or two. Better yet, bring one to the class and let him tell great fish stories while he teaches the craft. Visions of hundred pound

---

"Course evaluations indicated that we spent too much time indoors and not enough time in hands-on learning."

---

yellow catfish and blue cats that will twist your fingers off ... Even the illegality of the net under construction is appealing. Two large balls of #15 cotton twine and 30 net-tying needles from Memphis Net & Twine's mail-order catalog will cost maybe $10.00. The white oak is free, growing in some second-growth woodlot behind school, perhaps. Knowledge of how to split it and shape it is free, too, but takes some looking for. And the questions ought to come naturally: what was the fishing like? what was the river like, and the people who lived by it?

Next stop, 1930, before they dammed the rivers. Then people still fished long woven baskets like giant minnow traps, baiting with cotton seed meal or spoiled cheese. With a class or two of students looking, you might find one stored on the rafters of an old barn, or still in use in some private pond. The same fisherman who used hoop nets all his adult life probably learned to make these baskets as a youngster, and can do one for you or with your class. Best of all are the descriptions and the stories of the fish traps. Whole rivers, then running, were funneled down by wings into millraces ten feet wide or so, and when the water would color and rise after a rain, fish by the boatload would come sliding out on a series of inclined slats called fingers. Not just your everyday catfish and shad and the like, but fish long gone from the rivers like great sturgeon and twenty pound eel as big around as your leg. On first frost in central Alabama, they had to mesh the traps to hold the eel on their annual downstream run. Why no more eel and sturgeon? The dams... How'd you catch 'em? What'd you do with 'em? What'd you do when the river was too high to use the traps? Can you see where they were?

Then you go on back to 1800 or so when most Alabamians were still Creek Indians and the first naturalists described their fishing. Back way beyond the first netting laws, when pioneer communities still had huge summer fish fries, the young men swimming long nets down a mile of river to meet another net while the grown folks set up the fires and tables and got the skillets hot. And even before that. Last year field researchers with the Office of Archaeological Research in Tuscaloosa studied a river in Randolph County of East Alabama prior to impoundment. Aerial photos taken during the drought showed the stone structure of as many as sixty fish traps in a ten mile stretch of river. Digging at the places where the trap wings touched the banks, they almost always found an Indian site. One yielded a Clovis, a paleo projectile point from sometime before the dawn of world history. Sometime in this process it dawns on the more outdoor types in class

ecology as intertwined, and communicating that through as immediate and vivid ways at your disposal. I have used variations on that theme for two years now on the university level, and know it works; one of the reasons I was excited about this course is that I feel sure it will work on other levels of education, too. Unfortunately I am no high school teacher, and this class of active or prospective teachers couldn't help but be aware of that. From them, especially the social studies teachers, I learned that enthusiasm and some fresh insights are not enough to make education work in the public schools: it takes a level of organization and preparation beyond that. It was a painful lesson, but I will profit by it. The other side of the coin, something I couldn't help but be aware of, as much as I liked the members of the class, was their strange attraction to canned units not of their making, experience or personalities. I know there is a time pressure element involved; but this seemed to me more part of the "mortmain" of the system, Education with a capital "E." I hoped an experiential component could break through some of this. The value of taking students through an experience I have already had is that education becomes as personal as Thoreau's journal at Walden, and achieves a new level of honesty. If I really "know" something in the sense of being able to do it — as in singing mountain ballads, say — I find

> *"The value of taking students through an experience I have already had is that education becomes as personal as Thoreau's journal at Walden, and achieves a new level of honesty. If I really "know" something in the sense of being able to do it — as in singing mountain ballads, say — I find an immediacy in my teaching of it that helps bridge the credibility gap between teacher and student."*

that common methods of fishing — gigging, netting, trapping, driving, poisoning, noosing, jiggerpoling and grappling, to use the local terms — in fact every fishing technique short of dynamiting and electric shock, is of stone age origin. Cultural transmission begins to take on tangibility at this point. A semi-retired commercial fisherman I spent some time with over the past couple of years surprised me one day with some old-style whittled toys to take home to my children. Things that danced and flip-flopped and whirled, made of string and wood. One was a functional Indian pump drill, lacking only the stone point, but not recognized as being a drill at all by the fisherman, just a toy his grandfather had made. How is it that an Indian tool becomes a pioneer toy? This sort of history is visible and cumulative. That drill works as well in each year's class as it did the last.

The inescapable conclusion of such a history lesson is that commercial fishing on the rivers is an arduous but time-honored and rewarding life style. Only an unconscious culture destroys traditional jobs like this and a valuable local food supply by turning a river into a waste disposal system. The impact of the culture on the ecology is always reflected back again on the culture.

This historical model is simple, seeing the culture and

an immediacy in my teaching of it that helps bridge the credibility gap between teacher and student. From Doug Phillips in the Sipsey Wilderness to Ron Gager on Southside, I think that was the key to the successful part of every weekend.

This concludes my part of the article. In discussing this course I have surely exaggerated my component of it and slighted the other contributors. I leave it to Professor Crew to rectify that imbalance, and possibly to talk about History with a capital "H."

Part II: The Secondary Education Component

The primary objective of the education component of the weekend program was to instruct teachers in experiential learning and to help them see applications to their classes and school programs. The rationale was that the most effective way to learn about experiential education is to experience it, then analyze and draw implications from the experiences. This approach was used whenever feasible and whenever the instructors would conceive ways to do so. The disciplines of history and folklore were used as the content through which experiential learning was primarily demonstrated, thereby avoiding the age-old problem of separating methodology and content.

To encourage students to engage in the reflective phase of experiential learning, class members were asked to keep a diary of reactions to their experiences. A limited amount of class time was used for students to interact and to discuss course experiences. "Free time" and "after hours" during the weekends also proved to be fruitful times for such discussions.

The overall theme of the first weekend, "Experiencing the Environment," was chosen for several reasons. Not only did this approach fit the chronology of the historical theme, as described by Professor Brown, but the more experiential thrust was to experience the natural environment, to have a wilderness experience. A part of the Outward Bound philosophy of experiential learning was implemented by placing teachers in a challenging situation through the back-packing, camping-out experience in the wilderness. Several teachers were not quite sure how well they would be able to cope, and after they found that they could, there was a tangible sense of personal achievement, and since it was also a group effort, a unifying process.

The wilderness experience was also used as a base to inform and sensitize class members to the educational potentialities of school camping and outdoor education for elementary and secondary schools. Three staff members, Doug Phillips, Tracey Leiweike from IDEAS, and I, had been involved in programs of this nature and we shared these experiences with the class.

Over the span of the first three weekends, as time permitted, the class was introduced to the nature and theory of experiential learning through presentations, through follow-up discussions of selected readings from the professional literature, and through the process of drawing implications from the on-going activities during each weekend.

This overview of experiential learning, albeit brief, ranged from the views of Carl Rogers to group process, from simulation and open-ended inquiry to experience-based or action learning processes.

During the second weekend, classroom applications were enhanced by interaction with sponsors of two *Foxfire* replicas in Alabama, Tommie Harrison, from the Shelby County schools, and Bob England, from the Bibb County schools. An added dimension was the opportunity to talk with high school students from Bibb County who were involved in publishing Sparrow Hawk. Eliot Wigginton was there to inform and inspire; the replications were there to demonstrate that it can be done in Alabama, on limited budgets and by hard work.

The major theme of the third weekend, "Experiencing the World Through Work," was certainly highlighted by the presence of Lance Lee and the apprenticeship approach to experiential learning. It also provided the opportunity to share with the class my long-time interest in the values of productive work for adolescents, both in terms of its potential for experiential learning as well as an effective means for linking adolescence to adulthood. As part of this, the class read the current literature about the *Walkabout* model, sponsored by *Phi Delta Kappan*. The class was interested in the *Newsletter* from the *Walkabout* Task Force, especially the description of various experience-based programs in operation.

A local person, Mary Dodd, presented information about the Executive Internship Program in operation in the Birmingham City Schools. The Executive Internship Program is a national program in which the secondary student works full time as an intern with a local executive for a semester and receives academic credit.

For the weekend, "Experiencing the City," students were asked to read inquiry materials about cities from the High School Geography Project and the Sociological Resources for the Social Studies. The consultants for both the City and Regional Planning Weekends also brought excellent materials for examination by the class. Ron Marley's Regional Planning dealt extensively with urban areas. In retrospect, his information would have been excellent preparation for "Experiencing the City" and probably should precede the city weekend in any future course.

The final weekend was devoted to sharing experiential teaching units, analyzing and critiqueing course experiences, and talking about future plans. At the beginning of the course, each class member was asked to develop an experiential teaching unit, to teach the unit during the fall semester, and to share the plan and the results of its implementation during the final weekend. Those who were not teaching were asked to develop an experiential unit that they would like to teach. Class members enjoyed this sharing of experiences, and the staff was impressed with the quality of the units, several of which were highly innovative.

Student evaluations of the course were very positive. Class members enjoyed and learned much from interaction with different consultants each weekend. Permanent

> *"Student evaluations of the course were very positive. Class members enjoyed and learned much from interaction with different consultants each weekend. Permanent friendships were formed among class members.*

friendships were formed among class members. There was a deep commitment to experiential learning and to the development of an experiential learning center at Tannehill Park. The group also wanted to continue this involvement beyond the end of the course, and a decision was reached to establish an informal association of experiential education and to have occasional meetings for interested participants.

Depending on one's perspective, each staff member saw areas for improvement. From my view, not enough attention was given to classroom applications, to appropriate materials, and to alternative school programs. At times, partly due to time constraints, instructors tended to become didactic and propagandistic, and probably too much was attempted in too short a time. Not enough time was allowed for class interaction. In some ways, having so many class instructors complicated coordination and continuity.

In spite of whatever shortcomings were perceived, the spontaneity and intensity of this initial venture in experiential education, both for the instructors and for the students, more than compensated for deficiencies in planning and implementation. In the final analysis, the course appeared to have an impact that few courses have.

Part III: A Student's Perspective

My perceptions of the experiential course are from the point of view of a student who found it to be one of the most stimulating educational experiences I have had in my program. There were secondary teachers of social science, English, biology, home economics, business and agribusiness; and also, an elementary school teacher, two college teachers and a number of full-time graduate and undergraduate students, most of whom were pursuing degrees in some area of education.

Many of the participants in the course were interested in learning more about the natural environment, and two or three had taken wilderness education courses previously. Others had directed experiential learning projects in their schools, and several were interested in folkcrafts, but most of the students had had little exposure to experiential or outdoor education. Only a few had participated in any backpacking and camping activities.

By the end of the experience, however, we had a strikingly altered clientele, and that is perhaps most evident in the types of projects the participants had carried out. Two groups of teachers had organized overnight camping trips with their pupils, one to Tannehill Park with emphasis on local history and English experiences and the other to Talladega National Forest with development of the disciplines of science and creative writing. Both experiences were carefully structured by the teachers, who planned numerous group and individual activities including tours of historical sites, scavenger hunts, nature sensitivity walks, story-telling sessions, and journal-writing periods. The pupils were also responsible for preparing their own meals and cleaning up afterwards. Once back in their schools, the pupils related their experiences to information they had been studying and finished developing such projects as short stories, poems, and written reports. The teachers reported both successful and unsuccessful aspects of the trips, noting precautions they could have taken such as providing extra large amounts of food when feeding teenage boys, and the like. On the whole, however, the teachers involved felt that the trips were highly successful in achieving the goals they had set up.

Other teachers planned experiential units with one-day field trips as enrichment or central activities. One group of junior high pupils studied such aspects of their local natural environment as water supply and conservation, forest resources, wildlife, national parks and reserves, and local vegetation, following these efforts with a one-day trip to Tannehill State Park. The pupils were responsible for mapping out the area, directing the bus driver to the park, taking pictures, and pointing out historic sites, types of architecture, wildlife, vegetation and signs of pollution. Another teacher's class in civics discussed different kinds of city governments, held a mock election, studied the many services rendered by a city, and then took a field trip to discover the services, sights and sounds of their own town. They also mapped their town and then planned an ideal city.

A junior high teacher of gifted classes involved her pupils in short trips to several different interesting locations, including a cemetery, and showed them how to analyze one square foot of ground for its natural and man-made phenomena. She also developed a Learning Center packet of experiential materials for those of us in the class. The elementary school teacher took her boisterous youngsters on a carefully-planned field trip to a nearby Indian burial ground and museum as part of a unit on Alabama history. These pupils referred to what they had seen and done frequently in the daily discussions that followed, showing that they had gained a vital interest in the subject.

There were also internship and community service projects. An instructor in nursing set up a program whereby her student nurses helped to implement the federal handicapped children's law (P.L. 94-142) in the public school system. A high school social studies teacher set up what she called mini-internships in which her students spent one hour per day for one week working with such city officials as the sheriff, probate judge, tax assessor and probation officer. A business class participated in a local Trade Day, deciding what they would sell and for how much, setting up the booth, taking turns with all the jobs and closing the booth.

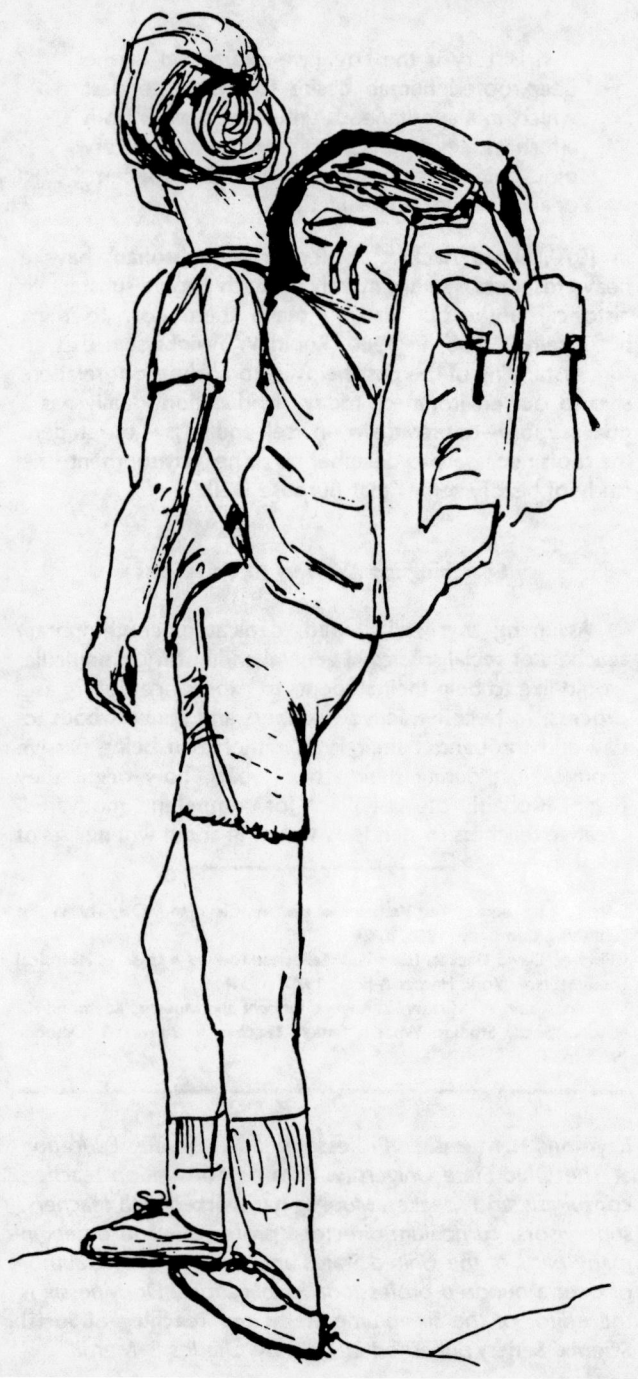

A teacher who was working with the culturally disadvantaged planned a sequence of three outdoor excursions to give the pupils insight into themselves and their natural environment. Her first excursion involved a "trust walk" in which blindfolded pupils were supposed to trust themselves to the guidance of others, but that project failed and led instead to a discussion of trust and the lack of it. The second trip found the pupils a little more helpful to one another as they tried to follow the course of a stream that flowed past the school and into a swampy area. These pupils seemed to have gained more than just an understanding of their physical surroundings.

In addition to the varied outdoor education projects, some teachers worked from the cultural journalism concept, one directing a student-written local history and another a "Roots" project in which students traced and wrote up their geneologies. A home economics teacher had her students research a craft, but their purpose was to recreate it rather than write about it. The class developed a resource file of community residents skilled in quilting, a file of terms, historical incidents and patterns used in the art, and a list of materials needed, and in addition, they began making their own quilts. A science class did structured interviews with older relatives or adults to fine out what lifestyles were like before our country depended on petroleum for so much of its energy needs.

One of the most elaborate service projects was carried out by several classes working together. An enterprising teacher used the combined efforts of his conservation, welding and advanced agribusiness classes to convert two military surplus four-wheel-drive weapons carriers into a cross country off-the-road fire truck and an equipment and manpower transport vehicle. The fire truck was complete with 500 gallon water tank, high pump, pressure hose and fire fighting equipment when the students finished with it.

Some of the projects were difficult to classify but nonetheless exciting. A social studies teacher had his class make a large dugout canoe following the procedures used by Indians, and that class also planted and cultivated a small wheat field using the methods of the early pioneers. The following semester the class intended to harvest their wheat, take it to the Tannehill Gristmill for milling, and use the home economics facilities to bake bread with their home-grown flour. One park commission chairman submitted a plan for the development of an outdoor performing arts center which is actually going to be constructed.

These were just some of the imaginative projects that were created in response to the stimulating learning situation developed in this course. The many rich experiences afforded us, the dynamic speakers and guests, the harmony between what staff members "practiced" and what they "preached" all contributed to a positive atmosphere and a growing cohesiveness in the group. By the end of the course, we all felt a common bond, and we made commitments to try to keep the group alive and working toward the development of experiential education projects throughout the state.

Experiencing History

By Raymond H. Muessig

Introduction

"History is more or less bunk," Henry Ford observed. Said Carl Sandburg, "I tell you the past is a bucket of ashes."

As taught for decades in too many traditional classes throughout our nation, history has ranked high on the "Hate Parade" of innumerable people, both during and after their formal schooling. Frequently the *content* of history instruction has consisted of a potpourri of endless names, dates, places, battles, and treaties. Many of the facts memorized by hapless students have been unimportant and even untrue. The customary *method* has followed a lecture-assign-read-study-recite-test-regurgitate-grade sequence. To a considerable extent, *learning* has meant a dreadfully small percentage of the happenings remembered, incompletely and often inaccurately at that.

Probably the last place for competent, motivated, creative teachers to start is by worrying about writing lists of behavioral objectives, referring to criterion-referenced and standardized tests, "covering" all of the content in adopted textbooks, adhering rigidly to mandated courses of study, and other such albatrosses that have been hung around their necks by various bureaucracies.

A fundamental problem is that subject-centered history teaching has focused on the *product* (end-result, outcome) of historical research and writing and not on the *process* (the way of working and thinking, the system of inquiring and analyzing). Although many historians are responsible for the emphasis of ends (answers) over means (questions), some of the brightest and the best servants of Clio (the Muse of history)—especially those interested in historiography (methods of historical investigation)—, have championed a more balanced approach for some time. In 1956, for example, Fritz Stern made this observation:

... History is the cognitive expression of the deep-rooted human desire to know the past which, in a spontaneous untutored way, is born afresh with every child that searches the mystery of its being. History springs from a live concern, deals with life, serves life. ...[1]

In 1970, David Hackett Fischer wrote, "historians have a heavy responsibility not merely to teach people substantive historical truths but also to teach them how to think historically."[2] And, in 1980, Robin W. Winks said that an "understanding of the past helps us to analyze our relationship to our environment today. If education ideally has a dual purpose—to provide joy in itself and to give the student the tools necessary to decipher his or her environment—the study of history serves that purpose well."[3]

Searching for Answers to Questions

Assuming that enlightened, dedicated, contemporary teachers of social studies in general and history in particular would like to help their students to *experience history as a process*, to become active searchers and thinkers both today and throughout their lives, rather than being passive sponges just during their school years, how might they begin? Probably the last place for competent, motivated, creative teachers to start is by worrying about writing lists of

---

[1] Stern, Fritz, editor. **The Varieties of History.** Cleveland, OH: The World Publishing Company, 1956, p. 24.
[2] Fischer, David Hacket. **Historians' Fallacies: Toward a Logic of Historical Thought.** New York: Harper & Row, 1970, p. 316.
[3] Winks, Robin W. 'History,' in Rogers, Vincent and Muessig, Raymond H., editors. "Social Studies: What is Basic?" **Teacher,** v. 98, no. 3 (October 1980), p. 43.

Raymond H. Muessig *is Professor of Social Studies Education at The Ohio State University. As a demonstration teacher, consultant, and speaker, Muessig has worked with teachers, supervisors, curriculum directors, professors, and others in many parts of the United States and in Canada. The author of over a hundred professional publications, Dr. Muessig is the editor of the six-volume* **Study and Teaching of Social Science Series,** *published in 1980 by Charles E. Merrill.*

behavioral objectives, referring to criterion-referenced and standardized tests, "covering" all of the content in adopted textbooks, adhering rigidly to mandated courses of study, and other such albatrosses that have been hung around their necks by various bureaucracies. Rather, taking into consideration the needs, interests, talents, problems, and aspirations of their students and the nature and potential experiential resources of the local community, teachers could encourage class members to frame appealing, challenging questions that learners—individually, in small groups and committees, and as a total class—could investigate as historical detectives.[4] Questions generated by students might be trivial or significant, humorous or serious, proximate or far-reaching, bland or controversial, just as long as they launch an active, purposeful, historical pursuit after defensible answers. Examples of some possible questions have been provided below to give teachers a feeling for the approach being recommended here. An attempt has been made to order the following questions from simple to complex, concrete to abstract to demonstrate that different individual students, groups of learners, and classes can begin at different levels and advance their understandings, skills, appreciations, and values by tackling increasingly demanding questions. Additionally, comments have been inserted under questions for clarification and amplification purposes.

Where is the oldest grave marker in our city?

This is a down-to-earth (pun intended) question that could motivate students at various instructional levels to begin an active historical quest. If each individual student were to decide to try to answer this question on his or her own, in time, when experiences are compared, class members might discover that there may be different ways of tracking down answers to a given historical question and that there may be different answers to the same question, depending on a historian's frame of reference, the accessibility of data to different researchers, the patience and thoroughness of an investigator, the way a sleuth "adds up" the facts, and so on.

But, let us consider briefly different techniques individual students might employ to locate the oldest grave marker and the extent to which they could take advantage of their environment. One person might rely on a kind of trial-and-error procedure, walk, hike, ride a bicycle, or take a bus; go to all of the oldest cemeteries, look around; and record the date of the oldest grave marker she or he finds. Using the "Yellow Pages" of a telephone directory, a second individual could call all of the cemeteries in the city for leads. Another student might talk with older people, including relatives and family friends, seeking advice with respect to where to look. Still another historical detective could visit a local, county, or state historical society to uncover clues. A fifth amateur researcher might spend some time in a public, college, or university library. And so on. Their investigations could bring class members into contact with a number of people and could take them to many parts of their community. Some budding scholars might even attempt to document their findings with rubbings, photographs, xerographic copies of records, etcetera, resulting in bulletin board displays, interest centers, and the like. Resource persons could be invited to class sessions, possibly including an archaeologist. Many rich and varied experiences could result from endeavors to respond to the first question suggested here. As a follow up—for various reasons and with different possible experiential rewards—teachers might form committees to locate the city's oldest living person, standing building, operating business, and the like.

What was the most important event in Our Town's History?

Questions such as this could bring out the resourcefulness of students and encourage them to evaluate their data. Using the facilities of newspapers, historical societies, and various libraries, class members could learn to use, and to become more familiar with the use of, card catalogs, clipping files, photograph collections, microfilm, microfiche, computers, histories, biographies, diaries, memoirs, documents, maps, ad infinitum. Superlatives such as "Worst" and "most" could fuel enthusiastic discussions often difficult to resolve. Considerable incidental learning might occur as students search for and exchange information.

What are some of the things that have attracted people to Courtesyburg?
For what reasons have people moved away from Courtesyburg?
What do you think are the most useful explanations for Courtesyburg's immigration and emigration?

"Multiple causation" is one of the key concepts in contemporary historiography. In their lectures, some traditional U.S. history teachers have told their classes that slavery was *the* cause of the Civil War. An approach more likely to stimulate students to think would be to ask, "how many *causes* can you identify that resulted in the Civil War?" Pressing class members to evaluate the importance of contributing factors further enriches learning.

---

[4] For additional background and methodological ideas, please read Muessig, Raymond H. "Suggested Methods for Teachers," in Commager, Henry Steele and Muessig, Raymond H. **The Study and Teaching of History.** Columbus, OH: Charles E. Merrill Publishing Company, 1980, pp. 104-119.

What are some of the things that the people of Friendlyville used to do and/or believe that they no longer do and/or believe?

Heraclitus observed that change is the basic condition of life and that there is nothing permanent except change. Through their manifold experiences with history, students may discover that change has been an important part of the human condition and that the rate of change may differ from time to time, place to place, ingredient to ingredient.

In-depth, tape-recorded interviews with community residents of different ages in homes, schools, libraries, museums, churches and synagogues, places of employment, recreational sites, hospitals, convalescent facilities, retirement villages, and so on could contribute to experiential growth in many ways, but students' interactions with others are especially germane to a class study of changes over time in activities and beliefs. Having conversed with people in different settings, learners might write insights they have gained on a time line, drawn on unrolled butcher paper and taped on the walls around the classroom. During their discussion of entries on the time line, class members could observe that technological changes have occurred more rapidly than have those of an ideological nature, that the pace of change has accelerated in Friendlyville in more recent decades, and the like.

Has Happytown had an interdependent relationship with different nations of the world in the past? To what extent does Happytown have an interdependent relationship with various countries at the present time? How likely is it that Happytown will have interdependent global relationships in the future?

What resources have been the most important to the residents of Helpful County in the past? What resources are the most important to the people of Helpful County at the present? What resources are likely to be the most important to the citizens of Helpful County in the future?

What are some of the most difficult problems that have faced the residents of Port Sunshine in the past? What are some of the most difficult problems facing the people of Port Sunshine today? What are some of the most difficult problems likely to face the citizens of Port Sunshine in the future? Are any of the past, present, and future problems related to each other? Why, or why not?

How might you describe the quality of life in Pleasant City in the past? How would you characterize the quality of life in Pleasant City today? What do you think the quality of life is likely to be in Pleasant City in the future? From past to present to future have there been and may there be more gains or losses on the whole in the quality of life in Pleasant City? Why?

Historian Michael W. Curran has written that "history and historical understanding are essential if we are to make informed judgments about the present and act reasonably responsibly in trying to shape a world in which we want to live."[5] Committed, innovative history teachers can and should provide opportunities for experiences in which youth come to perceive past, present, and future relationships through real-life inquiry in the immediate community. By seeking their own answers to their own questions concerning interdependent relationships, the use of resources, personal-social problems troubling local citizens, the quality of life, etcetera, students can establish past-present-future connections that reinforce Shakespeare's line in *The Tempest:* "What's past is prologue." They may also identify some of history's limitations when they find certain possible future concerns for which the past and the present provide few or no precedents.

Conclusion

"Nothing ever becomes real till it is experienced . . .," wrote John Keats. Isadora Duncan said, "What one has not experienced one will never understand . . ." Experiencing history as a process, through active questioning and searching for meaningful answers—especially by tapping readily available and vivid resources in the immediate community—offers students "an arch to build upon," as Henry Brooks Adams put it.

---

[5] Curran, Michael W. "A Historical Perspective," Chapter 3 in Muessig, Raymond H. and Gilliom, M. Eugene, editors. **Perspectives of Global Education: A Sourcebook for Classroom Teachers.** Columbus, OH: College of Education, The Ohio State University, in press.

MELDING CLASSROOM INSTRUCTION WITH Real-World Problem-Solving

by John E. Gannon and
G. Winfield Fairchild

Introduction

Excellent opportunities exist for the instruction of environmental biology at field stations across the country. Field stations offer the potential for experiential learning in a diversity of natural environments. Students normally enroll in two courses offered intensively over a short time period ranging from five to ten weeks. The learning experience, when condensed into such a short time frame, can become a disjunct helter-skelter dash through field exercises and laboratory methods without the proper development of an overall theme and sense of direction. However, with extra attention given to course planning and time budgeting, a fusion of basic and applied concepts can be achieved.

In our experience, the key to the integration process is directing the student's acquired knowledge and techniques toward solving a real environmental management problem. Our objective was to integrate a sound academic foundation with experience in resource management problem-solving, thereby better preparing students to act responsibly and effectively in resolution of environmental problems in their own communities, irrespective of their future as aquatic science professionals or as lay citizens.

Exposure to an applied problem can be structured formally by integrating field ecology with environmental impact analysis. Successful courses have been given which actually involve the students in the multi-disciplinary approaches and mechanics of environmental impact assessment, culminating in the writing of an Environmental Impact Statement.* Student activities can also be structured more informally, but still be designed to provide meaningful answers to a resource management question during the limited time frame of the course.

This paper presents some instructional experiences the authors have had teaching limnology (freshwater ecology) at the University of Michigan Biological Station during the summers of 1973-1978, and 1981-1982. Students were a mix of upper division undergraduate and graduate students, and typically took two courses in an 8-week period in mid-summer. Most courses met two full days per week. The basic approach, however, is adaptable to field stations elsewhere and to a wide range of field-oriented courses.

Course setting and format

The University of Michigan Biological Station is located on Douglas Lake in Michigan's lower peninsula near the Straits of Mackinac. It is close to diverse freshwater habitats, including inland lakes, streams, rivers, bogs and other wetlands and two of the St. Lawrence Great Lakes, Michigan and Huron. Inland lakes, which received the most emphasis in the course, range in size from small bog ponds to three of the largest lakes in the state and exhibit a full range of human impact from negligible to heavily developed.

Most summers, following registration but before the first day of formal class, the students, instructor, and teaching assistant went on a half-day hike to an undeveloped lake accessible only on foot. Only the simplest equipment (dip nets, plankton nets, and white enamel pans) was brought along for qualitative biological examination. Students were

---

John Gannon is *Associate Director of the State University Research Center at Oswego, New York.* **Win Fairchild** is *Assistant Professor of Biology at Central Michigan University, Mt. Pleasant, Michigan. They collaborated on this instructional approach while teaching at the University of Michigan Biological Station.*

*Haynes, J. M., G. W. Thorburn and J. E. Gannon 1983. Environmental impact assessment: Melding classroom instruction with problem-solving experience. J. College Science Teaching: in press.

> "Each team was charged with presenting an interpretation of data for one of the lakes."

asked to wander the shore, wade and sample at will. Then the group was reassembled on the shore and the instructor and teaching assistant led an informal discussion with questions about the lake's ecological characteristics. The trip was designed to brush away the cobwebs from aesthetic senses numbed by the academic year and to get students to begin asking questions about lakes as environments for aquatic organisms and their sensitivity to human impacts.

The first half of the course (about four weeks) introduced students to the basic limnology of lakes. The daily format varied depending on the distance of field work from the Biological Station. Several hours of morning lecture were typically followed by a field study. Lunch was often eaten in the field. Laboratory activities were usually reserved for the afternoon and were sometimes supplemented with discussions on methods.

Inexperienced students are often bewildered by the wide array of field sampling gear and laboratory apparatus they are exposed to in limnology. To minimize misuse and fumbling, an intensive introduction to limnological gear was included early in the summer session. Operation of each instrument was demonstrated and the advantages and disadvantages of its use were discussed informally. Equipment use in the field was demonstrated *in situ* on Douglas Lake, using the Biological Station's pontoon boat. Students collected samples with the apparatus and were instructed in the importance of collecting data in an organized and careful manner.

Following the introduction to limnological methods, a comparative survey was initiated, usually of five lakes representing broad differences in limnological features. Five teams were chosen by the instructor and the teaching assistant. Each team was composed of a mix of graduate and undergraduate students, and individuals with pertinent skills (e.g., taxonomy, chemistry) were divided among the teams as equitably as possible. Each team's responsibilities for data collection rotated at each lake (Table 1). Moreover, to assure that all necessary data were collected each person was designated as team leader on a rotational basis. In this manner, all class members obtained experience in field sampling, team leadership and organization. Although the scheme in Table 1 is rather simplistic, we found it to be exceedingly effective. Providing ample opportunity for experiential involvement by the less aggressive and less experienced students is rarely given the attention it deserves in most instructional modes.

Table 1. A simple but effective rotational scheme for allowing each student in a class of 25 to experience all field sampling techniques and to assume team leadership for data collection. Roman numerals (I-V) indicate teams of five students each. Letters (a-e) indicate which student on each team is the leader and responsible for data collection on each sampling trip. The scheme can be easily modified to accommodate different class sizes and different team assignments.

Team Assignment	Lake A	Lake B	Lake C	Lake D	Lake E
Physical	Ia	Vb	IVc	IIId	IIe
Chemical	IIa	Ib	Vc	IVd	IIIe
Biology 1	IIIa	IIb	Ic	Vd	IVe
Biology 2	IVa	IIIb	IIc	Id	Ve
Biology 3	Va	IVb	IIIc	IId	Ie

The site was found to be poorly suited for commercial development.

Most of the physical and chemical data were processed on the day of collection. The majority of biological samples were preserved for later analysis. Evening taxonomic work sessions were conducted on an informal basis, and teams were expected to analyze their biological samples outside of class time. This approach generated a comprehensive set of physical, chemical, and biological data in a relatively short period of time. Tables of data were prepared by the students, checked by the instructor and teaching assistant, typed on ditto masters, and distributed to the class.

Each team was then charged with orally presenting an interpretation of the data for one of the lakes. Students usually supplemented class data with past records of the lake and its surrounding watershed, and drew extensively upon available literature in support of their ideas. Presentations were a lively, all day affair and served as an excellent vehicle for crystallizing concepts of lake structure and function.

During the second half of the 8-week course the students addressed an applied resource management question concerning a local lake or stream. Based on student's interests and expertise, groups of two or three students were organized to work on various aspects of a problem. Invariably, these groups comprised a different mix of students than was assembled during the first half of the course. Field work was a coordinated effort during class time. Laboratory analyses and data interpretation were largely performed by the students outside of class. During this period class activities focused on stream limnology and sessions were designed to allow students to spend maximum time analyzing data on the applied problem. The students submitted written reports on their part of the applied project at the end of the course, and usually became involved in presenting their findings to an interested group of citizens or public officials.

Case History Examples

We have found that a thorough understanding of the local area is critical to selecting problems which are both current and feasible as applied projects. Contacts with individual citizens, lake associations, public interest groups, and state and local agencies have been of particular value. The permanent staff of the biological station can often assist the instructor in making pertinent contacts in the local community. Especially when the class was able to meet with an interested citizen or organization at the outset, the project suddenly became more than an instructional exercise and generated considerable enthusiasm. The following are three examples of the range of projects possible:

One class worked on a small (17 ha) reservoir on one of Michigan's best trout streams. The reservoir and surrounding land were owned by a person who wished to develop the area with shoreline homes. Students worked on lakeshore soils and their suitability for on-site wastewater treatment, water volume retention time in the reservoir, and a comparison of water quality and fish populations upstream and downstream. The site was found to be poorly suited for development because the lakeshore soils were sandy with low capacity to absorb wastewater nutrients and high potential for erosion. Findings were presented to the owner and the land has not been developed to date.

Another class project was generated by the proposed removal of a dam from a local trout stream. Measurements included stream flow and water

The rotational scheme (Table 1) insured that all students gained experience with field sampling techniques.
Photo courtesy of John Gannon

> **Because the students were working on a real problem, they perceived their work as important**

Students were encouraged to establish dialogue with citizens and public officials who had a knowledge and concern for the environmental problem that was the focus of the student's investigation.

Photo courtesy of John Gannon

chemistry, stream morphology and bottom substrate type, bottom-dwelling organisms, riparian vegetation and land use. It was concluded that dam removal at the lower end of the river would have little effect on trout habitat improvement, as most of the upper reaches had sluggish currents, silty sediments and high water temperatures that would be little affected by dam removal. Class members participated in presenting results of the study to a local planning commission at the end of the summer session.

A third class worked closely with a lake association on the feasibility of dredging as a lake restoration technique. The lake was shallow and had soft, flocculent sediments. After examining features of both the lake and surrounding land, the class concluded that dredging was an ecologically feasible technique for improving the lake's recreational attributes, but suggested alternative upland disposal of dredge materials over previously proposed disposal sites in wetlands adjacent to the lake.

Evaluation and Conclusions

The lake comparison series at the beginning of the course forced the students to collect, analyze and interpret a comparatively large set of information. The discussion of relevant concepts and techniques must therefore be planned carefully to keep pace with the lake measurements. Some students initially were frustrated and overwhelmed with so much data, and benefited from a little extra direction and encouragement. Then, as their integration of information increased, the enthusiasm heightened, and they were able to work more independently.

The applied problem provided reinforcement learning of the techniques and principles covered in the first half of the course. Because the students were working on a real resource management problem, they perceived their work as important. Consequently, they executed their assignments with greater accuracy and punctuality, developed better cooperative and leadership attributes, exhibited more originality and expended more effort than was actually required. Despite the hard work, response to the course has always been very positive. When asked if any portion of the work load should be reduced in the future, the response has always been a unanimous no.

The challenge for the instructor is to provide problem-solving experiences without unduly sacrificing basic environmental principles and theories. We believe biological field stations offer the setting, atmosphere and the intensive type of course where the melding of classroom instruction with real-world problem-solving can best be achieved.

The View from the Classroom

Editor's Note:

At last fall's AEE conference in Colorado, I talked with a group of teachers about what it's like to be experiential educators in a classroom setting. They were Tom Herbert, a social studies teacher in Concord, New Hampshire, Mike Loughery, an English teacher in Denver, Deborah Eads, a middle school science teacher in Nederland, Colorado, and Ava Heinrichsdorff, an English teacher at the Colorado Springs School, a private school with an experiential philosophy. Excerpts from their conversation are printed here:

* *

Peggy: How did you decide to become a teacher?

Mike: During my senior year in college, I realized I'd never been West of Chicago and I had a fascination for Indians and Navajo Indians in particular so I took a job teaching on the Navajo reservation. At this time I only had a degree in English and no education credits and merely taught as a vehicle to get myself on the reservation. I did that job for one year and left the reservation because I wasn't paid much more than a stipend. At that point I decided that education might be a good vehicle for disenfranchised or disadvantaged people to further themselves so I decided to look at schools in Albuquerque that I might teach in. But I found that I needed teaching credentials to teach in most schools, so as I framed houses I began the process of collecting education credits.

Ava: After a divorce I found that I needed a marketable skill. I had coached a horseback riding club, I had taught photography, archery, and had led a high school discussion group at the Unitarian Church and I knew I felt comfortable in a teaching relationship. It seemed reasonable to get that credential and keep on doing what I knew I like to do.

Tom: I decided in 4th grade that I was going to be a social studies teacher because I had such a good teacher in 4th grade. I went away from that but I ended up coming back to it. I tried being a college administrator in between.

Deb: I worked in outdoor programs but I felt that I could have more impact on students if I saw them for longer than a month. I really like the energy level of middle level students. They don't feel like they're too old to play and have fun and I enjoy teaching when everyone is having fun as well as learning.

Peggy: What made you decide to teach experientially rather than in a more traditional way?

Ava: I've never really thought of teaching any other way. I didn't know until quite recently that it had a name. It's what people called apprenticeship in the Renaissance and it's what good teachers have always done. Teaching experientially wasn't a decision that I made. I just knew that knowing something in your body and applying it through all kinds of activities is what makes something fun to learn and worth learning and gives you that exhilerating, "Wow, look what I can do" feeling. The most exciting thing for a teacher is to see students just delighting in their own new powers.

Tom: I teach experientially because it fits my personality and my personality fits it. I couldn't just stand up and lecture. I'm too much of a ham and I like to get involved with the kids. That's a key point. I learn a lot more about the kids and they learn a lot more about me. The interactions we have are a lot more meaningful if we get away from a straight lecture or text book approach. I also think that what they learn in class is much more significant. It lasts a lot longer if they are involved in what they learn.

Deb: I looked at the way that I learn and didn't learn and in retrospect I find that I learn best by doing. What I remember most from my own schooling is the times that we did something - going on marsh walks or birding, cooking and sewing in class, or doing art projects, playing sports, putting on plays. I feel that I got so much more out of those activities than sitting and reading history books. I think you learn more by doing the subject instead of just reading about it. That's not to cut out the necessity of learning to read and

"In the course of an entire year, you get to see everyone have their 'Eureka!' experiences."

write well in all subjects, but there is an important place for doing as well as for reading and writing. We need to balance out our learning and teaching styles.

Mike: I had heard of experiential education through an Outward Bound experience that I had. I had learned the value of risk-taking, and of challenging learning environments for myself and thought they would be really applicable to the kids I was working with who were dropouts. I did some wilderness trips and also some urban adventures with the kids I was working with at that time. I found that the challenging situations that I was able to set up were very motivating for the kids. From there I developed some cultural journalism programs and also some internship programs.

Peggy: What are some of the advantages of teaching experientially in a classroom setting?

Deb: The greatest advantage is being able to see the students for a whole year, rather than for 5 to 23 days in a special program. In the course of an entire year, you get to see everyone have their "Eureka!" experiences. When I see students for a year I start to build a closer bond with the students and there's a much higher trust level. You can discuss things, be it science or problems the student is having. I don't think I can get that kind of rapport with students after just seeing them for five days.

Mike: I get a lot of satisfaction in seeing kids who have not been able to apply themselves or motivate themselves or hold expectations for themselves do those things when there are learning situations that seem to fit their needs, in this case experiential learning. For example, I can remember one kid I had who, for all practical purposes, was illiterate. I sent him and another girl on a cultural journalism interview down to talk to a Mexican rug weaver. This kid came back about 3 or 4 hours later with eyes lit up, really excited about what he had just done and about transcribing the tape. The tape provided some great English exercises for the kid for the following weeks and he was willing to work on them. I've also seen other kids who ended up with more self esteem and confidence because of experiential learning situations in which they were forced to bring forth some skills and develop talents which they had never used before or had refused to use. There's the excitement of the kids which I haven't seen when I've taught traditionally.

Peggy: Tom, you take the kids outside and do many of the same ropes-course type of activities as many outdoor programs, but why do you choose to be in a classroom instead of working outdoors all the time?

Tom: I've been asked to do that a number of times, but I don't want to give up my regular classes. So many of the kids in school don't take an outdoor program. I like dealing with all kinds of kids and if you want to reach the mainstream of the kids you have to teach in a classroom situation. Our outdoor program can only handle 40 kids a year. I get 90 kids each semester in my 3 regular classes - that's 180 each year.

Then there is the larger educational issue: do people only learn experientially outdoors in the woods? When the outdoors is the setting, there's always the danger that the experiential education is getting left outside in the woods. The kids have to tie it back into the rest of their lives and one way to do that is to teach experientially in a classroom. I think that working in a classroom experientially validates experiential education in other educators' minds. A lot of people would see that you can do it outdoors, but wonder if you can do it within 4 walls in a 50 minute period. By trying to do that, we validate this philosophy, and that means that we will not only be having an impact on students, but on other staff who also then have impact on their students and the ripple effect goes out. And the more we do it, and the more different ways we can do it, the wider that ripple is.

The other thing is that if I were to just do outdoor things it would kill my family life. The divorce rate is too high among outdoor experiential educators. Being a teacher gives you family time because of the long vacations. The vacations also make it possible to arrange for new experiences to enrich your own life and your teaching. And, while teaching doesn't pay much compared to many professions, it is certainly more stable and lucrative employment than most outdoor leadership type of jobs.

Peggy: What are the disadvantages or disappointments that you've experienced in the classroom setting?

Ava: I don't know if it's a disadvantage or a challenge, but you have to work a little harder if you're teaching academic things like English or history experientially because it isn't the way we learned. We have to pay a little bit better attention to our preparations and to finding out what communities and natural environments surrounding the school can offer in order to teach experientially. It takes a lot of energy and planning to remember to teach this way and not to drop back into the traditional teacher-centered kind of things we were raised on and which comes quite naturally on the days when we're winging it because we didn't get our preparations done creatively enough.

Tom: It does take a lot of energy and time and creativity and generally a teacher doesn't have a lot of time to be creative. There are so many demands on you that sap your time and energy - papers to correct, meetings you have to go to, counseling sessions with troubled students, hall or cafeteria duty... there's no time to bounce ideas off other teachers to see if they'll fly. That's how I get so many of my ideas - I steal them or I modify them.

Deb: I agree that experiential education is hard work. It's really time-consuming. A lesson plan that I write one year to fit one group doesn't work the next year because it doesn't fit that group the same way. And I don't have the energy every day to develop new plans.

Another problem is that other teachers often question what you're doing. They have no background in terms of college courses or workshops to understand the experiential methods of teaching. They often say things like, "That makes the kids feel nice, but are they really learning anything?"

Peggy: How do you react to something like that?

Deb: I shut my doors. It used to make me angry and now I feel that I'm more accepting of that attitude because I think that it is good for kids to be exposed to different teacher's styles. If in one class the teacher lectures a lot and if in another class the teacher has them read a lot, that's good for some students' learning styles. In my class they're doing a lot and that's important for another learning style. So hopefully, as a community effort of teaching, we're all balancing each other out. But sometimes I wish I could go up to some of the other teachers and shake them and yell "Just try it!" or put them through a "Eureka" experience themselves to make them realize the power of this way of learning.

Mike: I've also found it hard to convince colleagues that my teaching is effective and is as

> "When the outdoors is the setting, there's always the danger that the experiential education is getting left outside in the woods."

valuable as what they're doing. It's hard to keep doing what is perceived as being strange activities for the kids. You don't get any pats on the back. Also, sometimes it's difficult when you have kids who are intimidated by leaving the textbooks and ditto sheets behind. They don't always want to take a risk and it's hard especially in a small room with 30 kids. With all the reports that have come down the pike in the last few years it's becoming harder and harder to do something which is perceived as being out of the ordinary.

Peggy: Tom, you've received various awards - selection by USA Today as one of the outstanding teachers in the country, selection as social studies teacher of the year. Have these given you more credibility for teaching experientially in your school?

Tom: Oh, I suppose the awards made some difference in the administration's perception, but I think I have my own credibility because I make sure I touch base with the administration. I make sure they know what I'm doing. I say, "This is my plan," or "This is my problem," or "I see these as the options, and this is the one I'd like to do if you don't have any problems with it." They usually say, "Fine, do it and let us know if you need our support." I think they appreciate the fact that I work hard and that creates the credibility that I need to do some crazy things.

Ava: In most schools the great disadvantage of trying to teach experientially is the constraint of the schedule. Fortunately, the Colorado Springs School has changed its scheduling so that we can teach experientially and become a model of experiential education and on those days when we're our best we do that.

Deb: Another disadvantage is evaluating experiential learning. How do you grade someone as to how sensitive they are to their lab partner's needs or how well they cooperate and work with a group to get a job done? It is easier to evaluate in more traditional ways such as tests.

Peggy: What advice do you have for someone considering a career as a classroom teacher with an experiential philosophy of education?

Tom: I would want them to know that teaching is a rewarding career. I teach because I want to know that what I have done has helped other people. I want to have mattered.

My advice to anyone considering this career is to first become a good teacher. Be a good, caring teacher and the experiential techniques will come. You have to care about other people, be willing to go that extra mile. You have to be willing to expose your humanity. That is what kids are longing for. They don't need another 45 minute teacher. On the other hand, I see teachers who are all over kids and have kids over their houses every weekend and I don't mean that either. There has to be a line between teacher and student, but you have to be a caring, approachable role model too.

I think it's important to realize that kids learn in different ways and teaching experientially isn't the only way to be a good teacher. One of the very best teachers in our school is a stand-up lecturer. He's 64 years old and I tell every student of mine that they must take one of his courses before they graduate. As a professional association, it's important for us in AEE to toot our own horn, but not to the exclusion of hearing the rest of the band.

Ava: An important piece of advice I would give is to make sure that your courses and activities have a lot of academic integrity. They have to be tough, they have to be demanding, and the experience has to bring out of each student a much more intense and a much more brilliant academic and scholarly effort than that student would have produced without the enhancement of the experiential aspect of whatever it is that you're doing. Also, since this kind of education isn't exactly the accepted, normal thing, you have to be smart in making sure that this first class, scholarly achievement is displayed in the right places. Make sure that parents, administrators, and other teachers are regularly awed by what your best students have produced. Make sure that your students themselves never take your course as a "blow-off" course. Create the reputation for each of your courses as really, really tough but worth it. Make sure your students feel tremendous pride in what they're doing and out of that pride let commitment come.

That's extremely important and that's a job that never ends because you always have a new clientele. You shouldn't let two months go by without paying very active attention to selling experiential education through observable, measurable, displayable results.

For teachers who want to teach experientially in a school where it's never done, there are several approaches you can take. One is to lobby hard for experiential education. Get together with some other teachers and become advocates with all the same public relations things I've already mentioned. And be very, very grateful for anyone who facilitated any of your programs and make sure that lots of glory is shed back on that person or all those people.

On the other hand, if you run into a great deal of resistance and have very few people on your side in your system, you might want to consider just being the best teacher you could possibly be in your own sphere without necessarily calling it anything or saying, "I am an experiential teacher." It doesn't have to be labeled to exist and chances are when you look around you, even in the most traditional setting, the really best teachers are experiential, or are doing some experiential things. When our school first began in 1963 we had girls in uniform who stood in front of their chairs until told, "You may be seated," at the beginning of every class and who lined up for assembly and walked in two by two to a march played by our music teacher. How traditional can you get? Even then, we were a very good school and we were on the forefront of experiential education because we had team taught, interdisciplinary courses, we had senior independent projects which were a month long and which took place all over the country and in some other countries, and we had a community service program as part of a course on current issues. So, being a traditional school does not mean you can't be experiential and it doesn't mean you can't be good. You don't have to look avant-garde all over the place to be doing very valid things. So I would suggest that people considering being classroom teachers with an experiential philosophy don't get into an all-or-nothing frame of mind. It just creates an adversary situation that nobody needs.

Deb: I have just one piece of advice for people who want to be experiential classroom teachers: Do It! Then keep your chin up and stick to your ideals.

Experiential Learning in Political Studies

by David M. Purdy

How should I teach a course that deals with the politics of over 80,000 governments (that's how many the USA has) and to what end?

That was my dilemma in teaching a Political Science course called State and Local Government, not exactly the sexiest sounding subject among the course listings in our, or any other, college catalogue. Although the course is considered essential by other departments at our school and while state and local issues and politics are actually closer to us than the American national government, the subject matter seems remote and uninteresting. How could I make it both immediate and interesting so that students would be well-informed and able to exert some influence over decisions that affect us all?

First I had to decide my goals for the course. Peeled away to the core, I wanted my students to understand how the political process works and why things turn out the way they do. In other words, how it is decided who gets what. That is, after all, what the study of politics is, and that can be extremely interesting and informative.

Next question: how best to achieve that? My answer: get students as close to real life situations as possible. At the same time, have them gain a grounding in abstract knowledge and generalizations by drawing on the scholarship of the field in order for them to be able to test or apply these generalizations.

Previously, I had come to the conclusion that simple information transfer was not adequate as a goal, and the traditional use of a text and tests certainly does not, as we know, have lasting results in terms of significant retention. Besides, the question had to be asked, "Retention to what end?"

David Purdy is a professor at Unity College in Maine.

Structure of the State and Local Government Course

Unity College is situated about 30 miles from Augusta, capital of Maine, and I decided to take advantage of its accessibility. At first, it was just visits by the class; then my encouragement to select a Maine issue for the subject of a term paper. I am excited about dealing with political issues in Maine, particularly environmental ones since in that area Maine is one of the most progressive in the nation. However, I lacked the imagination to make learning in the course systematically experiential. I was still tied to the text.

I still use a text, but as a reference. I still take the class to Augusta, but now I give them a set of scavenger hunt type of questions instead of a tour. For example, they might have to find a lobbyist. Who does the lobbyist represent? What does she or he do?

In class I explain that the course will be divided into four parts, two dealing with state politics, one with community politics in towns and cities, and one with big city politics. A paper will be required for each of the first three parts. The final exam will test in a traditional way for the fourth segment, since Maine has no big cities. There are thus four requirements for grades. I pass out a syllabus which, in addition to standard items, contains a weekly class schedule and a set of questions which link material in the text to issues which will be selected by students. I also explain that the text will be used as a reference book with the material in the pertinent chapters to be applied to a real issue, a Maine issue.

At this point nobody knows what I am talking about. So I explain that for paper number one, the whole class will write on the same issue, one pre-selected by me which has been resolved. I place on reserve in the library original

> "Students are pleasantly surprised to find the whole of Maine's state government open, accessible, friendly, and most willing to be helpful."

documents, newspaper clippings, editorials, position papers - anything and everything - to do with the issue. The students attempt to sift out the role and power of the governor, legislature, department agencies, the courts and interest groups and other participation by the public; apply generalizations made in the text; and attempt to draw conclusions as to why the issue was resolved as it was. In class sessions we discuss the questions relating the issue to the text. The questions are designed both for specific information and interpretation.

The first paper is really a prelude to the second one which is designed to be the major project of the semester. Students select their own topics although I help with a list of hot Maine issues. If students are from states other than Maine, which most of them are, I encourage comparative studies. Among the issues selected during the past semester were hazardous waste disposal, land use law enforcement, prison overcrowding, protection of agricultural land, funding for the fish and game department, and hydro development, all of which were reflected in bills introduced into the legislature.

The weekly schedule calls for class time to be used to discuss the statement of the issue, find library sources, make an outline, develop a list of resource persons to interview and set up interviews. Students begin the daily reading of newspapers for articles and editorials. We get copies of bills and schedules of public hearings. I give them a map of Augusta and a list of useful telephone numbers and they're on their own. I then suspend classes for a time and meet with students individually or in small groups to help them with clarification or assist them on the next step.

Students may work in pairs. In fact, I encourage it. What I ask for in this case by way of evaluation, in addition to the paper, is a self evaluation stating specifically what that person contributed to the paper. This tends to mitigate the occasional temptation to duck responsibility and leave it to your buddy. I encourage the small team approach for various reasons. It is efficient for interviewing, each one alternating asking questions and taking notes. It eases the transportation problem, and it assists mightily in increasing one's confidence, from calling on the telephone to sitting in the Attorney General's office, telling him that the Department of Environmental Protection thinks that he should move with more dispatch in the matter of land use law violation cases, and asking how he responds to that.

I ask the students to do four things: research and understand the issue, interview and obtain perspectives from participants in the issue all the way from the governor's office to interest groups, apply the generalizations in the text that do apply to this issue and predict or explain the outcome based on the students analysis of the relative influences in the process. The student's conclusion need not be correct. What I am looking for is an intelligent understanding of the process.

Students often show befuddlement about the process. I say, "Welcome to the crowd!" They are, in fact, doing what any good political science scholar or investigative reporter does. Conclusions must, after all, be drawn from the apparent mysteries behind President Reagan's meeting with the Chinese, Assad's relationship with Arafat, Mayor Koch's bargaining with the feds, as well as Governor Brennan's nod to the paper companies in omitting from his river's protection bill sections of wild rivers preferred by them for potential hydro development dams.

The third paper deals with community politics emphasizing the issue of planning and focusing on the city of Bangor which is currently undertaking a major redevelopment effort. This time I bring the chief participants to them. Following reserve reading, again consisting of newspaper articles, documents, editorials, and other flotsam, the students interview people such as the mayor and chief of city planning who will have a role in the decision-making. The meeting is designed to test textual generalizations in this specific case. Example: does the city planner really, as the text says, see the city council as the tool of downtown interests? Students again must reach a decision as to the probable outcome of the planning issue in a paper.

In addition to the experiential aspect of the State and Local Government course, students see the films "Hyde Park" and "Tighten Your Belts, Bite the Bullet", both excellent documentaries, and read the book *Boss* by Mike Royko.

The Environmental Politics Course

I also teach another course in which the students are immersed in experience, but it is offered during a three week mini-term, and the class meets every day for half a day. We work on the same issue in small teams of no more than four, conduct whole class interviews, invite speakers, and roam the capital city. Students are universally enthusiastic about this course, called Environmental Politics. If there is a complaint, it is that the session is short by a few days. Between logistical and other mechanics and getting a grounding in library research, it takes time to get started. It is probably fair to say that in this course I do no teaching at all in the traditional sense. I conduct beginning and concluding seminars, and I am routinely available with more than a little knowledge and know-how gained from past classes. Of course, I read the final papers and issue grades, but this tends to be a delightful experience.

Advantages of Teaching Politics Experientially

1. Students are pleasantly surprised to find the whole of Maine's state government open, accessible, friendly and most willing to be helpful. State officials and legislators respond generously to apparent student interest, and this surprises students. Perceptions are changed all around. Self-confidence improves noticeably. This, to me, is the most important accomplishment of the course.

2. Accompanying this is an ease and sophistication in, (a) dealing with people who are now considered friendly human beings and not distant abstractions in some vaguely superior position of authority and (b) doing library research.

3. I accomplish my main goal without contributing to information overload to brains already flooded with sheer information or to a situation where students are asked to solve complex questions in five minutes that have taken scholars years to assimilate.

Drawbacks

1. Our semester system contains traditional class periods which means that students must do a sophisticated job of planning their time and finding their way to interviews. Add to that the fact that most of our students are committed to one or two science labs a week or to the requirements of our Outdoor Recreation program which is experientially oriented.

2. While some students grasp the situation quickly, many students have a great deal of trouble using the text as a reference and linking the material therein to a real life issue. I find myself explaining the requirement over and over. What

> **"Students often show befuddlement about the process. I say, "Welcome to the crowd!" They are, in fact, doing what any good political science scholar or investigative reporter does."**

I am asking is a sophisticated skill, and I am eager to get through to the group, but some students never do pick it up. As I reiterate I get more specific, sometimes getting mechanical, citing chapter and verse, leaving little to creativity. Moreover, some students are dilatory, not aware of the need for pacing and planning, and therefore get a slow start. Thus, I also have to act as cheerleader. I am sure that some students think that I am unnecessarily trying to complicate their lives.

Conclusion

In all, I am excited about my approach. It is much more difficult to impart learning using the method I have described. After all the pushing and hauling during the semester, I am invariably exhilarated by the progress students show, not only in their research results but in the personal growth I see. I am now looking forward to the fall semester when I will attempt an experiential orientation in my course in American Government.

V. Service Learning

Editorial

RECLAIMING A WASTED RESOURCE: YOUTH

by Jim Kielsmeier

A smothering sense of dread filled me not long ago as I read the summary of the report on youth unemployment for the summer of 1982 by the U.S. Conference of Mayors. I remembered living near the 14th Street corridor in Washington, D.C. in 1968 when it and other parts of the city went up in flames ignited by the spark of Martin Luther King's assassination.

As I read the staggering projections, I wondered, "What incident will trigger the bombshell of anger and frustration that will be the outgrowth of these figures?"

- Youth unemployment rates higher this summer than anytime since World War II in 125 of the nation's largest cities.
- Minority youth unemployment rates projected up to 80% in several cities, over 50% in 23 cities, and ranging between 21% and 60% in three out of four cities.
- More than 1.35 million teenagers out of work in the summer of 1982, despite vaunted private sector involvement in creating employment.
- Dramatic increases in school dropouts and in long term unemployment.
- Soaring youth crime rates.

In a society where self-worth is clearly related to employment or educational achievement, the anticipated psychological devastation to individual young people, along with economic distress, is appalling.

Shortly after I put down the article, two college student advisees came into my office, bright-eyed with confidence and excitement. They were receiving academic credit for an independent study we had engineered together with the lofty title of "Recreation for Special Populations". Emmaus Home, a church operated institution for mentally retarded women, was their internship site. More than experiential learning, commonly defined, was obviously taking place as their journals revealed.

> For one thing I've appreciated my own mental and physical capabilities a lot more and realize what a wonderful feeling it is to be able to share part of myself with them. I feel that as much as I have given to the women—they have given it back to me twofold—I've never really had the confidence in myself that I should have had, and working with these ladies has not only helped me build my confidence but has made me realize that I do have some self-worth.

The students were intent on offering service to people in need. They were wonderfully accepted at Emmaus Home and very helpful to the staff.

In return, without anticipating it, they received gifts of learning and self-esteem. They had experienced what it means to be important in the life of another person and their grade for the course would only be an insignificant post script.

Their sense of personal worth was not a product of a "warm fuzzy" or "stroke" dutifully administered by a Rogerian counselor. This was a genuine achievement related to flesh and blood needs—and the students knew it.

Several observations can be drawn from these two incidents, one so foreboding, the other so encouraging.

From the one comes the conclusion that to exclude the young from meaningful work or service is to wreak havoc upon them and society in general. From the other comes proof that the youth of our culture are great untapped reservoirs of talent and energy.

Forms of experiential learning that include service as the preeminent goal can serve a vitally important function in our society, rescuing youth from defeating isolation and placing them in situations where their energy and talent can bear fruit.

The dynamic of synergy found in service learning—when both parties benefit—is created because each party needs the other. As Lyn Baird makes clear in her article in this issue, it is a "process of mutual risk and involvement" made possible when the quality of service rendered is given as much attention as the learning goals of the experience.

Results can be powerful, as Jonathan Kozol projects in his call to arms for a youth army of literacy trainers. "The adult illiterates will discover the *word*. Their teachers will discover the *world*. Together they will repossess their shared humanity."

Unfortunately, our profession is not clearly identified with the notion of serving first and learning second—public relations materials notwithstanding. Adventure skills, hands-on experiences, and "programmed rituals in the wilderness" are important learning devices.

Free-standing, however, these methods have little to say to the unemployed masses of discontented, idle young people on our streets this summer. Not any more today than in the summers of '69 and '70 when, as Outward Bound instructors, we marched confused, alienated Newark kids in the mountains for 26 days and sent them home—half of them before they finished the courses—to a community seething with racism, illiteracy and joblessness.

Perhaps we need to focus beyond our preoccupation with dramatic or life-saving service closely identified with Kurt Hahn and Outward Bound. As Bob MacArthur suggests in his article, we should address the need for encouraging compassion through experiences of "epic service," or continuing service over the long haul.

My bias is that we balance Hahn with mentors such as Robert Greenleaf and Alec Dickson in our search for clarity of purpose and process.

A friend who had shared some of the vision and toil of the 60's recounted with me the backgrounds of the people still active in idealistic pursuits. Nearly all had been deeply involved during their transition-to-adulthood period of life in some form of experiential service activity such as the Peace Corps, National Student Volunteer Program, Vista or the Civil Rights and Anti-War Movements—or Outward Bound and Foxfire.

We, like others, concluded that formative experiential service activities are important in the journeys of people who remain committed to building better societies rather than better bombs. We also noted that there are very few "graduating seniors" from present day programs like Vista and the Peace Corps and that, under the present Administration, these numbers will continue to dwindle.

Still emerging, however, are leaders of experiential education programs who have had experiences of significant service and who are redirecting their skills from "pure" experiential education programs to the leadership of service-learning projects. They are the people who have "returned from the mountain" as Alec Dickson would say and some are writing in this issue of the *Journal*.

Service-Learning is a way of combining the methods of experiential education with the needs of society. It is serving and learning and it is a way of creating the world. Young people need real employment and real service opportunities—and communities need genuine work and service accomplished.

I am convinced that the ideas and models are there to be applied or adapted (this *Journal* is full of them). What is not there too often is creative program leadership. If ours is an information rich and experience poor society, experiential educators are the wealthy—the experience rich. We have climbed to summits of human endeavor never considered by most and have skills that not only allow us to experience the world but to act upon that experience and to lead others in acting.

We have drawn close to the human spirit and embraced it—as we have embraced our natural environments—but have too often pulled back when it has meant shaping our society.

There are three keys to effective leadership of service-learning programs: commitment, experience and creativity. Nearly all who read this are eminently qualified to offer leadership by virtue of possessing the last two criteria. Regarding the first, as the saying goes, "If not you, who? If not now, when?"

And if there is any doubt about the "when", check out what's happening with kids in your community this summer.

> ***Jim Kielsmeir*** *is director of projects for the American Youth Foundation in St. Louis. He is guest editor of this special* Journal *issue on service-learning as well as a trustee of the Association for Experiential Education.*

AN ADDRESS DELIVERED AT THE NATIONAL CONFERENCE OF THE ASSOCIATION FOR EXPERIENTIAL EDUCATION IN TORONTO, OCTOBER, 1981

Return
FROM THE MOUNTAIN

by Alec Dickson

Over thirty years ago—before the names of people like Kolb, Lawrence Kohlberg, and Piaget had entered my consciousness and possibly when even Ivan Illich and Paulo Freire were known only to their parents and family—a colleague and I sat down in a small house on the slopes of Mt. Cameroon.

We were gripped by a double sense of urgency—first about our own immediate future, because the program that we had been sent by the government of Nigeria, whose servants we were, to implement amongst the local tribe had collapsed, stillborn, and therefore at any moment an official telegram might arrive posting each of us to some remote area so that we would not see each other again.

But the second reason for a sense of urgency lay in the fact that there were only three or four years to go before Nigeria would become totally independent of British tutelage. It was about education that we talked.

It seemed to us that schooling had become the enemy of community development: that whilst the old tribalism might be crumbling here and there, a new division perhaps more far-reaching in its implications had arisen— the separation of the schooled from the illiterate.

Its consequences were many— the brain drain, the exodus of educated youngsters from the villages, the severance of the ties that had bound them to their community, the rush to Lagos, the capital, and other main cities, and the search for a job, preferably in government service. Schooling in general had become a process of systemized selfishness.

And there was, too, an emasculating effect. In the past the young men had hunted, they had farmed, they had wrestled, if necessary they had been ready to defend their village against external enemies. But now their attitude was best summed up by a French-speaking Cameroonian student who reported to me one morning with such a small cut on his finger that I had to put my glasses on to look at it, and announced, "Monsieur, je suis gravement blessé!"

We were not unique in thinking these thoughts. But our arrogance probably lay in the fact that we were determined to see what we could do about it. We talked all day, I typed all night, then rushed still clad in my pyjamas to the small post office, somehow cajoled a rather astonished African postmaster to do something absolutely contrary to the postal code, namely to cut the seal, insert my letter, seal up the bag again to catch the one mail a week that went by air from our station in the remote southeast of Nigeria back to the capital and the Secretariat where power lay.

By one of those happy accidents, it reached the desk of a very senior British official at the same moment as a coded signal from New York arrived via London, "Understand Soviet delegate tabling motion censoring United Kingdom on its trusteeship of the West Cameroons stop Please send material for a reply." Cynically the official replied that the government was on the point of implementing a program for community development leadership training.

When news reached us of the dispatch of this telegram, we said to the government, "Now you will have to give us the authority and money to implement the program."

Because my colleague had come back from his last leave fired by his experience as an auxiliary instructor at a training institution at Aberdovey in Wales inspired by a German-born genius called Kurt Hahn, and curiously named Outward Bound, an adaptation of this approach formed the basis of our program.

The geographical setting was superb—a secluded bay with primaeval forest sweeping down to the edge of cliffs. At one end of the bay was an old German lighthouse resembling a Bavarian castle and on the cliff-edge, castle and on the cliff-edge, overlooking caves and grottoes, stood an old pre-First World War German plantation manager's house. Behind this lay millions of acres of bananas, and towering up inland loomed the largest mountain in West Africa—the same height as Mt. Eiger in Switzerland—Mt. Cameroon.

Here, it seemed to us, were all

Alec Dickson, *a founder of community service programs on several continents, directs Community Service Volunteers in Britain.*

Photo, right, students practicing agility at the Man O-War Bay Training Center in Nigeria, a project started by Alec Dickson.

"The experience 'out there' must prepare students to face the situation at home."

the concomitants of adventure. One could scarcely have found a better spot.

But in the wings were waiting sceptical British colleagues, chuckling with derision at the idea that young educated Nigerians would actually respond positively—particularly those

Students at Man O-War Bay Training Center returning by native canoe.

who came from perhaps 400 or 500 miles inland and had never seen the sea, at the notion that on the very first day they would be learning to swim and in two weeks' time be scaling that mountain. Why the thing was ridiculous!

I held out, but about two weeks before the opening of our first course some of this withering scepticism of my colleagues began to erode my confidence. So I made my way to the only senior high school existing in that part of the Cameroons to try out the idea on the African students.

I described the genesis of Outward Bound and the adventure training at Aberdovey and how manliness and stamina and endurance and courage were linked with service to the community. I went on to say how a rocket would be fired if there were a ship in distress, how a lifeboat would be launched and, donning oilskins and sou'westers, the students would go out to rescue its crew. With a rhetorical flourish, borrowing from Winston Churchill, I added, "Into the storm and through the storm."

Then I sat down and awaited the first question. "Please, sir, are students allowed to keep their waterproof clothing at the end of the course?" I realized then that some of the attitudes that we would be confronted with would be different from those at Aberdovey and other Outward Bound centers in Britain.

Because time was against us— we had, metaphorically, our eyes on the clock, with only three or four years to go before Independence—and because I was not convinced that within 26 calendar days one could alter human nature, we decided to take those in whom it seemed, in the eyes of others, that there was already some spark of leadership. They might be in the employment of the government, in the employment of missions, in private companies, they might be young teachers, young principals even, or forest guards, or in the railway administration.

But they would be those who were being watched for potential promotion—and all that we claimed to do was to create a sense of awareness. To create a sense of awareness that they had a greater potential in them to overcome difficulties and to contend with problems than they thought they had. That they had the capacity to understand the real nature of the problems of Nigeria. Above all, that they had a duty even, to do their best to do something about those problems.

And there was something else, which was indigenous and which was accepted by the government of Nigeria—that was the meaning and value of community development. The notion that young people owed something to their community—this was deeply implanted. It was precisely this that was endangered by the educational system which we had introduced and which was welcome enough to many young students.

How could we now show them that, shedding their shirts, setting an example with pickaxe and shovel, or taking a lead in a literacy campaign or a health campaign did not mean loss of dignity? This was true leadership.

After they had overcome the shock of discovering that they were going to learn to swim, that they were going to climb Mt. Cameroon, we transported them 200 or more miles to some part of Nigeria where they would be plunged into service with a rural community, because that was what the government felt Nigeria needed.

And, frankly, it corresponded with my own feeling about what was needed—leadership in community development.

But that did not prevent us from having fun; from exposing them to intellectual challenges every evening in discussion, in debate on what the real problems were facing their country. Also, on the last night we would ask every student to stand up and commit himself to what he would do on his return. And that is why I have called my talk today "The Return from the Mountain." Not personal survival on the peaks—but revival of the community on return.

On what we thought would be the penultimate course, we agreed to a request from the government that this particular course should not be for young adult men, but we would take the cream of the high school students—and certainly it was the cream that came to us from all over a vast country, a country of 80 million.

I remember the evening when we told them that they would not be sleeping in the old plantation manager's house, they would be bivouacking a mile or so from the house on the edge of the cliff. Dusk falls rapidly in the tropics; as the sun went down one could hear them cutting timber—but that did not matter because there were trees in profusion.

At this point I drew from my pocket a letter from the Director of Customs and Excise in the capital, Lagos, and read it out. It said that they had the whole coast of Nigeria to patrol and they could not be everywhere. It stressed that the area where we were was very exposed to smuggling. Out at sea canoes from Fernando Po smuggled in brandies and wine. Only two or three miles to our west, from the French Cameroons, in came scent and out went motor tyres and tobacco from Nigeria and the British Cameroons.

Could we, if we were doing any night operations, keep an eye open for the smugglers who were normally just local fishermen increasing their income by a little silent canoe work? So I read it out and added, "If you do hear a canoe come in quietly, be on watch on behalf of the government of Nigeria, apprehend the malefactors (they spoke good English, no need for me to simplify what I was saying), but don't use your cutlasses," because each student was equipped with what in some countries might be called a machete and this was what they were using to cut the wood for their bivouacs that night.

"Don't attack them because one doesn't want a death and then a court case with the possibility of your facing all sorts of manslaughter charges."

"We've got the message," they said, and then night fell.

I retreated in the darkness, hurried back to my quarters, my wife was waiting for me with cooking pots, I grated my fingers underneath, smeared black all over my face and arms, put a handkerchief over my head and then, with two or three African staff members, we went down to the jetty, got out our canoe, filled it with a petrol can full of stones, and took a torch because, unlike real professional smugglers, it was essential that we make the students aware of our arrival.

So as we came quietly under the cliff edge we rattled the stones, we shone the torch every few seconds and eventually we heard excited talking. Obviously they were alert. A few minutes later we beached the canoe, crept out, and then there was a gigantic shout and from behind stones and boulders students fell upon us.

I was brought to the ground with what we in Britain call a first-class rugby tackle by an extremely saucy and impertinent 17-year old who shouted in my ear as he clutched my arms and feet, "You wicked man—defrauding the government of Nigeria!" I was dragged up the cliff-edge, hurricane lamps and Coleman lamps were brought; by then some of the black was beginning to wear off my face.

"Oh! Oh! It's the Principal!"

Well, we all fell over ourselves with laughing and it was a good exercise and nobody had been hurt. Their preparedness to do

"Whilst the old tribalism might be crumbling, a new division had arisen between schooled and illiterate."

battle on behalf of the government showed just that brand of patriotism that would make a good independent Nigeria.

The laughter was short-lived. Three days later a group of students returned from ascending Mt. Cameroon, 13,300 feet high, appalled, because in a sudden upswirl of cloud, two of the students had been lost. Despite the fact that that very day the Prime Minister of Western Nigeria was due to pay a ceremonial visit, instantly we mobilized every member of the staff—black and white—and set out to climb the mountain.

But now we were faced with a tropical thunderstorm, lightning, bitterly cold rain, and darkness terrifying even to us adults. Our own lives were in danger. Despite the police being alerted, native hunters searching, the days went by, and telegrams between the government and our training center flowed in each direction.

I did the only thing possible and submitted my resignation to the government of Nigeria. As day followed day and a week went by, the search was abandoned and so was hope.

Then on the evening of the seventh day, when I had gone down to the jetty to pull up the canoes, suddenly my wife came rushing down the path. A radio message had been picked up. At the remotest of all plantations on the far side of the mountain, two boys had been found.

They had stumbled into the camp having survived seven days on a diet of grass and prayer, on courage and companionship. Each came from a town background and had gone through a daunting and terrible experience. They had triumphantly vindicated the training they had had by never losing self-confidence, by their implementing every tenet of the philosophy of the center, every technique that the course had tried to impart, all that one might have hoped.

But that was the end of a chapter in my life. I did not withdraw my resignation and I returned to Britain, to be faced with unemployment for myself and a great many other things besides.

A quarter of a century, quite a long time, passed and then a letter arrived one day on very impressive government notepaper from Col. Dr. A. Ali, Federal Commissioner of Education, Nigeria. To be in charge of education at all levels in a country with a population of 80 million, this means something. A real doctor, a fellow of the Royal College of Physicians, his previous assignment had been to introduce, despite a good deal of student opposition, a program of national social service by every university graduate from every university in Nigeria.

Would I come back to Nigeria, review the original program which still bore, at any rate as its telegraphic address, the extraordinarily romantic title which we had discovered as belonging to this particular locality, 'Man O' War Bay.'

Well, how could one refuse such an invitation? And, most particularily, in the knowledge that Col. Dr. Ahmadu Ali had been the 17-year old who brought me down with the rugby tackle a quarter of a century before in the smuggling simulation exercise.

The program had experienced the geographical dismemberment of its original base as that part of the country had been ceded by a referendum to the Republic of the Cameroon, had experienced the ferocity of the Biafran Civil War, the assassination of three Heads of State. Yes, they had gone through most things which our friends in the United States had gone through, but telescoped into about fifteen years.

And still, the program had survived. Indeed, it had greatly expanded. Now there was a sea school close to the capital, a mountain school in the hills of northern Nigeria and a traveling team which conducted courses in different parts of the territory.

To survive was something—but it seemed, moreover, to have flourished. Many governors of provinces, one or two generals, police commissioners, secretaries of state, numerous top level civil servants were alumni of the Man O' War Training Center.

And yet, and yet. . . . Virtually nothing of the message or its meaning had been absorbed into the general educational system of Nigeria. Still less into the teaching or ethos of the universities which had proliferated from one to nearly fifteen during the intervening years.

The adventure component, it seemed to me, had swollen to absorb practically the entirety of the training. And the provision of some experience of community development or community service, had woefully shrunken.

Even the physical challenge had become almost indelibly bound up with an obstacle course composed of ropes etc. which an intelligent and indubitably well-meaning Peace Corps Volunteer had set up some twelve years previously. Yet now it operated as an obstruction to more innovative approaches and more imaginative thinking on the part of the staff.

True, the idea of solo expeditions had been introduced. But this seemed to me, at least, to promote an attitude which should not necessarily have been emphasized: that individual stamina and personal initiative might be more important than cooperation between Muslim and Christian and a sense of their mutual dependency, in times of trouble, upon one another.

Students still certainly valued the experience, but they hugged it tightly to themselves. The characteristic was now self-discovery, benefitting oneself from the experience—not passing it on to others.

My wife and I watched, one afternoon on the beach near Lagos, two ex-students working as beach lifeguards, and as one vigilantly watched in case any bather got into difficulties, the other rested. We thought how sad that neither saw their role as teaching swimming, better still, life-saving to some of the hundreds of kids from the city disporting themselves in the water.

Somehow the course had remained a treasured personal experience; not a stimulus to communicate their skills, the vision that they had themselves received, to others.

During this visit I went around and saw State Governors, the Heads of Defense Forces, and it seemed exciting when the Chief of Staff of the Nigerian Air Force said that he would warmly welcome courses in survival training for pilots who, through engine trouble, made forced landings in wilderness areas.

This seemed to offer exciting possibilities to the program. How to secure water, how to avoid heat exhaustion, how to get direction from the stars, how to send up smoke signals, how to carry out self-medication or trap small animals. Exciting possibilities. . . .

But to no one did the thought occur that help might be looked for from local nomads or remote pastoralists. Still less that the willingness of these scattered peasant communities to help members of the Defense Forces in trouble might be contingent on the Defense Forces themselves giving assistance to remote peasant communities, who,

"**They had survived seven days on a diet of grass and prayer.**"

of all Nigeria's citizens, receive fewest benefits from the government.

The traveling team seemed to be a tremendous idea. Yet how much greater still it would have been if it had taken advantage of local needs, if it had positively exploited current situations of crisis.

For example, a course in the Sahara area, to bring home to young and not-so-young government officials how great was the need for special measures to offset the effects of drought and the encroaching desert, plus practical participation alongside the peasants in well-digging. A course beside Lake Chad itself for junior and perhaps senior Army personnel, from the Engineers, the Medical Corps, and the Education Corps, to concentrate on the problems caused by the receding waters of the lake, stranding the population of nearly half a million who were totally dependent upon this inland sea for their livelihood.

A course to be located amongst plantation workers of Nigerian origin, recently expelled after abominable mistreatment from Equatorial Guinea, on how to integrate refugees even of one's own nationality on their return from a long period in another country.

A course for police cadets to discover how, if they were to be functionally efficient, they would require to win the respect and cooperation of the local people and this respect and cooperation could only be earned by their attitude and assistance to the local community.

Nearly all the courses operated on the assumption that Nigeria was still predominantly a rural country, whereas in fact it now depended upon an oil economy with sprawling great cities and towns.

What might be the urban challenges for the sea school, situated only thirty minutes away from the center of the capital of Nigeria? What were the urgent problems they might be tackling?

Well, if they could get the Captain's permission, they could board a ship in the harbor (at one time 200 ships lay at anchor waiting to discharge their cargo of cement). They could discuss with the crew what they thought about Nigeria. They could go to the Port Authority and hear about congestion in the unloading of ships. They could spend a night or two with the Marine Police or Port Security guards

Can service be a substitute for the work ethic in a time of massive youth unemployment?

and learn how they went about their task of preventing pilfering of cargoes.

They could acquire, perhaps, some equivalent of the brigantine at Harbor Front in Toronto and enable their students to play a leadership role in giving kids from Lagos a taste of real seamanship, with visits along the coast to neighboring countries such as Togo and Ghana.

They could canoe across the short expanse of water to the grim federal prison, Kirikori, and conduct the service on Sundays amongst prisoners, some of them condemned to death, and visit others. Coming ashore, they might undertake a survey of adult beggars and destitute children, importuning customers outside the big departmental stores, and then make recommendations to the relevant authorities.

They might offer to organise a campaign on behalf of the medical officer of health against rats, blocked drains, involving an examination of the situation and persuasion of the local population, many recently arrived from rural areas where habits that seem natural in remote villages are singularly unsanitary in highly populated areas.

And now, perhaps one might think I have turned hostile to the concept of adventure training. Not in the least. I remain convinced that exposure to a totally new experience, the shock of being confronted by conditions you've never faced before —this is infinitely valuable.

Indeed, in the United Kingdom it is doubtful whether reconciliation is possible in Northern Ireland until or unless we can translate physically, for a period of time, mixed groups of young people, as Katimavik does in Canada, to other geographical areas where they learn cooperation rather than confrontation. It makes for a better life for all.

But never forget that what matters is the return from the mountain to the communities whence they came, and the fact that the experience "out there" must prepare them to face the situation back at home.

If we could wrench as many as possible of our British-born young people of West Indian parentage from Brixton and plunge them into a totally new setting for a brief while, how vital could be the consequences! But where to? Candidly, I'd like to see them not only in the Black Hills of North Dakota but also in Baltimore, where elderly Jewish residents are more likely to call on the predominantly black students of the Northwestern High School for help or a friendly chat than to rail against them as threats to person and property.

That is, since the students and staff of this remarkable high school set up their Community and School Together project. In a recent issue of *Synergist* there is an excellent account of this program.

Or to the South Bronx High School where in a desolate, slum wilderness of New York, a frontier spirit is moving students into new experiences of learning, serving and leading in their own urban environment. Sister Maryann Hedaa, in an article which the National Center for Service Learning in Washington will soon publish, describes marvelously how urban adventures can be devised that not only increase academic skills but promote a concern for the needs of others and the readiness to serve the entire community. Seventy percent of the students are Hispanic and the rest are black.

In my present work in Britain we have, at the request of chief constables, plunged many hundreds of police cadets into situations of need which have indubitably made them more sensitive in human relations. In one of Kurt Hahn's memorable phrases, we should "aim to make the brave gentle, and the gentle brave."

Two of those cadets, because things did not go according to plan, stand out in my memory. Aged 18, each was six foot tall, each played rugby football, each had undergone adventure training, each had the Duke of Edinburgh's Award. One had been hand-picked by his seniors for this special assignment, the other of his own accord wanted above all to have this particular form of experience. An interval of five years separated their involvement. I myself briefed the first one, negotiated and set up the project and additionally established lines of support, and suggested varied emergency support measures. In the light of what happened with him, I took even greater care with the second.

You are curious, of course, to know what the assignment was. It was to become a homeless youth in a strange city for a month, and then to report subsequently to the authorities on what might be done to help such young people. Well, the effect was explosive and very nearly disastrous. Despite outstanding physique, police training and the additional experience of outdoor adventure, each in fact was terrified. The first sustained almost a nervous breakdown within 48 hours and the second, in a voice that broke with fear on the

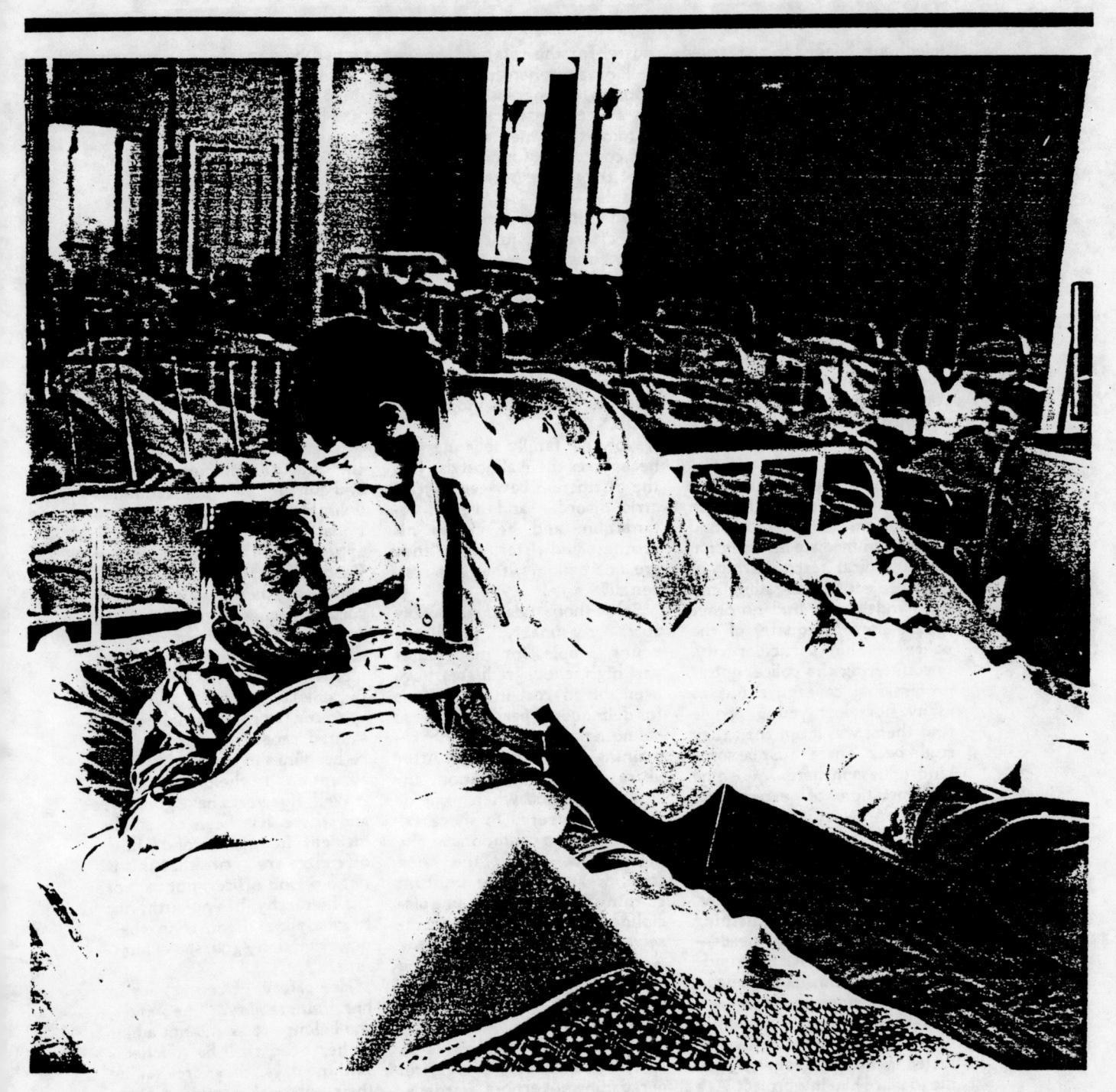

A Community Service volunteer, Keith Drake, working at Powick Hospital, Worcester, England.

"After the disadvantaged, who could we reach? What about bureaucrats?"

telephone, begged to be rescued after a night and a day on the project.

Now I would readily concede that to be alone, quite alone, at night in a great city—London in the first instance, Birmingham the second—cities strange to each of them, could of course be frightening. So how *do* you prepare young men to cope with a challenge of this kind? The classic measures to promote machismo had all been included in their training.

Perhaps we need to look very closely at the extent to which courage developed in one set of circumstances can be successfully transferred to another context.

There was one common factor in the experience of both which drove them to surrender and required immediate intervention and a radical restructuring of their project. It was falling into the hands (I can find no other phrase more adequate) of the police of that particular city. Encountering the police, not as professional colleagues but as many homeless young people find them, was more than they could bear. There must be some kind of lesson here . . . some manifestation of experiential education. What it is, I leave to you.

To bring about discovery at first hand of the problems of society, of one's own character, one's capacity to do something practical about human needs—well, one doesn't have to go quite so close to the brink of danger.

This last summer my sixteen-year-old godson, quiet, studious, bespectacled, from a highly protected middle-class family, asked me to place him in a project. As a train took him northwards to the midlands of Britain and to a hostel for the retarded, he was full of apprehensions. Natural enough, for there is within all of us a deep, instinctive fear regarding those mentally afflicted. Of course he found on arrival that they were both loving and lovable.

On coming out of the hostel one afternoon, just as schools were finishing for the day, he encountered a group of local boys who, pointing at him, shouted, "Loonie, Loonie!" His cheeks went scarlet with humiliation and indignation. To be taunted as a lunatic? Certainly this was for him his moment of truth.

Now his family tells me that he lectures them almost daily on the distinction between psychiatric disorder and mental retardation, and he chides his brothers and sisters . . . "they are not patients, they are residents!"

Some thousands of reasonably able, reasonably intelligent young people, for the greater part high school graduates, have been able to work in institutions for delinquents perhaps because delinquency is Britain's only remaining growth industry! After years of experimentation, including a period when some of them volunteered to share exactly the same conditions as the delinquents—to eat the same food, wear the same uniform clothing, submit to the same discipline as the inmates themselves, a secular variant of the worker priest, a task demanding some courage—we now see more clearly what their most effective roles can be.

One role quite simply is to spread the concept of service, persuading governors, wardens, superintendents, directors, principals of such institutions to trust them to take out a group of delinquents, involve them in help to the local community and see to it that they all return the same evening.

Here it is a proselytizing function, communicating the excitement and satisfaction of service to others. It isn't necessarily an easy task to win over support from the long-established staff in correctional institutons—still less the staff of other kinds of institutions whom you are asking to accept service from young people of this background, when their mentor may be only a few months or a year or so older than the average in the group.

The second discovery has been the value of switching the sexes and putting full-time feminine volunteers in all-male correctional institutions. A tremor of apprehension went through the Prison Department in London when they heard we'd received such a request from the governor of one of the maximum security correctional establishments (known in Britain as Borstals).

Young women would be assaulted, raped even; there would be headlines in the press and an abrupt end to the program.

Well, five years have gone by, and there has been no single incident. In a split second young offenders are aware that this is not a prison officer, not part of the hierarchy, has no authority to discipline them, is in their power, and my god, she is feminine.

Her safety, of course, lies in her vulnerability. "She's ours, she belongs to *us* and not a hair of her head shall be touched!" Within days they are taking their **personal**, profound problems to her, problems that they wouldn't dream of discussing with any male member of the prison staff.

Eventually the scales dropped from our eyes and from the eyes of others in authority—couldn't this process be reversed and some young offenders be released while still serving their sentence, to experience what it means to be wanted by others? So today, some 200 young offenders, ranging in age from 17-21, are brought to our office under escort.

Whatever their offence, be it robbery or grievous bodily harm, by the time they reach our office they are beginning to have second thoughts. They are distinctly apprehensive. Will they find themselves faced by three-headed monsters in a locked ward of a mental hospital?

But the retarded young people they encounter want, on the contrary, to hug and be hugged. When they reach out their arms to touch the young offender and clasp him in a mutual embrace it is as though they have taken him prisoner. Placing them with the physically disabled, a spastic kid, a young paraplegic, someone suffering from cerebral palsy —the young offender's immediate reaction is "Poor little devil, poor little beggar", ('beggar' isn't the actual word they use, but one very similar), he'll never walk, will he? He's a prisoner for life, isn't he? What have I to complain about? Why, I'll be free in four months time."

And that is the beginning of wisdom—the discovery that there are others worse off than oneself, that the chip on your shoulder and the feeling that you have been hard done by in life is minimal compared to what these kids have to put up with. Already, within a week, one is dealing with a different being.

After reaching out for the disadvantaged, we asked ourselves what further category might we seek to involve? The blind we had taken, and Borstal boys—say, what about bureaucrats?

Now, after months of negotiation with central government departments, we have begun to take young civil servants, especially released for a six months 'sabbatical', to come out from behind their desks and encounter problems not on paper but as people.

"My mind is moving in the opposite direction from Hahn's."

The first, a highly intelligent young woman in her late 20's, came from the Home Office (after the Treasury, that is the queen of ministries in Britain). We plunged her into a refuge for battered wives (actually that is quite a different atmosphere than is normally prevalent in the Home Office).

Well, one can always get a laugh by describing her very first action which was, in fact, to put the agency's files in order. You might say, well, one would expect that of a bureaucrat. But in fact it was a very sensible thing to do. The agency drew grants from local government and central government, and one day they might be asked to show their financial sheets and how they had accounted for the grants they had received. So it wasn't quite the stereotype that one might take it for.

But in the following six months, she succeeded in mobilizing local help for the refuge, obtaining free toys for the kids who come with the battered women, free furniture from a furniture factory, and two small buses donated by Rotary and Chambers of Commerce.

Looking through the window one day she saw an elementary school scheduled for closing because of the falling school rolls. How could she secure the transfer of this property belonging to a Board of Education to her voluntary agency? That would mean all sorts of hassles with the local authorities. But wait . . . what about that student who had had a crush on her at college ten years ago . . . hadn't it been architecture he had been studying? Where could he now be? A telephone call to the Registrar of Durham University —he was working in a planning office in London. Contact was reestablished, and in three weeks planning permission had been secured for transfer of the school to the refuge to accommodate their frequently unruly children.

"What did you get out of this?" I asked this obviously up-and-coming young civil servant when the six months ended. "I've learned to ask people for their help," she said. "At the Home Office I recorded minutes of ministerial meetings, drafted replies to parliamentary questions, approved grants and occasionally not approved others, helped prepare future bills for legislation, all of which entailed discussion with colleagues. But I never had to go out to total strangers and say, 'For God's sake, help me!'"

"Never forget that what matters is the return from the mountain."

I thought, on balance, that what she had learned was a fair exchange for what she had given. She went back to her ministry enriched by quite new insights that could only be gained by this kind of experience. And now, hopefully, we'll get many more.

And so to the title that I had orginally suggested for this session.

"What are the criteria for experiential education?" I asked one advocate.

"Well," he replied, "it would be an experience which enables students to gain new psychological insights, acquire knowledge of administrative techniques that they normally wouldn't have come by, polish up a foreign language or two and, oh yes, to be financially independent of their parents."

Working in a brothel in Bremen you'd certainly polish up your foreign languages, indubitably gain new psychological insights, almost certainly acquire management techniques and you might even earn more than your dad.

Is this what experiential education is about? Surely there is one acid test that has been overlooked. Has any other human being in the neighborhood, the nation, or the whole wide world benefitted from the way this student chose to spend that time at his or her disposal? If some experiences ennoble an individual, others can corrupt him. That is why I would like to see an ovelap between experiential education and service learning, the adventure culminating in service, the service itself an adventure into unknown territory.

I want to pose a much, much tougher issue during this conference. How do we, in fact, infect the educational system as a whole with our philosophy? Universities no less than schools.

Historically what has happened is very interesting. When I got to know Kurt Hahn at Gordonston School, he was feeling that the whole process (he

A Community Service volunteer with a mongoloid child in her arms at a mental hospital in the northwestern section of England.

had initiated) was too expensive both in time and money. It was five years from the age of 13 to 18 in a boarding school and to send a son to a boarding school for five years cost a hell of a lot of money then, and it would cost still more today.

So these five years meant by definition that this costly and long experience was confined to a few sons of the rich. Could the essence of this be distilled into a shorter period and made available to many more thousands? (The phrase "character training" was used then. I think there might be some self-consciousness in academic circles today if one were to use this phrase. Now one speaks of the development of the whole person, a rounded personality, awareness of values.)

So Hahn went from the school setting to discover, together with Lawrence Holt, how this experience could be imparted in highly concentrated form in a month, available for young people irrespective of their fathers' incomes.

My mind is moving in the opposite direction. How can we get the essence of this experience reinjected back into the ordinary educational system so it is shared by hundreds of thousands of young people?

Most of us think it possible— at least I do—to balance courage with concern. But there are other questions. How do we reconcile competitiveness (best grades, best marks, best colleges which count for so much in our society) with compassion?

How do we balance intellectual challenge with the development of character? How do we convert educational institutions into resource centers of help to the community.?

Last of all—what does this mean in the face of the massive unemployment that now engulfs tens of thousands of our school-leavers in Britain (and America)? What kind of experiential education can help them to cope with the discovery that apparently nobody wants them?

Can service in any way be a substitute for the work ethic which we have valued so highly up until now?

Fanning the Flame

by Lyn Baird

At the heart of the concept of service-learning is the belief that human beings long to establish truly mutual relationships. John, a student, wanting to participate, wanting to make a difference in the lives of others, offers himself as an extra pair of hands and an extra ounce of energy. He hopes not to change people, but to enlarge their possibilities.

To do this he must seek to understand them and their aspirations. He must participate in their lives, even to the point of risk and sacrifice. Perhaps the greatest risk he takes is the risk of changing himself. Those with whom he has volunteered to work also give, share, risk, and sacrifice—on *his* behalf. He needs them as much as they need him.

Through this process of mutual risk and involvement, the realization that we need each other hits home. Seemingly opposite concepts—giving and getting, acting and reflecting, serving and learning—begin to merge.

For this special issue of the *AEE Journal*, I was given the charge of describing the concept that gives the National Center for Service-Learning its purpose, and outlining some of the resources available to people interested in pursuing the concept further.

In 1969, five years after the President and Congress de-

Lyn Baird *is director of the National Center for Service-Learning in Washington, D.C. Prior to assuming this position in 1978, she served for seven years as deputy director.*

clared the war on poverty, the Office of Economic Opportunity launched the National Student Volunteer Program (NSVP). Its purpose was to link the needs of the poor to the resources of our educational system and the growing demands of students and educators for an active role in the struggle for racial and economic equality. The basic goals remained the same when, in 1971, NSVP became part of ACTION, the federal umbrella agency for volunteer programs. The National Student Volunteer Program was re-named the National Center for Service-Learning in 1979.

The new name, with its emphasis on service *and* learning, drew attention to our interest in the potential of volunteer programs not only for bettering the lot of the poor, but for fostering growth and development in those who provide service.

When NSVP was established 13 years ago, service-learning was a new idea. Initially, we were able to identify about 100 colleges that had some organized student volunteer effort. Today the Center is in contact with 20,000 secondary and post-secondary educators and community workers who endorse service-learning.

In responding to the rapid growth of voluntary action and experiential learning programs in the nation's schools and universities in the 1970's, our role was not so much to ignite the fire as to fan the spark. Clearly, the growth that has taken place is a tribute to the strength of the idea and the commitment and creativity of those who work with and believe in the programs of service-learning.

Service-learning achieves its full value only if it leads to an enduring lifestyle of continued personal development and concern for others. A one-shot inoculation of service will not provide lasting immunization against the social malady of self-interest. The impulse to serve needs to be nurtured over time.

By building opportunities for service into all levels of education, community service programs provide for vital growth. Twenty-two-year-olds tackle more challenging projects than they did at 16, and 16-year-olds undertake more demanding tasks than they did at 11.

An integral part of building an effective service-learning program is structuring a means of accountability and evaluation. Unguided experience does not teach. Students need a structured opportunity to assess their own progress, just as the persons receiving service need a voice in what service goals should be, and whether those goals are being met. With well structured goals and agreements between parties, programs can create an atmosphere of seriousness and productivity.

We are not advocating programs in which students perform menial or ordinary tasks while peering over the shoulders of those who are involved in actual service. Nor are we referring to programs whose sole purpose is to provide students with a learning experience. These would make the service activity a surrogate for the classroom and would encourage students to treat people as objects to be used, experimented

171

upon, and profited from. They would yield little real benefit to the poor.

Only reality can prepare students to cope sensitively and compassionately with the real world. The nature and quality of the service needs as much attention as the learning goals that we seek. Students and communities must work together to understand what is both common and different in their objectives, so that all can achieve the maximum benefit from the relationship, and so that none is exploited or given short shrift.

Serving-learning as a supplement to traditional classroom courses is of tremendous value in developing insight, skill, and commitment. It enlivens and enriches intellectual development with challenges and lessons from real life that can be powerful and convincing.

As educators have demonstrated repeatedly, service-learning knows no peer as an antidote to the closed environment that results when students of similar backgrounds are cloistered together.

From community service, students develop the social skills necessary to be effective in working with others. They practice decision-making and problem-solving skills, and perhaps most importantly, learn how to learn from experience—a skill that will serve them throughout their lives.

Finally, service-learning experiences contribute to personal growth. Confronted with values that often differ from their own, students come to a deeper understanding of themselves and their role in society. They learn about the needs and abilities of others as they become aware of their own worth. They gain in confidence, courage, and self-reliance.

It is the innate efficiency of service-learning that has attracted educators and program directors over the years. With careful planning, educators can assure that improvement in the quality of either the service or the educational attainment will signal improvement in the other. Tremendous amounts of constructive energy can be unleashed on behalf of those who need it most, and all are enriched.

Over the last decade, several other factors have contributed to the growth of service-learning. One is a new concern with career preparation. Another is the frequent failure of traditional methods of preparing young people for the transition from school to work and from dependent adolescence to responsible adulthood.

Still another factor is the dawning recognition of how

Resources of the National Center for Service-Learning

Seminars:

Training seminars, which are offered about eight times a year in different areas around the country, give managers of service-learning programs in public, private, and parochial high schools, and in two and four year colleges, an opportunity to come together with others like themselves to exchange ideas, resources, and program models.

Advanced seminars are offered as well. These seminars generally focus on one major issue (such as program evaluation) of interest to experienced program managers.

All of the seminars are tuition free. The only costs to participants are for transportation and living.

Consulting:

The Center maintains a pool of consultants that includes educators and community agency personnel with extensive experience in service-learning programs. These consultants are prepared to help schools launch new programs, or evaluate and strengthen existing efforts.

Publications:

The National Center develops and distributes, free of charge, publications on various aspects of service-learning programs. Some manuals are aimed at specialized audiences (high school officials or community agency staff) while others describe administrative subjects, such as how to plan or evaluate a program. The Center also assembles packages of information on particular service-learning issues such as fundraising and legal concerns.

Three times a year the Center publishes *Synergist*, a 56-page technical assistance journal for educators who work with programs that integrate course work and community service. *Synergist* aims to demonstrate how service-learning in general, and local programs in particular, improve the quality of life for the least privileged members of society, and the quality of learning for all students.

To obtain more information on NCSL's services, call 254-8370 in the Washington, D.C. area, or call toll free 800-424-8580, extension 89, or write the National Center for Service-Learning, ACTION, 806 Connecticut Ave., N.W., Room 1106, Washington, DC 20525.

much students can contribute in an era when needs are increasing faster than the supply of either funds or adult volunteers.

The spread of the concept of service-learning has been very encouraging. To document this decade of growth, the Center conducted a national survey in 1979. Whereas ten years ago the idea of connecting community service to high school courses was relatively unknown, the survey revealed three years ago that 14 percent of all high schools—public and private— had curriculum-related community service programs. Nearly two thirds of these programs award academic credit for the learning that students gain from their service experiences.

In a typical high school program, 119 students put in five hours of community service and three hours of related classwork each week, although variation in these characteristics is extensive.

Recognition of the utility of service-learning at other developmental levels is increasing. More elementary and junior high schools are arranging service projects for younger students; more post-secondary institutions are relating service-learning to the needs of non-traditional, older learners who are returning to or beginning college with considerable life experience under their belts.

Part of what we are seeing is a growing awareness that the value of serving others is relevant for people of all ages. Balancing growth of the self with concern for others *can* become a habit.

It we assume that education should prepare students not only to earn a living but to find satisfaction in other aspects of their lives, service-learning helps them see the lasting importance of service to society.

The lives they carve out will be more likely to include service to others. And the service they perform will be carried out with more skill, greater awareness, and a deeper compassion.

Other Resource Organizations

Council for the Advancement of Experiential Learning
Lakefront North, Suite 300
Columbia, MD 21044
(301) 997-3535

CAEL is a privately funded educational association formed to foster post-secondary experiential learning and to evaluate its effects. The organization provides consultation, training, and on-campus workshops.

National Commission on Resources for Youth, Inc.
36 West 44th Street
New York, NY 10036
(212) 840-2844

Since 1967 NCRY has served as a national source of information on youth participation programs. NCRY seeks out creative local programs and shares their insights and experiences (through publications, films, workshops, technical assistance, and a quarterly newsletter).

National Society for Internship and Experiential Education
1735 I Street, N.W., Suite 601
Washington, D.C. 20006
(202) 331-1516
(800) 424-2933

Founded in 1971, NSIEE is a non-profit membership organization. Its services include a newsletter, annual conference, peer assistance network, professional liability insurance, regional workshops, internship directories, and other publications.

The National Youth Work Alliance
1346 Connecticut Avenue, N.W., Suite 502
Washington, DC 20036
(202) 785-0764

NYWA is a non-profit organization concerned with the development of social services for youth, particularly those that involve youth participation in the delivery of services. The organization offers numerous technical assistance publications, a newsletter, and an information clearinghouse service.

VOLUNTEER: National Center for Citizen Involvement
1211 N. 19th Street, Suite 500
Arlington, VA 22209
(703) 276-0542

Created in 1970 to stimulate and strengthen volunteerism, VOLUNTEER offers support services to a growing network of more than 300 local voluntary action centers. These centers often are valuable resources in finding placements for students. VOLUNTEER also publishes a journal, information portfolios, reference lists, and case studies.

THREE Examples OF SERVICE LEARNING

THE CHANGING ROLE OF SERVICE IN OUTWARD BOUND

by Robert S. MacArthur

In the summer of 1975 in Jackson, New Hampshire, Cindy Shannon and her sister jumped into a river to retrieve the unconscious body of a fellow swimmer who had hit his head on a submerged rock. They pulled him to the surface and administered artificial ventilation, keeping him alive until the local rescue squad arrived to take him to the hospital. Both women had been trained in Senior Life Saving, but Cindy's additional training earlier that summer at Dartmouth had provided a valuable preparation for the rescue. As the newspaper reported, "Ironically, she was recently telling her family about a swimming rescue dramatization she took part in, in the Outward Bound Program, and of how 'realistic' it seemed at the time."

The life saving drama of rescue lies at the heart of Kurt Hahn's philosophy of service, and preparation for that moment of need has been central to Outward Bound training since the program began.

Today, however, the opportunities for rescue are remote. The proliferation of para-professional rescue units and the length, location, and structure of the Outward Bound course itself have meant that Outward Bound groups may not be called upon or may not be available when emergencies do arise. As a result, the centrality of service in Outward Bound has retreated with the lack of compelling applications.

Clearly, Outward Bound must redirect and rededicate itself to the concept of service, a review which must begin with an institutional commitment. Two sources may provide impetus and nurture for this redirection—a closer look at Hahn's philos-

---

Robert S. MacArthur *is director of the Outward Bound Center at Dartmouth College in Hanover, New Hampshire.*

ophy of service and the models provided by various service-learning programs outside of Outward Bound.

For the purposes of this article we shall look at the Outward Bound Living/Learning Term and the William Jewett Tucker Foundation at Dartmouth College as examples which highlight the major issues involved.

Dramatic Service

Self-denial in a life saving adventure epitomized for Kurt Hahn the essence of service. It was the highest form of duty to one's community and country. The drama of rescue, linked to the youthful passion for adventure, also provided a compelling curriculum for an educational equivalent of war. As Geoffrey Winthrop Young expressed on the occasion of the christening of the training ship Garibaldi at Aberdovey in 1943,

> Twice in a lifetime we have seen war produce in quite ordinary men and women heroic qualities of courage, endurance, and self-sacrifice and make permanently better citizens of those whom it did not destroy. And twice we, who have been concerned with education, have had to recognize that our ordinary systems of education had failed to educe those chivalrous qualities, in any considerable degree, in peace time. (1)

Twenty years later William Sloane Coffin, visiting Outward Bound in Great Britain to gather information for the Peace Corps, queried Hahn about the primacy of adventure in his training.

> Knowing that Outward Bound tried to link compassion with adventure by training people for rescue operations primarily on the sea and

in the mountains, I wanted to know if he felt this kind of experience could readily be translated, say, into the slums; could it be relived in the humdrum of every day life. "Aren't you afraid of the lure of the dramatic?" I asked. "Not at all," he answered. We can make the glamour of war fade only by introducing drama into the life of the nation at peace. The young hunger for adventure. They long to be tested, to prove their reserves. This longing can be driven underground, but there it will remain in unconscious readiness for a false prophet who will turn the scale in favor of violence. (2)

Hahn's recognition of youth's hunger for adventure and his ability to mobilize that passion are often cited among his foremost contributions to education. A good example comes from the public school he founded at Gordonstoun and the formation of the Gordonstoun Watchers. After an initial attempt to motivate his students to service as lookouts on the rocky coast, he invited

> "Outward Bound must redirect itself to the concept of service."

two Captains of the Coastguards to visit the School. In full regalia they told the boys they were needed to assist in manning a rescue station.

The response was positive and the Watchers were constituted to sit at their post, "looking into the darkness in patient readiness lest a stranded vessel should burn an inefficient flare." Fire service and mountain rescue were added later, and each boy was required to join one of the three and undergo the requisite training. (3)

Hahn has been criticized for his pessimistic persuasion that many, if not most, of the passions of youth are poisonous. Hence, adventure becomes a means of keeping these passions at bay, like cold showers after the morning run. As Robert Skidelsky notes, one impetus for the rescue service at Gordonstoun was the challenge to keep a community of adolescent males spiritually healthy, to overcome the deformities of puberty." (4) Hahn never defines the term, but we can understand it to mean the sexual drives and preoccupation with self which are characteristic of the age.

While this attitude seems somewhat archaic to middle class minds today, it has been a central tenet behind Outward Bound's effectiveness in work with adjudicated and emotionally disturbed youth.

Epic Service

William Sloane Coffin's question to Hahn about the applicability of dramatic service to settings other than the mountains or the sea, leads us to explore a less visible form of service, one which Hahn never fully embraced, but one which is, nonetheless, important to a renewal of service in Outward Bound. In a lecture delivered in 1965 Hahn told the General Assembly of Unitarian and Free Christian Churches,

> I have mentioned voluntary bodies trained for dramatic rescue. We should take equally seriously those epic labours of love which are undertaken by young people; helping old people, the spastics, the blind, the deaf, helping in hospitals, helping to preserve the treasures of nature. I mention Alec Dickson's Community Service and the great work done by Voluntary Service Overseas which he founded. (5)

We shall use the phrase "epic service" to refer to those labors in which the need is not as acute, the adventure less physical, and the action less dramatic than rescue service.

It appears that Hahn's recognition of "epic service" came late in life and was influenced by others, notable among whom was Alec Dickson. In a dinner conversation at the Toronto conference of the Association for Experiential Education, Dickson corroborated the notion that Hahn's primary allegiance was to "dramatic service." When Dickson had first described to Hahn the work of his students in community institutions in Nigeria, Hahn had failed to appreciate the relevance.

Hahn's ambivalence toward "epic service" appears in the development of the Moray Badge. In 1936 he sought to expand the influence of Gordonstoun through a county award scheme in which young people would complete the three-fold tasks of physical training, an expedition, and a project. It was the local education authority in Hertfordshire, however, which insisted on adding the service component as the fourth requirement of the Badge, a decision which occasioned Hahn a great deal of misgiving.

> The giving of service was an accepted part of the natural order of living at Gordonstoun but he felt strongly that to make it a condition for an award of any kind was to court distortion of motive and was likely to lead to a debasement of the whole idea. (6)

On the other hand, Hahn later wrote that "a personal renewal in the young can take place only 'if voluntariness is supported by compulsion.'" (7)

The Peace Corps provides another example of a program which influenced Outward Bound's concept of service through "epic labours." Freddie Fuller, who became warden of Aberdovey in 1952, participated in the training of Peace Corps volunteers in Puerto Rico and returned to England convinced that it would be possible to devise a course in an urban setting which would be as demanding as those conducted on the sea and the mountains. The result was City Challenge at Leeds.

> The boys undertook an exciting programme of physical education which included drownproofing, canoe rolling, trampolining, and judo. Small groups in turn manned the casualty reception points of local hospitals, worked in a hostel for down-and-outs, assisted with play groups largely composed of immigrant children, and restored order in the homes of people who had rejected all the normal services. Finally they created a splendid adventure playground on waste land in a new housing estate. (8)

In highlighting the discussion thus far, it will be useful to compare our observations about service to the contemporary Outward Bound course. We are struck immediately by differences which inevitably impact the nature of service.

- The Outward Bound course takes place in the wilderness and is primarily a mobile experience; this is in contrast to the residential setting of the boarding school. (9)
- Occasions for dramatic rescue on the course have been reduced by the mobile patrol's remoteness from people and by the growth of para-professional rescue groups which will be the first called in an emergency.
- The length of the Outward Bound course today is 6-26 days compared with 6-26+ months at Gordonstoun. There is less time for service.
- The age of Outward Bound students is rising as the organization commits itself, consciously or unconsciously, to a marketing approach which is consumer-oriented rather than program-oriented.
- Outward Bound has been affected by a cultural shift from duty to personal growth, from self denial to self indulgence.

Tucker Foundation

Participating in the Outward Bound service project at Dartmouth, Marcia spent two hours each week tutoring two male inmates of a nearby correctional facility. Through piano instruction, she literally brought music into their lives. At first, their appreciation alone was justification for the time she invested.

It soon became apparent, however, that they offered her much more.

Both men were her age. She was attracted to the first who was serving time for illegal possession of drugs, and she wondered about the fine line separating his circumstances from her own.

She was repelled by the other, a convicted rapist who began writing her love letters, and she wondered how she could continue to tutor him. Why do people commit such acts? How have family, faith, and schools failed them? What is the role of the correctional institution—to punish, to isolate, to rehabilitate? What role was she playing through her visits? What values of her own were at risk? Why has she been impelled into this situation by her school?

Marcia's experience is an outgrowth of an institutional commitment on the part of Dartmouth College to develop conscience as well as competence through the liberal arts. In 1951 the Trustees established the position of the Dean of William Jewett Tucker Foundation and an independent endowment to support it.

Named after the last preacher president, the Foundation embodies the Trustees' conviction that the College's "moral and spiritual purpose springs from a belief in the existence of good and evil, from faith in the ability of men to choose between them and from a sense of duty to advance the good."

In addition to offering traditional chaplaincy services, the Foundation today provides opportunities to hundreds of students annually to serve and learn in a variety of settings—big brother/big sister programs, tutorials for children and adults, fellowships in social service agencies, work projects for Upper Valley needy, and visitations to the elderly and the handicapped.

Service has played a central role in conveying the purpose of the Foundation since its inception, although each Dean has emphasized the Foundation's mission differently in accordance with the circumstances of the day. The current Dean, Warner R. Traynham, characterizes the Foundation in these terms.

> The Provost has said that the focus of this institution is the life of the mind. That life is surely broader than simply the power to analyze and reflect, the capacity to discover and imbibe knowledge. It is also a function of the mind to appreciate, to apprehend significance, to commit to purpose, to perceive obligation and to care. (10)

Traynham's predecessor, Charles F. Dey, knew Outward Bound through Josh Miner, a colleague on the faculty of Philips Academy, Andover who had taught at Gordonstoun and had been instrumental in bringing Outward Bound to this country. Dartmouth's historic strengths in the outdoors,

"We may turn to epic service as a vehicle well suited to our times."

among which was the formation of the first collegiate outing club in 1909, further commended Outward Bound to Dey as a program which would enhance the Foundation's purpose and diversify its programs.

Among the factors he cited in proposing the Center was the role which colleges and universities might play in leadership development for programs of alternative national service—Peace Corps, Vista, Neighborhood Youth Corps, and the like.

In the Tucker Foundation, then, we see an institutional commitment to epic service where the service is harnessed explicitly to learning. "The activity should include prior preparation, reading and research, seminars and writing, and analysis and recommendations following return to campus." (11) Also, many of the programs included at their core a residential unit where students had responsibility for cooperative living and where they could gather in the cycle of the day to share and reflect on their experiences.

Outward Bound Center

Two programs have provided the major activity of Outward Bound on campus. The Outward Bound Laboratories are weekend experiences through which students can apply classroom learning. The Labs occur in urban and institutional settings as well as the outdoors.

Through these sessions the Outward Bound Center serves as an experiential learning resource to the campus. Values clarification, team-building, interpersonal skills, communication skills, and the opportunity to interact with professors outside of the classroom are incidental but purposeful to the primary goal of enriching academic learning. Occasionally the Labs are designed around service.

The Outward Bound Living/Learning Term is an intense eleven week course which involves twelve students and two instructors each quarter of the year. Activities include all the components of a standard Outward Bound course; cooperative living on campus; an academic course taken in common; human relations training; and a service project outside the college. The program is demanding because students must also complete their normal academic requirements at the same time.

Following the pattern of Salem and Gordonstoun, service begins with an inward focus toward the members of the Living/Learning community and extends outward to the communities of the Upper Connecticut River Valley. Within the house, students learn service to their peers. Household chores, food preparation, and budget management form the basis for much service activity, but the human relations sessions provide the greatest opportunity for reaching out to others.

Constructive feedback to individuals on their behavior demands sensitivity, tact, and support, a service that is available in few other settings on campus. Occasionally, in fact, the College counseling office refers to Outward Bound students who can benefit from the supportive group environment.

Turning outward, the Living/Learning students engage in a variety of activities with individuals and agencies.

- tutoring inmates of a nearby correctional center, as was illustrated in the case of Marcia
- teaching outdoor skills and group problem solving techniques to junior and senior members of Partners, a program which pairs an adult with a young person in need of positive role models
- teaching outdoor skills to seventh and eighth graders of a rural elementary school, a project which culminates in an overnight camping trip
- assisting in the renovations and winterizing of an urban community center
- accompanying mentally retarded adults on field trips and camping ventures
- conducting a short term behavioral modification program for residents of a center for emotionally disturbed youth
- visiting elderly residents of a convalescent home or patients at the Veterans Administration.

Some of the characteristics of these projects may prove useful as guidelines for redirecting service efforts in other programs, as for example the shorter Outward Bound courses.

1. The relationships are reciprocal. Students learn from neighboring residents, as the students offer skills, information, and recreation.
2. The time frame is realistic. Students work 3-4 hours weekly over a 6-8 week period. This is sufficient time for the project to be significant while manageable for all parties involved.
3. Students must be accountable to relationships outside of academia. This accountability may serve as an alternative to the drama of rescue.
4. Most of the projects are based on person-to-person interaction as differentiated from the trail maintenance or trash removal projects of many mobile courses.
5. Many projects force students to confront abilities and disabilities, a favorite theme of Hahn. The ages of many mentally retarded adults are the same as the students, or older, while their behavior is obviously younger; the elderly whom students visit may be losing health or mind while the student is exercising both vigorously; an amputee at the VA may give the student pause to reflect as he prepares for his marathon event.
6. The project often forces students to apply outdoor skills they are learning, to develop planning and organizational abilities, to teach, and to evaluate.
7. The projects are often part of a larger institutional commitment between Outward Bound and the community agency; the student takes his or her place in an on-going relationship between organizations.
8. On occasion the service project has been integrated within the core academic course, providing a more highly structured service-learning process.

For many students the service component is the highlight of the Living/Learning program, in large part because they have participated in a commitment outside of the college and outside of themselves. They have contributed some small measure of welfare to another and have learned in the process. They have experienced the kind of education that former Dean Dey characterized as truly liberal, one which

> would enable students to test themselves against the stark realities of poverty, ignorance and oppression; to discover that to individual human beings they can make a difference; to find out how desperately the world needs their talents; to reap the personal fulfilment that comes from investing those talents in a significant enterprise; to strengthen those inner spiritual resources which give meaning and purpose both to life and to a liberal education. (12)

...To Seek a Newer World

While preparedness for the drama of life saving service should remain a pillar of Outward Bound, it should be supported by more concerted training for its application after the course, as, for example, in Cardio Pulmonary Resuscitation. And with the retreat of opportunities for dramatic service, Outward Bound must examine its commitment to service as an educational process and as an institutional goal.

Traditional approaches to outdoor skills can be expanded so that students plan, organize and teach others what they have experienced.

We may turn to the concept of epic service, alluded to more than developed by Hahn, as a vehicle well suited to our times. We may look to the early themes of Hahn, sewn in the soil of Salem and Gordonstoun, to find the image of health-giving centers. And we may see for the Outward Bound schools a more definitive practice of the healing arts—physical fitness, diet, specific

"Epic labours of love" by young people was Alec Dickson's expansion of the call to service.

skills in emergency care, stress management, and the supportive dynamics of the small group.

Specific strategies for the Outward Bound schools might include restructuring program elements in mobile courses to include person-to-person service; developing ongoing institutional relationships locally through which transient students may pass, serve, and learn to mutual benefit; developing significant service components in semester length courses; and developing an after-course focus on service through deliberate empowerment of centers and networks of alumni.

We must also look to the examples of other service-learning programs. The Tucker Foundation has served as one such source for Outward Bound at Dartmouth. There are numerous other models offered by service-learning programs in dialogue with the AEE. We must seek collaboration with these groups to learn from their experience in the realms of epic service and to provide the ignition to serve which the Outward Bound short course can do effectively.

The moral equivalent of war can be achieved through rescue service, but in the absence of drama the on-going duty of citizenship must be sustained by other means. It is our task as educators to rediscover the forms of epic service and the health-giving arts, to raise them up to transform ourselves and our institutions, and to present them as a worthy pursuit for a new generation.

Footnotes

1. Hogan, J. M. *Impelled Into Experiences* (Yorkshire, 1968), pp. 67–68.
2. Coffin, William Sloane, Jr. *Once To Every Man* (Atheneum: New York, 1977), p. 183
3. Skidelsky, Robert *English Progressive Schools* (Penguin Books: Baltimore, 1969), p. 205
4. *Ibid.*, p. 204
5. Hahn, Kurt "The Young and the Outcome of the War" (Lindsay Press, 1965), p.23
6. Hogan, *Op. Cit.*, p. 21
7. Hahn, Kurt, "Juvenile Irresponsibility" in the Gordonstoun Record (6.12.1961); quoted by Hermann Röhrs in "The Educational Thought of Kurt Hahn"—Röhrs and Tunstall-Behrens, *Kurt Hahn* (London, 1970), p. 126
8. Hogan, *Op. Cit.*, pp. 113–114
9. See issue paper by Tom James, "Service—What Is It? and Why?" Colorado Outward Bound School, 1980. Also James, Thomas *Education at the Edge* (Denver, 1980), pp. 74–78
10. Traynham, Warner R. "Concern for Pigs and Moral Purposes" Tucker Foundation Broadside, Fall 1979, p. 4
11. Dey, Charles F. "William Jewett Tucker Foundation, A Report of Stewardship 1967-1971" p. 9
12. *Ibid.* p. 2

THREE Examples OF SERVICE LEARNING

PROJECT LEADERSHIP PAIRS YOUTH WITH INNER-CITY CHILDREN

compiled by H. Dean Evans
and Roberta Bowers

One of the most direct application's of Robert Greenleaf's concept of the "servant leader" is a service project for high school students initiated by the Lilly Endowment, Inc., and the American Youth Foundation in Indianapolis.

Over a period of a year, a group of 55 high school students learn to serve as positive role models for some 130 inner-city elementary students from schools with a high percentage of economically disadvantaged parents. Called "Project Leadership-Service", the project began in 1979 and is funded by the Lilly Endowment, Inc. in Indianapolis.

It is based on two principles. First, high school students can be influential, positive role models for elementary students who learn best by example. Second, exemplary high school students can benefit from experiences which give them the satisfaction of helping others.

The project begins in April of each year, when a Youth Advisory Committee sifts through applications from juniors attending the 33 high schools in Marion County, selecting 55 students. Those selected mirror the ethnic composition of the city with an equal number of male and female participants.

First, the students learn about inner-city life in Indianapolis and the important role of the servant-leader in community affairs. They meet the mayor in one session and are introduced to matters that vitally concern the city's residents, such as employment and transportation facilities.

Because they will spend the next school year serving as role models for inner-city elementary students, the high school students learn about the social services provided to Indianapolis residents. They spend a day accompanying caseworkers from the welfare department on routine visits to the homes of the welfare clients. Following these home visits, students discuss child abuse and measures taken by city agencies to see that each home is properly heated in the winter regardless of the occupants' ability to pay. Family life and the lack of healthy family relationships are studied with emphasis on the diverse types of families which exist today: one-parent households, families with one or both parents unemployed, and stepparent families.

Other meetings are designed to provide the high school participants with personal skills such as journal keeping, reflection, and communication. Communication skills which include listening, reacting, and writing are especially helpful to the high school students when they begin to interact with the elementary students.

Elementary school students who will participate in the project are chosen in May. All of the approximately 130 elementary school students will be sixth graders in September in schools that do not go beyond the sixth grade. They are potentials leaders for their schools, just as the selected high school students are potential leaders.

Younger and older students meet each other in the spring, but it is during a summer leadership camp that true bonds are formed.

Camp Miniwanca

Camp Miniwanca is owned and operated by the American Youth Foundation headquartered in St. Louis, Missouri. The camp is built in a forest which grows on sand dunes and is located approximately forty miles north of Muskegon near Shelby, Michigan.

The leadership conference begins with a six-hour bus trip from Indianapolis first for the high school students and four days later for the elementary students. The four days that the high school students spend at camp prior to the arrival of the sixth graders are spent pre-

---

H. Dean Evans *is director of Project Leadership-Service in his capacity as senior program officer for elementary and secondary education at the Lilly Endowment, Inc.* Roberta Bowers *is program assistant for the project, as well as an English teacher in the Indianapolis Public Schools.*

paring for interaction with the sixth graders.

During this time, the seniors go through an accelerated version of the same leadership training that the elementary students will receive. The only difference is that the experience of the seniors emphasizes understanding the needs of eleven- and twelve-year olds as well as leadership development.

On the fourth day at camp, the sixth graders arrive. Two or three sixth graders are assigned to each senior. Although adult staff members are at camp, the seniors have total responsibility for the sixth graders in their cabins and accompany them to all activities.

For the next seven days, seniors and sixth graders learn to be leaders together. Upon returning to Indianapolis, the seniors will be the oldest students in their schools as will the sixth graders. Therefore, both groups will have opportunities to apply the skills learned at camp.

At the same time, another level of learning is taking place. Sixth grade leaders-to-be are observing, imitating, and talking with exemplary high school students. In addition to teaching leadership skills, the camp curriculum includes language arts instruction. High school students read, write in journals, and keep a daily calendar with elementary students.

On the low ropes course, both groups learn to trust one another, to cooperate in solving problems, and to make decisions which are implemented immediately. Individual differences and worth are noted as all processes are discussed thoroughly.

Participants extend themselves by undertaking difficult tasks on the high ropes; by exercising daily in preparation for a marathon run; and, for some, by learning to swim. Self-esteem grows for seniors and for sixth graders as knowledge and experiences increase. Students also study citizenship, music, communications, crafts, singing, acting, and canoeing. They learn about the natural environment, repelling, compass reading, and astronomy.

The last night at camp is special. The seniors and sixth graders spend time reflecting silently on the dunes. A campfire is built on the top of "Old Baldy," the largest dune, and another is built at the bottom. Candles light the way down. Hand-in-hand, the students participate in singing and speaking at each campfire and as they trek down "Old Baldy." All participants are invited to share their thoughts.

The following morning the sixth graders leave—many tearfully. The seniors spend their final day at camp relaxing, "debriefing," and planning for their return home. How will they use what they have learned about leadership? How will they serve and lead their younger brothers and sisters during the next school year in Indianapolis? These questions are addressed during the last day at camp.

Teaching Staff

The American Youth Foundation (AYF) staff includes resource people who are experts in outdoor education, communication, water skills, language arts, music, theatre, and crafts. This resource staff made up of outstanding adult leaders is responsible for the major seminars on leadership skills at camp. Resource people are additional role models for elementary and high school students.

The service staff is made up of college juniors who participated in an AYF leadership conference at Camp Miniwanca when they were high school seniors. These students assist the resource staff in teaching the basic seminars. They also perform auxiliary cleaning, cooking, and planning duties.

Teachers who work in the project elementary schools are invited to camp also. The teachers ride the buses to and from camp with the sixth graders. On the bus they lead pre-camp activities. However, once they arrive at camp, they participate in a seminar designed for them which is conducted separately from the elementary and high school students' conference.

The teachers do plan a one-day's nature study lesson for the elementary students. This day, which occurs midway in the conference, gives the teachers an opportunity to practice what they have learned. It also provides a break for the seniors who have been with the elementary students twenty-four hours each day up to this point.

After Camp

From September until April following the camp conference, the senior participants continue to meet approximately once every three weeks. The seniors determine what the programs for these meetings will be. Therefore, the programs vary from year to year.

Seniors have chosen to study the institutions of correction which includes a trip to the Indiana School for Girls and a dialogue with the girls. It also includes a tour of the Indiana State Reformatory at Pendleton, Indiana, and a time to converse with inmates. Staff representatives and ex-offenders from a local rehabilitation center have spoken to the group along with the director of the Juvenile Justice Task Force. High school participants have visited the municipal courts in session and stood behind the judge's bench. They have also chosen to attend a meeting of the City-County Council and the Indianapolis Board of School Commissioners.

Another meeting focused on student rights and crime in the schools. Two Indiana University school law professors discussed student rights. This was followed by a presentation by Marion County Prosecutor, Steve Goldsmith, who told how rights can be taken away if they are not enjoyed in a responsible way.

At another meeting, a panel of media representatives debated media issues with the students. In March, the group traveled to the Marble Hill Nuclear Energy Plant in New Washington, Indiana, to study the advantages and disadvantages of nuclear energy.

In addition to continuing to learn about their community, the high school students maintain close ties with their elementary counterparts after camp. They do this by talking on the telephone, by writing notes, and by planning activities with the younger children. Groups of high school and elementary students from Project Leadership-Service appear at most high school football games, the Haunted House, the Children's Museum, and local pizza parlors.

In addition, the high school students volunteer to assist in the project elementary schools. They help with craft activities, holiday programs, and school work. In one case, they worked with the teachers at a school to plan and participate in a walking tour of downtown Indianapolis for all of the sixth graders.

Dr. Victor Smith of the Indiana Department of Public Instruction did a thorough evaluation of the camp segment of Project Leadership-Service which included the use of formal tests, scales, and the informal comments of students. (Victor A. Smith, Ed.D., "An Evaluation Report on the Project Leadership-Service Conference," August, 1981).

Formal results indicated that students left camp motivated to serve in their community. They understood the connection between service and leadership and felt they had increased their knowledge in many skill areas. In addition, both high school and elementary school students departed from camp with improved attitudes about themselves.

More interesting than the formal results which are available through the American Youth Foundation are the responses volunteered by the students to open-ended questions on the post-test evaluation forms. Some of these responses follow.

"Helped me get this new idea about myself: I can't think of other words: servant-leader."

"Made me think about the fact that we're all leaders."

"Helped me to understand that even though I am a leader, I have to let others help do the job. I can't always do it myself."

"Helped me get this new idea about myself: I am as much of a leader as anyone, and I should put all my potential into projects."

THREE Examples OF SERVICE LEARNING

"YES"— UPBEAT PROJECT BUOYED BY STUDENT INITIATIVE

by Joy Hardin

The phones ring a lot at Youth Educational Services.

"YES! your youth group can go on a river rafting trip with our Discovery Program."

"YES! we'd love to be donated a volleyball for our recreation program with inmates."

"YES! we're the place that adopts grandparents."

"YES! The Greenpeace Y.E.S. program says the blue whales are coming through this weekend."

"YES! people here will support a call-in campaign to have the six o'clock news interpreted in sign language."

"YES! there is a tofu burrito sale for Nutrition for Kids today."

"YES! several of our kids' programs would probably like to deliver singing Valentines for your fundraiser."

Youth Educational Services (Y.E.S.) was named so people could say "Yes" to the needs of others in the community. Begun 14 years ago with a tutoring project, Y.E.S. is currently composed of seventeen programs. All were initiated by students and are directed by students. Yearly, over 250 volunteers from Humboldt State University and the Arcata community work with over 1,000 program participants. Funding is primarily from student activity fees.

I came to work with Y.E.S. searching for a form of community-focused experiential education that empowers university students to make a difference in the lives of others. I knew that small group wilderness adventures were one dramatic experience of the power of working together. Could service learning be equally compelling? Could people discover their capabilities confronting complicated human problems like aging, environmental insensitivity and social inequality?

My first six months as director of Y.E.S. have given me enormous hope. I am filled with images of what can be done . . of service beyond picking up litter . . . of service that is no less absorbing and mutually beneficial than other small group adventures.

I am personally convinced that the process of student-directed service learning is virtually identical to other forms of experiential education. A volunteer enters a *demanding, unfamiliar environment*. People take *risks* when they make commitments to individuals and groups offering service. Volunteers see the *consequences of their actions* when real people depend on them. And people recognize their *interdependence* when they feel their common humanity with persons whose lives are unlike their own.

The first part of this article shares with you some illustrations of this process at work in Y.E.S. . . tells you some stories. The second part of the article focuses on the uniqueness of student-directed and student-initiated programs. I close with some observations on starting points for student directed service-learning.

Illustrations

It's Saturday night in the sparsely furnished attic of the Y.E.S. house. Twenty-two children and adults jubilantly share

---

Joy Hardin is executive director of Youth Educational Services, a student project at Humboldt State University in Arcata, California.

games, stories, popcorn, and laughter. The occasion is the Together-in-Sign slumber party, where the common language is American Sign. The younger people are deaf and hearing impared children. The older people are their adopted big brothers and sisters who either study sign language or rely on it themselves.

The evening has different high points for different participants. With his hands, Dennis, a deaf volunteer, fluently and expressively tells the "Three Bears" to a raptly attentive group. Three pre-schoolers are heralded for their popcorn making. Six year-old Daniel, labelled "unable to communicate" and a "behavior problem" risks taking his turn answering a heavy question for both big and little brothers and sisters—"What is the hardest part of communicating with your parents?"

In three years Together-in-Sign has grown from three volunteers to twenty (and a waiting list). It began when a mother called the Y.E.S. Together program and requested a "big sister" who spoke sign. It became a free standing-program as the volunteers working with deaf children stumbled into the issues of the deaf community and needed more support. Advisors are a professor from the Speech and Hearing Department, and professional interpreter and advocate from an agency focusing on the needs of persons with handicaps.

Earlier that week, many of the 35 seniors who are Adopted Grandparents and their volunteer "grandchildren" gathered at Redwood community park for an old-fashioned box-lunch auction and picnic. Adopt-A-Grandparent is a thriving example of mutualism.

A favorite story about the program is told by the senior center staff. They had referred an elderly, housebound woman to the program. They were a little hesitant about a volunteer being comfortable with her, as her body was deteriorating rapidly and her language was quite limited. A volunteer had agreed to try visiting her. The senior center worker called the housebound woman to find out how the visit had gone.

"Oh, she came all right," her voice was frail. "And I liked her right well. I think I can help her, too. She's far from her family you know . . ."

The volunteer student's remarks on the visit were virtually identical: "I think I could really help her."

The objects of one's compassion sometimes comes as a surprise. Over at the county jail, the women inmates saw films for the first time in two years. There had been much concern that volunteers from Inmates Need Daily Exercise and Education to Develop (INDEED) wouldn't get in to show the films because the guards are worried about security right now. They're expecting a new inmate, a prisoner whose terrorist friends have taken the lives of five prison guards in facilities where she has been housed. The volunteers talked about their frustration with not being allowed to offer recreation for over six weeks this winter. But there was also a note of

Can service learning be as compelling as wilderness adventures? Y.E.S. at Humboldt State says "Yes!"

empathy for the men and women who work at the jail, and fear for their lives.

Far from the boiling whitewater rivers he has worked on since he was twelve, Jim Ritter, the director of Discovery, is as nervous as he remembers being since before Clavey Falls rapid on the Tuoloumne, where he once dumped. Two foundation representatives are coming to meet with him today. Jim's non-stop efforts of the last three months have been to get the river rafting program for special needs youth funded to continue to the summer. He now has a shot at getting money for one new raft. Previously, Discovery has depended on donated discards of the river companies. Those "retreads" are of marginal strength for a full summer of use. Jim debates about wearing his constant river hat to such a meeting, and prepares his notes.

Manila is an isolated community on a once-awesomely beautiful spit of land battered by the Pacific ocean and by the crashing decline of lumber and construction industries. Kids Club of Manila's series of clubs—Teen Outdoor, Girls Club, Saturday Recreation,

Monday Recreation and Tutoring—are an oasis in the boredom of the young people. This week the Girls Club is sponsoring Jazzercise as a fundraiser. Will anyone come? Will it be a success like the previous mother-daughter dinner where girls abandoned their teenage postures and RAN down the road to reserve their spots at the table? Jazzercise is the most current variation of a theme of Y.E.S. Tutoring Center by night.

At a neighborhood meeting in a housing project, Hazel talks about four generations of her family that live there and the events all the tenants come out for. "Halloween, now that's a big time. And this year the kids all rode the bus and went up to the campus, too: they were sure excited about *that*." The 5-H program volunteers had realized that college students sequestered in dormitories missed having trick-or-treaters. So they brought the small-sized ghouls and goblins to the dorms. Y.E.S. had dorm dwellers telephoning asking "Do you think three pounds of candy corn will be enough?"

Student Impetus

Student-initiated programs and student-directedness are the particular aspect of Y.E.S. that differentiates it from the swelling numbers of service learning programs. Many other programs place students in existing agencies/projects.

Y.E.S. grew out of students' desire to be fully involved in decision making, planning and implementation of social action initiatives. The specific projects change—maybe one a year dies or moves out onto its own. The duration varies: for example, the tutorial program has existed for 14 years; a car-pool program lasted only a year. Some programs live in the community after "growing up and leaving home:" a citywide recycling center, a health education curriculum in the public schools, an appropriate technology demonstration house, and a crisis phone line are among those still thriving.

New programs are proposed to the Y.E.S. board of directors, which consists of directors of current Y.E.S. programs and administrative staff.

In addition to the funding Y.E.S. receives from student activity fees, United Way contributes about 3%, 4-H supports several programs, especially with insurance; and the university provides an executive director. There is an internal paid staff of 2½ positions. Directors receive miniscule stipends unless they are work-study eligible.

Some programs that remain under the Y.E.S. umbrella are re-defined frequently. Welfare Outreach, for example, was begun to help determine peoples' eligibility for food stamps and medical aid. This year, welfare regulations have tightened down so vociferously that very few people not already enrolled are eligible. In response, Welfare Outreach is reorganizing to address the entire problem of food for local people. Volunteers have begun collaborating with the local food bank, while other volunteers

---

"**C**hallenges more subtle than a rockface. Challenges of making it happen to benefit others."

---

are starting a food buying club.

Because Y.E.S. is small and the communication between directors informal, it can function like the ultimate integrated neighborhood, a microcosm of the community. Monday evening the 25 student directors share dinner followed by a formal meeting. There and in the cramped office spaces, concerns surface about the people served by their programs. Other directors respond from their knowledge of resources.

Problem solving can sometimes be immediate and personal: for example, a friendship program pairing volunteers and persons with developmental disabilities has no volunteer to match with an adult labelled "retarded" who now lives independently. Another director suggests she be invited to join the newly forming food buying club. She does.

The problem solving and support amongst the directors focuses on a different set of issues as well: how to organize and lead volunteers, and how to share the ownership of the program with volunteers and participants.

There is a sequence of challenges for

developing the leadership of students involved in Y.E.S.

1) The immersion stage is *volunteering*. Students are asked for a two-quarter commitment of at least 4 hours a week. They are oriented by returning volunteers and participants and introduced to the folks they will be directly involved with. For example, teenagers in Manila show new and returning volunteers around their community, and all ages participate in planning the events of the quarter. New volunteers usually choose to work in an established aspect of the program.

2) Stage Two—Volunteer *takes charge of a specific part* of their program. For example, a new Horizons Unlimited volunteer took responsibility for producing participant-designed Christmas cards. Another volunteer coordinated sales.

3) Stage Three—Volunteer develops and *leads an ongoing aspect* within the program. For example, a volunteer just back from NOLS joins Kids Club of Manila and organizes a teen outdoor program.

4) Stage Four—Volunteer *directs the program*. This is a big step in commitment. Besides taking responsibility for keeping the program going, the position requires an active role in the board of directors of Y.E.S., a share in the decision making for a whole organization. Further, directors are responsible for coordinating with the confusing array of related agencies and services throughout the county.

5) Stage Five: Volunteer *expands or reorients* the program, or begins a new one. For many, this is the crux of student initiated service-learning.

One Student's Dream

Because the whole process of students dreaming a dream and making it happen is so critical to Y.E.S.'s approach, I offer a case study of Austin Smith, the founding father of Discovery.

Austin has been involved with Y.E.S. for over six years. He has spent his time running a giant Y.E.S. tutoring project, river guiding, getting bummed out by education courses, leaving school and coming back.

Austin was a poor city kid. His first experience with anyplace "wild" came by tagging along with his neighbors, who lived in a center for people with muscular dystrophy. His first river trip came in high school. He got to go as part of a special experiential program for problem youth. Around the same time, he was kicked out of his home. He landed in a neighborhood youth corp with the choice of working for the police department or for a day care center. "You didn't have to cut your hair to work in day care," Austin recalls, "so I took it." His interest in working with kids was born.

Despite his immediate love affair with rivers, Austin saw little of rivers until much later. "Going down on my own in rubber duckies was all I could get. I couldn't afford ARTA's whitewater school, but I wrote

Dreaming a dream that includes others. That's what Austin did.

them anyway. They sent me a job application instead."

So Austin became a river guide. "I saw that upper middle class people were my only passengers. I didn't even see any kids like myself when I was younger."

Back in school in Humboldt County, debate raged over the creation of Redwood National Park. Environmentalists and natural resources majors lined up against loggers who saw their livelihoods threatened. Austin recalls the moment of the Discovery program's conception: a spirited argument with his room mate on the park issue. "I found myself taking the loggers' point of view. Parks are supposedly for people to use, but only people with time or money ever do. I kept thinking inner-city kids would never use a National Park up here.

His idea was of a program that would get excluded kids out in the land of the redwoods. Austin talked to ETC (Environmental Traveling Companions), a Bay area program that included handicapped persons in the groups it took out. After training with them, Austin located one local supporter, drew up goals, proposed and received a budget of $75 from Y.E.S., "made up fliers, and put up some of my hottest whitewater shots on the kiosk. I sat out on the quad (campus center) talking; the photos drew them in. I had 25 people at the first meeting."

For the next three months, training and equipment became foremost. "Student Legislature gave us $800 for equipment. The agreement was, if we didn't get three boats donated by April 1, we'd return it all." Two days before the deadline, the third boat was promised.

Less than six months after Austin's argument with his room mate, Discovery was on the river. Three years later, Discovery's current director, Jim Ritter, is

"The process of student-directed service learning is virtually identical to other forms of experiential education."

going for it again, partnering with 4-H to get a full-scale summer program going. "It's a direction I never would have thought of taking the program," Austin says. "I always worried about what will happen when I leave. Now I guess I can go."

What has it all meant for Austin? "The experience of having an idea and making it work is really rewarding. I feel like I could start something anywhere I go. Now I *know* a community will respond. (It was) a personal accomplishment, of course, maybe even more than if I'd been paid to do it. It's one of my peak experiences."

Starting Points

Where to start? Nobody like Austin is approaching you? I offer a few suggestions for *beginning* service learning programs that may "grow" the students to be the directors and initiators of the next stages.

1) Programs that offer one-to-one relationships provide high initial reward to volunteers and less pressure on student directors. The matching process requires a lot of care but once matched, programs partially run themselves. First-time directors can organize group activities and challenges to supplement the one-to-one relationships.

2) Tutoring has been (and remains!) such a star of service learning because it combines that one-to-one, highly personal relationship with an external focus, a program for tutor and tutee to solve together. I saw similar tangible magic in art students partnering in the woodshop one-to-one with severely handicapped people who had never previously designed or made any object for their home.

3) The pleasure of sharing the thing you most love to do is heightened and deepened by doing it with people vastly different from yourself. Students talk about getting their "kidfix" and "having an excuse to do what they love to do anyway." One volunteer who never before had had contact with people labelled "disabled" talks with great animation about how his "little brother" and he work on motorcycles together. Therefore, a starting point may be a strong shared interest of several volunteers.

4) The challenge of student-directed service learning is that of "making it happen." Therefore, more small projects within programs and more small programs, mean more leadership roles. For example, Y.E.S. currently has three different big-brother/big-sister types of friendship programs. Our experience is that even 20 volunteers is too big; roughly each 4-6 volunteers need a clear area of ownership and challenge.

I got involved in service learning programs because I wanted to see if the bonds of love and support, and empowerment of groups and individuals could happen all the time, instead of only through sharing a physical adventure. I wanted the kind of community and power I knew were possible by the end of a women's expedition, and I wanted it to happen in the city. My first immersion, working in Boston, convinced me it could happen amongst artists, designers, people labelled severely handicapped, their parents and caretakers.

Six months at Y.E.S. suggests it can happen amongst just about any volunteers who have sufficient back-up and support to go for it.

And my experience at Y.E.S. suggests that challenges more complicated and subtle than a rapid or rockface—challenges of making it happen to benefit others—can catalyze incredible efforts.

Seeking Roots
FROM HAHN TO GREENLEAF

by Anthony Richards

Because of its eclectic nature, experiential education appears to have no specific or finite roots. We say that experiential education can be whatever we want it to be. There is hardly any aspect of education, both within schools and without, that cannot be approached experientially. The diversity of experience-based learning has contributed to its strength and persistence. But it also makes it so difficult to ascertain roots that some experiential educators ignore them and continue with a "blind faith syndrome" (Wickman, 1980).

Not only can the knowledge and understanding of the roots of a program help to develop new ideas, but it can also help to give that program a base of credibility. Kurt Hahn has been credited with pioneering an aspect of experiential education through the creation of such programs as Outward Bound, the Duke of Edinburgh Award Scheme, United World Colleges and many others. One of his main themes in these programs was service learning. This article will discuss the role played by Kurt Hahn and the concept of service in the area of service learning.

During the 1930's Kurt Hahn delivered a number of speeches which were aimed at promoting the educational ideas he was developing at the time. The speeches contained the common theme of problems with the youth of the day. He illustrated these problems by listing six declines

---

Anthony Richards *is associate professor of physical education and director of experiential education at Dalhousie University in Halifax, Nova Scotia. A native of London, his understanding of Kurt Hahn is based on extensive research on both sides of the Atlantic.*

by Robert Sigmon

Service-learning terminology has emerged in the past ten years, and—as in the case of many traditional Christmas carols—the authors are unknown. The great carols belong to the public, a product of folk traditions at their best. Service-learning represents the coming together of many hearts and minds seeking to express compassion for others and to enable a learning style to grow out of service.

The term service-learning is now used to describe numerous voluntary action and experiential education programs. Federal laws now use the phrase. Its diffusion suggests that several meanings now are attributed to service-learning. If we are to establish clear goals and work efficiently to meet them, we need to move toward a precise definition.

Robert Greenleaf, author of *Servant Leadership: A Journey into the Nature of Legitimate Power and Greatness*, defines service as it is used in this service-learning formulation:

"One who serves takes care to make sure that other peoples' highest priority needs are being served. The best test, and difficult to administer, is: do those served grow as persons; do they while being served, become healthier, wiser, freer, more autonomous, more likely themselves to become servants? And what is the effect on the least privileged in society; will they benefit, or, at least, will they not be further deprived?"

Robert Sigmon *is assistant director of the Wake Area Health Education Center in Raleigh, North Carolina. He has helped develop and manage service-learning programs in South Carolina, North Carolina, Georgia and Tennessee.*

which were the social diseases of the time (Richards, 1981).

Hahn felt that it was the responsibility of education to redress these declines which have been identified as: decline of fitness due to modern methods of locomotion; decline of initiative and enterprise due to the widespread disease of spectatorites; decline of memory and imagination due to the confused restlessness of modern life; decline of skill and care due to the weakened tradition of craftsmanship; decline of self-discipline due to the ever present availability of stimulants and tranquilizers; and the decline of compassion due to the unseemly haste with which modern life is conducted.

These are all issues which can be discussed in the 1980's. The pertinence and relevance of the solutions are being revived some fifty years later. However, it is the last of the declines which is of particular interest to service learning.

Hahn's solution was to provide deliberate ways of including activities which developed compassion. These were generally in the form of service projects.

Hahn believed there were three ways to enlist the service of the young:

> Persuasion, compulsion and attraction. You can preach at them: that is a hook without a worm; you can order them to volunteer: that is dishonest; you can call on them—"you are needed": and that appeal will hardly ever fail (Hahn, 1961, p. 12).

This approach of appealing to the young by the call that they are needed is an approach which has met with success for many years.

Another unique observation made by Hahn when introducing the service project was the fact that human to human interactions were so much more potent than human to thing interactions. This came about as a result of two inspiring writings. The first was the parable of the Samaritan which Hahn often quoted in his speeches. In fact he coined the phrase samaritan-ethic as being the value which was manifested during spontaneous acts of compassion. The other writing was that of William James and his search for a moral equivalent to war. This captured

Learning flows from the service-task(s). To serve in the spirit of the Greenleaf definition requires attentive inquiry with those served and careful examination of what is needed in order to serve well. As a result, learning objectives are formed in the context of what needs to be done in serve others.

Based on my work designing, managing, and evaluating programs with service and learning dimensions, and with a spirit of inquiry about how any of us serve well and are served well by our actions, I suggest the following three principles for those in similar positions:

Principle one: Those being served control the service(s) provided.
Principle two: Those being served become better able to serve and be served by their own actions.
Principle three: Those who serve also are learners and have significant control over what is expected to be learned.

(The above paragraphs were excerpted from an article by Robert Sigmon in the Synergist, spring 1979, titled "Service-Learning: Three Principles".)

Calling Robert Greenleaf "the only wise revolutionary I have ever known," Noel Perrin, head of the Department of English at Dartmouth, states that Greenleaf's "ideas on leadership would, if adopted upset most of our institutions—and remake them in truly human form."

I share Perrin's enthusiasm. Unknown to Greenleaf, he has been my mentor for about ten years and has been instrumental in shaping my views on service-learning.

Who is this man who contends that only those who serve also lead? Following a distinguished career with American Telephone & Telegraph in management research, development, and education, in 1964 he retired to new careers in writing and consulting. His writings focus on the young and how institutions can provide better opportunities for young people to serve and be served. He urges institutions—business, church, government, schools—to spend as much energy producing servant-leaders as they do accountants, doctors, lawyers, and business administrators. He and his wife Esther, an artist,

Hahn's imagination and he responded by saying that not only did the service projects provide this equivalent but they were capable of releasing the highest dynamics of the human soul, even more so than war.

Service, in one form or another, appeared in all of Hahn's educational programs. There were various levels of service which ranged from community service and estate work to serving each other in school and the coastguard and mountain rescue service. However, as far as Hahn was concerned, the ultimate service was to save another man's life. He referred to this as the Aristocracy of Service.

> # Hahn decried the decline of compassion which was "due to the unseemly haste with which modern life is conducted".

The philosophy of Kurt Hahn is sometimes referred to as "Hahnism" (Richards, 1981). It came across the Atlantic to North America in an uncontaminated form as Outward Bound in 1961. It has been through Outward Bound that Kurt Hahn is best known on this continent. However, there are several other programs which bear his stamp and have their roots with this man.

Colorado Outward Bound was established at Marble and operated from a base camp. The service component within the program was confined to "estate work" which was very necessary in the early days in order to clear the land and develop the physical plant.

The introduction of the mobile course was a turning point in the American Outward Bound. It was no longer possible to perform conventional service projects either in the form of "estate work" or as a service to people, because these courses were conducted in wilderness settings away from any form of civilization.

There have been various attempts at including service as an integral part of Outward Bound courses but these have invariably been contrived projects such as trail clearing or garbage removal. Whereas these have served a useful purpose, they have not brought out the highest dynamics of service, which involves people to people interactions.

Hahn's first service project was the development of the coastguard service. This required the boys to sit for extended periods of time in the coastguard hut, alone and watching attentively, squinting to see an inefficient flare that might signal a ship foundering (Hahn, 1944). It was the vigilance of the watchman and the readiness to be of service, which was vital to the process.

A similar project exists in the State of Oregon where high school students must attend a cardio-pulmonary resuscitation (CPR) course. Each student has to pass this course successfully in order to graduate from high school, the theory being that every young man and young woman will be ready to serve should a cardiac arrest occur.

Whereas readiness to serve is vital, it soon wears thin if there is no opportunity to use the skills. It is the action phase of a rescue service, CPR training or fire fighting service which is the most exciting. The hands on action also releases the "highest dynamics of the human soul". How can projects be created that guarantee "call-outs" or deal with real emergencies?

There are two areas that service learning may be experienced with people who are in real need of service as genuine person to person interactions. A number of projects can be seen in schools and youth organizations which devote their time to helping people in the community, working in hospitals, caring for older persons, designing barrier-free access to buildings for the disabled, and many others. Whereas these projects do not involve the saving of life, which Hahn referred to as the aristocracy of service, they do contribute to the increase in quality of life.

The other area which illustrates a high

HAHN

level of service is best illustrated by the recent innovation by the Round Square Conference. This Conference comprises a group of schools which have their roots with Kurt Hahn. They have entered into a program in which they train their senior students to help with flood relief in India. The training takes place in the schools throughout Europe with skilled staff. The advantage of the project is that a "call-out" is guaranteed. Every July there are floods in India and help is needed. The students are mobilized and flown to the trouble spots where they work for the summer period helping to rebuild the devastated communities.

The basic principles of Hahn's service projects are very sound and his desire to "help the young achieve a balance of power in their inner lives so that the love of man can take charge", is possible today. However, it requires similar creative leadership to design projects which stir and excite young people.

The 1980's will be a decade where action is of prime importance. The challenge is to create an aristocracy of service which demands and guarantees action.

References

Hahn, Kurt. *Ten Years of Gordonstoun*. Welshpool: County Times Publication, 1944.

Hahn, Kurt. *Service by Youth*. Address to directors of Bournville Co. Ltd., April 1961.

Richards, A. *Kurt Hahn: The Midwife of Educational Ideas*. Unpublished dissertation, University of Colorado, 1981.

Wickman, T.F. Babies and Bathwater: Two Experiential Heresies. *Journal of Experiential Education*, Spring 1980.

GREENLEAF

now live in a Quaker retirement center, where he is working on three new books.

His concept of the servant as leader was developed over the years and crystalized when he read Herman Hesse's *Journey to the East*, a story that shows how a group disintegrates with the disappearance of the servant who had sustained the members with his spirit as well as his menial labor. Greenleaf contends that great leaders are those who are servants first, *i.e.*, who lead because of a desire to serve rather than to gain power or personal gratification.

Greenleaf cites historical examples of servant leaders, including Thomas Jefferson, and predicts that in the next 30 years leaders will come from the "dark skinned and the deprived and the alienated of the world" rather than from elite groups who have not learned to listen and respond to the problems of those to be served.

In his chapter on "Servant Leadership in Education," Greenleaf returns to his theme of the need for secondary and post-secondary schools to prepare the poor "to return to their roots and become leaders among the disadvantaged." He states that the goal of a college education should be to "prepare students to serve, and be served by the current society."

Greenleaf also devotes chapters to "The Institution as Servant," "Trustees as Servants," "Servant Leadership in Business," "Servant Leadership in Foundations," "Servant Leadership in Churches," "Servant Leaders" (profiles of Abraham Joshua Heschel and Donald John Cowling), "Servant Responsibility in a Bureaucratic Society," and "America and World Leadership."

Greenleaf shows a way of putting together two overworked words (service and leadership) into a fresh perspective. In *Servant Leadership* he offers experiential learning managers a holistic framework for understanding the significance of service-centered learning for individuals and institutions.

(*Excerpted from "Preparing Servant-Leaders" by Robert Sigmon, Synergist, winter 1980.*)

> "Robert Greenleaf's ideas on leadership would remake our institutions in truly human form."

FIGHT *Illiteracy* WITH VOLUNTEER YOUTH

by Jonathan Kozol

One out of five American adults cannot read these words and could not possibly have written them.

According to a Ford Foundation study carried out in 1979, twenty percent of the adult population of our nation is illiterate. *Newsweek* later translated this percentage into numbers: 23 million men and women could not read or write at all. Updated by more recent studies, the figure should be raised now to 25 million.

The U.S. Department of Education estimates that 57 million American adults are not able to carry out most basic tasks essential to effective participation in the life and the economy of our society.

This means 35 percent of our entire adult population is functionally illiterate—cannot read enough to understand a modestly sophisticated want ad, nor write with sufficient competence to fill out a cogent application for a job.

Entirely apart from the financial cost of mass illiteracy (prison maintenance for illiterate adults, heightened welfare, and lowered productivity alone amount to $13 billion a year) the human price is far too great for any wealthy nation to accept without a passionate endeavor to redress extreme injustice by the greatest possible investment of our national determination and resources.

What does it mean to be illiterate in the 1980's?

It means that you cannot read the warnings in factories that have been posted, by federal

"We can be those who alter history."

law, in order to protect your health, e.g., "Warning! This chemical is dangerous if inhaled or if it should come in contact with the skin. If this should be the case, immediately wash the area involved and ask for medical advice."

How can you ask for medical advice if you don't even understand the sign?

It not only means that you cannot read advertisements for a job but also that, if you get the job, you probably will lose it and seldom will qualify for promotion.

You cannot read the documents to which you sign permission in the hospital for surgery that you do not even understand.

What will it take to call a halt to this ongoing and increasing tragedy? What do we need to do?

Mobilizing Students

After several years of watching laudable literacy programs in all sections of the nation and recognizing that all of them, up to this date, have reached only four percent of those in need, I am convinced that we must draw at last upon that one most energetic and least recognized resource—the secondary students and the college undergraduates of the United States.

What I have in mind, in briefest terms, is nothing less than a national mobilization of young people, guided by teachers, credentialed by their schools or universities, and released for a substantial period of time—at least one full semester and one summer of hard work—in order to form a literacy army of devoted teachers for the 25 million illiterate men and women of the nation.

We make this kind of sacrifice in time of war. We do it in times of flood or disease. Now we must do it also for the pestilence of mass illiteracy within our land.

I propose an all-out literacy campaign, in which the vanguard of the struggle would be represented by at least three million youthful volunteers, supported by competent senior citizens wherever possible, and guided in their efforts by the classroom teachers—above all, teachers of English and of related language arts who would otherwise be

---

Jonathan Kozol *won the National Book Award in 1968 for* Death at an Early Age. *His book on literacy,* Prisoners of Silence, *was released in 1980. He has been a teacher of English at South Boston High and is now professor of English and literacy at the University of Massachusetts.*

working with them in the public schools.

I propose that those who volunteer for such a task—if they are teachers—ought to receive the very same salary and credits that they would be paid if they were in the classroom. Students ought to receive full academic credit for the time that they devote but ought to be prepared to work, for this brief period only, for a token salary—basically, no more than a survival stipend. (I will discuss the sources of support later in the article.)

What could be more wise, more sane, and more profoundly educational in value than to give up a single semester of "The

> "We must draw upon that one most energetic and least recognized resource: students."

Problems of Democracy" to go out instead into the world around the school in order to try to *solve* one of those problems?

When they return, those teachers and those students, I suspect, will have no difficulty in uncovering subjects to involve them in exciting class discussions. At last our students will be freed from the ironic task of being compelled to join in class debates on problems that they cannot possibly understand and have no chance to alter or correct.

By this means young people from all segments of the population will live for a short time on an equal basis with the poorest people in the land. The volunteers will be poor, but those they seek to help will have been poor forever. The volunteers will be living without the extra cash to see a movie, but their students will be people who have not seen a movie in ten years.

The adult illiterates will discover the *word*. Their teachers will discover the *world*. Together they will repossess their shared humanity.

The question, of course, instantly will be posed: "How can these totally untrained adolescents possibly teach so many of those who are totally illiterate?"

My own response, as a teacher of reading and professor of education for a total of twelve years, is perhaps a bit iconoclastic: The teaching of reading is, without question, a complicated challenge, *but it is not neurosurgery*. It is a difficult labor, but it is not an occult skill nor a sacerdotal mystery.

Two weeks of drill in intensive phonics, with a strong emphasis on the learners' active words—words that already count the most to them (and words that already form a part of the rich and often unexpected oral vocabulary of virtually all people in this land)—will initiate the task we have at hand.

I do not speak with mindless optimism. These words are based upon a fresh and vivid memory from my own career. When I was a very young man with no experience of any kind at all in formal teaching skills, I was instructed to teach reading to illiterates in a course taught in the basement of a small black church in my community.

This course lasted only 14 days and depended heavily upon a single phonics method and an intensive emphasis upon our obligation to elicit—for the purpose of our lessons—only those words which mattered most to those whom we would teach.

In the course of three months of painstaking work with illiterates that followed my brief training, all but two out of a class of 16 pupils were able to move from total illiteracy to a very solid fifth grade competence.

With no further experience or training, I became, two weeks later, a fourth grade teacher in the Boston Public Schools. Almost immediately I was made one of the reading experts in my school.

I would argue that there was nothing unique about my competence, or energy, or preparation. What worked for me can certainly work for those young student literacy workers whom I believe we shall find within the classrooms of our universities and high schools.

A few more specific details of the plan. I suggest, for a number of obvious reasons, that whenever at all practicable, each of our prospective volunteers ought to be ready to live *within* the neighborhoods in which they work.

They ought to work in rather small teams—15 or 20 people at the most—teams that represent an ethnic mix and thereby help to ward off any danger of a missionary style.

Team leaders, to lend both personal and pedagogic reinforcement, ought to be found not only among the public classroom teachers but also among those veteran literacy workers who are already involved in VISTA, Literacy Volunteers of America, and other national groups, and among community leaders and many of the active literacy experts in the major libraries of the United States.

In the cities, literacy workers might well live and work in newly created literacy houses—slum buildings left behind by landlords who desert the city but whose neglected houses may be rapidly repaired by common efforts of a neighborhood block committee and a group of older experts and young student volunteers. It is hard to imagine a better way to build a prior sense of common cause.

Certain groups also might

choose to work not in the rural slums or urban ghettos but in the state and federal prisons. The highest single locus of illiterate adults is in the prison population.

The ideal approach does not attempt to impose *external* motivation upon the illiterate adult but instead releases the intrinsic motivation that is already there. It does so (as I have suggested above) by releasing words that form a part of that rich and virtually limitless oral vocabulary already existing among even the most inarticulate people in the land.

The result of this work is what the literary world calls oral history stories, specifically, that are narrated *to*, not *by*, the literacy teacher. It is the kind of material that often is shared during long evenings of engrossing and openended conversation between a student volunteer and several of the oldest citizens of a communtiy.

Oral history is returned, thereby, in edited and mass-duplicate form, to those people—the students of *our* students—who offer forth these stories in the first place. Their own experience is given back to them as literature; their own word is returned to them on paper. This, then, after proper editorial work, might well become the starting point for little more than 100 hours of one-to-one or small-group literacy lessons on the part of thousands of devoted volunteers.

The traditional library story-hour thus has been turned around: The people tell us their story, and we return their soul to them in words.

Sources of Support

Who will support us in a venture of this kind?

A vast amount of backing, I believe, will come from almost every element of the business sector: insurance companies that now incur enormous costs for accidents that take place constantly in factories where laborers cannot follow, nor even hope to comprehend, written instructions; sophisticated industries that, even in a period of unemployment, cannot find the competent employees to fill a whole new category of sophisticated (and nonmenial) entry-level jobs; the major publishers and the print media that now lose millions of prospective customers (i.e., prospective readers) to television; and those who are concerned with national defense,

The highest locus of illiterates is within prison walls. Community Service volunteer in England.

prison recidivism, street crime, and increasing welfare costs.

It is a long, long time since student ethics, corporate interests, and popular concerns have found themselves allied around a single issue of such sweeping magnitude and national importance. Admiral Hyman Rickover recently observed, "One third of our naval recruits are a danger to themselves and to the ships on which they serve"—by reason of their inability to read instructions.

Is this proposal for mobilizing students a fantasy, a daydream, an ideal?

Dozens of teachers, in all sections of the nation, already have been working with their students, at both university and high school levels, in precisely the kind of program I have just described. Like the pacesetting teachers of all ages, they have moved forward on their own, taking permission where they find it and pursuing the excitement of their students when they can arouse it.

The stunning news, so far as the mass media is concerned, is that so many students are entirely willing and determined to participate in projects of this kind, with or without a stipend or class credit, in order to redress an obvious and unquestioned evil in their midst.

Teachers in Indiana, in Connecticut, and—on a very large scale—in Miami, have been conducting literacy-action programs with their pupils now for several years. From all reports, their success is impressive, their funding-problems few, and the challenge of recruitment far less serious than most acquiescent readers of the press and viewers of television probably would expect.

The media myth of student selfishness and apathy is just exactly that: a *myth*. During the past three years, I have been traveling and talking with young people in all regions of the country. I am convinced that there is a groundswell of essential decency within the students of the nation—students who are now in high school, or in their college years, and who are no longer willing to allow the agencies of mass dissemination to tell them how they feel.

I speak at thirty or forty high schools, colleges, and universities each year. I listen to the students and I talk with them late into the long evenings. Despite the worst the press can say, they do not sound "defeated, broken, avaricious." I go to New Hampshire, Michigan, New Mexico, South Carolina. Everywhere I go, the message is unchanged. Their conscience, their convictions, and their passions are intact.

Sometimes, admittedly, it is difficult at first for a teacher to elicit the real and honest voices of the young. At one high school, not long back, I asked the students how they felt about participation in an active, adult literacy struggle of the kind I have described.

The answers, at first, were all the same.

"Students don't care about those issues anymore," one pupil said.

"How do you know that?" I replied.

"Well", another student said, "the campus is quiet all around the country nowadays."

"Students are doing their own thing," another pupil said. Then she repeated that all too predictable but, somehow, never quite convincing statement of defeat: "They're into their own heads."

"How do you know that?" I inquired once more.

"Well, I read it in *Newsweek*," she replied.

The other students smiled.

I asked those students, a few minutes later, how many might be willing to give up a school's semester to participate in a local literacy effort if they could get class credit for their time. Before I left, half the students present had put down their names, addresses, and phone numbers on a sign-up sheet. I gave it later to one of their more energetic teachers.

Challenge to Teachers

This is a challenge to thousands of vigorous, hopeful, and imaginative teachers in our public schools. It is a challenge to raise high the stakes, then to break down that challenge into something tangible and real and near at hand: neither a sweeping nor an inconceivable endeavor, but one to which young people in their school or in their class or in their town can easily react and readily direct their personal passions and imaginations.

It must be a battle big enough to matter, but one which is still small enough to win.

Small beginnings lead to eloquent undertakings. We have to begin with challenges and problems that our students can imagine, analyze, and understand—and logically believe that it is in their personal power to confront.

Is the entire plan too radical? Is it, for that matter, a *truly* radical idea?

It is radical only when we lose all sense of history. Two hours of research and ten minutes of reflection will demonstrate to those who have forgotten, or perhaps who never knew, that childhood or, in this instance,

---

> "The people tell us their story, and we return their soul to them in words."

195

"adolescence"—as definitions of an antiseptic, morally isolated, school-mandated period of inert preparation—are relatively new and arbitrary concepts that did not exist prior to recent times.

"Adolescence", as the degrading definition of a docile and unquestioning consumer for a million-dollar industry of junk commodities and a billion-dollar industry that is defined as "public school," is not a definition that emerged out of a forehead of a Greek or Roman god.

Childhood in the passive and inert sense that we know that term today is not a biological given of our human nature.

Both concepts are arbitrary, antihuman and perhaps quite dangerous inventions of the Sixteenth Century. Prior to that time, childhood, as we think of it nowadays, did not exist at all. Children, once beyond the years of infancy, were treated, dressed, and acted pretty much the same as adults, with proper allowance made for their frail bodies and small size.

With the invention of childhood as a unique condition—like some form of illness—lasting generally into and after adolescence, the role of children underwent a drastic change. Little by little, as the Sixteenth Century progressed, children came to be regarded as they would be viewed for most of the next several centuries: "little packets of charming but incorrigible mischief, lovable at best, infuriating at their worst, in either case ingesting food and drink and other commodities of sundry kinds—contributing little and consuming much." (For additional information on "the invention of childhood" in the Sixteenth Century, see *Centuries of Childhood* by Phillipe Ariès. New York: Vintage Books, 1962.)

Children were regarded as "preparatory adults," "humans in training," small problems patiently waiting to be big ones.

Childhood, including adolescence, became a moratorium on life, a holding pattern, a time in which young people were obliged to spend about one quarter of their projected biological existence in rote drill and readiness for the next three quarters, which they might or might not ever live to know. Youth was thus defined as a preparation *for* life, not as a portion *of* it.

The concept, then, is (a) recent, (b) historical in origin, (c) totally outdated and archaic. It is neither god-given nor decreed by nature. It is the product of the highly imperfect imaginations of absolutely ordinary human beings: a product suited to another age, contrived to meet the needs of other centuries, but manifestly no longer useful to our own. Any concept that was contrived by men and women can be revised by men and women, too.

This, then is our challenge. It is the ultimate challenge for those of us who speak of literacy action or, indeed, of any other form of service learning on the part of those young men and women whom we teach.

It is for us to seize, perceive, and ultimately reconceive a concept which is, simultaneoulsy, a definition and a degradation of our pupils—one which serves to stifle the best within them while it holds them back from serving those who need their energies the most.

Students and teachers need not be the docile objects of historic process. We can also be its active subjects, catalytic and compassionate progenitors of moral change. We can be those who alter and empower history, rather than those who sit still in a quiet cell and watch it all pass by.

The choice this time does not belong to those who edit the daily newspapers and the weekly magazines, or cut the tapes and clip the films at CBS and ABC and NBC. The choice belongs to you and me.

Oral history and illiteracy can be linked as the words of the people are returned to them in writing. Reid Chapman tells a Salt student about his life in Kennebunk, Maine.

VI. Interns and Apprentices

Editorial

by Tim Stanton, Guest Editor

INTERNSHIP EDUCATION: PAST ACHIEVEMENTS/ FUTURE CHALLENGES

Alice laughed. "There's no use trying," she said, one can't believe impossible things."
"I dare say you haven't had much practice," said the Queen. "When I was your age I always did it for half an hour a day. Why sometimes I've believed as many as six impossible things -- before breakfast."
Lewis Carroll

Would you believe that almost every college and university, and many, if not most, high schools offer internships or other experiential learning opportunities to their students? Would you believe that in many institutions these experiences are now required of all students and that nationally one in seven students is involved in field experience education? That's the "conservative estimate" of the National Society for Internships and Experiential Education, extrapolated from data developed in statewide surveys in Kentucky and Michigan, and from their experience of more than 10 years' service to practitioners of this form of education.

What is internship education? It is a form of learning as old as our civilization, which has recently been rediscovered and reintegrated into modern educational practice. It includes all experiences wherein students learn by taking on responsible roles as participants in organizations, observing and reflecting while they are there. Expected outcomes of such experiences include increased self-esteem and personal growth derived from successfully meeting new interpersonal and intellectual challenges, acquisition of particular skills and knowledge, exposure to various work roles and career choices, and service to a particular community or group.

Internship experiences are found in every sort of organization -- non-profit agencies, corporations, government, policy institutes, neighborhood centers, etc. They are open to high school students (and recently even junior high students), undergraduate and graduate students, continuing education students, faculty, executives, unemployed youth. There are internship opportunities for everyone.

Internships can be paid or volunteer, part-time or full-time. They last anywhere from a few weeks to a year or more. They may be arranged and sponsored by educational institutions (for credit, career awareness, etc.), by work organizations (for personnel recruitment, professional advancement, etc.), by independent organizations and government agencies (to enable students to explore issue areas, policy making, etc.), or simply to provide extra hands for needed tasks. Name an activity and there's probably an internship related to it.

Long before the creation of schools and universities, learning-by-doing was the only way to learn. Craft guilds, apprenticeships, and the continued, informal passing-on of wisdom, skills, and lore were the essential means of teaching. Distinctions between learning and doing, between scholarship and work arose with the creation of the first universities. Only then did education evolve toward the theoretical, abstract, removed-from-the-practicalities-of-life model, which became paramount by the mid-point of this century.

Early colleges in the United States, patterning themselves after their European sisters, developed curriculum which was widely separated from the needs of a newly established nation. It was not until the founding of Rensselaer Polytechnic Institute, in 1824, that field experience learning was organized and sponsored by an educational institution. In this case students made field trips to factories and coal mines to examine first-hand their subject of study.

Passage of the Morrill Act (1862) represented the first national mandate for systematic application of knowledge. In each state the "agricultural and mechanical arts" were to be studied and shared with those on the farm who needed and would use them. "Field" work became a natural and integral part of "land grant" students' curricula.

The Settlement House movement of the late nineteenth century added to the trend toward practicality in education and the connection between it and the needs of society. Colleges and universities sponsored human service centers through which students served individuals and groups adjusting to the disruptions of migration and industrial urbanization, an early form of "service learning."

With the inception of professional education, the traditional internship was born. William Osler, Professor of Medicine at Johns Hopkins University, required his medical students to perform autopsies and observe his treatment of patients, a revolution in medical education at the time. Eventually other professions followed the doctors' lead developing "practice teaching," "moot court," "social work practica," etc.

Starting in 1906 a few, scattered undergraduate colleges, such as Northeastern, Antioch, and Benoit began experimenting with "cooperative education," requiring their students to supplement their liberal arts learning with alternative semesters of work or service. Internships and field experience education had developed a small, but firm toe-hold in U.S. education, which it maintained into the early 1960's.

What accounts for the recent, exponential growth in internship education? As in so many aspects of life in the United States since 1960, educators were suddenly forced by events, by changing technologies and cultural mores, to shake loose from their traditions. True believers among them began to identify "learning-by-doing" as an answer to a variety of social concerns and educational problems.

In response to the call, "If you're not part of the solution, you're part of the problem" students and faculty rejected the notion of a removed, cloistered curriculum, and worked to combine community service with learning. In the social sciences particularly, internships and practica were developed to relate studies directly to the social problems they were meant to address. Students exercised their social commitment and compassion through volunteer work in neighborhoods and communities surrounding their campuses. Faculty found a means to support their activities with seminars and credit.

Field experience education was seized by other educators and students as a means of reducing the Grand Canyon-like gap that traditional education had erected between learning and career development. Internships were developed to enable students to take on adult roles in a society that was establishing ever increasing education and professional certification prerequisites for joining the work force.

Not to be left in the dust, liberal arts faculty began to perceive internship experiences as important to both their disciplines and their students' rising clamor for relevance in the curriculum. Through "field studies" and internships the students were offered opportunities to develop critical thinking, problem-solving, communication, and learning-to-learn skills, which faculty grudgingly admitted could be more effectively acquired and practiced in the field than in the classroom.

Then there were the educational critics and reformers. Inspired by the philosophies of Dewey, Goodman, Whitehead, etc. and armed with the theories and findings of Coleman, Rogers, Friere, Kohlberg, Kolb, etc. they saw the purpose of education as holistic, developmental and political; to enable students to become whole and complete persons, equipped with both "critical consciousness" of themselves and their place in society and the tools, knowledge, motivation, and roles with which to effectively participate in the world and improve it. For these people linking theory and practice through field experience and critical reflection was the only means of effective, progressive education.

Finally, and most recently, field experience education has been utilized by those working to provide equal access to education and career advancement for such groups as adult learners, women, racial minorities, handicapped students, and unemployed youth. Internships and assessment and crediting of experiential learning have become a means of recognition and certification of the skills and knowledge possessed by individuals previously under-served by and under-represented in traditional education.

Thus we find ourselves today surrounded by a large and expanding variety of field experience-based learning opportunities. Whether labeled service learning, cooperative education, field study or internships, (just to list a few of the names currently in use), these experiences have transformed our thinking about learning and doing and the relationship between the two, and fundamentally changed curriculum and instruction in our educational institutions.

Given this considerable achievement, what are the next challenges to be faced by practitioners of this form of education and training? How can programs become fully institutionalized and available to every interested learner? How can coherence and professional discipline be brought to a "field" as dynamic, diverse, pioneering, and fragmented as experiential education? The contributors to this issue of the *Journal* suggest at least a few directions for our attention.

Jon Wagner describes a program model which effectively integrated three traditions of experiential education -- group process, simulation, and field experience -- into academic, university sponsored field studies. He notes the importance of combining these traditions to enhance and ensure student learning from experience. His article reminds us of the breadth of this field we call experiential education, its differing and often separate traditions and strands, and the potential benefits available to us through combination and integration of our differences.

Dennis Pataniczek and Carol Johansen examine the new roles internship education requires of both students and faculty and the need to better understand these differences in order to maximize benefits to all concerned. Joan Chan, supervisor of interns at New York's Downstate Medical Center, describes the role interns take in her program and the significant contributions they make to patient care, noting the means she utilizes for providing training and supportive supervision. Samuel Mungo describes an internship program designed to combat later "burnout," a common problem of those in the helping professions. Gale Warner, ex-intern, eloquently outlines her internship with the Hidden Villa Environmental Project, and articulates many feelings, problems and benefits she derived from her experience.

Each of these writers touches upon another serious challenge to field experience educators -- our need to develop more complex and more accurate methods with which to define and describe what interns, faculty, and field supervisors do to ensure learning for the student and service for the host organization. A first step may be simply to examine field experience itself. David Thornton Moore describes two dimensions of interns' experiences that contribute to learning: the substantive knowledge gained and the social relationships experienced on the job. He suggests that increased understandings of these categories of experiential learning would enable field experience educators to both better articulate what interns actually learn and begin to break down the troublesome dichotomy between classroom and field learning. Judith Kleinfeld, in the Idea Notebook, offers a helpful suggestion for discovering the content and extent of student learning without undertaking an ambitious research project.

And there are still other serious challenges before us. Perhaps later issues of the *Journal* and other publications should address some of the following issues.

- --When are learners ready for field experience education? More specifically, how do we determine which particular program model and strategy is most appropriate for an individual learner at any particular individual stage of personal development? What type of program best serves adult learners? Under-prepared learners? Adolescent learners? Primary school learners?
- --What is the most appropriate relationship between field experience learning and traditional, disciplinary learning? Should one dominate the other? Can they serve and support each other?
- --Can we define and develop professional development tracks for practitioners of field experience education, internship coordinators, etc.? How and where may they effectively sharpen their skills, and extend their abilities to apply their experientially gained skills and knowledge?
- --Finally, and perhaps most importantly, what is the ultimate purpose and value of this form of learning and teaching? What sort of citizens do we hope to develop as a result of an internship program? Were field experiences learning to become a dominant pedagogy in U.S. education, what sort of schools would we have, or would we have any? What sort of society, and what values do we wish to promote as a result of our effort?

The next two decades of development in field experience education should be no less critical, nor less difficult than the last two. I believe they will also be equally productive and rewarding for all concerned. How many impossible things can you believe before breakfast on December 31, 1999?

Tim Stanton is Director of the Field Study Office and Lecturer in the College of Human Ecology at Cornell University.

AN INTRODUCTION TO INTERNSHIP EDUCATION:
New Roles for Students and Faculty

by Dennis Pataniczek and Carol Johansen

Internship education has emerged as a vital component in the professional and pre-professional training programs available in many, if not most, institutions of higher education today. Such internship education or field-based education is different in its very nature from traditional academic learning for both students and faculty members and thus will require different roles and yield different benefits than on-campus academic learning situations. It is vital to understand these differences in roles, for such an understanding will enhance the internship education process and maximize its benefits to all concerned.

Internship or field-based education, for the purposes of this discussion, is defined as direct involvement in nonclassroom settings, sponsored by an institution of higher education, and jointly and cooperatively supervised by agency and university personnel. Internships may be full-time or part-time; compensation may be monetary or not. In either case, academic credit is earned by documenting the achievement of selected learning goals and objectives.

New Roles for Students

Students involved in university sponsored internships are learning experientially

Dennis Pataniczek is Faculty Advisor and Assistant Professor, ESCAPE Field Study Project, University of Oregon. Carol Johansen is Field Coordinator, Wallace School of Community Service and Public Administration, University of Oregon.

which differs from traditional classroom learning in that experiential learners are actively involved in doing, while classroom learners' involvement is often more indirect. In addition, experiential learners are asked to **set their own goals for learning** and task accomplishment while traditional classroom learning goals are usually set by the instructor prior to the first class meeting. Assessment of the learning is also different, since those involved in field-based learning are asked to reflect on their experience, to **engage in self assessment**, and to utilize such reflection and self assessment in setting further learning goals. In contrast, nearly all formal assessment in traditional classrooms is completed by the instructor. Whether or not reflection and self assessment occurs is frequently considered extraneous to the real (graded) learning experience.

Therefore, in their role as learners, those involved in internship education are expected, by the very nature of experiential learning, to engage in goal setting, reflection, self assessment, and revising both task and learning goals several times during any given internship experience. In addition, often by necessity, interns are required to **integrate newly learned concepts, procedures, and skills with prior learning from on-campus courses** and other experiences in order to effectively perform the tasks expected of them.

Another role often new to students in internship education is that of entering a **collegial relationship with agency personnel.** Such collegiality is expected by agency staff members, and it affords the intern professional development opportunities available to full-time staff members such as obvious on-the-job training as well as staff meetings and professional meetings and conferences.

Most interns find themselves in new roles of **giving and receiving feedback.** Because interns often come to agencies armed with the latest in theory and the newest techniques, they may be asked to make observations on current agency practices from their own fresh perspective. From the feedback they receive from agency staff and supervisors, interns learn to identify their own strengths as well as areas for improvement and are frequently encouraged to take risks in order to develop further competence and confidence.

A final and often unrecognized new role for student interns is the opportunity to act as a **liaison between the university and the community.** Student interns find themselves representing their programs, department, and university to the agency and, in turn, representing or at least reporting agency concerns back to campus.

Benefits to Students

The benefits to students who assume these roles as interns are numerous. It is recognized that such benefits may vary among individual internship situations and programs, but the authors believe that the following represent significant benefits across internship settings.

Perhaps first and foremost among these benefits to students is **direct experience in the world of work.** Such documented and supervised experience is invaluable to students when they seek employment; participation in an internship experience provides a definite advantage over those applicants who have no such comparable experience. Such an internship enables participants to apply often highly abstract theories in practical real-life situations; in short, internships can help to make classroom learning "come alive."

A second obvious benefit for students is that internship education offers opportunities for both **career exploration and preparation.** Internships provide students with a clear sense of what it is like to work in a given profession, with people who have chosen that profession. Training is provided by those directly involved in the field, and student interns frequently have contact with those in a given profession who make decisions regarding the employment and dismissal of those having chosen a particular career. Such persons offer distinct and often highly valued perspectives regarding "next step" future training experiences. In addition, career preparation through internships enables students to make decisions about future coursework and professional development based on real experiences with testing their own skill and knowledge level.

Another difference exists for student learners who are engaged in internship education. Students **learn skills involved in the documentation of their own learning.** It is essential to understand that academic credit is earned not for the intern experience itself, but rather for the learning that accompanies and results from it. Such learning must be articulated and documented, and interns are actively engaged in this process. This facet of the learning process provides invaluable practical training in accountability.

When internships involve concurrent seminars composed of fellow interns, another role emerges for students: that of peer facilitator. In such seminars, students share their own experiences, but also question one another, often rigorously. Such questioning results in students articulating more clearly the rationale for actions as well as becoming more clear regarding their own learning and task accomplishment.

In addition to the different roles expected of interns earning academic credit, direct participation at an institution or agency provides the student intern with a wealth of additional opportunities for role-taking which are not commonly available through other learning contexts. These opportunities are briefly discussed below.

Perhaps the central feature of internship education is that students are expected to **be active participants** in their role at their agencies. From being an active participant in choosing the agency at which they will serve as interns through involvement in goal setting and learning contract negotiation and beyond, active involvement is expected and demanded by agencies. Interns are expected to "jump in and get their feet wet" from the onset, with a minimum of observation and passivity.

Professional behavior on the part of the student intern is expected according to the norms at the sponsoring agency. Interns receive an initiation into the professional work world via orientation, interactions with agency colleagues and supervisors, and staff meetings. A central part of this expectation of professional behavior involves interns' contributing their own ideas, being innovative, and locating and utilizing available resources. Interns often find they are appreciated for the fresh perspectives they offer to the agency as well as for the gaps in agency service and/or expertise which they help to fill. Accountability to the agency is also expected of interns; such accountability helps interns to learn another important aspect of professional behavior.

Internship education provides students with effective and meaningful learning experiences, because internships are supervised and evaluated. In simpler terms, an internship experience, because it offers **opportunities for students to test skills and to learn from mistakes with feedback and support,** offers an attractive alternative to the "school of hard knocks."

Finally, and of utmost importance, is the **opportunity for the student intern's personal growth.** It is the authors' belief that internship education provides an unequalled opportunity for students' competence and confidence building. Students often leave internships seemingly totally different persons from when they entered; they gain a sense of direction, a belief in themselves and their careers, and a confidence that comes only after a "trial by fire."

Such benefits do not accrue to all student interns. Some learn lessons much different than those above, and some will even decide not to pursue careers in a given profession based on internship experiences. The authors contend that such a situation is actually of long-term benefit to both the student and the profession. However, for most student interns who assume and maximize the new roles expected of them in the internship setting, these benefits and more will come.

Briefly summarized, internship or field-based education requires students to be active participants in the entire learning process. The student assumes a role of collaborator and colleague with both agency and university personnel.

New Roles for Faculty

Because students' new roles in internship education do not come naturally or easily to most students, faculty members who supervise and/or coordinate intern programs assume new roles as well. Faculty **become facilitators of learning** rather than merely purveyors of knowledge. They must communicate intensively and extensively with students, agency personnel, administrators, and other faculty in order to assist students in arranging their internships and learning from the experience. Students in the field are applying classroom theories and experimenting with different methodologies. Their reactions to their experiences are immediate and they demand explanations and help with the problems that arise. Faculty must be prepared and willing to meet such demands. Such intervention and interaction enable faculty to point out strengths or deficiencies in students' work.

As facilitators of learning, faculty have the opportunity to use new and creative methods of teaching. They experience themselves in new and different roles in their institutions. Experiential education offers an opportunity for faculty to **work with students and faculty from departments different from their own.** Quite often students from various academic disciplines will undertake a project in the field. The result is that faculty must work together with these students as advisors/facilitators, enabling them to share perspectives and teaching responsibilities with each other.

Faculty who facilitate internship education **have a high degree of visibility and responsibility in their teaching roles.** Faculty are indeed on the front line, at times the firing line. If students make mistakes in the field or have been poorly matched to the learning internship or if the agency has not been prepared to work with interns, faculty must accept much of the responsibility. On the other hand, students' success becomes faculty success. Students who feel they have achieved little in traditional graded academic classrooms and find they excel in the field tend to relate their achievements to faculty who work with them in the field.

Another new and often challenging role for many faculty is that of **performing liaison and public relations** functions between the campus and the community. The fact is that faculty who are visible in the community become informal spokespersons for the institutions they represent. Community leaders, business owners, government officials, legislators, and taxpayers look to field faculty for information about happenings on campus. Being on the front line means having to offer explanations for what students or administrators are doing on campus. However, there are definite benefits to this front line position. If field faculty place well-informed, hard-working students in appropriate internships, then the community at large is quick to perceive that the faculty and the institution are doing its work well and that students today are certainly receiving a solid and beneficial education. Many taxpayers, parents, and power brokers translate the effectiveness of students' education to the students' ability to get jobs, keep jobs, and contribute to their communities. Faculty members involved in such ventures are vital links in disseminating information about such programs and students' contributions to the community.

Internship education also offers faculty members **opportunities for enhancing their own career goals.** Faculty participation in internship education may result in access to agency or business owned technology which is lacking in on-campus settings. Many institutions rely heavily on theory without practice due to the expense of maintaining up-to-date equipment. By developing solid internship programs, faculty can **arrange with sponsoring agencies for use of their equipment** in exchange for person-power output.

Participation in internship education can also **open up new possibilities for consulting.** Faculty in the field are easily accessible to agency personnel and are in the position to offer advice and help. Such avenues of consulting are seen by many institutions as service consulting rather than entrepreneurial. The community at large often views this service as a positive effort of schools to involve themselves more with the community in which they are located.

Participation in internship education can also **complement traditional faculty roles in research and publication.** Faculty who are on-site at agencies on a regular basis will develop a new and cooperative relationship with agency personnel and will find a warmer welcome for conducting research. Data becomes more accessible, and the possibility of collaborative research efforts emerge.

Briefly summarized, the faculty role in field-based education broadens the concept of the facilitator of learning. Field-based education offers faculty a range of teaching methods in unlimited settings. The benefits of being able to adopt curriculum and teaching methods to individual students and learning situations are obvious. The expanded faculty roles of communicators and outreach representatives of their institutions are new and potentially exciting. Working with faculty from many departments on campus and working with community leaders and professionals outside of academia is a gratifying challenge. However, it has been the authors' experience that seeing students grow and achieve before their eyes is the most satisfying role with the greatest benefits.

Such benefits for faculty who work with interns may come years after the internship when students report that they have lasting memories of what they learned through their internship and that it had real impact on their lives. While not everything that students learn is "positive" in an affective sense, applied learning does give the opportunity to sift through information, theories, and methodologies on a personal and individualized level.

Internship education, then, can play an extremely positive role for both students and faculty members at institutions of higher education. Institutions which support internship education and other field-based programs are viewed by students and the public as being responsive to their needs. When significant field-based learning opportunities are offered to students, an expanded definition of service is developed for both faculty and the academic institution. Such service--to students, to faculty, and to the public--when documented and disseminated, can only mean increased public support for the institution from its community.

Educating Interns in a Child Life Program:

The Agency Supervisor's Perspective

by Joan M. Chan

When I first met Marie, she was awaiting her fourth cadaveric kidney transplant. Who was this ghostlike, yet fiery elfin child who hobbled along dragging a cumbersome, plastic right leg that never seemed to belong to her? A little girl just 7 years old. What brief passage in my textbooks had ravaged her childhood? Marie bore a mindless, indifferent fluke of nature: cystinosis, a rare, fatal, genetic disease. Marie was two years old when discovery of cystine crystals deposited throughout her body confirmed the diagnosis of Fanconi syndrome.

When Marie was 5 years old, she received her first kidney transplant. Rejection and transplant nephrectomy ensued. Within the next 2 years, surgeons would perform two additional kidney transplants: both kidneys were rejected. During this period, complications of angiography led to Marie's right, below-the-knee amputation.

The dry, unyielding, haunting facts of Marie's chronic deterioration speak for themselves. She experienced numerous hospitalizations and separations from her family. Massive nose bleeds, precipitated by Marie's incessant nose picking, terrified her mother and led to seven emergency hospitalizations and transfusions. Each Monday and Thursday, for a minimum of 4 to 5 hours, Marie underwent hemodialysis. My job as a Child Life intern was to help Marie negotiate the maze of pain, helplessness, terror, anger, and annihilation itself, locked within her experience.

Excerpt from log of Patricia Taner Leff

Joan M. Chan is Director of the Child Life Program and Clinical Assistant Professor in the Department of Pediatrics Downstate Medical Center, Brooklyn, N.Y.

Working with hospitalized children in the Child Life Program at State University Hospital, Downstate Medical Center, Brooklyn, New York, is a unique field placement for student interns. Since the Program's inception in 1973, our two main goals have been:
1. to be a model therapeutic play program for pediatric patients,
2. to provide supervised field work experiences for student interns in a health setting.

Students knowledgeable in child development theories with previous experience in working with healthy children, and interested in examining a potential career in the health field seem attracted to the setting. They are young adults striving to obtain maturity and adulthood. Many are uncertain of the profession they wish to enter, but are anxious to gain knowledge of various types of vocations. Child Life, a relatively new profession, offers a good introduction to the health care setting.

"Interns must develop the ability to be reflective, non-interfering, empathetic, growth-promoting therapeutic agents."

> "As hospitalized children bring their damaged organs and illnesses to us for healing, they also bring themselves: a growing, developing infant, toddler, pre-schooler, little boy or girl, a young adolescent."

State University Hospital is a tertiary care facility situated in a high risk urban area. Our internships are designed to help college students understand the implications of hospitalization for children (and their families) from infancy through 18 years of age. We expect interns to adopt a holistic approach to help ease the psychological and developmental stresses of our patients. They supplement the professionals in fostering growth and development of patients through play activities. As an agency supervisor, my responsibility is to help the interns make significant contributions to the Child Life Program, gain a thorough understanding of the special needs of hospitalized children and their families, and achieve personal growth. I accomplish this by continued and careful sharing of knowledge regarding patient care and professional issues, and by providing ongoing support.

All pediatric patients suffer pain, discomfort, emotional distress when they are hospitalized. However, not all children can express their feelings or relate in the same manner as when they are well and intact. Patients often enter an unfamiliar institution with strange sights and smells, staffed by unknown people who often inflict pain. There are those suffering from chronic, often life-threatening conditions who are frequently re-admitted for lengthy or repeated stays. As hospitalized children bring their damaged organs and illnesses to us for healing, they also bring themselves: a growing, developing infant, toddler, pre-schooler, little boy or girl, a young adolescent. They bring their own fantasies, feelings, and fears concerning their illnesses, others' abandonment of them, mutilation, and death. In addition they bring the wishes and fears of their families reacting to the profound stress of their child's illness.

For example, in our hospital, we have children with tracheostomies, with congenital heart disease requiring open heart surgery, with end-stage renal disease requiring hemodialysis treatment or transplantation, or with various forms of cancer. Our patients, families, staff (including interns) are faced with the prospect of death for a more extended period than in the past. Along with prolongation of life, we have thus become increasingly concerned with the quality of life, the impact of severe illnesses on children, the impact of multiple separations from the family.

Play (including manipulation of materials, art, creative writing, medical doctor play) is the primary tool in the Child Life Program, because it has an important role in learning, coping with stress, and in gaining some aspect of control and mastery. Play is natural for children. In the hospital, it brings normalcy to an otherwise confusing environment. To develop a therapeutic milieu, we have designed a playroom to provide the space, materials and personnel to give support to children and their families. The patients often express their feelings about their illness, and/or handicap and hospitalization in this safe, child-oriented environment, where no painful treatments or procedures ever take place. There is a free choice of materials, and play activities are conducted by professionals supplemented by interns.

Objectives in Educating Our Student Interns

We have developed several objectives in educating interns in order to help our sick and handicapped children, both humanely and scientifically.

In the hospital setting, opportunities are afforded to help interns:
1. Deepen their understanding of the meaning of human development (i.e. physical, neurological, mental, personal and social).
2. Recognize the special and individual needs and reactions of hospitalized children and their families during a crisis period.
3. Develop appropriate techniques to encourage therapeutic play with sick and handicapped children.
4. Develop an ability to communicate with hospitalized patients, their parents and other members of the health team.
5. Develop the ability to be reflective, non-interfering, empathetic, growth-promoting therapeutic agents with sick children and their families.
6. Understand the diverse needs and background of other members of the intern group, thus working cooperatively with them.
7. Observe how illness and hospitalization interrupt the growth and development of children.

Selection Process

Prior to acceptance in the Child Life Program we ask that each intern be interviewed by their campus internship program co-ordinator and read our Student Volunteer Manual, which contains information about the goals of the program, description of patients and wards, requirements, guidelines for observing, recording, etc. Then, if they are still interested, and deemed appropriate to the Child Life internship, they may be referred to me, as agency supervisor, for an interview.

In order to provide a meaningful educational experience for our interns, and in view of the lengthy time (a minimum of 4 eight hour days a week for a semester) a careful selection of the intern must be made. A very strong commitment to the Program's goals is elicited in the initial interview prior to acceptance. The student is also asked to spend some time observing patients, their families, and other staff and interns in a playroom session prior to making a decision. In addition to the educational requirements, interns must exhibit a degree of enjoyment of children, and sensitivity to their needs through warmth, understanding, flexibility and creativity. They must also demonstrate satisfactory relationships with adults and emotional stability. As an agency supervisor, my priorities are both to provide quality patient care as well as positive educational experiences for our interns.

Role of the Intern

The goal of the intern is to contribute to the optimal well-being of our pediatric patients. By focusing on the child rather than the child's illness, interns establish and maintain interpersonal relationships through observation, play, and conversation, thereby helping sick children and adolescents to understand what has been done to them in medical and nursing care. To do this effectively the student needs to be knowledgeable and understand the significance of the child's medical diagnosis, the age of onset, course and severity of the illness. As supervisor, I discuss these issues with the interns during the pre-conferences held before each play session. In addition, each intern is expected to elicit further information about the child's medical and psycho-social situation, and to assess needs and develop treatment goals by speaking with other health professionals, the patients themselves, and family members.

Effective communication skills can only be carried out if the intern has a good understanding of the psychological reactions as well as the physiological status of the child. A trusting relationship is established through satisfying and constructive verbal and non-verbal interchange. This is often a difficult task, however. Interns must learn to recognize such behaviors as egocentricity, constricted interests, heightened anxiety, emotional dependence, and insecurity as normal reactions of hospitalized children and their families.

In their advocacy role, interns are expected to support sick and/or handicapped children's rights. Patients need to be informed in developmentally appropriate ways about the nature of their illness and treatment to help them cope and function. Interns accomplish this by providing play or activities for patients to express feelings about their illness, family relationships and attitudes toward staff. Interns' reports of these activties enable the professional staff to be better informed and to help patients cooperate more appropriately with their treatment.

The type of assignment made to each intern depends on past educational experiences, personal level of maturity and needs of the Child Life Program. Generally, the role of the student is limited to direct involvement with individual or small groups of children in the Playroom. After some experience, when the interns have assimilated the goals and philosophy of the program, and have developed skills and techniques in therapeutic play, they are assigned to individual bedside activities with terminally ill children. Interns are given a choice in these assignment.

As a student progresses in the internship, she is expected to assume responsibility for the maintenance and supervision of the playroom, materials and equipment. They are also expected to contribute a special project to the program in the form of creating preparation materials for procedures and surgery, creating puppet shows, or developing patient educational materials. The project is tailored to the intern's special interests and talents.

To prevent interruption of normal development which often takes place during hospitalization, on-going assessments of the needs of patients and their families as well as re-evaluation of relationships are carried out and recorded by the interns. In their attempts to help the family be a partner in the health care team, interns observe and discuss with other health professionals various techniques in handling crisis situations. Because of their continued presence on the wards, they are able to observe how parents and children are given information, treatment alternatives, and possible outcomes.

Supervision

The support networks we provide in Child Life are individual and group supervision. This support is necessary because of the stress created by working with children who have complex, chronic illnesses (and their families). In the Child Life Program supervision is given through group conferences 30 minutes prior and 30 minutes after each play session. In the pre-conferences, interns' assignments are made and background medical, psychosocial information is provided for every child expected to attend the playroom or those to be given bedside activities. The specific handicap (with any special limitations) of each child is discussed, along with the plan of treatment for the day, and suggestions for suitable and favorite play materials. Every attempt is made to assign the same intern to the same child during the child's entire hospital stay. In order to maintain consistency and continuity of treatment, interns write up their activities after every session for review by the supervisor.

The post conference is held after every session. The supervisor generally makes an opening remark to elicit a general reaction to the play session. Interns are also asked to make pertinent observations of their child's behavior through play, interactions between parents and child, communication between other personnel (administering treatments) to the child, and to describe their reaction to the situation. The supervisor gives recommendations for play materials and alternate ways of handling the child during the play session. At this time interns may also question or seek ideas as to what sort of guidance to give parents as they consider effects of medical treatments and decisions and reflect on their reactions.

It is not unusual for interns to feel uneasy and guilty about revealing to the entire group observations and information they have obtained. The supervisor tries to help them accept the need for developing skills in the critical evaluation of the medical, emotional, developmental and social data they observe. Every attempt is made to help the interns see that discussion and objective evaluation of their experiences are part of the learning process, and need not imply punitive or unfavorable criticism of the child, family, or the intern.

Individual supervision is offered to interns through a one hour weekly session. Prior to these meetings interns are required to hand in their written logs containing their feelings and reactions to the hospital setting, patient assignments, relationships with supervisors and/or peers. It is during these conferences that the interns' emotional reactions to the internship and professional aspirations are explored. Priorities are also clarified so that interns may be helped to function more effectively.

I am pleased with myself as I notice myself being firmer with my handling of the children. If a child is in the wrong, like grabbing a toy away from another, I've learned to immediately intervene and say "We do not grab it out of another child's hand -- you will get your turn when --- is finished. In the playroom we share all the toys." I used to be aware of all these rules, but was always afraid to enforce them. One of my fears was that the children would not listen to me and they would dislike me. It's still a little hard for me to do this, but I am much farther along from where I started out. Also, I gather that I used to be more afraid of children than I am now. Both being too overpowering or weak in front of children was of major concern to me. I find when you are sure of yourself and your actions the child will pick it up immediately -- if you are insecure the child will also pick it up and make life miserable. The child needs someone solid and sure in order for him to feel safe and comfortable. Is it a wonder that neurotic parents breed neurotic children? The children respond better toward a person who is comfortable and sure of what they are doing and saying. I find this is so in my case.

Understanding their own individual needs, weaknesses and strengths requires a great deal of self-examination on the part of the interns. Sorting out thoughts and feelings is a joint process for interns and the supervisor. We try to encourage expression of feelings, so that interns may sharpen their awareness of how stress affects their patients, the families, and themselves.

> When I first heard today that Eddie died, the words had little effect on me. Maybe I didn't really believe it. In the morning, I know I walked slower when I heard Eddie died, but I don't know what I thought. It started hurting when I saw the effect it had on other people. I didn't know how to talk about death. Or have any way of expressing my feelings, except crying to myself.
>
> Excerpt from log of
> Donna Cohn, former intern

"I didn't know how to talk about death."

In addition, the socio-cultural background of our patients is often very different from that of the interns. This needs to be shared and related to patient adjustment problems.

> Stacey said that her mother would not come to pick her up (on discharge from the hospital). This thought alone caused her to be a very insecure little girl. She now avoided talking about mother altogether; she had given up hope. The child knew her mother very well -- she was constantly feeling the pain of abandonment. Mother left Stacey in the hospital for fourteen days after she was supposed to be released. During that time she changed her phone number and left her job. It took the police to find her and issue her a warrant to pick up the child. Stacey was going home. She had to come back to the clinic every Friday morning. If she didn't go for treatment, the statistics said that she would be dead within a year. I knew as she left the hospital her case would be out of our hands. Mother called the hospital later in the week. She said that she was not bringing Stacey back but would look for a hospital closer to her home. Stacey went home in December. She received no treatment that I am aware of. This November she became a statistic. I question if treatment could have cured Stacey. I wonder if she could have led a normal life. I try to hold back my anger -- to hold back feelings of hate for a woman I don't even know. I try to understand. Sometimes I don't even want to try.
>
> Excerpt from log of
> Nancy Cincotta, former intern

Evaluation

Evaluation of each student's progress is a continuous process interwoven with the functions described above. It begins with the supervisor's first meeting with the intern. Immediate impressions are obtained during the two playroom observations sessions. The manner in which the interns conduct themselves, how they respond to their assigned families, how they accept supervision and how they relate to other staff members and to other students are continually assessed. Gathering and sharing this information with the interns is important in helping them in the role of Child Life assistant.

At the completion of their clinical experience in the Child Life Program, interns are given a final evaluation of their performance and are requested to complete an evaluation of the program.

Relationship between Campus Coordinators and Agency Supervisors

Open, direct communication between campus internship coordinators and agency supervisors is critical to a successful internship program. The need for an on-site visit by the campus coordinator to the agency hosting interns prior to placement cannot be overemphasized. The coordinator and the agency supervisor should develop a close working relationship and set parallel goals and objectives for their respective activities with the student interns.

In addition, before sending a student to the agency for an interview the campus coordinator should provide the supervisor with information on the potential intern's academic record, and an assessment of the student's level of functioning, adaptability, maturity, and ability to function under stress. Without this information the agency supervisor will have difficulty determining whether her internship will be appropriate and ultimately successful for both the program and the intern.

Interns usually spend more time in their field placement than on campus, thus diminishing, if not eliminating sustained contact with faculty. (Hopefully contact on some regular basis will be established and maintained with the intern by the campus coordinator.) As a result, the agency supervisor must also make a great investment and commitment to developing an intense and mutually satisfying relationship with the interns in order to help them make substantial contributions to the program and emerge with a positive sense of self.

I am currently a registered pediatric nurse. My decision to pursue a nursing profession came after four years of liberal arts and early childhood education courses at Brooklyn College. The turning point came when I joined the Child Life Program five years ago as an intern for part of my clinical experience required by Brooklyn College. The Child Life Program contained all the ingredients necessary to help formulate my personal and professional life. Some of the ingredients were as follows: working with different types of children on a long and short term basis; group discussion after each session with close supervision; ongoing supervision with Mrs. Chan to deal with the problems and crises that arise while working in the hospital setting; a feeling of contribution and growth in the program and in myself. Without my involvement in the program I seriously doubt I would be in the health profession today.

*Excerpt from the log of
Linda Cohen Wollman, former intern*

References

- Adams, M.A. "A Hospital Play Program: Helping Children with Serious Illness." *American Journal of Orthopsychiatry,* 1976, 46 (3), 416-424.
- Blom, G.E. "The Reactions of Hospitalized Children to Illness." *Pediatrics,* 1958, 22, 590-600.
- Bolig, R. "Child Life Workers: Facilitating their Growth and Development." *Journal of Association for Children's Health Care.* 1982, 10, 3, 94-99.
- Brown, L. "Supervising Child Life Students: Practice of Hospital Supervisor." *Journal of Association for Children's Health Care,* 1982, 10, 3, 100-102.
- Chan, J. and Leff, P. "Parenting the Chronically Ill Child in Hospital: Issues and Concerns." *Journal of Association for Children's Health Care,* 1982, 11, 9-16.
- Chan, J. and Cincotta, N. "Training Students to Work with Terminally Ill Children in a Child Life Program." *The House Staff and Thanatology,* Ed. de Bellis, 1982, Arno Press, 111-117.
- Freiberg, K. "How Parents React When Their Child is Hospitalized." *American Journal of Nursing,* 1972, 7, 1260-1272.
- Leff, P. and Chan, J. "Reflections of a Medical Student in a Child Life Program." *Journal of the Association for the Care of Children in Hospitals,* 1977, 5, 3, 18-24.

PERSPECTIVES ON Learning in Internships

by
David Thornton Moore

Talking about learning in internships is harder than many people think. In years of research and reading about students who work in a real-world setting for educational credit, I have heard participants -- both students and teachers -- make claims like these: "I learned a lot about people"; "I learned how to be more confident"; and, "I learned all about city government." Pressed to elaborate on these statements, many of my respondents began to stutter: "Well, you know, like how to get along with different people, you know?" These disappointingly vague answers do not necessarily indicate that, in fact, the students learned nothing of substance in their field experiences (although, regretfully, that may be the case). Rather, this inarticulateness points, I suggest, to the lack of a clear and productive vocabulary for describing what one has learned by working.

Many practitioners and writers in the field of experiential education implicitly assume or explicitly claim that activity in non-classroom settings leads to two basic forms of learning: personal growth, or development in such "affective" areas as self-concept, attitudes about school and work, and social interaction skills; and practice or retention of academic and practical skills. For the purposes of this paper, I will set aside the question of personal or affective growth in classroom and internship environments. Instead, let us focus here on the intellectual, cognitive, mental domain of learning.

Some of the classic theoretical treatments of experiential learning contribute to the common assumption that "academic" learning happens in classrooms and is at best "tested" or refined through engagement with non-school, experiential activities (Coleman, 1977; Kolb, 1976). This apparent belief that classroom learning and field learning are clearly dichotomous, that they may be complementary but exceedingly different experiences, worries me. Obviously, in some respects they are very different at times: in purpose, in social organization, in skills required, in outcomes. But several years of first-hand research in internship sites (Moore, 1981, 1982) convinces me that the lines between the two formats are not so clearcut as some people suggest. In fact, the two often overlap.

There are two important dimensions of comparison in the relationship between academic learning and field learning. The first concerns the kinds of mental work one is expected to perform in either setting. The second involves the forms of social relations in which one engages while participating in a particular learning environment.

"Mental Work" in Internships

To some extent, the first dimension is about "subject matter," or the substantive knowledge the intern encounters and uses in the process of working in class or placement. That substance may be about local government, or business principles, or computational skills, or the structure of a complex organization. Any of those "subjects" may be handled either in a classroom or in a workplace. What concerns me more than substance, however, is process: What is the student expected or able to *do* with it? How does the student engage and use the facts, skills, principles, values, procedures or worldviews that make up the social stock of knowledge in the environment? There are several ways of talking about the mental work that a person does in a classroom or placement setting. Bloom (1956) proposes a taxonomy of educational objectives for school in which he outlines six progressively complex forms of intellectual performance:

— knowledge (remembering, by recognition or recall, of ideas, material or phenomena)
— comprehension (understanding the literal message in a communication)
— application (correct and appropriate use of knowledge)
— analysis (breaking knowledge down into component parts and detecting relations among them)

David Thornton Moore is Director of Cooperative Education at the Gallatin Division of New York University.

> "Is the knowledge presented to the learner as fixed, masterable, indisputable? Or can the student-intern add to the knowledge, reorganize it, transform it, even reject it?"

— synthesis (putting together elements to form a whole)
— evaluation (making judgments about the value, for some purpose, of ideas, solutions, materials, etc.)

This framework for categorizing levels of knowledge-use has been used extensively in the development and study of school curricula. In similar ways, it could be used to understand the forms of thinking performed by interns in work or other non-classroom environments. I have no particular stake in the Bloom taxonomy; there are other schemes that help one to analyze mental operations (cf. Piaget in Wadsworth, 1971; Bruner, 1973; Luria, 1976). The point here is not so much to propose a specific theory as to raise the questions: Is the knowledge presented to the learner as fixed, masterable, indisputable? What operations is the learner expected, enabled, forbidden to do with the knowledge? Can the student-intern add to the knowledge, reorganize it, transform it, even reject it?

Typically, knowledge in schools is defined in advance, presented as certain, displayed intact on cue (cf. Mehan, 1979). Especially at the lower grades, but even into college, students ingest facts and ideas, store them whole, and present them back to the teacher. The knowledge acquired in this way may get more and more complex, but it remains fixed and external to the student. In some instances, of course, a student may be encouraged to invent knowledge, or at least to transform it.

Knowledge-use in internship settings appears to vary somewhat more than that in classroom, according to our observations in thirty-five different workplaces where students participated in an experiential learning program. In many sites, interns are presented "facts" as immutable, unchallengeable, once-and-for all.

Item: A student placed in a curriculum development firm was asked to calculate the "readability levels" of some new texts. She was shown the formula for determining the grade-level of a passage, and then set about figuring it for a set of entries. Her supervisor presented the formula as fixed, necessary (if slightly silly); the student was not permitted to invent a different method.

In other situations, students undertook complex tasks which demanded considerable flexibility and creativity of intellect.

Item: An intern in a city councilmember's office decided, after running into problems locating information, to reorganize the legislative files. He set up a system for receiving, categorizing, storing and retrieving information about the substance and progress of various bills passing through the Council. To complete the job, he had to understand not only filing techniques, but also the important dimensions of legislation, the kinds of things people would need to know about bills.

In our extensive observations of student-interns, we also discovered that the "reflection" component of thought, so often claimed by experiential educators to be missing from the "real world," in fact appears more frequently than we expected. While it is true that people working in a business or other organization do not often stop to discuss the abstract, generalized implications of their work, or to apply explicit theories to their practices, we nonetheless found a number of instances in which workers did formulate general principles, did articulate working theories, did consider alternative approaches to complex problems. Theorists such as Coleman and Kolb both seem to have a picture in mind of an intern diving into a practical arena with no preconceptions about the field, with no hypotheses about the way things will work; they suggest that the new worker uses a "trial and error" strategy. To some small extent, that may be true. But to a larger extent, we find that the student-worker approaches each new problem with some working framework, some set of hunches or principles or guidelines that shape her strategy. Those approaches may emerge from the student's own thought processes and experiences, or may be presented in advance of the work by other members of the organization. The fact is that most productive organizations cannot afford too many mistakes, and so will structure the task environment for the intern clearly enough to avoid costly errors. That means that the student, in first encountering the task problem (in the phase we called "establishing"), has to get some more or less general information about the nature of the job, the kinds of skills and knowledge one needs to perform it, and the

> "There is always some room for inventiveness; there is always some control."

criteria by which performance will be judged. In many cases, that "establishing" included rather extensive discussion of the theoretical or conceptual underpinnings of the work.

Item: In a hospital speech clinic, before the student ever had a chance to work directly with children, she first heard about the kinds of speech defects the clinic handled, about their possible causes and treatments, about diagnosis, about the kinds of materials used in different cases; then she observed systematically as the professional speech therapist worked with several kids, and discussed the cases and the treatments afterward.

Even when the "establishing" phase of the work did not explicitly cover theories or general strategies, the "processing" phase often did. By processing, we meant those activities through which the student received monitoring and feedback on her performance on a task, and opportunities for reconstructing the problem and designing a new approach. Feedback of one form or another was very common in the worksites. The "reflection" type of processing was seen less frequently, but definitely occurred.

Item: A student-intern working as a reporter for a small community newspaper received a general assignment from his editor, to do a piece on graffiti artists in the neighborhood. She gave him broad instructions about how to locate his subjects and how to interview them; but she left the construction of a first draft up to him. When he presented his rough copy to her, the editor sat down with him and reviewed it carefully, asking questions about specific points but also making more general comments about the way one puts together a feature article.

The common wisdom about knowledge-use in internships, as I argued above, is that practical experience may be good for practice of academic learning, may be effective in the process of knowledge retention; but that it is not good for academic, intellectual, complex learning, for the acquisition and manipulation of difficult and respectable theories and concepts. Hundreds of hours of observation in thirty-five internship sites convinces us that the common wisdom cannot be held universally true. We watched students acquire and use some very complicated and "scholarly" knowledge: about the institutional relations among segments of the municipal bureaucracy; about the etiology and treatment of speech disorders; about the principles of consumer protection law. But more than that, we saw students perform very advanced forms of mental work, kinds of thinking we rarely witness in school classes: the interpretation of a tangled situation involving tenants and landlords, and the construction (synthesis) of a strategy for seeking relief for the tenants; the evaluation of manuscripts submitted to a writers' agent; the *ad hoc* production of systematic and coherent answers to children's questions in a history museum. To be sure, we also observed people doing some terribly mundane thinking: answering phones and taking messages; performing a specific procedure for separating blood in a hospital lab; even walking dogs. The point is not that internships always encourage higher forms of learning -- just that they *can*, given the right circumstances.

Experiential educators should not succumb to the academic myth that systematic, rigorous, complex mental work occurs only in classrooms; or that practical experience is good only for practice and retention. Rather, they should pay close attention to the kinds of mental operations interns will be encouraged and expected to perform in the course of doing their work. Thinking in the real world may indeed supplement and reinforce school-based learning; but it can also do far more to develop valid and important learning in its own right.

Social Relationships in Internships

The second dimension of comparison between academic and experiential settings centers on the kinds of social relations in which one engages while participating in a particular environment. For educational purposes, those relations have two kinds of significance. First, the forms of personal growth a person undergoes in the course of a given experience is integrally connected to the ways she engages in interactions with others. Through our observations, we came to realize that claims about "building self-esteem" and "developing a sense of responsibility" in experiential learning programs make sense only if the real-world interactions move the person in those directions. We saw students engaged in work that could hardly build self-esteem, for example: walking dogs or cleaning cages in an animal shelter; typing reams of envelopes to mail out brochures in a museum; filing. In other situations, however, we saw students interact with supervisors and co-workers in highly responsible, rewarding ways: taking charge of a tour of elementary school students in a history museum; helping a senior citizen ward off eviction by a greedy landlord; teaching a child with a stammer how to enunciate certain new sounds. In each of these cases, the critical fact was that the intern was performing a task that demanded responsible behavior; other people counted on the student to come through as expected; and they often let her know that the job had been important to them. In classrooms, students rarely have the opportunity to be truly responsible -- not just punctual or obedient, but to have others actually count on them for something meaningful.

The second significance of social relations in learning environments concerns the extent to which people can participate in the definition, creation, use and transformation of knowledge. This question touches on the sociology of knowledge: Who gets to know what? and Who decides that? The issue combines role theory with learning theory. In some situations, knowledge is distributed among roles in a fixed and hierarchical way: The people at the top know more and control the knowledge-access of those below them. In other situations, social relations are more level, more collegial, and all participants have roughly equal access to the various kinds of facts, skills and ideas in use.

Traditional school classrooms generally manifest the fixed and hierarchical form of social relations and knowledge distribution. The teacher possesses the important knowledge, and decides when and how to transmit it to the students; for their part, the students have the role obligation of taking in the requisite knowledge and displaying it on command. One indication of this kind of social relation in classrooms is that teachers ask questions to which they already know the answers (cf. Mehan, 1979). Their only purpose can be to check and control the behavior and learning of the students. In fact, Mehan argues that much of the learning students do in classrooms has to do with social relations: They have to learn how to "behave" in the various contexts that make up the school day. Of course, that kind of learning and performance is important in any social context.

Internships, as contrasted with classrooms, represent a wider range of social relations. Frequently, workplaces look very much like classes in certain respects: The boss knows, tells the worker, and the worker does as told.

Item: At County Hospital, a student working in the blood lab was shown how to operate the centrifuge to separate blood for testing. He repeated that mandated procedure again and again, recorded the results in the appropriate form in a notebook, and forwarded that information to the necessary places. He did not improvise, experiment or transform the knowledge he was given.

In some situations, the knowledge used by the intern was tremendously complex and subtle, and highly responsible in its application -- but the student was still given little latitude in the definition and use of knowledge.

> "Frequently, workplaces look very much like classes in certain respects: The boss knows, tells the worker, and the worker does as told."

Item: In a municipal consumer protection agency, a student worked on the complaint phones, taking calls from consumers and helping them solve their problems. The job required broad knowledge of consumer laws and agency procedures, a sensitivity to the caller, and an ability to interpret specific situations in the light of labyrinthine regulations. Still, the supervisor of the phone room claimed that there were rather definite and immutable procedures to be followed, and that the student could not be allowed to invent new approaches or advance new interpretations.

On the other hand, some interns came to occupy a full and virtually equal position in the work environment, to participate completely in the definition and use of knowledge. In these more "democratic" or "collegial" settings, knowledge was regarded as more flexible, more situational, more expansive than in the other places. People analyzed practical and theoretical problems together, and collaborated in finding the information and methods best suited for their solution. Experience and knowledge always counted for something, of course, but newcomers could contribute as well as veterans.

Item: The student who worked as a tour guide in a history museum spent a good deal of time being gradually inducted into that role; she progressed from passive observer to helper to performer of limited segments to a complete guide. In the process, she also improvised new styles for handling certain kinds of situations, certain questions and behaviors from the students she led; she was encouraged to add her own understanding to the construction of the tour guide role.

Item: Students working in the office of a progressive member of the City Council were treated as competent (if beginning) members of the staff, and were helped to take on more and more responsibility for their own work. They were shown how to find and use information, not given answers. Moreover, they were prompted to treat constituents the same way: to help callers mobilize their own resources to solve their problems, rather than to solve the callers' problems for them.

There is a strong connection between the dimensions of mental work and social relations, and it lies in the kinds of thinking (and, by extension, learning) that people are expected and enabled to do in the course of performing certain activities. In their most simplified forms, the two dimensions can be described in polar terms. The types of mental work or knowledge-engagement done in either classrooms or internship sites can be regarded as falling somewhere between these two extremes:

a) rote/algorithmic: knowledge is fixed and certain, and is used according to a mandated procedure;

b) creative/transformative: knowledge is fluid and situational, amenable to addition or change; higher operations are required;

Similarly, the types of social relations found in classrooms and work sites may be described as combinations of the following opposites;

c) hierarchical/controlled: the distribution of knowledge is static and top-down, and the higher-ups determine what the others will know;

d) collegial/participatory: knowledge is widely distributed across roles, and all members can participate in its creation and use.

No single context falls clearly into one extreme or the other. There is always some room for inventiveness; there is always some control. These dimensions, however, may be useful conceptual tools for the practitioner who is trying to think systematically about the nature of a learning environment, whether a classroom, a work site, a family home or a playground. The concepts pull us away from oversimplified, rigid claims about the kinds of learning that can occur in different types of environments. They can help experiential educators relieve themselves of the burdensome assumption that out-of-school learning is somehow inferior or subordinate to academic learning.

People operating in the "real world" do not work totally without theory or principle, without

> "We saw students perform very advanced forms of mental work, kinds of thinking we rarely witness in school classes."

systematic bodies of knowledge and skill, without complex mental processes. First-hand experience in those work roles can -- *if* it is properly set up, monitored and enhanced -- spark forms of learning that are fully as developed, sound and rigorous as anything encountered in classrooms. That is not to say, once again, that all work experience is educational in these terms. Nor is it even to say that creative knowledge-engagement and collegial social relations are always "better" than rote and hierarchical. Clearly, there are times when knowledge *is* in fact certain and fixed, and when top-down control is perfectly functional and appropriate. My point in this paper, rather, has been to propose that both practitioners and researchers in experiential education consider these dimensions -- the ways we use knowledge, and the ways we relate to others -- in locating, developing, monitoring and supplementing non-school learning experiences.

References

- Bloom, Benjamin, ed., 1956, *Taxonomy of Educational Objectives: Handbook I: The Cognitive Domain*. New York: Longman.
- Bruner, Jerome S. (Jeremy M. Anglin, ed.), 1973, *Beyond the Information Given*. New York: W. W. Norton.
- Coleman, James S., 1977, Differences between experiential and classroom learning. In Morris T. Keeton, ed., *Experiential Learning*. San Francisco: Jossey-Bass.
- Kolb, David, 1976, *Learning Style Inventory*. Boston: McBer and Co.
- Luria, A. R., 1976, *Cognitive Development: Its Cultural and Social Foundations*. Cambridge, MA: Harvard University Press.
- Mehan, Hugh, 1979, *Learning Lessons*. Cambridge, MA: Harvard University Press.
- Moore, David Thornton, 1981, Discovering the pedagogy of experience. *Harvard Educational Review* 50:2 (May 1981), pp. 287-300. 1982, Students at work: Identifying learning in internship settings. *Occasional Paper #5*, Washington, DC: NSIEE.
- Wadsworth, Barry J., 1971, *Piaget's Theory of Cognitive Development*. New York: David McKay.

Acknowledgement

The research for this paper was supported by a generous grant from the National Institute of Education (NIE-G-79-0147) through the Center for New Schools.

Integrating the Traditions of Experiential Learning in Internship Education

by Jon Wagner

Theories about experiential education have been proposed since antiquity and vigorously debated since the emergence of higher education in the Middle Ages (Chickering, 1977; Houle, 1976). In the last few decades, however, the more general tradition of learning from experience has found practical expression in three different models of formal instruction: group process, simulation-games, and field experience. The growing popularity of experiential education in secondary schools, colleges and universities (Keeton and Tate, 1978; Hamilton, 1980) raises a number of important questions about these models: What differences exist between them? In what circumstances can each model contribute most effectively to educational enterprises? And, what possibilities exist for integrating them in practice?

While these questions can be addressed theoretically, I would like to consider them here in terms of educational practice. To do so, I will examine the process by which all three traditions of experiential education were effectively integrated within a particular educational experiment: the Field Studies Program at the University of California, Berkeley. Before describing that process -- and its implications for more general issues of educational reform -- let me outline each of these three traditions in more detail.

Three Models

Experiential learning generated through "group process" builds upon the interpersonal interaction of individuals in a group setting. These interactions can be examined as analogs of interpersonal relations which exist in the world beyond the group, or as representations of individual predispositions.

As an educational vehicle, "group process" has been refined through the development of T-groups, sensitivity training sessions, leadership workshops, group psychotherapy and the like (Milman and Goldman, 1974; Borman and Lieberman, 1976). In developing "group work" as an instructional vehicle, practitioners drew upon a history of social research into the dynamics of group behavior, particularly as it is manifest in the workplace.

The institutional applications of group process work are presently so varied as to almost defy unifying classification (Cooper, 1973), though several attempts have been made to do so in recent years (Klein, 1978; Lennung, 1978). As a tradition of experiential learning, however, group process activities remain an approach subscribed to by an identifiable constituency of supporters and professional practitioners (Cooper and Alderfer, 1978).

Simulation-games represent a second model of experiential learning which has developed greatly in the last few decades. This approach has been used in learning programs related to physical education, military training, city planning, theater performances, social studies, international affairs, architecture, industrial engineering, psychology, economics, and business management, as well as other more specialized areas too numerous to mention (Shubik, 1960; Guetzkow, 1962; Zuckerman and Horn, 1970).

As vehicles of experiential education, simulation-games rely on "gaming" activities to engage students in distinctive patterns of action and interaction (Coleman, 1968). The patterns are structured to develop skills and understanding which can be transferred beyond the immediate context of the game, and to simulate important external realities.

A third model of experiential education emphasizes the integra-

---

Jon Wagner is the Coordinator of Professional and Community Services at the School of Education, University of California, Berkeley.

> "Students were confronted with a dual challenge: to develop familiarity with their field setting, and to question the assumptions of that understanding through group discussion with their peers."

tion of academic inquiry with off-campus student experience in work, travel, volunteer service, or some other non-academic endeavor. Students may participate, for example, in cross-cultural exchanges, outdoor or wilderness trials, or community service activities, all of which are organized and recognized as an integral part of their undergraduate education (Chickering, 1977). In other cases, students combine ongoing work experience or internships with academic study in related areas (Duley and Gordon, 1977). In some institutions, provisions are also available for crediting -- through a process analogous to "advanced placement" -- the learning which students have gained through direct experience before they even enroll, a format which has proved to be particularly valuable to older, returning students (Meyer, 1975; Moon and Hawes, 1980).

All three models refer explicitly to a common body of theory about experiential learning. As Keeton and Tate have described it,

> *Experiential learning refers to learning in which the learner is directly in touch with the realities being studied. It is contrasted with learning in which the learner only reads about, hears about, talks about, or writes about these realities, but never comes into contact with them as part of the learning process. (1978:1)*

Chickering (1976:63) offers a parallel definition in which experiential learning "means that learning that occurs when changes in judgment, feelings, knowledge or skills result for a particular person from living through an event or events."

Given this broad conception, theoretical aspects of one model of experiential learning can certainly be applied to the other two. And they are. Citations to a few general formulations -- such as those provided by Agyris and Schon (1974); Kolb and Fry (1975); and Coleman (1976) -- appear with great frequency in the literature associated with each of the three different models. In addition, practitioners in each of the three traditions all state that they are working within the experiential context of learning which John Dewey identified, described and promoted during the early part of this century. In theory, then, there are grounds for a great deal of agreement and integration.

In practice, however, there are grounds as well for disagreement and disintegration. For example, all three models emphasize the educational value of analyzing direct experience, but they occupy different positions along the social environmental continuum which runs between the classroom and the world beyond. The group process model underlines what individuals can learn by examining closely interaction process within the instructional setting itself. Simulation-games make explicit but symbolic connections between exercises in an instructional setting and real problems of the world. The off-campus model calls attention to the educational value of participation in non-academic setting themselves.

The three models also draw implicitly upon different traditions of scholarship and research. Practice in group process is associated most closely with theory and research in social psychology, and the sociology of small group interaction, both of which are cast within a "clinical" context (Janowitz, 1978).

The simulation and gaming approach, in contrast, is seen more in terms of "experimental" science, whether it be in psychology, physics or biology (Dawson, 1962; Meier, 1961). Off-campus approaches to experiential education are commonly practiced in anthropology, sociology, botany and zoology (Chickering, 1977). While each model of experiential education can call upon a rich tradition of scholarship, distinctions between such traditions are still very much alive. "Clinicians," "experimenters," and "field workers," are not known for working closely together.

In practice, these implicit distinctions between the three models have usually overshadowed their theoretical commonalities. As a result, professional and institutional segregation of the activities they inspire is the rule, rather than the exception. Instruction in physical education, the natural sciences, art, or architecture, for example, may rely heavily on laboratory simulations, studios and the like, and yet ignore the interpersonal group process in which students are engaged, as well as related opportunities for field experience. Group process workshops, on the other hand, are rarely designed to build upon student reports of the off-campus situations in which they are involved on a continuing basis. And, the educational agendas for programs emphasizing off-campus experience all too frequently ignore the lessons to be learned from examining group process and the conceptual and technical understanding which can be enhanced through directed simulations and games.

What are the costs of this specialization and segregation in the design of experiential education programs? Are there techniques and concepts in one of the three models which could be productively examined or used by those working in the other two? Could these different traditions be integrated in practice within a particular program? And, if so, how would it look?

Off-Campus Experience

The Field Studies Program at the University of California, Berkeley, was an interdisciplinary academic unit for administering and developing field-based and experiential instruction (Heskin, 1977). Founded in 1971, the Program underwent a number of important changes in the ten years during which it operated on the Campus. While these did not fundamentally alter its administration as a Program of "experiential learning," they brought into the Program elements of each of the three models described above.

The Program began as a clearinghouse through which students interested in community work were matched with community organizations and agencies which needed volunteers. Another of its "clearinghouse" functions was to refer students to Campus faculty members with whom they might pursue related projects of independent study for academic credit. In both respects, the Program's design was elaborated within a climate of reaction to the traditional lecture-discussion format of instruction which Coleman (1976) has identified as "information assimilation," and which dominated--and still dominates--the Campus.

In its first year of operation, the Field Studies Program directed over 600 students to off-campus placements, as well as sponsored a series of voluntary discussion sessions in which they could review with their peers the nature of their field experience. Fourteen work-study students were hired to coordinate both seminars and field placements. The Program was administered by a full-time director and supervised by the chair of an Academic Senate committee established to encourage instructional improvements on the Campus. The program was funded by that same committee and a small, extramural grant.

At the end of the first year, however, changes were made in the Program's design and operation which turned it from a clearinghouse into a unit of academic instruction. First, a Faculty Governing Board was established by the Chancellor to oversee the Program and to provide formal connections with the academic affairs of the university. Second, the voluntary discussion sections previously run by work-study students were transformed into required academic seminars, each of which focused on a particular topic (e.g. alternative schools, child care, community mental heath, consumer protection, women, criminal justice, media, labor, and public advocacy). And third, while the Program continued to employ eight work-study students to assist in the coordination of seminar and field placements, six other individuals were hired as "teaching associates" to actually conduct the seminars under the supervision of sponsoring faculty members. In recruiting for these associate teaching positions, the Program administrators and the Faculty Board looked for graduate students and Ph.D.'s who also had a background of professional experience as lawyers, child care administrators, social workers, city planners, psychotherapists, etc.

Taken together, these developments increased the deliberation with which the Program addressed both the Campus and the field. The Faculty Governing Board took an active interest in ensuring that students were academically challenged by their off-campus experience, and not just "sent out into the field to do as they wished." At the same time, the teaching associates brought questions from both their academic disciplines and professional fields to the students enrolled in their seminars. The reaction to traditional instruction which had initially inspired the Program was tempered by the academic environment in which it had to survive, and yet provisions were made to preserve an educationally productive tension between off-campus experience and campus-based instruction (Hursh and Borzak, 1979).

Up until its recent demise--a result of budget cuts to the University and Campus-wide reorganization--the Program continued to offer a dozen or so courses, each of which combined an academic seminar with student participation in related field internships. Seminars enrolled from fifteen to twenty students and met once a week for three hours. Students worked in their internships--which were arranged for them by seminar instructors--for another ten to twelve hours each week. In its last few years, courses focused on the media, child development, public advocacy, international economics, business and labor history, publishing, criminal justice, urban animal behavior, art, fiction writing, and environmental aesthetics.

In conducting these courses, Field Studies teachers worked from two quite different kinds of "texts." One of these was a set of assigned readings which were organized according to a week-by-week thematic syllabus, much like readings for more traditional academic courses. Other "texts," however, were provided by the students themselves through written and oral reports of their field experience. While the academic content and focus of the course was determined by the instructor, the manner in which that content was examined owed a great deal to the students' observations of the field settings in which they were engaged. Both written evaluations by students and a series of outside evaluations (Lunsford, 1973; Pilisuk, 1976; Scriven, 1978; and Goodman, 1982) confirmed the fact that the process worked and that the Program was effective in challenging students to integrate field experience with academic inquiry.

To understand this effectiveness, however, it is important to note that the Field Studies Program was more than "field-based." Initially designed around opportunities for field internships, the Program quickly incorporated two other features which were essential to the educational effectiveness it achieved in working with student, off-campus experience.

Group Process

The first of these changes had to do with the conduct of seminar discussions. From the start these had emphasized student participation and initiative, for two reasons: leadership for establishing the Program in the first place came largely from students, and the first seminars were organized and conducted by work-study students themselves. Within the first few years, however, responsibility for conducting the seminars was transferred from work/study students to "teaching associates" and leadership passed from students to Program Administrators and the Faculty Governing Board.

Field Studies courses continued to encourage students to become self-conscious about learning from their own experience and that of their peers. This approach was refined and elaborated with models such as group psycotherapy, Quaker meetings and the women's movement providing ideas for incorporating a broad range of individual experience into group formats without losing sight of a collective focus. Incorporation of elements from each of these models into the Field Studies Program occurred as a result of personnel appointments. For example, the director was a professionally trained social worker experienced in group process in a variety of settings. She hired a number of instructors who had been trained as psychotherapists and community mental health workers. Similarly, several instructors in the Program had become skilled in feminist group practice and these individuals provided other teachers with examples from their own specialized experience as to tactics for encouraging successful discussion. Group process skills were disseminated throughout the staff during the Program's continuing series of in-service workshops on teaching/learning strategies.

How did group process skills contribute to the Program's effectiveness in field-based instruction? First, seminar discussion tactics were borrowed from group process work to help students articulate and analyze their field experience. A "check-in" period, for example, during which each student would report briefly on internship developments which had taken place during the past week, became a common feature of courses offered through the Program. "Check-in" reports could be relatively straightforward for individual students, and yet challenging and stimulating to the group as a whole. A student interning in a corporate public relations office, for example, might simply comment that her "host" organization was currently responding to a local labor strike. Another student in the class, however, might be interning in a union involved directly or indirectly with the strike. Still a third student might be working for a local newspaper which was covering the strike. What might appear as a matter-of-fact to each of these students, could become much more problematical in the context of reports from the other two. By providing a "safe" context in which to make such reports, the instructor could broaden student concerns beyond those of their individual field internships. By underlining differences between these individual reports, the instructor could further challenge the group into original intellectual work.

"Check-in" reports were also used to examine personal and professional interests related to the course. In the "Public Advocacy" seminar, for example, a student commented during "check-in" on his growing reservations about the effectiveness of public interest law and his future in that area. As other students questioned him about this matter, however, it became clear that his concern was more with the lack of financial rewards for public interest law in comparison with corporate law. "They just don't make as much money as they should," he said. Several other students questioned how much importance should be granted to money in making a career choice, but the initial speaker critiqued their comments in response: "Look, you're just like me. You took this course because you wanted to be a lawyer in the first place. We're all interested in money."

At this point the instructor intervened in what had moved from a "check-in" process to a group discussion, and asked the class several questions about the social and economic organization of legal work. How are lawyers in different branches of law paid for their services? Why are they paid in different ways? Has this always been the case? What exceptions can be identified to the generalizations we would like to make about these matters? And what are the consequences of these different patterns of remuneration for how the law is

> "The field experience approach was refined and elaborated with models such as group psychotherapy, Quaker meetings, and the women's movement."

practiced? She concluded her series of questions by asking them if they knew the salaries paid to different people in the legal offices in which they served as interns, and the source of funds which supported the offices themselves. To the group's surprise -- but not to hers -- no one actually knew. Once this had been established, she asked them to take that upon themselves as a research assignment for the coming week. As a result of the group process and her intervention, a student's personal concerns about his economic future had become the starting point for examining the economic structure of legal work, a project to which the students would be contributing data from the field settings in which they served as interns.

At issue in integrating field work with group process was a question about the domain of student experience which could be appropriately examined within the conduct of a Field Studies course (Borzak and Hursh, 1977). Should students be asked to limit their comments about the field to "observations" which might be externally verifiable, or should they be encouraged to comment about the broader phenomena of their "experience" in the field? Should the comments of their peers be treated simply as "data" about the field, or should they be challenged by reference to the personal and professional ambitions which students brought to the field, the course, and the seminar itself?

The Program remained committed to the broader context of educating its students -- asking about an individual's "experience" as well as her or his "observations" -- but it drew upon group process traditions to preserve the focus and structure of the seminars themselves. "Check-in" sessions led to challenges and further discussion. Individual reports and testimony were compared with each other within the collective context of the seminar. "Feed-back" and "evaluation" sessions were conducted at the end of each seminar, not only to summarize content, but also to comment on the manner in which it had emerged during the session itself. Instructors moved back and forth in their efforts to facilitate effective group process, calling upon the class at one moment to respect what each individual had to say, then encouraging the class as a whole to critically examine these reports in the light of course content and assigned readings.

The broad domain of student experience embraced by the group process of Field Studies seminars also carried over into personal exchanges between students and Program instructors. The assignment of a "journal," for example, was used not only to challenge students to articulate their field experience, but also as a vehicle for communication between the student and teachers. While it was common in journal reviewing to direct students to readings related to the issues of their field work, these exchanges were also seen as occasions for raising questions about personal and professional development. In response to a student's description of difficulties encountered with discipline in a child care center, for example, an instructor might write something like the following:

You seem to be having some difficulties with the exercise of your authority in the field. That's perfectly understandable, considering the place where you are working, but why don't we talk about what you can learn from these difficulties and how you can move beyond them. Perhaps you'd like to focus your term paper on this issue.

Exchanges similar to this might occur in the seminar itself, or between an instructor and a few students within a tutorial session arranged to clarify term papers. It is important to note, however, that attention directed to student "experience" in the field and in the seminar was not offered as therapy. An effective therapeutic strategy would have to grant priority to personal development and attend to *whatever* issues a student was confronted with at the time. In Field Studies courses, on the other hand, the experiential domain was broadened primarily *around the issues of the course itself*. If a student was ill, or had a death in the family, or was having a problem adjusting to dormitory life, that was the student's own "personal" problem. If, on the other hand, the student was troubled by matters directly related to the focus of the course -- e.g. poor leadership in field settings, difficulties encountered in dealing with clients or supervisors, or the inability of an organization to do what it intends to do -- these were taken as appropriate topics for classroom discussion. Students enrolled in the courses were thus confronted by a dual challenge: to develop personal familiarity with their field setting, and to question the assumptions of that understanding through group discussion with their peers.

Instructional Simulations

In its last years of operation, the Field Studies Program drew upon yet a third tradition of experiential learning to improve the effectiveness of its course offerings. As with group process, elements of the simulation and gaming model were not taken in whole, but rather borrowed piece-meal in response to the instructional demands of a particular course.

The incorporation of simulations and gaming exercises into the more general Field Studies instructional mix was made explicit in 1976 in a search for an "academic coordinator" to assist the Program director. The individual selected on the basis of this search was given responsibility for conducting the Program's in-service workshops. Given his background and interests, these at first focused on the use of instructional simulations and gaming exercises in field-based education.

In one such workshop, for example, the academic coordinator scheduled a presentation from a professor of architecture who had developed a number of classroom simulations for his undergraduate studio course (Lifchez, 1979). Even though the Field Studies Program offered no architecture courses of its own, Field Studies teachers discussed the manner in which similar simulations could enhance instruction in their own courses.

In bringing this third tradition of experiential education into its own instructional activities, however, the Program made good use of a valuable resource already on hand: the professional work with which many of its teachers were engaged as a complement to their part-time appointments in the Program. The instructor for the media and writing courses, for example, was a practicing professional journalist; the instructor for the course on public advocacy, a lawyer; and the instructor for the courses in child development, a child therapist.

This professional experience provided Program instructors with a rich background for developing field-related instructional simulations. In the media course, for example, instead of asking students to prepare a proposal for their final paper, the instructor required that they write an actual "query letter," such as that used by a professional journalist in submitting proposals to commercial publications. In the public advocacy course, students were introduced to legal interviewing skills through an in-class simulation. Similarly, in the child

> "Simulations gave in-class experience some of the potency usually reserved for experience in the field."

development course, students were asked to make recommendations regarding prepared scenarios of "problem children," much as they would have to if they were to administer a child care center in the field.

These interactive simulations helped the Program integrate field experience with critical inquiry in three important respects. First, they helped students develop an appreciation of social phenomena as "rule governed" behavior. As such they illuminated the larger social world as a phenomenon itself, as something to be examined rather than a given (Mills, 1959; Berger and Luckmann, 1967). Second, the in-class simulations helped students try out a variety of unfamiliar roles which they encountered in their field work, some of which they might actually have to take on themselves within their internships. In this latter regard, simulations provided a context intermediate between normal classroom discussions and the "real" situations of student involvement in the field (Argyris and Schon, 1974). And third, they gave in-class experience some of the potency usually reserved for experience in the field. Given the variety of field placements with which students in a particular class were involved, in-class simulation and gaming exercises performed an important integrative function. They had the power to bring a group of quite different students close together for a short period of time in performance of a common, course-related task.

A "mock court" exercise in the public advocacy class was a particularly effective example of this kind of simulation, and in their course evaluations, thirteen of fifteen students enrolled stressed the importance of this exercise in giving them a sense of the class as a whole.

Principles and Practice

This history of the Program's pedagogy is necessarily abbreviated and suggestive. There are areas in which the three models of experiential education were interdependent, confounded or superimposed. It is also impossible to identify all the contributions which each made to the overall instructional effort of the Program. And, it should be noted, instructors in the Program did not self-consciously identify with *any* of the three models of experiential education outlined above. That is, they made use of instructional elements without participating as "members" of the traditions they represent. In their own minds they were Field Studies Program teachers, not "experiential educators."

If other programs seek the

same kind of integrated approach to experiential education which characterized the Field Studies Program, these practical, institutional resources must be kept clearly in mind. Simply placing students in the field and in classrooms, for example, may not provide the kind of "experiential learning" that we would like to associate with experiential education (Ehrensaft and Wagner, 1981). In much the same way, asking seminar instructors to pay attention to group dynamics and simulations may have little effect unless the teachers have previous training in those areas or are willing and in a position to learn about them directly from their peers. A career in which an individual has managed to integrate both academic inquiry and field experience provides a model within the teacher's own experience for the kind of integrated inquiry in which students are to be thoughtfully instructed. And finally, a peer culture which supports individual teachers as well as collective inquiry about teaching effectiveness represents a Program resource of inestimable value. Without practical resources such as these, agreement about the theory of experiential learning may be of little consequence in ensuring that a program's instructional goals are actually achieved.

Another way of summarizing these observations is to underline the fact that whatever else it might be, the campus is also a workplace. Field Studies teachers were successful at providing integrated experiential education to Berkeley students because of their individual talents and the resources that they were given or invented for themselves. But that they even tried was tied closely to the fact that every day, and, in many ways, it was their job to do just that.

References

- Agryis, Chris and Schon, Donald, *Theory in Practice: Increasing Professional Effectiveness*, Jossey-Bass, San Francisco, 1974.
- Berger, Peter and Luckmann, Thomas, *The Social Construction of Reality*, Doubleday, New York, 1967.
- Borman, Leonard D. and Lieberman, Morton, eds., "Special Issue," *Journal of Applied Behavioral Science*, vol. 12, pp. 261-463, July 1976.
- Borzak, Lenore and Hursh, Barbara, "Integrating the Liberal Arts and Preprofessionalism Through Field Experience: A Process Analysis," *Alternative Higher Education*, no. 2, pp. 3-16, 1977.
- Chickering, Arthur W., "Developmental Change as a Major Outcome," in *Experiential Learning*, ed. Morris Keeton, pp. 62-107, Jossey-Bass, San Francisco, 1976.
- Chickering, Arthur W., *Experience and Learning: An Introduction to Experiential Learning*, Change Magazine Press, New Rochelle, N.Y., 1977.
- Coleman, James S., "Academic Games and Learning," *Proceedings of the 1967 Institutional Conference on Testing Problems*, ETS, Princeton, NJ, 1968.
- Coleman, James S., "Differences Between Experiential and Classroom Learning," in *Experiential Learning*, ed. Morris Keeton, Jossey-Bass, San Francisco, 1976.
- Cooper, Carl L., *Group Training for Individual and Organizational Development*, S. Warger, Basel, 1973.
- Cooper, Carl L. and Alderfer, Clayton, Advances in Experiential Social Processes, John Wiley and Sons, Ltd, New York, NY, 1978.
- Dawson, Richard E., "Simulation in the Social Sciences," in *Simulation in Social Sciences: Readings*, ed. Harold Guetzkow, Prentice-Hall, Englewood Cliffs, NJ, 1962.
- Duley, John and Gordon, Sheila, *College-Sponsored Experiential Learning -- A CAEL Handbook*, Educational Testing Service, Princeton, NJ, 1977.
- Ehrensaft, Diane and Wagner, Jon, *Integrating Theory and Practice in Experiential Learning*, TIES/Field Studies, University of California, Mimeographed, Berkeley.
- Goodman, Oscar, "Cultural Understanding and Field-Based Learning," , External Evaluation of the Cultural Literacy Project, Field Studies Program, University of California, Mimeographed, Berkeley, 1982.
- Guetzkow, Harold ed., *Simulation in Social Science: Readings*, Prentice-Hall, Englewood Cliffs, NJ, 1962.
- Hamilton, Stephen, "Experiential Learning Programs for Youth," *American Journal of Education*, vol. 88, no. 2, pp. 179-215, February 1980.
- Heskin, Alan D., "The Field Study Program," *Alternative Higher Education*, vol. 2, pp. 119-33, 1977.
- Houle, Cyril O., "Deep Traditions of Experiential Learning," in *Experiential Learning*, ed. Morris Keeton, pp. 19-33, San Francisco, 1976.
- Hursh, Barbara and Borzak, Lenore, "Toward Cognitive Development Through Field Studies," *Journal of Higher Education*, vol. 50, no. 1, 1979.
- Keeton, Morris and Tate, Pamela, "The Boom in Experiential Learning," in *New Directions for Experiential Learning: Learning by Experience -- What, Why, How*, ed Morris Keeton and Pamela Tate, pp. 1-8, Jossey-Bass, San Francisco, 1978.
- Klein, Edward B., "An Overview of Recent Tavistock Work in the United States," in *Advances in Experiential Learning Social Processes*, ed. Carl L. Cooper and Clayton Alderfer, pp. 181-202, John Wiley and Sons, Ltd, New York, NY, 1978.
- Kolb, David A. and Frye, R., "Toward an Applied Theory of Experiential Learning," in *Theories of Group Processes*, ed. Cary Cooper, John Wiley and Sons, New York, 1975.
- Lennung, Sven-Ake, "A Classification of Experiential Social Processes: A European Perspective," in *Advances in Experiential Social Processes*, ed. Cary L. Cooper and Clayton Alderfer, pp. 29-38, John Wiley and Sons, New York, NY, 1978.
- Lifchez, Raymond, "Seeing Through Photographs: Projections and Simulation," in *Images of Information*, ed. Jon Wagner, pp. 217-232, SAGE, Beverly Hills, CA, 1979.

- Lunsford, Terry F., *Evaluating Field Studies at Berkeley,* TIES/Field Studies, University of California, Mimeographed, Berkeley, 1973.
- Mills, C. W., *The Sociological Imagination,* Oxford University Press, New York, 1959.
- Pilisuk, Marc, *Campus-Community Education: An Evaluation of the UCBerkeley Undergraduate Field Studies Program,* TIES/Field Studies, University of California, Mimeographed, Berkeley, 1976.
- Scriven, Michael, "Report to the Vice Chancellor, Ira M. Heyman," , 1978.
- Shubik, Martin, "Bibliography on Simulation, Gaming, Artificial Intelligence and Allied Topics," *Journal of the American Statistical Association,* vol. 55, pp. 736-751, 1960.
- Wagner, Jon, "Field Study as a State of Mind," in *Field Study: A Sourcebook for Experiential Learning,* ed. Lenore Borzak, pp. 18-49, SAGE, Beverly Hills, CA, 1981.
- Zuckerman, D. and Horn, R., *Guide to Simulation Gaming for Education and Training,* Information Resources, Lexington, Mass., 1970.

VII. Research and Evaluation

National Assessment of Experiential Education: Summary and Implications

By Dan Conrad and Diane Hedin

> Experience is never limited, and it is never complete; it is an immense sensibility, a kind of huge spider's web of silken threads suspended in the chambers of consciousness and catching every airborne particle in its tissue.
>
> (Henry James, quoted in Pitchett, 1979, p. 3)

James' poetic characterization serves to put the Project and this report in perspective. As experience is too immense, too complex, illusive, even too mysterious a phenomenon to fully comprehend, so also is it the case with what is learned from it. There is no pretense in this report that its tables and numbers have miraculously captured that "sensibility" which has eternally eluded the poet. The report's more pedestrian aim has been to capture some small particles of experience, to reduce some part of the mystery to a size and form that can be grasped, understood, manipulated, and from which conclusions may be drawn and lessons learned.

Overview of Project

Case for Experiential Education

The arguments for experiential education are rooted in a concern for the total development of young people—social, psychological, and intellectual. This development is seen as jeopardized by a social milieu that increasingly isolates young people from the kinds of experiences, encounters, and challenges that form the basis for healthy development and that add purpose and meaning to formal education. The aim of social development—the development of active, concerned, involved citizens—is jeopardized by practices which isolate the young from adult society and deny them an active and valued role it it. The aim of sound psychological development—of persons who have a clear sense of who they are, what they believe, and what they can do—is jeopardized by lack of opportunity to demonstrate one's worth and to test, stretch and challenge who one is and can be. The aims of intellectual development and academic learning are jeopardized by equating education with classroom instruction in an education process that produces graduates who are "information rich and action poor" (Coleman, 1974), who have had insufficient opportunity to test and apply that information, and who have not been prepared to continue learning from the experiences of everyday life outside of school.

More by default than desire or design, the schools have been left to play a central role in the total development of America's young people. Few educators have been at ease with the responsibility. Some have chosen to deny its broadest implications and to focus on the schools' more narrow and traditional aims of developing cognitive skills and transmitting the accumulated experience and wisdom of the society. Others have accepted a broader view—some from a sense of cultural necessity and some from a belief in the interrelationship of all dimensions of development—that no one aspect can be achieved in isolation from the others. Among the latter are numbered many of the advocates of experiential education.

DIANE HEDIN is an Associate Professor at the Center for Youth Development and Research, University of Minnesota, St. Paul, Minnesota.

DAN CONRAD IS Director of Community Involvement Program, Hopkins Public School, Hopkins, Minnesota, and also lectures at the Center for Youth Development and Research on the St. Paul campus of the University of Minnesota.

Background of Project

While strong endorsements of experience-based education abound, there is relatively little "hard" evidence to demonstrate or document the impact of such programs on student participants. Little effort has been made to systematically test the assumptions underlying the endorsements or to investigate empirically which specific forms of experiential programs may be the most effective in realizing the hypothesized benefits.

The Evaluation of Experiential Education Project was undertaken to begin filling that gap—to assess the impact of experiential education programs on the psychological, social, and intellectual development of secondary school students. Equally importantly, it aimed at using this data to identify the program variables that are most effective in facilitating such development.

The project was initiated by the Commission on Educational Issues and co-sponsored by the National Association of Secondary School Principals, the National Association of Independent Schools, and the National Catholic Education Association. It evaluated 27 experiential programs in independent, public, and parochial schools around the country. Over 1,000 students participated in these programs. A preliminary study was also conducted involving nearly 4,000 students in 33 programs.

Primary funding for the Project was provided by the Spencer and Rockefeller Foundations with additional support from the General Mills Foundation. The Project operated out of the Center for Youth Development and Research, University of Minnesota, under the direction of Drs. Diane Hedin and Dan Conrad.

Defining Experiential Education

For purposes of this research effort, experiential programs are defined as "educational programs offered as an integral part of the general school curriculum, but taking place outside of the conventional classroom, where students are in new roles featuring significant tasks with real consequences, and where the emphasis is on learning by doing with associated reflection."

Selection of Programs

The programs included in the study are of four major types: volunteer service, career internships, outdoor adventure, and community study/political action.

Within each type, individual programs differ in terms of **length** – from four weeks to nine months; **intensity** – from 2-4 hours each week to full time; nature of **reflective component** – from none to a daily seminar related to the field experience; **student characteristics** – from ages 12 to 19, from good students to poor, and from low income to highly affluent; its **voluntary or compulsory nature** – with nearly all programs being voluntary.

The school programs included in the study were not randomly selected, but chosen because of a demonstrated record of excellence—and as being representative of the major type of experiential programs. It seemed prudent to study only the most well-conceptualized and established programs to discover the effects of experiential programs.

We assumed, in addition, that the teachers and administrators involved in exemplary projects would be the persons best able to define, articulate, and specify the fundamental outcomes for experiential education. Furthermore, this research effort was committed to an approach which was practical, understandable, and applicable to everyday life in schools. Thus, a "Panel of Practitioners" (the educators who ran the programs being studied), along with the research project co-directors, were responsible for defining the issues to be studied, for helping to select and develop assessment tools, for implementing the research

---

The Evaluation of Experiential Education Project was undertaken to assess the impact of experiential education programs on the psychological, social, and intellectual development of secondary school students.

---

design, and for helping to interpret the data collected. It would be impossible to overestimate the contribution of this Panel to the conceptualization and implementation of the research effort and the interpretation of the data collected. Such cooperation and counsel made this a shared effort throughout, one in which all felt a commitment to its success.

Selection of Issues

The first step of the research process was to survey the directors of 30 experiential programs. They were asked what they believed to be the actual effects of their programs on students, what each had directly experienced, seen, and heard.

There was a striking similarity in this "testimony of concerned observers." They described a core set of outcomes which each of them had observed whether they represented programs in small towns of large cities, work with low income or affluent youth, or programs featuring outdoor adventure, service, internships, or political action. The important implication was that there are common threads that unite a variety of exemplars of experiential education.

Among the observed effects reported by the directors were 24 which appeared with high regularity. This list was redrawn as a questionnaire and in May, 1978, administered to nearly 4,000 students in 33 programs. The students were asked which, if any, of the outcomes represented what they personally had gained from their program. A summary of the results of this survey is presented in Table 1 which is an abridgment of that found in Chapter Three of the final report. On 14 of the 24 items there was an average agreement level of over 80% across all programs. The most frequently cited outcomes fit into three major categories—social, psychological, and intellectual growth. These became, then, the major areas of investigation for the project itself.

Table 1

What Students Learn in Experiential learning

Composite Profile of Students Responses from 30 Experiential Programs (N=4,000)
The first 10 and last 4 of 24 items

ITEM (in rank order)	Agree*	Disagree*	Don't Know
1. Concern for fellow human beings	93	4	3
2. Ability to get things done and to work smoothly with others	93	4	3
3. Realistic attitudes toward other people such as the elderly, handicapped, or government officials	88	4	8
4. Self-motivation to learn, participate, achieve	88	7	5
5. Self-concept (sense of confidence, sense of competence, self-awareness)	88	7	5
6. Responsibility to the group or class	86	7	11
7. Risk-taking—openness to new experiences	86	7	8
8. Sense of usefulness in relation to the community	85	8	6
9. Problem-solving	86	9	5
10. Risk-taking—being assertive and independent	86	9	5
21. Use of leisure time	60	26	14
22. Narrowing career choices	54	34	12
23. To become an effective parent	52	29	19
24. To become an effective consumer	46	32	22

*Strongly agree and agree are combined, and disagree and strongly disagree are combined.

The Research Questions

In regard to **social development**, the research questions were as follows: to what extent do experiential programs have a positive impact on students': a) level of personal and social responsibility; b) attitudes toward others; c) attitudes toward active participation in the community; and d) involvement in career planning and exploration. In regard to **psychological development**, both general self-esteem and self-esteem in social situations were assessed, as was moral development. Finally, in regard to **intellectual and academic growth**, students were asked for self reports on learning—were tested on problem-solving and, as mentioned above, tested for levels of moral reasoning.

In addition to looking at the general effects of experiential education on student participants, we also were interested in determining the ways in which different program forms (community service, internships, policital action, community study, and adventure education) and formats (length, intensity, characteristics of the individual field experience) affect student learning. For example, do shortterm experiences of three to four weeks show any effect on attitudinal change? Does the intensity of the program—two hours versus ten hours per week—affect student outcomes? Are some types of programs, e.g., community service, more likely to promote a sense of social responsibility or interest in community participation? To what extent do the characteristics of each student's individual experience affect the results?

The Research Method

Test Instruments. The overall effects of social, psychological and intellectual development were operationally defined as scores on the test instruments and questionnaires employed in the study. The specific instruments used to measure psychological development were the Defining Issues Test (moral reasoning), the Janis-Field Feelings of Inadequacy Scale (self-esteem in social situations), and the Rosenberg Self-Esteem Scale. Social development was measured by the Social and Personal Responsibility Scale (social responsibility), three semantic differentials (attitudes toward others) and the Owens' Career Exploration Scale (career maturity). Intellectual development was investigated through the Problem Solving Inventory and through self reports of participants. The test battery included both standardized tests and adaptions of standardized tests. Two of the tests, the Social and Personal Responsibility Scale and the Problem-Solving Inventory were original instruments designed specifically for this study.

Because the outcomes being measured were elusive, triangulation of the data appeared to be the most reasonable approach. Each outcome was looked at from several different angles: paper and pencil tests; systematic observations of parents, teachers, and community supervisors; student journals and writing samples; case studies of individual students and programs; and a host of unobtrusive measures.

Design. All students were pre and post tested on or near the first and last days of the program. Six of the experimental groups (at least one in each program type cluster) also had comparisons. These were not random controls, but the students in each were comparable to those in their experimental pair in terms of age, grade-in-school, geography, grade-point-average, socio-economic status, classroom programs, and were tested pre and post at the same time as their experimental pairs.

Analysis. The data were analyzed in two phases. In the first, pre-post results were compared for each experimental and control group individually, by experimental and control groups combined, and by direct comparison between the four experimental-control pairs available for the study. In the second phase, specific features of the programs were examined to assess their influence on pre-post change scores. The specific elements investigated were: type, length, and intensity of the experience, existence of a reflexive component, student demographic characteristics, and the specific characteristics of individual experiences (e.g., how interesting, how demanding of responsibility, etc.). The analytical tools employed included t-tests of significance, analysis of variance, and multiple regression.

Findings: Impact on Students

The results from the formal measures employed in this study demonstrated that the experiential programs did have a positive impact on the psychological, social and intellectual development of the student participants. This conclusion, while true in general, masks significant patterns of effect and effectiveness which are summarized below.

Psychological Development

An important finding in research in schools is that studying the formal, academic curriculum does not automatically lead to personal and psychological growth. In fact, there is a body of research documenting the largely negative impact of schooling on such variables as self-esteem, interest in learning, and personal autonomy (Sprinthall & Sprinthall, 1977). Proponents of experiential education have argued that psychological growth is more likely to be achieved through their approach to learning. They believe that placing students in well-planned experiential confrontations with practical problems is an effective mode of promoting personal growth. In summary, psychological growth requires challenge, conflict, support and significant experience.

Did the findings of this study coroborate this theoretical argument for experiential programs? The answer is clearly **yes** as discussed below.

Moral Reasoning. Students in two experience-based programs and one comparison group (from the same school) were administered the Defining Issues Test (DIT) pre and post. This is a paper-and-pencil test designed to measure levels of moral reasoning as detailed by Lawrence Kohlberg. All three groups received identical instructions in Kohlberg's theories, the only difference being that the two experiential groups were simultaneously involved in service activities in the community.

The test results showed that both experimental groups attained significant gains in their moral reasoning scores while the comparison group did not gain. This finding substantiated that of several other studies which have likewise shown the combination of significant role-taking experiences and active reflection to be an effective means of promoting growth in this aspect of development.

Experiential programs can effectively promote the psychological development of adolescents and do so at least somewhat more effectively than classroom-based programs. The impact is strongest when the experience is most intensive, most dissimilar from ordinary school activities.

Self-Esteem. Students in experiential programs did show increases in self-esteem and to a degree slightly but consistently greater than those registered by comparable students in classroom-based programs.

On the Janis-Field Scale, which focuses on the confidence one feels in social situations (e.g., meeting new people, speaking in front of a class), 20 of the 27 experimental groups increased, 10 at a level of statistical significance (.05). On the Rosenberg Scale, which deals with more general feelings of self-worth (e.g. "I feel I have a number of good qualities"), 23 of the 27 experimental groups increased, 9 at a level of statistical significance. Students in the comparison groups also registered some gain in self-esteem consistently on the Janis-Field Scale (3 or 6 groups increased, 2 significantly). In direct comparison, the experimental groups had greater increases on both scales, but this advantage was statistically significant only on the more stable Rosenberg Scale.

Among program types, the highest absolute levels of self-esteem, even on the pretest, were registered by students entering career internships. It may be that such programs attract students who are relatively more sure of themselves, at least enough to test themselves in adult career roles. The most consistent pre-post gains were registered by students in outdoor programs—both in comparison to other experiential programs and to their own gains on the social and intellectual dimensions of growth examined in the study. Since no other program category showed such consistent results, it suggests that intensive outdoor experience may have a particularly strong effect on self-esteem. This may result from the intensity and uniqueness of such experiences and/or from the fact that evidence of achievement is clearly seen by, matters to, and is immediately reinforced by both teacher and peers.

In summary, the results from the Defining Issues Test and the two measures of selfesteem lend support to the hypothesis that experiential programs can effectively promote the psychological development of adolescents and do so at least somewhat more effectively than classroom-based programs. The data further suggest that the impact is strongest when the experience is most intensive, most dissimilar from ordinary school activities and, in the case of increased moral reasoning, when there is a combination of action and systematic reflection.

Social Development

In the past decade, there has been a great deal of public concern about the level of personal and social responsibility exhibited by teenagers. Charges of increased privatism, hedonsim, and aimlessness among adolescents have become commonplace, along with findings that they feel a strong sense of powerlessness in relation to the larger society and no sense of having a significant role in it (Hedin, 1979). Experiential educators have argued that it is precisely this lack of a significant role in the community and society that has bred apathy, cynicism, and powerlessness. They counter by suggesting that placing students in responsible roles in which their actions affect others will help them develop more responsible attitudes and behaviors.

This section summarizes the findings relevant to this hypothesis: that responsible action in an experience-based program would have a positive impact on students' levels of personal and social responsibility, have a positive influence on their attitudes toward adults and others, lead them to feel more inclined to participate in their communities and, relatedly, help them plan for and to explore potential adult careers.

The results reported below clearly show that experience-based programs can have precisely those effects. Despite the inevitable differences between specific programs, there was a strong and consistent showing of positive impact among the experiential programs as a whole. Furthermore, these gains significantly discriminated between these programs and the comparison groups. The latter tended to decline or show no significant change on most of the scales and subscales relating to social development. These results are outlined below according to the specific scales employed.

Social and Personal Responsibility Scale (SPRS). The overall results from the total SPRS scale indicated general positive movement by the experimental groups and no change by the comparisons. The experimental groups combined had a mean increase of almost 2 full points (+1.92, P=<.0001) while the combined comparisons declined (−.09, P=NS). More precisely, 23 of 27 experimental groups increased, 13 by at least 1.50 mean points and at a level of statistical significance. Of the 4 groups which did not increase, 2 had the highest pretest scores of any of the groups and were still among the highest on the posttest; the other 2 were very low income groups who generally tended to do poorly on paper and pencil measures. In contrast to the above, 5 of the 6 comparison groups declined, 2 at a level of statistical significance.

There were some differences by program types. Career Internship programs showed the largest positive gains (an average of 2.58 points); Community Study/Action was next (1.77); followed by Service (.63) and Outdoor programs (.30).

SPRS Subscales. The SPRS contained five subscales relating to sense of **duty**, **social welfare** orientation, **social efficacy**, sense of **competence** and assessment of **performance**. the combined total of all experimental groups showed significant positive change on all five subscales while, among the comparison groups (combined) there was no significant change on any subscale except Social Welfare—in which there was a statistically significant decrease. Nine of the experimental groups showed positive change on each subscale. There were only two instances of significant positive change among the comparison groups, both on the Competence subscale.

Overall, the strongest changes were toward taking responsible **action** as opposed to having more responsible **attitudes**; and, among attitudes, toward having more **personally** responsible attitudes as opposed to **socially** responsible attitudes. This finding is consistent with most research on attitudinal and behavioral change which suggests that changes in behavior tend to precede rather than follow changes in attitude. It also suggests that the traditional model in citizenship education, that instruction in proper attitudes about personal and social obligations will lead to responsible behavior, may need revision. While the evidence from this study can only be suggestive of that conclusion, it is further strengthened by the fact that most of the comparison students were in social studies classes which were deliberately, and apparently ineffectively, aimed at improving attitudes toward taking personal and social responsibility.

One further point from the Social and Personal Responsibility Scale data bears mention. Students in service programs had the highest pretest scores on the SPRS followed by those in career internships, outdoor programs, and community study. The advantage for students in service programs was largely accounted for by their higher scores on the sense of duty and the social welfare subscales. This would be consistent with the fact that these students had volunteered for programs in which helping and serving others is the major task (in contrast, students in outdoor programs had the lowest social welfare pretest-and posttest-scores). Students in Career internships had the highest scores on the performance and competence subscales which seems consistent with their choosing placements where they would be working independently with and as adults. It also coincides with their being the highest-ranked students on the two measures of self-esteem reported earlier.

Attitudes Toward Adults. A common critique of modern socialization practices is that young people are locked in an adolescent ghetto separated from meaningful interaction with adults. The implicit assumption is that separation breeds suspicion, if not hostility, and that greater contact with adults would promote more positive attitudes. This latter hypothesis was confirmed by the results of this study. Students in the experiential programs entered into collegial relationship with adults that are atypical of most school and work settings. These students tended to show large, consistent changes on the semantic differential scale toward more positive attitudes toward adults.

Study data also suggest that the traditional model in citizenship education,—that instruction in proper attitudes about personal and social obligations will lead to responsible behavior,— may need revision.

There was a positive change in 22 of the 27 experimental groups, and the combined mean change for all the experimentals was +1.45 which was statistically significant at P=<.0001. This mean change of near 1.5 was made on a scale of only 7 possible points. Students in comparison groups, conversely, showed an overall decline of −.74 mean points spread over 5 of the 6 groups.

It is clear, from the above, that the adolescents do not automatically think more highly of adults merely because they have moved a little closer to that status themselves. It depends on what they are doing during that time. Remaining in a classroom with an adult teacher appears not to be a situation which raises their esteem of adults. Associating with adults on a collegial basis outside the classroom does, however, seem to have such a positive effect

Attitudes Toward Others. A further contention of the proponents of experiential education is that when students are involved with persons they don't ordinarily encounter, they will come to value them more highly. The data, from a 10-item evaluative semantic differential scale, clearly indicates that community participation has a positive effect on students' evaluations of the people with whom they have been interacting. In the direct contrast between experimental-comparison pairs, each experimental group increased significantly while each of the comparison groups showed a decline. The difference was significant for the individual and the combined comparisons (the latter at <.001).

> At the time of the pretest, students in experiential classes valued the general notion of "being active in the community" less highly than did students in traditional classes.

Considering specific groups or categories, students initially valued hospital and little kids most highly, followed by old people, business persons, police and, dead last, junior high kids. On the posttest the ratings of all these categories had increased significantly—except for hospitals toward which there was a small increase and for business persons toward which there was a slight decrease in valuation.

The small increase in valuation of hospitals may reasonably be explained by the fact that the high pretest rating (the highest of any category) left little room for positive change. The decrease in relations to business persons is less easily explained. Perhaps it is the nature of interaction, not interaction per se, that creates more positive attitudes. In the case of internships, students perhaps tended more to be observers than participants, a situation that could account for the lack of change.

In any case, the fundamental finding of this portion of the study is that students do tend to show increased appreciation for the people with whom they associate in their off-campus experiences.

Attitudes Toward Being Active in the Community. A further hypothesis of experiential educators is that direct participation in the community will lead students to value such activity more highly and increase the likelihood of their seeing themselves as accepting community responsibilities in the future. The first part of the hypothesis was tested through a semantic differential with pairs such as smart-dumb and useless-useful. The second was tested by single continuum from "something I will do" to "something I won't do." The results from both scales confirmed the hypothesis.

At the time of the pretest, students in experimental classes valued the general notion of "being active in the community" less highly than did students in traditional classes. The highest rating was given by students in service programs followed by the comparison group and then students in community study, career internships, and outdoor programs. By the time of the posttest the situation was reversed. All of the comparison groups decreased, while 20 of 27 experimental groups increased. The strongest gains were by students in community study and outdoor programs, and the least gain by students in career internships. It must further be noted that for 4 of the 6 comparison groups the value and importance of community participation had been a deliberate (and seemingly unattained) emphasis of the in-school course.

A further question was whether students' evaluation of being active in the community carries over to (at least reported) inclination to actually do it. The data here revealed that secondary students rather strongly assert that they will be active in their communities. However, from a position of virtual equality on the pretest, the experimental students increased and the comparison students declined. A direct comparison between experimental and control groups showed the difference in change scores to be statistically significant.

> By the time of the posttest the situation was reversed. All of the comparison groups decreased, while 20 of 27 experimental groups increased.

Career Exploration. One common critique of adolescent socialization is the inability of many youth to make a smooth transition from school to work. Many teenagers appear to have very little information about the myriad of careers available, and they fall into the trap of thinking that an interest in some activity implies a lifelong pursuit of one single occupation. An often expressed goal of experiential learning programs is to increase a young person's knowledge about work and career options. To learn whether this goal was achieved, students were given the Career Exploration Scale.

The data from this scale show that 24 of 27 experimental groups registered a positive gain, 13 at a level of statistical significance. Measures were also registered by the six comparison groups, with 2 at a statistically significant level. The combined change scores for both experimental and comparison groups were significant, though the absolute level of increase was substantially greater for the experimental groups.

The Career Exploration Scale contains two subscales. The first measures Career Action, or the degree to which students have been actively engaged in exploring careers. The second asks about information they have gained about a career field. Analysis of these subscales revealed that the greater overall increase for experiential students was largely accounted for by greater gains on the Action subscale. All 27 experimental groups increased on the Action subscale, 16 significantly so. In contrast, no comparison group showed significant gains on this subscale and 2 actually declined. The gains on the Information subscale were about equal for the experimental and comparison groups. Apparently facts can be effectively conveyed either in or out of the classroom. But the experiential approach adds the dimensions of active involvement in potential career choices.

Some interesting differences emerged from examining individual program scores. The highest pretest mean was attained by affluent 12th graders in an independent school and the lowest means by either junior high or low income students. It does appear that active planning and exploring of careers is related to both age and income—with older and more affluent students having the advantage.

In summary, the data support the hypothesis that participation in experiential programs does, or at least can, contribute to the social development of adolescents.

Among types of programs, those offering career internships did have the largest increases—most particularly a medical careers program for low income minority youth and a program featuring semester-long, full time internship experiences. However, community study, service, and outdoor programs also showed strong increases even though they had almost no organized or explicit focus on careers. It may be that when young people want to learn about careers, they actively seek such information, on their own, in their field experiences.

In summary, the data discussed in this section support the hypothesis that participation in experiential programs does, or at least can, contribute to the social development of adolescents. Students in experiential programs increased significantly in social and personal responsibility, gained more positive attitudes toward adults and others with whom they worked, and felt more positively toward being active in the community. They also showed increased information about, and activity in exploring, careers. The data also show that such increased are not necessary and inevitable outcomes of any and all experiential programs. There were almost always exceptions to the general trends suggesting there were dynamics operating within the programs that require closer analysis. Such analysis will be presented following the discussion of intellectual development.

Intellectual Development

Theorists of learning and intellectual development from Aristotle through John Dewey to James Coleman have stressed the necessary relation of experience and education. Experience serves both as the source of knowledge and as a process of knowing. Education is of, by, and for experience. The study examined this relation by looking both at academic learning and intellectual development.

Amount Learned. Because the programs varied widely regarding academic objectives it was not practical to directly test the academic learning assumptions through any general test of facts or concepts. Instead, students were asked how much they felt they had learned in their experiential program compared to what they learned in an average class in

Students tend to feel they learn more from experiential programs than from regular school classes.

school. Seventy-three percent of the students reported learning more (41%) or much more (32%) in their experiential program, with 25 of 27 programs having mean responses that rounded off to 4 ("learned more") or higher. The mean responses of the other two were somewhat over 3 ("learned about the same"). Only 9% of the students reported learning less.

While all programs received high ratings on this dimension, there was a rather large spread between the higher and lower ranked programs which invited some speculation about the differences between them. Of the 12 highest ranked programs, 11 had a clearly defined seminar/reflective component, an element which characterized less than half (7) of the remaining 15 programs. Looked at from another perspective, 8 of the 12 programs with highest ratings involved students who might be expected to have a low opinion of regular classes. Four were composed of students in special alternatives for economically and educationally disadvantaged students, and four others involved students who had opted out of regular school for a full semester (one year) to participate in an experience-based program. These factors did not characterize any of the lower-ranked programs. Finally, the higher ranked programs were longer and more intensive than the lower programs.

The data indicate, therefore, that students tend to feel they learn more from experiential programs than from regular school classes and that this is most pronounced when the experiences are longer (at least 12 weeks), more intensive (at least 2 hours daily), include a formal reflective component and, to a lesser extent, involve students who may be disenchanted with traditional classroom programs.

Problem Solving. The primary measure of intellectual development used in the study was the Problem Solving Inventory. This Inventory presented students with 3 interpersonal problems and led them through the steps in problem solving outlined by John Dewey. Student responses were scored, pre and post, according to the number of alternatives listed, the degree to which they took responsibility for solving the problem, the degree to which they justified a decision according to its consequences, and the level of empathy and complexity of thought shown in the overall analysis of the problem.

Experiential education programs can and do have a positive effect on student learning and intellectual development. This is most strongly the case when the program features a combination of direct experience and formal reflection on that experience.

On the whole, neither the experimental nor comparison students showed significant increases on the first three indices. This appeared, however, to be more a factor of test weariness than lack of program effect. Only one program showed significant increases in the alternatives and consequences indices, and this program was unique in the degree the students faced problems similar to those in the stimulus stories and to which problem solving per se was a central focus of their seminar sessions. One other finding of interest on these dimensions is that in nearly half of the cases (48%), students selected other than their first alternative listed as their "best choice." This suggests that the request for further alternatives did help elicit the best thinking of students and confirms the common sense notion that one's first impulse does not always represent one's best judgment.

The heart of the Problem Solving instrument is its Empathy/Complexity Index. This Index assesses the ability and/or inclination of the respondents to empathize with the key "other" in the story, the level of need upon which s/he focuses, and the complexity of analysis applied to the problem. The pretest means were quite similar for all groups, with 27 of the 33 experimental and control groups having means that sounded off to level 4 (conventional, stereotyped thought and concern). On the posttest there was general movement by experimental students toward level 5, a more complex pattern of thought with a focus on relational concerns. This is discussed more fully below.

The Complexity/Empathy Index did clearly discriminate between experimental and comparison groups and between types of experiential programs. In terms of mean changes, 21 of the 27 experimental groups increased, 8 increasing at least a one-third step on the seven point scale. Five of the 6 comparison groups decreased and one showed a non-significant increase.

Most interesting was the pattern between types of programs. To test a hypothesis, programs were divided according to the degree in which students were 1) directly confronted with interpersonal problems similar to those in the stimulus stories and/or 2) where problem solving was a deliberate focus of accompanying seminar sessions. These turned out to be critical variables in promoting change in complexity/empathy. Programs which featured both conditions registered an average mean increase of .59 points. Programs in which all students had one condition and some (not all) had the other, showed an average increase of .22 points. Programs in which both conditions were only partially present showed an average mean gain of .17. Programs in which students had neither element showed an average decrease of −.15.

The data reported in this section suggest that experiential education programs can and do have a positive effect on student learning and intellectual development. This is most strongly the case when the program features a combination of direct experience and formal reflection on that experience.

The pre-post test data clearly show that experiential education programs can have a positive impact on students' psychological, social and intellectual development.

Summary

To recapitulate what has been said thus far, the pre-post test data clearly show that experiential education programs can have a positive impact on students' psychological, social and intellectual development. Students in experiential programs tended to increase significantly, both in absolute terms and in relation to students in classroom programs, in the major scales employed in this study. These included tests of moral reasoning, self-esteem, social and personal responsibility, attitudes toward adults and others, career exploration, and empathy/complexity of thought.

While the results were extremely positive on a general level, they were not invariably so. That is, on every scale there were important differences among the experiential programs. The discussion shifts, thus, toward examining the dynamics within individual programs that could account for the differences in obtained results.

Findings: Correlates of Effectiveness

The second major focus of the Evaluation of Experiential learning Project was to identify the program practices which were most effective in facilitating development in students. The factors examined for effect were 1) general **program features**: nature of off-campus experience, length, intensity, and reflective component; **student characteristics**: age, grade point average, and socio-economic status; and **characteristics of individual experiences** including the degree of autonomy, amount of direction, how interesting and varied they seemed to participants, and the like.

The safest conclusion that can be drawn from the data is that no single practice or set of practices guarantees effectiveness from all students. Within every program and every type of program there were students who gained a great deal and others who did not. There were some clear patterns however, patterns which suggest interesting hypothesis concerning the effective operations of experiential programs.

Program Features

As described earlier, there were four general types of programs in this study: service, outdoor adventure, career internships, and community study/action. In actual practice, however, few of these were pure types, with elements of one or more (e.g., service) being found in more than one category of program. It may have been this factor as much as anything that resulted in there being no discernible relation between program type and student growth. While service programs appeared to do somewhat better than others on rankings of programs on intellectual and social development, the advantage virtually disappeared in a regression analysis which controlled for other program and student characteristics. Other elements, however, did appear to make a difference.

Among other program features, the presence of a formal (and at least weekly) seminar proved to be the single strongest factor in explaining positive student change. This was particularly true on measures of social and intellectual development. Interestingly, there was no clear relationship between a seminar and growth in measures of personal growth such as self-esteem. Perhaps students can make personal meaning of their experiences on their own, but if this meaning is to affect their broader social attitudes and intellectual skills, systematic and directed reflection must be added.

Other factors which consistently related to positive student change were length and, to a lesser degree, intensity. Experiences lasting a full semester (18 weeks) were relatively stronger than shorter experiences, as were those in which students were in field placements 2 or more hours, 4-5 days per week. Of these two factors, that of length was stronger than intensity though even in combination they were not as powerful predictors of change as was the presence of a seminar. It must be emphasized, however, that **all** of these factors collectively did not predict more than about 5% of the variance (by regression analysis) in pre-post change scores.

Student Characteristics

The student characteristics analyzed were age, grade-point-average, and socio-economic status. These were even less influential than program features, accounting for only about 3% of the variance between pre-post scores. Among the characteristics, only age showed any influence at all, with older students showing somewhat greater growth than younger students, especially on issues of social development. Neither student GPA nor socio-economic status were at all significant in predicting change. One other relevant fact which should be mentioned is that there did turn out to be a positive reaction between maturity (as measured by the Complexity/Empathy Scale) and the degree of approval given to an experience-based program.

The general finding of no strong relation between student demographic characteristics and program effectiveness does support one common contention of experiential education: that such experiences can benefit a wide variety, if not all kinds, of students.

No single practice or set of practices guarantees effectiveness from all students. Within every program and every type of program there were students who gained a great deal and others who did not.

Characteristics of Experience

One of the major problems in educational research and evaluation is that the assumption often has to be, or at least is, made that the program has been implemented as described and that all students participating in it have had the same experience. That neither is usually the case can be attested to by anyone closely associated with educational programs. Thus it was an aim of this study to go beyond gross program descriptors and examine more directly the specific experiences of students within the programs. It proved to be a fruitful search.

Compared with program features and student characteristics, the specific characteristics of an individual's experience proved the more powerful predictors of pre-post gains. While the former two categories combined explained no more than 8% of the variance in change scores, the latter consistently accounted for from 15 to 20 percent of variance. The finding lends credence to the notion that individuals experience educational programs idiosyncratically and that this is especially likely to be true in experience-based programs. The specific pattern of impact is outlined below.

The first issue examined was the relation between characteristics of experience and general rating of the program. The characteristics contributing most strongly toward a student rating their program as "excellent" or "good" was that the experiences were rated as being "interesting" and that the student felt s/he was "appreciated for their work."

While feeling appreciated and doing interesting things contributed to favorable program ratings, these characteristics had little or nothing to do with whether students grew from their participation in a program. The factors which contributed most strongly to pre-post gains were, rather, a mixture of features describing a combination of autonomy (e.g., "did things myself") and a collegial relationship with adults (e.g., "discussed experiences with teachers"). The 13 characteristics which made any appreciable impact on student growth are listed, by rank, in Table 2.

Table 2

Relative Effect of Characteristics of Experiences on Mean Gain Scores for All Tests Combined

Rank	Characteristics of Experience
1	Discussed experiences with teachers.
2	Did things myself instead of observing.
3	Adults did not criticize me or my work.
4	Had adult responsibilities.
5	Developed personal relations with someone on site.
6	Had freedom to explore own interests.
7	Discussed experiences with family and friends.
8	Felt I made a contribution.
9	Had a variety of tasks.
10	Was free to develop/use own ideas.
11	Got help when I needed.
12	Made important decisions.
13	Had challenging tasks.

It should be noted that the characteristics that the experiences were "interesting" did not make this list. Even more significantly, characteristics which describe a more typical student-adult relationship (esp., "given enough training to do my tasks" and "I was given clear directions") did not contribute to pre-post gains and, in fact, correlated negatively with them on several scales.

The most important implication for secondary schools is that experience based programs should be adopted and expanded. This is a significant departure from the overwhelming trend in public education to return to "the basics".

The characteristics of experience were further examined to see if certain ones contributed more to one kind of growth than another. In Table 3 the strongest contributors to social growth are listed next to the strongest influences on indices of personal development.

As evident on the following page, it turned out that the characteristics suggesting autonomy (e.g., "free to develop and use own ideas") were more influential in promoting personal growth (e.g., self-esteem) than in social growth (e.g., responsibility). Conversely, the characteristics suggesting a collegial relationship with, and even guidance by, adults, showed the opposite pattern of influence. In short, personal growth was stimulated most by dealing autonomously with challenging tasks while social development accrued more from interaction with adults—as long as it was in a non-student role.

Analysis of student responses to an open-ended question asking them to explain why they rated their program as excellent or good revealed another interesting pattern. The majority of responses described personal benefits to the participant (e.g., "personal sense of improvement") while only a small minority cited more socially-relevant gains (e.g., "affected another person," or "increased understanding of others' needs").

It goes only slightly beyond the data given to argue that the analysis suggests that students will rate a program highly if the experiences are interesting, if they're shown appreciation for their effort, and if they sense some personal gain from the experience. Similarly, students will make the strongest **personal** gain when they are given some autonomy to act on their own and to use their own ideas. In

In many areas of the country, declining enrollment and declining resources have led school systems to discontinue all but the most traditional classroom instruction. This study indicates that dropping experiential programs is a serious mistake.

expanded. This is a significant departure from the overwhelming trend in public education to a return to "the basics". The usual—and in our view—narrow meaning of "the basics" is classroom instruction in symbolic representation of experience. The consistent finding that classroom instruction in a traditional mode, as represented by the comparison groups, showed no improvement in personal and intellectual development in contrast to consistent, strong growth for experiential programs should lead educators and the general public to rethink the notion that only classroom instruction is legitimate and effective. The strong positive showing of the experience-based programs do warrant schools offering such experiences. At the very least, experiential programs currently in existence should be maintained. In many areas of the country, declining enrollment and declining resources have led school systems to discontinue all but the most traditional classroom instruction. This study indicates that dropping experiential programs is a serious mistake. On the contrary, well-constructed programs, as those in this study, warrant a significant and expanding role in secondary schools.

Development Focus for Education

The first implication—that experiential programs are effective in promoting development and should be adopted by secondary schools—assumes that development is a legitimate aim of education.

It is through a peculiar misuse of the English language, or perhaps a symptom of something deeper, that the comprehension of symbols and the manipulation of mediated experience has come to be identified as learning the "basics". Such an interpretation of what is fundamental ignores the source of learning (experience), the nature of the

If significant experience is truly a critical element in development, it ought not be restricted to isolated doses in the later school years but be a central focus from the elementary years and on.

learner (especially development), and the purpose of learning (personal growth and social improvement). Theorists such as John Dewey (1902/1964) and Lawrence Kohlberg (1972) have made cogent arguments for considering development to be the aim of education; research on the effects of schooling (Heath, 1978; McClelland, 1973) has demonstrated the predictive power of personal development (in contrast to academic achievement) for adult success; the present study and others have shown the viability of promoting such development through deliberate educational interventions. It would seem more than reasonable for educators to act on this information. The aim and effect would not be the denigration of more traditional goals, but to imbue them with new vitality and purpose. For experiential educators as well, a focus on development can provide both a framework for organizing activities and a goal—that of promoting social, psychological, and intellectual development.

The Need For Experience

Educators who are serious about development as an aim of education may also have to be serious about adopting experiential methods for achieving that goal. Developmental

It would seem more than reasonable for educators to act on this information. The aim and effect would not be the denigration of more traditional goals, but to imbue them with new vitality and purpose.

theory, from the time of Dewey to the present, has stressed that development requires interaction, transaction, conflict, cognitive dissonance, consequential choices and action on behalf of those choices. The more that children and adolescents are isolated from broad, varied, and significant experiences in the social environment, the more must schools encourage such involvement to successfully work toward facilitating development.

Furthermore, if significant experience is truly a critical element in development, it ought not be restricted to isolated doses in the later school years but be a central focus from the elementary years and on.

Finally, the provision of more meaningful participation cannot be met by the schools alone. The findings of this and other studies that experiential programs can promote development must not be overdramatized. It would be foolish to argue or believe that a change in school practice is enough to substantially counter the effects of impoverished experience and prolonged childhood and adolescence. Ways must be found to share the educational mission with the broader society and to provide opportunities for children and youth to be more seriously involved in their communities.

Changes in Teacher Education

Education through experience, and for human development, implies a new kind of teacher training. Needed is an emphasis on understanding adolescence and human development in contrast to the current emphasis on teaching a discipline. Needed also is increased knowledge of, and involvement in, the wider community by teachers themselves—partly for increasing their capacity to facilitate experiences within it, and partly for their own renewal and continued development.

Table 3

Relative Influence of characteristics of Experience on Social and Personal Growth

Social Development	Rank	Personal Development
Discussed experiences with Teachers	(1)	Did things myself instead of observing.
Discussed experiences with family and friends	(2)	Free to develop and pursue own ideas.
Adults did not criticize me or my work	(3)	Had challenging tasks.
Had adult responsibilities	(4)	Developed personal relations with someone at site.
Made important decisions	(5)	Free to explore my own interests.
Felt I made a contribution	(6)	Discussed experience with teachers.
Had a variety of tasks	(7)	Felt I made a contribution
Free to explore own interests	(8)	NS
Developed personal relations with someone at site	(9)	NS

contrast, positive change in social attitudes and reasoning skills requires more interaction with adults—where the involvement is collegial, not patronizing, and when they can initiate the contact.

In summary, it was found that the most powerful predictors of growth were the **characteristics of the experiences** of individual students, with features suggesting autonomy being most productive of personal development and features suggesting a collegial relationship with adults and others being most productive of social development. Among **program** features, the most powerful positive factor was the existence of a regular seminar. Of somewhat less influence was length of program (especially if 18 weeks or longer); even less influential was intensity (better if 2 or more hours 4-5 days a week). There was a small positive relationship between age and growth on social and intellectual measures. No significant relationship was found between student growth and general type of program, on the characteristics of student GPA or socio-economic status.

One final word may be the most significant of all. 95% of the participants in experiential programs rated their own program as either excellent (49%) or good (46%). Perhaps no further comment is needed.

Implications

It is not presumed that this study has definitively answered the central questions of educators. Nonetheless, its findings, combined with others reported within it, do contain implications that merit consideration and application even before "all the facts are in." Central among these are: 1) the demonstrated value of continuing and expanding experiential programs; 2) the importance of a developmental focus for education; 3) the need for direct experience to meet developmental goals; 4) needed changes in teacher education; and 5) the possibility and need for simultaneously working toward personal growth and social improvement.

Value of Experiential Education

The clearest and most significant conclusion of this study is that experiential programs are a powerful educational vehicle for promoting personal **and** intellectual development and can do so more effectively than classroom instruction. The most important implication for secondary schools is that experience based programs should be adopted and

Personal Growth and Social Improvement

> As the material of genuine development is that of human contacts and associations, so the end, the value that is the criterion and directing guide of educational work, is social. The acquisition of skills is not an end in itself. They are things to be put to use, and that use is their contribution to a common and shared life. (Dewey, 1934/1964, p. 11)

Americans have always had an enormous faith in education: that it would improve the individual and also make for a more prosperous, more just society. The above statement by John Dewey may serve as a gentle reminder that both goals are essential for either to be achieved. Perhaps one of the greatest strengths of experiential education is that it provides the opportunity to work on both goals simultaneously. As the individual grows from direct experience in the community, so may the community benefit, and not just in the long run, from the participation of youth in it. The study indicated that personal growth is a more automatic outcome of experiential education than is social development. To accomplish the dual goals of personal and social improvements, a new kind of relationship between student and teacher is necessary—a collegial mentorship.

There is much left to be learned about human development, about experiential education, and about how to bring about a better society. This study and the others cited within it do not tell us all we need to know. They provide a beginning and some idea of how to proceed. Again, John Dewey (1932) said it best:

> The sources of educational science are any portion of ascertained knowledge that enter into the heart, head and hands of educators, and which, by entering in, render the performance of the educational function more enlightened, more humane, more truly educational than it was before. But there is no way to discover what is 'more truly educational' except by the continuation of the educational act itself. The discovery is never made, it is always making.
> (pp. 76-77)

Further Questions for Practice and Research

William Perry is fond of pointing out that people are bigger than the theories used to explain them. In like fashion, issues of education and human development are larger than can be contained in or investigated by one study. Therefore, it would be well to cite some important issues that require further examination.

Impact on Others and the Wider Community

If students are truly involved in significant experiences with real consequences, it should then be possible to detect the effects of their activities on others and on their communities, as well as on themselves. While the assertion is rather commonly made that experiential education programs can contribute to meeting the real economic, social and educational needs of communities and the nation (National Commission on Resources for Youth, 1974) relatively little evidence has been assembled to date. An investigation into the social and economic impact of youth participation would seem particularly important as discussion of the utility of a national Youth Service Program grows more serious (Landrum, 1979).

Who Benefits?

Important questions remain concerning who benefits most from experience-based educational programs—and why. For example, to what degree is maturity, or advanced development, a cause or a consequence of learning through experience? If the exercise of autonomy leads to growth, is the demand for it a factor of the experience or setting itself, or do certain kinds of individuals carve out autonomous roles within the experiences made available to them? Is there a relation between cognitive style and ability of propensity to learn from experience? What are the specific skills and habits that enable a person to learn and grow from experience? Can these be isolated, and then taught and learned in the way that skills in learning from symbols have been? Such questions require a deeper, more focused examination of individuals and specific experiences than was possible or intended in this study.

How to Guide Experience and Reflection

As instructive as it may be to know that experience must be accompanied by reflection, it is not practically useful without more precise information on how best to structure, guide, and encourage such reflection. In addition, more information is needed to identify the kinds of off-campus activities which are most effective for achieving particular developmental and academic goals. One important issue, for example, is whether work-study (and other job experience) programs have effects similar to programs located in the general academic curriculum such as were the focus of this study.

Effect on Academic Knowledge and Skills

The antidote to being information-rich and experience-poor is not to reverse the condition. More insight is needed to understand how direct experience and personal development may enhance the traditional academic aims of schooling—and vice-versa.

Long-term Effects

The investigation of the impact of experience on development must be enriched by the study of, in Dewey's terms, "its influence upon later experiences," the degree to which "they promote having desirable future experiences" (1938/1962, p. 27). Clearly it would be important to know if patterns established in the program—of learning from experience, of participating in the community, of exercising autonomy—were continued. Also of interest would be students' assessment of what aspects of their experiences seemed particularly valuable a year or two after as opposed to during or immediately following the experience.

Research Methods

An important problem in the investigation of experiential education has been the lack of appropriate methods and instruments. The Social and Personal Responsibility Scale and the Problem Solving Inventory were developed to help fill this gap. The results indicate they were useful measures and merit further development and refinement.

Results from this study demonstrated that paper and pencil tests can be useful in detecting important effects of experiential education. They also demonstrated some of the limitations of this approach. Evidence from this and other studies suggests that such measures are less than satisfactory for some students, particularly those with a history of negative experiences with testing. In addition, such measures do not adequately capture the small individual changes, the critical incidents, the nuances, the sense and sensibility of experience. Thus additional techniques must be developed and used. Interviews, observations, analyses of journals, enthnographies, and case studies could be used both to triangulate and to see beneath the findings from paper and pencil measures. Such measures could uncover, in Dewey's terms, "the qualitative characteristics of things as they are originally and 'naturally' observed" (1929/1960, p. 90).

Programs

An important aim of the study was to include schools that would represent a variety of program orientations (service, career internship, community study, outdoor adventure); of school types (independent, parochial, public); geographic area and type of community (urban, suburban, small town); of program structure (seminar—non-seminar, short and intermittent experience to long-term and intensive); and of student populations (poverty level to affluent, low to high grade point average).

Within these general guidelines, the chief criteria for inclusion in the study were that the program have a reputation for excellence, have been in operation for at least four years, that it be an integral part of its school's academic program, and that there be a local interest in being included. Potential participants were identified out of the project directors' working knowledge of experiential programs, nominations from the sponsoring organizations (NAIS, NASSP, NCEA), and recommendations from the National Commission on Resources for Youth, Inc., and from the National Center for Service Learning. Of the schools finally contacted, only three chose not to be included. Of those who were included, three were unable to complete the testing (one independent, one parochial, and one public). The latter were replaced by schools which applied on their own initiative and met the criteria for inclusion.

The final roster of programs were as representative as might have been hoped for. The chief imbalances were an underrepresentation of schools from the West and South and of programs which had outdoor adventure (a la Outward Bound) as an exclusive program focus. By all other criteria the programs were relatively balanced.

It must be noted, and cannot be too strongly emphasized, that any success achieved by this project was in no small measure due to the efforts of the individual program directors and administrators. They were responsible for identifying the key outcomes of experiential learning, defining the focus of the study, administering the tests themselves, and helping to interpret the data. Without such capable, willing, and energetic people there is no possible way that a study of this scope could have been carried out short of a twentyfold increase in staff and budgets—and then it's doubtful.

Schools included in the Project are: **Independent:** Dana Hall School, Wellesley, MA; Francis W. Parker School, Chicago, IL; Carolina Friends School, Durham, NC; Duluth Cathedral High School, Duluth, MN; **Parochial:** St. Benedict's Preparatory School, Newark, NJ; Bellarmine High School, Tacoma, WA; Ward High School, Kansas City, KS; **Public:** Eisenhower High School, Hopkins, MN; Mitchell High School, Colarado Springs, CO; Minneapolis Public Schools; Allegheny Intermediate Unit, Pittsburgh; St. Paul Open School; South Brunswick High School, Monmouth Junction, NJ; Rochester, Minnesota Public Schools; Bartram School of Human Services, Philadelphia, PA; Beverly Hills High School; Ridgewood High School, Norridge, IL; Kirkwood High School, Kirkwood, MO; North Central High School Indianapolis, IN.

Editor's Note: A preliminary report of the Evaluation of Experiential Learning Project was published earlier in the AEE Journal under the title: "Johnny Says He Is Learning . . . Through Experience," spring 1977, Vol. 2, No. 1. We are pleased to offer here the complete results of the study.

A summary of this study and/or the **Project Instrument and Scoring Guide** are available at a cost of $3.00 each from the Center for Youth Development and Research, 48 McNeal Hall, University of Minnesota, St. Paul, MN 55108.

The Judicial Process as a Form of Program Evaluation

by James Ellsberry

Traditional forms of program evaluation have been supplemented successfully by a judicial inquiry. It adds to both the evaluative process and to the opportunity for participation of a wide segment of the community.

"The jury recommends that no major changes be made in the structure of **Learning Unlimited**...although more rigid structure might reduce some of the abuses within the program, the jury felt that it would not compensate for the loss of the individualized approach to learning."

This quote has been extracted from the findings of an impartial jury called together to hear testimony regarding the need for stricter guidelines and procedures to be implemented as part of an innovative program named **Learning Unlimited.** Perhaps it seems strange to think of putting a school program on trial, but at North Central High School in Indianapolis, Indiana, this "trial" has become an accepted part of the total process of program evaluation. As an alternative program, **Learning Unlimited** has scheduled the burden of accountability by employing a very broad and aggressive approach to the whole problem of program evaluation.

The general belief held by staff and administration has been that, any single means of gathering and reporting data is vulnerable to attack by critics. To avoid this pitfall, evaluators compared full and part-time **Learning Unlimited** students to students enrolled solely in the traditional school on the basis of grade point average, a variety of standardized test scores, and rating scales designed to measure such things as personal efficacy, mastery of life skills and the effectiveness of instructional methods. External consultants conducted formal interviews to evaluate perceptions of the students, staff, administrators and parents of

---

James Ellsberry is presently Assistant Principal at North Central High School in Indianapolis, Indiana. He has an M.S. in guidance and administration from Indiana State University and an Ed.S. in guidance from Michigan State University. He is a writer, lecturer and educational consultant in the areas of staff development, evaluation, individualized instruction and experiential learning.

---

students in **Learning Unlimited** regarding program outcomes. Follow-up questionaires have been mailed to program graduates and there have been the annual judicial inquiries. The valuable role of the judicial inquiry as a meaningful part of a comprehensive approach to evaluation is the theme of this article.

Dr. Robert Wolf of Indiana University was the first to adapt the judicial process of the legal profession to the educational setting. The beauty of the judical inquiry is its inherent versatility. There are three very good reasons why the inquiry process is so attractive as a form of evaluation. First of all, it is an effective method of investigating both sides of an issue in an open forum. Second, it is a unique public relations tool because it permits the active involvement of a diverse audience and large numbers of participants. Third, and probably most important, it affords an exciting opportunity for

---

The beauty of the judicial inquiry is its inherent versatility.

---

teaching and learning. All these advantages and it's fun! It has become an eagerly awaited annual event for staff and students of **Learning Unlimited.** Many of the adult participants from previous inquiries volunteer to serve as jury members a second time. Familiar faces can be seen in the audience from year to year. It has become an occasion for students, teachers, parents of students in the program, administrators, and community resource people to come together for the expressed purpose of program improvement through evaluation.

Ten Basic Steps for Organizing
a Judicial Inquiry

Step One: Identifying the issues. This can be accomplished by a simple questionaire survey or telephone interview to determine primary concerns of students, teachers and parents. Or, the administrator may select

the issue for presentation. Some of our past issues reflect the concerns of parents and students are:
  Is the school providing adequate basic skill preparation for college?
  Is the educational value of community-based learning worth the cost and time involved?

The role of the judge is very important. It is up to him to enforce the rules of the trial. A local judge, an attorney, or the school's debate coach would be among those who would be competent choices to serve in this position.

Not only must the issues be identified, but the pro and con positions must be clearly stated. For example: the pro side would state and build a case to prove the graduates of our high school are adequately prepared academically for college. The con side would state and try to prove that the graduates of the school are not adequately prepared for academic competition in college.

Step Two: Participant teams may be selected in a variety of ways. The inquiry can become a class project through a course like business law, speech or government. It can be conducted as a student council project to improve the school. Though participation does require a considerable investment of student time, students need not be experienced in debate or legal procedures. They can be taught these skills in preparation for the inquiry. It is advisable to grant students school credit for the inquiry experience as partially

Students should be selected to become an "expert" at each of the various components that make up the inquiry. Outcomes for learners are substantial. Skills needed include: gathering pertinent data, developing trial tactics, organizing and sequencing the presentation, learning communication skills of interrogation and debate, and developing an effective closing statement.

fulfilling the objectives of a course, and it is easy to justify credit, for students gain expertise in areas such as research, organization, analyzation and public speaking—all of which contribute significantly to academic as well as personal growth. In addition, granting credit gives students an incentive to make the commitment of time and effort necessary for a successful endeavor. Team captains should be selected and an effort made to divide the responsibilities by delegating or voluntarily dividing the chores in preparation for the inquiry.

Identifying persons who can provide expert testimony to support their position is another important skill that student participants must develop. Parents, teachers, students, or local businessmen and women are listed among the resources that can be used to provide supportive testimony during the trial.

Step Three: Selection and preparation of the site. The physical setting for the inquiry should be created as though prepared for a dramatic production. An auditorium is fine, provided all participants can see and hear. Visit a courtroom and try to simulate the arrangement by placing, for example, the judge in a raised, central position. The jury and pro and con teams must be seated so that they can be clearly seen and heard. This may require a number of microphones.

Step Four: Selection and preparation of the judge and jury. The judge and jurors play key roles in the inquiry. A local judge, lawyer or your school's debate coach would be a competent choice. The judge defines the rules of the trial and enforces them. For example, he or she determines what is admissible as evidence, the order of events and proceedings, and the sequence of pro and con redirect testimony. He or she must also maintain order in the audience. Inquiry rules and proceedings may vary to fit your purpose and should be determined by the judge in collaboration with the pro and con teams.

We have selected jury members in two different ways. First, we have selected jury members who are not familiar with the school and therefore are neutral and objective. They have represented a variety of groups and areas of expertise. Jury members have included college professors, attorneys, an adolescent psychologist, parents, teachers, counselors and student council representatives from neighboring school districts. The second method of jury selection is to invite those persons known to be emotionally involved with the school program—people who already have a great deal of information about school—or perhaps persons who need more information, such as a school board member or central office administrator. Both advocates and adversaries of the program make excellent jury members because of their information-base and concern. However, for this same reason they should not be expected to be neutral and unbiased.

The jury needs no instruction prior to the event, provided one member is appointed jury foreman and given the responsibility of managing the jury assignment. A form to guide and standardize their reactions during the trial can be distributed to jury members.

Step Five: Training the student participants. This is time-consuming and essential. Students may visit a courtroom or secure assistance from local volunteers, such as a lawyer or debate coach. Students will need assistance with:
1. Gathering data to prove their position.
2. Developing strategies and tactics to use during the trial.
3. Organizing and sequencing presentations.
4. Learning the communication techniques of interrogation, debate, and the use of emotional, humorous and intellectual appeals to convince the jury.
5. Understanding the rules, like when to legitimately object to evidence or testimony being presented.

Certain students should be selected on each team to become expert at each segment of the previously mentioned tasks. For example, one student might be selected to **write** the opening and closing statements while another member is selected to **present** the statements at the inquiry.

Step Six: Building the case. Each team is free to pursue any method necessary to prove the validity of their position and destroy the validity of the other position. The only caution needed here is the responsibility of the faculty sponsor to approve all material and witnesses before the trial. The purpose of this restraint is to avoid embarrassing innocent persons or entering unsubstantiated statistics into the hearing proceedings.

This process is valuable for students because they are forced to seek out potential data by interviewing prospective witnesses, reviewing existing program evaluation information and perhaps generating their own research project to prove their position.

There are three primary sources of data:
1. The testimony of an expert witness (parent, student, teacher or other participants in the issue).
2. Research, the result of a questionnaire, test scores, attendance records, program statistics, etc.
3. Media, exhibits, slide presentations, visuals, tape recordings (for example, one of our teams used a telelecture this year during the trial that enabled them to interview a program graduate at a university 200 miles away).

In the excitement and competition of the final few days prior to the trial, the battle plans and sequence of events are changing almost daily for both teams.

Both teams develop a battle plan, including dividing the major issue into subissues and outlining the sequence of events and the time to be allotted for each presentation. Staying within the time limits predictably is a problem.

Step Seven: Practice session for both participant teams. This is an opportunity to refine the skills of the presenters and guarantee that both the pro and the con teams are pursuing parallel paths of the issue.

There are to be no surprises! Both sides must share with each other a list of witnesses, sequence of events, and subissues leading to the closing statements. In the excitement and competition of the final few days prior to the trial, the battle plans and sequence of events are changing almost daily for both teams. As witnesses refuse to testify or new witnesses are secured or valuable new data uncovered, both teams are revising the battle plans.

Occasionally, witnesses are reluctant to be negative toward the school or program on trial. The faculty sponsor must reassure the witness that their contribution will be viewed as helpful to the school, rather than destructive, because the negative testimony makes possible new, creative solutions to the problems.

Step Eight: Promoting the event. Promotion of the inquiry can be a public relations paradise. Selected individuals may be sent invitations by students or school officials. Parents, relatives, counselors, ministers, neighbors and school and community officials may be invited to attend all or part of the trial.

Usually the media is especially interested in covering the trial, due to the novelty of the procedure and

---

The general reaction from the public has been that we the program, must have nothing to hide or we wouldn't risk public inspection.

---

interest in schools. This is an opportunity to get public recognition of the school's or program's willingness to be accountable. The general reaction from the public has been that we the program, must have nothing to hide or we wouldn't risk public inspection. There have also been expressions of admiration for the courage of school officials in risking the inquiry process.

A brochure announcing the event and explaining the process aids in recruiting an audience and it helps the audience to the understand the purposes of the inquiry.

Step Nine: The trial is finally in session. With careful planning and thoroughness on the previous eight steps, the trial is in the hands of the judge, jury and student participant teams. Relax and enjoy it!

Step Ten: After the trial, the decisions of the jury are first distributed to the pro and con teams. The results and jury recommendations are also distributed to decision makers, which may include school board, central office administration and parent advisory groups. Any or all of these may wish to assist in an action program to implement the recommendations and thus, resolve the issue. The school is never bound by the decisions of the jury, nor must the administrator adhere to the recommendations, but from our past experience, the jury has, in all cases, contributed valuable, new insights and solutions.

How to Creatively Evaluate Programs

By Alan Warner

"After awhile we set sail for Hearn Island. A crowd of people gathered to watch us leave. The crew was very efficient, no one raised their voice or made a false move. The wind was brisk and blowing straight into the entrance, which is about forty feet wide. We made seven tacks to get clear. Everyone got quite a charge out of it and we waved good-bye as the tourists snapped pictures" - From the journal of a troubled youth who participated in an adventure challenge sailing program.

"Hypothesis (2) stated that there would be a significant difference on the post and follow-up testing intervals between the experimental and control groups of the youth sample on the Self-Esteem Measure and the Behavior Rating Form. Planned comparison as well as the two way overall analysis of variance supported this hypothesis" - From an evaluation research study of an adventure challenge program for troubled youth.

Alan Warner has recently completed a doctorate degree focusing on the evaluation of experiential education programs. He is now the Coordinator of the Cornwallis House Psychiatric Day Centre in Kentville, Nova Scotia.

I find it hard to believe that these quotes describe similar outcomes in two experiential programs which are nearly identical in their educational philosophies, goals, and practices. The discrepancy makes one suspicious that something is askew. My experiences, both in a whale boat on the open ocean and in the library of a prestigious university, confirm this suspicion. There is an enormous gulf between research and practice which has produced a weak research literature that practitioners ignore. In turn, experiential programs have missed the opportunity to get meaningful feedback from evaluation research. Numerous people have called for more evaluation research with well controlled research designs and greater scientific objectivity. But we do not need to repeat the mistakes of the past on a more sophisticated scientific level. Instead, we need to understand the past gap between research and practice and then move beyond it to explore new directions and ideas for evaluation research.

Differences Between Research and Practice

A review of the evaluation research literature over the past twenty-five years in experiential education (Warner, 1982 and Conrad, 1979) indicates a preoccupation with attempts to show that programs develop positive personal attitudes among participants. Most of these studies use paper and pencil psychological tests and written questionnaires. If one reads only the empirical research, it would be easy to conclude that the goal of experiential education is to improve participants' self-confidence. In contrast, if one reads the literature focusing on the development of experiential education philosophy or the material on innovations in program development, one quickly realizes that there is much that the researchers have ignored. There has been very little empirical work addressing the interpersonal, social, or intellectual goals of experiential programs. Studies rarely look at how specific variables in the experiential learning process interact with each other and contribute to the total impact. Why is there such a discrepancy between the empirical research and practice in both style and content?

Evaluation Research as Propaganda

The basic reason for the discrepancy is that evaluation projects have been typically undertaken for and by persons outside the field. Program administrators and staff have supported the development of formal empirical research projects largely because they have wanted "facts" which can be used in the battle to attract funds and participants. The logic is: "we believe our program is effective and if we can prove it, then we will have a strong argument in our efforts to get more support". The primary expectation for research has been that it provide information which can be used as propaganda in a political context. Most administrators in experiential programs were once front line staff and their hearts are in programming and staff development, not research.

This perspective has resulted in practical choices which have relegated evaluation to a lowly position in experiential education. A typical pattern has been for a program to contract out evaluation projects to researchers or graduate students, which has meant less time, worry, and involvement for the program. Clinical and educational psychologists have undertaken a large portion of the projects. Unfortunately, many applied psychologists have had a bias toward using paper and pencil tests which provide quick and easy measures of personality traits and attitudes. The researchers' biases have matched the administrators' needs in that attitude tests do not interfere with programming, yet they produce clean numerical results. One can say that "our program" increased self-confidence on the "Zickepheus Self-Esteem Scale", and then produce numbers to prove it. Hopefully, the funding source will be impressed and the program will continue.

> "Experiential educators have fought bitterly against traditional educational principles in the past only to accept similar standards as basic research principles."

This pattern has left experiential education with a weak empirical research foundation. Even when research designs are well controlled, many social scientists question the value of psychological tests because of their empirical deficiencies in reliability, validity, and ability to predict behavior (Mischel, 1969 and Abelson, 1972). Many people question whether constructs such as self-concept, which only have an indirect relationship to behavior are useful in understanding how interventions alter behavior. Others question whether assessment techniques which measure abstract concepts and depend on participants' verbal and cognitive skills should be the primary means of evaluating experiential education programs committed to learning through concrete action and experience. Finally, this type of study provides little information to program administrators and staff or to experiential educators elsewhere.

If "our" program increases participants' self-confidence, so what? It tells us that the program may be doing something right, but then we probably believed that previously. If our program does not increase self-confidence according to the tests, we now believe that either the research methods were flawed or that our program is not living up to our general expectations. This type of information does not help to develop or improve a program, hence it is not likely to impress administrators or staff, reinforcing the belief that research and evaluation is of little practical value.

Could this type of study still be valuable as a political tool to gain support even if the approach is questionable on practical and scientific grounds? I would argue that if the goal is to sell a program, it is probably more productive to put time and effort into developing sophisticated promotional materials and building positive relationships with decision-makers as opposed to implementing evaluation research projects. A program is rarely funded on its scientific merits. Bureaucrats and politicians who have a positive perspective on a program and its approach will be very accepting of data documenting the programs' benefits. However, they probably would have supported the program regardless of the data. Decision-makers who have other ideas and agendas will likely refuse to accept the data and can always point to flaws in the research methodology. The Reagan administration's past refusal to accept the large quantity of scientific data linking industrial smoke emissions to the environmental damage caused by acid rain is an excellent example of the use of political as opposed to scientific criteria in decision-making. In short, the political justification for outcome oriented, attitude research projects is also weak.

Toward Creative Evaluation Projects

Evaluation research can be of significant benefit to the experiential education movement if we move beyond the limitations and assumptions inherent in past research trends. We have to give up the notion that evaluation research should be undertaken for persons and agencies outside of one's program and the field. The key step is for experiential educators to initiate evaluation projects with the primary expectation that they can document strengths and weaknesses in present practices and provide information to assist in program development. Reflection is a key ingredient in learning through experience - it is time that experiential educators embrace this basic principle as it applies to program development through evaluation research.

Five types of research strategies seem to be particularly deserving of attention and development if the experiential education movement is to build a stronger research base.

First, evaluation research must be *developmental* so that it is an integral part of the process of building the program from the outset. Research and practice

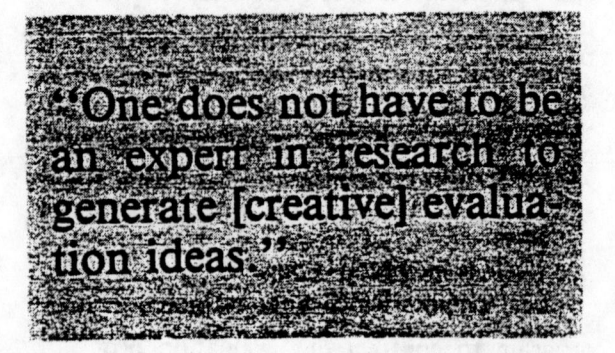

"One does not have to be an expert in research to generate [creative] evaluation ideas."

> "It is paradoxical that an education movement which places so much emphasis on learning as process focuses its research efforts on documenting products."

must be the two steps in the learning process for both staff and participants. For example, one issue in adventure programming is the leader's role in encouraging a small group to work together to solve problems. It could be a valuable evaluation process to specifically chart the sequence of conversation among group members as they work through a series of planning sessions for an expedition. The charting process identifies which members of the group are dominating conversation and provides insight into group leadership. It also gives the leader feedback on his or her role in the conversation. Finally, if the communication pattern is charted in a standardized fashion, the results can provide information about leaders' roles across programs, which in turn can be correlated with other variables and outcomes. A series of studies can document how group leaders structure and facilitate group conversations and whether different leader strategies produce different outcomes. This information can in turn have practical implications for the group process issues that are addressed in staff training. Most importantly, this type of evaluation tool can have benefits at multiple levels because it is built into the process of the program. In contrast, the standardized test requires a break in the experiential learning process in order for participants to complete it.

A second important research strategy is to alter our evaluation focus from producing general data on outcomes to providing specific information on *processes*. It is paradoxical that an education movement which places so much emphasis on learning as a process focuses its research efforts on documenting products. It is of both practical and theoretical interest to begin to explore which components and processes in programs produce particularly valuable learning experiences. We could begin to address the question as to how the best components from a number of programs could be combined. We could begin to generalize from data gathered in specific studies to come up with principles which are important to include in new program components.

Some of the recent research demonstrates the potential for looking at specific processes. For example, researchers have begun to explore the characteristics and qualities of an experiential education program which seem to produce personal and social growth (Conrad and Hedin, 1981). Another possibility would be to explore the stages and experiences a person goes through on the "solo" component of many adventure programs. Participants could be asked to keep journals during their time alone and a system could be set up to analyze the content across individuals and programs. One could address questions as to the best length and placement of a "solo" in a program. Developing this type of methodology would take work and time relative to giving a psychological test, but it would produce valuable information.

A third strategy which could improve evaluation research would be to shift the focus from documenting subjective attitudes to examining concrete *behaviors* and *accomplishments*. Experiential education has been strong in recognizing the importance of working at both levels simultaneously, yet empirical research efforts have not lived up to the standard set by the educational philosophy and practice. For example, adventure programs claim that troubled adolescents become cooperative and socially responsible as a result of their program experiences. There are numerous possibilities for testing this notion by looking at practical behaviors. Evaluators might look at the young peoples' drinking patterns before and after their experiences. One could examine whether participants became involved in positive work or recreation activities after their programs. These evaluation possibilities could also lead to program developments. The focus on follow-up behaviors might draw attention to the importance of reintegrating adolescents into their communities and provide ideas on how best to work with them at home.

One might also want to carefully examine the development of cooperative and socially responsible behaviors across an adventure program. For example, we observed and coded the levels of positive, passive, negative, and non-involvement of elementary students on a series of standardized initiative games across a residential outdoor program (Warner, 1984). The measure provided a quantitative behavioral index of changes in group cooperation over time.

Despite the need to shift our focus to behavioral measures, attitude tests do have a place in that they provide one type of general outcome measure which can be correlated with specific program characteristics, components, and modifications. However, they are of little practical value if they are not accompanied by behavioral data focusing on specific learning processes.

A fourth research need is to develop evaluation measures which are themselves *experiential* and model the types of learning emphasized in experiential programs. For example, it would seem quite possible that students might behaviorally demonstrate increased cooperation during initiative games following an adventure program, but might not change their responses on a paper and pencil test, which measures cooperative attitudes toward others. In addition, a written test might not be appropriate for students who are turned off by traditional academics and impersonal questionnaires. It is important that we develop creative experiential measures which mirror our learning experiences.

My work with the "Chocolate Game" is an example of the development of a measure which provides a meaningful learning experience for the participants while documenting changes in behavior among group members (Warner, 1982). The game models for young people the frequent social dilemma each person faces when deciding whether to cooperate in group or social situations. The Chocolate Game is played in small groups and each individual is put in the position of having to make an individualistic or a cooperative choice with the pattern of choices across the group determining how much free chocolate each child receives. A cooperative choice returns a moderate amount of chocolate to the person and maximizes the total reward for the group if everyone cooperates. An individualistic choice maximizes the personal reward at the expense of others if most of the group members cooperate. But the greater the number of individualistic choices, the lower the total reward for the group, until finally, if everyone makes individualistic choices, no one receives any chocolate. The game is played across a series of days and can be used to assess the level of group cooperation.

The game provides an interesting example of the impact research can have on practice. We originally introduced the game in the schools as an evaluation tool but a number of teachers are continuing to use it as an educational tool with their classes after the completion of the research project. Experiential measures are required if evaluation research is to more carefully and critically investigate the power of experiential methods.

A final research need is to *diversify* our efforts in terms of the types of evaluation methods which are being developed and utilized. The field is still very young and it is not clear which procedures will prove most fruitful. For example, we need to explore the possibilities for sophisticated peer evaluation along with the possibilities for retrieving important information from journals and interviews. Surely there are also applications for ethnographic procedures which have been developed in sociology. We might also need to explore the applications of rigorous behavioral research procedures developed for applied behavioral analysis. The potential is particularly striking, given the narrow range of much of the past work.

From Ideas to Action

Assuming that there is the willingness to move beyond past limitations and focus on new approaches, where do we start? Who can do the work? There are no quick and easy solutions which is one reason that evaluation research has been weak in the past. A good place to start is with projects that are designed to meet specific needs in specific programs. Projects should be a part of the program and should build a strong link between research and practice. Staff have to come to see research and evaluation as a priority if more creative and powerful projects are to be developed. One does not have to be an expert in research to generate the types of evaluation ideas which are outlined in the examples. One does need to be creative and have a full understanding of specific program needs and general experiential learning processes. Administrators and staff may need external help available from universities to implement projects, but they should not abdicate the responsibility for making decisions on evaluation goals and criteria.

Dr. Douglas Heath in his keynote address to the 1983 AEE conference emphasized that experiential educators are on the creative edge of the discipline. It is time to apply some of this creativity to research and evaluation, rather than borrow quick and easy techniques from other disciplines. Experiential educators have fought bitterly against traditional educational principles in the past only to accept similiar standards as basic research principles.

If we are to diminish the discrepancy between research and practice which was highlighted by the opening quotes, we must integrate them in training settings. Meaningful and creative evaluation research learning must be built into graduate and undergraduate experiential education programs. Experiential education students would in turn be able to serve as resource persons for programs committed to developing practical approaches internally. Even if a person is oriented toward leadership or program development, training in research and evaluation is critical to increasing the individual's awareness of the possibilities and roles for research in practical work.

The challenge is to move toward research approaches which are developmental, process-centered, behavioral, experiential, and diverse. It will not be easy to build creative and powerful, evaluation research methodologies. The easiest way is not always the way by which one learns the most.

References

- Ableson, R. "Are Attitudes Necessary?", in B.T. King and E. McGinnes (Eds.), *Attitudes, Conflict and Social Change*, New York: Academic Press, 1972.
- Conrad, Dan. "Experiential Education: A Summary of the Theoretical Foundations and a Critical Review of Recent Research." Center for Youth Research and Development, University of Minnesota, St. Paul, Minnesota, 1979.
- Conrad, Dan and Hedin, Diane. "National Assessment of Experiential Education: Summary and Implications:, *Journal of Experiential Education*, Vol. 4, Fall, 1981.
- Mischel, W. *Introduction to Personality*, New York: Rhinehart and Winston, 1969.
- Warner, Alan. "A Social and Academic Assessment of Experiential Education Trips with Elementary School Children," Dalhousie University, Halifax, Nova Scotia, 1982. (Doctoral thesis)
- Warner, Alan. "Using Initiative Games to Assess Group Cooperation," *Journal of Experiential Education*, Vol. 7, No. 1.

Idea Notebook

PRACTICAL EVALUATION FOR EXPERIENTIAL EDUCATION

by Judith Kleinfeld

Evaluations of experiential education programs typically take one of two roads. There is the high road -- formal, scientific evaluation with experimental groups, comparison groups, pre-tests, and multiple measures. There is the low road -- questionnaires asking program participants what they liked and didn't like about the program activities, staff, special speakers, session lengths, and so forth.

In practice, few programs carry out formal scientific evaluations. They are too expensive in program funds and staff time. Questionnaire evaluations are common. But most program staff, with little training in research methods, draft questionnaires which yield little useful information.

We developed an education-based evaluation strategy for the Alaska Department of Education to use in evaluating a group of experiential education programs the Department operated. A variety of programs were included, most funded by the state legislature under the general rubric of "leadership development." Our strategy was to design an easy-to-use, inexpensive way of finding out whether students are actually learning from an experiential program or just having a good time. Most important, this evaluation method would add to, rather than steal time from, the educational experience. We wanted to help students think about what they should be learning from the program before the experience begins, and to help them reflect upon what they have gotten out of the program when the experience concluded.

The most popular program we looked at, Alaska Close-Up, gives high school students a first-hand look at state government operations. The program is designed to increase students' understanding of and participation in public affairs. Modeled on the national Close-Up program, the Alaska Close-Up program brings high school students and teachers to the state capital, Juneau. Students observe legislative sessions, hear agency and other speakers, meet their state legislators, and sometimes testify before legislative committees. Students also participate in simulation games, such as "log-rolling" where they enact the roles of legislators attempting to pass bills of importance to their constituents.

Another example is the Rural Student Vocational Program, designed to provide work experience for Eskimo and Indian students from isolated villages. Students who grow up in these villages see few jobs other than schoolteacher, doctor, health aide, secretary, fire-fighter, and construction worker. The Program brings them to an Alaska city for two weeks and places them in a job. Students spend regular working hours at the job site observing the occupational routines and helping with the work. They receive a stipend of $100 to simulate a paycheck.

Despite the popularity of the programs, we questioned how much education was taking place. First, students were not prepared for the expensive experience they were having. The Eskimo and Indian high school students traveling to the cities for work experience, for example, usually learned little about how the workplace was organized and what they could expect to do on a job before the experience began. We sus-

---

Editor's Note: In response to the often expressed need for experiential educators to document what they are doing, this is the first in a series of articles explaining practical research ideas.

Judith Kleinfeld *is a Professor of Psychology at the Institute of Social and Economic Research, University of Alaska.*

pected that many floated through the experience without learning, for example, how supervisors communicated work demands and expectations, how one part of a business affected another part, or what characteristics led to job success.

Second, most programs had few follow-up activities to help students reflect upon what they had experienced and make sense of it. We suspected, for example, that Alaska Close-Up students, exposed to a few exciting days of speeches from legislative aides and talks with state senators about how important their participation in government was, came away with a Pollyanna-ish view of how state government operated.

Talking with program directors about these matters, however, was unproductive. The usual response was defensiveness. Whatever the evaluation strategy we developed, it was critical that program staff believe the results. Program staff would be most likely to believe the results, we felt, if they did the evaluation themselves. Also, an outside evaluation would only apply to the particular year the evaluation was done. An on-going evaluation effort, done routinely by staff, would be far more useful.

Most of the experiential programs we studied already did conduct their own internal evaluations. Typically they used questionnaires. Alaska Close-Up, for example, asked students to rate on a one to five scale various program activities -- the speakers they heard, the luncheon with their elected representative, program staff, and so forth.

These questionnaires told the program staff which events students liked. They did not tell the program staff what students had learned. Giving such a questionnaire to evaluate an experiential program was like giving an English test that asks students to rate on a one to five scale how much they had learned about punctuation.

Conrad and Hedin's study (1982) of the effects of experiential learning programs indeed found that whether students rated a program highly had little to do with how much they had gained from the program as measured by objective tests. Students rated programs highly when they felt the experience was "interesting" and when they were "appreciated for their work." Students learned from the program primarily when they did things rather than just observing them and when they had a chance to reflect upon and discuss the experience.

Education-Based Evaluation

Our alternative approach to evaluation was based on prevailing theories of how people learn from experience. Educators in the field emphasize that a program must do more than provide students with a rich experience. The program must also help students think about the experience and figure out what it meant. As Joplin puts it, "Experience alone is insufficient to be called experiential education, and it is the reflection process which turns experience into experiential education." (1981:17)

Joplin has proposed a particularly useful model of the stages of effective experiential education:

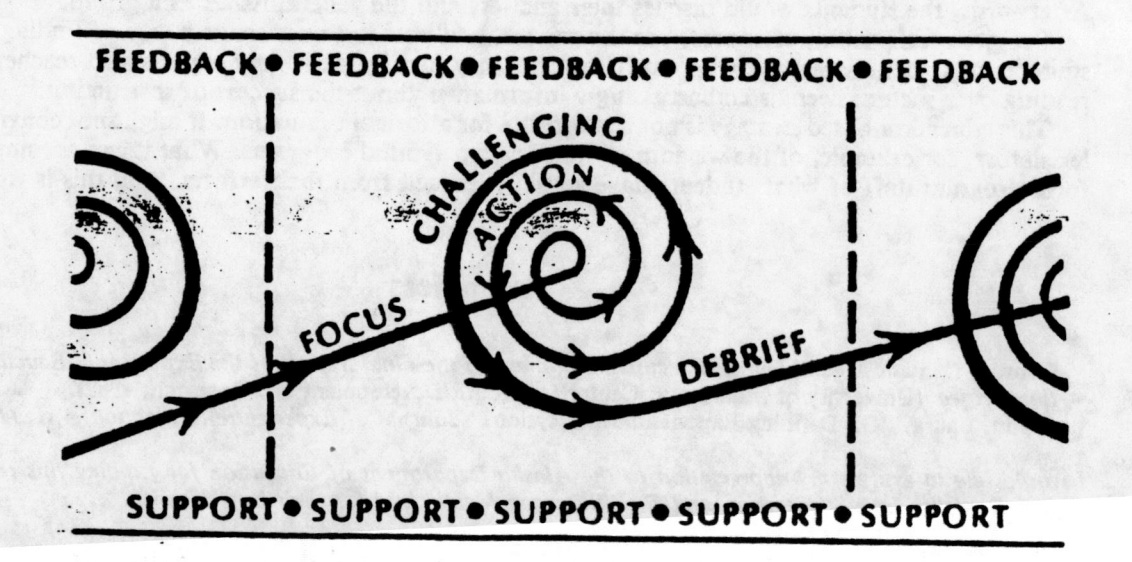

The model has three stages:

1. **Focus.** Program staff must clearly define what students can learn through the program experience and direct students' attention to it.

2. **Action.** The essence of experiential education is direct experience and participation.

3. **Debrief.** Students identify and discuss what they learn. In this stage, they form concepts and make generalizations which they can test in new situations.

The evaluation strategy which we proposed was to link these stages of experiential education to evaluation activities. Specifically:

1. Focus Stage Combined with Evaluation Pre-test:

Program directors use focusing activities to direct students' attention to what they should be learning from the program. The focusing activity doubles as a pre-test of what students already know about the area.

2. Debrief Stage Combined with Evaluation Post-tests:

Program directors use debriefing activities to help students think about what they have learned. The debriefing activity doubles as a post test.

We will illustrate how a program director could use this approach to evaluate Alaska Close-Up. When students first get together in the capital of Juneau, they would be asked to do a written simulation game such as the following activity:

EXAMPLE OF CLOSE-UP EVALUATION

(Students receive a copy of a pending bill with a list of arguments for and against the bill.)

1. Decide whether you are for or against this bill. Suppose you want to tell legislators what you think. However, you are at home and you don't want to spend more than half an hour and $5.00 on this project.

    a. Name as many different ways to communicate your views as you can. Be specific. (Don't just say "send a letter." To whom would you send a letter? What other ways could you use to send a message?)

    b. What do you think happens to these kinds of communications?

    c. How much influence do you think your communication will have?
       ☐ a lot   ☐ some   ☐ not much   ☐ none at all

2. Suppose this bill is very important to you. You are willing to spend several days and several hundred dollars to get the bill passed or defeated.

    a. What kinds of actions would you take? (Name as many as possible and be specific.)

    b. How much influence do you think you will have?
       ☐ a lot   ☐ some   ☐ not much   ☐ none at all

After the Close-Up experience, students would be asked this set (or a parallel set) of questions again. Afterwards, the students would discuss their answers and the general issues as a group.

Program staff could, of course, use the pre-test and post-test answers as a way of finding out whether students had actually learned what staff thought they had learned. Any experienced teacher knows that reading over such answers is embarrassingly informative about the success of instruction.

This education-based strategy is not a substitute for a formal evaluation. It might not convince skeptical legislators, for example, of the wisdom of funding experiential programs. What it can accomplish is to inform program staff of what students have actually learned from their efforts. And this is worth doing.

References

- Conrad, Dan and Hedin, Diane, *Executive Summary of the Final Report of the Experiential Educational Evaluation Project* (University of Minnesota: Center for Youth Development and Research, 1982).
- Joplin, Laura, "On Defining Experiential Education," *Journal of Experiential Education*, 4, 1, (1981).

I would like to express my appreciation to the Alaska Department of Education for funding this research and to Denise Daniello, Lois Stiegemeier, and G. Williamson McDiarmid for their help with it.

RESEARCH UPDATE: The Effects of an Experiental Aerospace Program on Career Maturity

by Betty B. Burkhalter
and James P. Curtis

Too many students fail to see meaningful relationships between what they are being asked to learn in school and what they will do when they graduate from the educational system. Thus, an experiential environment, actively involving industry, government, and education, is one approach to provide students with the needed balance between theory and experience. Based on this need for a partnership among industry, government, and education, the Alabama Space and Rocket Center along with a number of aerospace industries and government agencies, sponsored an experiential program to provide intense career exploration for high school students. The hypothesis was that students participating in the Experiential Career Exploration Program in Science and Technology would achieve greater gains in career maturity than students who participated in a regular vocational career exploration program.

Sixty students were chosen of the 5,000 original applicants from vocational centers throughout Alabama. The experimental group participated in five days of intensive career exploration activities at the Space and Rocket Center while the comparison group participated in traditional career exploration programs at their respective vocational centers. The students in the experimental group participated in activities such as solving problems in a neutral buoyancy simulator, engineering an apparatus that would enable an egg to drop ten feet into an egg carton without breaking, using a computer to learn information related to possible careers, and meeting with and observing astronauts in training.

The Career Maturity Inventory (CMI), designed to measure an adolescent's specific competencies involved in making career decisions, was used to measure the impact of the program. After participation in the program, those students in the experimental group were more decisive, independent, and involved with respect to choosing a career alternative. They demonstrated a greater ability to realistically appraise career capabilities, to come to terms with the working world, to identify the relevance of various activities for planning work, to cope adaptively with adversity, and to select appropriate paths to reach a desired goal. A similar change did not occur with the comparison group.

Based on the results of the Experiential Career Exploration Program, the United States Summer Space Camp Program is being developed to serve approximately 1400 students throughout the country each summer. It is the on-going mission of the Alabama Space and Rocket Center to motivate the youth of America to become interested in science and technology careers and to develop a broader understanding of space technology. Persons from education, industry, and government have become partners to assure that this mission is achieved through the experiential approach to learning.

This research was done by Bettye B. Burkhalter, Auburn University, Alabama, and by James P. Curtis, The University of Alabama. A detailed report on this program is pending publication in the Journal of the British Interplanetary Society, London.

JOHNNY SAYS HE IS LEARNING... THROUGH EXPERIENCE

by DIANE HEDIN and DAN CONRAD

This is the first of a series of articles reporting on aspects of program evaluation. The Evaluation of Experiential Learning Project described here is of national scope and major import.

Learning to get things done and to work with others, to solve problems, to accept the consequences of one's actions, to gather and analyze information, to become more open to new experiences, to feel and act like a useful member of the community, to develop greater self esteem, to become more self-motivated, and to be more concerned about others. Where are these taught or learned in the secondary school curriculum? According to 4,000 students in some twenty public, private, and parochial school systems across the country, they are taught and learned in the experiential programs in which they are enrolled.

This report of early research is one of several by the Evaluation of Experiential Learning Project, a major effort co-sponsored by three national educational organizations (National Association of Secondary School Principals, National Association of Independent Schools, and the National Catholic Education Association) and funded by grants from the Rockefeller Family Fund and the Spencer and General Mills Foundations.* The Project, directed by Diane Hedin and Dan Conrad of the Center for Youth Development and Research of the University of Minnesota, is just completing the first and pilot phase of its study.

The purpose of this article is to describe the evaluation effort, to describe its early evaluation results, and to describe the educational practice being studied.

A. FIRST RESULTS PROVE IMPRESSIVE

The Evaluation Effort: At the heart of the Project is its "Panel of Practitioners," teachers and administrators from twenty diverse school systems from Beverly Hills, California, to Newark, New Jersey.* With the assistance of seasoned educational evaluators like Ralph Tyler, they are responsible for defining the issues to be studied, for helping select and develop instruments, for implementing the design, for helping interpret the data collected — and for keeping the whole study practical, understandable, and applicable to everyday life in schools.

In June 1978, at the Spring Hill Conference Center in Wayzata, Minnesota, the Panel examined the data collected during the pilot phase of the study. They admit to being surprised, even overwhelmed, by what they found. The biggest surprises were how very positively both teachers and students rate their experiential programs, the significance of the things they report being learned in them, and the extraordinary level of agreement between students and teachers about these program outcomes. Furthermore, the findings held constant across the broad range of programs represented in the study (internships, volunteer service, political action, outdoor adventure, etc.)** and for extremely diverse schools and student populations throughout the country.

Early Evaluation Procedures and Results: The first evaluation effort of the Project was to survey people who direct experiential programs. In January, 1978, they were asked what they could most confidently claim to be the actual effects of experiential programs on students. They were asked not what they believed *should* happen, but what they had *directly* experienced, seen and heard. The

---

Diane Hedin, *is the Associate Director of the Center For Youth Development and Research at the University of Minnesota.*

Dan Conrad, *is an instructor at the Center for Youth Development and Research at the University of Minnesota.*

*The originator of this effort was Bill Berkeley of the Commission on Educational Issues.

*Schools included in the Project are: *Independent:* Dana Hall School, Wellesley MA; Francis W. Parker School, Chicago, IL; Carolina Friends School, Durham, NC; Duluth Cathedral High School, Duluth, MN; *Parochial:* St. Benedict's Preparatory School, Newark, NJ; Bellarmine High School, Tacoma, WA; Ward High School, Kansas City, KS; *Public:* Eisenhower High School, Hopkins, MN; Mitchell High School, Colorado Springs, CO; Minneapolis Public Schools; Allegheny Intermediate Unit, Pittsburgh, St. Paul Open School; South Brunswick High School, Monmouth Junction, NJ; Rochester, Minnesota Public Schools; Bartram School of Human Services, Philadelphia, PA; Beverly Hills High School; Ridgewood High School, Norridge, IL; Kirkwood High School, Kirkwood, MO; North Central High School, Indianapolis, IN.

**The study encompasses virtually all forms of what is termed experiential education with the notable exception of work-related or vocational programs.

result represents an important study in itself, being a report of "concerned observers" looking critically, if not disinterestedly, at experiential education. Among the vast array of observed effects were twenty-four which appeared with amazing regularity. Together, they comprise an imposing list of outcomes which schools everywhere hope to achieve, but less often do (or even dare to claim): improved self esteem, learning responsibility, learning to solve real-life problems, etc. (see Table 1). Given the current level of pessimism in American education, it is encouraging, even startling, to see such confidence about the effects which at least one educational practice seems to be having.

This original survey sets the stage for the next and more critical step in the evaluation process. Believing that the consumers of a "product" are usually more reliable judges of its value than its producers or salesmen, this list of observed effects was presented to all the students in each of the programs. This survey was taken in the Spring of 1978. The students were informed that the list represented what some people had said might be the effects of experiential programs, and students were asked: "Which, if any, of these things have you personally learned or gained from the activities in your own experiential program?" The researchers knew from previous studies and their own experience that students' perceptions of the purposes of a course are often considerably different from and their evaluations less effusive than those of their teachers. Therefore they expected not more than a fifty percent level of agreement between teachers and students on the effects of the programs. In fact, however, only one item "to become a more effective consumer," (46%) failed to meet this level of agreement, but becoming a more effective consumer was a deliberate emphasis in only two of the programs surveyed. More than half (14) of the items achieved an average agreement level of over eighty percent across all programs. These items are the ones listed in the opening paragraph of this article, plus "learning responsibility to the group or class," "learning responsibility for my own life," "gaining more realistic attitudes toward other people," "increased knowledge of community organizations," and "risk-taking — openness to new experiences (see Table 1)." Each of the other items, such as learning communication skills, learning about community problems and resources, learning about careers, etc., received eight to one hundred per cent agreement in those programs where they were a deliberate emphasis. With apparently good reason, the participants in these experiential programs think they are pursuing something worthwhile in education.

TABLE I
WHAT STUDENTS LEARN IN EXPERIENTIAL LEARNING
COMPOSITE PROFILE OF 20 EXPERIENTIAL PROGRAMS (N=4,000)

ITEM (in rank order)	Agree*	Disagree*	Don't Know
1. Concern for fellow human beings	93%	4%	3%
2. Ability to get things done and to work smoothly with others	93	4	3
3. Realistic attitudes toward other people such as the elderly, handicapped, or government officials	88	4	8
4. Self-motivation to learn, participate, achieve	88	7	5
5. Self-concept (sense of confidence, sense of competence, self-awareness)	88	7	5
6. Responsibility to the group or class	86	3	11
7. Risk-taking — openness to new experiences	86	7	8
8. Sense of usefulness in relation to the community	86	8	6
9. Problem-solving	86	9	5
10. Risk-taking — being assertive and independent	86	9	5
11. Accept consequences of my own actions	85	9	6
12. Gathering and analyzing information, observation, reflecting on experience	84	8	7
13. Knowledge of community organizations	82	7	11
14. Responsibility for my own life	80	10	9
15. Awareness of community problems	78	13	9
16. Assume new, important tasks in community and school	78	14	8
17. Communication skills (listening, speaking, presenting ideas through variety of media)	77	11	7
18. Awareness of community resources	71	13	16
19. Realistic ideas about the world of work	71	18	11
20. Learning about a variety of careers	70	22	8
21. Use of leisure time	60	26	14
22. Narrowing career choices	54	34	12
23. To become an effective parent	52	29	19
24. To become an effective consumer	46	32	22

*Strongly agree and agree are combined and disagree and strongly disagree are combined.

Not only is there substantial agreement between students and teachers about what is learned in experience-based programs, but community people who supervise the students, ranging from free clinic counselors to television network executives, also reported that they observed student progress toward these twenty-four outcomes. In one school's program (Beverly Hills High), the students' supervisors were asked to respond to the same questionnaire as the students. The only difference between the student and supervisor rating was that the latter ratings were more positive, with a much higher incidence of "strongly agrees" appearing in their responses.

As interesting and significant as the above results might be, they represent only the beginning of the work of the Evaluation of Experiential Learning Project. The next step will be to subject these observations to more rigorous examination. In their June meeting, the Project's staff and Panel of Practitioners gave final form to the formal research design, focusing their investigation on seven issues suggested by the preliminary study: self concept, responsibility, problem solving, attitudes toward others, learning about the community, communication skills, and career development. These issues will be examined through standardized tests, project-designed instruments, systematic observations (by teachers, supervisors, parents, and outside observers), case studies, and a myriad of unobtrusive measures. Testing will begin in the Fall of 1978 and continue throughout the school year. The aim will be to confirm, qualify, or refute the direct reports of teachers and students. In addition, they hope to determine what kinds of programs produce what results, what classroom and community activities best help assure their being attained, and what kinds of evaluative techniques are most appropriate to these practices. Among the products of the Project will be its research report, a portrait of individual programs and students, a compilation of ideas for program and class activities, and a handbook of evaluative tools which individual schools can use to assess the effectiveness of their own experiential programs.

The Educational Programs Studied: The early findings of this Project suggest that direct community experiences may be an important means for nurturing certain kinds of growth and development in students. That similar findings came from such a diverse range of programs is especially interesting. What the programs have in common is that they all engage students in new and challenging roles outside the school. That they all should report similar results suggests that the researchers may be uncovering effects that are generic to experiential education. If that is the case, not everyone should be surprised. The notion that *people learn some things best by doing them* (and that adolescents need significant and challenging tasks) is as old as John Dewey, if not Plato. That secondary schools should include experiential learning programs in their general curricula has been an important recommendation of every major commission on youth, education, and citizenship of the last decade. Yet, until now, no one has systematically investigated the assumptions underlying the recommendations, tested the claims made for the programs, or tried to spell out very clearly just what is learned through them. This lack of systematic investigation may explain why, for many educators, such programs remain in the category of things that sound good but may turn out to be more troublesome than worthy.

More exhaustive research is needed, and it is forthcoming. In the meantime, the early accounts of what students (and their teachers, administrators, and community supervisors) report to be the effects of experiential learning programs are certainly encouraging. If these results persist through subsequent research, experiential education will have to be viewed as an effective means for achieving some of the highest goals in education.

B. THE RESEARCH DESIGN

That secondary school should include experiential programs has been a recommendation of every major commission on youth, education, and citizenship of the last decade. Yet, until now, no one has systematically investigated the assumptions underlying the recommendations...

The jargon word for our overall approach is "triangulation." That is, when looking for phenomena that are hard to find, and where standardized tests are not adequate in themselves, and when breaking new ground, an acceptable level of confidence can only be achieved by examining each element from several different angles. In our study we will be examining each chosen issue by at least three different methods — each of these *in addition* to our grounding in theory, our comparison with other research and the continuing reports by concerned observers. The basic tools are standardized tests, project-designed instruments, systematic observations (parents, teachers, supervisors), case studies, and a host of unobtrusive measures. A profile of the overall approach to each topic (e.g., "social responsibility") is depicted below.

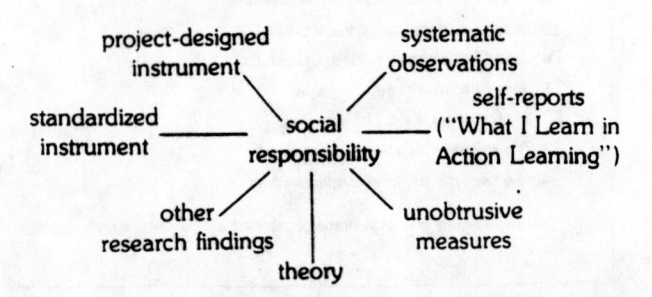

```
     project-designed          systematic
         instrument            observations
                                           self-reports
standardized ─────── social ─────── ("What I Learn in
 instrument       responsibility      Action Learning")
          other  /        \  unobtrusive
    research findings      measures
                     theory
```

The **research questions** that will be addressed are:
1. What are the immediate effects of experiential learning on students?
2. What are the long-range effects on students?
3. What factors make for successful and unsuccessful learning experiences in these programs?
4. Who (students and staff) are involved in the programs and do they have certain characteristics that are related to success in experiential learning?
5. What goes on in the programs — what do students do, both in and out of the classroom; what are the costs; how is the program administered; etc.?

In Chart I (see next page) the pattern of multiple measures for gathering information on each of these questions is outlined.

The **research design:** All the schools will administer, pre and post, the following standardized instruments with student in their programs: Rosenberg and Janis-Field Self Esteem Scales, a Semantic Differential on the type of person(s), such as government officials, the elderly, the handicapped, that the program focuses on; and the Crites Career Maturity Scale.

The following project-designed instruments will also be administered to all students pre and post: Personal and Social Responsibility Scale and the Problem Solving Assessment Inventory. Two other project-designed instruments will be administered as post-tests only, the Experiential Learning questionnaire and the Community Problem Inventory.

For those programs that have two different groups of students during the school year, all of the above instruments will be administered to both groups. The design for these schools is one of the strongest available for educational research. It is described as:

E_1 Pre Post
E_2 Pre Post

In some schools, randomization and true control groups can be used, creating from the above pattern a true experimental design.

Some schools cannot use this basic design because students are in the program for the full year, or the program is only offered once during the school year. In these cases, a pre and post test will be administered only once and a comparison group will be used. The design will be:

E_1 Pre Post
C_1 Pre Post

In addition to the instruments that will be given to students as described above, each school will also administer the parent and community supervisor questionnaires at the end of the course. Finally, all schools will record unobtrusive data throughout the school year in the notebeook described earlier.

Five programs will participate in the follow-up study of former students, using a revised version of "What I Learn in Action Learning" Questionnaire and personal interviews of selected former students.

Case studies of students and programs will be compiled and written by several members of the Panel of Practitioners and Project Staff if funding is available. A book of student portraits is the anticipated final product. The book will be organized around the theoretical framework for experiential learning, with anecdotes and short case studies of individual students to illustrate, enliven, and humanize these rationales.

While all the programs will collect all the data described above, some will collect additional information according to their special emphasis. For example, at Mitchell High School in Colorado Springs, the staff is particularly interested in assessing growth in student responsibility, and have designed a instrument to do that. At several schools in Minnesota — the Minneapolis Schools and Eisenhower High School, Hopkins — moral development is a program goal and the Rests' Defining Issues Test will be given to those students. Collecting these additional data will increase the richness and depth of the study.

With apparently good reason, the participants in these experiential programs think they are pursuing something worthwhile.

Editor's Note:

This article reports on an important on-going study being made of experiential learning in secondary education. It also serves as the first in a series planned by the Journal's editors to examine the crucial issue of evaluation and assessment for experience-based education programs. Subsequent articles in the series will address methods for achieving sound program evaluation and significant research in the field which can help all of us better assess the contributions we are making to education as a whole.

The first segment of this article was published in the November, 1978 issue of the N.A.S.S.P. Bulletin and is reprinted with N.A.S.S.P.'s permission. We have added the description of research design for this study as excerpted from the "First Year Report," Evaluation of Experiential Learning Project, Center for Youth Development and Research, University of Minnesota. Additional information about the study can be received by writing the authors at the Center (48 McNeal Hall, 1985 Buford Avenue, St. Paul, Minnesota 55108).

CHART I

ISSUES AND OUTCOMES	STANDARDIZED MEASURES	PROJECT-DESIGNED MEASURES	UNOBTRUSIVE & INDIRECT* MEASURES
What are immediate effects on students?			
Self Concept	Rosenberg Self-Esteem Janis Field Scale	Supervisor Questionnaire Parent Questionnaire	Attendance Anecdotes Indicators of Distinctive Performance Teacher ratings using maturity checklist Disciplinary Actions
Responsibility		Personal and Social Responsibility Scale Supervisor Questionnaire Parent Questionnaire	Attendance Assignments Disciplinary Actions Extension of Experience Anecdotes
Problem-Solving		Problem-Solving Assessment Inventory	Anecdotes Skills
Attitudes Toward Others	Semantic Differential	Parent Questionnaire Supervisor Questionnaire	Anecdotes Assignments
Facts about the Community		Community Problem Inventory	Assignments Skills
Communication		Problem-Solving Assessment Inventory Supervisor Questionnaire Parent Questionnaire	Anecdotes Skills Assignments Indicators of Distinctive Performance
Career Development	Crites Career Maturity Scale		Extension of Experience Skills
What are the long-range effects on students?		Revised Form of "What I Learned in Action Learning" Interviews with sample of students	Occupation students currently in or preparing for? Number of times former students visited or contacted program?
What factors make for successful learning experiences?		Experiential Learning Questionnaire Intentional/Unintentional Activities Worksheet completed by each school	
Who is involved in program? Students General Profile of Students Case studies of selected students		Student Background Questionnaire Interview Schedule for Student	
Staff		Case* Study	All forms of unobtrusive measures
General Profile of Staff		Staff Profile Questionnaire	
What happens in the program? General Profile of programs		Program Profile & Program Administration Questionnaire	Assignments
Case Studies of Selected Programs		Interview Schedule for Program Case Study*	Requests for information about program Letters from supervisors Extension of Experience Program Administration

Evaluating Experiential Learning Programs:
The Case Study Approach

by Robert Stevenson

Editor's note

This article is part of a series on the evaluation of experiential education. Other articles of interest on this topic are: "How to Creatively Evaluate Programs" (Summer, 1984), "Using Initiative Games to Assess Group Cooperation" (Spring, 1984), and "Practical Evaluation Ideas" (Fall, 1983).

* * * * * *

Perhaps your staff wants to make certain aspects of their program more effective...

Or maybe your funding agency requires specific information about what students gain from your program...

Or perhaps you have a paper due in a graduate class and you wish to research an issue of particular interest to you...

In all of these cases, evaluation is serving different audiences and purposes. The specific purposes need to be clarified before decisions can be made about what type of evaluation strategy would yield the most appropriate information. The case study approach is appropriate for many of the intentions underlying experiential educators' wish to evaluate a program. Unfortunately, however, this approach is often not considered.

Why a Case Study Approach?

Frequently, evaluations conducted for accountability or funding purposes demand exclusive attention to precise questions, usually concerning the "products" or outcomes of a program. Sometimes, however, in the case of these "political" evaluations, but more commonly for "in-house" evaluations, the focus may be more open-ended and subject to negotiation and/or clarification as the evaluation proceeds. Such evaluations also may be more concerned with the processes or internal dynamics underlying various program characteristics rather than measurable outcomes. It is this second situation that may be conducive to the use of a case study approach.

There are two main advantages of the case study approach:
1) It provides the opportunity for evaluation questions to emerge during the process of collecting data rather than being precisely determined beforehand.
2) In-depth information can be obtained about such things as
- specific incidents and the processes that created them
- individual students and their perceptions of particular incidents and learning situations
- the operation of the program as a total entity

Of course, these advantages are not attained without some costs. One disadvantage is the problem of making empirical generalizations to other programs. As Wehlage (1981) pointed out, the kind of generalization that can be made from case studies differs from the law-like relationships stated for the reader by empirical evaluations. The consumer of the case study evaluation is left to establish the transferability (by analogy) to other

---

Bob Stevenson is a doctoral candidate in the Department of Curriculum and Instruction at the University of Wisconsin-Madison. He has a master's degree in experiential education for which his thesis involved the case study approach.

contexts — whether they be the "same" program offered in a different setting or to a different group of students, or a new program yet to be implemented. Thus, while the neglect of sampling procedures precludes statistical comparisons of programs, generalized insights may be drawn from a case study of one program that are useful to the planning of a similar program — or for that matter to the planning of staff development in either program. In fact, this immediacy of use has been suggested as one of the positive attributes of case studies (Adelman, Jenkins & Kemmis, 1976).

A second disadvantage is the need to tolerate some ambiguity at the beginning regarding the type of conclusions the evaluation will seek. This may be a problem if funding is sought to conduct the evaluation, or especially if answers to certain kinds of questions are desired, such as the effect of a program on Kohlberg's stages of moral development. Otherwise, progressive focusing as salient issues emerge during the evaluation may not be a significant hindrance.

Relevant Features of Experiential Education

There are a number of inherent features of experiential education programs that lend themselves to a case study approach, provided that the questions being asked of the evaluation are compatible with the methods applicable to case studies. These features include:
1) the idiosyncratic attributes of every program and the uniqueness of each individual's experiences within a program;
2) the highly interactive social setting in which experiential learning takes place and the complex multiple realities that constitute a student's experiences of such a setting;
3) the multidimensional and problematic objectives that characterize most programs; and
4) the lack or primitive state of appropriate instruments for measuring the kind of outcomes to which experiential education is usually aimed.

Case studies attempt to unravel the complexities of human intentions and behaviors that surround an educational program, by focusing in-depth on the unique experiences of individuals (i.e. teachers/instructors and/or students/participants) and their construction of reality. They seek to enrich our understanding by not only describing, but also explaining; by addressing not only the overt and the intended but also the covert and the unintended. Since a variety of techniques are used, each of which may tap a different reality or outcome, the chances of capturing the essence of a program are enhanced.

Planning a Case Study

There is no standard methodology associated with the case study approach, but rather a commitment to using a variety of data gathering techniques. These techniques generally include: structured observations (as a participant or non-participant); structured observations (of simulated or real situations); interviews (using varying degrees of structure); and content analyses of documents (such as curriculum statements and student journals), photographs and films (including student-produced) and discussions (from audio recordings). In addition, paper-and-pencil instruments are often administered to provide further data for cross-checking with that obtained from the sources described. The actual techniques chosen will depend upon, as well as determine, the nature and scope of the particular evaluation (Adelman, Jenkins & Kemmis, 1976). For example, considerable time is necessary for an ethnography, while interviews and document analyses are more likely to suit a short-term evaluation. At the same time, however, the lack of ethnographic observations will limit the kind of issues that can be investigated and the behavioral insights that will result. Conversely, interviews provide an opportunity to explore the intentions underlying observed behaviors.

Three interrelated and recurring stages have been identified as characterizing this type of evaluation:
1) an exploratory search, usually involving observations and informal interviews, for common or salient issues or incidents;
2) a more directed and intensive inquiry into selected questions; and
3) a search for underlying principles and patterns leading to the construction of an explanatory framework. (Parlett & Hamilton, 1972)

These stages indicate that data collection and analysis are interwoven because questions may not be clear until the "initial analysis of impressions, perceptions and tentative conclusions has been done" (LeCompte & Goetz, 1983).

Some qualitative researchers argue that the pre-specification of evaluation questions and a theoretical framework for collecting and analyzing data

> "Case studies attempt to unravel the complexities of human intentions and behaviors that surround an educational program by focusing in-depth on the unique experiences of individuals and their construction of reality."

creates an unnecessary bias in what one sees and finds. While adoption of such a stance might represent an ideal aspiration, an evaluation setting can be entered with one's preconceptions either explicit or tacit. If preconceived ideas are explicated, then a conscious effort can be made to compensate for their possible influence by, for example, looking for disconfirming data. Additionally, some tentative questions, which can be revised as necessary, help guide information gathering (as everything cannot be observed), and prevent the evaluator from being trapped into a false sense of comprehensive understanding of a program when, in fact, only the perspective of the most accessible and cooperative participants have been uncovered (Peshkin, 1982). This approach does not preclude a gradual shift from relatively unsystematic observations, focused only by broad questions or ideas, to more systematic forms of observation and recording.

Beginning a Case Study

A case study evaluation can begin with either a very open-ended question or a more focused one; that is, at the first or second stage of the three stages described. An open-ended question is appropriate when: little is known about the program to be evaluated but there is a desire to increase general understanding; or there is a vague feeling that some sort of problem exists (Dobbert, 1982). Examples of such questions with which an evaluation of an experiential education program might begin are: What is it like to be a participant on Outward Bound? What unanticipated outcomes are occurring in cross-age tutoring? Why are some students ambivalent about their internships? When a particular problem, question or hypothesis already exists, a focused evaluation can be undertaken from the beginning (Dobbert, 1982). Examples might include: What specific incidents are triggering a student's change of approach in peer counselling? What role should students play in planning an internship to facilitate their social development? Do students consider moral issues as they engage in community service? In either situation it is useful to list some sub-questions or sub-issues that might relate to the major evaluation question and help guide observations and/or interviews.

The initial evaluation questions(s) may be derived from one's personal knowledge or from a theoretical framework. If the former, then potentially relevant theories should be researched in order to identify a suitable framework for guiding the evaluation. Relevant theories, in relation to some of the questions suggested above, might concern the process of experiential learning, social and moral development, the structure and function of groups, or conflict resolution in interpersonal relationships. In either case, theories should continually be reviewed throughout the study and evaluation questions refined in light of examining both the literature and the data being collected. Irrespective of the type or source of the initial questions(s), the evaluator should accept that different, but more critical, questions may emerge at any time. Thus, a focused question may even need to be replaced by a more open-ended question.

Analyzing and Synthesizing the Data

Theory assumes an important role in analyzing the data, particularly if a reasonable level of interpretation or explanation is to be attempted. In the first instance, theory may suggest useful categories into which the evaluator can try to organize the data. The recourse to a theoretical frame of reference is necessary for offering an explanation of the relationship which produced the patterns expressed in the categories. In either of these analyses the selected theory (or theories) may prove inadequate in organizing and interpreting the data, since a theory is based on previous knowledge. Thus:

> "Reasoning should proceed both from theory to the data at hand in order to generate new insights about that data and from the data to theory

in order to question or to test or add to and improve the theory's explanatory ability." (Dobbert, 1982)

In analyzing and synthesizing the data, three procedures should be borne in mind:
1) the evaluation questions and frame of reference employed in collecting data at any stage should also be used as the focus for analyzing that data;
2) underlying patterns or recurring themes, both within and across data sources, should be sought, guided initially by the evaluation questions but remaining alert for the unexpected; and
3) data from different sources should be cross-checked for collaboration or contradictions — a critical step in testing for validity.

Another important means of validating data is to invite the subjects involved to comment on the evaluator's account of the situation and indicate any aspects with which they disagree. Some researchers then argue that the proposed interpretation must be negotiated before either further abstractions can be drawn or the disputed description or explanation can be reported.

Reporting

In theory, a variety of forms for reporting a case study can be used. Besides the usual written report, film, mixed-media presentations, photographic essays, oral reports (including role-play) and semi-journalistic reports can be found. In fact, case studies have the distinct advantage of presenting "evaluation data in a more publicly accessible form than other kinds of research reports" (Adelman, Jenkins & Kemmis, 1976). Despite the frequent length of written reports, their narrative form and less technical language allow a wider audience to make judgements about a program. It should be emphasized, however, that the possible lack of any statistical analysis does not mean that anyone who can write is capable of conducting a useful case study evaluation. Considerable skills of synthesis, creative organization, and fluency with prose are required. Not everyone possesses or can learn such skills.

Irrespective of the format selected, a number of reporting principles should be followed, especially when a report is to be made "public." First, pseudonyms or other means should be adopted to protect subjects from identification. Finally, descriptions as far as possible should be differentiated from interpretations so that readers are able to draw their own inferences from the "raw" data and access whether the evaluator's are valid.

Conclusion

A case study evaluation, through its in-depth concentration on a single program, can provide a holistic picture of the operations of an experiential learning program in which unique and unanticipated features can also be revealed. Furthermore, such information can be made available in a non-technical, highly readable (and/or visual) form that enables a diverse audience to "vicariously experience the program" and then reach their own judgement (Fehrenbacher et.a., 1978).

Although generalizations in the form of verified propositions cannot readily be drawn from case study data, readers are able to decide the generalizability to situations with which they are familiar. Thus, the products of this approach to evaluation offer the opportunity not only to yield insights that can improve one's own program, but also — if shared — to stimulate thinking and discussion among educators, and to enhance communication with non-educators, concerning the processes involved in experiential learning.

I am indebted to Fred Neumann whose extensive comments on an earlier draft prompted a major change in my approach to this paper.

REFERENCES

- Adelman, Clem; Jenkins, David; & Kemmis, Stephen. *Re-thinking Case Study: Notes From the Second Cambridge Conference*. Centre for Applied Research in Education, University of East Anglia, 1976. (mimeo)
- Dobbert, Marion L. *Ethnographic Research: Theory and Application for Modern Schools and Societies*. New York: Praeger, 1982.
- Fehrenbacker, Harry L., Owens, Thomas R. & Haenn, Joseph F. "Student Case Studies as Part of a Comprehensive Program Evaluation." *Journal of Research and Development in Education*, 1979, 12(3), 63-69.
- LeCompte, Margaret D. & Goetz, Judith P. "Playing With Ideas: Analysis of Qualitative Data." Paper presented at the American Educational Research Association Meetings, Montreal, Canada, 1983.
- Parlett, Malcolm & Hamilton, David. "Evaluation as Illumination: A New Approach to the Study of Innovatory Programs." In Glass, G. (ed.), *Evaluation Studies Review Annual*, Vol. 1, 1976, 140-157.
- Peshkin, Alan. "The Researcher and Subjectivity." In Spindler, George (ed.), *Doing the Ethnography of Schooling: Educational Anthropology in Action*. New York: Holt, Rinehart, & Winston, 1982.
- Wehlage, Gary. "The Purpose of Generalization in Field Study Research." In Popkewitz, Thomas S. & Tabachnick, B. Robert (eds.), *The Study of Schooling: Field Based Methodologies in Educational Research and Evaluation*. New York: Praeger, 1981.

VIII. Practical Ideas

How to Process Experience

By Larry K. Quinsland and Anne Van Ginkel

The class has just returned from a tour of the advertising agency. On the return trip students have been enthusiastic and animated. Their excitement is obvious. Upon entering the classroom, the teacher (fully cognizant of the "Nation at Risk..." report) asks the students to please get their multiplication tables out and to practice quietly by themselves. He has just committed a major faux pas in experiential learning theory.

"What is this grave error?" you might ask.

***

Larry K. Quinsland and Anne Van Ginkel are Professors at Rochester Institute of Technology (RIT) in the College of the National Technical Institute for the Deaf (NTID). In addition, Larry Quinsland is a 1983 recipient of a grant award from the Mina Shaughnessy Scholars Program through the Fund for the Improvement of Post-Secondary Education (FIPSE) and in that capacity is touring major post-secondary programs for deaf students within the U.S. and Canada for the purpose of disseminating his work in experiential learning and deafness.

After facilitating a two hour series of ropes course activities, the instructor has assembled the participants in a circle and begins the "processing" session:

"Well...how do you feel about this experience?..."

"...(silence)..."

"How about you, David?..."

"...uh...I don't know..."

"Paula?..."

"...um..." (shrugs shoulders)

We've all been there. We know the students/participants have "experienced" something. We saw it in their expressions, heard it in their exchanges. So why can't they talk about it?

***

The above two examples illustrate the two most common missed opportunities in an experiential instructional sequence. The first example illustrates a missed opportunity to explore, through structured processing, the new learnings that occurred. The second example, although careful to include "processing" as part of the instructional sequence, fails due to an inability to "connect" with the participants. In other words, David and Sue had great difficulty responding because the facilitator did what many of us do automatically... ask the most difficult questions first!

But why do we need to process in the first place? And, why are some questions more difficult to answer than others?

This paper is designed to explore the concept of "processing" as an integral component of experiential learning and to suggest a method of approaching the design of processing activities.

Experiential Learning Models - Something in Common?

It is important to recognize that experiential learning is defined in a great variety of ways and that a universally acceptable definition does not exist. This paper begins with the premise that *all learning is experiential ... but some learning (in an educational sense) is more experiential than others.*

A variety of experiential learning models have been proposed and serve as the basis for continuous debate among interested professionals (for examples, see Coleman, 1973; Kolb, 1974; Gager, 1977; Williamson, 1979; and Joplin, 1981). Greenberg (1978) has transcended the academic debate and suggests something of use to the practitioner: "Which theories (of learning) we choose may not be as important as choosing something." In other words, it is critical for anyone in the position of facilitating experiential learning to have a conceptual foundation (e.g. model) upon which to test one's ideas and to base the planning of learning activities/ contexts/ events/ situations. For the experiential educator to achieve and maintain credibility within the academic community, it is essential that she be able to justify her actions at any given time while facilitating learning. She must be able to succinctly explain why she is doing what she is doing and to what end she is working. Readers without this conceptual base are encouraged to search for a model that feels right, perhaps beginning with an examination of the models cited above.

Although it is not the intent of this paper to explore the range of experiential learning models in depth, it is important to point out the components which are common to each. Although the language differs, each experiential learning model refers to some form of action, some form of reflection and some form of application. Processing is the reflection component, the pause for each learner to consider what is important about that thing which was recently experienced. The model we will use in this paper is illustrated in Fig. 1. Although the model is self-explanatory, it is important to emphasize two points: 1. The designer/facilitator necessarily expends energy in planning before the learner becomes involved; and related to this, 2. a processing activity is a pre-planned part of the learner's experience. In addition, it is strongly recommended that a processing activity be designed to address all types of learning including cognitive [knowledge], psychomotor [skills], and affective [feelings], and not artificially limit the focus of the learner's experience through consideration of only one aspect of development (see Quinsland & Yust, 1982).

Processing is an activity which is employed for the purpose of encouraging the learner to reflect, describe, analyze, and *communicate* in some way that which was recently experienced. Communication implies action. The communication can be written or oral - to oneself, to another individual, or to a group. Written processing activities might be in the form of a journal which is structured to elicit a description of events, an analysis of the experiences, and a description of impressions. Other verbal processing activities might be designed to encourage the sharing of the salient parts of the experience. The critical suggestion here is that something be done with the reflection so that the individual is forced to assume responsibility for that which was encountered and learned.

By utilizing active participation and active processing, the learning event will become "more experiential." In a relative educational sense, the learner will be more "in-touch" with his/her own learning through forced bridging or meaning-making which is caused by the processing.

Cognitive Hierarchies

Bloom (1956) outlined a taxonomy of cognitive processing or thinking levels

```
Designer's Experience              Learner's/Participant's
Define Objective                   Experience

    ↓
Design Strategy                    Prior Learning
    ↓                                  ↓
Design Processing Activity
    ↓
Design Follow-Up
    ↓
Evaluate Consistency of
Objective and Strategies           Expectations Established
    ↓                                  ↓
Implement ¹                        Experience/Activity/Event ²
    ↓                                  ↓
Evaluate Strategies and            Process ²
Refine if necessary⁴                   ↓
                                   Follow-Up ²,³
- - - - - - - - - - - - - - - - - - - - - - - - - - -
    ↓                                  ↓
Define New Objective               New Experience
    ↓                                  ↓
Etc.                               Etc.
```

Fig. 1 Experiential Learning Design Model

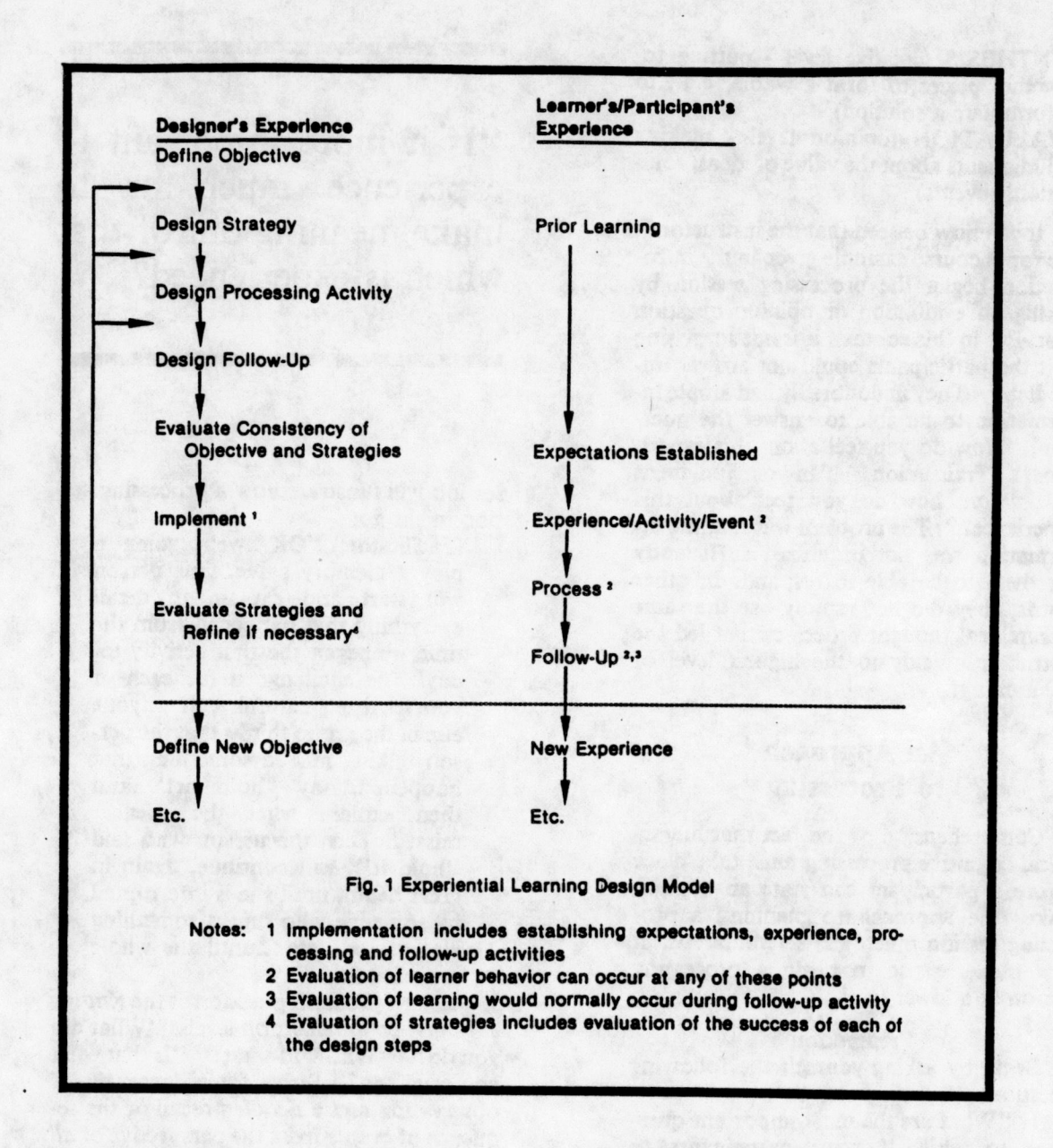

Notes: 1 Implementation includes establishing expectations, experience, processing and follow-up activities
2 Evaluation of learner behavior can occur at any of these points
3 Evaluation of learning would normally occur during follow-up activity
4 Evaluation of strategies includes evaluation of the success of each of the design steps

which is helpful in the planning and sequencing of processing activities. Many other cognitive processing models exist (for examples see Lewin, 1951; Piaget, 1971; and Bruner, 1973). Bloom's six levels of thought were most recently described and utilized in an experiential learning context by Moore (1983) in his analysis of the forms of thinking required of interns in work or other out-of-classroom environments. The following six levels of thought are listed from the most basic thinking level to the most complex; i.e., in terms of complexity of thought, the lowest level is first.

KNOWLEDGE (memory level - remembering information by recognition or recall)
COMPREHENSION (understanding level - interpreting or explaining knowledge or learnings in a descriptive literal way)
APPLICATION (simple usage level - correct use of knowledge; e.g., to solve rote problems or answer rote questions)
ANALYSIS (relationship level - breaking knowledge down into component parts and detecting relationships between them; e.g., identifying causes and motives)

SYNTHESIS (creative level - putting together pieces to form a whole; e.g., to formulate a solution)

EVALUATION (opinion level - making judgments about the value of ideas, solutions, events)

It can now be seen that the instructor in the ropes course example given in the introduction began the processing session by asking an evaluation or opinion question first. Put in this context, it is not surprising that the participants could not answer immediately. They undoubtedly had ample information to be able to answer the question, "How do you feel about this experience?" (Translation = "In your judgment or *opinion*, how do you feel about this experience?") The problem was that the information was not organized sufficiently for them to be able to respond. In other words, they did not rapidly use the same hierarchical thought processes that led the instructor quickly to the highest level of questioning!

An Approach to Processing

Comprehension of the fact that hierarchical cognitive processing must take place before a participant can state an opinion makes the approach to planning a processing session much less serendipitous. It now makes sense to begin a processing session at a lower level.

Preparation

Begin by asking yourself the following questions:

1. "What are the most important questions to which I want participants to respond?"
2. "At what level are these questions?"
3. "What questions should I use to lay the foundation for the important questions to be more easily answered?"

With a little practice this planning process can become almost automatic. However, the difference that this small amount of pre-planning can make in your processing sessions can be dramatic!

Example

The following example of a processing

"Is it more important to experience much or to make meaning out of that which is experienced?"

---

session will illustrate how a processing session might go:

(Facilitator:) "OK...we're going to play a memory game. One person will start and explain in detail everything that happened from the time we began the first activity today. The challenge is for each of you to listen carefully. If anyone else in the group thinks that the person talking missed something that happened...say 'hold it!'...and then explain what the speaker missed. Then the person who said "hold it!" will continue, again in great detail, until she is interrupted by someone who thinks something was missed...etc....until the whole story is told..."

Begin a processing session at the *Knowledge* and *comprehension* levels. "What did you do?" "Who said what?" "Is that what you saw, too?" Strive for a consensus of observation and a *detailed* recall of the sequence of events from the perspective of *all* observer/participants.

Once that is taken care of, it is possible to move on to *application* and *analysis* level questions:

"Did all groups/individuals try to solve that problem in the same way?"..."What did Mary Lou's group do that allowed them to finish so quickly?"..."Compare Kent's strategy to Gary's..."

Next, move to the *synthesis* level and discuss possible solutions to problems faced:

"What other ways could you use to attack that problem?"..."Think of other things you could do to make your next attempt more successful"..."Invent a piece of equipment or a tool that would make that task easier."

After this preliminary "cognitive guidance" has occurred, it is appropriate to ask, "How do you feel about this experience?" The participant has now been guided through the cognitive levels to the point where *evaluation/opinion* questions can more easily be answered:

"Do you agree or disagree with Bill's approach to the problem?"..."What do you think about...?" ..."What are the most important...?" ..."What did you learn?"

An interesting consideration in planning processing activities around cognitive hierarchies is the development in participants of the ability to make transitions from lower to higher levels of thought. Maybe this is the essence of "getting in touch with" one's feelings.

Cautions/Suggestions

It might be valuable to share some cautions and to provide some suggestions in utilizing this cognitive model of processing experiential learning activities. Note that these are based on the experiences of the authors in experimenting with processing techniques:

- In a given processing session, it is not always necessary to structure questions to hit upon all levels. Even though it is recommended that questions be put in sequence by level going up the hierarchy, it is important to know that it is all right to jump down in level if it is felt that the answers lack sophistication and require more lower level preparation.
- It is important to be aware of variations in the development of thinking skills; e.g., children do not all develop the ability to think abstractly or beyond a concrete level at the same age. According to Piaget (1971), children will generally be able to think abstractly around the age of eleven, but some will demonstrate this ability before or after this age.
- When asking questions, be sure to provide enough "wait-time" for each learner to think. A wait of 20 or 30 seconds before one of the learners risks a response is awkward at first. However, wait-time should not be avoided because it is uncomfortable. Too often the facilitator answers his own question because of *his* discomfort with silence or his need to get the answer he is expecting, while stealing from the learner the time needed to organize her thoughts. Awareness of this is particularly important at higher levels of questioning.
- Know the level of the question you are asking *before* you ask it. That is the only way that you will know if the response is appropriate. For example, a typical response to the question "What did you learn...?" is often a description of what happened (knowledge or comprehension levels) rather than a judgment (evaluation level) by the learner of what he has internalized from the experience.
- Keep a mental checklist of learners responding to your probes. Be sure to challenge *all* participants at each level of questioning used.
- Time is often an important planning consideration. You may have to make alterations and shorten some learning activities to be able to facilitate a processing session well. This is a quantity vs. quality issue; i.e., is it more important to experience much or to make meaning out of that which is experienced?
- Journals are excellent processing tools. Processing questions can be assigned periodically with responses to be recorded in a personal journal. (Remember to organize questions in sequence by level.) A journal writing activity (e.g., one-hour of alone time with specific questions to ponder) can be followed by a group processing

activity. This type of group processing is often extremely lively due to the learner's advance opportunity to reflect upon her experience and to organize her thoughts.

- A successful technique with which to end an "experiential" lecture or demonstration is to have each learner turn to the person next to her and to share "...5 things I learned during this activity which I will take with me when I leave." A variation of this is to have participants summarize the learning activity and what was learned in a "Dear _____ letter" to the facilitator.

- When posing synthesis level questions calling for creation of alternative solutions, and when it seems as if no more ideas are forthcoming...ask for two more! Participants often select the alternatives or solutions generated by this challenge to be the best.

- During the initial knowledge/comparison level questioning, it is sometimes helpful to ask the learner to rephrase what the person before him said before proceeding with his own response. This tends to stimulate learners to be more attentive and sensitive to each other and to quickly draw members of the group together.

- When processing affective responses to an experience, the facilitator should be aware of the possibility that learner responses might be limited by an inadequate vocabulary base. The language of feelings must often be taught by the facilitator during processing by supplying a word for the emotion being implied by the learner's description of the effect of an experience.

Processing is an essential component in any successful experiential learning activity. In fact, it is *the* unique component which makes the learning which takes place "experiential" in an educational sense. The practitioner can experience much enjoyment, intellectual stimulation, and professional satisfaction through effective planning and use of processing in her learning environment. It is hoped that the perspective on processing presented here will provide the incentive for facilitators of experiential learning to experiment in their unique learning environments.

References

- Bloom, B., ed. *Taxonomy of Educational Objectives, Handbook I. Cognitive Domain*. New York: David McKay, 1956
- Bruner, J. S. *Beyond the Information Given*. New York: W.W. Norton, 1973.
- Coleman, J.S. "Differences Between Experiential and Classroom Learning." In *Experiential Learning: Rationale, Characteristics and Assessment*. Edited by M.T. Keeton. San Francisco: Jossey-Bass, 1976.
- Gager, R. "Experiential Education: Strengthening the Learning Process." *Voyaguer* (Newsletter of the Association for Experiential Education) I (October 1977).
- Greenberg, E. "The Community as a Learning Resource." *J. of Experiential Education* I (Fall 1978): 22-25.
- Joplin, L. "On Defining Experiential Education." *J. of Experiential Education* IV (Spring 1981): 17-20.
- Kolb, D., et al. *Organizational Psychology*. Englewood Cliffs, NJ: Prentice-Hall, 1974.
- Lewin, K. *Field Theory and Social Science*. New York: Harper, 1951.
- Moore, D. T. "Perspectives on Learning in Internships." *J. of Experiential Education* VI (Fall 1983): 40-44.
- Piaget, J. *Science of Education and the Psychology of the Child*. London: Longman Group, Ltd., 1971.
- Quinsland, L.K. & Yust, W. "Growing Up Deaf: Developmental Perspectives on Experience and Learning." Paper presented at the 10th Annual Conference of the Association for Experiential Education, Arcata, CA, 10 September 1982.
- Williamson, J. "Designing Experiential Curricula." *J. of Experiential Education* II (Fall 1979): 15-18.

Acknowledgements

This paper was made possible by a grant from the Mina Shaughnessy Scholars Program through the Fund for the Improvement of Post-Secondary Education (FIPSE), U.S. Department of Education.

The authors also wish to acknowledge the assistance of Professors William Yust and Gary Long of the National Technical Institute for the Deaf at Rochester Institute of Technology for their critiques during the evolution of these concepts.

Chicken Gizzards and Screams in the Night

The Making of a Successful Simulation

by David Morrissey Moriah

Unless your program's instructional staff is committed to and practiced in using your risk management plan, even the best of such plans is of dubious value. To bring staff, and even student/participants into the quest for safer activities, many adventure-based programs utilize an "arranged" accident as a training technique. The staged event may be announced as such before it happens, or it can be presented as real.

While this approach has tremendous potential, it also harbors the possibility of being a total flop, or worse, the cause of a real accident as the event unfolds. To maximize the effectiveness of simulations and to avoid hazards, a systematic approach should be used. However, because very little has been written about the subject, many programs plunge into simulations armed with little more than rudimentary knowledge and a bottle of ketchup to smear over the "victim."

The following guidelines have been gleaned from my eight years in the field with the North Carolina Outward Bound School and with an outdoor education program operated through the Cornell University Physical Education Department.

OBJECTIVES

There are three major objectives for simulations:
1. DO THEM FOR A SPECIFIC REASON.
2. PLAN METICULOUSLY - DON'T WING IT!
3. DEBRIEF CAREFULLY AND THOROUGHLY.

DEFINITIONS

A simulation for our purpose is defined as a feigned accident presented to a group as a problem for them to solve. Every attempt should be made for it to be convincing, perhaps even shocking, depending upon the purpose for doing it.

In almost all instances, it should be known to all from the beginning that it is a staged accident. The details may be a surprise to the group, but at no time should anyone believe it's the real thing.

SAFETY CONCERNS

Remember, any rescue/emergency training contains the risk of an actual accident. This is especially true where panicky reactions and/or inexperience in dealing with emergencies can lead to poor decisions,

---

David Morrissey Moriah was Director of the Outdoor Education Program at Cornell University until August 1984.

careless movement, improper handling of victim, etc. The most important part of preparation is playing out all "what ifs" relating to potential accidents. During the event, an instructor should carefully monitor the group (including watching for signs of shock) and be ready to intervene at any time.

PREPARATION

1. Define the results you wish to achieve. Decide these first and construct an event to accomplish these specific purposes. Some suggested purposes include:
   - Motivating the students to learn first aid/emergency procedures
   - Providing skills training in first aid/emergency procedures
   - Bringing the students together through a common challenge
   - Providing a high energy, meaningful adventure
   - Demonstrating the complexity and difficulty of a rescue operation

In addition to using the accident to accomplish any of the above purposes, the simulation should always be used to emphasize the need for clearly designated leadership and the value of having a prearranged organizational plan for emergencies.

2. Determine the Accident Type. Keeping the purposes in mind, consider a wide variety of accident scenarios. The accident should be consistent with the environment and activities of the program. Here is an excellent opportunity to bring life to safety issues which have hitherto only been talked about. Instead of one more lecture about driving program vehicles safely, for example, why not haul a van from the junkyard and fill it with "victims" for your staff to cope with?

Of course, a simple one-victim injury is probably best for novices, but it is only the beginning of possibilities. For a large or advanced-level group, a second victim or hysterical friend of the victim adds a nice complication. A "plant" in the group can start acting obnoxious or offering bad suggestions.

A variation which has become quite popular at Cornell staff trainings is a simulation series called the "Bloody, Gory, Hall of Fame." We began with the desire to 1) expose the staff to a wide variety of possible accidents in a brief training period, and 2) provide many hands-on opportunities to each member of a large staff. We then designed several ten to fifteen minute dramatic accident simulations which small groups (of three to four participants) rotate through over a period of one to two hours. While it is obviously difficult to teach first aid skills in this amount of time, we have found it a valuable opportunity to test ourselves under fire.

A search for a victim is another possibility. Remember, it can take longer (or shorter) than you thought, and coordination of the group is quite difficult. Selecting terrain appropriate to the participants' level of experience and ability is a crucial consideration. For staff and more advanced participants, a long carry can almost always be a valuable exercise, especially over difficult terrain. If the accident was not taken seriously before the carry, it won't take long for the mood to change. Carries frequently bring out stress, are more difficult than a group expects, and end with a real feeling of accomplishment.

3. Plan the Event. After deciding the type of accident simulation suitable for your purpose, visit the site where it will take place and study it. Visualize the event. Ask yourself such questions as: What will be the effect of changing weather conditions? Is there a possibility of passers-by stumbling upon the scene?

It's quite embarrassing to have police cars and ambulances screeching to your simulation. Notify authorities and rescue squads in advance if there's any chance they would be alerted during the event.

Brief all "actors" well in advance. As a group discuss all "what-ifs." Fine tune the event to fit the strengths and weaknesses of the victim and other role-players. If the part doesn't "feel right" to the actor, it won't be convincing or effective for the participants.

Finally, plan a realistic way to get the instructors or group leaders out of the picture so the participants are forced to deal with the accident. This is especially tricky in a simulation where the group will be looking to the designated leadership to take charge. One solution is to have the leader or leaders be the victims. (This can have direct benefits. In 1978 two Outward Bound Instructors were knocked out by lightning, and the patrol they had just trained in resuscitation techniques revived them using CPR.)

ACTION

1. Theatrics: Do it with gusto, but don't overact. Props such as fake blood and chicken bones should be realistic. Acting should be appropriate to the injury. Try using a victim the group doesn't know so they won't know what kind of reaction to expect.

Realism here is the key to success of the entire event. A giggling victim will destroy the operation. Use an injury the victim has actually had once, or if hypothermia is to be the problem, go straight into the icy waters. A good actor works right into the part.

(SAFETY NOTE: If there's any possibility that the victim may actually become endangered (as in the hypothermia example stated above), a "positive check-in system" must be arranged. That is, don't wait for the victim to say, "I'm in trouble!" Have a periodic signal (eg. codeword, hand signal) for the victim to indicate that s/he is alright.)

2. Observation. At least one instructor should be in a position to act as an observer. The primary role is to monitor safety. Secondarily, this is an excellent opportunity to watch everything for later feedback to the group. Take notes. Say nothing unless it is critical for immediate safety.

This role is often incompatible with being the victim, so a complication arises in the effort to place the designated leaders in positions where they won't be looked to for leadership in simulations. Sometimes the only way to arrange this is to hide behind a tree! The best way is merely to tell participants the various roles instructors are playing.

DEBRIEF

Allow adequate time for the debrief or don't do the event. Call it off early if necessary. The importance of a good debriefing cannot be overemphasized.

The observing instructor should facilitate a discussion immediately after the activity is ended. Have a plan in mind and stick to it. The tendency is to drift toward specific treatments. Steer discussion away from that. Here is a suggested discussion plan:

1. Air feelings. Let everyone release feelings. A feeling statement is "I felt angry/frustrated/inadequate..." It is not "We should have done..." Be a strong facilitator to be sure everyone has a chance to get it all out. It's not unusual for participants to experience strong emotional reactions. By drawing it all out early, you may be able to head off potential inter- or intra-personal crises.

2. Factual chronology. Bring everyone to the same knowledge level **without analysis.** There will be a strong tendency to begin evaluating the operation right away. However, an objective description of what happened is critical, especially if there were multiple victims or if activities were happening in different places.

3. Analysis. The group will draw most conclusions themselves, so facilitation becomes more relaxed. Have a list ready of your major observations to be sure all are covered. Watch for these tendencies:

a) The group and/or individuals will berate themselves. It may be necessary for you to point out that mistakes are to be expected even with experienced groups, and to focus on what they have learned for the next time.

b) Excess attention will be given to first aid treatment. Insights into organizational and leadership issues may be neglected. Remind them they can always look up first aid in a book, unless no one remembers they have a book!

WRAP-UP

A well-run accident simulation inevitably leads to spirited discussion and a flood of insights into self, group, and emergency procedures. Designing and conducting the event is a skill in itself, and the staff which planned and executed it should find it valuable to conduct **its own** debriefing and evaluation.

It will probably involve more time and attention to detail than you ever imagined, but after you clean up the chicken bones, you're certain to be glad you did it.

Idea Notebook

DESIGNING PROCESSING QUESTIONS TO MEET SPECIFIC OBJECTIVES

By Clifford E. Knapp

The ultimate goal for experiential educators is to assist participants in learning from their experiences. Participants should be taught how to apply the skills, concepts and attitudes they have learned to future life situations.

Experiential educators can improve their ability to process or debrief experiences by being clear about their objectives and then by planning strategies to meet them. Processing is a method for helping people reflect on experiences and for facilitating specific personal changes in their lives. The skill of processing primarily involves observing individuals, making assessments about what is happening, and then asking appropriate questions.

There are many personal and group growth objectives that can be achieved through adventure and other types of experiential programming. Among the more important objectives are: communicating effectively, expressing appropriate feelings, listening, appreciating self and others, decision making, cooperating, and trusting the group. If the leader has one or more of these objectives in mind, the observations, assessments, and processing questions may be better directed toward achieving these ends. The underlying assumption of this article is that if the leader and participants know where to go and how to get there, the participant is more likely to arrive. The following questions, organized by specific program objectives, are designed to assist leaders in more effectively processing experiential activities for personal and group growth.

Communicating Effectively

1. Can anyone give an example of when you thought you communicated effectively with someone else in the group? (consider verbal and non-verbal communication)
2. How did you know that what you communicated was understood? (consider different types of feedback)
3. Who didn't understand someone's attempt to communicate?
4. What went wrong in the communication attempt?
5. What could the communicator do differently next time to give a clearer message?
6. What could the message receiver do differently next time to understand the message?
7. How many different ways were used to communicate messages?
8. Which ways were most effective? Why?
9. Did you learn something about communication that will be helpful later? If so, what?

Dr. Clifford E. Knapp is an Associate Professor of Curriculum and Instruction at the Lorado Taft Field Campus - Northern Illinois University.

Expressing Appropriate Feelings

1. Can you name a feeling you had at any point in completing the activity? (consider - mad, glad, sad, or scared) Where in your body did you feel it most?
2. What personal beliefs were responsible for generating that feeling? (What was the main thought behind the feeling?)
3. Is that feeling a common one in your life?
4. Did you express that feeling to others? If not, what did you do with the feeling?
5. Do you usually express feelings or suppress them?
6. Would you like to feel differently in a similar situation? If so, how would you like to feel?
7. What beliefs would you need to have in order to feel differently in a similar situation? Could you believe them?
8. How do you feel about the conflict that may result from expressing certain feelings?
9. How do you imagine others felt toward you at various times during the activity? Were these feelings expressed?
10. What types of feelings are easiest to express?... most difficult?
11. Do you find it difficult to be aware of some feelings at times? If so, which ones?
12. Are some feelings not appropriate to express to the group at times? If so, which ones?
13. What feelings were expressed non-verbally in the group?
14. Does expressing appropriate feelings help or hinder completing the initiative?

Deferring Judgment of Others

1. Is it difficult for you to avoid judging others? Explain.
2. Can you think of examples of when you judged others in the group today?...when you didn't judge others?
3. What were some advantages to you by not judging others?
4. What were some advantages to others by you not judging them?
5. How does judging and not judging others affect the completion of the activity?
6. Were some behaviors of others easy not to judge and other behaviors difficult?
7. Would deferring judgment be of some value in other situations? Explain.
8. Can you think of any disadvantages of not judging others in this situation?

Listening

1. Who made suggestions for completing the activity?
2. Were all of these suggestions heard? Explain.
3. Which suggestions were acted upon?
4. Why were the other suggestions ignored?
5. How did it feel to be heard when you made a suggestion?
6. What interfered with your ability to listen to others?
7. How can this interference be overcome?
8. Did you prevent yourself from listening well? How?
9. Did you listen in the same way today as you generally do? If not, what was different about today?

Leading Others

1. Who assumed leadership roles during the activity?
2. What were the behaviors which you described as showing leadership?
3. Can everyone agree that these behaviors are traits of leaders?
4. How did the group respond to these leadership behaviors?
5. Who followed the leader even if you weren't sure that the idea would work? Why?
6. Did the leadership role shift to other people during the activity? Who thought they were taking the leadership role? How did you do it?
7. Was it difficult to assume a leadership role with this group?
8. Why didn't some of you take a leadership role?
9. Is it easier to take a leadership role in other situations or with different group members? Explain.
10. Did anyone try to lead the group, but felt they were unsuccessful? What were some possible reasons for this? How did it feel to be disregarded?

Following Others

1. Who assumed a follower role at times throughout the activity? How did it feel?
2. How did it feel to follow different leaders?

3. Do you consider yourself a good follower? Was this an important role in the group today? Explain.
4. How does refusal to follow affect the leadership role?
5. What are the traits of a good follower?
6. How can you improve your ability to follow in the future?

Making Group Decisions

1. How were group decisions made in completing the activity?
2. Were you satisfied with the ways decisions were made? Explain.
3. Did the group arrive at any decisions through group consensus? (some didn't get their first choice, but they could "live" with the decision)
4. Were some decisions made by one or several individuals?
5. Did everyone in the group express an opinion when a choice was available? If not, why not?
6. What is the best way for this group to make decisions? Explain.
7. Do you respond in similar ways in other groups?
8. What did you like about how the group made decisions? What didn't you like?

Cooperating

1. Can you think of specific examples of when the group cooperated in completing the activity? Explain.
2. How did it feel to cooperate?
3. Do you cooperate in most things you do?
4. How did you learn to cooperate?
5. What are the rewards of cooperating?
6. Are there any problems associated with cooperation?
7. How did cooperative behavior lead to successfully completing the activity?
8. How can you cooperate in other areas of your life?
9. Did you think anyone was blocking the group from cooperating? Explain.

Respecting Human Differences

1. How are you different from some of the others in the group?
2. How do these differences strengthen the group as a whole?
3. When do differences in people in a group prevent reaching certain objectives?
4. What would this group be like if there were very few differences in people? How would you feel if this were so?
5. In what instances did being different help and hinder the group members from reaching their objectives?

Respecting Human Commonalities

1. How are you like some of the others in the group?
2. Were these commonalities a help to the group in completing their task? Explain.
3. Were these commonalities a hinderance to the group in completing their task? Explain.
4. Do you think you have other things in common with some of the group members that you haven't found yet?
5. How did this setting help you discover how you are similar to others?

Trusting the Group

1. Can you give examples of when you trusted someone in the group? Explain.
2. Is it easier to trust some people and not others? Explain.
3. Can you think of examples when trusting someone could not have been a good idea?
4. How do you increase your level of trust for someone?
5. On a scale of 1-10, rate how much trust you have in the group as a whole. Can you explain your rating?
6. What did you do today that deserves the trust of others?
7. How does the amount of fear you feel affect your trust of others?

Closure Questions

1. What did you learn about yourself?
2. What did you learn about others?
3. How do you feel about yourself and others?
4. What new questions do you have about yourself and others?
5. What did you do today of which you are particularly proud?
6. What skill are you working to improve?
7. Was your behavior today typical of the way you usually act in groups? Explain.
8. How can you use what you learned in other life situations?
9. What beliefs about yourself and others were reinforced today?
10. Would you do anything differently if you were starting the activity again with this group?
11. What would you like to say to the group members?

Idea Notebook

USING INITIATIVE GAMES TO ASSESS GROUP COOPERATION

Editor's Note: This is the second in a series of articles in the Idea Notebook section of practical evaluation techniques for experiential educators.

by Alan Warner

Experiential educators need to develop evaluation research measures which are an integral part of programming and provide practical information about key variables in the experiential learning process. Here is a specific technique involving initiative games that we have successfully used to assess the level of group cooperation among eleven to thirteen year olds in a school setting. The basic approach would be applicable to any age group but the specific tasks might have to be modified.

We developed a precise observational system for coding individuals' behavior in small groups of five to seven students while they tackled a series of initiative tasks.* The basic notion is that students who are able to work cooperatively will demonstrate a higher level of positive involvement on these tasks relative to students who are less cooperative.

The first step was to select an appropriate set of initiative tasks. We needed to come up with a series of roughly equivalent tasks because we wanted to assess changes in positive involvement within a group across time. Equivalent tasks are required because a problem cannot be repeated at a later date once participants are aware of the solution. We initially experimented with a large number of tasks before selecting nine tasks to pilot test intensively in order to standardize rules, adjust task difficulty, and examine behavior patterns.

Task difficulty had to be carefully monitored. If a task was too easy, the group would finish quickly and there would not be time for a sufficient number of observation periods. If a task was too difficult, the group would give up and complain. Task orientation was also a dimension which had an important impact on student behavior patterns. Some tasks have an individual orientation (e.g., Nitro Crossing, Electric Fence) in that participants typically complete the task one at a time to arrive at a group solution. Other tasks have a group orientation (e.g., Hanging Teeter Totter, Peanut Butter Bog, Points of Contact) in that the solution is reached only if the whole group is physically involved simultaneously. We ended up selecting the three group oriented tasks identified above for our study and used them as pre-treatment, post-treatment and follow-up tests.

The observational procedure required that an observer watch each group member during the task on a regular rotating basis. Each student was observed for five seconds and the observer then had five seconds to make a coding decision on a standard form. The observer had to decide whether the individual exhibited positive, passive, negative, or non-involvement with the task during the observation interval. Positive behavior was defined as physically or verbally doing something which contributed to the solution of the task. Negative behavior was saying or physically doing something which impeded progress towards the solution of the initiative task. Passive involvement consisted of a student focusing his or her eyes on the others in the group; whereas non-involvement was defined as staring away from the group. More precise definitions are available in the staff manual for those readers interested in duplicating this measurement technique in an accurate, reliable way.**

SAMPLE OBSERVATION FORM

	Observation Cycle I								Observation Cycle II							
Student Name or Description	Kate	Jon	Marcy	Mike	Ann	Keith										
Positive	✓	✓			✓											
Negative				✓												
Passive				✓												
Non-involvement			✓													

	Observation Cycle III								Observation Cycle IV							
Positive																
Negative																
Passive																
Non-involvement																

The observation and recording intervals were cued for the observer by a specially prepared tape played through a cassette recorder with an earphone attachment. The tape defined ten cycles of observation periods with seven subjects per cycle. For smaller groups, the observer skipped the appropriate number of observation periods per cycle. Inter-observer reliability was checked by having two observers independently code behavior for the same group. Observers were able to attain a high level of agreement after a series of training sessions.

We successfully implemented the procedures with treatment and control groups and demonstrated that our experiential trips did significantly increase the level of positive involvement on the tasks. However, the potential applications for the methodology are more important than the specific results. The measure takes time and energy to develop, but it provides a practical assessment of cooperation which is compatible with a large number of programs.

*Detailed descriptions of a variety of initiative tasks are available in *Initiative Games,* by B. Simpson, available from the Colorado Outward Bound School, and *Cowtails and Cobras,* available from Project Adventure.

**Further details are available by writing to the author c/o Cornwallis House, Miller Hospital, Kentville, Nova Scotia, Canada B4N 1M7.

Alan Warner recently completed a doctoral degree focusing on the evaluation of experiential education programs. He is now coordinator of the Cornwallis House Psychiatric Day Centre in Kentville, Nova Scotia.

NOTEBOOK

Some Simple Initiative Tasks
by Jeff Witman

The initiative tasks which follow have been successfully utilized with developmentally disabled individuals as a lead-up to more complex cooperative tasks. They've also proven effective as "ice-breakers" for programs combining disabled and non-disabled individuals.

1. **Rock Climb:** The challenge is to have every group member reach the top of or get up on to a boulder.
2. **Trail Barriers:** The challenge is to move around/over/through barriers placed on a trail. Barriers could include: a brush pile, a fallen tree, a puddle.
3. **Jungle Co-op Mean:** Components of a meal or snack are hidden in various areas. The group is divided to search for the various objects (e.g., breakfast: a) cereal, b) eggs, c) silverware and utensils, d) milk and juice). Emphasis is placed upon the importance of each group's accomplishment of their task toward the success of the meal/snack.
4. **Creek-Cross:** The challenge is to utilize natural objects (e.g., branches, rocks) to form a bridge across a small stream.
5. **Total Silence:** A hunter is passing only a few yards away. The group (deer) must be completely silent and freeze until the hunter passes by.
6. **The King's Reward:** The king has offered a thousand gold coins to the group which can encircle the greatest number of trees. Begin with one and see how many you can enclose. To count, a tree must be taller than the tallest member of your group.
7. **Mother Nature's Revenge:** The challenge is to completely rid a picnic or other outdoor area of litter/debris for an inspection visit by Mother Nature, who's promised a 6-week delay of Spring if not completely satisfied.
8. **Guard the Treasure:** The group pairs up into twos. Each pair stands back to back. The treasure is placed between their backs. (Treasure is a ball or pillow.) Each pair has to get over a fallen tree and finally over a distance of twenty feet.
9. **The Bomb:** The bomb, a balloon, is thrown up among the group. The group has to keep the balloon up (not catching it) for as long as possible.
10. **Kick the Stick:** Assemble group in a line (using wide open area) approximately five feet apart. First person kicks a stick to the second person and on until the stick reaches the opposite end of the line. (Divide by teams or time the event.)
11. **Bucket Brigade:** Object is to fill a container, using several smaller containers, by passing smaller containers from source of water to large container and back. Variation: put out campfire using a bucket brigade.
12. **Space Walk:** The challenge is for the entire group to remain in contact with the life-line (a length of rope) during a hike.

Processing of the activities has worked particularly well when Polaroid photos of the sequence of an activity have been taken and reviewed.

The Idea Notebook

The "Idea Notebook" is a new section of the **Journal** designed to give readers an opportunity to share practical ideas that have worked for them. To submit an idea, send two copies (typewritten on 8½ x 11 inch paper and double spaced) to AEE, Box 4625, Denver, Colorado, 80204. Articles for this section should be less than 800 words. Ideas on any topic related to experiential education are welcome. Upcoming issues will focus on Experiential Education with Special Populations and Experiential Approaches to Environmental Education.

An Initiative Problem and a "New Game"

Touch My Can
Object: For a group of about 10-12 students to make physical contact with a can while avoiding physical contact with one another.

The Rope Push
Halve your group and ask each half to stand on either side of a marker line (chalk line or rope). Hand them a 60-80 foot length of rope (any diameter or material) so that each side has an equal amount on their side of the marker line. Mark the center of the rope with a piece of tape. At this juncture they are probably ready for a good old Tug-of-War, BUT the object this time is, at the end of a one minute time limit, to have more of your rope on their side than they have of the rope on your side! WHAT? That-s right, this is a rope push, not pull. Here are a couple of rules to ease the transition from tradition to chaos:

> No one on either team is allowed to cross over and touch the other team's turf or person (no purposeful contact). Tugging on the rope is taboo — only push. Throwing the rope is not allowed.
>
> Judging this evenly is well nigh impossible, but who cares and a tie is usually well received by all except the most die hard competitors. This confused melee is worth trying again, so suggest taking a minute or two to develop team strategies and subtrefuges of sneaky initiative ideas.

These ideas are taken from "Bag of Tricks," a quarterly newsletter with new ropes course, initiative, and game ideas available from Karl Rohnke, P.O. Box 69, Hamilton, MA 01936.

Time Flies When You're Having Fun

Tom Herbert (Concord High School, Concord, New Hampshire) covers the clocks in his classroom and confiscates watches as his sociology class enters the room. As the students squirm, not knowing when the bell will ring, they come to realize our cultural dependence on scheduled and precise time.

Experiencing a Handicap

Gruffie Clough (Denver, Colorado) wanted her students to understand what it is like to be handicapped. Each student was greeted at the door one morning with a wheelchair in which the student had to remain for the entire school day. The wheelchairs were borrowed from a local agency such as Easter Seals.

Nothing Artificial
David C. Mellen

Photosynthesis or maple syrup—which would you prefer studying? Measurement, proportions, percentages, convection, boiling point, buoyancy, density, specific gravity, and precision should all be covered in science and math. Perhaps I can outline here how much sweeter they are to study through a maple sugaring project. To study this "industry" is also to study its people, for sugaring is richly steeped with culture. Taken as a whole, this project touches many topics and may motivate students toward everything from writing to physical labor.

Step One—the psych:

Find a sugar house for a field trip. Write to the U.S. Department of Agriculture Forest Service or your state agricultural service for assistance. Take your class in late February or early March to see the operation in full swing. Arrange ahead for a complete tour—everything from tapping and collecting to testing the final product. Interview the people that do this yearly —why do they work so hard?

Step Two—the prep:

In the fall, choose a site for your operation, identify the trees you will use, and prepare your boiling apparatus. Outdoors with even crude protection from wind and rain is preferrable to indoors where the huge amounts of steam will produce more destruction than syrup. Sugar maples are the preferred tree, but red maples and even birch trees will make syrup.

A wood burning stove with flat top and large firebox will do fine in combination with an evaporating pan. The larger the pan the better and using a small second pan for the final step (indoors perhaps) is a good idea. You may not be able to copy the dividers and fins you will see in the professional evaporators on your tour and you may have trouble finding pans constructed from stainless steel or English tin. These are something to work toward for future years; use any old clean pan for now.

Step Three—tapping & collecting:

Tap shortly after Washington's birthday (depending on your location) with a 7/16 inch bit boring 7-8 centimeters into the tree at a slight slant for drainage. Tap height is not critical and one tap for every 25 centimeters of tree diameter is allowable on a healthy tree. Do not plug the holes when you're through—they are small enough for the tree to close as it heals, and plugs retard the healing. Taps may be purchased, cut from tubing, or whittled from pithy pranches like sumac (poke the soft center out to make them hollow). Plastic gallon jugs may be slit near the top and slipped onto the taps for collecting; tie them up by the handle to prevent the jugs from falling off the taps as they gain in weight. The jugs and any containers used to store the sap must be washed with diluted clorox before collecting and whenever cloudy, smelly sap is found growing—yes growing! That is your bacteria and sanitation lesson. Sap must be stored in a cool place or used immediately. The sap looks like water but spill some inside and your custodian will surely join the lesson by pointing out the difference.

Students should be assigned a tree or trees. Many will bring sap from a tree at home. Don't miss this chance at data collecting and record keeping. Students may bar graph the amounts collected daily from their trees. A class high-low temperature graph plotted daily may be made on plastic. The horizontal axis should be marked of by the day in the same scale on both graphs so students may lay the plastic temperature graph over their bar graph and check for correlation. And of course—it's liters and Celsius now!

Step Four — "cauldron boil and cauldron bubble:"

Syrup will sour if too thin and crystalize if too thick. How do you know when it is just right? This is an ideal question for students of science to wrestle with (even better since it has more than one good answer). The proper density is 1.32 kg/liter. To test density students can measure the volume of a sample and put it on a balance. A 10 ml sample should be 13.2 grams. They could then learn about specific gravity and try an even simpler test—a hydrometer should float in a sample at the 1.32 mark. Since expansion and contraction cause this to vary, taking syrup temperature and computing the adjustment is necessary if you wish to facilitate precision. If you're a social studies teacher full of compassion for students who cannot handle this technical approach, send them out to interview an old timer. With legwork and patience they will discover a technique worthy of **Foxfire**. It's so simple science teachers will either groan or smile.

There is a lot to do during the boiling-down process. Sap should constantly be added, scum should be skimmed, the fire needs continual stoking, and a cautious eye must always be on the foam and thermometer. Foaming over can be halted with a squirt of cream, and frequent temperature checks will warn you as the critical moment draws near. Inattention at this point spells disaster—scorched syrup and perhaps a ruined evaporating pan. One way to help prevent this is to make this a yearly project and revive the guild system. With a master, journeyman, and apprentice (or two) on hand at all times, you may self-perpetuate the project with high standards and guarantee success.

Boiling point is an important concept to understand for successful sugaring. The day you plan to finish off your syrup, check the boiling point of distilled water. It will vary with altitude and barometric pressure. Your syrup is ready for final testing when it boils at 4.1 degrees Celsius over the boiling point of pure water.

It may take anywhere from 32 to 60 liters of sugar maple sap to boil down to 1 liter of syrup. The average proportion is 1:40. Do your students understand the concept of percentage? What percentage of the sap is maple syrup? This percentage should be figured for every batch of syrup since it will vary considerably. As the season progresses the ratio will generally increase until the buds begin to burst, the sap becomes cloudy, and the resulting "buddy" syrup is not worth the effort.

Sap contains more than sugar and water. Many of the minerals dissolved in sap will precipitate during boiling. Keep this secret at first and you may find students arguing over who threw sand in the syrup. This "sugar sand" is a combination of malate of lime or nitre and various other impurities. It should be removed immediately while the syrup is very hot and will filter most easily. Strain the hot syrup through a layer of wet white felt or multiple layers of cheese cloth.

Maple sugar candy might be the ultimate challenge for this project. With extreme care, the boiling process may be continued until the syrup is boiling at 10 degrees Celsius over the boiling point of pure water. Pour it into molds and it will crystalize into candies. It boils down fast at this point—you may end up with a burned mass of "caramel."

Step Five - ending with class:

This may be the hardest logistic problem of the project, but if you can pull it off it is unforgettable: a pancake breakfast with globs of grade A fancy, grade A, and, oh well, grade B maple syrup (hide the grade C).

Hindsight - why bother?

A maple sugaring project is a lot of work for everyone involved. The beautiful thing about it is that it combines hard work and fun while integrating learning. Most any old timer will tell you that sugaring is a labor of love. Students who are intensely involved may discover a love of labor that could become the most valuable lesson they ever learned. A difficult, successful, and rewarding experience can carry great impact. With sugaring, the success is obvious and the reward is sweet.

David C. Mellen is a science teacher at Bacon Academy in Colchester, Connecticut, and director of "Experience It," a non-profit, trip camp.

Bridging the Generation Gap

As a homework assignment, students can be asked to interview their parents. They are to ask questions about a place or time which was important to their mother or father when he or she was a child, teenager, or young adult. The students return to class with their questions and answers, then brainstorm additional questions that they can ask their parents in order to get more details. (What songs were playing on that juke box in the soda shop? What kind of a car did you drive to get there?) As students interview their parents in some depth, the details usually begin to cluster around a special event or a typical time. Once they have collected enough details, students write a short story in the first person, telling the story through their parent's eyes. This assignment has the benefit of getting students to talk with their parents and also prepares them for later interviews with adults in the community.

Dave Bernstein and Greg Trimmer use this assignment with English and cultural journalism classes at Minnechaug Regional High School in Wilbraham, Massachusetts.

Simulating Literary Experiences

It is sometimes difficult to think of ways to include an experiential approach in the study of literature, which is a vicarious look into the lives of others. Two New Hampshire teachers try to simulate the problems and experiences of characters in the books.

One of Peggy Walker Stevens' classes reads **Dove**, an autobiographical account of a teenager who sails around the world alone. The greatest problem for the author was coping with loneliness during his trip. Students get a taste of this loneliness by being blindfolded at school and driven to an isolated wooded area where they are alone with only a notebook and pen until they are picked up 4 hours later. This "mini-solo" has a big impact on many younger teenagers who seldom spend any time alone. They can begin to understand what it is like for the author of **Dove** to have spent months by himself at sea.

Louise Hickey brings unfamiliar settings of books to life by having the students prepare meals similar to those eaten in that time period or in that region. Following the reading of "MacBeth" students research the food of Shakespearian times and the traditional dishes of Scotland. They have prepared a feast of baked turkey (a whole boned turkey breast in a pie shell), Shrewsbury cakes, cider, and Scotch eggs (hard boiled eggs wrapped in sausage and deep fried).

Since most New Hampshire students are unfamiliar with the southern dishes described in **To Kill a Mockingbird**, students found recipes and prepared Smithfield ham, black eyed peas, grits, and "Charlottes" (as served in **Mockingbird**).

Administrators are invited to the meals—a good way to gain support for creative ideas.

Got a Local Problem? Study It.

Branford, Connecticut has a huge mountain of "trap rock," extruded waste material from the activity of Tilcon Tomasso, a local company that produces road-paving material. As a result of a recent Project Adventure Academic workshop, Joan Bailey of Branford became excited about using the "mountain" as a focus for an experiential unit. She approached the company and was received enthusiastically. As part of an interdisciplinary science-economics unit, students will study the plant operations, "mountain" composition, and local geology. The class will produce a contour model of the town and a slide tape of the company's operations. Ecological recommendations will be part of the slide tape.

The company has donated maps, chemicals, company assayist time, jeeps, drivers, film and development costs.

This idea comes from Dick Prouty, a staff member of Project Adventure in Hamilton, Massachusetts.

Organizing Brainstorms

By Kate Friesen

There must be many different definitions for the phrase, "covering a topic", ranging from reading a chapter and answering questions to developing an entire curriculum based on the topic. It is easy for me to reject the extreme of reading a chapter. I am a believer in interdisciplinary education and a strong advocate of experiential education. However, to create a high quality experiential curriculum can be boggling! There is so much relevent material to find and organize. Project possibilities sound intriguing. Skills must be developed and improved. A worthwhile experience must happen. It is a difficult challenge to the most inspired teacher to make the four or five weeks the best possible learning experience for students. It is easy to be part way through week three and find it is too late to carry out some of the better ideas.

Having been in frustrating situations of getting good ideas too late, or discovering that I was conducting a very teacher-directed classroom, I began to develop a pattern to my brainstorming. I worked out a step by step, cover-all-angles system to allow my brainstorming binges to wander, to center, to start from a new perspective, and to center again. The results are themes of study that are well thought out. They involve many disciplines using a variety of learning styles, they are experiential, and they include opportunities for developing some essential skills.

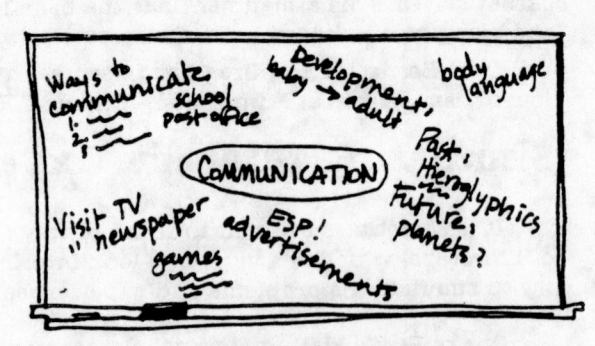

Step I: The Initial Brainstorm

I begin with a chalkboard or a large piece of paper, and some friends. I write the topic, **Communication**, in the center of the space. We all stare for a bit—then ideas begin. I write everything that comes to anyone's mind. A possible beginning point can be concepts that should be learned. What do we feel a student should learn by the end of the five weeks? For example, in the study of **Communication**, I might want students to be able to list at least eight methods of communication. I might want them to be able to explain how a telegraph system works. Several general or specific concepts can usually be identified. From concepts, we think of some activities. Some activities may be directly related to our list of concepts that should be learned. Other activities aren't directly related, but I write them anyway.

Another category we make sure to brainstorm is resources. We think in terms of field trips, (the TV station, the post office), and people in the community who could visit us or direct us to other experts (musicians, deaf or blind people). We think of libraries and media resources. We also think of careers (radio announcers, language interpreters), of natural resources (what is needed to construct a telephone?). We raise questions of values (how important is it to construct a multi-million dollar TV satellite?). We ponder things we know little about (intergalactic communication, systems of communication used by human infants or honeybees). Everything that concerns the topic is written down somewhere on the board.

The space is cluttered. There is a lull. Step II can begin.

Step II: Organizing by Perspectives

Organizing by perspectives is a series of different ways to arrange the ideas we have just written down. New ideas will also emerge.

1. Organize by discipline

In the first attempt to order cluttered ideas, I list disciplines — history, math, music, creative writing, reading, and so forth. I take ideas we've written already and see where they fit in. This also provides a structure for new ideas. Once, the topic was electricity and I saw that the column under "music" was empty. The idea of electronic music emerged and later some students became interested in lear-

---

Kate Friesen is currently enrolled in a program at Cornell University leading to a Master's degree in Science and Environmental Education. She has taught 3rd and 4th grade at The Colorado Springs School.

ning how music is amplified. I don't think it is terribly important to make a theme multidisciplinary. An activity in each discipline can be too contrived. However, going through this process provides me with another route along which to brainstorm and often I have come up with ideas I like.

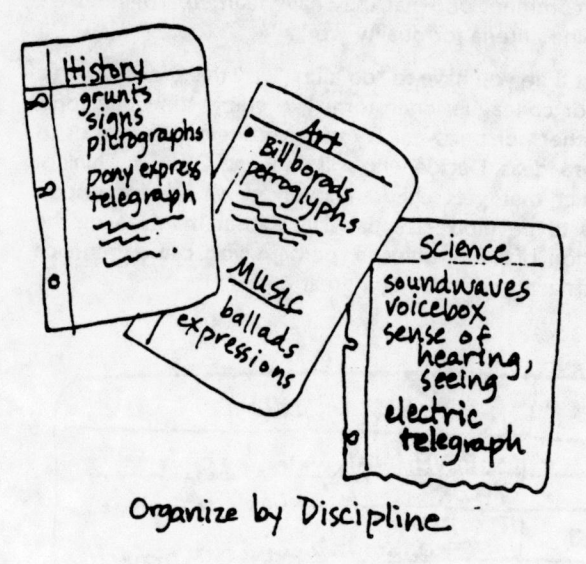

Organize by Discipline

2. Organize by responsibility

By this time I am getting a pretty good idea of some things that might happen in this theme of study. I have some ideas of projects I definitely want to try, and other ideas that sound like fun, but that are not imperative to do. At this point, sometimes it is appropriate to organize the theme by responsibility. One year when my class studied the pond ecosystem, I decided to be responsible only for some of the scientific aspects of the theme. I would direct investigations into organisms and their food chains, life cycles of aquatic animals, and so forth. My students, however, after participating in a group brainstorming session, were each responsible for an independent project concerning the pond. Some measured its circumference and diameter. Some took the temperature of water in different depths and areas of the pond and had to devise a way to get a temperature reading from the middle of the pond. Others made detailed paintings, poems, and set up experiments. Students worked on their projects during school and at home and presented them to the class later.

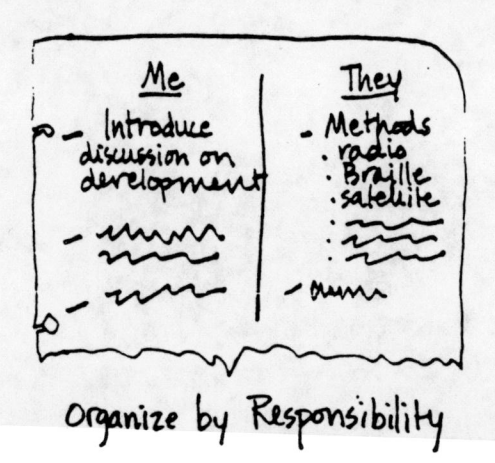

3. Organize by logical sequence

Some themes lend themselves to a sequential approach. In these cases, I decide which concepts and activities should happen before others. A lesson in electrical circuits must be scheduled before the class begin to construct a buzzer communication system with the next classroom. Some activities are redundant and should only be used by a few who need remediation. At this point, weekly and daily lesson plans will begin to fall into place.

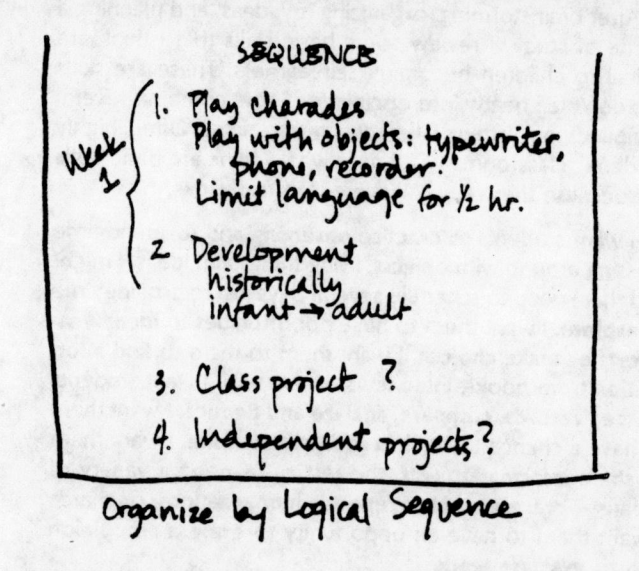

STEP III: Experientialize It

Again, review your plans which by now have taken some real shape. Most likely, there are already some opportunities for students to DO something with the topic, but think again if there is a major class project that can be done. In a study of architecture, can you design and build a playhouse? in a study of American Colonial life, can you barter items you have made with other classes in a town meeting? In a study of nutrition, can you make a cookbook? Can you get involved in a world hunger project? In a study of communication, can you start a school newspaper, a radio station, or a postal service? Are you really doing something meaningful to real lives in each theme of study? Children become involved in experiences. Significant learning happens when children are involved.

Experientialize It

STEP IV: Using Skills Beyond Disciplines

After brainstorming, organizing my ideas, and planning a theme of study, I review some basic skills that I think are critical to children becoming self-learners. These are skills that don't fall neatly into disciplines. Some combine several disciplines, and others fall between disciplines. Often, highly academic classrooms will ignore what I think are basic skills just because they're not "covered" in textbooks.

I want students to **practice observing** and to spend time messing around with objects, living things and ideas. I might find that I need to schedule several days just to provide time **to explore**. I want them to have opportunities to **identify interests** or **make choices**. I want them to learn to **find information** from books, interviews, and media. I want students to **keep records, compare, analyze** and **deduce**. I want them to have a chance to **work in groups and alone**. I want them to **share information** with the rest of us using a variety of means — oral and written reports, dramatizations, or charts. I want them to have an opportunity to **express an opinion** and to **evaluate work**.

Many of these skills can be practiced through independent projects. I sometimes ask students to choose a project or an interest that relates to our topic. I will plan with him or her a set of expectations for which they are responsible. I will ask that they find sources of information, order it, share it, and comment on what they have learned. Together we determine criteria for quality work.

Next time you have to "do a unit", try this process with a friend or colleague. Brainstorm like crazy. View the topic from other perspectives. Try categorizing by disciplines to get more ideas. Decide who will do what. Order it. Think of a project that gets children involved. Check for opportunities to develop essential skill. Rather than feeling the frustration of being diffused, perhaps you can experience the satisfaction of refining a great idea!

Beyond Disciplines

THE Idea NOTEBOOK

by Bert Cohen

With his book of two folded pages of ditto paper in hand, Seth approaches Lee. "Do you want to listen to a book I made?" Twenty seconds later Seth is through reading and off to staple his book together.

I wasn't aware that kids were reading their books to each other. I would have mised this if I hadn't started my observation time. I thought I didn't have time to stop my "teaching" and observe my first graders write. I was wrong.

I'd been aware for years that I would like to really see what is happening in my classroom. As I reflected on how kids were writing, I was aware of the large gaps in my awareness. That's when I made the announcement to the class. "As you know I'm interested in learning about how you write. In order to learn more, I am going to start each of our writing times by looking at you working. I'm going to set the timer for seven minutes. During this time I will be making notes about what you are doing. Please do not come to me or ask me questions as I want to concentrate on what you are doing."

This practice has been working well — with a few exceptions. One day I was about half way through my observation time. I heard Seth say to Jonathan, "The stapler is empty." I saw Seth start toward me. "Mr. Cohen." I ignored Seth. "Mr. Cohen." I looked the other way and concentrated on Glenda writing her books. A tug on my shirt sleeve, again, "Mr. Cohen." I walked to the other end of the room and looked at Melissa showing Jennifer her book. Time passed with two more "Mr. Cohens" and then at last the kitchen timer rang. My seven minutes were up. I acknowledged Seth, who by then was at his seat with his hand up.

I learned two things: one, make staples available to kids, and two, it pays not to break your observation time for answering questions. Kids have learned well that I don't talk during my observation. The kids even protect me now. The other day Jim came into our room from the class next door with a lunch pail in hand to see if it belonged to anyone in my class. Melissa said, "Don't talk to Mr. Cohen now. He's watching how we write and won't talk to you."

What I see frequently is not dramatic, yet it enables me to move in the direction of helping kids learn to write and have ownership of their writing.

It had also been my feeling that I wanted to start kids reading books to each other. When I saw Seth reading his book to Lee, I began to notice Melissa was also reading her books to Jennifer, and Latika read her book to four different friends at her table before putting it down to start a new story. It was clear the kids were ahead of me. By observing, it seems I can teach with a lighter touch. In the case of having kids read their books to each other, I had only to merely encourage a process that had already started.

Observation also helped me eliminate some of my directive teaching methods. For example, it was the start of writing time and Lara had her dot to dot book on her desk which she had been working at the indoor rainy day recess. My normal tendency would be to give a reminder that recess was over and we were writing now; however, it was my observation time and since I wasn't talking to kids, I noticed that after three minutes Lara had finished her dot to dot, stapled a book together, and was writing. This brought me to reflect and notice how much kids will do given the right atmosphere. I find I am directing less and supporting kids more. I notice more of what they are doing and build on it.

Noticing what kids do has become a part of the day I look forward to. It has a calming effect on me and the class. I find a creative challenge in discovering what I will be focusing on as I observe the class. It is like a painter looking at a landscape, what features will be picked out to create the picture? What part of the writing process will emerge for me to focus on? The surprise of seeing Seth reading to Lee brings me back with renewed energy to continue discovering the process kids use to learn. It is nice to know that there are a few minutes each day where I can focus on seeing kids write.

Bert Cohen *teaches at the Little Harbor School in Portsmouth, New Hampshire and is also a veteran staffer with the Live, Learn, and Teach program at the University of New Hampshire in Durham.*

THE Idea NOTEBOOK
by Sherrod Reynolds

Every English teacher is confronted with the paragraph, how to introduce it, teach it, make it palatable not only to students, but to themselves. Here is one way to take some of the boredom out of this most essential writing tool.

Have students write a *chronological* paragraph describing how to get somewhere within the immediate vicinity. Then have them exchange papers and attempt to follow the directions given without help from the authors. Once they have found that place, they are to sit down and write a *descriptive* paragraph using either a spatial or an associative approach. Upon returning to the class, these new papers are given to a third student who must attempt to discover the place described in the paper. When they find it, they must then write a *pro/con* paragraph arguing whether the description was accurate, clear, and well presented.

This exercise may be done in steps, or all at once, depending on how advanced your students are. If the first paragraphs are so bad that no one could follow the directions accurately, then I would suggest a little more ground work before trying again.

Sherrod Reynolds, *former Foxfire associate and frequent contributor to the Journal, is currently studying and consulting in Boston.*

Idea Notebook: The Encouraging Teacher

by Mike Pegg

I believe we can be Encouragers in our daily lives and work. We can be Creators rather than Complainers, find positive solutions rather than simply discuss problems, and choose life rather than death. I believe we can build a more Encouraging World.

Maybe it sounds old-fashioned today. I believe in teachers. Why? During my life I have been saved, supported and helped to make transformations by all kinds of teachers. One message I hear continually from people on my courses, 'Yes, I had a teacher who gave me courage to take new steps in my life.' So I believe in teachers: they can inspire people and help to create a better world.

The Encourager's Values

Teachers can offer a child many wonderful things in the classroom: life-experience, facts, knowledge. But maybe the most important is the gift of encouragement. The teacher can be, after the child's mother and father, the third most significant person in the student's life. Many of us still remember positive and negative messages given to us by teachers at school. Teachers can help to encourage or destroy a child: the child can either leave school with hope in his heart or trying to restore his shattered confidence.

Teachers have positive intentions and struggle to guide children through school. But their efforts will be defeated unless we radically rethink and develop new goals in education. I believe we can take six steps to introduce more encouragement into education.

1. We can change the aims of education to, 'We want to help children to learn the basic educational skills, find their strengths, find enjoyable work and learn life-skills for keeping themselves healthy and creative during their future lives.' We will then give young people the confidence, knowledge and tools they need to play a positive role in modern society.

2. We can give children the chance to choose where they want to learn. After mastering the basic educational skills; reading, writing and arithmetic, they can choose to stay in their present school or, for example, learn in the Traditional School, Open School, Free School, etc., run by teachers who share the same educational philosophy. Children could choose to learn in any of a variety of authorized schools in their area.

3. We can give like-minded teachers the chance to set up their own school with colleagues who share the same educational philosophy. But there would be two conditions: they must define what they offer the students and some students must want to attend. The teachers would then be able to build a school where people want to be there, agree on common goals, do creative work and reach their goals.

4. We can devote the final year of a young person's time at school to helping him to find enjoyable work or making a satisfactory transition to further study.

5. We can offer teachers a philosophy and practical tools they can use to encourage children and build a positive and effective school.

6. We can offer young people the chance to learn life-skills which they can use to keep themselves healthy and creative during their future lives.

Since 1980 Mike Pegg has been teaching two-day Encouragement courses for 14 and 15 year-old students in Swedish schools. Create-Your-Own-Work courses are also being set up to help unemployed high school leavers create their own jobs or find satisfying work in a changing society.

The Encourager's Work

Imagine you are a teacher beginning a new term with your class at school. Here are several practical things you can do to support your students. Take the ideas you like and use them in your own way to create a positive atmosphere and do effective work in your school.

1. Decide, 'I want to be an Encourager, not a Stopper, in my school. I want to help the children to learn the basic educational skills, find and use their strengths, find enjoyable work and learn life-skills they can use to keep themselves healthy and creative during their adult lives. I want to encourage my colleagues and work to build a school where both students and teachers want to be there, have common goals, do creative work and reach their goals; which is one model people can follow to build a healthy school.'

2. Get 'The First Four Minutes' right when you meet your colleagues or students. Make people feel safe, wanted and important. Look at them, give them 100% attention, listen to them and show you have heard what they said. My math teacher at school could destroy a positive atmosphere in four seconds. Striding into the classroom after the summer holidays, he announced, 'Stop talking, be quiet, do as you are told. The holidays are over and it is time to begin working. Turn to page 32, read to page 36, then we will have a test.' Another of my teachers began by saying, 'Welcome back to school. Maybe none of us wanted to return. So let us begin by going around and each person saying what they enjoyed best during the summer holidays and what they would like to learn during the coming term. I can start myself and then we will go around the class.' Guess which teacher got us to do the most creative and effective work.

3. Try to find and win the leaders in the class. If you win the leaders, they will win the other students for you. How? Try various ways and find a style which fits for you. For example, Peter, a 15 year old Swedish boy, strolled into the classroom for my two day 'Learning for Life' course wearing an Arsenal football scarf and demanding to know, 'What is this course about?' I walked across to him, touched his scarf and said, 'Arsenal! Is that a football team? I support Derby.' 'Derby!' he exclaimed, 'They play in Division 2 don't they?' 'Yes', I replied, 'Maybe we can discuss football later. Would you like to know more about the course? I aim to teach people ways they can do what they want in their lives without hurting other people. And I would like you to help me with the teaching later.' Peter threw himself into the activities, especially the first warm-up game called 'Fruit Salad', role-played a head teacher and a spluttering moped, and acted as a good model for his friends in the class. Every person needs to feel important and get time and attention. If someone like Peter cannot get it from his teacher by doing positive things, he will certainly get it by doing negative things: such as arriving late for lessons, complaining of headaches or starting fights with other students. Winning the leader in your own way will release you from the policeman role. You will then have more time, energy and opportunity to encourage the other students in your class.

4. Give the students enjoyable exercises they can do to discover their strengths, creativity and plans. For example, Peter made a list of 'Thirty Things I Enjoy Doing,' which looked like this:

Thirty Things I Enjoy Doing
1. Playing football
2. Watching TV
3. Mending cars
4. Reading car magazines
5. Being with my friends

Peter's poster gives a clue to his strengths and also provides material which can be used to invent special projects to help him learn the basic educational skills. He can, for example, compile a journal of the cars he mends, measure and draw the engines, research the car's history, describe which company produces the car and where its factories are located, and illustrate his journal with photographs from American Magazines. Peter will be pursuing his interests while also practicing reading, writing, grammar, mathematics, technical drawing, history, geography, design and creating a finished product.

5. Hold a Personal Meeting with each student in your class. Set aside at least half-an-hour early in the term to study their 'Enjoyment Poster' or other exercise, discuss their hopes and make plans for the term. Personal Meetings will offer the opportunity to make a good relationship with each person in your class.

'But I have not got the time', you might argue. Invent different methods for seeing the students if you find it difficult to meet each student by themselves. Put them in small groups, talk with two or three students who are friends, invite the class leaders to visit your home one evening or during the weekend. Charismatic teachers can win the students in ten seconds and quickly make a positive relationship with each person in the class: but some teachers feel more comfortable spending quality time alone with each student. This method can in fact save time during the term. Why? As I mentioned before, every person longs for time and attention from the teacher and, if they cannot get it in positive ways, they will grab it by causing trouble during the lessons. Holding Personal Meetings can help you to build good relationships with the students, save time and release you to perform effective teaching in the classroom.

6. Encourage each student in your class. Here are some practical suggestions.

a) Have positive eyes when looking at a person or marking his work. Try to consider: What has he done right? What can he do better next time? And how? How can I put this in a way he can accept and use to improve his work? Build on the student's strengths and give positive alternatives for tackling his weaknesses.

So when does Peter 'come most alive'? When he is fixing cars, playing football, playing the guitar? What is he doing right then? In the case of mending cars, he is: Doing what he wants; setting a goal; doing what he enjoys; using his strengths; daring to experiment; doing one thing fully at a time; enjoying the journey towards his goal.

How can I encourage him to do more of these things during his future life? I can start by helping him to set personal aims, search for enjoyable work and support him until he reaches his first goal. The next step is to teach Peter how to keep himself healthy, creative and alive during his adult life. More about this later.

b) Make an Encouragement Book which describes the student's strengths. Class Registers often refer to misbehaviour, late arrivals and refusal to do homework, but teachers may find it refreshing to compile another kind of class book (see illustration).

MY ENCOURAGEMENT BOOK

NAME	WHAT HE ENJOYS DOING	WHAT HIS STRENGTHS ARE	WHAT HE WANTS TO DO IN HIS LIFE	HOW I WANT TO ENCOURAGE HIM
PETER	He enjoys mending cars, playing football, playing music, reading car magazines etc.	He is a fighter. Works hard when doing things he enjoys and can make finished products.	He wants to be a car mechanic, buy his own motorbike and perhaps have his own garage.	I want to show him I care for him, help him to set goals, and help him to find satisfying work.

c) Give the students positive alternatives to help them grow as people and improve their work in school. Imagine Peter has destroyed a lesson by starting a fight in class. Blaming him in front of his friends will make him resentful and reinforce his role as a troublemaker. Criticizing Peter will have the opposite effect from the one you intended: he will develop the art of being a problem child. Why? Because it is the way he can be a big guy in school.

What can you do instead to get Peter to change and to continue building a positive and effective atmosphere in the class? Before exploding, it is important to ask yourself three question: What is the

result I want to achieve with Peter? How can I do my best to achieve this result? When do I want to try? Here are four guidelines you may like to follow:
- Stand up for yourself without knocking down Peter.
- Describe your rules for working in the classroom and give your reasons for these rules.
- Give Peter a positive alternative concerning how you would like him to behave in the future and describe the consequences for him in choosing the positive or negative road.
- Keep trying to find a positive solution in which, as far as possible, everybody can win.

You can take a stand when Peter disrupts the class or talk with him during his Personal Meeting. You may wish to say, 'I believe you are a powerful person, Peter. You can choose to be positive or negative, creative or destructive, help people or hurt people. We both know this. I like it when you are positive because you have such a lot to give people, for example, when you role play in sketches or sing your songs for the class. I would like you to help people rather than fight. What do you say?' Build on Peter's reply and make an agreement concerning how to improve his behaviour during lessons.

Miracles seldom occur overnight: it requires support and patience if Peter is to grow. My own experience with disturbed teenagers is they often respond to honesty and being given a new road to follow. But do not be afraid to set clear limits and stick to the consequences if a student refuses to change. As a teacher you are responsible for making the rules and helping each child to learn in the class. You may need to use "tough-love" to protect this atmosphere: but you also need to be seen as fair and giving difficult students, such as Peter, a way to return and take a constructive role in the class. This is hard work. It calls for standing up for yourself, love, creativity and asking a student to choose which way he wants to go in life. But when it succeeds the rewards are enormous.

IX. Book Reviews

BOOK REVIEWS

Experiential Education Policy Guidelines
Experiential Education: A Primer on Programs

Reviewed by Mary Jensen

Experiential Education Policy Guidelines. The National Center for Research in Vocational Education, The Ohio State University, Columbus, Ohio 43210, Research and Development Series No. 160, 1979.

Experiential Education: A Primer on Programs. The National Center for Research in Vocational Education, The Ohio State University, Columbus, Ohio 43210. Information Series No. 162, 1978.

Since 1976, the National Center for Research in Vocational Education has been conducting research in experiential learning programs. Such programs, which expand on traditional education, offer youth a change to explore careers and gain experience in actual work environments. Two recently published guides will be helpful to those interested in starting, or already involved in existing, experiential education programs.

The first of these is *Experiential Education Policy Guidelines*. This brief report resulted from a year's study of policy issues in education. Sixteen policy guidelines are presented which will call attention to details of all phases of program operation from pre-program planning through program evaluation. Each recommendation is accompanied by a narrative which develops concisely the pros and cons of such issues as "pay or no pay for experiential learners," "credit or no-credit," "displacement of workers in time of economic hardship," etc. Fair representation of learner, educator and business/labor views is made, although the brevity of discussion occasionally leaves the reader's appetite whetted for more specific information. Clear communications among all those involved in experiential education programs is emphasized throughout, so that all may benefit. *Experiential Education Policy Guidelines* is well organized for quick identification of key points and contains an extensive bibliography for readers desiring more information.

The second volume is *Experiential Education: A Primer on Programs*. The contents of this book are divided into three sections. The first section provides an overview of experiential education programs. Seven general program models ranging from "Supervised Volunteer Work" to "Experienced Based Academic Programs" are described. Forty abstracts of exemplary programs which fit into these seven models are found in the third section of the book, while narratives describing the manner in which policy has been developed for the programs comprises the second section. The section on policy-making contains few surprises, however, the abstracts provide numerous examples of how experiential education programs actually operate. Abstracted are programs which represent a variety of funding patterns, client populations, progammatic goals, and relationships with the community, business, and labor sectors of society. Readers will be interested in rudimentary cost analysis information which indicates that some programs actually pay for themselves. Information about published material relating to specific programs is given in each abstract. Like its companion volume, *Experiential Education Policy Guidelines, A Primer on Programs* is well organized and easy to read. Both volumes can be obtained from the National Center for Research in Vocational Education, The Ohio State University, 1950 Kenny Road, Columbus, Ohio 43210.

Mary Jensen is affiliated with the School of Health, Physical Education, and Recreation at Ohio State University in Columbus, Ohio.

Book Review:

by Barbara Shoup

The Experiential Taxonomy: A Different Approach to Teaching and Learning. By Norman W. Steinaker and M. Robert Bell.

The natural characteristics of a person drawn to the experiential approach in teaching and learning are, at the same time, uniquely effective and limiting. I would suspect that most experiential educators are rooted firmly in the real world, because they are concerned with making things happen. As humanists, they work to mesh the intellectual and affective needs of their students with curricular requirements.

There is something of the adolescent in all of us who teach experientially. Just as the adolescent nature passionately refuses to be told about the world, stubbornly demanding to learn through experience, we teachers often bypass the easier route of predicting educational outcomes through the careful study of theory. We are determined that each person, each learning situation is unique. Like our students, we do not like to be told what will work and what won't.

So, we often find ourselves coming to theory through the back door. In my own experience, I have come to a sort of a layman's theory of my own which I find hard to articulate. I am like Robert Pirsig in **Zen and the Art of Motorcycle Maintenance** trying to define "excellence." I know it when I see it. Describing learning situations to educators better versed in educational theory than myself, I am often surprised to learn that what I have been doing fits neatly into one of the basic theories educators have been testing and developing over the past 60 years or so.

To be fair, theory has its drawbacks, too. Perhaps teachers and educational theorists remain at loggerheads because theory so often neglects to speak to the realities teachers face every day in the classroom. **The Experiential Taxonomy: A New Approach to Teaching and Learning**, by Norman W. Steinaker and Robert M. Bell is one of those rare books where logistics and theory meet and translate into a workable plan. In the preface, the authors claim that their Taxonomy "...is a deceptively simple yet pedagogically...sound instrument." I think they are right.

In a style and format that is readable and to the point, the authors not only present their experiential taxonomy; they justify its need, trace its development, and illustrate its usefulness as a model for curriculum development. They tie the taxonomy to learning principles and to creativity, critical thinking and problem solving. Since evaluation is built into the taxonomy, this issue is treated as thoroughly as program planning and the execution of learning experiences.

One of the things that makes the book both believable and exciting is that the authors have tested their taxonomy in a variety of settings. This research in the field has enabled them to make pragmatic suggestions for implementation that will be helpful to teachers who must always be concerned with fulfilling curricular requirements set forth by their school systems.

The experiential taxonomy provides a strong defense against those critics who insist on equating experiential education with the experimental, permissive free school concept of the late 60s. Because experiential learning does not fit into the traditional structure of most schools, educationally conservative educators and parents often assume that there is no structure at all and this has provided the basis for their sharpest criticism. But experiential educators have known for quite some time that this type of learning is, in fact, highly structured. We have argued that we have a different kind of structure. **The Experiential Taxonomy: A New Approach to Teaching and Learning** gives shape to what all good experiential programs have come to on their own. The book offers an organizational format for building an experiential approach to learning that can be used with any subject matter, with any age. Reading it, I thought: this is what we have known, intuitively, all along.

This struggle toward creating a structure that defines and demands and at the same time allows the creativity and freedom of movement of each individual has been one of the greatest and most constant dilemmas of experiential educators. So often, we see programs that begin with real promise either side step, ultimately, the crucial issue of the balance of academics and experiences or slip slowly but surely back toward a more and more traditional format. Having the experiential taxonomy available to educators to help them plan a program rather than chancing their coming to a sense of it, eventually, through trial and error, is a great step forward for the "science" of experiential learning.

Book Review:

by Al Adams

Cheez! Uncle Sam: What Price Justice?

Nagel, Ed. **Cheez! Uncle Sam: What Price Justice? A Resourceful Struggle on Behalf of Freeing Our Children.** Santa Fe, New Mexico: S.F.C.S. Publications, 1978. 220 pp.

Cheez! Uncle Sam is a refreshing oasis in the arid educational climate. It is also a nostalgic reminder of ideals which have been diluted and energies which have been coopted since the late sixties. Ed Nagel portrays the Santa Fe Community School as the "mouse that roared," with the concomitant characteristics of a righteous cause and amazing victories that are produced by clever tactics and unswerving persistence. His allegory about ASA, the mouse, and his limburger trials while fighting the "fat cats" provides Nagel with the opportunity to editorialize in the third-person and also adds a pleasing artistic/esoteric touch. This stylized story is judiciously interspersed with accounts from Nagel's 1970 journal and quotations from the kids, staff, well-known educators, newspaper stories and legal documents that bring the reader up-to-date through 1977. **Cheez!** is a lovely and, at the same time, tragic story that will be an inspiration to progressive educators, while forcing them to look critically at their current ideologies. Radical educators will feel reaffirmed.

The first half of this book is more engaging and, perhaps, more universally relevant, than the second half. It is here that Nagel describes the kind of school S.F.C.S. wants to be and the kind of school it is. Consisting of about sixty students (most of whom are from low-income families) from ages two to twenty and twelve staff members, it is a "free school" that began in 1967. Much of this section focuses on what is wrong with public schools where students are "prisoners" and school officials are "educrats." It contains a plethora of quotations from Holt, Neill, Illich, Kozol and Herndon as Nagel joins them in constructing a rationale for creating alternative schools. Some of the resulting rhetoric appears to be passe, but more because it is old than because it is no longer accurate. It once again builds a compelling case for making the school fit the child rather than shaping the child in a preconceived mold. The subsequent discussion of the learning needs of kids reasserts that, rather than being processed (Cheez!), kids must have the freedom to explore the process of learning and that we must nurture their "response ability" and their self-respect. It also supports teaching the "3 R's" and therefore cannot be dismissed as "one of those free schools which sacrifices kids for the sake of an ideal by producing incompetents." In short, this section is a substantive review for all of us as we reconsider our own assumptions about kids, what education should be and our accompanying **modus operandi**. I feel that this segment is more relevant than the remainder of the book because it really is about kids, and it is at this level that significant change has to start. Without the commitment to address the individual needs of kids, the politics of how to fight the system are all but superfluous.

Each state's statutes are different, so Nagel's discussion of S.F.C.S.'s legal battles cannot be considered a "how to" manual. However, there are many issues in this section that are important to all of us. First, we must realize that any new or alternative program will be viewed through a much more critical lens than existing programs. In fact, this suggests a sometimes successful strategy of turning that same lens in the direction of the status quo. Next, we must deal with the question of who is ultimately responsible for a child's education. The New Mexico state legislature (House Bill 254) agreed with S.F.C.S. that parents have the right to that responsibility. What is the relationship between the state and nonpublic schools? The New Mexico Supreme Court agreed that the state has no authority in this area. The power of the state and the amount of money and time required to fight bureaucratic injustice is also a staggering realization. Lastly, the importance of solidarity and mutual support, in this case from the Rio Grande Education Association, Holt, Kozol, Dennison, the Harvard Center for Law and Education, the A.C.L.U. and the National Association for the Legal Support of Alternative Schools, is a crucial lesson to be heeded. Although S.F.C.S. has challenged the state bureaucracy on twelve separate issues and has won in each case, Nagel leaves us with a sobering conclusion:

Al Adams, is the Academic Dean of the Colorado Springs School.

"Every single battle described in this book has resulted only in **temporary** setbacks for the system; the conditions that precipitate oppression continue. As a result, without exception, each bureaucratic program continues to exert almost unbearable pressures upon the people of this school through the sheer weight of their **recognized authority**. True, the oppression is less blatant, the "issues" are less offensive, the costs are less significant; by the same token, the public is less concerned, the issues less newsworthy, the challenges required "cost" more: it's a cold war siege, and the system is winning." (Page 178).

It is unlikely that S.F.C.S. or any other radically alternative school would enjoy a successful birth in 1980. Given the current economic insecurity that abounds in the U.S., the "back to basics" movement and the accompanying "looking out for number 1" mentality, most of the radical educators of the late sixties have either opted out of education or have been coopted by the system. In many ways S.F.C.S. is a vestige of bygone days. However, the evolution of our society over that past ten years seems to buttress rather than to detract from Nagel's call to reform. Future shock is upon us, and today's conventional schools are doing little to help young people learn to live with and even to exploit change. Today's is the first generation in U.S. history that cannot be assured of doing better economically than its parents (see Tom Hayden's article in the February 1979 issue of **The Independent School Bulletin**). What are we doing to help kids cope with the prospect of getting a smaller piece of the pie? Our society is becoming increasingly depersonalized by the bureaucratic leviathan, and the "robots" who leave most schools, conform far too placidly to the system. Public education is accused of being too expensive, is characterized by a duplication of services, does not use community resources efficiently and thus, speaks more eloquently than ever to the need to "de-school" society. In short, the stakes are as high today as they were when John Holt wrote **How Children Learn.** Perhaps they are even higher, given the lethal combination of a precarious global balance of power and the rise of "psychological/narcissistic man" (see Christopher Lasch's **The Culture of Narcissism,** W.W. Norton and Co., N.Y., 1978).

Although the small size of the type in **Cheez!** is not thoroughly appealing, the specifics of the various legal battles become somewhat redudant and the rhetoric is occasionally vitriolic, it has few other shortcomings. Perhaps its greatest virtue, poignantly captured by Nagel's very readable style, is its uncompromising and uncompromised spirit. Just as S.F.C.S. is the "mouse that roared," we too must be convinced of our capacity to become "mighty mice" in our own realms - even in 1980.

Books
IN REVIEW

Cognition and Curriculum:
A Basis for Deciding What to Teach
Elliot W. Eisner. New York: Longman, Inc., 1982

Reviewed by
William G. Larmer

Those who have found themselves out of step with the movement which would reduce the curriculum to the "basics" will be especially indebted to Elliot Eisner. *Cognition and Curriculum* takes up where *Experience and Education* left off, and Eisner extends Dewey's seminal thinking to provide an even firmer foundation for a curriculum based on experience. He presents a straight-forward and disciplined rationale for a holistic curriculum founded on sensory experience which, he maintains, provides the foundation for all concept development. Concepts are developed and communicated by humans through a variety of forms of representation -- forms which might include words, pictures, objects, mathematical formulas, music, physical movement, or some combination of these. The ability to skillfully use a variety of forms of representation to decode and encode meaning is the overall goal of a curriculum based on sensory experience.

The rationale for an experience-based curriculum is established by Eisner in the opening chapter. Attacking the "Back to the Basics" movement, the author contends that a singular emphasis on the development of fundamental language and computational skills has had the effect of drastically limiting the scope of the curriculum. A broader perspective is needed, and instead of aiming exclusively at the limited goals of increasing achievement scores in language and mathematics, the school curriculum should be "...grounded in a view of how humans construct meaning from their experience" (p. 21).

Experience serves the additional purpose of uniting the cognitive, affective and psychomotor domains of learning -- domains which have been artificially separated in the typical departmentalized curriculum.

Conventional measures of achievement would provide only a limited assessment of an experience-based curriculum. Eisner points to the need to assess the broader aspects of schooling, such as the quality of learning experiences, and the ability of students to employ a variety of forms of representation in understanding and expressing concepts. In Chapter IV, the author calls for innovative methods of evaluating these subtle and complex elements of the curriculum.

Eisner provides a theoretical framework for considering the merits of experiential learning. Such thinking is sorely needed if educators are ever going to progress beyond piecemeal modifications to an already fragmented curriculum. *Cognition and Curriculum* will stand as a significant contribution to the field of curriculum.

Books in Review

Teaching as a Conserving Activity
Neil Postman, New York:
Dell Publishing Company, Inc., 1980

Reviewed by Bert Horwood

Neil Postman is probably best known for his book, with Charles Weingartner, *Teaching as a Subversive Activity*. Now, as a solo effort, he has given us what appears to be the "vice versa" of that earlier work. Closer inspection shows that the book is a serious critique of current popular trends in education and promotes a conservative view in the best possible sense of that term.

The book is organized in three sections. The first is a concise statement of the theme of the work. Postman argues that when social and cultural changes are likely to be destructive of the ability of the young to control their destinies, then the schools have a role to play as bastions of the traditional intellectual knowledge and skills. He uses a cybernetic model, like that of a thermostat, as a theme to illustrate the ways in which schools should dampen the more extreme swings of technological change.

The second section of the book is devoted to articulation of the problems which Postman sees. Here he argues that there is a media environment which surrounds us all from our earliest days. The media environment sends strong continuous messages which constitute the "first curriculum." He shows that the messages are not compatible with a self-sustained independent society; and that students are not developing the critical power to recognize the effects of the media environment. Similarly, Postman argues that the biases and excesses of extreme technicalization (his word) can best be countered by the schools where humane considerations may be conserved. He is equally aware that there is a Utopian fallacy that schools can cure all ills and right all wrongs. This notion is attacked with the same incisiveness as was the technical thesis; and such matters as sex education, prayer in schools, and psychotherapy in schools are given short shrift.

By this stage, Postman has managed to assault every major sacred cow in the

---

Bert Horwood is on the Faculty of Education, Queen's University, Kingston, Ontario.

educational field. The impression might be very negative except for the thermostatic theme. The role of a thermostat is to control the temperature somewhere by turning off a heater when the temperature is too high, or by turning it on if too cold. A thermostat, like Postman, is never satisfied for long in a dynamic system. He does provide a series of interesting suggestions by which schools might have the kind of cultural thermostatic effects needed to offset the other biases. One powerful suggestion, premised on the idea that a curriculum ought to have coherence, is that schools should adopt a curriculum that is essentially historical. The *Ascent of Man* curriculum, named from the remarkable TV series and book of that title by Jacob Bronowski, would enable students to find the roots of their culture through thoughtful and critical study of all of the accomplishments of humanity: arts, sciences, explorations, governments, philosophies, religions. The thrust of this idea is not to teach as facts a selected set of instances from the past, but rather to practise students in the same kinds of thinking that have brought us from earliest times to our present state. Under such a scheme students should have a sense of the whole scope of human experience and be able to see themselves in ways other than shadows of television images.

Postman also provides substantial suggestions for a "conserving" curriculum that would emphasize the study of language as a way of getting knowledge. Unlike back-to-basics proponents, he argues for studies in language that go far beyond fundamental communication and literacy. His position is nothing short of letting kids in on the epistemological implications of language. Similarily, he argues that the social implications of language should be explored fully and profoundly in the language curriculum. Finally, there should be an education in the media. Postman pictures this as a critical analysis of the values and structures within the information businesses today. He suggests, to give one example, a comparison of the implicit messages in television programs and commercials. This is not to generate curriculum for the sake of being "with it," but is to use the power generated by the previous curriculum ideas to counteract the pervasive and otherwise hidden TV curriculum. Postman rounds out his set of proposals by describing classroom and evaluative practices which are compatible with the main thesis that schools should conserve and stabilize.

All of this is written in an eminently readable style. The arguments are well supported, the proposals clearly exemplified. Postman is deliberately provocative but in a cheerful good-humored way that keeps the book from being heavy. In a few places he trips over his own cybernetic model, but these inconsistencies are only minor drawbacks in an otherwise well-crafted work. I heartily recommend it as good reading for those interested in participating in the debate about the appropriate directions for education.

Now let's give the last word to Postman himself (p. 12):

> ".... I have tried to make my argument clear, and I should be very interested to know what its refutations are, for that is how conservation begins. Perhaps we do not require a new 'movement' after all. Only a good conversation."

BOOK REVIEW

by PETER T. KLASSEN

Growing up Suburban, by Edward A. Wynne, University of Texas Press, 237 pp., $10.95, 1977

Growing up suburban is an experience that has been possible only in the recent past. In an attempt to give the best to their children, parents have moved to clean, open spaces in suburban tracts. In the process, their environment has changed from one of diversity to homogenized sameness and restricted access. It may be considered heresy to say "the king has no clothes", but this homogeneity is developing a new group of socially and culturally deprived, the suburban raised youth.

In his book, Ed Wynne tries to address the effect of suburbia on youth development. I found Wynne's preface very accurate in appraising the value of the book.

> "It is likely that this book will quickly become obsolete. It is an early work on an important, dynamic subject that will inevitably become the focus of growing concern. And, as an early work, it may be surpassed by future events, more data, and increasingly refined analyses. Still, there must be a starting place."

According to Wynne, of the twelve hundred entries in a current bibliography on suburbia, only ten percent relate to education, and amazingly, only five to ten of the entries even touch on the relationship between the suburban social and physical environment and the child-rearing patterns in suburban neighborhoods and schools.

Growing Up Suburban is a starting place for looking at that relationship between suburban life and the environmental influences on education. During his opening chapter, Wynne clearly states the concern.

> "As children mature, they should attain increasing competency in meeting the challenges of adult life: finding satisfying work, earning a living, initiating and carrying through a successful marriage, raising healthy children, maintaining friendships and participating in community life. We should not assume that competency in meeting such challenges is necessarily related to academic skills — beyond some minimal level. In other words, prolonged attendance in typical modern schools and college is not enough. To really achieve such competency, children, adolescents must be raised in environments that stimulate them to develop adaptive and realistic attitudes, significant coping skills, and the potential for judicious and profound commitment."

With this strong opening Wynne continues to list symptoms and problems which support his position that we need to worry about the perceptions of youth growing up in the suburban environment. He compares the current suburban setting with traditional rural and urban settings. His conclusion: "Children in post-industrial suburbs are uniquely isolated from diversity."

One of the basic competencies needed in adult life, Wynne emphasizes, is the need to negotiate, compromise, and work in cooperation with others. As the antithesis of this social competency, Wynne sees suburban schools where students may achieve very well on cognitive skills, on individualized instruments and tests, but have extremely limited learning experiences that help develop skills in working in communities and in accepting the need to compromise one's personal desires in order to recognize others' personal desires.

Moving from description of the problems to suggestions for solution, Wynne presents the example of students working on the production of a play. The remainder of the book presents some interesting considerations of the fundamentals and functions of community, discipline and a role for student volunteers.

In his section on volunteer activities as an important learning experience, Wynne develops clear, strong support both in terms of developing community and the effect service has on participants' self concept after the extended dependency of suburban adolescents.

However, Wynne finds it hard to break out of the confines of "school." The idea that suburban school environments could include the diversity of the real world is left undeveloped. The diversity of the world and the need to cooperate that made the urban and rural environment such a rich learning environment is not included as a resource for students' use through outdoor education, work cooperatives, and the wide variety of experiential programs. Instead, Wynne spends time developing rationale for enriching the ceremonial recognition of students and faculty and making graduation meaningful through final tests before graduation.

Wynne provides us a clear summary of the current state of suburban education and its environment; the difficulties which we face and the needs of its students when we focus beyond the cognitive skills and test scores. During the second part of his book, Wynne seems to lose sight of the connection between a diverse, multifaceted living environment and the potential for experientially enriching the learning of students through using out of "school" resources and experience. While I may or may not agree with the proposed solutions and ideas, I found *Growing Up Suburban* worth reading; the first half for its description, and the second half for its stimulation in clarifying my own ideas as opposed to Wynne's solutions. I would recommend it as an important starting point for those involved in experiential education in the suburban setting.

PETER T. KLASSEN, is an instructor at the College of DuPage, Glen Ellyn, Illinois.

Books
IN REVIEW

Educating for a New Millennium: Views of 132 International Scholars, Harold G. Shane with M. Bernadine Tabler, Phi Delta Kappa Educational Foundation, Bloomington, Indiana, 1981. 160 pages.

Reviewed by Dan Conrad

"Everyone knows a great deal, we all know which way we ought to go and all the different ways we can go, but nobody is willing to move."

Over one hundred years ago Soren Kierkegaard thus chided his fellow Danes with a phrase that loses no pungency by being moved to our time and directed at our educational system. Article after article predicts the doom or depicts the gloom of American education. Study after study reports declining achievement and interest, the finding of 'no difference' for this or that method or school, the lack of relationship between success in school and success in life.

Expert panel after expert panel reviews all this and dutifully reports out its list of recommended reforms which it more or less compellingly urges upon us. Meanwhile, educational practice drifts listlessly backward becoming more like it used to be than it actually used to be. The reforms that are tried are such paltry antidotes to the problem as to be aptly characterized by an administrator-friend of mine as "rearranging the deck chairs on the Titanic." The inability or unwillingness to act on our own information and to follow our own advice is surely one of the more baffling wonders of our age.

Among the reforms urged by commentators

Dan Conrad *teaches at the University of Minnesota and is affiliated with the Children's Theatre Company and School in Minneapolis.*

and commissions, none is more commonly recommended than that education be made more real, more involving, more experiential. The idea that young people need to leave their straight-backed chairs and vault the ramparts of their sterile compounds to wrestle with real-world problems reverberates like a shepherd's horn in the Alps. The Report of the President's Science Advisory Panel headed by James Coleman, the NASSP report on American Youth in the Mid-Seventies, the National Commission on the Reform of Secondary Education, the National Task Force on Citizenship Education, the Office of Education study on The Education of the Adolescent, the Phi Delta Kappan task force on The New Secondary Education, the Carnegie Council on Higher Education, Alvin Toffler in Learning for Tomorrow — and more — all plea for educational methods that involve students in direct and engaging experiences in the real world outside the school. Now Shane and Tabler add their recommendations for reform and give headline billing to the suggestion of "extending learning into the real world" and promoting "genuine student participation in society's problems and processes."

Readers of this Journal who are pure experiential learners and cannot bear the thought of reading another book on education — or even a review of one — but who need basic reinforcement for their view can stop at this point. *Educating for a New Millennium* can legitimately be cited in your next report or proposal as offering support for a call for more experiential education. It's authors do it, however, from a more interesting base than underlies most educational anlysis. It is that base which makes their argument for experience unique and compelling.

The book is subtitled: "Views of 132 International Scholars" — which is what it purports to be and at least partially is. The idea behind the study and book is the sort that makes the reader

Educational practice drifts listlessly backward becoming more like it used to be than it actually used to be.

wish he'd thought of it first. The authors were commissioned to find out and summarize what distinguished scholars in the natural and social sciences are concerned about these days and ask them to identify the concepts in their fields "that young people should understand if they are to survive in the troubled years ahead... and need to learn in order to live more humanely with their fellow citizens."

The persons interviewed represent a kind of "Who's Who" of international scholarship: Albert Baundra in psychology; Geoffrey Barraclough and Lawrence Cremin in history; Hughes de Jouvenal in law; Edward T. Hall in anthropology; Duncan Macrae, Jr. in political science; E. O. Wilson in science; Walter Heller in economics; and 124 more from all parts of the world.

The first half of the book summarizes the views of these persons and is by far the most compelling part of the book. Their view of the future gives little cause for comfort: "as the world begins more and more to resemble a ricocheting bullet as it careens from disaster to disaster." The dangers listed are already present: global conflict, terrorism, hunger, increasing pollution, inequality, overpopulation, competition for depleted resources, threat of nuclear holocaust, unstable economies, thought control, and the strain which all of these place on democratic ideology and institutions.

There is scant evidence here of a sanguine hope that the problems caused by technology will be readily solved by the routine application of more technology. Rather the call is for a realistic appraisal of the fix we're in, for greater understanding of the workings and effects of technology, for values that promote survival, and for the knowledge and skill and will to deal with our problems and prospects imaginatively, humanely, and productively. The central dilemma is identified as "that almost everyone wants to get more than they have" with the attendant requirement that we must, as psychobiologist W. Jackson Davis is quoted as saying:

> ...move forward, not backward, into a simpler life. We are going to face the future without as much energy, but with a population that has been generated by energy. If we don't change our values, then the depletion of energy and resources will do it for us.

The mission of education, in the face of the alarming potential for global disaster, has seldom been more movingly expressed than it is here by the French jurist Hughes de Jouvenal:

> Our goals for education should not be to turn out cogwheels, but to develop in each child the richness of his humanity, potential for self-realization, and social skills. Or as Immanuel Kant said, to help him to achieve 'all the perfection of which he is capable.' The future challenges us to create an apprenticeship in acquiring an entirely new mode of thinking.

There are many other issues discussed: the need for an "anticipatory curriculum," for understanding and valuing interdependence, for literacy in science and facility in the scientific method, for a sense of history and a willingness and capacity to examine values. But most of all it is an urgent call for an educational program that gives students the blunt truth about the seriousness of our situation and provides the knowledge, skill, and will to creatively and effectively act on what we know.

This is where experiential education comes in. It is the peculiar merit of this approach that it takes

"Half a good book is certainly better than none."

people out of the passive and circumscribed student role, provides practice in creative problem solving, presents real moral dilemmas, gives people the chance to test themselves against challenges that matter, involves them in new relationships and unfamiliar cultures, requires people to take responsibility for their own actions, and calls for what Herbert Thelen termed "the humane application of knowledge."

The potential for experiential learning is not lost on the authors or panelists. They urge that "real world experiences must become an integral part of schooling in the future" and quote, amongst others, Erik Wilkerson of the University of Glasgow to the effect that:

> We need to stop thinking of schooling as preparation for life. It is necessary for students to accept an apprenticeship in the affairs of society so that they can get inside what's going on and be involved in the perpetual struggle to improve society.

That pretty much sums up the first half of the book and just a bit from the second. It's unfortunate that there is a second half, for the remainder is as soporfic and conventional as the beginning is fresh and challenging. There is the usual revision of the Cardinal Principles and the call for a new paradigm for education (what would we do without Kuhn?). The latter is complete with distracting diagrams, flow charts with feedback loops, and the *di rigueur* cubic representation of the relationship of everything to everything.

By the time one has waded through the sample lists of goals it is harder than ever to figure out how any of this — including the (diagramed) call for regional centers of educational consultants — has to do with the views (and the passion) of those nearly forgotten 132 scholars. If one perseveres to the last chapter one is rewarded by encountering enigmatic generalizations ("The sciences... bring order out of enormous quantities of data, a process that transmutes them to arts"), oddly-worded entreaties ("social justice must be improved"), ominous enjoinders ("learners must be protected from the effects of 'junk information'"), and amusing malapropisms ("we can stand back and take a *Weltenschauung*... of the globe in all its aspects").

The awkward educationese of the second half of the book does not negate the value of the rest, but clearly diminishes it some. The gulf between the two parts made this reader wonder if the authors were impelled to these recommendations by what they learned from the interviews — or if they were filling up space with a random sampling of their own predilections. At the least one wishes that proportionately more space had been allotted to the information and ideas gleaned from the interviews.

This is a reasonably good book that might have been outstanding. But, come to think of it, even a reasonably good book on education is a rarity nowadays — and half a good book is certainly better than none. For this reader it has provided some useful ammunition, as in: "in a summary of the views of 132 international scholars it is recommended that...." But it does more. It (the first half) challenges you to examine why you do what you do, suggests high stakes and a critical mission for education — and dares you to accept it.

That our world is in critical danger, that education must be revitalized and reformed, that experiential approaches to learning must be a part of the reform — all this has been said before. But it needs to be said again, again, and again until more people are "willing to move."

Guest Editorial: Becoming "High-Risk" Educators

by Maryann Hedaa, C.N.D.

The 1970s ended with headlines that spoke out loud of our dilemmas and struggles with human values. Major papers proclaimed: 11 DEAD IN CINCINNATI AND THE BAND PLAYED ON, and editorials commented on the fact that there were few choices left to prevent mob violence. New York's **Village Voice** welcomed the Christmas season with a headline "suited to the selfish spirit of our epoch: REMEMBER THE GREEDIEST!" During the same week **Time** magazine honored India's Mother Theresa and her gentle efforts to help the poor of the world. Loren Eisely captured the "end of a decade spirit" when he wrote, "We find ourselves with one foot poised at the threshold of the stars and with almost limitless power at our command, yet we tremble over that which we created." So, we approach the 1980s trying to reconcile the polarization of human values: self-survival versus compassion; power versus powerlessness; action versus reflection; isolation versus involvement; individualism versus service; observation versus participation; materialistic acquisitiveness versus voluntary simplicity; outer appearance versus inner realities. Where in this paradox of human values are those risk takers willing to speak out—touching compassion, involvement and service? Where are those risk takers willing to act—to risk love and compassion across the barriers of race, economic status, popular opinion, religion and personal comfort?

During the past decade, the experiential education movement has fostered an approach to learning that involved elements of risk taking, interpersonal relationships in a community setting, reflection on direct actions, and a high level of student participation. The 1970s witnessed the emergence of a wide variety of experiential learning programs that served diverse populations in areas throughout North America.

The decade before demands that we move beyond the elements of our programs. No longer can we merely stress the merits of high-risk education, we must become high risk educators who are willing to assume the risk in speaking out—of compassion, involvement and service.

As high-risk educators, we will challenge ourselves to remain an educational community rather than become an educational commodity. We will resist becoming another large-scale educational institution in the sense that we become resistant to change—self-perpetuating, dehumanized, and seeing our movement as an end rather than as a means to an end. As high-risk educators, we will challenge the current and popular "banking system" of education, whereby education becomes an act of depositing knowledge, in which students are depositories and the teacher is the depositor. We will challenge both the public and private sectors of education that foster "a culture of silence" among our young. We must continue to offer experiential programs that will challenge young people to "an energetic participation" in dealing with their own lives, learning and decision making.

The task of the experiential educator in the 1980s will be to challenge public institutions to become more responsive to human needs and values and to remember what a human person really is. E.F. Schumacher states it beautifully in **A Guide to the Perplexed:** "First of all, we come from a spiritual level into this earth. We are from a Creator Spirit. Secondly, we are social beings, we don't come alone. We are put in a social context. And third, we are an incomplete being. We have been sent to complete ourselves. As a spiritually arrived at being, we are called to love a Creator Spirit. As a social being, we are called to love our neighbor. And as an incomplete being, we are called to love ourselves. If these human needs are not fulfilled—persons become unhappy, destructive, isolated, confused, vandals and maniacs."

The Buddhists have a nice expression: "Buddhism is the finger pointing at the moon. The moon is the thing, Buddhism simply directs your attention to it." So with us, experiential education is simply a finger pointing at the moon.

Sister Maryann Hedaa, C.N.D. is Program Director of Urban Adventures, a new experiential learning program for special populations in New York City.

Books in Review

Mindstorms
Seymour Papert
New York: Basic Books, 1980

Reviewed by

Peggy Walker Stevens

Experiential educators are often heard claiming that they improve students' problem-solving abilities. Meanwhile, at every educational level in the United States, there is increased talk of such topics as brain growth, critical thinking, problem-solving skills taught with and without computers, and the development of high level thought processes in "gifted and talented" students. Harvard Graduate School of Education held a large conference on the topic last summer and turned away hundreds of people for lack of space. Most of the major education journals and magazines have devoted a recent issue to the topic of thinking skills and many curriculum materials are being repackaged under the claim that they teach problem-solving and critical thinking.

How does the philosophy and practice of experiential education fit in with all this? Do we indeed improve students' problem-solving and thinking skills and, if so, how? Can the use of computers for teaching problem-solving be experiential?

I have become interested in these and related questions and would like to share a review of one book which set me to thinking about thinking. At the end of the review, I have listed other books about thinking and problem-solving skills. If you read one of them, please share it by writing a short book review (300-600 words). In fact, reviews of thought-provoking books are always welcome. Just send them to the AEE office.

****

Seymour Papert is a mathematician at M.I.T. who has developed a computer language for children which is called LOGO. Papert feels that subjects like higher mathematics and physics seem difficult and foreign to most people because they have no experience base upon which to draw in order to help them make sense of these subjects. He sees the computer as a powerful tool for allowing young people to have concrete experiences with concepts that have always been abstract.

Before reading *Mindstorms,* I had never even turned on a computer. After reading the book, I bought two more copies to share with friends and signed up for the only computer course that I could find (70 miles away) which included LOGO.

Children use LOGO to program the computer to draw pictures. In learning how to command the computer to do what they want, they learn many principles of geometry. For example, I watched third graders trying to get the computer to draw a square. The easiest set of commands would have been to type into the computer:

FD 50 (tell the arrow to go forward 50 tiny steps)
RT 90 (tell the arrow to make a 90° turn)
FD 50 (tell the arrow to go forward 50 tiny steps in the new direction)
RT 90 (tell the arrow to make a 90° turn)
FD 50 etc.

However, third graders don't know that a square has four 90° (right) angles. I watched a group of them form a square by typing in:

FD 50 (tell the arrow to go forward 50 tiny steps)
RT 5 (tell the arrow to make a 5° turn)
RT 5 (tell the arrow to make another 5° turn)
(Repeat the instruction "RT 5" another 15 times)

Eventually, one member of the group had the insight to suggest that they could say RT 90 once instead of RT 5 eighteen times. No one told these children that a square has a 90° angle; they learned it through direct experience, by trial and error problem-solving.

This is only the simplest of examples of what children can learn to do with LOGO. Two eighth grade boys who had been doing LOGO for only two months showed me a program that had sperm whales spouting water as they moved across the computer screen, and two girls let me see their program called "French Lace" which featured 10 colors racing around the screen at once with an intricate and delicate pattern the final result. Again, in both of these examples, students were able to concretely experience concepts that had previously been abstract ideas.

Advocates of LOGO make sometimes startling claims about the impact computers can have on education when they are used to let children improve their problem-solving skills. Among the more conservative statements was that of the school superintendent in the district where I observed the children programming in LOGO. "These students will never need to take geometry when they get to high school," she told me. "But don't tell the high school math teachers I said that."

I feel that it is important to admit that I couldn't finish reading *Mindstorms*. Papert describes how advanced students of LOGO will learn physics concepts such as velocity through direct problem-solving experiences on the computer. Never having had a course in physics, his ideas became too complex for me. Still, I recommend the book to anyone interested in teaching computers experientially. As a colleague who runs an experiential program for high school students with a variety of emotional, motivational, and learning problems told me, "As good as the results are that I get from the ropes course, I get better results from using computers." Reading *Mindstorms* is a good way to begin exploring the potential of computers for your students.

****

Other Suggested Books on Thinking Skills
Lateral Thinking by Edward de Bono.
New York: Harper and Row, 1970.
Conceptual Blockbusting by James L. Adams.
New York: W.W. Norton and Co., 1980.

X. Higher Education

Impelled into Experience: The United World Colleges

by David Sutcliffe

"We can scarcely hate any one that we know" - William Hazlitt.

"L'education peut tout" - Helvetius

The thoughtful international educator may not wish to swallow Hazlitt or Helvetius whole, but he cannot deny his critical dependence on experiential education.

International Education

Derek Heater, in his book *World Studies*, has carefully analyzed four different dimensions of international education.
1. the "objective" study of relations between nation-states,
2. the study of the interrelatedness of world affairs,
3. the "Domesday" model which emphasizes the "perilous condition of the world, the imminence and

---

David Sutcliffe is Headmaster of the United World College of the Adriatic, Trieste, Italy.

immanence of universal ecological or nuclear suicide,"
4. the "integrated" model which, with the aid of psychology, sociology and politics, sheds light on conditions that foster peace at all individual and community levels of human activity.

Sharply clear, the moment one advances beyond the first model, is that we are concerned with values and the formation of attitudes, that international education is morally committed. Committed, however, to which priorities and whose ideals?

The problems are not far to seek!

Professor T.H.B. Symons, Vanier Professor of Trent University, Canada, speaking at the Thirteenth Congress of the Universities of the Commonwealth in 1983, commented that we are, towards the end of the Twentieth Century, still dealing with the same three basic questions that concerned John Ruskin and the great socio-cultural thinkers of the Nineteenth Century:

1. the preservation of nature and of ecological balance, in the face of man's rapacity;
2. the exploitation of man, by man;
3. the exploitation of the less developed parts of the world by the more developed.

And now the nuclear threat infuses them all with the urgency that comes from our renewed awareness of living in an apocalyptic age.

All these issues are ultimately at the heart of all international education. International education is the chief hope and most probable instrument of their final resolution.

Mixing young people together at an impressionable age from diverse, deeply different traditions, cultures, races, religions, is a bold gesture of confidence in their ability to work out new values without loss of personal or cultural identity. As international educators, we make assumptions when we bring them together, but it is for them, not us, to determine these new values.

Students from India and Italy on a Social Service visit.

The United World Colleges

Kurt Hahn, the founder and spiritual father of the United World Colleges, was quite clear about the essential value of experience: "It is immoral to coerce young people into opinions, but it is negligent not to impel them into experience." Of course we cannot ingenuously claim that we are entirely neutral in the experiences which we arrange. In my judgement the success and the strength of the United World Colleges lie in their clear statement of aims and the uniformly high motivation of their students.

The concept was born when Kurt Hahn, in the mid-fifties, visited the NATO Defense College, then in Paris. If middle-aged military officers, enemies a few years earlier, could within six months achieve such a strong sense of shared commitment, how much more could be done with younger people over a longer period! Sixteen to nineteen was judged to be the "magical age" - when boys and girls, growing into adulthood, are thirsty for new experience, adventurous, idealistic, open to change, still free of the pressures of career choice and specialization, responsive to challenge and to trust, aware of their roots, yet young enough to accept the disciplines of residential community life, and the comprehensive demands of an educational programme which would stretch them intellectually and emotionally beyond anything they had yet dreamed of.

The Atlantic College was founded in 1962. Five Colleges have followed - The UWC of South East Asia, (1972), Lester Pearson College of the Pacific, Canada (1974), UWC of Southern Africa, Swaziland (1979), UWC of the American West, New Mexico (1982) and the UWC of the Adriatic, (also 1982).

UWC students are aged between 16 and 19. They come from 100 different countries to spend their last two years of high school before entry to university and further education. Entry is by special selection and scholarship. Committed in principle before their arrival to the UWC ideals, they find them tested, proven, and in almost all cases strengthened, in two years of intensive experience.

An Education in Attitudes

It is an education in attitudes. "A classroom approach to the instilling of ideals is absolutely ineffective save in the case of the altogether outstanding educator," wrote Atlantic College's first Headmaster, Desmond Hoare, perhaps a shade dogmatically! The Colleges value and stress hard intellectual effort - the competitive nature of university entry world-wide leaves them little choice in the matter - but the lessons to be learned from shared experience, in the dormitories, on the playing fields, in cultural activities, but above all in the "rendering of trained service to those in need," are the key-notes of the UWC philosophy. The law of the situation creates its own rules - young people respond to reality and to need. "There are three ways of trying to capture the young. One is to preach at them - that is a hook without a worm. The second is to coerce them and to tell them "You **must** volunteer" - that is of the devil. The third is an appeal which never fails: "You are needed." (Kurt Hahn).

Service

The students at Atlantic College man coast rescue services on the dangerous Bristol Channel coastline and have saved 160 lives since 1962; students at Pearson College are the crews for lifeboats and mountain rescue patrols; students in New Mexico provide wilderness patrols; students at all the United World Colleges undertake social service with the needy, the physically and mentally handicapped, the elderly, the young in trouble with the law. In seeking to develop active qualities of compassion, we are engineering a "confrontation to undesirable human attitudes." The experience is international. No country has a monopoly of compassion. No country is free of social problems. Comradeship and inter-personal understanding come, not from being together, but from doing things together.

"The United World Colleges are a bridge between home and the world, between the single loyalty to one's own country and the twin loyalties to country and mankind."

Academic Programme

The academic programme of these Colleges, the International Baccalaureate, is unusual in the remarkable degree of its acceptance world-wide for university entry. It is probably unique in its CASS requirement - Creative, Aesthetic and Social Service - under which all students are obliged to engage in community service each week to qualify for the final Diploma. Launched experimentally in the mid-1960's, now offered at some 200 schools world-wide, and with a growth rate of about 25% annually, the Diploma requires students to follow six courses over two years, three at Higher Level (strong Advanced Placement standard), three at the Subsidiary Level. They must include the mother language and literature, a foreign language, the study of man (history, philosophy, economics), a natural science, mathematics, the sixth option being art or music, or a second foreign language, a second science or a second study of man subject. The principle is one of choice within a given framework. All however also follow a compulsory common course in the Theory of Knowledge, and all must submit an "Extended Essay" of some 4000 words on an individual topic drawn from one of their six main courses. The United World Colleges are a bridge between home and the world, between the single loyalty to one's own country and the twin loyalties to country and mankind. The International Baccalaureate is the bridge from the secondary school to the university. Is it conceivable that the Carnegie Commission could have made its report without reference to it?

The Acorn and the Oak Tree

It requires powerful devotion to belief in the power of the acorn to grow into an oak to think that six colleges, with an output of some 900 graduates a year, will have much influence on the pressing problems of the world. But about the existence of "international education" on a much wider scale there can be no doubt. What however of its content, its purpose and achievements? Can the United World Colleges offer a few markers on the way forward?

I think of the young Chinese student in Atlantic College who left an economics class in protest because what was being taught was not "economics"; his classmates took up matters vigorously with him over lunch - the most silent but most attentive listener at the table was his teacher of economics. I think of the Ethiopian boy, one of a family of 13, all on the borderline between survival and starvation, who spent two years at the Adriatic College unable to visit his parents or even to communicate his experience, because they are illiterate - he was even unable to visit them in the interval between UWC and taking up a scholarship in Canada in engineering because of military service which would have involved him in war with the country of a College friend - he sent his Japanese roommate to Ethiopia to assure his parents that all was well with him. I can compare the stunned bewilderment of our American students in 1963 at Kennedy's death with the tears of our Indian students when Mrs. Ghandi was assassinated. I remember how our students in Wales taught deaf and dumb young people the techniques of scuba diving, so that, with their rapid sign language, these young people found themselves for the first time in their lives enjoying an advantage over their fellows; or our students in Italy helping the adult mental patients in a hospital to prepare masks for Carnival so that they, too, could take part for once on equal terms. Alison, a young delinquent with a hopeless family background, was spending eight weeks at Atlantic College on a special course. One of our American students, Elizabeth, was her personal tutor. One afternoon, Alison decided on dramatic suicide. Seating herself at the cliff edge, she refused all entreaties to come back, letting herself go further and further over the 90 foot drop. "Fetch Elizabeth quickly". Elizabeth came, and, with that special authority which 18 year olds have over those two or three years younger (usually so much greater than that of professional social workers): "Don't be silly, Alison. Come with me". Alison scrambled up and walked off with Elizabeth, taking her hand.

I recall a young Israeli of stubborn, dogmatic views at Atlantic College who found that he was to spend his second year sharing rooms with a German. He fought this situation bitterly until I told him that he must either accept it or leave the College. Eighteen months after he had completed his examinations, he wrote to me -

"In Atlantic College I lived among folks of 51 different countries and there I found that I felt closer to the Arabs than to people of any other nation. Now I can point myself out as one of the few Israeli who **understands** the Palestinians and Arabs - we Israeli ex-students, people in conflict with other nations, have strong national feelings alongside a longing for peace and an end to our sufferings."

As the Falkland crisis

> "No country has a monopoly of compassion. No country is free of social problems. Comradeship and inter-personal understanding come, not from being together, but from doing things together."

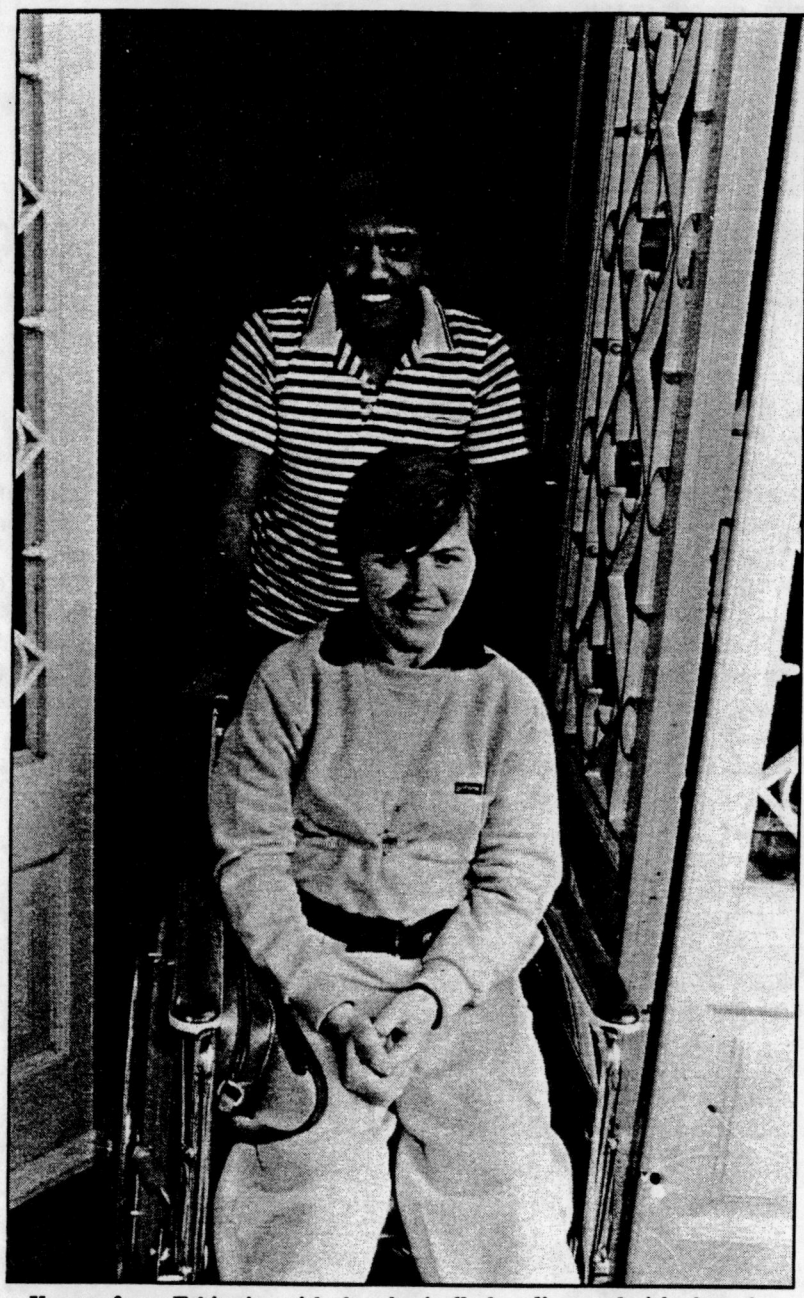

Kenzu, from Ethiopia, with the physically handicapped girl whom he visited each week during his two years in Italy.

developed in the South Atlantic, I received a letter from an Argentinian ex-student studying in the United States: He wrote:

"During this last week, I've been receiving very distressing news from my country. All young men born in 1962 have been called into the army. Most of my friends are under arms.

As you may see, I'm forced to choose - either defend my country if need be or follow my deeply entrenched principle of internationalism. As an ex-student of Atlantic College the latter should be the option, but as a national of Argentina the former path seems more appropriate. During this week's turmoil, my Atlantic College experience has been dominant. I will never be able to put up a finger against UK, which received me and kept me so well whilst I was a student at A.C.

My doubt is, how strong can my feelings be for international understanding, if war is declared and my friend and relatives are ordered to fight. This is followed by a second doubt, namely how practical is it, in the short term, to think about the ideals so cherished by the UWC organization? In the long term, I have no doubt, they will succeed, but what sort of sacrifices are we expected to make so that these ideals become realities?"

Shakespeare's King Lear cried out to the blinded Gloucester on the heath: "You see how the world goes," and Gloucester answered: "I see it feelingly."

Can we teach our young people, with Gloucester, to "see the world feelingly?" This, surely, must be the mission of international education as a whole, as it is already of the United World Colleges.

STUDENT ORIENTATION IN WILDERNESS SETTINGS

by

Michael A. Gass
Pamela J. Kerr
University of New Hampshire

I. INTRODUCTION

As an established institution in American society, higher education has played an extremely influential role in shaping the lives of its participants. Not only do colleges and universities positively affect the vocational futures of students, but also their intellectual, emotional, moral, and social growth (Ramist, 1981). Both entrance into and graduation from college are seen as major accomplishments in an individual's life. The experiences gained from attending college, both academic and non-academic, are often viewed as the maturing processes that develop and shape the future lives of individuals.

While higher education does hold a valuable position in our society, it is also a separate society in itself, with its own rules, values, social groups, and expectations. Adjustment to the environment of college can be extremely difficult, as stated by Astin (1975) in the following passage:

> "The influence of college is pervasive, especially for the 18-year-old leaving home for the first time. The freshman is at once deprived of the influence of parents and confronted with relationships that may be based on remarkably different beliefs and backgrounds. Sex, drugs, alcohol, and political activisim loom as opportunities or threats, and the student may experience the first real challenge to his or her academic skills. College can change (in the four-year period) values, attitudes, aspirations, beliefs, and behavior."
>
> (pp. 5-6)

Colleges and universities have generally referred to the difficulty students have in adapting to college as "freshman stasis" or the "retarding effect on a freshman of the cultural shock of entering a college or university following the more controlled environment of school or home which generally contributes to poor academic performance." (International Dictionary of Education, 1977)

II. ORIENTATION PROGRAMS

In an attempt to combat freshman stasis and assist in the ongoing development of students at institutions of higher learning, colleges and universities have been involved in providing entering and ongoing orientation programs since 1888 (Bonner, 1972). Traditional orientation programs have continued since that time to represent the most common method used by universities for assisting incoming students in their adjustment to the college environment. The methods used most often in these programs have taken on the form of university credit and non-credit courses, programs designed to involve significant others with the student and/or advising/preschool sessions.

While the popularity of such programs exists, there are a number of major concerns pertaining to the validity and the effects of college orientation efforts. For example, orientation programs have been criticized for lacking the intensity to influence students to perceive or integrate material for use in adjustment (Oppenheimer, 1984). Baker and Nisenbaum (1979) have also pointed out that many students use programs for social purposes and their ability to teach actual transitional skills is limited beyond this single focus.

In order to provide more effective methods of student orientation, a number of schools have implemented alternative or supplementary programs. One such type of program is the wilderness orientation program. Since the inception of the Dartmouth program in 1935, over forty institutions of higher learning have implemented programs that utilize wilderness components (Gass, 1984). The reasons for these programs are quite different in focus. Some colleges use the program as a means to acquaint incoming students to the school's outing club program, whereas other institutions provide it as a means to insure a more positive transition to college life and a method of reducing attrition.

While the foci of these programs do vary, most wilderness orientation programs have been developed with the same purpose in mind as traditional programs - to ease the transition of the student to college and provide a means of facilitating student developmental growth. And despite the fact that wilderness orientation programs purposely choose to place incoming college students in an environment quite different than traditional programs, the goals of both programs are also the same. In investigating the literature on traditional and wilderness orientation programs, the authors have generally found the following factors central to the mission of all orientation programs, whether they be traditional or alternative in structure:[1]

1) Attachment to a positive and meaningful peer group.
2) Significant interaction with faculty members (both in quality and quantity).
3) A clear focus on career development and major course of study.
4) A challenging and stimulating academic program.
5) Adequate preparation for college work.
6) Compatability between student expectations and

      university actualities.
7) Positive use of campus facilities and high involvement in campus activities.
8) Positive self-concept.

III. WHY OUTDOORS?

Given that the focus of orientation efforts are to provide programs that directly relate to some or all of these eight factors, why have some colleges and universities chosen to conduct their orientation efforts in a wilderness environment? While the specific answers to this question vary between institutions, most colleges and universities have found this environment more conducive in reaching the goals of their program. Some of this belief is embodied in a brief statement by Smith (1976).

> "Briefly, it is believed that the (Outward Bound) experience will be translated into changes in the participants' attitudes toward themselves and others. The participant will become more aware of his capabilities and limitations, will expand his capabilities, will more readily assert himself against the challenges from the environment, become more self-reliant and better able to deal with other people. There is further contention that the enhancement of these psychological characteristics has secondary effects on the achievements of participants. That is, the student or worker will do better in school or on the job, assume positions of leadership and demonstrate positive adjustment."

Using the elements of a model designed by Walsh and Golins (1976), another explanation can be presented which further illustrates the effect adventure experiences can have on individuals. While a more descriptive representation of the model occurs in their work, it basically illustrates that the elements of adventure experiences, when utilized in their unique physical and social environment, lead to a state of "adaptive dissonance." By dealing with these challenging tasks and the associated anxieties which accompany them, the indivdual adapts and changes. As stated by Walsh and Golins (1976):

> "The answer is deceivingly simple: the learner finds it rewarding to solve reasonable (i.e. concrete, manageable), and consequential problems holistically within a supportive peer group and in a stimulating environment. It makes one feel good about oneself and those who have assisted. Since the learner does not have the opportunity to master such problems ordinarily, he enlarges and has a more congruent perception of himself (reorganization of the meaning of experience). These new attitudes, values (affective skills) make us more likely equipped and ready to tackle

subsequent problems (reorganization of the
direction of experience). If one does something
he has wanted do which he could not, or has not
done before, he has reorganized the meaning or
significance of his experience or existence and
the ability to direct the course of subsequent
experience." (pp. 12-13)

The ultimate goal of this model, as well as other theories that describe the elements, interactions, and benefits of adventure experiences, is their relevance in the participant's future. It is quite obvious that these programs that do not transfer beyond the wilderness experience are extremely limited in educational value.

IV. PROGRAM MODELS

To illustrate the actual implementation of orientation programs that use the wilderness, two program models at the University of New Hampshire will be briefly described. The purpose of the Fireside Experience Program is to aid in the ongoing development of students while they are members of the university community. The focus of the Summer Fireside Experience Program is to assist students in their entrance and adjustment to the college environment.

A. THE FIRESIDE EXPERIENCE PROGRAM

History and Goals of the Program

In the late seventies, the University of New Hampshire began to perceive the need to take a more active role in the ongoing learning process of undergraduate students, especially in the areas of intellectual values, identity, and interpersonal development. Based on the knowledge of student developmental needs and the ability of adventure experiences to have a positive impact on individuals, the Associate Dean of Students at the University proposed and implemented the Fireside Experience Program. Unlike the existing University Outing Club, whose role was to teach outdoor skills and organize recreational outdoor trips, the Fireside Program was founded to meet two fundamental needs of the institution.:

1) Create an environment for students that would
help facilitate the acquisition of problem-
solving skills and employ a methodology which
focused on helping students learn how to think.

2) Provide a program that would have a positive
impact on the nature of a student's experience
at the institution, increasing student satisfaction, and aiding the development of cooperation various segments of the campus, students,
faculty, and staff.

Based on these needs, six goals were developed as the focus for all Fireside experiences. Each of these goals is presented below with a rationale focusing on the reasons for its implementation.

GOAL 1: To provide a forum for students, faculty, and staff to participate as co-learners in a vigorous learning environment.

RATIONALE: By bringing students together with faculty and staff members as co-learners, students gain the opportunity to be involved in the "process" of problem solving. In the traditional student/teacher relationship, students are often denied the opportunity to witness how a faculty member arrived at an answer. Fireside activities place participants in positions where they must make decisions as a group, analyze various options, and follow a plan.

GOAL 2: To encourage in students responsible behavior while working as a group member.

RATIONALE: The design of the Fireside Program dictates that participants exercise self-control, consideration of others, and good judgement related to understanding one's own strengths and limitations. The success of the experience is often the result of the cooperative posture of group members. The focus of these activities is the transfer after the experience has ended into other areas of the student's life where responsible behavior is required, thus contributing positively to the general life on campus (see Section V).

GOAL 3: To offer a wide variety of "vigorous learning environments"[2] to the university community.

RATIONALE: Many students who attend UNH have had limited exposure to an urban environment. These students may view a weekend in Boston or New York with a sense of fear and apprehension, similar to that which is exhibited by other students facing their first overnight in the wilderness. The Fireside Program recognizes that a student can learn in a variety of settings and that what may be a vigorous learning environment for one student may not be for another.

GOAL 4: To use the wilderness as a natural setting for the study of male/female roles.

RATIONALE: The wilderness provides an excellent setting for participants to gain an understanding of the limits inherent in traditional sex role stereotyping. The program encourages participants to transcend these limitations and explore new perspectives relative to the roles of men and women in a variety of settings.

GOAL 5: To provide non-alcoholic programs on weekends for students.

RATIONALE: Like many institutions of higher learning, the University of New Hampshire is continually involved in addressing the issue of alcohol in campus life. This has become especially true with the drinking age being raised to the age of twenty-one. The Fireside Program offers a non-alcoholic weekend experience for students and focuses on asking them to examine the role of alcohol in their lives (e.g. the reasons why the students use alcohol, the role of alcohol in relating to peers).

GOAL 6: To provide learning experience in leadership positions for students.

RATIONALE: Much of the education in the traditional school setting does include experiential components of learning. The Fireside Program places its staff into positions of involvement and responsibility that require problem-solving skills, intellectual growth, and practical application. Through the guidance of faculty, staff and participant observers, student leaders attain levels of development that would be impossible to achieve through passive forms of learning.

Structure and Administration of the Program

The Fireside Experience Program is administered through the Dean of Students Office and the Outdoor Education Program in the Department of Physical Education. Approximately sixteen to twenty-four weekend trips occur during the academic year. These trips take place in a variety of "vigorous learning environments" (e.g. sea canoeing in salt water bays, exploring and performing volunteer service in downtown Boston, rock climbing on precipitous granite cliffs) and consist of two student leaders, ten student participants, two faculty participants, and one participant observer.

The program is operated by a director funded through the Dean of Students Office. This individual is responsible for overseeing the twelve to fourteen Fireside student leaders and organizing weekly class sessions and one staff training per semester. Student leaders are awarded two credits per semester for a class entitled "Outdoor Leadership" offered through the Department of Physical Education. Requirements for the course consist of leading one or two trips a semester, attending staff trainings and weekly three-hour class sessions, and conducting two-hour seminars on leadership development. Each staff member must possess current defensive driving, CPR, and Advanced First Aid or EMT certifications.

Faculty in the Department of Physical Education support the program by assisting the Director, advising the student leaders, and offering feedback during pre-trip meetings. A participant observer, generally a former staff member, is also involved with each trip by offering feedback to the student leader.

B. THE SUMMER FIRESIDE EXPERIENCE PROGRAM

History and Goals of the Program

In 1982, based on the need to assist incoming students in their adjustment to the University and the success of the Fireside Program, the Summer Fireside Experience Program was developed. This five-day program is offered to incoming freshman students prior to their entrance into the University. It is somewhat different from the Fireside Program in two central aspects. First, the elements of the curriculum focus more specifically on the factors central to the mission of orientation programs stated earlier (e.g. attachment to a positive peer group, beneficial interaction with faculty members, preparation for college work). Second, since the needs of the entering student are different than those of the student already connected to the university community, the primary goals of the Summer Program are also differernt. Listed below are the goals of the Summer Fireside Experience Program and in parentheses, the activities that are used to reach these goals during the five-day program:

1) Present a variety of new and challenging tasks enabling each to set goals, make decisons, learn how to work with others and examine personal strengths and weaknesses. (Intitiative tasks, bushwacking, rock climbing, solo, night discussions, expedition planning, and goal setting sessions.)

2) Provide experiences which will place a premium on positive interaction with faculty members. (Long distance run, night discussions with a variety of faculty members, and rock climbing.)

3) Place students in an environment which will enable them to match personal expectations, plan for an intended major and thoughts concerning possible career plans with opportunities available to them at the University. (Solo, night discussions, and goal-setting sessions.)

4) Give students an awareness of how they cope in stressful situations and present comparisons to the University setting. (Rock climbing, backpacking, night discussions, initiative tasks, long-distance run, and solo.)

5) Provide the opportunity for students to begin a positive personal relationship with the University. (Service project, interactions with faculty.)

6) Provide the opportunity for students to begin healthy relationships with peers through

shared, challenging activities. (Initiative
tasks, expedition planning, rock climbing,
night discussions, and long-distance run.)

7) Plan activities which will increase an
individual's self-concept and their
responsibility for their own behavior. (Night
discussions, service project, rock climbing,
initiative tasks, camp responsibilities,
solo and expedition planning.)

<u>Structure and Administration of the Program</u>

Besides minor variations, the administrative structure of the Summer Fireside Experience Program is the same as the Fireside Experience Program offerd during the school year. While the Dean of Students Office and the Department of Physical Education jointly support this project, the student leaders instructing the trips are paid and do not receive academic credit for their services.

Along with the five-day program prior to school, a number of follow-up experiences are provided to strengthen the goals of the program. Some of these experiences include rock climbing reunion trips with faculty members one or two weeks into the first semester, and subsequent weekend experiences where goals set during the five-day experience are reviewed and revised if necessary. Informational materials are also mailed to students on areas discussed during the summer session (e.g. self-help materials, a description of the tutoring services available at the University).

V. TRANSFER INTO THE COLLEGE ENVIRONMENT

While both of the previously stated programs provide powerful learning experiences for participating students, the primary focus of these programs is the effect they have on the adjustment and ongoing development of the college student. Wilderness orientation programs without application or relevance to these two goals are of limited value. In planning such experiences, it is imperative that instructors/program directors implement the various elements of their wilderness activities based on how they will positively affect the orientation and developmental growth of the college student.

This effect of utilizing particular experiences to enhance future learning experiences is referred to as the transfer of learning, or simply, "transfer." Gass (1985) has identified the following techniques as ways that programs can enhance the transfer of learning from adventure experiences:

1) Design conditions for transfer before program
activites actually begin.

2) Create elements in the student's learning
environment similar to those elements likely
to be found in future learning environments.

3) Provide students with the opportunities to
practice the transfer of learning while
still in the program.

4) Have the consequences of learning be
natural--not artificial.

5) Provide the means for students to internalize
their own learning.

6) Include past successful alumni in the
adventure program.

7) Include significant others in the learning
process.

8) When possible, place more responsibility
for learning with the student.

9) Develop focused processing techniques that
facilitate the transfer of learning.

10) Provide follow-up experiences which aid in the
application of transfer.

Based on these techniques, both programs have implemented methods that focus on the transfer of learning elements into the college environment. Every activity within each adventure experience is structured to reach at least one of the stated goals of the respective program and to insure that the transfer of learning from this activity occurs. An example of this can be seen in the goal of positive peer interaction with the Summer Fireside Experience Program. Here activities such as initiatives and rock climbing are not done to make students better rock climbers. The main purpose of these activities is to create a strong group of peers to begin the school year with and learn the skills associated with developing strong, positive, and well-founded friendships in the college setting. As stated previously, a focused effort is made to transfer these behaviors from the wilderness experience where they were learned to the college environment they are entering.

VI. CONCLUSION

In an effort to assist students, colleges and universities continue to utilize orientation programs to aid in the adjustment and ongoing development of students. In exploring methods to improve these efforts, some institutions have implemented wilderness orientation programs.

An example of these efforts that use the wilderness include the Fireside and Summer Fireside Experience Programs at the University of New Hampshire. Initial research on these programs has shown their effectiveness in reaching their goals in student adjustment and development. Other positive findings have been reported by Stogner (1978) at Ferrum College and Hansen (1982) at the University of Missouri-Columbia. However, none of these studies have been replicated and their isolation exemplifies the lack of research on such programs.

If the true validity and potential of wilderness orientation programs are to be realized, a number of changes must occur in the present structure of these programs. It is the authors' contention that the following four suggestions can lead to wilderness orientation programs that are well-established and supported within their respective college and university structures:

1) Beginning and existing programs must familiarize themselves with the vast amount of information available on incoming and ongoing student orientation. Efforts must be made to synthesize appropriate elements from traditonal programs into approaches that utilize adventure experiences.

2) A stronger focus needs to be taken to insure the transfer of program elements from the wilderness into the student's college environment.

3) Greater efforts must be made in researching the validity and generalizability of these programs. Future research also needs to investigate the effects of different adventure experiences on students and how long the effects of these programs last.

4) Greater networking needs to occur between programs. The sharing of information, program techniques, and resources can only strengthen the ability of programs to reach their intended objectives.

BIBLIOGRAPHY

Astin, Alexander W. Preventing Students From Dropping Out. San Francisco, California: Jossey, Bass, 1975.

Baker, Robert W. and Nisenbaum, Steven. "Lessons From an Attempt to Facilitate Freshman Transition into College." Journal of American College Health Association, Blume 28, October 1979, pp. 79-80.

Bonner, Don. "Evaluating the Effects of Using Upperclassman Trained in Group Dynamics to Lead Small Process Freshman Orientation Groups." Washington, D.C.: National Center for Educational Research and Development (DHEW/OE), Regional Research Program, December 1972.

Calder, Cheryl, et. al. Fireside Manual. Durham, New Hampshire: University of New Hampshire, Second Edition, 1983.

Gass, Michael A. The Value of Wilderness Orientation Programs at Colleges and Universities in the United States. Durham, New Hampshire: University of New Hampshire, 1984. (ERIC Document Reproduction Service No. ED 242 471).

Gass, Michael A. "Programming the Transfer of Learning in Adventure Education." Journal of Experiential Education, Vol. 8, No. 3, Fall 1985.

Hassinger, James. Of Living and Learning. Durham, New Hampshire: University of New Hampshire, 1976.

Oppenheimer, Bruce T. "Short-Term Small Group Intervention for College Freshmen" Journal of Counseling Psychology, Volume 31, No. 1, 1984, pp. 45-53.

Ramist, Leonard. College Student Attrition and Retention. College Board Report No. 81-1. New York, New York: College Entrance Examination Board, 1981. (ERIC Document Reproduction Servic No. ED 200 170)

Walsh, Victor and Golins, Gerald. "The Exploration of the Outward Bound Process." Denver, Colorado: The Colorado Outward Bound School, 1976.

Are Good Teachers Born or Made?
A Canadian Attempt at Teacher Midwifery

by Bert Horwood

Most of us have a natural teaching method. It is a kind of personal composite of the teaching methods of our own teachers. Anyone who has watched children playing school has witnessed the process at work. The sum of these accidental influences, as filtered through individual personalities, yields the kind of teachers that folks say are born to it. If this chancy process is the only source of good teachers, then teacher education programs are mostly vain. But if the quality of a teacher can be influenced by intentional experiences and reflection, then teacher education has a critical function. Being a teacher of teachers, I hold the assumption that deliberate instruction can influence a teacher's future work. But I also recognize that this is accomplished with sufficient difficulty that birthing is an apt metaphor for the process of making teachers.

The problem is to devise a program which will purposefully promote the growth and development of young men and women to enhance their abilities and willingness to teach both in the natural, familiar ways **and** in ways other than those by which they were taught. Such intervention is absolutely necessary if a teacher is to be able to go beyond the influence of some sixteen years of conventional schooling. And further, the intervention must be of such a kind that empowers the student to become an independent and self-directing professional. The process of teacher birthing must not create intellectual or emotional dependency.

Bert Horwood is a member of the Faculty of Education, Queen's University, Ontario.

What are the general ingredients that could provide such a program? The candidates must aspire to the knowledge needed to teach experientially and be ready to make the effort. We demand that those who would influence the growth and development of others not evade their own growth and development. A program with this kind of challenge must be contrived so as to build progressively on prior experience and on the substantial body of knowledge and skill already present in the students. For experiential teachers to emerge, it is essential that the program practice what it teaches. It must be its own exemplar. The program becomes an extended rite of passage, a kind of birth process through which the natural impulse to grow is channelled and disciplined to yield persons able to operate independently on new levels. And in this respect, if not in much more profound ones, the educating of teachers in experiential modes is a kind of pedagogic midwifery. Our graduating teachers are both born and made.

The Program

In our jurisdiction, the majority of teachers are educated on a consecutive pattern. The intending teachers come to studies in education already holding a bachelor's degree, as a minimum. A one-year post-baccalaureate academic program including supervised practice teaching in schools yields the successful aspirant a further degree, the Bachelor of Education (B.Ed.), plus the government's teaching license. In our case we wanted to combine such a teacher education program with studies especially emphasizing the methods and values of outdoor and experiential education. Candidates were to be able to work effectively as professionals both in schools and in alternative settings like outdoor education centres, parks interpretive programs and social service agencies.

Fortunately, the Faculty of Education at Queen's University of Kingston, Ontario, provided fertile ground for the growth of such an enterprise. There, the B.Ed. Program already contained recognizable experiential components. For example, there was a service learning project required of all candidates and there were well-established electives in adventure education and in outdoor and experiential education. Another advantage was the presence on the faculty of Bob Pieh and Margueritta Kluensch, both of whom have strong commitments to the goals of the program and great experience in conceiving and starting innovative educational enterprises. Finally the Faculty appeared to be facing a probable shortage of applicants, and fresh programs likely to appeal to persons who might not otherwise be attracted to teacher education received administrative approval.

With these favorable circumstances in place, the Co-operative Program in Outdoor and Experiential Education (Co-op OEE) came to be. It was clear that the intent of the program provided a kind of double qualification which could not be fitted into the single academic "year" without making crippling substitutions. Therefore, the Co-op Program was designed to add components before and after the usual academic year (September to April).

Students register for the opening phase of the program on the first of May in any given year. There follows a ten-day residential orientation to experience-based education using wilderness and rural settings. A practice teaching experience is included. Students then scatter to their internship settings which constitute the first work experience component of the program. The internships placements are mostly arranged by the students themselves, subject always to faculty assistance and approval. Generally there are two internships through the summer. The first is commonly in a school-board operated outdoor centre for roughly six weeks. The second placements are more diverse, ranging from summer camps, parks and museums to adventure and adaptive programs for special populations.

Both internships are thoroughly supervised. The co-operating agencies provide an on-site supervisor who is closely connected to the student's work on a day-to-day basis. The faculty supervisors try to visit each site, geography permitting. Faculty members also monitor assignments in the form of weekly journal entries. A learning contract is set up by each intern to provide a combination of self-direction and accountability for the internships.

The first phase of the Program concludes with a five-day residential interval at the end of the summer to bring a degree of closure and to prepare for the start of the second, or B.Ed. phase. The second residential includes a major debriefing of the work experience and a solo. There is usually time, too, for some course counselling and other related work preliminary to beginning the fall term.

The B.Ed. phase completely fills the academic and practical requirements for basic

"There are encounters with a remarkable array of able experiential educators who dream dreams of excellence and then bring them to life."

teacher certification in the Province of Ontario. The usual foundational and curriculum studies, student teaching and service learning are included as the central core. Originally, all Co-op OEE students were required to have some academic background in environmentally related Sciences and included Environmental Science as a teaching subject in their B.Ed. schedules. Later this expectation was dropped. The Co-op Program takes advantage of electives in the B.Ed. offerings to provide students with special studies in group process, an outstanding course in curriculum design, and work in wilderness crisis management. The electives also provide a framework to continue weekly classes, including a shared meal, in the programs and methods of experiential education. All of this makes for a very full autumn and winter.

The Co-op Program concludes with a third

phase running immediately at the end of the winter term. This phase includes a mobile comparative study of experientially based programs and a final internship. The comparative study tours programs and institutions of proven quality and has features resembling an expedition. Staff and students travel in two vans for approximately three weeks on a loop including the States of New York, New Jersey, Connecticut, Massachusetts, Maine, New Hampshire, Vermont and then home. There are a multiplicity of outstanding programs, environments and people who hospitably agree to receive us. Urban and rural programs emphasize environmental education issues. Farms and schools integrate therapy and education. We meet folks in New York City and Gloucester, Mass. and the New Jersey Pinelands who cherish and promote their cultures in exciting ways. The visits provide vivid contrasts between schools in central Newark and the National Headquarters of Outward Bound Inc. And throughout them all, there are encounters with a remarkable array of able experiential educators who dream dreams of excellence and then bring them to life. The comparative study forms the climax and highlight of the Co-op Program.

The final internship, dangerously diffuse and anti-climactic, frequently works to enhance career development. Students often use the opportunity to test their competence in fields as yet untried. And it is common enough for the final internship to turn into longer term employment. The students are widely scattered all over North America and sometimes abroad at this time and the dispersion is basically terminal. No class has ever reconvened after the final internship.

In these ways, the usual teacher education program has been made into a kind of sandwich filling between an opening orientation and work experience phase and a final overview of practice in the field with terminal work experience. Graduates are armed with full teacher credentials and class-room competence as well as extensive practical and academic experience in other forms of experience-based education.

Conclusion

The chief value in any program description lies in generalizable lessons that it may have for others. The Co-op OEE Program at Queen's is unique for its combination of education for the schools and for alternative settings, with an experiential thrust, in a single coherent program. There seem to be several elements critical to success. First, is the absolute need for the program to be its own model. Nothing less carries conviction that experiential modalities are worth using. And nothing less reveals the fine balance that can be achieved among academic, social and personal considerations. Second, there must be a hospitable environment for the program. Not only must the home institution have the resources of staff and material, but a wide network of co-operating agencies is required for the internships. Third, the candidates must be widely recruited and carefully selected. There is delicate point of readiness that comes from the applicant's background and ambitions. Some persons may have a work history that would make much of the program redundant. Others may be inadequately prepared to make the most of the opportunities. Careful candidate selection using academic transcripts, resumes, references and personal interviews is vitally important. The ideal gender ratio is equal numbers of men and women. That goal is rarely achieved (of late, men are in short supply) but it is an important complication in the recruiting task.

Finally, this program illustrates the need for the kind of curriculum adaptation and compromise which does not violate the integrity of the competing models of teacher education. And in the adaptation, the students should not be squeezed in the competition for their time and energy. In making such accommodations we are adding another chapter to the fascinating, if uneasy, history of collaboration by academic institutions in experiential education. The collaboration is made more difficult in times of financial constraint.

The Co-op OEE Program is the realization of a vision of what experiential teacher education could be. Here, intellectual demands are integrated with personal and group challenges leading, sometimes painfully, to professional growth. The successful graduates are able to work in a variety of experiential settings. Whether born, made, or both, they are empowered to responsibly but vibrantly follow their own dreams.

PROBE: PROBLEM-BASED TEACHER EDUCATION

by

Richard J. Kraft, John D. Haas, and Homer Page
University of Colorado-Boulder

More than a few politicians, members of the general public, and even some teacher educators would suggest in 1986 that the title of this paper should be the Problems in Teacher Education, rather than Problem-Based Teacher Education. The Federal and State Governments have placed the reform of teacher education high on their agendas over the past few years and although the current critics may not be as strident as Lyons, who stated that "teacher education...is a sham, a mammoth and very expensive swindle of the public interest, a hoax, and an intellectual disgrace" (Lyons, 1979, p. 125), they are, nevertheless, seeking a major overhaul of the system.

Among the major reforms being discussed and implemented in various states are: the elimination of the undergraduate Education major (allowing only liberal arts subject majors), the movement of all basic teacher education to fifth-year programs (i.e. post-baccalaureate), "fast-track" entrance to the profession by "testing out" of required certification courses, the use of multiple tests for both entrance to and exit from teacher certification programs, recruitment of better quality teachers through scholarships and payback fellowships, new public school/university partnerships, and other organizational and structural reforms. Few of the political or educational reformers, however, have probed beneath the surface of these "convenient" policies that merely tinker with existing rules, regulations, and administrative structures. In their haste for the "quick fix," rarely do they confront the philosophical and methodological underpinnings of the teacher education process itself. Without examination of basic assumptions, it is doubtful that effective and lasting changes in teacher education programs will occur. What is more likely is a set of cosmetic, political alterations of present arrangements similar to those that emerged from A Nation at Risk -- longer school years and school days, more credits for high school graduation, more homework, and more frequent testing.

HISTORICAL BACKGROUND

Three years ago, prior to the current outcry over the need for reform in teacher education, the University of Colorado-Boulder (CUB) took a critical look at its program. After a year of careful analysis and planning, a new experimental design emerged which has come to be known as PROBE, an acronym for Problem Based Education.

Traditionally the teacher education program at the University of Colorado-Boulder has been similar to those found in most American colleges and universities, with theory preceding practice, courses in Educational Foundations and Psychology, General and Special Methods, Special Education, and Communications coming in advance of school-based student teaching.

During the late 1960s and early 1970s there were efforts at CUB to add more "humanistic" components to the program, which in turn was followed by an influx of Federal funds to implement a "module" approach to "competency-based teacher education." By the time of the school reform movements in the early 1980s, the CUB program had reverted to its traditional, course-based mode. These efforts, however, were not without some lasting changes. CUB abolished its undergraduate majors in Education in 1980, several years prior to the call to do so by many state and national commissions. It placed students in "alternative" student teaching settings in addition to traditional public school classrooms. Many CUB instructors attempted to tie the university classroom instruction to the realities of the public schools through teaching their university classes in the schools, and assigning classrooms. Still, the basic university-based, course-based lecture program remained the dominant mode. That program is still in place and handles the majority of teacher certification students, while the new PROBE experiment involves only twenty to thirty students each year.

The failures of previous attempts at reform and the felt need for a different program for "older" adults (ages 23 to 50 or older) who were returning to the university to obtain secondary school teaching certificates, prompted a group of faculty to meet extensively during the 1982-83 school year to design a new program. Many factors led to the PROBE model, but among the most important were the previous history of reform at the University of Colorado-Boulder, the nature of the research university environment, the outstanding intellectual quality and maturing of returning students, the desire to model a teaching/learning environment which could be used in the schools, and the university faculty members' skills, interests, and philosophies.

GOALS AND OBJECTIVES

One of the basic characteristics of PROBE is its continuing evolution as a program, and this necessitates the constant review of goals and objectives. The following list has been developed over the three years in which the program has existed, but is regularly scrutinized and revised.

1. To identify and define educational problems and to search for information to resolve and manage them.

2. To think critically about education and schooling, and gain a knowledge and skill base to resolve problems.

3. To become a competent member of a small group, and to function productively as part of that group in learning, research, and teaching.

4. To develop self-awareness and the ability to cope with the emotional reactions of self and others.

5. To become a self-directed learner with abilities in the selection and use of appropriate resources, the management of personal working time, and self-

evaluation skills.

6. To be aware of and be able to work in a variety of educational settings.

7. To develop the skills and to learn the methods required to diagnose learning needs and to manage the educational problems of learners, including their cognitive, physical, emotional, and social aspects.

8. To be aware of the "culture of the classroom" and of the school, and the role of the teacher as a professional in this environment.

9. To become aware of the stresses and demands placed upon teachers, and to develop strategies for coping with them.

10. To participate in the life of the school community as an active member and to perceive one's self as an educator.

11. To identify the forces operating on the classroom and on the school, and to conceptualize the school as part of the broader society.

12. To move through the stages of Teacher-as-Person, Teacher-as-Learner, Teacher-as-Teacher, and Teacher-as-Member-of-the-Broader-Society.

In addition to these broad goals, the PROBE program has a range of more specific objectives too numerous to list here, but all related to the goals presented above.

STUDENT SELECTION

In its initial year, 1983-84, PROBE admitted a range of students from twenty-one-year-olds in their senior year to mature adults, who were seeking to change occupations. While all the students succeeded in completing the program, the staff felt that the younger students had a more difficult time adjusting to the self-directed nature of the program, while the mature adult learners were, for the most part, able to adapt rapidly to this significantly different learning model. The relatively unstructured learning environment was too great a shock for those who had been institutionalized for sixteen consecutive years, and the staff had a difficult time weaning them away from their expectations of lectures and tests. It was as a result of this experience that the program decided to limit PROBE students to age 25 or older, generally with experience in other professions or with children in the home or other settings.

The range of students in the three years of the program has been exceptional, with a median age of 32 and students up to the age of 55. All candidates must present at least a Bachelor's degree, and many have presented M.A.s, with several having the doctorate. Work in one's major discipline must have been completed prior to coming into the program, although students are permitted to take one course concurrently, as long as it does not interfere with their participation in tutorial groups or work in the schools. A majority of the students have come from the sciences and mathematics, and this has made them most desirable to the schools of the region, many of which are facing shortages in these areas. Like students in the regular teacher education program, they must pass a Basic Skills examination, but they must also have a 3.00 grade point average for acceptance, yet most have a 3.5 average or better. The following occupational and educational groups have been represented in the first three PROBE classes: engineering, business, homemaking, law, veterinary medicine, airline hostess, herpatology, philosophy, chemical engineering, outdoor education, environmental education, and the military.

At least as important as the "paper" requirements for admission are the personal characteristics and abilities of applicants. Using a mock tutorial case-study all candidates are screened for such demonstrated abilities as independent learning, imaginative problem-solving, and ability to work productively in a small group. Such characteristics as emotional stability, capacity for self-evaluation, responsibility, and motivation to enter the teaching profession are weighed prior to admission. The mock tutorial case-study experience is used in combination with the more traditional academic criteria to determine admission to the PROBE program. The tutorial has proven to be an excellent device for revealing motivation, personality, and interpersonal skills.

EXPERIENCE-BASED LEARNING

A deep commitment to the role of experience in learning underlies PROBE, as was pointed out in the section on the philosophy of the program. The PROBE faculty takes seriously the need for practice or experience to precede theory. PROBE candidates are thus placed in the schools from the first day of the program, and are in and out of the schools and other settings on a daily basis throughout the full nine months. While initial placements are with the help of the University staff, the candidates themselves soon move into the role of structuring their own visits, observations, tutoring, mini-teaching settings, and student teaching settings. If a student is unable or unwilling to rapidly move into this pivotal role of finding one's own learning environments, the staff will initially aid them, but soon suggest that they are not funcitoning well in the self-directed learning mode expected of PROBE students. In three years, only a handful of the seventy-five participants have had much difficulty in this area.

While students are encouraged to begin their school/classroom experiences in regular public secondary schools, since this is the final destination for most of them, they are also encouraged to range far beyond the confines of suburban, white, Anglo-Saxon junior and senior high schools, and visit pre-schools and elementary schools, as well as inner-city secondary schools. Visits to alternative private and public secondary schools provide another view on the practice of schooling, as do observations in teen parenting centers, juvenile delinquent homes, and parochial schools. Wherever children and teenagers are to be found in our society is where the PROBE candidates are encouraged to observe, aid, teach, and reflect. Since by state law all teachers must have completed a 400-hour student teaching experience, there is the expectation that some time during the fall or spring semester such an intensive experience will take place. For most candidates this occurs in the spring semester, but program flexibility permits it to occur whenever the individual is ready, and it may begin as early November or as late as April. While PROBE candidates according to an evaluation done after the second year, appear to be considerably more at ease about their intensive student teaching experience than the younger, more traditionally trained undergraduate, they did ask for more actual teaching experiences prior to being submerged for eight weeks in a "student teaching" setting. With this request in mind, in the third year of the program, a mini-teaching week was instituted in early October, so that students could experience a fuller range of responsibilities, from lesson planning to classroom management, than was the case in the observational and tutorial settings.

The experiential aspect of the PROBE program, then, consists of continuous contact with schools, children, and learning environments from the beginning of the academic year in September until the end of the program in May. The PROBE students thus get to experience the full academic year in the schools, with its planning, organizing, teaching, examining, and other activities. Such a field-based component is often not possible in programs geared more to the university setting. There is also the opportunity to do observation and mini-unit teaching in a range of different settings, and to do in-depth student teaching in at least two different environments. Students have taught in regular public junior and senior high schools, parochial schools, juvenile justice centers, teen parenting schools, alternative public and private schools, outdoor education centers, Indian reservation schools, and overseas dependent schools.

Dewey spoke constantly of the need for the interaction of experience and reflection, while the Brazilian philosopher, Paulo Freire, speaks of the praxis of action and reflection. Experiences in the schools and other settings can be educative or mis-educative. With this and other considerations in mind, PROBE planners included the "Tutorial Group" as a component of the program. This has become that critical place where the teacher candidates reflect upon their experiences, react to each other's experiences, and apply old and new experiences to the analysis and solutions of case studies.

TUTORIAL GROUPS

A critical part of the PROBE model is the small-group tutorial setting. Twice a week in the fall term, and once a week in the spring, the teacher candidates meet with eight to ten fellow students and two tutors. The pair of tutors consists of a regular faculty member of the university and a teacher on leave from the schools. The tutorial group serves a variety of functions. It is a laboratory where students develop interpersonal skills and look at their own personalities and abilities. It is a place for peer evaluation, in which students regularly critique each other's presentations and overall involvement in the program. Traditional teacher education programs seldom teach persons how to listen or to give or receive criticism, but these are important components of the PROBE tutorial group. The ability to give accurate and candid feedback within the safety of the tutorial group aids the future teachers for the day when they must evaluate and give feedback to their students in the schools. Since individually and collectively the students are responsible for their own learning, educational planning is also learned as part of the tutorial group process.

Not only is the tutorial process new to the vast majority of students in the program, it is also new to the professors or tutors as they are called. One of the major reasons that the tutorial model was chosen was to change the teaching behavior of faculty members. Many teacher education reform movements have faltered when individual faculty members insist on continuing their particular classes in a lecture mode, even though the rest of a program might have adopted a very different mode. One of the first decisions made by the PROBE planners was to eliminate all courses in the regular teacher education program and move to the small tutorial groups in their place. This of course meant that in many cases the tutor/professor would not be an "expert" in the many topics to be dealt with in the case studies and thus would be forced into the role of generalist and facilitator, rather than as lecturer on his/her area of expertise. The tutor becomes a model of the self-directed learner and problem solver, rather than the expositor of a fount of knowledge, so ubiquitous in regular university classrooms.

The tutorial role is often difficult for both the tutors and the students. It is always easier to just "tell them the answers," than to help the students to define the problems and find the answers for themselves. The facilitation role, which has become such an important part of the counseling movement, is rarely seen in academic classrooms so there are few examples from which to learn. Such roles as hinting, shaping, reinforcing, and encouraging, while occasionally part of more didactic approaches used in higher education, are not the major focus of a professor's teaching behavior. The tutorial approach is what might be called "guided discovery," and the tutor permits the student to make mistakes, but does not let the frustration reach a level at which learning becomes paralyzed.

It is through the tutorial groups and the experiences in the schools that the teacher candidates receive regular course credits from the University and complete all the state requirements for certification. Although the students do not take specific courses in methods, evaluation, foundations, psychology, and others, they do cover all these topics in their tutorial groups and/or in their school/classroom experiences. Since the springboard for analysis and discussion in the tutorial group is the case study, these are intentionally general, encompassing many related topics and suggesting many others.

PROBLEM-BASED CASE STUDIES

Once it had been decided to develop an inquiry-oriented model for teacher education, the problem-based case study was a natural vehicle on which to focus the process of inquiry. The Harvard Business School has used the case study method successfully for many years, but used highly detailed cases developed at great cost, and containing most of the information needed by the student buried within the case. The McMaster Medical School cases, however, are very short, often only a paragraph or two, and the student researcher is forced to find the information needed to analyze and "solve" the problems in a wide range of learning resources. The PROBE staff, working as it was with no special or external funding, decided that for both practical and philosophical reasons, the McMaster model was more suitable. The case studies have been written by faculty tutors, graduate students, teachers in the schools, and some by PROBE participants.

Although each case study is short (usually a page or two), embedded in the problem situation are many interrelated topics. Some of the topics are "obvious" while others can be inferred from a careful reading of the narrative, and still others uncovered by the students were not even imagined by the authors. The "solutions" are seldom few or simple, and students bring to the tutorial groups evidence for their preferred solutions from a wide-ranging variety of sources: their own background of experience, recent experiences in schools/classrooms, and material from their readings in books and journals. Among the many resources which students consult in dealing with the problems are the following:

1. The PROBE library of books donated by faculty members along with two or three "texts" purchased for each participant.

2. The PROBE tutors.

3. Public school teachers, counselors, and administrators.

4. The University library.

5. The School of Education faculty and resource center.

6. Fellow students at the University.

7. School children and sometimes their parents.

8. Other educative agencies in the society such as churches, youth centers and clubs, courts, migrant programs, juvenile homes, city and county agencies, cultural centers, and others.

9. Pre-schools and elementary schools, even though PROBE is currently a secondary teacher training program.

10. Rural schools, alternative schools, inner-city schools, and others which have special characteristics.

11. Videotapes, tape recordings, films, and other media.

Students or groups of students bring their "findings" back to the tutorial group for presentation and discussion. Some of these presentations are videotaped for critique by the tutorial group or for use as models for succeeding programs. Following the completion of each case, the tutor and tutorial group discuss which of the PROBE objectives and which state certification objectives have been achieved and at what level.

The search for "solutions" to the various problems is carried out individually, in pairs, or even by a whole tutorial group. Students are encouraged to work together to seek out information and to consult a wide range of resources. Once they have analyzed a problem in depth and have marshalled evidence to support their tentative solutions, they must organize a mode of presentation for delivery at the next scheduled tutorial group meeting, and be prepared for reactions and critiques by the tutors and their fellow group members.

The case study approach represents an alternative to the traditional ways of viewing knowledge. Instead of individual courses with bodies of knowledge and prescribed textbooks, the PROBE model uses problem case studies from which the students derive, analyze, and present the same topics found in the required courses in the regular program. The major differences are that the knowledge topics do not occur ("come up") in tidy parcels such as educational psychology or communications, and that knowledge is acquired to analyze and solve problems rather than in a logical typology. This approach to learning is much like that described in Robert Pirsig's <u>Zen and Art of Motorcycle Maintenance</u>, in which each hypothesis opens up countless other hypotheses, and problems are never "solved," but rather the learner is involved in a continuous search.

EVALUATION

Evaluation occurs throughout the PROBE academic year as continuous feedback is critical to both the students and the tutors. The basic purposes of evaluation in this program are to facilitate student learning and to modify the program, not to compare students or rank order them. Although students receive grades at the end of each term as required by University regulations, the evaluation is continuous and not an anxiety producing "final examination." Students are actively involved in regular self-evaluation, as this is consistent with the self-directed learning format used in PROBE. Tutorial group members also evaluate each other, and of course the tutor gives regular and systematic feedback throughout the term.

Observation of the students in the tutorial groups and in the various school settings become part of the evaluation process, as do the various written products of the students. Formal and informal presentations in the tutorial group, along with a range of activities in the school setting are part of the overall evaluation. Precise definitions of satisfactory and unsatisfactory performance are not stressed in the program, but after three years' experience in the program, there appears to be extremely high correlations among the evaluations of fellow students, the tutors, and teachers in the schools. Except for a few cases, these external evaluations are similar to those given by the students themselves. Rather than emphasize performance levels on tightly specified learning criteria, PROBE prefers a descriptive profile on how each student is achieving, and what needs to be done in the future.

CONCLUSION

PROBE is in its third year and it is still too early to proclaim it an unqualified success. Graduates from the program seeking teaching positions have all been employed, most in school districts with vast numbers of applicants for each opening. Student evaluations of the program have been overwhelmingly positive, with the few negative criticisms serving as prods to change. Numerous school districts have sought to work closely with PROBE, and the U.S. Department of Education recently selected it for one of its grants as a special demonstration project. Formative and summative evaluations of the program keep it in a state of change, but the overall model appears to be sound. No single component of PROBE is unique, but we believe that the combination of ingredients in a single year-long program is worthy of consideration as an effective alternative to current teacher educaton programs.

BIBLIOGRAPHY

Lyons, Gene. "Why Teachers Can't Teach." Texas Monthly, 7 (September, 1979), pp. 122-128, 208-220.

Association for Experiential Education
C.U. Box 249 Boulder, CO 80309 (303) 492-1547

EXPERIENTIAL EDUCATION AND THE SCHOOLS, edited by Dick Kraft and Jim Kielsmeier. Second edition printed in a larger and more readable format. A 343 page book containing some of the best articles taken from the past AEE journals. This book addresses a variety of issues including national reports, general theory, cultural journalism, experiential learning, research and evaluation, and practical ideas.

THE THEORY OF EXPERIENTIAL EDUCATION, edited by Dick Kraft and Mitch Sakofs. Revised and expanded second edition of a 298 page collection of articles which address the historical, philosophical, spiritual, and psychological foundations of experiential education.

COMMON PRACTICES IN ADVENTURE PROGRAMMING (CP) One of the best single documents available concerning common practices in adventure programming. In addition to detailed procedures, this book includes helpful forms, information sheets, questionnaires, evaluation instruments, directories, and bibliographies. CP is an indispensible resource for individuals and organizations working in all types of adventure programs with all types of populations.

ETHICAL ISSUES IN EXPERIENTIAL EDUCATION, by Jasper Hunt. This book provides the reader with an overview of the philosophical questions surrounding ethics, an exploration of specific ethical dilemmas facing adventure program leaders, and a methodology for resolving ethical problems.

THE DIRECTORY OF ADVENTURE ALTERNATIVES IN CORRECTIONS, MENTAL HEALTH AND SPECIAL POPULATIONS. Contains a state-by-state, as well as alphabetical, index of adventure alternative programs which utilize adventure programming as a part of their therapeutic process.

EXPERIENTIAL EDUCATON IN HIGH SCHOOL "Life in the Walkabout Program", by Bert Horwood with foreward by Maurice Gibbons. This book is a stirring ethnography of Jefferson County Open High School, an institution based on the revolutionary idea of high school as a rite of passage from adolescence to adulthood. A book for all educators and an important contribution to literature of experiential education.

THE NORTHEAST DIRECTORY OF PROGRAMS is a 35 page index that lists over 100 experiential education programs/agencies in the northeast.

To order your copies of the publications, use reverse side of form, or write to the AEE office for further details.

AEE PUBLICATIONS LIST

CU Box 249
Boulder, CO 80309
(303) 492-1547

BOOKS	Member	Non Member
Common Practices in Adventure Programming	$20.	$25.
Experiential Education in High School	$9.	$12.50
Ethical Issues in Experiential Education	$12.50	$15.
Experiential Education and the Schools	$14.	$16.
The Theory of Experiential Education	$12.50	$15.
The Directory of Adventure Alternatives in Corrections, Mental Health, and Special Populations	$7.50	$10.
The Northeast Directory of Programs	$5.	$7.

PUBLICATIONS	Member	Non Member
The Journal of Experiential Education (three issues annually)	Free	$18.
The Membership Handbook	Free	$5.
The Membership Directory	Free	$15.
The Jobs Clearinghouse (one year/postage included)	$15.	$25.
AEE Journal Index (Subject, Title, Author)	$6.	$6.
AEE Journal Back Issues (if available)	$6.	$6.

Postage & Handling

4TH CLASS (1-4 WKS DELIVERY)
Single book — $2.50
Multiple books — 10% of total

1ST CLASS (2-5 DAYS DELIVERY)
Single book — $3.50
Multiple books — 20% of total

BOOK ORDER FORM

TITLES   PRICE
1. _____
2. _____
3. _____
4. _____

U.S. FUNDS ONLY

Total Cost _____
Post & Handling _____
Overseas add $4.00
TOTAL _____

SHIP ORDER TO:

Name _____
Address _____
_____
City _____
State/Province _____
Zip/Postal Code _____ Country _____